PRINCIPLES OF
BUDGETARY AND
FINANCIAL POLICY

PRINCIPLES OF BUDGETARY AND FINANCIAL POLICY

Willem H. Buiter

The MIT Press
Cambridge, Massachusetts

First MIT Press edition, 1990
© 1990 Willem Buiter

First published in 1990 by Harvester Wheatsheaf, a division of Simon & Schuster
International Group.

Printed and bound in Great Britain

Library of Congress Cataloging-in-Publication Data

Buiter, Willem H., 1949–
    Principles of budgetary and financial policy / Willem Buiter.
        p.   cm.
    ISBN 0-262-02303-2
    1. Fiscal policy.   2. Debts, public.   3. Crowding out (Economics)
4. Budget.
        I. Title.
HJ141.B85   1990   89-13024
    336.3—dc20   CIP

This book is dedicated to
Jenny, Frank and Moniek,
the first of the new generation

CONTENTS

Acknowledgements   ix

1 Introduction   1

Part I Setting the scene

2 Allocative and stabilization aspects of budgetary and financial
  policy (1984)   25

3 A guide to public sector debt and deficits (1985)   47

Part II Issues of measurement

4 Measurement of the public sector deficit and its implications for
  policy evaluation and design (1983)   105

5 The arithmetic of solvency (1987)   145

Part III Crowding out

6 'Crowding out' and the effectiveness of fiscal policy (1977)   163

7 Debt neutrality, redistribution and consumer heterogeneity: a
  survey and some extensions (1988)   183

8 Debt neutrality, Professor Vickrey and Henry George's 'Single
  Tax' (1989)   223

9 Debt neutrality: a brief review of doctrine and evidence (with
  James Tobin) (1980)   229

10 Long-run effects of fiscal and monetary policy on aggregate
   demand (with James Tobin) (1976)   252

11 Fiscal and monetary policies, capital formation, and economic
activity (with James Tobin) (1980)   287

Part IV   The fiscal roots of inflation

12 A fiscal theory of hyperdeflations? Some surprising monetarist
arithmetic (1987)   359

13 Can public spending cuts be inflationary? (1988)   368

Part V   Fiscal and financial policy in developing countries

14 Some thoughts on the role of fiscal policy in stabilization and
structural adjustment in developing countries (1988)   407

Index   449

ACKNOWLEDGEMENTS

I should like to acknowledge the following permissions received to reproduce articles in this book which were originally published elsewhere.

Chapter 3 'A guide to public sector debt and deficits', *Economic Policy*, 1, no. 1, November 1985, pp. 13–79, Cambridge University Press.

Chapter 4 'Measurement of the public sector deficit and its implications for policy evaluation and design', *International Monetary Fund Staff Papers*, 30, no. 2, June 1983, pp. 306–49

Chapter 6 '"Crowding out" and the effectiveness of fiscal policy', *Journal of Public Economics*, 7, 1977, pp. 309–28, Elsevier Science Publishers, Physical Sciences and Engineering Division.

Chapter 8 'Debt neutrality, Professor Vickrey and Henry George's "single tax"', *Economics Letters* 29, 1989, pp. 43–7, Elsevier Science Publishers, Physical Sciences and Engineering Division.

Chapter 9 'Debt neutrality: a brief review of doctrine and evidence', with James Tobin, in G.M. von Furstenberg (ed.), *Social Security Versus Private Saving*, Ballinger, 1979, pp. 39–63. Reprinted with Permission by the American Council of Life Insurance.

Chapter 10 'Long-run effects of fiscal and monetary policy on aggregate demand', in J. Stein (ed.), *Monetarism*, 1976, Elsevier Science Publishers, Physical Sciences and Engineering Division.

Chapter 11 'Fiscal and monetary policies, capital formations, and economic activity', with James Tobin, in G.M. von Furstenberg (ed.), *The Government and Capital Formation*, Ballinger, 1980, pp. 73–151. Reprinted with Permission by the American Council of Life Insurance.

Chapter 12 'A fiscal theroy of hyperdeflations? Some surprising monetarist arithmetic', *Oxford Economic Papers*, 39, 1987, pp. 111–18, Oxford University Press.

1 · INTRODUCTION

Fiscal policy is once again at the center of the economic policy debate all over the world. Professional economists and economic policy-makers try to make sense of a bewildering variety of data generated by often badly managed national, regional and global economic laboratories.

Among the open issues that (should) trouble the sleep of those responsible for the design of monetary, fiscal and financial policy are the following:

How can we reconcile the 'twin deficits' of the United States, i.e. the more or less simultaneous emergence of deficits in the current account of the balance of payments and in the Federal budget, with the recent development in Britain of a large current account deficit in the balance of payments at the same time as the public sector budget was moving into surplus?

Are public sector budget deficits monetized sooner or later, i.e. do they eventually spell inflation? Is a correction of the fiscal deficit a necessary condition for a sustained reduction in the rate of inflation?

Is it true, as argued by (among others) Milton Friedman and Robert Barro, that (to a first approximation) the only relevant aspects of the budget are the volume and composition of public spending on real goods and services and that the choice of financing method (taxation, domestic credit expansion or borrowing) is irrelevant? Does financial crowding-out of private saving, capital formation and/or the current account surplus by public sector debt remain a concern?

What remains of the Keynesian arguments for countercyclical budget deficits? Going beyond the above-mentioned first approximation, is the neo-classical tax-smoothing argument (that, since non-distortionary taxes do not exist, planned or expected distortionary tax rates should be smoothed to minimize the efficiency losses inevitably involved in financing the government's spending program) the only remaining rationale for countercyclical budget deficits?

How do we assess the solvency of a government? How do we evaluate the consistency of the government's spending and revenue-raising plans with its outstanding debt obligations and its inflation objectives?

How does the pursuit of internal or external stabilization objectives through fiscal means affect the government's structural (or allocative) and distributional objectives?

These and similar issues have been a central concern in my research since I was a graduate student at Yale in the early 1970s. A representative sample of my work on fiscal and financial policy is brought together in this volume. The 13 essays that follow this Introduction develop four major themes and are organized into five parts.

The first theme, which pervades the essays in each of the five parts, is that the stabilization role of fiscal policy cannot be analyzed separately from its allocative and distributional roles. Variations in any given fiscal instrument (public spending category, tax rate, etc.) will affect the balance between aggregate output and absorption or demand, will alter the key relative prices (static and intertemporal) and rationing constraints faced by private agents, and will alter the distribution of resources.

The second theme, which is the central topic of Part II ('Issues of Measurement') and crops up repeatedly in each of the other parts, focuses on the measurement of public sector activity over time. Giving priority to issues of measurement and accountancy does not merely reflect the fact that, fundamentally, economists are bookkeepers with ambitions (or pretensions). Without measurement there can be no science. Also, the way we measure things, organize data and try to map them into their theoretical counterparts will color our understanding of the processes we are monitoring.

The snapshot, single-period view of the government's corner of the flow-of-funds accounts known as the public sector deficit is now generally recognized to possess very little informational content about anything of interest to an economist, such as impact of fiscal policy on demand, crowding-out pressure, etc. Part II considers how (and to what extent) a longer-run perspective on the government's finances can be summarized in a single comprehensive government balance sheet or its flow counterpart, something which, by abuse of language, we might call a 'permanent deficit'.

The third theme concerns 'crowding out', the displacement of private economic activity by public economic activity. When we investigate this multi-dimensional concept, it soon becomes apparent that both the direct and the indirect or general equilibrium effects of public sector actions on private economic behavior can be reinforcing or complementary ('crowding in') rather than offsetting or substituting ('crowding out'). Part III ('Crowding Out') contains a wide-ranging theoretical analysis of this issue and presents some tentative empirical evidence on the importance of financial crowding out.

Financial crowding out concerns the consequences of financing public sector deficits by borrowing. The fourth theme, emphasized in Part IV, but also present in Parts I, II and V, deals with the implications of choosing the alternative financing mode, domestic credit expansion or, in closed economic systems, monetary financing.

The government budget constraint (or budget identity) shows that any excess of expenditure over current revenues has to be met by asset sales, borrowing or domestic credit expansion. In conjunction with the government's (intertemporal) solvency constraint limiting the extent to which additional net debt can be incurred, this means that domestic credit expansion is endogenously or residually determined once the government fixes its expenditure and taxation plans, and assuming it will not default on its debt. What does this fiscal view of the ultimate determinants of monetary growth and thus of the rate of inflation tell us about policies to achieve a lasting reduction in the rate of inflation?

All four themes (the need to consider jointly the stabilization, allocative and distributional consequences of fiscal and financial policy; measurement issues; crowding out; and the fiscal origins of inflation) are introduced in a non-technical manner in Part I ('Setting the Scene'). In the final Part V ('Fiscal and Financial Policy in Developing Countries') we see how the tools and concepts developed under these four theme headings can be applied under the extreme conditions generated in the laboratory of developing countries facing severe internal and external disequilibrium.

We now turn to a more detailed review of the essays included in this volume.

1.1 SETTING THE SCENE

The two papers of Part I (Buiter, 1984b; 1985) are broad-ranging, non-technical papers aimed at a wider public. The first of these (Chapter 2) was my inaugural lecture at the London School of Economics (LSE) in 1983 (minus a section on public sector solvency and the consistency of fiscal, financial and monetary plans, dealt with at length in Chapters 3 and 4 in this volume). As I never got around to preparing the inaugural lecture for publication in *Economica* (the normal practice at the LSE), I am pleased to have this opportunity to reissue this rather uninhibited paper here.

The paper deplores the still prevalent split between approaches stressing the stabilization role of fiscal and financial policy and approaches stressing its allocative and distributional aspects.

The incentive- and distributional effects of non-lump-sum taxes, transfers and subsidies and the incentive- and distributional effects of exhaustive public spending (complementarity or substitutability between public and private consumption and investment, conventional public goods issues, etc.) tend to be studied in universes where stabilization issues are ruled out a priori. (Stabilization here refers to policies designed to affect — and, one hopes, to minimize — gaps between actual levels of output and employment and their socially efficient levels, and to policies aimed at influencing the rate of inflation.) Competitive Walrasian economies, especially when endowed with complete contingent markets, do not permit consideration of the kinds of market failure that generate a potential use for stabilization policy. For example, except for policies aimed at influencing misperceptions-induced departures from the full information equilibrium, there can be no stabilization policy in New Classical models. In such economies, the consideration of financing problems, i.e. the issues involved in choosing the mix over time of various kinds of taxation, borrowing and monetary financing, for a given program of public spending on goods and services, reduces to a standard neoclassical exercise in optimal taxation. With the usual convexity assumptions, the general neoclassical policy prescription ('When in doubt, smooth it out') emerges predictably for conventional distortionary tax rates, especially when objective functionals are time-additive, when there is ample contemporaneous separability and when certainty equivalence rules (see, for example, Barro, 1979; and Kydland and Prescott, 1980). Similar results obtain for the inflation tax rate (see, for example, Phelps, 1973; Mankiw, 1987; and Barro, 1987).

The key Keynesian insight that market economies can get stuck in persistent non-Walrasian equilibria characterized by widespread under-utilization and waste of human and non-human resources has not yet made its mark on those studies in public finance that look seriously at the structure of taxes, duties, tariffs, transfer payments, benefits, subsidies and public sector charges or at the composition and nature of exhaustive public spending programs.

Approaches that take seriously the possibility of significant and persistent failures of the invisible hand and emphasize the influence of fiscal, financial and monetary policy on aggregate demand (and through that on the levels of output and employment) have suffered from two weaknesses. The first is the rather coarse characterization of the spending and tax instruments and of the way in which they affect private sector behavior. Even in a demand-constrained equilibrium, it is likely to make a difference whether a given reduction in current tax revenues is achieved through a cut in personal income tax rates, corporate profit tax rates, capital gains tax rates, tariffs, etc. By the same token, the composition of an increase in public spending may be as important as its magnitude for the determination of its short-run and long-run effects.

Second, the economic mechanisms generating and supporting the non-

Walrasian equilibria are often spelled out poorly or not at all. Note, however, that the failure to generate the equilibrium as the outcome of a dynamic process unfolding in real time (and not in auctioneer's time) is shared by the Walrasian competitive equilibrium; no amount of repetition of the phrase 'all trades perceived to be mutually advantageous are exhausted' can substitute for an explicit analysis of how we get there from here.

Progress has been made, however, on the 'microfoundations' of Keynesian macroeconomics. It is well-known that efficiency-wage phenomena in the labor market (see, for example, Akerlof and Yellen, 1986) can generate persistent equilibria with socially inefficient unemployment of labor. When combined with imperfect competition in product markets (see, for example, Akerlof and Yellen, 1985a; 1985b; 1988; Buiter, 1988b) and with any plausible mechanism for generating *nominal* price or wage stickiness (e.g. menu costs or other real costs of nominal price adjustments, as surveyed in Rotemberg, 1987) such models provide, in principle, the microfoundations of demand management and of stabilization policy. Another promising approach to the microfoundations of Keynesian economics and to stabilization policy is through explicitly game-theoretic models (such as Cooper and John, 1988; or Shleifer and Vishny, 1988) stressing strategic complementarity, spillovers and externalities as the mechanism for generating Keynesian demand externalities or through the related models of search with externalities explored by Diamond (1982; 1988). Blanchard and Kiyotaki (1987) also belongs to this family. None of these new approaches to non-Walrasian economics has as yet come close enough to the institutional reality of modern market economies to permit a recognizable positive or normative analysis of public spending, taxation, borrowing and monetary financing. The very limited intertemporal structure of the current crop of new-Keynesian models is a further obstacle to a serious analysis of budgetary issues, many of which are inherently intertemporal. This will no doubt change in the future as this promising branch of enquiry develops further, but as of now we are stuck between the Scylla of the study of relevant spending and tax structures in uninteresting models and the Charybdis of the study of rudimentary tax and public expenditure options in more interesting models.

Virtually every change in exhaustive public spending programs, tax structures, benefit coverage, entitlement and enforcement will redistribute resources between (groups of) individuals, households, regions, social classes, etc. The often highly aggregative models of modern public finance may miss much that is important to human welfare.

The simple sequential general equilibrium models, such as the neoclassical growth models with an overlapping generations (OLG) structure on the household side, that are now often used for policy-oriented analyses of public finance issues, can lull the profession into a comfortable neglect of

6 *Introduction*

important distributional issues. The most extreme example of this approach, the so-called representative agent models popularized especially by Lucas (see, for example, Lucas, 1978; Lucas and Stokey, 1983; 1987), lose even the very limited ability of simple OLG models to address intergenerational redistribution and focus on pre Friday Robinson Crusoe economies in which distributional issues cannot arise.

While in this relative neglect of distributional issues the fashionable wing of the economics profession reflects, as ever, the spirit of the times, it is both short-sighted and unnecessary. The computational capacity to analyze dynamic models with non-trivial heterogeneity among households, workers, etc., does exist (see, for example, Auerbach and Kotlikoff, 1987). While many of the applied computational general equilibrium models remain awkwardly static (even when they purport to analyze intertemporal issues involving public sector deficits, external borrowing and domestic capital formation), there are now a number of examples (such as Feltenstein, 1986) showing that this, too, may be a potentially fruitful approach to the analysis of public finance issues with non-trivial distributional aspects.

Chapter 3 considers the three main worries associated with public sector debt and deficits. These are the link between public sector debt, deficits and inflation; the issue of public debt, deficits and solvency; and public debt, deficits and financial 'crowding out'.

Sargent and Wallace (1981) is the starting point of the analysis of the monetary implications of public sector debt and deficits. In a closed economy with an exogenously given primary (non-interest) government deficit, there is assumed to be an upper bound on the public debt–GDP ratio. When this ceiling is reached, further borrowing by the government is constrained to be no more than the product of this debt–GDP ceiling and the growth rate of nominal GDP (in the case of nominally denominated public debt) or the product of the debt–GDP ceiling and the growth rate of real GDP (in the case of index-linked public debt). For simplicity, consider the case where the real interest rate and the growth rate of real GDP are exogenous. Money financing (i.e. the increase in the stock of non-interest-bearing high-powered money or base money) is endogenously or residually determined by the path of the primary deficit, the debt–GDP ceiling, the real interest rate and the growth rate of real GDP. Even if inflation is proximately a strictly monetary phenomenon (most dramatically in the case where the base money–GDP velocity of circulation is constant and real GDP is exogenous), monetary growth is a fiscal phenomenon. If the interest rate exceeds the growth rate of GDP, current reductions in money growth which are not the reflection of reductions in the primary deficit imply increased borrowing and an increase in the debt–GDP ratio. Any given debt–GDP ceiling will be reached earlier (or, in the case analyzed by Sargent and Wallace, the debt–GDP ratio at any given future date, T say, will be higher) than it would have been without the current reduction in monetary financing. If the debt–GDP ratio at T is maintained forever after, then higher monetary growth after T is the consequence of lower monetary growth before T, in the absence of any fundamental fiscal correction (i.e. absent any reduction in the primary deficit).

In a comment on Sargent and Wallace's paper (Buiter, 1984a) I pointed out that the correct deficit for measuring the 'eventual monetization' implied by the fiscal stance could differ quite dramatically from the conventionally measured Public Sector Financial Deficit (PSFD) and a fortiori from such mysterious and mystifying measures of public sector financial transactions as the Public Sector Borrowing Requirement (PSBR) in the United Kingdom. Consider, for example, the case where the current debt–GDP ratio is to be stabilized. Rather than recording current interest payments, the deficit measure relevant for eventual monetization would take the market value (measured or imputed) of all public sector non-monetary liabilities (net of non-monetary assets) and multiply them by the (long) real interest rate net of the growth rate of real GDP. Only the consumption component of exhaustive public spending should be recorded, but a correction should be made for any shortfall of the government's cash rate of return on its capital assets relative to the government's opportunity cost of borrowing. If the current value of the (consumption) primary deficit is a poor indicator of its future value, a 'permanent' (consumption) primary deficit measure should be constructed. If the act of stabilizing the debt–GDP ratio were to change future expected inflation rates, the market value of outstanding stocks of long-dated nominal debt can, of course, change dramatically (as emphasized by Minford, 1985). Similar valuation changes can occur if expected future real rates are affected. These issues were addressed also in Buiter (1982) and in Buiter (1983), the latter included in this volume as Chapter 4.

Sargent and Wallace also pointed out that many familiar money demand functions (including the linear and the log-linear ones) imply the existence of a long-run 'seigniorage Laffer curve'. The same steady-state amount of real revenue can be appropriated by printing money either with a low or with a high proportional growth rate of the nominal money stock (and therefore ultimately with either a low or a high rate of inflation). Restricting ourselves to 'unimodal' long-run seigniorage Laffer curves with a unique seigniorage revenue maximizing rate of inflation, Sargent and Wallace's conclusion that a reduction in monetary growth now implies a higher rate of monetary growth in the future need not hold on the 'slippery slope' of the Laffer curve, when inflation is above the revenue-maximizing level. These issues are considered further in Buiter (1987a; 1988d; 1988e), included in this volume as Chapters 12–14.

It is important to note that the seigniorage or inflation tax revenue of the Sargent–Wallace model is the *anticipated* inflation tax revenue only. Governments capable of surprising holders of long-dated nominal debt with a burst of unanticipated inflation, or a fortiori with a price-*level* jump (say through a devaluation or, in a New Classical Wonderland where goods prices behave like forward-looking financial asset prices, through a competitive market-clearing general price-level jump) can impose an (unanticipated) inflation levy. Finally, both anticipated and unanticipated inflation are likely to affect the primary deficit; the Tanzi (1978) effect of (hyper)inflation on public sector outlays and revenues may, in countries with very high inflation, outweigh the familiar effect of 'bracket creep' on progressive income tax revenues when the general price level rises.

One important aspect of the fiscal–monetary nexus which the essays in this volume do not consider is the strategic or game-theoretic interaction between the fiscal and the monetary authority. The Sargent–Wallace scenario, after the debt–GDP ceiling has been reached, can be thought of as representing the situation of a dominant fiscal authority forcing an accommodating monetary authority to monetize whatever residual financing requirements it has. This may represent institutional reality in France and, perhaps to a slightly lesser extent, in the United Kingdom where the monetary authorities are *de jure* and/or *de facto* subordinate to the Treasury. The central banks in many developing or semi-industrial countries also tend to be agencies for the fiscal authorities without independent authority.

The scope for independent action of the Federal Reserve Board of the United States is somewhat greater than that of the Bank of England, and the former's influence and indeed leadership in fiscal and financial matters in general are also no doubt enhanced by the fact that budgetary authority in the United States is fragmented between the executive and legislative branches of government. The contrast in this regard with the United Kingdom's unitary state and the absence of any effective separation of powers is striking indeed.

At the extreme end of the spectrum of monetary independence in the industrial world is the West German Bundesbank. A reversal of the Sargent–Wallace ideal-type, with the central bank in a leadership role, setting the amount of seigniorage it is willing to extract and leaving the fiscal authority with the passive role of adjusting its primary deficit to the central bank's monetary target may well be appropriate for a positive analysis of this case.

When the government cannot run Ponzi games, i.e. cannot forever finance the entire interest bill on its outstanding debt simply by borrowing more, we can derive in straightforward fashion the public sector solvency constraint or present value budget constraint. This says simply that the present discounted value of future primary surpluses plus the present discounted value of future new issues of high-powered money should be (at least) as large as the value of the outstanding public debt. The 'no Ponzi game' restriction seems reasonable when (on average) the interest rate is expected to exceed the growth rate in the future.

The government's solvency constraint can be used as a systematic, forward-looking accounting device for evaluating the consistency of the authorities' fiscal, financial and monetary plans. When a discrepancy is shown to exist, various 'permanent deficit' measures can be constructed to indicate the magnitude of the long-run adjustments that will have to be made to spending plans, revenue projections or future planned recourse to seigniorage, in order to achieve feasible plans.

If neither spending, nor revenue, nor monetizations plans can be revised to fill the hole in the government's solvency constraint, a partial or complete default on the government's outstanding debt is indicated.

The brief review of financial crowding out in Chapter 3 anticipates later work (Buiter, 1977; 1988c; 1989; Buiter and Tobin, 1979; Tobin and Buiter, 1976; 1980), which together constitutes Part III of this volume.

It is well known that in otherwise conventional Keynesian models with demand-determined output and sluggish price adjustment, forward-looking financial markets can help create conditions under which the unanticipated announcement of a *future* fiscal expansion causes a recession between the announcement date and the implementation date: the anticipation of higher future short interest rates raises the current long rate of interest, causes the exchange rate to appreciate and may also depress Tobin's q. (see, for example, Blanchard, 1981). The only minor innovation as regards financial crowding-out in the paper is in Appendix 3B which analyzes a simple aggregate demand–aggregate supply model with an augmented Phillips curve and a government budget identity. Even the unexpected announcement of an immediately implemented increase in exhaustive public spending can be contractionary in this model if the government's financing rule is sufficiently biased towards debt.

Finally, the paper repeats the well-known but nevertheless systematically ignored warning of Blinder and Solow (1974) that there are no 'model-free' measures of fiscal stance. Neither the government deficit, not its change, nor the inflation-, growth-, investment- and cyclically-corrected, demand-weighted deficit is a measure of the expansionary thrust (short-, medium- or long-run) of fiscal policy in any model of the economy that I am aware of. Similarly, none of the (doctored or undoctored) deficit measures are reliable indicators of the magnitude or even the sign of the effects of fiscal policy on interest rates, capital formation or the current account of the balance of payments (see also Kotlikoff, 1988).

1.2 ISSUES OF MEASUREMENT

Part II consists of two papers, the first of which (Chapter 4) was written while I was a visiting scholar with the Fiscal Affairs Department of the International Monetary Fund during the summer of 1982. I have always been struck by the willingness of this institution (and its big sister across the street) to encourage and support heterodox research by consultants and advisers, even when the policy implications of this work did not appear to fit in comfortably with current operational practice and/or institutional conventional wisdom.

The paper considers in considerable detail the construction and interpretation of the comprehensive wealth accounts or solvency constraints of the public, private and external sectors. Focusing on these accounts, rather than on the current flow of funds, compels the policy-maker to take the long view. An important part of stabilization policy consists in the restructuring by the government of its comprehensive balance sheet, consisting of its tangible and intangible assets and liabilities, in such a way that private agents (who might otherwise be constrained in their spending behavior by cash flow constraints, liquidity constraints, lack of collateral or other capital market imperfections) can also take the long view and are enabled to act as if they, too, are constrained only by their permanent income.

Basic differences in the 'opportunity sets' of the private and public sectors mean that the government is the natural borrower or borrower of first resort when the economy is hit by shocks that drive current income below permanent income. Such shocks often increase the incidence and severity of liquidity constraints in the private sector and worsen the quality of the private balance sheets, thus reducing their collateral value. Because of its monopoly of the power to tax, to regulate and to declare some of its liabilities legal tender, governments have access to the capital markets on terms that are superior to those available to most private agents. By borrowing (a device for singling out non-liquidity-constrained private agents) or by printing money during periods when liquidity constraints bite more widely and more deeply than usual and by retiring this debt or the additional money through higher taxes during times when liquidity constraints are less prevalent, the government can improve the intertemporal allocative efficiency of the economy as a whole. This argument for fiscal stabilization would hold even if reductions in demand did not have Keynesian consequences in the form of wasted idle capacity and underutilization of labor. They are, of course, reinforced by Keynesian failures of goods and labor markets. The political economy issues associated with temporary borrowing or monetization (the time-consistency of such fiscal-financial strategies) is an issue that is not addressed in my work. The design of political institutions that will support wise stabilization policy (especially 'reversible-in-present-value-terms' deficit financing) is an important issue, but there is no need to wait for its resolution before we can begin to think systematically about the nature of optimal stabilization policy. The analysis of optimal policy under the assumption of full credibility (or ability to pre-commit) also makes us more aware of the costs of the inability to pre-commit and may act as a spur to institutional reform.

The construction of the solvency constraints is, of course, no substitute for the modeling of economic behavior. The paper emphasizes this repeatedly. It comes up, for example, when it is pointed out that the 'human capital' relevant to the behavior of the private sector is the human capital of those currently alive, while the present discounted value of future taxes on labor income in the public sector's solvency constraint includes the labor income taxes paid by future generations. Only when those currently alive are linked to these future generations through a chain of operative intergenerational gifts or bequests will the future tax streams constraining private and public behavior be the same.

The short Chapter 5 is an excerpt from a much longer paper (Buiter, 1987b), written as a background paper for the preparation of the 1988 *World Development Report* of the World Bank. It is included here to demonstrate the practical uses that can be made of the government's solvency constraint, even with very limited data and unlimited reluctance to make projections about the likely future behavior of public spending, conventional tax revenues and inflation tax revenues. It contains calculations for the main industrial countries of the constant or permanent primary surpluses (as a percentage of GDP) required to stabilize the public debt burden. It also shows that in recent years seigniorage (measured as the ratio of the change in the base money stock to GDP) has been a negligible source of government revenue in all the major industrial countries with the notable exception of Italy.

1.3 CROWDING OUT

Part III, 'Crowding Out', is the longest in the volume. It contains the most careful statements about why and how public debt and deficits matter and emphasizes the distinction between 'financing issues', i.e. the choice between tax financing, money financing and bond financing of a given 'exhaustive' public spending program, and 'public expenditure issues', the analysis of the consequences of variations in the size and composition of the exhaustive public spending program for a *given* financing mode. Didactically, it is probably best to analyze the consequences of variations in public spending in a balanced budget setting, with lump-sum taxes (if they are available) or broadly based distortionary taxes (if lump-sum taxes are not available) varying endogenously to maintain budget balance. A bond-financed increase in public consumption spending would then be viewed as the sum of two distinct kinds of fiscal policy actions: a balanced budget increase in public consumption expenditure and a tax cut financed by borrowing.

After developing a taxonomy of 'crowing out' in Chapter 6 (Buiter, 1977), the 'microfoundations' of debt neutrality and its absence are developed in Chapters 7 and 8 (Buiter, 1988c; 1989). Chapter 7 is the only essay in this volume to make serious technical demands on the reader. Some early empirical tests of the debt neutrality proposition are reported in Chapter 9 (Buiter and Tobin, 1979) and the economy-wide consequences of alternative fiscal-financial strategies when there is absence of debt neutrality are analyzed in two further joint papers with James Tobin, Chapters 10 and 11 (Tobin and Buiter, 1976; 1980).

The search for sufficient causes for absence of debt neutrality involves the study of individual and aggregate private consumption behavior. Having obtained an aggregate consumption function for which taxes today and taxes (equal in present value) tomorrow are not equivalent, we can embed it in a simple dynamic aggregative general equilibrium model and analyze the consequences of public debt and deficits for the behavior of the economic system as a whole, i.e. for interest rates, saving, capital formation, inflation and, in open economic systems, for the trade balance and real and nominal exchange rates. The two 'microfoundations' essays in Part III (Chapters 7 and 8), while written about a decade after Chapters 10 and 11 (which deal with general equilibrium aspects of crowding out and crowding in), are logically prior to them, as they provide sets of conditions under which (something like) the *ad hoc* aggregate consumption functions of Chapters 10 and 11 can be rationalized. Part III would likewise be incomplete without the simple aggregative general equilibrium models of Chapters 10 and 11 and the means they provide for doing systematic policy analysis.

Chapter 6 grew out of my Ph.D. thesis. It develops a taxonomy of 'crowding out' which I still consider useful. Apart from the *degree* of crowding out or crowding in (crowding out is seldom an all-or-nothing phenomenon) and the *time horizon* under consideration (impact or short-run, intermediate or long-run), the main distinction is between *direct* and *indirect* crowding out. Direct crowding out (or crowding in) refers to effects of public actions (mainly exhaustive spending) that occur because these public actions enter directly as arguments in private utility functions or production possibility sets. Examples are public consumption or investment spending that may be complementary with or a substitute for private consumption or investment spending. Such public actions affect private behavior even at given prices (including interest rates) and without directly affecting the private budget constraints.

Indirect crowding out refers to the consequences of public actions that affect private behavior either by altering private budget constraints or by influencing the prices faced by private agents. The effect on private consumption behavior of the substitution of borrowing for current lump-sum taxes, holding constant the magnitude and composition of the exhaustive public spending program, is an example.

This issue is explored at length in Chapter 7. Following Barro's (1974) famous restatement of the proposition, first formalized (and rejected as implausible) by Ricardo (1817; 1820), that operative intergenerational gift and bequest motives would effectively turn an overlapping generations economy with finite-lived households into a single infinite-lived representative household whose consumption behavior would not be affected by intertemporal redistributions of lump-sum taxes, I had made two earlier attempts at a more satisfactory formalization of these ideas (Buiter, 1979b; 1980). While Buiter (1979b) had serious flaws, Buiter (1980), which benefited from the work of Carmichael (1979; 1982) (see also Buiter and Carmichael, 1984), contained a satisfactory analysis of the case of 'one-sided' intergenerational caring (i.e. the case where a person cares directly either about his children or about his parents but not about both). It also contained the proposition that stationary competitive equilibria with an operative child-to-parent gift motive are inefficient (the interest rate is below the growth rate). The reason for this is that parental utility, while valued positively, is discounted by the child. Contrary to the case of the infinite-lived representative consumer, therefore, earlier consumption (by earlier generations) is valued less than later consumption (by the current generation).

The case of 'two-sided' intergenerational caring was still not handled satisfactorily in Buiter (1980). It was the work of Kimball (1987a; 1987b) that provided an elegant solution to this problem. His approach is reproduced, essentially unchanged, in the first part of Chapter 7. His model of consumer behavior is then embedded in a neoclassical growth model in the style of Diamond (1965) and is used to analyze the implications of deficit financing, unfunded social security retirement schemes and variations in exhaustive public spending.

The second half of the paper reviews, reinterprets and extends the Yaari–Blanchard–Weil OLG model. The absence of debt neutrality in the Blanchard (1985) OLG model with uncertain lifetimes was initially attributed to the presence of uncertain lifetimes and (effectively) finite horizons for private consumers. This in contrast to governments, whose effective time horizons (assuming they do not repudiate the debts incurred by themselves or by previous governments) are infinite. Weil (1985; 1987) showed that even when each individual consumer lives for ever, debt neutrality will be absent if there is a positive birth rate and if there is no operative intergenerational gift and bequest motive. In Buiter (1988a) I showed that not only was the assumption of uncertain lifetimes not necessary for debt neutrality in the Yaari–Blanchard–Weil model, it was not sufficient either. In that model a positive birth rate is both necessary and sufficient for absence of debt neutrality. The reason is that in the Yaari–Blanchard–Weil model with its constant (age-independent) instantaneous probability of death, all survivors, regardless of age, have the same life expectancy. With a zero birth rate, postponing lump-sum taxes on labor income therefore does not alter the choice set of any of the agents that are currently alive. If, on the other hand, different survivors have different life expectancies, then postponing lump-sum taxation on labor income will redistribute resources towards those with shorter time horizons. In most cases, this will boost aggregate consumption. A positive birth rate means, even with common (possibly infinite) horizons for those currently alive, that by postponing taxes part of the tax burden can be shifted to the new-born, thus boosting the consumption of those already alive.

The general insight is that for debt neutrality to break down, changes in the pattern over time of lump-sum taxes should redistribute resources between heterogeneous consumers. Representative agent models therefore preclude the possibility of absence of debt neutrality. Capital market imperfections only provide a mechanism for departures from debt neutrality if they affect different private agents in different ways.

Recently, Bernheim and Bagwell (1988) have shown that if all private agents in the economy are linked, directly or indirectly, by operative gift motives, not only will intergenerational redistributions of lump-sum taxes be neutral, so will all distortionary fiscal actions except for variations in the volume or composition of exhaustive public spending. Given typical marriage patterns (ignored in Kimball's and my own work) such comprehensive interpersonal caring is argued to be quite likely, although the likelihood of interior solutions for voluntary interpersonal giving remains an unknown. Kimball's finding — that in his model without strategic gift and bequest motives, no one would make positive voluntary transfers to related contemporaries (siblings, first cousins, second cousins, etc.) — suggests that corner solutions may be quite likely. Regardless of the issue of the likelihood of interior solutions for voluntary transfers between private units, I confess to being uncertain as to what to make of this analysis. In particular, I worry about what appear to be assumptions about strategic behavior by households that seem incompatible with 'small' households taking prices, government behavior and voluntary gifts by all other households as parametric.

The short Chapter 8 (Buiter, 1989) points out that the breakdown of debt neutrality (in the absence of operative intergenerational gift motives) when there is a positive birth rate assumes (implicitly) that the taxes that are being redistributed over time and between generations are lump-sum taxes on *labor* income. If instead the tax falls on the income from a non-human factor ('land') whose ownership claims are priced efficiently, then, if all land is owned by generations currently alive, changes in the inter-temporal pattern of taxation do not permit current generations to shift the tax burden to future generations nor do they permit short-lived households currently alive to shift part of the tax burden to households with a longer life expectancy. In the absence of slavery, the human capital of future generations is not owned by anyone alive today and postponing lump-sum taxes on labor income will indeed make those currently alive better off.

Chapter 9 was written jointly with James Tobin, who has had such a major influence on my perception of the substance and process of economic discourse. After reviewing the history of economic thought on the subject (an exercise that left me permanently in awe of the formidable analytical skills of Ricardo), we present some econometric consumption function estimates to test our view on the irrelevance of debt neutrality. The econometric testing of propositions derived from intertemporal optimizing models has made rapid strides since 1979 when this paper was written. Both estimation methods based on the intertemporal first-order conditions of a representative optimizing agent (so-called 'Euler equation' methods; see, for example, Hall, 1978; and Hansen and Singleton, 1983) and methods based on closed-form decision rules (for example, Leiderman and Razin, 1988) have been used to test the debt neutrality hypothesis, directly or by implication.

It is fair to say that many (though by no means all) of the recent tests have failed to reject the null hypothesis of debt neutrality. This leaves in a bit of a quandary those who, like myself, believe that public debt and deficits matter for reasons other than a neoclassical desire to smooth the time pattern of distortionary tax rates. Still, even if the debt neutrality proposition were correct, there would be no cost (other than possibly in terms of suboptimal distortionary tax rate smoothing) to the government acting as if debt is not neutral. The converse obviously does not hold. If debt neutrality fails, a government acting on the mistaken belief that debt is neutral could do real damage.

Chapter 10, also written with James Tobin, was the first paper to be published with my name on it (albeit in second position). The first part is a 'sensitivity analysis' of Blinder and Solow (1973), which studied the long-run effects of public spending and tax changes under different financing rules. In a fixed price-level Keynesian model with demand-determined output and taxes an increasing function of output, bond financing of deficits (with public spending exogenous) will tend to generate instability unless a larger volume of public debt lowers the primary (non-interest) deficit by more than it increases the interest burden. This will happen only if debt has a strong positive effect on consumption demand (no debt neutrality) and a weak effect on the demand for money. We consider alternative spending rules that may stabilize the debt process by reducing exhaustive spending when interest payments increase. The last part of the paper analyzes money and debt financing in a full-employment, flexible price level model in which an endogenous capital stock generates variations over time in the level of capacity output.

Chapter 11, again written with James Tobin, consists of two parts. The first is an extensive, non-technical discussion of crowding out, debt neutrality, monetary neutrality and monetary superneutrality. The second

16   *Introduction*

part develops a class of dynamic stock-flow models that are then used to analyze some fiscal and financial policy issues in closed and open economic systems.

The models are so-called 'end-of-period' equilibrium models (see Foley, 1975; and Buiter, 1979a), rather than 'beginning-of-period' equilibrium models, so the goods market equilibrium condition (*IS*) and the asset market equilibrium conditions (*LM*, etc.) are dimensionally commensurate. While both beginning- and end-of-period models can be used to tell essentially the same story, the latter have the expository and didactic advantage of clearly showing the current period flow-of-funds (government and external deficits) entering into the current period market-clearing conditions.

The private sector behavioral relationships (asset demand functions, investment function, etc.) are not derived from optimizing first (or last) principles but are based on sound *ad hoc* judgement. Expectations are taken to be predetermined in the short run, although in steady state (a neoclassical balanced growth path) expectations are realized. Impact effects of fiscal and financial policy are derived for Keynesian and full-employment versions of the model and long-run comparative static propositions are derived for the full employment version of the model. It is my belief that such models, while currently somewhat out of fashion, have a lot of useful mileage left in them.

1.4 THE FISCAL ROOTS OF INFLATION

The two papers in Part IV, 'The Fiscal Roots of Inflation', take up some unfinished business in Sargent and Wallace's analysis of the eventual monetization of fiscal deficits (Sargent and Wallace, 1981; Sargent, 1982). Once the public debt burden has reached its upper limit, monetary growth is residually determined given the primary public sector deficit, the real interest rate and the real growth rate. In his application of this approach to four historical hyperinflations, Sargent (1982) attributed the hyperinflations to excessive fiscal deficits and argued that a credible reduction in the fiscal deficit was a necessary condition for ending these hyperinflations. While I do not necessarily disagree with this diagnosis, it cannot, unfortunately, be derived from and supported by the formal model of Sargent and Wallace (1981). With rational expectations, this model cannot generate a hyper-inflationary outcome. In Chapter 12, which contains a continuous-time analogue of the discrete-time model of Sargent and Wallace, I first reproduce their finding that their model either has two stationary (constant inflation) equilibria (for low fiscal deficits as a proportion of GDP), or one or none (for large fiscal deficits). Of these two stationary equilibria (in the case of low deficits), the low-inflation equilibrium is on the friendly side of the long-run seigniorage Laffer curve, while the high-inflation equilibrium is on the unfriendly or slippery slope of the long-run seigniorage Laffer curve. With rational expectations the low inflation equilibrium is locally unstable and the high inflation equilibrium is locally stable. (The price level and thus the inflation rate are taken to be non-predetermined in the Sargent–Wallace model, so the existence of a locally stable stationary equilibrium creates problems of non-uniqueness.) When the deficit gets to be so large that no stationary equilibrium exists, the non-convergent, 'explosive' solutions are in fact 'implosive' ones. We *cannot* get a process of forever rising inflation and falling real money balances. That would put us further and further on the wrong side of the (non-steady-state) seigniorage Laffer curve; the deficit could not be financed at all and no solution would exist.

There appear to be solutions with a forever falling (and increasingly negative) inflation rate and a forever rising stock of real money balances (or seigniorage tax base). As we now are on the efficient side of the seigniorage Laffer curve, the deficit can be financed. Unfortunately, a forever rising stock of real money balances (indeed one which rises without bound) is inconsistent with equilibrium in the Sargent–Wallace model. On the (perhaps doubtful) principle that you cannot start what you will not finish, the 'hyperdeflation' solution is then ruled out. Excessive deficits imply that there exists *no* solution, not a hyperinflationary solution in the Sargent–Wallace model with rational expectations.

Sargent has suggested interpreting a move from the (locally unstable) low inflation equilibrium to the (locally stable) high inflation equilibrium as a hyperinflation. There seems to be little in common between, on the one hand, a transition in the Sargent–Wallace model from one steady rate of inflation to another steady rate of inflation (both supported by the same deficit–GDP ratio) and, on the other hand, the explosive, runaway hyper-inflations of the historical record. The inflation rate corresponding to the high-inflation steady state will, for reasonable money demand functions, also be orders of magnitude below the peak inflation rates experienced during historical hyperinflations.

If the rational expectations assumption is dropped and replaced, say, by adaptive expectations, the low-inflation steady state (in the moderate deficit case with two stationary equilibria) may become locally stable and the high-inflation steady state locally unstable. While this eliminates Sargent's interpretation of a hyperinflation as a transition from a low-inflation steady state to a high-inflation steady state (for a given deficit), the divergent, explosive solution in the case of large deficits when there is no stationary equilibrium now is indeed a hyperinflation. This, of course, is merely Cagan's (1956) original model.

There are bound to be ways of tinkering with the money demand function, the primary government deficit or the price formation process, that will make hyperinflations consistent with rational expectations. The current crop of straightforward Cagan-style money demand functions augmented with price-level- and inflation-rate-independent primary government deficits does, however, force one to make a choice between hyperinflations and rational expectations.

Chapter 13 also focuses on countries in which further increases in the internal and external debt burden are impossible and monetary financing has become the residual financing mode. While the paper also explores the slippery slope of the seigniorage Laffer curve, its main point can be made most transparently when the government still operates in the range where higher inflation generates larger seigniorage revenue.

Public spending cuts aimed at reducing the primary deficit and thus the rate of inflation may have the opposite effect if the spending cuts take the form of reductions in productive public expenditure. I refer to such spending as public sector investment, although there are categories of current public expenditure that may have similar characteristics (education, maintenance of infrastructure, public administration, tax collection, etc.).

A reduction in public sector capital formation will, *ceteris paribus*, reduce the deficit one-for-one. Set against this *expenditure effect*, there can be a *direct revenue effect*, reflecting the consequences of a lower public sector capital stock on the direct cash returns the government obtains from its ownership of the public sector capital stock. In addition, there are *indirect revenue effects*, which comprise the implications of a lower public sector capital stock for domestic output and thus for production-, income- or sales-related tax revenues. Note that the direct and indirect revenue effects exclude the Keynesian revenue effect which will obtain if output is demand-determined and a reduction in public spending reduces aggregate demand and thus GDP and GDP-related tax revenues.

A lower level of productive public sector capital expenditure may therefore end up increasing rather than reducing the public sector deficit and thus increasing rather than reducing the public sector's 'demand for seigniorage revenue'. It may also, by reducing income, reduce the demand for real money balances and with it the private sector's 'supply of seigniorage revenue'. This adverse *money demand effect* creates further scope for an adverse response of inflation to ill-conceived policies aimed at reducing the public sector deficit by cutting public expenditure.

1.5 FISCAL AND FINANCIAL POLICY IN DEVELOPING COUNTRIES

The last part of this volume contains a single longish paper, Chapter 14, which is a synthesis of two working papers written for the World Bank as background papers for the preparation of the 1988 *World Development*

Report (*WDR*). It clearly reflects the many discussions I have had on these issues with Sweder van Wijnbergen.

In this paper we come full circle, in terms of the concerns expressed in Chapter 2, by considering the whole gamut of stabilization, allocative and distributional aspects of fiscal and financial policy. The application here of the methods and theories developed in the earlier essays to the problems of restoring internal and external balance and of achieving structural adjustment in developing countries, should serve to emphasize the wide applicability of these approaches.

The paper analyzes in a non-technical manner the role of fiscal policy in the restoration of internal and external macroeconomic equilibrium and in achieving structural adjustment, i.e. major changes in the patterns of intersectoral and intertemporal resource allocation.

The external transfer problem and the associated internal fiscal and real resource transfer problems, as well as some of the distributional issues that are likely to arise, are discussed with special emphasis on possible causes of the breakdown of the internal and external transfer processes. Again the concepts of sectoral and national solvency are seen to be useful for the evaluation of the mutual consistency and feasibility of fiscal, financial and monetary plans. The strengths and weaknesses of some operational methods for evaluating the consistency of fiscal plans and inflation objectives (see, for example, Anand and van Wijnbergen, 1987) are also evaluated.

Each of the subjects discussed in this volume is very much 'alive', both as an area of academic and intellectual investigation and as a policy issue. I very much hope that the reader will share the sense of excitement and indeed of fun that I experienced while writing these essays.

1.6 REFERENCES

Akerlof, G. and J. Yellen (1985a) 'A near rational model of the business cycle, with wage and price inertia', *Quarterly Journal of Economics*, August, pp. 823–38.

Akerlof, G. and J. Yellen (1985b) 'Can small deviations from rationality make significant differences to economic equilibria?', *American Economic Review*, 75, September, pp. 708–20.

Akerlof, G. and J. Yellen (1986) *Efficiency Wage Models of the Labor Market*, Cambridge University Press, Cambridge.

Akerlof, G. and J. Yellen (1988) 'How large are the losses from rule of thumb behavior in models of the business cycle?', mimeo, May.

Anand, R. and S. van Wijnbergen (1987) 'Inflation and the financing of government expenditure in Turkey: an introductory analysis', World Bank mimeo, revised, June.

Auerbach, A.J. and L.J. Kotlikoff (1987) *Dynamic Fiscal Policy*, Cambridge University Press, Cambridge.

20   *Introduction*

Barro, Robert J. (1974) 'Are government bonds net wealth?', *Journal of Political Economy*, 82, November–December, pp. 1095–117.
Barro, Robert J. (1979) 'On the determination of the public debt', *Journal of Political Economy*, 87, October, pp. 940–71.
Barro, Robert J. (1987) 'Interest rate smoothing' University of Rochester, NY, mimeo.
Bernheim, B. and K. Bagwell (1988) 'Is everything neutral?', *Journal of Political Economy*, 96, April, pp. 308–38.
Blanchard, Olivier J. (1981) 'Output, the stock market and interest rates', *American Economic Review*, March.
Blanchard, Olivier J. (1985) 'Debt, deficits and finite horizons', *Journal of Political Economy*, 93, April, pp. 223–47.
Blanchard, Olivier J. and N. Kiyotaki (1987) 'Monopolistic competition and the effects of aggregate demand', *American Economic Review*, 77, September, pp. 647–66.
Blinder, A.S. and R.M. Solow (1973) 'Does fiscal policy matter?', *Journal of Public Economics*, 2, pp. 319–37.
Blinder, A.S. and R.M. Solow (1974) *The Economics of Public Finance*, The Brookings Institution, Washington, DC.
Buiter, Willem H. (1977) '"Crowding out" and the effectiveness of fiscal policy', *Journal of Public Economics*, 7, pp. 309–28 (also Chapter 6, this volume).
Buiter, Willem H. (1979a) *Temporary and Long-run Equilibrium*, Garland Publishing, New York.
Buiter, Willem H. (1979b) 'Government finance in an overlapping generations model with gifts and bequests', in G.M. von Furstenberg (ed.), *Social Security vs. Private Saving*, Ballinger, Cambridge, MA, pp. 395–429.
Buiter, Willem H. (1980) '"Crowding out" of private capital formation by government borrowing in the presence of intergenerational gifts and bequests', *Greek Economic Review*, 2, August, pp. 111–42.
Buiter, Willem H. (1982) 'Deficits, crowding out and inflation: the simple analytics', Centre for Labour Economics, London School of Economics, Discussion Paper no. 143.
Buiter, Willem H. (1983) 'Measurement of the public sector deficit and its implications for policy evaluation and design', *IMF Staff Papers*, 30, June, pp. 306–49 (also Chapter 4, this volume).
Buiter, Willem H. (1984a) 'Comment on T.J. Sargent and N. Wallace: Some unpleasant monetarist arithmetic' in B. Griffith and G.E. Wood (eds), *Monetarism in the United Kingdom*, Macmillan, London, pp. 42–60.
Buiter, Willem H. (1984b) *Allocative and Stabilization Aspects of Budgetary and Financial Policy*, London School of Economics, London (also Chapter 2, this volume).
Buiter, Willem H. (1985) 'A guide to public sector debt and deficits', *Economic Policy*, 1, November, pp. 14–61, 70–9 (also Chapter 3, this volume).
Buiter, Willem H. (1987a) 'A fiscal theory of hyperdeflations? Some surprising monetarist arithmetic', *Oxford Economic Papers*, 39, March, pp. 111–18 (also Chapter 12, this volume).
Buiter, Willem H. (1987b) 'The current global economic situation, outlook and policy options, with special emphasis on fiscal policy issues', CEPR Discussion Paper, no. 210, November.
Buiter, Willem H. (1988a) 'Death, birth, productivity growth and debt neutrality', *Economic Journal*, 98, June, pp. 279–83.
Buiter, Willem H. (1988b) 'The right combination of demand and supply policies:

the case for a two-handed approach' in H. Giersch (ed.), *Macro- and Micro-Policies for More Growth and Employment*, Kiel Institute of World Economics, Kiel.

Buiter, Willem H. (1988c) 'Debt neutrality, redistribution and consumer heterogeneity' in W.C. Brainard *et al* (eds), *Essays in Honor of James Tobin*, MIT Press, Cambridge, MA (also Chapter 7, this volume).

Buiter, Willem H. (1988d) 'Can public spending cuts be inflationary?', CEPR Discussion Paper no. 225, April (also Chapter 13, this volume).

Buiter, Willem H. (1988e) 'Some thoughts on the role of fiscal policy in stabilization and structural adjustment in developing countries', Centre for Labour Economics, London School of Economics, Discussion Paper no. 312, June (also Chapter 14, this volume).

Buiter, Willem H. (1989) 'Debt neutrality, Professor Vickrey and Henry George's "Single Tax"', *Economics Letters*, 29, pp. 43–7 (also Chapter 8, this volume).

Buiter, Willem H. and J. Carmichael (1984) 'Government debt: comment', *American Economic Review*, 74, pp. 762–5.

Buiter, Willem H. and James Tobin (1979) 'Debt neutrality: a brief review of doctrine and evidence' in G.M. von Furstenberg (ed.), *Social Security versus Private Saving*, Ballinger, Cambridge, MA, pp. 39–63 (also Chapter 9, this volume).

Cagan, P. (1956) 'The monetary dynamics of hyperinflation' in M. Friedman (ed.), *Studies in the Quantity Theory of Money*, Chicago, University of Chicago Press.

Carmichael, J. (1979) 'The role of government financial policy in economic growth', Ph.D. thesis, Princeton University.

Carmichael, J. (1982) 'On Barro's theorem of debt neutrality: the irrelevance of net wealth', *American Economic Review*, 72, March, pp. 202–13.

Cooper, R. and A. John (1988) 'Coordinating coordination failures in Keynesian models', *Quarterly Journal of Economics*, 103, August, pp. 441–63.

Diamond, Peter (1965) 'National debt in a neo-classical growth model', *American Economic Review*, 55, December, pp. 1126–50.

Diamond, Peter (1982) 'Aggregate demand management in search equilibrium', *Journal of Political Economy*, 90, pp. 881–94.

Diamond, Peter (1988) 'Credit in search equilibrium' in Meir Kohn and Sho-Chieh Tsiang (eds), *Finance Constraints, Expectations and Macroeconomics*, Oxford University Press, Oxford, pp. 36–53.

Feltenstein, Andrew (1986) 'An intertemporal general equilibrium model of financial crowding out: a policy model and some applications to Australia', *Journal of Public Economics*, 31, October, pp. 79–104.

Foley, Duncan (1975) 'On two specifications of asset equilibrium in macroeconomic models', *Journal of Political Economy*, 83, April, pp. 305–24.

Hall, Robert E. (1978) 'Stochastic implications of the life cycle-permanent income hypothesis', *Journal of Political Economy*, 86, December, pp. 971–88.

Hansen, Lars P. and K.J. Singleton (1983) 'Consumption, risk aversion and the temporal behavior of asset returns', *Journal of Political Economy*, 91, April, pp. 1269–86.

Kimball M. (1987a) 'Making sense of two-sided altruism', *Journal of Monetary Economics*, 20, September, pp. 301–26.

Kimball, M. (1987b) 'Making sense of two-sided altruism' in Kimball, 'Essays on intertemporal household choice', Ph.D. thesis, Harvard University, Chapter 2.

Kotlikoff, L.J. (1988) 'The deficit is not a well-defined measure of fiscal policy', *Science*, 241, 12 August, pp. 791–5.

Kydland, Finn and Edward C. Prescott (1980) 'A competitive theory of fluctuations and the feasibility and desirability of stabilization policy' in Stanley Fischer (ed.), *Rational Expectations and Economic Policy*, Chicago University Press, Chicago, pp. 169–87.

Leiderman, L. and A. Razin (1988) 'Testing Ricardian neutrality with an intertemporal stochastic model', *Journal of Money, Credit and Banking*, 20, February, pp. 1–21.

Lucas, Robert E. (1978) 'Asset prices in an exchange economy', *Econometrica*, 46, pp. 1429–45.

Lucas, Robert E. and Nancy L. Stokey (1983) 'Optimal fiscal and monetary policy in an economy without capital', *Journal of Monetary Economics*, 12, pp. 55–93.

Lucas, Robert E. and Nancy L. Stokey (1987) 'Money and interest in a cash-in-advance economy', *Econometrica*, 55, May, pp. 491–513.

Mankiw, N.G. (1987) 'The optimal collection of seigniorage: theory and evidence', *Journal of Monetary Economics*, 20, September, pp. 327–41.

Minford, Patrick (1985) 'Comment', *Economic Policy*, 1, November, pp. 64–8.

Phelps, E.S. (1973) 'Inflation in the theory of public finance', *Swedish Journal of Economics*, 75, pp. 76–82.

Ricardo, David (1817) *On the Principles of Political Economy and Taxation*, London.

Ricardo, David (1820) 'Funding System' in Piero Sraffa (ed.), *The Works and Correspondence of David Ricardo*, Vol. IV, Cambridge University Press, Cambridge (1951).

Rotemberg, Julio J. (1987) 'The New Keynesian microfoundations' in Stanley Fischer (ed.), *N.B.E.R. Macroeconomics Annual 1987*, MIT Press, Cambridge, MA, pp. 69–104.

Sargent, T.J. (1982) 'The ends of four big inflations' in R.E. Hall (ed.), *Inflation: Causes and Effects*, University of Chicago Press, Chicago, pp. 41–97.

Sargent, T.J. and N. Wallace (1981) 'Some unpleasant monetarist arithmetic', *Federal Reserve Bank of Minneapolis Quarterly Review*, 5, Fall.

Shleifer, A. and R.W. Vishny (1988) 'The efficiency of investment in the presence of aggregate demand spillovers', *Journal of Political Economy*, 96, December, pp. 1221–31.

Tanzi, V. (1978) 'Inflation, real tax revenue and the case for inflationary finance: theory with an application to Argentina', *IMF Staff Papers*, Vol. 25, September.

Tobin, James and Willem H. Buiter (1976) 'Long-run effects of fiscal and monetary policy on aggregate demand' in J. Stein (ed.), *Monetarism*, North Holland, Amsterdam, pp. 273–309 (also Chapter 10, this volume).

Tobin, James and Willem H. Buiter (1980) 'Fiscal and monetary policies, capital formation and economic activity' in G. Von Furstenberg (ed.), *The Government and Capital Formation*, Ballinger, Cambridge, MA, pp. 73–151 (also Chapter 11, this volume).

Weil, P. 'Essays on the valuation of unbacked assets', Ph.D. thesis, Harvard University.

Weil, P. (1987) 'Love thy children: Reflections on the Barro debt neutrality theorem', *Journal of Monetary Economics*, 19, pp. 377–91.

PART I

SETTING THE SCENE

2 · ALLOCATIVE AND STABILIZATION ASPECTS OF BUDGETARY AND FINANCIAL POLICY

2.1 INTRODUCTION

The subject matter of this paper is the principles that should govern the design of budgetary and financial policy. While some of what I shall be saying will have a faint tinge of originality, much of it will — or should be — familiar. My excuse for restating the obvious is a growing concern about the low level of public and political debate on the vital subject matter of fiscal and financial policy design, both in the United Kingdom and in the rest of the industrial world, and about the failure of academic economists to make much of a contribution to this debate.

One would expect the public debate about fiscal and financial policy to focus on the subjects outlined, for example, in Atkinson and Stiglitz (1980, p. 8). Among the most important are:

1. The distribution of wealth and income.
2. The supply of and demand for public goods.
3. 'Merit wants' and the legitimacy and limits of government paternalism.
4. Externalities in production and consumption.
5. Appropriate responses to departures from the textbook ideal of perfect competition.
6. Policy responses to incomplete futures and insurance markets.
7. The failure of markets (especially the labor market) to clear.

The trivialization of the public debate about budgetary and financial policy becomes evident at the international level when the International Monetary Fund lectures finance ministers and heads of central banks on a theme that, with only slight exaggeration, can be summarized as follows: public sector deficits, and especially increases in public sector deficits, are bad always and everywhere, regardless of circumstances, and discretionary spending cuts and/or tax increases should be implemented to reduce these deficits always and everywhere regardless of circumstances (de Larosière, 1982). The messages emanating from the Commission of the European Communities in Brussels and from the Secretariat of the OECD in Paris are only slightly less unqualified.

The economics profession itself must bear a large share of the blame for this trivialization of the debate about fiscal and financial policy. The academic study of fiscal and financial policy is split into two virtually non-communicating sub-disciplines. Certain individual economists may work in both sub-disciplines, but even for them the compartmentalization within their own research tends to be almost complete. The two sub-disciplines in question are the 'microeconomic' theory of neoclassical public finance and the 'macroeconomic', neo-Keynesian theory of stabilization policy.

There are excellent standard textbooks, such as Prest and Barr (1979) and Musgrave and Musgrave (1976), which cover fiscal stabilization policy in a relatively short and self-contained section without any attempt at integrating it with the main part of the book. Blinder *et al.* (1974) has one hundred pages on fiscal and financial stabilization policy in which is heard not a discouraging word about distribution, incentives, incidence, dead-weight losses, excess burdens, externalities, natural monopolies, merit wants or public goods. This is followed by one hundred pages of discussion on incidence and economic effects of taxation which is predicated on an assumption of continuous full employment of resources. The recent leading text on neoclassical public finance, Atkinson and Stiglitz (1980), which has already been referred to, limits its consideration of stabilization and macroeconomic policy to the statement that 'no attempt is made to cover stabilization and macroeconomic policy' (p. 4). Macroeconomic approaches, which almost invariably specify exhaustive public spending as consisting of digging holes in the ground and filling them in again and which limit their perspective on taxation to its impact on current disposable income and on the magnitude of a multiplier whose microfoundations tend to be implicit and therefore insecure, can no longer be taken seriously. Neoclassical analyses of public finance issues which are conditioned on an assumption of continuous full employment of resources and perfect capital markets (except for imperfections introduced by the government itself, e.g. through taxation) belong firmly to the realm of inapplicable economics. Unfortunately, the two half-truths do not together make a whole truth; one does not teach a person to walk using two legs by first teaching her to balance and hop along on the left leg only and then on the right leg only.

There are a few hopeful signs that this sorry state of affairs may be changing slowly. More tax, transfer and subsidy parameters are making an appearance in our classroom macroeconomic models. We now include in our teaching the effects of payroll taxes, value added taxes and other indirect taxes or subsidies on the notional demand for labor; direct taxes, transfers and subsidies and benefits are arguments in our notional labor supply functions; the distinction between before- and after-tax interest rates and rates of return plays a role in investment, saving and portfolio allocation in some recent macroeconomics, etc. Most of this, however, amounts to no more than paying lip service to A-level supply-side economics, with the greater realism of the tax-transfer-subsidy structure being purchased at the price of removing all interesting non-Walrasian features from labor, output and capital markets.

Much the more interesting and promising work aimed at integrating the two worlds of budgetary and financial policy follows the considerably harder route of explicitly building up a non-Walrasian equilibrium approach within which a role for stabilization policy (or its absence) can be derived from first principles instead of being imposed at a very late stage when its relationship to economic fundamentals has been lost completely in the semi-reduced-form equations that make up all policy-oriented macroeconomic models.

Two distinct, but in my view potentially complementary, approaches can be identified, one developing the asymmetric information paradigm, the other emphasizing imperfect competition. Examples of the second approach are Weitzman (1982) and Hart (1982a). The former is exemplified by papers of Stiglitz and Weiss (1981; 1983) and Webb (1981; 1982). They show how non-cooperative behavior and asymmetric information can create the same problems of adverse selection and moral hazard in credit markets that were first observed and analysed formally in insurance markets. A prima-facie case for government intervention in the financial mechanism is thus shown to exist. At the same time applications of the asymmetric information paradigm to the labor market (Weiss, 1981; Grossman and Hart, 1981; and Hart, 1982b) have established the logical possibility of non-Walrasian and socially sub-optimal and inefficient equilibria (some of which may even look like 'Keynesian' rationing equilibria) being generated as the outcome of optimizing, decentralized, non-cooperative behavior.

Since the most interesting role and widest scope for stabilization policy will be generated by the coexistence and interaction of significant imperfections in credit or capital markets and in the labor market, these developments are very exciting indeed. Rather than speculating on developments that may occur (or are likely to occur), I shall retreat to safer ground and discuss with some more confidence a few firmly established facts and a few controversial propositions.

Equity and efficiency should be the ultimate concerns of budgetary and financial policy, as of all policy. For our purposes, we can think of equity as the distribution of income and wealth — between individuals, households or other groups, categories or classes in the same and/or different generations. Efficiency considerations can, following the traditional approach, be subdivided into allocative efficiency and stabilization efficiency. Stabilization policy is policy aimed at influencing (and, one hopes, minimizing) deviations from full employment equilibrium. Allocative policy aims to influence the full employment equilibrium configuration itself. According to this definition there can be no stabilization policy in the instantaneous equilibrium models of the New Classical School. It is possible to modify the definition by differentiating between a 'full information' equilibrium (i.e. an equilibrium in which agents possess complete information on all relevant contemporaneous and past endogenous and exogenous variables) and an incomplete information equilibrium. Even in the hyperactive invisible-hand models of the New Classical School, alternative budgetary and financial policy rules can, in general, alter the information content of currently observed endogenous variables such as prices and thus influence the deviations of the actual from the full information equilibrium (Turnovsky, 1980; Weiss, 1980; Buiter, 1980b; 1981; King, 1982). Such 'stabilization' policy can then be distinguished from allocative policy actions or rules which aim to influence the full information equilibrium itself.

I hope that this paper will convey my strong conviction that the distinction between allocative and stabilization policy, ingrained though it is in our thinking, fundamentally makes no sense, even conceptually. In practice (i.e. both in the real world and in the 'practice' of the abstract models we work with), virtually every budgetary or financial (including monetary) policy action will have distributional, allocative and stabilization consequences. It is true, unfortunately, that budgetary or financial actions are often undertaken with just specific distributional, allocative or stabilization objectives in mind and with complete disregard for the inevitable side effects.

Consider, for example, the proposal to cut exhaustive public spending and reduce taxes at the same time in such a way as to keep the public sector deficit constant. The objectives are the allocative ones of freeing resources for private absorption and of creating more favorable tax incentives for the supply of effort. If there is any merit in the balanced budget multiplier theorem, this budgetary action will have contractionary stabilization consequences. The distributional consequences both of the spending cuts and the tax reductions are likely to be important but are seldom analyzed satisfactorily. Unintended longer-term allocative consequences are likely if, as in the United Kingdom since 1979, all cuts in public sector spending on goods and services have fallen on public sector capital formation.

In summary, there exist no 'pure' stabilization policy instruments. It takes a very convoluted set of allocative policy actions to leave the degree of underutilization of resources unaffected. Equity and efficiency are inextricably intertwined. In what follows I shall, for reasons of space, not be concerned with the distributional *objectives* of the authorities, although the distributional *consequences* of policies undertaken for allocative or stabilization purposes will not be ignored.

2.2 PUBLIC SPENDING ON GOODS AND SERVICES

The most general approach to budgetary and financial policy design would involve the optimal joint determination of the public sector's consumption and investment programs and their method of financing. Rather than pursuing such a grand design, Section 2.3 below is limited to a less ambitious consideration of some of the issues that arise in connection with the optimal financing of a given program of 'exhaustive' public spending on goods and services. The determination of the size and composition of this spending program is not considered there. In this section I only restate some home-truths about public spending and reproduce some familiar facts about recent developments in the United Kingdom. No attempt at systematic or complete coverage of the subject is made.

The presentation of public spending in the Financial Statement and Budget Report is almost completely uninformative. No distinction is made between exhaustive spending on goods and services, transfer payments and the cost of servicing the national debt. No distinction is made either between current or consumption spending and capital formation.[1] All of these belong to distinct functional categories. Lumping them together and specifying policy objectives in terms of the resulting aggregate is at best an example of incomplete policy design and in all likelihood represents a recipe for fiscal mismanagement.

The breakdown of total public spending on goods and services into consumption and investment is essential but fraught with conceptual and practical difficulties. Much of what is conventionally classified as final public spending on goods and services does not in fact constitute value added or net national product at all (i.e. is neither consumption nor investment), but should properly be classified as production of intermediate services which are used up as inputs in the production of true value added in both public and private sectors. Law and order and (on a favorable interpretation) defense fall into this category. Even though they may be essential intermediate inputs without which no value added could be created at all, they are not value added themselves and should be excised from the national income, expenditure and production accounts.

The official statistics on public sector consumption and investment contain many further ambiguities. Does 'current' expenditure on education represent investment in human capital, the consumption of enjoyable education services, or both? Is 'current' spending on health akin to depreciation, to net investment in human capital, to the provision of intermediate input services or to final consumption? If we ignore these deep

Table 2.1 General government expenditure, United Kingdom, 1973–82 (percentage of GDP at market prices)

	Goods and services	Current grants and subsidies	Debt interest
1973	25.1	11.2	3.7
1974	25.6	13.4	4.3
1975	26.3	13.6	4.0
1976	25.5	13.6	4.3
1977	24.2	13.5	4.4
1978	23.4	14.0	4.3
1979	23.2	14.1	4.6
1980	23.7	14.4	5.0
1981	24.5	15.5	5.3
1982	23.1	15.9	5.2

Source: *Economic Trends*, September 1983, and *Annual Supplement*, 1983.

issues and take the published data at face value, the following startling and worrying picture emerges from Tables 2.1, 2.2 and 2.3.

Since the early 1970s general government consumption has grown roughly in line with national income, with its share in GDP hovering just above 20 per cent. The Thatcher government has cut this rate of growth somewhat relative to that prevailing under the previous Labour government, but has not reduced the level of real spending. General government fixed capital formation has been in decline, as a proportion of GDP and in volume terms, since its peak in 1973. Note that this policy of shifting resources from the future to the present has had bipartisan support. Between 1973 and 1979 general government gross fixed investment declined steadily by 41 per cent in volume terms.

Since 1979 a further 40 per cent reduction has taken place. Of the 64.6 per cent reduction in real general government gross fixed investment between 1973 and 1982 only 10.6 percentage points can be attributed to the decline in public sector construction of dwellings. The nationalized industries have suffered a decline in gross domestic fixed capital formation since 1976, when the Labour government chose the politically most convenient way of implementing the expenditure cuts involved in the IMF package. Between 1976 and 1981 there was a real decline of 22 per cent. The period 1981–2 saw the first swallow of hope with a small (1.6 per cent) increase.

Capital consumption figures are notoriously imprecise. For what they are worth, the official figures in Table 2.3 suggest that net public sector fixed investment in assets other than dwellings was insignificantly different from zero in 1982!

Few would argue that the United Kingdom is overendowed with social

Table 2.2 Public sector consumption and gross domestic capital formation, United Kingdom, 1973–82

	General government consumption		General government gross domestic fixed capital formation		Public corporations' gross domestic fixed capital formation	
	at 1980 prices (1980 = 100)	as a percentage of GDP at market prices	at 1980 prices (1980 = 100)	as a percentage of GDP at market prices	at constant prices (1975 = 100)	as a percentage of GDP at market prices
1973	88.4	20.0	197.9	5.1	93.3	2.9
1974	89.8	20.7	185.1	4.9	106.2	3.4
1975	94.6	21.8	170.24	4.5	116.7	3.7
1976	95.5	21.3	164.9	4.2	120.4	3.7
1977	94.5	20.8	137.0	3.4	110.2	3.3
1978	96.5	20.5	121.5	2.9	103.4	3.0
1979	98.3	20.4	116.7	2.8	102.1	2.9
1980	100.0	21.3	100.0	2.4	100.0	2.9
1981	99.8	22.6	74.6	1.9	93.8	2.9
1982	101.2	21.4	70.2	1.7	95.3	2.8

Source: Economic Trends, September 1983.

Table 2.3 Net domestic fixed capital formation at current prices by the public sector, United Kingdom, 1973–82 (£ million)

	1973	1974	1975	1976	1977	1978	1979	1980	198	1982
Dwellings										
Public corporations	101	141	244	308	257	186	193	195	12	79
Central government	26	35	30	25	23	17	10	11	2	2
Local authorities	593	885	1,158	1,363	1,267	1,249	1,232	1,219	51	897
Other fixed assets										
Public corporations	298	542	840	990	511	216	231	213	-11	-116
Central government	568	684	904	996	829	772	962	1,013	1,0 8	1,304
Local authorities	1,564	1,674	1,515	1,417	877	540	536	286	-2 7	-1,173

Source: National Income and Expenditure, 1983.

overhead capital and infrastructure. The statistical evidence of increasing underinvestment and indeed of decumulation of capital documented in Tables 2.1–2.3 is reinforced by ample anecdotal and impressionistic evidence of a country lumbered with an antiquated, often obsolete and crumbling stock of social overhead capital. Not only does it contribute to the prevailing drabness and shabbiness of much of our living and working environment, it is also bound to constitute a major obstacle to sustained recovery and higher economic growth. Both cyclical and structural (or stabilization and allocative) arguments favor a major expansion of public sector investment in infrastructure.

Table 2.1 also documents some tendency towards trend growth in the share of transfer payments and subsidies in GDP and the effect of the post-1979 depression. High interest rates and the slump have also boosted debt interest service as a proportion of GDP. With even a modest recovery and barring major reversals in the anticipated downward path of world real interest rates, the debt service–GNP ratio is likely to decline again in years to come.

There is no single figure that summarizes adequately the many different facets of public sector size and the role and cost of public sector activity. Indeed, there is no sharp discontinuity separating public sector and private sector activity. The public sector is a very heterogeneous and multi-faceted collection of organizations, agencies and agents. Its boundaries with the private sector cover a very large gray area.

For certain purposes the volume of public sector exhaustive spending may be of interest. It measures public sector 'absorption' of goods and services; in a fully employed economy public sector absorption must 'crowd out' private absorption or increase the current account deficit. Efficient public spending policy involves the balancing at the margin of these private absorption losses against the benefits from public sector absorption. For other purposes public sector employment may be the relevant index of size. The total tax burden, or its breakdown into various subtotals, may be of interest. Efficiency considerations suggest focusing attention on excess burdens and dead-weight losses associated with non-lump-sum tax-transfer and subsidy schemes rather than on the share of taxes in national income and similar measures. The political economy of the budgetary process may well, however, be centered more around the total tax burden and the (actual or perceived) equity of its distribution than around the academic economist's notions of efficiency. Further information about the size of the public sector is conveyed by measures of the public sector capital stock and by other items in the public sector balance sheet.

Much harder to quantify is the scope of government activity in the economy through regulation, jaw-boning, red tape and other administrative interventions. A government regulation that every British worker should between 11 a.m. and 3 p.m. attend to her duties while standing on her head, would not register in any of the conventional indices of government size and scope but would represent a major intervention indeed.

Paying attention to the details of the size and composition of the government's spending program on goods and services is essential if we are to become serious about modeling what I have called 'direct crowding out' of private consumption and investment by public spending (Buiter, 1977). Direct crowding out (or 'crowding in') refers to substitution or complementarity relationships between public and private spending that occur not through changes in prices, interest rates or required rates of return engendered by changes in public sector activity, but through public sector consumption being an argument in private utility functions and through the public sector capital stock being an argument in private sector production functions. Direct substitution, in varying degrees, can be expected between, for example, public and private education, and between free school lunches and private lunches. Direct complementarity between public sector capital formation (roads) and private investment (factories) is likely to be important.

It is unfortunate that wide-ranging governmental cost–benefit analyses of the whole range of public spending programs effectively have to be conducted in secret. Since resources are scarce (or would be scarce given a sensible demand and supply management policy) every appropriation and every program should be the subject of critical scrutiny as a matter of course and on a regular basis, both as regards the appropriateness or degree of priority attached to the objectives and as regards the efficiency with which these objectives are pursued.

It is my belief that a critical reassessment of ends and means in public spending will reveal the need and scope both for greatly improved efficiency in the provision of public services, through higher-quality management and an attack on restrictive practices, and for a steady and sizeable increase in public sector consumption and capital formation, in real terms and as a proportion of GNP. While there is a case for a significant reallocation of resources within the public sector, there is an equally strong case for a reallocation of resources toward the public sector as a whole. Demographic developments such as the graying of our population and new developments in medical care, for example, argue for an increase in the share of total resources going to health care. Both on equity and efficiency grounds the case for the public sector supplying the health services and for funding this operation out of general revenues is overwhelming. With all its shortcomings, the National Health Service is the outstanding contribution of post-war Britain to the world's very small stock of workable ideas for improving the quality of life in an affordable manner.

Demographic trends notwithstanding, education is another area where there will have to be a significant increase in available resources if the

United Kingdom is to avoid becoming an industrial and intellectual back-water. Again equity and efficiency considerations suggest the public provision and financing of these services. The vast majority of teenagers are educated badly, whether one views education as a consumption good or as an investment in skills and knowledge necessary for economic survival, let alone prosperity. The proportion of the late teens to early twenties age group attending institutions of higher education has been lower in the United Kingdom than in any other industrialized country. Recent cuts in higher education spending have adversely affected both the quantity and quality of advanced training and research. Adult education (full-time and part-time) and retraining are seriously underfunded. The bill for such myopic policies is, of course, not presented to the nation immediately but it will surely have to be paid in due course.

Allocating additional resources to health and education, and to public sector capital formation in the form of spending on roads, bridges, tunnels, water supply, drains and sewers, railroads, airports, hospitals, facilities for the infirm, handicapped and aged, telecommunications, etc., may not in all cases be a *sufficient* condition for increasing and improving the effective supply of these goods and services. 'Throwing money' at these areas is, however, in my judgement, a *necessary* condition for improved performance in many cases.

A properly managed UK economy could generate much of the additional resources for increased public spending through growth in productivity at a high level of resource utilization, without any need for absolute reductions in the volume of private absorption or for larger current account deficits. Given my own priorities, I would favor an expansion of public spending on goods and services which, once the slack created by the recent depression has been worked off, is likely to involve at least a temporary real reduction in private absorption brought about through a rise in the overall tax burden. It will require skilful manipulation of the tax mechanism to achieve one's preferred division of this reduction in private absorption between cuts in private consumption and in private investment.

An attractive by-product of this proposed increase in exhaustive public spending is its favorable implications for employment, both directly through the creation of public sector service jobs and indirectly through increased public sector procurement of private sector goods and services (e.g. construction). All indications are that future employment growth will be primarily in the services sector — private and public, market and non-market. This reality is not fully recognized by the present government because of an ideological bias against 'things public'. It is not fully recognized by the Labour opposition because of its historical identification with traditional manufacturing and extractive industry and its resulting tendency to confuse the promotion of employment with the maintenance, even at very high costs, of existing jobs in industries embodying yester-year's comparative advantage.

2.3   FINANCING THE PUBLIC SECTOR SPENDING PROGRAM, OR WHEN ARE DEBT AND DEFICITS GOOD FOR YOU?

This section deals with some of the issues that arise in connection with the optimal financing of a given program of 'exhaustive' public spending on goods and services. Government financial policy is about the management of the public sector balance sheet, broadly defined. It includes the choice of taxation versus borrowing. It also concerns the composition or structure of taxes (lump-sum, direct, indirect, degree of progression, etc.) and the characteristics of the debt instruments issued by the government (interest-bearing or non-interest bearing, legal tender, maturity, degree of indexing, etc.). Monetary policy, exchange rate management and foreign exchange market intervention therefore belong to financial policy as much as open market operations or bond issues 'to finance the deficit'. It should be obvious that questions concerning the distribution of income and risk (intra-generational as well as intergenerational) are inevitably bound up with questions relating to the financing of a given real spending program (see, for example, Stiglitz, 1983a; 1983b). All the work I shall be discussing allows fully for the 'government budget constraint' — the identity that public spending must be financed through taxes, through borrowing, by creating high-powered money or by running down official foreign exchange reserves. Most of it follows the recent conventional wisdom of assuming model-consistent or 'rational' expectations.

Like any other kind of government intervention in the economy, government financial policy can be rationalized in one of two ways. The first is intervention for purely distributional reasons. While they are of major importance, I shall for reasons of space not pay any attention in what follows to the distributional objectives of the government. The distributional consequences of alternative financing rules will, however, be central. Indeed financial policy influences real economic variables largely by affecting the intertemporal and interpersonal (including intergenerational) distribution of income, wealth and risk. The second justification for financial policy is the identification of instance(s) of market failure or, more generally, failure of decentralized private action, together with the attribution to the government of the ability to undertake remedial welfare-improving actions that private agents either cannot undertake or do not find in their own perceived self-interest to undertake.

The market 'imperfections' central to an appreciation of the potential welfare-improving role of financial policy are capital market or credit market imperfections. Included in this are any restrictions on the ability of private agents to effect intertemporal transfers of purchasing power in either direction at the social intertemporal terms of trade. In the theoretical domain of our profession, as exemplified by the overlapping generations (OLG) model with finite lives and without operative intergenerational gifts and bequests, the incompleteness of the set of forward markets (or the absence of a full set of Arrow–Debreu securities) is due to the 'technological' constraint that the dead cannot consume goods and services and the legal constraint that private agents cannot impose binding financial obligations on the unborn. In real life this non-existence of certain forward markets is augmented by a wide array of capital market imperfections. Private agents are constrained in their spending plans by the illiquidity and non-marketability of certain assets such as pension rights and human capital (including expected future income tax cuts). Collateral requirements limit access to credit, etc.

These cash flow constraints, liquidity constraints, lack of suitable collateral, non-marketability of assets and a host of similar capital market imperfections need not take the form of strict credit rationing but may instead merely be reflected in a market price of credit that is in excess of its shadow price.

My inability to borrow on the same terms as the UK government is, of course, not in and of itself evidence of market failure. The recent applications, already referred to, of the theory of market equilibrium under asymmetric information to credit markets (see, for example, Webb, 1981; Stiglitz and Weiss, 1981; 1983), however, have shown how adverse selection or moral hazard can generate privately rational but socially inefficient equilibria that may be characterized by credit rationing, excessive spreads between lending and borrowing rates, etc.

Granted the existence of significant and persistent capital market imperfections, does the 'opportunity set' of the government differ from and in certain respects dominate that of private agents? Can the authorities do things private agents cannot or will not do? In the OLG model, there are two features that differentiate private and public opportunity sets. First, the institution of government is longer-lived than the individual private agents. Frequently endowed with eternal life, governments can in these models enter into implicit or explicit contracts that extend beyond the lifespan of any given generation. In this way governments can be a substitute for some of the non-existent forward markets. Second, the authorities have the power to tax, i.e. the power to impose unrequited charges or payments on individuals. For good reasons, governments are exceedingly jealous of this power and discourage private agents from assuming this prerogative — it is classified as theft when exercised on private initiative.

The power to tax enables the government to redistribute income between members of the same generation at a point in time, over time for (a

group of) individuals and between generations. This power to tax is also
the reason why, in an uncertain world, governments can borrow on terms
that are superior to those faced by private agents.[2] Total current and future
national income is, subject to political constraints on the tax burden, the
collateral for government borrowing. The risk of default through insolvency
(but not of discretionary or dishonest default) is therefore less for government bonds than for private debt. Most governments also have the power
to determine what shall be legal tender. Almost all have opted for a government monopoly of legal tender, thus adding directly to the attractiveness of
those of their liabilities designated as legal tender (their monetary liabilities)
and indirectly improving the quality of all public debt. Most of the other
differences between private and public opportunity sets referred to in the
literature derive from the greater longevity of the institution of government
and the government's power to tax.[3] The view of government financial
policy I am advocating has governments acting as (potentially) superior
financial intermediaries, changing the composition of private sector portfolios over time and altering private disposable income flows. Well-designed
policy interventions of this kind exploit governments' 'comparative advantage' in borrowing to smooth out income streams and facilitate risk sharing.
By exploiting their position as the 'natural borrower', or borrower of first
resort, governments can minimize the extent to which disposable income,
current cash flow and the portfolio of liquid, marketable or realizeable assets become binding constraints on private consumption, investment, production and portfolio allocation decisions.

This view of financial policy is at the opposite end of the spectrum from
the ancient 'debt neutrality' position as restated by Barro (1974) (see also
Buiter, 1979; 1980a; and Carmichael, 1982). Debt neutrality (i.e. invariance
of the real solution trajectories of the economy under changes in the
borrowing-taxation mix), prevails if financial policy cannot affect the intertemporal (including the intergenerational) distribution of income and of
risk and the intertemporal terms of trade. With infinite-lived households
or, equivalently, finite-lived households characterized by an operative
chain of intergenerational gift and bequest motives, with private access to
capital markets on the same terms as the government and with unrestricted
lump-sum taxes and transfers, public sector financial policy is irrelevant.
Relaxing any or all of these exceedingly restrictive assumptions causes this
Modigliani–Miller theorem for the public sector to break down and a
potential welfare-improving role for active financial policy to emerge.

Active financial policy is most easily defined as the orthogonal complement of passive financial policy. Passive financial policy I define as
balanced budget financial policy, i.e. a continuous or period-by-period
matching of receipts and expenditures.[4] Active financial policy permits,
under specified conditions, systematic, predictable and even persistent departures from budget balance.

Active financial policy, as just defined, has a wide range of functions and consequences, only a few of which can be considered here. By influencing the interpersonal, intertemporal and intergenerational distribution of income, it will affect risk sharing, the extent to which households can smooth consumption over the life cycle and capital formation. All this can occur and can be welfare improving in models in which goods and labor markets clear continuously and lump-sum taxes and transfers are possible.

2.3.1 Minimizing the excess burden of non-lump-sum taxes

If lump sum taxes are not feasible, the timing of distortionary taxes will influence the total excess burden or dead-weight loss imposed on the economy. The same will hold if tax collection costs in any given period are a more than linearly increasing function of the marginal or average tax rate in that period. Again this applies in labor and output market clearing models.

Recently Barro (1979; 1981) and Kydland and Prescott (1980) have applied a well-known 'uniform taxation' theorem in neoclassical public finance to the macroeconomic problem of optimal public sector debt and deficits in an economy with continuous full employment. In the absence of uncertainty and given suitable symmetry, homogeneity and separability assumptions, it is optimal to levy wage taxes at a constant proportional rate throughout an individual's lifetime (see Sandmo, 1974; 1976; Sadka, 1977; and Atkinson and Stiglitz, 1980). The argument assumes the non-availability of lump-sum taxes and subsidies. The original public finance literature on the subject was formulated in terms of the dead-weight loss or excess burden of fiscal programs involving distortionary taxes. Barro's papers also consider the further possibility of tax collection costs being an increasing and strictly convex function of the ratio of the net total tax take to the tax base. For a stochastic environment, Barro (1981) has argued that the deterministic constant planned tax rate solution translates approximately into a Martingale process for the tax rate τ, i.e. the *expected* future tax rate is equal to the current tax rate:

$$E(\tau_{t+i}/\Omega_t) = \tau_t \quad i \geq 0 \tag{2.1}$$

where E is the conditional expectation and Ω_t the information set conditioning expectations formed at time t.

In spite of many theoretical and practical objections to the strict 'uniform expected tax rates over time' proposition, the notion that it is optimal to smooth planned tax rates relative to planned exhaustive public spending because collection costs and/or excess burdens increase more than linearly with the tax rate, is likely to be robust. In the strict version of equation (2.1) the theory implies that a temporary increase in public spending unaccompanied by a matching increase in real output (the tax base) should be financed at least in part by borrowing. A transitory increase in real output will, given public spending, be associated with a budget surplus. The 'countercyclical' behavior of the deficit that will characterize the economy if the exogenous level of output follows a regular cyclical pattern and public spending is constant has nothing to do with Keynesian fiscal stabilization policy or the operation of the automatic stabilizers, however. These are considered next.

In a world with persistent labor market and/or output market disequilibrium, the capital market imperfections that are the *sine qua non* of financial policy spill over into the markets for output and labor. For example, the existence of the multiplier, which is due to the inclusion of current disposable income as an argument in the private consumption function, over and above its contribution to permanent income (calculated using social discount rates), reflects a capital market imperfection — the difficulty of borrowing against the security of anticipated future labor income. In a fixed price model with demand-constrained output and employment the operation of the multiplier amplifies the effect of demand shocks on output and employment. Financial policy entailing temporary deficits may be the appropriate government response.[5] These Keynesian arguments for running larger deficits (smaller surpluses) when effective demand is depressed and smaller deficits (larger surpluses) when effective demand is buoyant are familiar and valid. Tax cuts in the face of negative demand shocks (or the 'automatic' decline of taxes and rise in transfer payments when economic activity falls, which is written into most existing tax and benefit laws) help maintain disposable income. To the extent that disposable income rather than permanent income is the binding constraint on private demand, such active financial policy helps reduce fluctuations in output and employment. In Keynesian models, with workers off their notional labor supply schedules and possibly also firms off their notional demand curves for labor, avoiding demand-induced swings in real activity is sensible policy.

By reducing taxes (net of transfers) and increasing borrowing during the downswing, exhaustive public spending during the downswing will be financed to a larger extent by private agents who are not constrained by current disposable income — the purchasers of the bonds. Total consumption demand will therefore decline by less than if taxes, which I assume to fall equally on disposable-income-constrained and permanent-income-constrained private agents, had been kept constant during the downswing. When the economy recovers, the additional debt incurred during the downswing can be repaid out of higher than normal taxes. The demand effects of cyclical tax cuts during the downswing and tax increases during the upswing may not be symmetric if, as seems likely, more private agents are constrained in their spending by current disposable income during the downswing than during the upswing.

The smoothing out of consumption over the cycle permitted by counter-cyclical financial policy would be desirable because of its intertemporal allocative effects even if product and factor markets cleared. Its virtues are enhanced by the initial demand-disturbance-amplifying presence of labor and output market disequilibrium. Without labor and output market imperfections, successful stabilization policy permits consumption plans that are constrained only by a given permanent income. With labor and output market disequilibria successful stabilization policy, in addition, raises permanent income.

When used for cyclical stabilization, successful financial policy should not imply any trend increase in the real stock of debt or in the debt–output ratio. If long real interest rates are increasing functions of current and anticipated future deficits, the transitory and reversible deficits that are associated with countercyclical policy should have at most minor effects on long real interest rates. Short nominal and real interest rates can be controlled by temporary and reversible partial monetization of deficits. Thus, by raising the level of activity, countercyclical deficits absorb private saving in the short run without lowering the capital stock in the long run. If long real interest rate determination is more myopic, even short-run and reversible increases in deficits and debt may lead to significant crowding out of interest-sensitive private spending. Again such crowding out can be avoided by monetizing part of the deficit. Provided this monetization is reversed (and is *expected* to be reversed) in proper countercyclical fashion during the upswing, it should have no effect on trend monetary growth and thus on inflationary expectations. Without real resource scarcities, financial crowding out is merely bad financial policy.

The balanced budget multiplier theorem would appear to suggest that any desired response to demand shocks can be achieved without deficits by varying both exhaustive public spending and taxes net of transfers. I would argue that, to a first order approximation, optimal budgetary stabilization policy of this kind would involve varying taxes and transfers in response to demand shocks while leaving the path of public consumption and investment spending unchanged.

The government's spending program on goods and services should be designed to achieve the best feasible public–private consumption mix out of permanent national income. The tax-transfer-borrowing and money creation rules should be aimed at optimizing national permanent income, keeping private disposable income in line with private permanent income and ensuring an adequate share of disposable, realizable (financial) private wealth in total or comprehensive private wealth, which includes such illiquid assets as human capital.

42   *Setting the scene*

The above applies to the *optimal* design of exhaustive spending policies and financing policies. If, as in the United Kingdom today, certain categories of public spending (especially social overhead capital formation) have been cut to levels that are well below most reasonable notions of optimality, and if at the same time a 'Keynesian' fiscal boost to aggregate demand is desirable, both structural (or allocative) and stabilization purposes can be served by a larger volume of spending on goods and services.

2.4 CONCLUSION

I shall conclude by restating and re-emphasizing the grounds for a complete revaluation of conventional attitudes towards public sector deficits.

First, from a wide variety of perspectives, ranging from Keynesian to Classical, optimal or even merely sensible, budgetary policy is bound to be characterized by systematic, predictable and sometimes persistent departures from budget balance. Even in long-run equilibrium, zero is not a uniquely interesting figure for the budget deficit. A constant debt–output ratio *is* a requirement of stationary long-run equilibrium. The optimal value of this ratio is unlikely to be zero.

Second, the conventionally measured public sector deficit (level or change, at current prices, at constant prices or as a proportion of GDP) has a very high noise-to-signal ratio as an indicator of anything that might be of economic interest. The same holds, however, also for the cyclically corrected, full employment or high employment deficit. The use made of these statistics is a symptom of the search for the unattainable: a single-figure, model-free measure of fiscal impact or of some other relevant aspect of budgetary and financial policy.

Neither the 'raw' deficit nor the cyclically corrected deficit, neither the permanent deficit nor the constant net worth deficit[6] is a measure of the short-run impact on effective demand of fiscal policy. The first two deficit constructs also fail as useful measures of (changes in) potential short-, medium- or long-run financial crowding-out pressure. Indeed, in the absence of real resource scarcities, financial crowding out is simply evidence of bad financial policy. At full employment complete short-run crowding out of private spending or the current account surplus by public spending is unavoidable, no matter what the financial policy. Only the last two deficit constructs are useful indicators of the sustainability of the fiscal stance and of the consistency of spending, taxation, crowding out and monetary objectives; the 'raw' and the cyclically corrected deficit also fail as informative indicators of the eventual monetization implied by the fiscal stance.

The familiar point, emphasized in Blinder and Solow (1974), that there are no 'model-free' measures of short- or long-run fiscal policy impact

Table 2.4 Public Sector Financial Balance, United Kingdom, 1978–83 (percentage of market price GDP)

Financial Years	(1) Actual balance	(2) Year to year change	(3) Built-in stabilizers	(4) Cyclically-adjusted budget change
1978–79	−4.9			
1979–80	−3.6	+1.3	0.1	1.2
1980–81	−4.7	−1.1	−3.1	2.0
1981–82	−2.4	+2.3	−1.9	4.2
1982–83	−2.7	−0.3	−0.7	0.4
Sum of changes	—	2.2	−5.6	7.8
(Sum of 'weighted' changes)	$(0.2)^a$		$(-3.4)^b$	$(3.7)^c$

Notes: sources and methods.
Column 1: PSFD/GDP at market prices. *Source: Economic Trends.*
Column 2: Change from previous year in column 1.
Column 3: From *NIER*, February 1983, p. 8, Table 2, row 3 less row 1.
Column 4: Column (2) less column (3).
Figures in parentheses: From *NIER*, February 1983, p. 8, Table 2 (calculated as (a) sum of row 2; (b) sum of row 4 less sum of row 2; (c) = (a) − (b)).

cannot be fudged. A recent paper on the behavior of the UK economy since 1979 (Buiter and Miller, 1983) reproduces an attempt of the National Institute of Economic and Social Research to calculate the impact effect on demand of fiscal policy in the four years since 1979. The figures are given in Table 2.4. They suggest that the demand effect of the government's spending and tax program changes was to remove almost 4 per cent from demand in the economy. This characterization of fiscal policy as severely contractionary is consistent with the direct evidence of a major increase in the tax burden, documented in Table 2.5.

The 'demand-weighted' (i.e. adjusted for marginal propensity to spend on domestic output) cyclically corrected deficit shown in Table 2.4 (last line) is the proper index of the short-run (first-round) demand effect of fiscal policy only in a static, rather old-Keynesian and expectations-innocent model. The first best approach would be to simulate one's preferred model of the economy under different values of fiscal and financial policy parameters and to call the difference between the solution trajectories (or the statistics describing them) the measure of fiscal impact. Such proper measures of fiscal stance will therefore be model-specific, have time subscripts attached to them, and be functions of when a particular fiscal or financial action (or rule change) was first anticipated, of its antici-pated degree of permanence, and of the degree of confidence with which these expectations are held.

Table 2.5 The UK tax burden, 1978–83

	Average tax burden* (%)	Average tax rate of employee on average earnings** (%)	Marginal tax rate of employee on average earnings† (%)	Marginal direct tax rate of married couple in basic rate band† (%)
1978	34.11	47.0	54.6	33.6
1979	34.93	48.0	55.1	30.1
1980	36.64	49.0	55.4	30.2
1981	38.83	51.5	56.9	31.0
1982	39.81	51.4	57.3	32.4
1983		51.2	57.5	33.2

Source: A.W. Dilnot and C.N. Morris, 'The Tax System and Distribution 1978–83', *Fiscal Studies*, vol. 4, no. 2, May 1983, pp. 54–64.
* Direct and indirect taxes, national insurance, etc., contributions as a percentage of GDP at market prices, expenditure estimate.
** Direct and indirect taxes, national insurance contributions, etc., as a percentage of gross income (including employers national insurance contribution).
† Marginal rate of income tax plus employees national insurance contributions for a married couple in the basic rate band. *Source*: same as above.

This may seem like a tall order and perfectionism is indeed often the last refuge of those unwilling to stick their necks out. To admit that progress towards a better policy-oriented modeling of budgetary and financial policy will be difficult is not, however, to condone the continuation of the naive PSBR targeting that has been the cause of so much avoidable distress in the UK economy and elsewhere.

Putting together these comments on the PSBR with my earlier discussion of public spending, it will come as no surprise that I consider a complete rethink of budgetary and financial policy a precondition for a sustained recovery and for a lasting improvement in the economic determinants of the quality of life.

2.5 NOTES

1. Note that the distinction between consumption and capital spending matters not because it is proper to borrow in order to finance the latter but not the former. There is nothing wrong in principle with borrowing for consumption today by private or by public agents, as long as one plans accordingly for a level of future consumption that is lower than it would otherwise have been by an amount sufficient to cover payment of interest and maintain solvency. In the neoclassical regions of our profession there is a flourishing literature on consumption loan models which deals precisely with this subject.
2. Clearly IBM borrows on better terms than the state of Grenada. The insertion of the word 'most' before 'governments' and 'private agents' would, however, merely clutter up the text.

3. For example, Webb (1981) shows how government financial policy will be non-neutral in a world with asymmetric information, if it is less costly for the government to extract taxes from reluctant taxpayers than it is for private lenders to compel performance by dishonest borrowers.
4. Weakly passive financial policy permits balanced budget redistribution; strictly passive financial policy compels taxes and taxes net of transfers and subsidies to be the same. It is well-known that, for example, in the overlapping generations model of Diamond (1965), a balanced budget social security scheme implemented through lump-sum taxes on the young and lump-sum transfer payments to the old will depress capital formation. Most balanced budget intertemporal or intergenerational redistribution schemes can be reproduced in terms of their effects on all real endogenous variables by unbalanced budget policies involving public sector borrowing or lending. For example, the social security scheme just mentioned is isomorphic to government borrowing with debt service financed by new debt issues and by lump-sum taxes on the young.
5. First best policy would eliminate the market imperfections. The discussion assumes that this has been pursued as far as is possible.
6. For a discussion of the last two deficits, see Chapter 3.

2.6 REFERENCES

Atkinson, A.B. and J.E. Stiglitz (1980) *Lectures on Public Economics*, McGraw-Hill, New York, London.
Barro, Robert J. (1974) 'Are government bonds net wealth?', *Journal of Political Economy*, 82, November–December, pp. 1095–117.
Barro, Robert J. (1979) 'On the determination of the public debt', *Journal of Political Economy*, 87, October, pp. 940–71.
Barro, Robert J. (1981) 'On the predictability of tax rate changes', NBER Working Paper no. 636, February.
Blinder, A.S. and R.M. Solow (1974) *The Economics of Public Finance*, The Brookings Institution, Washington, DC.
Buiter, Willem H. (1977) ' "Crowding out" and the effectiveness of fiscal policy', *Journal of Public Economics*, 7, pp. 309–28 (also Chapter 6, this volume).
Buiter, Willem H. (1979) 'Government finance in an overlapping generations model with gifts and bequests' in G. von Furstenberg, ed. *Social Security versus Private Saving*, Ballinger, Cambridge, pp. 395–429.
Buiter, Willem H. (1980a) ' "Crowding out" of private capital formation by government borrowing in the presence of intergenerational gifts and bequests', *Greek Economic Review*, 2, August, pp. 111–42.
Buiter, Willem H. (1980b) 'Monetary, financial and fiscal policy under rational expectations', *IMF Staff Papers*, 27, December, pp. 758–813.
Buiter, Willem H. (1981) 'The superiority of contingent rules over fixed rules in models with rational expectations', *Economic Journal*, 91, September, pp. 647–70.
Buiter, Willem H. and Marcus H. Miller (1983) 'The macroeconomic consequences of a change in regime: the U.K. under Mrs. Thatcher', *Brookings Papers on Economic Activity*, 2.
Carmichael, J. (1982) 'On Barro's theorem of debt neutrality: the irrelevance of net wealth', *American Economic Review*, 72, March, pp. 202–13.
Diamond, Peter (1965) 'National debt in a neo-classical growth model', *American Economic Review*, 55, December, pp. 1126–50.

de Larosière, J. (1982) 'Restoring fiscal discipline; a vital element for economic recovery', International Monetary Fund, Washington, DC, March.

Grossman, S.J. and O.D. Hart (1981) 'Implicit contracts, moral hazard and unemployment', *American Economic Review*, Papers and Proceedings.

Hart, O.D. (1982a) 'A model of imperfect competition with Keynesian features', *Quarterly Journal of Economics*, no. 386, February, pp. 109-38.

Hart, O.D. (1982b) 'Optimal labour contracts under asymmetric information: an introduction', London School of Economics, ICERD Theoretical Economics Discussion Paper Series, no. 44.

King, R.G. (1982) 'Monetary policy and the information content of prices', *Journal of Political Economy*, 90, April, pp. 247-79.

Kydland, Finn and Edward C. Prescott (1980) 'A competitive theory of fluctuations and the feasibility and desirability of stabilization policy' in Stanley Fischer (ed.), *Rational Expectations and Economic Policy*, University of Chicago Press, Chicago, pp. 169-87.

Musgrave, R.A. and P.B. Musgrave (1976) *Public Finance in Theory and Practice*, 2nd edn, McGraw-Hill, New York.

Prest, A.R. and N.A. Barr (1979) *Public Finance in Theory and Practice*, 6th edn, Weidenfeld and Nicolson.

Sadka, E. (1977) 'A theorem on uniform taxation', *Journal of Public Economics*, 7, June, pp. 387-91.

Sandmo, A. (1974) 'A note on the structure of optimal taxation', *American Economic Review*, 64, September, pp. 701-6.

Sandmo, A. (1976) 'Optimal taxation: an introduction to the literature', *Journal of Public Economics*, pp. 37-54.

Stiglitz, Joseph E. (1983a) 'On the relevance or irrelevance of public financial policy', *NBER Working Paper*, no. 1057, January.

Stiglitz, Joseph E. (1983b) 'On the relevance or irrelevance of public financial policy: indexation, price rigidities and optimal monetary policy', *NBER Working Paper*, no. 1106, April.

Stiglitz, Joseph E. and A. Weiss (1981) 'Credit rationing in markets with imperfect information', *American Economic Review*, 71, June, pp. 393-410.

Stiglitz, Joseph E. and A. Weiss (1983) 'Incentive Effects of Terminations', *American Economic Review*, 73, December, pp. 912-27.

Turnovsky, S.J. (1980) 'The choice of monetary instruments under alternative forms of price expectations', *Manchester School*, March, pp. 39-62.

Webb, D.C. (1981) 'The net wealth effect of government bonds when credit markets are imperfect', *Economic Journal*, 91, June, pp. 405-14.

Webb, D.C. (1982) 'Default risk in a model of corporate and government finance', *Journal of Public Economics*, 17, April, pp. 287-306.

Weiss A. (1980) 'Job queues and lay-offs in labour markets with flexible wages', *Journal of Political Economy*, 88, June, pp. 526-38.

Weiss, A. (1980) 'The role for active monetary policy in a rational expectations model', *Journal of Political Economy*, 88, April, pp. 221-3.

Weitzman, M.L. (1982) 'Increasing returns and the foundations of unemployment theory', *Economic Journal*, 92, December, pp. 787-804.

3 · A GUIDE TO PUBLIC SECTOR DEBT AND DEFICITS

3.1 INTRODUCTION

Public sector deficits and the burden of the public debt are once again at the center of macroeconomic policy debate. In Britain the rhetoric and, to a somewhat lesser extent, the reality of the Medium-Term Financial Strategy (MTFS) adopted and pursued since 1980, emphasized the primacy of fiscal orthodoxy and sound money, the former being viewed as a pre-condition for the latter. In continental Europe, countries as diverse as the German Federal Republic, France, Italy, the Netherlands, and Belgium have felt compelled to make the control and reduction of public sector financial deficits a (often *the*) corner-stone of macroeconomic policy design, overriding traditional concerns with the use of fiscal policy and budgetary deficits as cyclical stabilization devices. In the United States, widespread professional concern about steadily growing structural federal deficits is now beginning to be shared by the administration and a major political battle to contain and cut back the deficit through spending cuts and/or tax increases is under way.

The concern about public sector debt and deficits is most easily under-stood when one first considers the extremely rarified set of conditions under which the magnitude of public sector debt and deficits would be irrelevant. Right away, it should be emphasized that 'debt neutrality' or

I would like to thank David Begg, Charles Wyplosz and Charlie Bean for helpful comments on an earlier draft. My two discussants, Patrick Minford and Torsten Persson, made many useful suggestions. The paper develops ideas in Blanchard, Buiter and Dornbusch (1985). Some throwaway remarks by Alan Walters at a conference in September 1984 prompted the discussion of negative multipliers in Section 3.5.

This paper was originally published in *Economic Policy*, 1, November 1985, pp. 13–79.

non-neutrality refers to the absence or presence of real effects from alternative ways of financing a *given* program of spending on goods and services, such as hospitals and defense. Since such expenditure pre-empts or exhausts real resource inputs, I refer to it as exhaustive public spending, in contrast with transfer payments (such as unemployment benefit) which merely transfer purchasing power, and can be regarded as negative taxes. Changes in public sector deficits caused by changes in exhaustive spending will (almost) always have real effects, the only exception being where public consumption or investment is a perfect substitute for private consumption or investment (Buiter, 1977). Barro (1974) has shown that, under extreme assumptions, changes in public sector deficits arising from a switch from tax to bond financing (borrowing) of a given real exhaustive spending program will have no real effects. Later, I will argue that these assumptions are hopelessly unrealistic. Thus, in general, there is no debt or deficit neutrality. The level of debt and deficits matters, and is a legitimate subject of public debate.

In what follows, I shall focus primarily on the consequences of adopting different modes of financing a given program of real exhaustive public spending. These modes are tax finance, bond finance, and base money creation. One reason why public sector deficits have a bad reputation is the view that, sooner or later, the government will resort to printing money to finance the deficit, and that this monetization of the debt will lead to inflation. This proposition is analysed in Section 5.3. A second fear is the doomsday scenario in which the attempt to finance persistent deficits by borrowing leads to a debt-deficit spiral in which the interest payments on an ever larger debt grow explosively. The threat of the bankruptcy of the Exchequer, and the danger of an ultimate repudiation of the public debt, are discussed in Section 3.4.

Section 3.5 addresses crowding out. For a given exhaustive spending program, will a switch from tax to bond finance, and a larger public deficit in consequence, lead to an expansion or contraction of the private economy? Here it is necessary sharply to distinguish two questions: the direction of the impact effect on private demand; and the supply potential of the economy to respond to any such change in aggregate demand. In Section 3.6, I draw together the implications of the preceding sections and discuss the meaning and relevance of various measures of fiscal stance that have been proposed.

3.2   PUBLIC SECTOR DEBT AND DEFICITS IN THE UNITED KINGDOM: SOME STATISTICAL FACTS

The main facts about the behavior of the public sector deficit and debt in the United Kingdom are given in Figures 3.1–3.4 and in Tables 3.1–3.4.

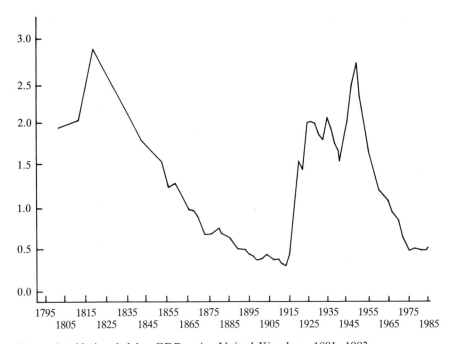

Figure 3.1 National debt–GDP ratio, United Kingdom, 1801–1983

Sources: National debt: Mitchell and Dean (1962); Mitchell and Jones (1971); *Annual Abstract of Statistics* and *Financial Statistics*, various issues. GDP, 1801–51: Mitchell and Deane (1962, p. 366); 1855–1983: Mitchell and Deane (1962, p. 367); and *Economic Trends*, various issues.

Figures 3.1 and 3.2 display very long time series for the debt–GDP ratio and the debt service–GDP ratio, respectively. Figure 3.1 brings out the familiar fact that governments incur most of their debt during or immediately following major wars and use peacetime conditions to reduce the debt–output ratio. The data since 1801 show that the period following the Napoleonic Wars saw the all-time peak of the debt–GDP ratio at 2.88 in 1821. From then until the beginning of the First World War, the debt–GDP ratio declined with only slight interruptions, reaching an all-time low of 0.29 in 1914. This reduction in the debt–output ratio between 1820 and 1914 was brought about partly by debt-retirement (from a peak value of £844.3 million in 1819 to a low of £620.2 million in 1912). A remarkable feature of this period is, however, that this decline in the debt–GDP ratio was accompanied by a steady, if gentle, decline in the general price level. Hence, although it is possible to reduce the real value of nominal debt through inflation (amortization), it was in fact real growth that accounted for the decline in the debt–GDP ratio. After the First World War the debt–GDP ratio reached a 'local' peak of 2.09 in 1924. It then declined

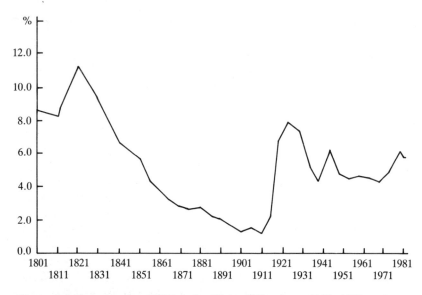

Figure 3.2 Debt service–GDP ratio, United Kingdom, 1801–1983

Note: Pre-1861 estimate of GDP is total gross national income from Mitchell and Deane (1962, p. 366). It applies to Great Britain rather than the UK and omits various services. It is therefore likely to understate GDP. The debt–service GDP ratio is consequently likely to be somewhat biased upwards before 1861.

steadily through the stagnation of the late 1920s and the onset of the Great Depression until it had reached 1.79 in 1930. From 1931 it increased to 2.07 in 1934 after which it fell again until 1940. The Second World War and its aftermath brought a new local peak of 2.72 in 1947. The ratio then declined steadily until 1975 when it reached 0.48. Since the mid-1970s it has remained roughly stationary around 0.50.

Figure 3.2 shows that the behavior of the debt service–GDP ratio for the United Kingdom paralleled that of the debt–GDP ratio from 1821 until 1941. The local peak reached in 1947 was, however, below that of the second half of the 1920s. Debt service declined by less than 2 percentage points of GDP between 1947 and 1973 after which it rose again to its 1946–7 level of 6 per cent of GDP in 1981 with a small decline since then. The stability of the debt service ratio between 1951 and 1971 relative to the decline in the debt ratio is accounted for in large measure by the increase in nominal interest rates over the period. Real interest rates were negative for much of the 1960s and 1970s.

A comparison of the UK's debt–GDP ratio and of its public debt service–GDP ratio with that of the other OECD countries is given in Table 3.1 and Figure 3.3. The debt–GDP ratio of the general government (central and local) in the United Kingdom in 1970 (86.2 per cent) was well above the

Table 3.1 General government debt–service (percentage of GDP)

	Debt outstanding		Debt interest payments	
	1970	1983	1970	1983
United States	46.2	45.8	2.2	4.6
Japan	12.0	66.8	0.6	4.4
West Germany	18.4	41.1	1.0	3.0
France	29.4	32.6	1.1	2.6
United Kingdom	86.2	54.2	3.9	4.9
Italy	44.4	84.5	1.7	9.1
Canada	53.7	55.5	3.8	7.2
Total seven major countries	39.6	50.8	1.9	4.6
Total larger OECD*	38.9	50.7	1.9	4.6

Source: OECD, *Economic Outlook*, December 1984.
* Australia, Austria, Belgium, Canada, Denmark, Finland, France, West Germany, Greece, Italy, Japan, Netherlands, Norway, Spain, Sweden, United Kingdom, United States.

average for the major seven OECD countries (39.6 per cent) and the average for the OECD as a whole. By 1983, the UK ratio, at 54.2 per cent, was in line with the major seven countries' average (50.8 per cent) and the OECD average of 50.7 per cent. The United Kingdom was the only major industrial country to achieve a significant reduction in its debt–GDP ratio between 1970 and 1983. Japan, West Germany, and Italy saw large increases while the United States was about constant over that period (but rising rapidly, and even explosively, towards the end of the period). All major industrial countries saw a rise in the debt–service ratio between 1970 and 1984. The increase was monotonic for all but the United Kingdom whose debt–service ratio peaked (at 5.6 per cent) in 1980 and has since fallen to 4.7 per cent in 1984, slightly below the provisional estimate of 4.9 per cent for the major OECD countries.

In Table 3.2, I present a decomposition of the change in the UK debt–output ratio since 1948 into three parts: new debt arising from the public sector deficit; erosion of the real value of existing debt from inflation; and changes due to real output growth. This is a purely arithmetic, *ex post* accounting exercise.

We see that the total change in the debt–GDP ratio between 1948 and 1984 of −1.94 can be almost exactly accounted for by the effect of inflation on the real value of the outstanding nominal government debt. The cumulative contribution of the deficits was to increase the ratio by 1.06, while real growth lowered the ratio by 0.98. The fact that *ex post* inflation accounted for virtually all of the reduction in the debt–output ratio since 1948 should not lead one to conclude that the way further to amortize the

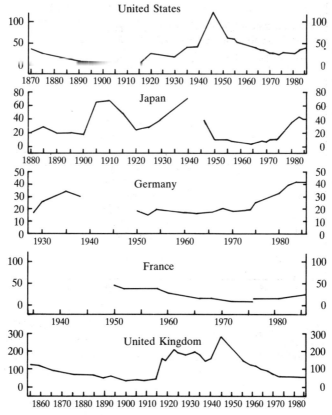

Figure 3.3 Historical public debt–GNP ratios for five major OECD countries

Source: OECD, *Economic Outlook*, 37, June 1985, p. 7.

Table 3.2 Decomposition of changes in UK debt–output ratio, 1949–83

Period	Change in debt–output ratio	Contribution of deficits	Contribution of inflation	Contribution of output growth
1948–60	−1.25	0.13	−0.77	−0.56
1961–70	−0.46	0.18	−0.34	−0.29
1971–80	−0.27	0.55	−0.71	−0.10
1981–84	0.04	0.20	−0.13	−0.03
1948–84	−1.94	1.06	−1.95	−0.98

Source: See Figure 3.1.
Note: The decomposition is not quite exact.

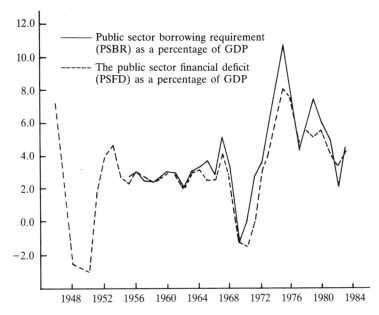

Figure 3.4 Public sector deficit–GDP ratio, United Kingdom

Source: Economic Trends, various issues.

public debt is to have another bout of inflation. Higher inflation could go hand-in-hand with a rising debt burden, for example if real output growth is low and real interest rates are high. Inflation, interest rates, and output growth are jointly endogenous variables and almost any pattern of covariation between them could be generated, depending on the nature of the exogenous variables driving the economic system.

Figure 3.4 shows the UK public sector financial deficit (PSFD) and the public sector borrowing requirement (PSBR), each as a proportion of GDP. Since the PSBR puts 'above the line' (counts as current receipts) the proceeds of certain asset sales which the PSFD properly puts 'below the line' (counts as financing), the latter is more informative. Table 3.3 reproduces the Bank of England's 'inflation corrected' PSBR, what the PSBR would have been if debt service had been costed not at nominal interest rates but at the actual real interest rates which prevailed.[1] When such inflation correction is undertaken, notice that the supposed PSBR explosion between 1969 and 1975 is almost eliminated, and that the cumulative inflation-corrected PSBR between 1967 and 1983 is considerably in surplus.

Table 3.3 'Inflation-corrected' PSBR, United Kingdom, 1967–83 (£ billion, March 1982 prices)

Year	PSBR (£ billion)	'Inflation correction' (£ billion)	'Inflation-corrected' PSBR (£ billion)	'Inflation-corrected' PSBR as a proportion of GDP at market prices
	(1)	(2)	(3)	(4)
1967	1.8	−0.8	1.0	2.5
1968	1.3	−1.2	0.1	0.2
1969	−0.5	−1.9	−2.4	−5.1
1970	0.0	−2.7	−2.7	−5.2
1971	1.3	−3.2	−1.9	−3.3
1972	2.0	−3.1	−1.1	−1.7
1973	4.1	−4.0	0.1	0.1
1974	6.4	−9.3	−2.9	−3.4
1975	10.2	−11.9	−1.7	−1.6
1976	9.0	−7.5	1.5	1.2
1977	5.5	−9.4	−3.9	−2.7
1978	8.5	−6.7	1.8	1.1
1979	12.7	−14.9	−2.2	−1.1
1980	11.8	−13.1	−1.3	−0.6
1981	10.6	−12.3	−1.7	−0.7
1982	5.0	−7.3	−2.3	−0.8
1983	11.6	−5.9	5.7	1.9

Source: *Bank of England Quarterly Bulletin*, June 1980 and June 1984.
Note: Construction of 'inflation correction' in Column 2: Net nominal stock of government debt held outside the public sector times percentage change in consumers' price deflator. An exchange rate correction is applied to assets and liabilities denominated in foreign currency.

3.3 DEFICITS, DEBT AND INFLATION

The fear that public sector deficits will eventually be monetized and thus lead to inflation is a deep-rooted one among economic policy makers, officials of treasuries, central banks, international organizations, and among the public at large. There are two distinct but not mutually exclusive views of the debt–deficit–inflation nexus. The first emphasizes the incentive for a government to reduce the real value of its outstanding stock of interest-bearing, nominally-denominated (non-index-linked) debt through an unexpected burst of inflation. The second, recently restated by Sargent and Wallace (1981), emphasizes the long-run inflationary consequences of a short- or medium-term switch from money or tax financing to debt financing of a given public spending program. This second view does not require inflationary surprises in order to be valid.

3.3.1 Amortizing the public debt through inflation

There are four ways through which governments can reduce the real value of their debt. First, at a given general price level and a given nominal price of bonds, they can run a budget surplus and repurchase existing debt. Second, they can attempt to reduce the real value of the outstanding stock of debt, at a given general price level, by pursuing or announcing policies that cause a drop in bond prices. Third, an inflationary policy can reduce the real value of the inherited stock of debt, even with a balanced budget and given nominal bond prices. Finally, a government can formally repudiate part or all of its debt. The discussion of this final option is left to the next section.

Why should governments wish to reduce the real value of their debt? We can distinguish distributional and efficiency reasons. The distributional issues are fairly straightforward. Those who hold the debt and those who pay the taxes that service the debt are not the same people. Typically, debt is owned (directly or indirectly through pension funds and other financial institutions) by people who are, on average, both older and richer than the representative taxpayer. The recurrent caricature of the toiling workers supporting the idle (retired?) rentiers is an exaggerated version of this distributional conflict. In the short run, debt debasement favors labor, and the young in general, at the expense of rentiers and older people. The efficiency argument focuses on the role of public debt in crowding out private saving and capital formation. If the authorities judge the domestic rate of capital formation to be less than the optimal rate, one possible remedy is to stimulate private saving by reducing the real value of the financial claims of the private sector on the public sector. Provided this can be achieved without a Keynesian slump in effective demand, such a policy will stimulate both private saving and investment.

A systematic view of the deficit–debt–inflation nexus starts from the consolidated government budget identity. This states that the excess of exhaustive government spending and debt service over tax receipts must be financed either by base money creation, or sales of debt (of any maturity), or by running down reserves of foreign exchange. This identity linking all public sector sources and uses of funds is often, somewhat misleadingly, referred to as the government budget 'constraint' or (worse) as the budget 'restraint'. The constraint lies not in the identity itself but in the limits we set, implicitly or explicitly, on the government's ability to borrow (i.e. on the real stock of debt or the debt–output ratio), in the lower bound we impose on the stock of foreign exchange reserves, and in the constraints, political or economic, imposed on the real value of the resources that the government can appropriate through seigniorage. By seigniorage I mean the government's ability to pay for real resources simply by rolling the printing presses. Thus the real value of seigniorage equals the increase in nominal base money deflated by the price level, or, equivalently, the proportional increase in base money multiplied by the outstanding real stock of base money.

Even in the era of floating exchange rates, official purchases of foreign exchange have not disappeared completely. Nevertheless, for simplicity of exposition I shall ignore fluctuations in official foreign exchange holdings. In that case the increase in the real value of the debt is just the sum of the real value of the budget deficit (net of revenue from real seigniorage) and the increase in the real value of the outstanding debt stock caused by a higher bond price or a lower general price level.

To simplify the presentation I shall assume that the short and long interest rates are related to each other through the 'expectations hypothesis' of the term structure. With risk-neutral operators in financial markets this implies that the expected rate of return on long bonds (including any expected capital gain or loss due to changes in the price of long bonds) must equal the yield on short bonds. It follows that the expected or planned change in the real value of the public debt is composed of three parts: the real *primary* deficit (defined as the real value of 'exhaustive' government spending, i.e. *excluding* debt service, less tax revenues); plus expected *real* interest payments (which by virtue of the 'expectations hypothesis' is simply the real value of the debt multiplied by the *ex ante* short real interest rate); less seigniorage. Consequently, a correctly anticipated policy of inflation will not affect the real stock of public debt outstanding unless it affects the real primary deficit, the *ex ante* short real interest rate, or the real revenue from money creation. An unanticipated inflation policy may in addition lower the real value of the public debt by causing private bondholders to underpredict the inflation rate or overpredict the increase in the price of long-dated debt.

The theoretical and empirical case for an effect of a fully anticipated and well-understood inflation policy on the *ex ante* real interest rate is open.[2] A reasonable bench-mark is to assume that higher expected inflation is fully reflected in nominal interest rates, leaving the real rate unaffected.

The extent to which the real primary deficit is affected by inflation depends on the institutional, legal, administrative, and political framework governing the determination of public spending and taxation. For instance, with a progressive and incompletely indexed tax system, there will be an increase in the real tax burden through 'bracket creep' when the general price level rises. Depending on the way in which they are implemented, a system of 'cash limits' may also lead to an (unexpected) reduction in the real value of public spending when there is an (unexpected) increase in the price level.

The implications of higher inflation for real seigniorage revenue are simplest to analyse when we assume that a particular inflation rate is maintained for a long time, in which case it is likely to be associated with an equivalent rate of monetary growth. Let the demand for real money balances be a decreasing function of the short nominal interest rate and of the inflation rate, and an increasing function of real national income. If real output and real interest rates are independent of the inflation rate, a permanently higher rate of money growth (with matching permanently higher rates of inflation and nominal interest) will have two effects on real seigniorage: first, seigniorage on a given stock of real money balances is higher since money is being printed more quickly; second, the outstanding stock of real money balances will in fact be lower, since higher inflation and nominal interest rates reduce real money demand. Hence the theoretical effect of higher inflation on real seigniorage is ambiguous, though we can say that if the inflation elasticity of base money demand (inclusive of induced effects on nominal interest rates) is below unity in absolute value then higher inflation will increase real seigniorage.[3]

I estimated a simple demand function for base money for the United Kingdom using annual data from 1948 to 1984. The dependent variable was (the logarithm of) the real monetary base m (the wide monetary base deflated by the GDP deflator at factor cost). Independent variables were a constant, a time trend t, current and lagged values of (the logarithm of) real output y (real GDP at factor cost), a short nominal interest rate (the three-month Treasury Bill discount rate up to 1960, the three-month Treasury Bill yield after 1960), a long nominal interest rate (the yield on consols or twenty-year securities), the rate of inflation π (the proportional rate of change of the GDP deflator at factor cost), and lagged values of the real monetary base.

The best estimate in terms of residual autocorrelation, parameter stability, and goodness of fit is given below. (Figures in brackets below coefficient estimates are absolute values of t-statistics.)

$$m = -3.47 - 0.253t + 0.956y - 0.516\pi + 0.67m_{-1} \qquad (3.1)$$
$$(10.1) \quad (9.9) \quad (10.3) \quad (12.4) \quad (16.9)$$

Sample period 1948–84; Standard error = 0.016; DW = 1.83; h = 0.54.

Equation (3.1) implies a semi-elasticity of real base money demand with respect to inflation of -1.56, which seems reasonable.[4] This implies that the annual UK inflation rate would have to exceed 67 per cent before higher inflation would start to reduce real government revenue from money creation. While historical and foreseeable inflation rates would seem to place the British economy in the range where higher inflation rates still boost total revenue from the 'inflation tax', the amounts involved are small. Table 3.4 shows the historical insignificance of seigniorage revenue in the UK economy. It would have taken an increase in the tax burden of only 0.55 per cent of GDP to do away with the need for revenue from seigniorage altogether. It therefore seems implausible to base a positive theory of inflation for the United Kingdom on the perceived need of successive governments to extend the tax base and find a further source of revenue. I would go further and argue that the fact that we have experienced (and are still experiencing) any inflation at all in the United Kingdom and the other industrial countries (albeit at rates well below the seigniorage-maximizing level) cannot be rationalized in terms of the optimal trade-off between

Table 3.4 Seigniorage as a source of revenue, United Kingdom, 1948–83

Period	Change in money base (% of GDP)	Change in money base (% of total tax receipts*)	Change in money base (% of general government taxes and NI contributions)	Money base (% of GDP, end of period)
1948–60	0.33	0.92	1.01	11.59
1961–70	0.39	0.97	1.07	8.96
1971–80	0.67	1.53	1.72	5.63
1981–83	0.21	0.43	0.48	4.94
1948–83	0.43	1.06	1.18	4.94

* Taxes, NI contributions, trading income, rent, royalties, interest, etc.

seigniorage and the other sources of revenue. Instead it seems likely that the increasing inflation rates and rates of monetary growth of the 1960s and 1970s were the by-product of policies aimed at maintaining capacity utilization rates and unemployment rates in the face of deteriorating supply-side conditions, and/or of attempts to exploit a non-existent long-run employment–inflation trade-off, regardless of the revenue implications of the increasing rates of monetary growth. In other words, the data support the screw-up theory of inflation rather than the optimal seigniorage theory of inflation.

Not only has seigniorage historically been an insignificant source of government revenue in the United Kingdom, but my estimate of the demand for narrow money suggests that the maximum possible yield of this tax is also small. With a constant semi-elasticity of -1.5, the seigniorage-maximizing annual inflation rate is 67 per cent and the maximal seigniorage in mid-sample 1967 is 2.74 per cent of GDP. This estimate leads one to conclude that *expected* inflation appears to be a costly way of raising additional government revenue. These calculations are little more than recreational and should be taken as indicative, at most, of orders of magnitude.

As noted above, anticipated inflation will generally not affect the real value of the stock of public debt, although there will, of course, be revenue from seigniorage. *Unanticipated* inflation is potentially the most important means by which a government can reduce the real value of its nominally denominated debt other than through formal repudiation or default. Unanticipated inflation reduces the real value of all debt (other than index-linked debt) and an unexpected decline in the price of long debt further reduces the real value of debt with longer maturities. Even moderate unexpected changes in the rate of inflation can have dramatic effects on the market value of long-dated non-indexed debt, if these changes are expected to persist. This can be seen as follows.

If the expectations theory of the term structure holds, and if short nominal interest rates are expected to be the same in the future as they are today, then long and short rates would be identical. Since the yield on consols (I) is simply the coupon divided by the bond price, it follows that a rise in the rate of inflation by one percentage point will in the bench-mark case of constant real interest rates, produce a fall in the price of consols of ($1/I$) percentage points. Thus if long rates are initially 10 per cent, a one percentage point increase in the rate of inflation will cause a 10 per cent drop in the price of consols.

More generally, the effect of an increase in the current and expected future short rate on the price of long bonds of any maturity must be negative. Higher current and expected future short nominal interest rates associated with higher expected future inflation, which was unanticipated at the time that the longer maturity nominal debt was issued, will not be reflected in the coupon rate or the issue price of these long-term bond issues. This will therefore lead to a fall in the market value of this debt, and effectively serve as an unexpected levy on bondholders. In the bondholders' balance sheet this will show up as a capital loss. From the government's point of view it is akin to amortization of part of its long-term debt.

In principle, even short-term debt can be amortized in this way, if it is possible to engineer an unexpected instantaneous discrete jump in the general price level. In an open economy, an unexpected discrete devaluation of the exchange rate might succeed if importers pass this on 'at a stroke', but for a country like the United Kingdom this is not an attractive option.[5] With very short-term debt, floating rate debt, and, of course, index-linked debt, the scope for governments to lower the *ex post* real rate of return on their debt through surprise inflation is quite limited. Moreover, Figure 3.5 shows that the average maturity of UK public debt has shrunk since 1945[6] (a phenomenon also occurring in the United States), thus making unexpected inflation even less effective as a means of liquidating real debt.

By issuing only index-linked debt, governments would explicitly relinquish the option of reducing the real value of outstanding debt through unexpected inflation, though seigniorage revenue – the expected inflation tax – could still be extracted. Thus indexation might make a government commitment to a policy of price stability more credible by removing the subsequent incentive to cheat on inflation which nominal debt provides.

3.3.2 Debt, deficits and monetization

The recurrent notion that deficits will, eventually, have to be monetized, has been formalized fairly recently in a paper by Sargent and Wallace (1981) (see also Buiter, 1982; and Sargent 1983). In a nutshell, the argu-

60 Setting the scene

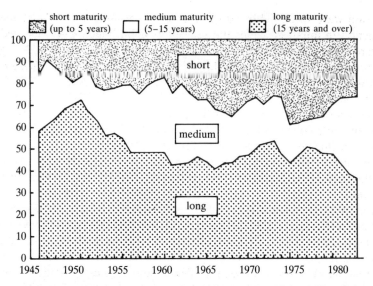

Figure 3.5 Maturity structure of the public debt, United Kingdom, 1945–83

Source: Annual Abstract of Statistics, various issues.
* British government and government guaranteed marketable securities. Nominal values at 31 March. Non-official holdings.

ment can be put as follows. Public sector deficits are financed either by printing money or by borrowing. After some date, T, the debt–output ratio is to be kept constant at b, for example because there is a limit on the private sector's willingness to absorb debt. With an exogenously given real *primary* deficit, money financing then becomes endogenous. It is the residual financing mode. The real interest rate, r, is assumed to be fixed and to exceed the trend rate of growth of real output, n. With the debt–output ratio constant after T, new issues of debt are just sufficient to offset the downward effects of inflation and real output growth on the debt–output ratio. Money growth μ after date T is therefore given by:

$$\mu = v[d + (r - n)b] \tag{3.2}$$

where v is the income velocity of circulation of money and d the primary deficit as a proportion of output.

To estimate the eventual monetization implied by the fiscal stance one must therefore calculate the 'inflation-and-real-growth-corrected' deficit as a proportion of GDP: $d + (r - n)b$. Note that the debt–output ratio b in this calculation is a sustainable and sustained debt–output ratio. Care must be taken not to identify it with the *currently observed* ratio of the market value of the public debt to output, when one wishes to estimate the inflation-and-real-growth-corrected deficit that would be observed if a lower rate of inflation were to be achieved unexpectedly. Assume such an unexpected reduction in inflation leaves the real interest rate unchanged and reduces current and expected future nominal interest rates one-for-one. At a given general price level, the real value of nominally denominated, long-dated debt will increase as a result of the decline in current and expected future short nominal interest rates (see the discussion of this issue in Subsection 3.3.1). Consequently $(r - n)b$ will increase because the price of long bonds rises even if real interest rates, the number of short and long bonds, etc., remain unchanged. In order to stabilize the debt–output ratio at its current value, surpluses (measured conventionally) will have to be run to counteract the increase in the real value of long-dated nominal debt as inflation declines.[7]

A number of conclusions can be drawn from Equation (3.2). First, if the real interest rate exceeds the real growth rate, a higher debt–output ratio will be associated with a higher proportional rate of growth of the nominal money stock, unless velocity falls (the demand for money per unit of output increases) so as to offset the higher debt service burden. If the real interest rate, instead of being constant, increased with the debt–output ratio, these conclusions would be reinforced (see Buiter, 1982). Thus, any financing policy prior to T that leads to increased debt accumulation (a higher value of b), will require higher real seigniorage after T, and thus, if money demand is less than unit elastic with respect to the inflation rate, a higher rate of growth of nominal money and, sooner or later, more inflation.

In Britain, the income-velocity of circulation of high-powered money has risen steadily since the end of the Second World War, from 5.00 in 1946 to 20.24 in 1983. Even in the most favorable case where velocity is constant rather than increasing with the rate of inflation, a UK government would be unlikely to choose to finance an increase in debt service due to a higher debt–output ratio by printing money rather than by raising explicit taxes. With a constant velocity of 20 and a real interest rate that is two percentage points above the trend growth rate of output, an extra ten percentage points on the debt–output ratio would require a 4.0 per cent increase in the rate of money growth and thus in the long-run rate of inflation. To finance the increased debt service at an unchanged rate of inflation by raising taxes would require an increase in taxes (or cut in transfer payments) equal to 0.2 per cent of GNP only. It would be very unlikely for an economy like the United Kingdom, with a well-developed financial system (reflected in a high money base velocity) and a reasonably broad tax base, to choose 'secular' money financing over tax financing. The situation is of course quite different for a number of Third World countries. Many of them have relatively rudimentary internal financial systems, reflected, among other things, in a much lower money base velocity. Many also have a very narrow tax base and the administrative and political constraints on raising taxes and cutting public spending may be more severe than in the industrialized countries. Even in Britain in the immediate post-war years, when money base velocity was about five, the cost of a ten percentage point increase in the debt–output ratio would (with a constant velocity) only have been a 1 per cent rise in the inflation rate. Note that the relative attractiveness of seigniorage versus explicit taxation is not affected if we recognize that the real interest rate is likely to increase with the debt–output ratio, as this affects the amounts to be raised through seigniorage or taxation equally.

3.4 DEFICITS, DEBT AND SOLVENCY

Every Chancellor's nightmare must be state bankruptcy in which the government defaults on its debt liabilities. To investigate this doomsday scenario, we can disaggregate the government budget identity (Appendix 3A provides a more formal treatment).

$$
\left.\begin{array}{l}
\text{Money creation} \\
+ \text{ Debt sales} \\
+ \text{ Sales of public} \\
\quad \text{sector assets}
\end{array}\right\} = \left\{\begin{array}{l}
\text{Exhaustive public spending} \\
\text{(current, plus gross capital formation)} \\
+ \text{ Debt interest} \\
- \text{ Taxes} \\
- \text{ Net income on public assets}
\end{array}\right. \quad (3.3)
$$

This highlights two revenue sources not yet discussed: first, income earned (which could be negative) on public sector capital; and second, income accruing to the government from its ownership of natural resource property rights (e.g. North Sea oil in the UK). The left-hand side of Equation (3.3) identifies one additional financing mode, the sale of public sector assets (such as the privatization of British Telecom). The right-hand side of Equation (3.3) is the public sector financial deficit (PSFD) and properly treats asset sales as part of the financing category on the left-hand side. In contrast, the public sector borrowing requirement (PSBR) treats sales of public sector assets as a negative entry on the right-hand side. The reason for this uninformative accounting is lost in history. For simplicity, I have omitted foreign assets and liabilities from Equation (3.3).

3.4.1 The solvency constraint

If the expected rates of return on all assets are equalized, we can sum over time the succession of single period budget identities like (3.3) to obtain the public sector's intertemporal budget identity or balance sheet. Letting *PV* denote the present value of an income stream:

$$
\begin{aligned}
&\begin{aligned}PV\text{ of exhaustive}\\ \text{current spending}\\ \text{program}\end{aligned} =
\left\{
\begin{array}{l}
\text{Public sector assets}\\
-\ \text{Public sector debt}\\
+\ PV\text{ of taxes}\\
+\ PV\text{ of seigniorage}\\
+\ PV\text{ of public sector}\\
\quad\text{capital formation}\\
-\ PV\text{ of terminal net}\\
\quad\text{liabilities}
\end{array}
\right\} = \text{Net worth}
\end{aligned}
\qquad (3.4)
$$

Tangible, and potentially marketable, public sector assets are public sector capital and ownership of natural resources, each valued at the present value of the income streams to which they give rise, which could be negative for loss-making operations. There are two intangibles on the asset side of the balance sheet: the present value of future taxes (net of transfer payments) and of future seigniorage. If public investment is undertaken up to the point at which the financial return equals the opportunity cost of funds, the present value of future public capital formation will be zero, and will disappear completely from Equation (3.4). By the same token, privatization of public assets (or nationalization of private assets) affects public sector net worth only if the sale (or purchase) price of the assets differs from the capitalized value of the subsequent income stream.

The final item in the intertemporal budget identity is the present value of the government's expected terminal net liabilities. (The government's terminal net liability is its net indebtedness at the end of the planning horizon.) This item permits us to turn the *identity* into a meaningful *constraint* on solvency. The government is solvent when the present value of its expected eventual net liabilities is zero.

When (as is currently [1985] the case) the real interest rate exceeds the long-run rate of output growth, a sufficient condition for this solvency constraint to be met is that the ratio of net marketable public sector debt to trend output remains bounded. That is what I shall assume below. Here, I merely note that when the rate of trend output growth exceeds the real interest rate a so-called Ponzi game is feasible: the government can keep financing existing debt service by further borrowing without insolvency. Cohen (1985) discusses this possibility in more detail.

However, I shall assume that in the long run the real interest rate exceeds the growth rate of output and impose the solvency condition that the present value of net terminal liabilities is zero. Consequently, the market value of the government's net non-monetary debt must be matched by the present value of expected future primary *current* surpluses and the present value of expected future seigniorage. Hence, assuming the return on public and private capital is the same, the solvency condition implies:

$$
\left.\begin{array}{l}
\text{Public sector net} \\
\text{liabilities as a} \\
\text{proportion of} \\
\text{current output}
\end{array}\right\}
=
\left\{\begin{array}{l}
PV \text{ of primary current} \\
\text{surpluses} \\
+ PV \text{ of seigniorage, all} \\
\text{as a proportion of current output}
\end{array}\right. \qquad (3.4a)
$$

The relevant discount rate in this set of present value calculations is the real interest rate minus the trend rate of output growth. Note again that the surplus/deficit measure is that on the government's *current* account. Unless the return on public sector capital differs from its opportunity cost, public capital formation can be netted out completely. Six short points should be made about the formalism of the solvency constraint before we turn to the theory and practice of debt repudiation.

First, Equations (3.4) and (3.4a) discount *real* values at *real* interest rates. An equivalent expression can be derived by discounting nominal values at nominal interest rates. Discounting real values at nominal interest rates would be an irrational procedure, although Modigliani and Cohn (1981) have argued that such behavior accounts for the undervaluation of the stock market in inflationary periods.

Second, consider what would happen if, contrary to my assumption, the natural rate of growth, n, exceeds the real interest rate, r. In that case the forward-looking present value budget identity is not defined. However, the debt–output ratio is perfectly well behaved for any finite primary deficit as a proportion of output, d, and the associated steady-state value of the debt–output ratio is simply $d/(n - r)$. There is no solvency constraint for this government. There are, obviously, 'physical' constraints such as the condition that, in a closed economy, government spending cannot exceed output. The choice of borrowing versus taxation depends exclusively on distributional criteria and on the relative efficiency costs of debt versus tax financing. In spite of a positive share of public spending in national income, taxes need never be levied and may indeed be negative for ever.[8]

Third, the solvency constraint permits us to take a forward-looking view of the 'eventual monetization' implied by the fiscal-financial program, discussed in the previous section. From Equation (3.4a) we get, holding the rate of monetary growth, μ, and the velocity of circulation, v, constant

$$
\mu = v(R - n)A \qquad (3.5)
$$

where R is the real yield on perpetuities and A is the present value of future primary current deficits as a proportion of output less the public sector net asset–output ratio. This equation simply solves Equation (3.4a) for the constant rate of growth of base money that is implied, as a residual to satisfy the solvency constraint, by the current and prospective future plans for the primary deficit and the initial stock of non-monetary debt. Note that the 'net liability' on the right-hand-side of Equation (3.5) is annuitized using the long real interest rate net of the rate of growth of output. If the policies summarized in Equation (3.5) are inconsistent with a constant velocity, we can rephrase the question in terms of the constant (permanent) share of seigniorage in GNP that is implied by the current spending and taxation plans and by the already outstanding net debt obligations. This simply amounts to dividing both sides of Equation (3.5) by the velocity of circulation.

Fourth, the various items in the solvency constraint are unlikely to be behaviorally independent of each other. The nature of these inter-dependencies is of course model-specific. For a Keynesian world, a cut in the spending program will reduce effective demand and output, reduce the tax base and, at given tax rates and interest rates, reduce the present value of taxes. Changes in the rate of inflation, brought about through changes in the seigniorage program, may alter the future capital intensity of production and thus the tax base. Many other linkages can be considered.

Fifth, the government's assets net of its liabilities were referred to as government 'net worth'. It might be argued that this involves a certain abuse of language. The right-hand side of Equation (3.4) is to a large extent a choice variable of the government (even ignoring the possibility of default), as the government can choose, within bounds, its tax-transfer program, its monetary growth targets, and its capital formation program. Whether or not we wish to use the term 'net worth', with its connotation of something parametric to the government, the mutual consistency of the consumption program and 'net worth' represents a valid solvency constraint.

Sixth, it is easily checked that *after-tax* rates of interest should be used to discount future flows of revenues and expenditures (see Buiter, 1984a). The stream of current and future taxes net of transfers that enters into the present value calculations should be total taxes net of transfers minus the receipts from income and capital gains taxes on the assets and liabilities appearing in the solvency constraint.

There has been no empirical attempt to implement the comprehensive balance sheet accounting outlined here. In a recent paper Hills (1984) presented estimates of some of the less conventional assets and liabilities. His 'full' balance sheet of the public sector is presented in Table 3.5. It includes estimates of the value of physical assets, but excludes much of the social infrastructure (roads, sewers, etc.); since very few of these social overhead assets yield any cash return to the public sector, exclusion is not a serious matter for the purpose of constructing the public sector comprehensive balance sheet. The value of natural resources is measured by future oil revenues, and a subset of the present value of taxes net of transfers and subsidies is included (corporate deferred tax and pensions deferred tax component, state pensions, unfunded public service pensions). Omitted are the rest of the present value of taxes net of transfers,

Table 3.5 Estimated full balance sheet for UK public sector (£ billion, March 1982 prices)

	1957	1975	1982
Assets:			
physical (including land and shares)	130	415	420
financial	35	45	35
future oil revenues	–	70	105
deferred corporation tax	–	10	–
deferred tax on pensions	10–15	35–45	60–65
Total assets	175–180	575–585	620–625
Liabilities:			
financial	195	150	135
state pension	235	390	430–455
unfunded public service pensions	20	90–115	120–140
Total liabilities	450	630–655	685–730
Net liability	275	55–70	65–105

Source: Hills (1984).

subsidies, etc., the present value of future seigniorage and the present value of the 'excess returns' (if any) from future planned public sector capital formation if public sector capital is used more efficiently, at the margin, than private capital. While one can quarrel with each and every one of Hills's figures, the need to go through an exercise of this kind in order to evaluate the feasibility and consistency of public sector fiscal–financial–monetary plans is beyond doubt.

If we take, for example, Hills's 1982 figure of a net liability of between £65 billion and £105 billion (at March 1982 prices) at face value, this means that for solvency the remaining items in the comprehensive balance sheet, but not in the Hills calculations, should add up to a net asset value of between £65 billion and £105 billion. These items are: the present value of future seigniorage; the present value of future taxes net of transfers, excluding debt service and the taxes and transfers already considered by Hills (oil revenues, state and public service pensions, etc.); *minus* the present value of public sector consumption; and the present value of any excess returns from future public sector investment.

With annual velocity of circulation constant at 20, a non-inflationary future (with monetary growth of 3 per cent, say) and a real interest rate of 3 per cent per annum would (in 1982) have given us a present value of future seigniorage figure of £13.9 billion. Doubling or halving this, it remains small beer (a mere 0.15 per cent of GDP in the illustrative example). The remainder amounts to between £51.1 billion and £91.1 billion in 1982. With the real interest rate two percentage points above the trend real growth rate, this represents the need for a 'residual'[9] permanent primary surplus of between 0.37 per cent and 0.66 per cent of GDP.

Adding back in the annuitized value of future oil revenues, the deferred tax component of pensions and taking out the annuitized value of public sector pension liabilities, raises the required total permanent primary surplus to between 3.1 per cent and 3.7 per cent of GDP. Interest payments on the public debt were 5.3 per cent of GDP in 1982. A conventionally measured public sector financial deficit of between 1.63 per cent and 2.2 per cent of GDP in 1982 would therefore have been 'sustainable' according to these back-of-an-envelope calculations. One can contrast this with the kind of sustainability calculation that ignores all intangible assets and liabilities and proceeds as follows. Interest-bearing public debt is 50 per cent of annual GDP in the United Kingdom. The trend growth rate of real GDP is, say, 2.5 per cent per year. Assume inflation is to be stabilized at, say, 5 per cent per year. The interest-bearing debt–output ratio will therefore be stabilized when new bond issues are 3.75 per cent of GDP. With the income velocity of circulation of base money constant at 20, say, the sustainable PSFD as a proportion of GDP would be 4.1 per cent. If a zero inflation scenario is envisaged, the sustainable PSFD as a proportion of GDP (ignoring any effects of lower inflation on the debt–output ratio and on velocity) would be 1.4 per cent.

3.4.2 Sustainable fiscal–financial–monetary plans

The 'balance sheet' solvency constraint in Equations (3.4) or (3.4a) in one sense tells us all there is to know about solvency. Feasible or consistent fiscal, financial, and monetary plans should satisfy this identity. Any particular set of plans or projections may, however, fail to satisfy it. If a government attempted to implement its spending, tax-transfer and monetization program, insolvency (i.e. debt repudiation) would occur to satisfy, *ex post*, the constraint that was violated *ex ante*. There are a number of alternative ways of measuring the extent or magnitude of the departure from solvency, each one of which emphasizes a feature of the plans already implicit in the balance sheet solvency constraint. Such measures of inconsistency can be expressed, for instance, as flow deficits or deficits as a proportion of output. This brings out the sustained or permanent changes in spending programs, revenue raising programs, or seigniorage plans, that are required to eliminate the *ex ante* discrepancy in the government's comprehensive balance sheet.

3.4.3 The 'permanent deficit'

Consider an inconsistent or infeasible fiscal–financial–monetary plan. This is characterized by a violation of Equations (3.4) and (3.4a). Such an excess or shortfall of spending over resources will not, of course, be observed *ex post*. Something will give to re-establish *ex post* equality, whether this takes the form of changing spending plans, net worth, or both.

The *permanent deficit*, F, is the real perpetuity equivalent or annuity value of the discrepancy in the government's *ex ante* comprehensive balance sheet. If S is the present value of spending plans and W is net worth then

$$F = R(S - W) \tag{3.6}$$

The *permanent deficit share* is $(R - n)(S - W)$ expressed as a proportion of trend output. While these *ex ante* 'permanent' deficits will not materialize *ex post*, let alone be permanent, they do represent the *permanent adjustment* that must be made, to spending, to receipts, or to seigniorage, in order to achieve solvency.

Two further informative deficit measures are the *constant net worth deficit*, F^W, and the *permanent income deficit*, F^P. The *current* level of public sector consumption spending can be said to be sustainable if it keeps net worth constant (*ex ante*). This will be the case when real public sector consumption equals the current expected real rate of return times public sector net worth. The *constant net worth deficit* is then given by:

$$F^W = c^G - rW \tag{3.7}$$

where c^G is government current spending.

If one's criterion for the sustainability of current consumption involves the maintenance of a constant (*ex ante*) ratio of public sector net worth to capacity output, the sustainable consumption level is given by $(r - n)W$ rather than rW. The constant net worth share deficit is then defined as $c^G - (r - n)W$, expressed as a proportion of trend output.

The level (share) of public sector consumption consistent with constant net worth (or a constant net worth share) will be subject to anticipated fluctuations over time if the short real interest rate varies over time. A permanent income approach to the sustainability of public sector consumption plans has been proposed by Miller (1983) and Miller and Babbs (1983). The highest indefinitely sustainable constant level of public sector consumption (or public sector permanent income) is given by RW, i.e. net worth times the real long interest rate rather than the real short interest rate. The *permanent income deficit* can then be defined as

$$F^P = c^G - RW \tag{3.8}$$

Finally, if a constant share of public sector consumption in trend output is taken as one's criterion for the sustainability of current consumption, the permanent income share deficit can be defined analogously to the constant net worth share deficit as $c^G - (R - n)W$, expressed as a proportion of trend output.

Each of these 'permanent deficits' measures the magnitude of the long-run inconsistency, expressed as a flow of spending or income, in the government's fiscal, financial and monetary plans, according to some notion of long-run sustainability. As presented here, the measures single out public current spending on goods and services (public consumption) from all other outlays and receipts. It should, however, be clear that the sustainability of *any* public spending program can be evaluated simply by transferring the present value of the relevant outlays (e.g., transfer payments plus subsidies) to the left-hand side of the present value budget constraint and redefining public sector 'net worth' appropriately.

None of these measures conveys any information about the short- or long-run stance of fiscal policy as regards its effect on aggregate demand. To obtain measures of fiscal stance or fiscal impact on the economy, an explicit model of the economy is required. The solvency constraint and the various permanent deficit measures are merely a useful accounting framework for organizing facts and plans about fiscal, financial and monetary policy, and for evaluating the mutual consistency of spending and revenue projections, public sector debt objectives, and monetary targets. Its behavioral content is limited to the (restrictive) assumption of certainty equivalence that permitted us to equate *ex ante* expected rates of return on all non-monetary assets. To make the forecasts of future tax receipts, transfer payments and real interest rates required to implement the present value and permanent deficit calculations, some model of the economy will, of course, in general be necessary.

3.4.4 Debt repudiation

What happens if current plans, projections and expectations add up to a violation of the solvency constraint? The government could achieve a consistent set of plans by cutting spending or by raising taxes. It could also try to fill the hole in its balance sheet by increasing the revenue brought in from seigniorage. An increase in the revenue accruing from the public ownership of capital would also help close the gap. Finally, if, at the margin, public sector investment yields cash returns in excess of (below) its opportunity cost, an increase (decrease) in the scale of the public sector investment program could do the trick. If a corrective combination of such policy measures is not implemented, the residual item in the present value budget constraint, the real value of public sector debt, will have to give.

We have already reviewed the option of reducing the real value of debt and debt service by inflation. This leaves the option of cutting real debt and debt service by repudiation or special taxation (capital levies, forced loans or conversions, and special levies on government debt). Arithmetically, repudiation (partial or complete) would seem to be a means for reconciling otherwise inconsistent spending and revenue plans. Why then do governments not make use of it more frequently? One reason is that repudiation or a massive capital levy is perceived as a breach of public faith and is politically and electorally unattractive. The point is well-made by the Committee on National Debt and Taxation (1927, pp. 295–6):

> We do not suggest that a levy would necessarily arouse feelings of the most violent kind. We are convinced, however, that it would be strongly resented ... exceptional circumstances are required to reconcile the owner of capital wealth to the levy idea. The opposition is no doubt founded partly on political suspicion and on prejudice: to impose a capital levy would be, as Mr. Keynes expressed, to insult a set of very strong irrational feelings in men, and such grounds of opposition are exceedingly difficult to overcome. It is possible that time may bring a change of ideas.

Second, repudiation or a major capital levy would not just represent a redistribution of wealth from rentiers to taxpayers, but would also be likely to have serious consequences for the private financial system. The enforceability of private contracts will be in doubt when the government is openly or effectively in breach of contract (implicit or explicit). Finally, if a government considers it likely that it may wish to borrow again at some stage in the future it will (since the terms on which it will be able to do so will reflect its reputation) weigh the advantages of current repudiation against the enhanced future cost of debt service should it repudiate now. Using the analysis made familiar in the literature on (Third World) external debt and repudiation, the rate of return payable on the public debt will include a risk premium reflecting the probability of default. Beyond some point, however, a further increase in the risk premium payable on the debt may make repudiation so much more attractive to the debtor that a rational lender would prefer not to increase his exposure. Credit rationing results: the government cannot borrow more on any terms.[10]

The preceding considerations make it seem unlikely that a government in one of the major industrialized countries would resort to wholesale repudiation of domestically-held public debt under peacetime conditions. In the aftermath of a war or following a major change in the political regime, however, rough treatment of private holders of public debt has not been uncommon.

In France in 1770, when the government faced the financial consequences of its participation in the American War of Independence, Abbé Terray effectively repudiated one-fifth of French government debt through a forcible refunding operation (see Kindleberger, 1984, p. 217).

Ricardo, in the years following the Napoleonic Wars, advocated a capital levy, and in Parliament said that such a tax was the best, in fact the only, way of handling the burden of accumulated wartime debt (Kindleberger, 1984, p. 62). This proposal was not taken up, however.

More recently, Germany has had two monetary reforms in the last sixty-two years, both of which involved a form of capital levy. After the hyperinflation in 1923, a mortgage on agricultural and industrial land served as backing for the new currency, the Rentenmark. The German monetary reform of 1948 consisted of a conversion of all money and debts at 10 : 1 (except for the first 60 Reichsmarks of currency per capita). Since private debtors had, for the most part, paid all their private creditors by then, the conversion involved mainly public debt. A further capital levy (or *Lastenausgleich*) of 50 per cent on the value of all real property and equity holdings was intended to correct at least in part the inequity as between owners of debt (which suffered a reduction in value of 90 per cent) and owners of real assets and shares of corporations. For political reasons, the capital levy was introduced in September 1948 separately from (and slightly later than) the conversion (Kindleberger, 1984).

For Italy, a capital levy to reduce the burden of the debt has been advocated recently by Basevi and Giavazzi (1983). The distinction between 'legitimate' or conventional tax increases and confiscatory capital levies is, of course, one of degree rather than kind and inevitably involves an element of subjective judgement. There would seem to be no economic or moral grounds for giving priority to safeguarding the owners of government debt against unexpected levies in preference to owners of real industrial and human capital. As regards the United Kingdom, with a debt burden which in 1985 is low by historical standards, with a safe middle-of-the-pack position among the major industrialized countries in terms of the *level*, and a uniquely favorable position as regards the *trend* of the debt–output ratio, the spectre of *de jure* or *de facto* repudiation should not haunt the holders of the UK public debt. Most other industrialized countries would seem to be in a similar position, although the high and rising debt burdens of Italy and Belgium (see Table 3.1) might be a cause for concern to those with a high propensity to worry.

'Selective' repudiation of the public debt (e.g., through an open-ended Ponzi-style rescheduling of externally held debt) has been more common. The Latin American foreign debt repudiations of the 1930s and the recent *de facto* external insolvency of Poland, Zaire, and a number of the smaller Latin American countries are reminders of the possibility of sovereign default — all the more so since none of these defaults involved the kind of dramatic political upheaval and change of regime that led to the repudiation of the Tsarist debt by the new Soviet regime and of the Batista debt by the Castro government in Cuba. Nevertheless, the conditions, whether political or economic, that have historically been associated with repudiation of externally held public debt, seem sufficiently different from those faced by today's industrialized countries that even such 'selective' debt repudiations seem rather unlikely.

3.5 CROWDING OUT

Even without fears of the eventual monetization of the deficit (and hence inflation) or of a future debt repudiation, there may be other worries about large deficits and debt–output ratios. It is often alleged that a debt-financed fiscal expansion will 'crowd out' private economic activity. I shall continue to focus on the consequences of substituting public borrowing for tax financing of a given exhaustive public spending program. Typically, these consequences include the effect on private saving, investment and the current account of the balance of payments, and in the longer run the capital intensity of production and the country's net external asset position. Before turning to these effects in detail, I deal with the assertion that the substitution of debt for tax finance will have no effects whatsoever.

3.5.1 The neutrality of debt and deficits

Barro (1974) has shown that, given perfect foresight, debt neutrality will obtain when three conditions are met: (a) private agents can lend and borrow on the same terms as the government; (b) private agents are able and willing to undo any government scheme to redistribute spending power between generations; and (c) all taxes and transfer payments are lump-sum, by which we mean that their basis of assessment is independent of private agents' decisions about production, labor supply, consumption, or asset accumulation. Under these extreme assumptions, any change in government financing (government saving or dissaving) is offset one-for-one by a corresponding change in private saving itself financed by the accompanying tax changes.

All three assumptions are of course hopelessly unrealistic. Condition (a) fails because credit rationing, liquidity constraints, large spreads between lending and borrowing rates of interest, and private borrowing rates well in excess of those enjoyed by the government are an established fact in most industrial countries. These empirical findings are underpinned by the new and burgeoning theoretical literature on asymmetric information and the implications of moral hazard and adverse selection for private financial markets (see Webb, 1980; Stiglitz and Weiss, 1981; Grossman and Hart, 1983; Williamson, 1984; Greenwald and Stiglitz, 1984; and Laffont, 1985); and by game-theoretic insights of how active competition in financial markets can yield credit rationing as the equilibrium outcome (see Eaton and Gersovitz, 1981a; 1981b; Sachs, 1984; Sachs and Cooper, 1984; and Ghosh, 1985).

Condition (b) fails because it requires either that agents must live for ever or else effectively do so through the account they take of their children and parents in making gifts and bequests. In reality, private decision horizons are finite and frequently quite short. Some households do not care about their descendants, others attach no weight to their welfare. Even among those who love their parents and children, the probability of child-lessness in current and future generations leads current savers to discount, at least in part, the welfare transfer which can be achieved across generations through gifts or bequests.

Condition (c) fails because in practice taxes and subsidies are rarely lump-sum. Explicitly or implicitly individuals can deduce the basis of the tax assessment and impute the relevant marginal tax rate to their decisions on consumption, work, and asset accumulation. Under certain assumptions, recognition of distortionary taxation can lead to a prescription for tax 'smoothing' over time to minimize the welfare burden or collection cost of the tax system; if so, it can provide an argument for temporary deficits or surpluses (Barro, 1979).

In any case, I conclude that the possible neutrality of public debt and deficits is little more than a theoretical curiosum. The models underlying the discussion of crowding out in the remainder of this section all rely on differences between public and private borrowing rates and opportunities, though frequently, as with the Keynesian multiplier, this dependence on imperfections in capital markets is only implicit. The distortionary nature of taxes will at times be important in the discussion that follows.

3.5.2 Old-fashioned Keynesian short-run crowding out

The 'short run' of old-fashioned Keynesian crowding out refers to the assumption that changes in the outstanding stocks (private non-human wealth, domestic capital, government debt, high-powered money, and net foreign assets) brought about by the flows (private saving, investment, government borrowing, monetization, and foreign investment) over the period under consideration are very small relative to the stocks and can be ignored. Expectations (of future interest rates, exchange rates, prices or demand) are also taken as given.

'Crowding out' in what follows refers only to what I have called elsewhere 'indirect crowding out'. 'Direct crowding out' occurs when government instruments affect private decision-making directly. For instance, government spending on health may be a substitute for private spending. 'Indirect crowding out' refers to the effects on the level and composition of output of a tax cut or a spending increase through effects on budget constraints, interest rates, exchange rates, wages or prices (Buiter, 1977). 'Keynesian' means that demand effects alone are considered. It is assumed that there is spare capacity on the supply side so that any increase in demand will happily be fulfilled.

Figure 3.6 depicts a familiar *IS–LM* diagram, the *IS* curve showing the level of output demand associated with a given level of interest rates and the *LM* schedule showing the combinations of output and interest rates which keep the demand for money in line with its fixed supply. Suppose there is a substitution of debt for tax finance. An income tax cut raises

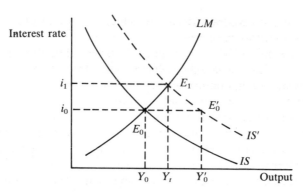

Figure 3.6 Effect of a tax cut

output demand, shifts the *IS* schedule to the right, and moves the equilibrium from E_0 to E_1. What is crowded out? In this example, private investment. The tax cut boosts consumer spending and total output, forcing a rise in interest rates to keep money demand in line with its fixed supply. The higher interest rates hit investment. Whether this crowding out should be attributed to the fiscal stimulus or to the unwillingness of the monetary authority to hold interest rates by expanding the money supply is a semantic question.

A different picture emerges when the tax cut takes the form of an investment subsidy. Now both private consumption and private investment are increased at E_1. Of course private investment is lower at E_1 than it would have been at E_0' (at the lower level of interest rates) but it is higher than at E_0.

Within this framework, can a bond financed tax cut actually be contractionary? Mankiw and Summers (1984) argue that taxes may affect money demand through their effect on the transactions variable. If disposable income is the relevant proxy for transactions,[11] a tax cut will boost money demand and shift the *LM* schedule to the left. In principle, this could outweigh the expansionary effect of the rightward shift in the *IS* schedule and leave the economy with lower output. Interest rates, of course, would rise unambiguously.

One final word on short-run Keynesian crowding out is in order. In an open economy with a freely floating exchange rate and facing perfect international capital mobility, crowding out is complete. A bond-financed tax cut stimulates domestic spending but also induces a nominal and real exchange rate appreciation which crowds out net exports by a matching amount, leaving aggregate demand unaltered.

3.5.3 Old-fashioned classical short-run crowding out

In the classical model, wage and price flexibility maintain the economy at 'full employment' even in the short run. Thus, in the simplest version of the model, output supply is simply fixed. Fiscal changes which stimulate some components of aggregate demand necessarily induce complete crowding out of other demand components to maintain total demand in line with the fixed total supply. In the Keynesian model, short-run crowding out is primarily the result of a failure to co-ordinate monetary and fiscal policy; in the classical model it is inevitable. It is of course possible to give a more sophisticated treatment in which fiscal changes, by changing *marginal* tax rates, alter microeconomic incentives and change full employment output. Such supply-side economics is not my chief concern here.

3.5.4 Old-fashioned Keynesian long-run crowding out

The 'government budget constraint' literature (Christ, 1968; Blinder and Solow, 1973; Tobin and Buiter, 1976) was generated by the recognition that bond-financed public sector deficits imply a cumulative growth of the outstanding stock of debt and that this 'intrinsic' dynamic would shift the *LM* and *IS* curves, if wealth effects on money demand and consumption demand are present and if government debt is perceived as net wealth at least to some extent. The simplest models ignored asset accumulation other than through public sector deficits (e.g., private capital accumulation and foreign wealth dynamics through the current account of the balance of payments). The Keynesian version continued to treat the price level as given and output as determined by effective demand.

Consider the case of bond-financed deficits. Regardless of the nature of the fiscal policy action (or other exogenous shock) that causes a deficit or surplus, as long as the deficit (surplus) persists, the *IS* curve will be shifting to the right (if consumption increases with wealth) and the *LM* curve to the left (if the demand for money also increases with wealth). Left to themselves, deficits feed on themselves. For simplicity, consider the case where taxes and transfer payments do not adjust to changes in the debt-service component of the budget. Higher debt means higher debt service at any given interest rate. It also produces a higher interest rate on the existing debt. After a disturbance, this economy can only ever settle down in a balanced budget equilibrium if debt issues, through a strong wealth effect on consumption, raise activity and the tax base by enough to raise income-related taxes by more than the total increase in interest costs. Explosive debt growth is certainly possible with this particular (perhaps rather implausible) specification of the fiscal policy rule: fixed values of government spending and tax rates.

Stability or instability is, however, a function both of the parameters describing the behavior of the private economy and of the parameters describing government behavior. For example, if the authorities had a fiscal decision rule which raised taxes or lowered transfer payments whenever debt service increased, stability would become much more likely. Assuming an increase in wealth raises demand overall (wealth effects on consumption are more powerful than those on money demand), stability of the debt-deficit process can be ensured by raising taxes sufficiently in response to the increased debt service. Even if an increase in wealth actually reduced demand (because of its effect on money demand and thence on interest rates), the debt explosion can still be smothered if taxes are raised by *more* than the increased debt service. There are many alternative debt-stabilizing tax-transfer functions, and the addition of exhaustive public spending to the arsenal of potential debt-stabilizing instruments only reinforces the conclusion that an explosive debt-deficit spiral is a *policy choice* rather than a deep structural property of the economy.

If tax revenues do not rise with the debt service, and *if the model is stable*, one can check that a bond-financed tax cut has a stronger expansionary effect on output in the long run than a money-financed tax cut. This is because in equilibrium tax revenues must be higher, and therefore the tax base larger, under bond financing than under money financing in order to pay for the higher level of debt interest as well as financing the tax cut itself. I do not consider this result, due to Blinder and Solow, to have much policy relevance. It amounts to a restatement of the (very strict) stability conditions for this model under the given specification of the public spending and revenue functions. If this model is to be stable under bond financing, then endogenous income-related tax revenues must outstrip the explosive intrinsic debt dynamics. This can only happen if a larger stock of bonds raises demand (and thus output) to such an extent that tax revenues grow faster than debt service.

The major weakness of this class of models is that the significance of a dynamic analysis (and a comparison of stationary equilibria) which extends into the long run the assumptions of nominal wage and/or price rigidity and demand-constrained output of the short-run Keynesian model, is not too apparent. A further problem has been that the focus on fixed price, zero-trend real growth models has at times led to the identification of stationary equilibria with balanced budget equilibria. Stationary equilibria are more generally characterized by stationary stock–flow and stock–stock ratios. Nominal asset stocks can grow (shrink) at the sum of the growth rates of the general price level and the level of capacity output. These shortcomings have been rectified in a number of places (see Buiter, 1979) by adding some version of an augmented Phillips curve to the Blinder–Solow model and thus combining short-run nominal rigidity with long-run nominal wage and price flexibility.

It should be intuitively obvious that adding an exogenous capacity constraint or full-employment output constraint to the *IS-LM*-government budget constraint model, worsens the prospects for stability under the usual specification of the taxation and public spending functions. The reason is that the tax base (the exogenous level of real income) cannot expand in the long run to offset the effect of higher interest payments on the deficit. Stability can now be achieved only if a larger stock of debt raises the general price level by enough to lower the real value of debt interest payments, even though their nominal value increases. If full-employment output is endogenous in the long run, say through private capital formation, prospects for stability under the given tax-transfer and spending rules are even dimmer. This is because debt-financing almost certainly raises real interest rates and, except in a Keynesian demand-constrained regime, lowers the incentive to invest. This reduces the tax base and thus increases the likelihood of debt-deficit instability.

The lasting insight from the government budget constraint literature is that it made it very clear that questions such as 'what is the effect on output of an increase in public spending by an amount *x*?', are badly (because incompletely) worded. One must specify both the *financing mode* and the *term* (impact, steady-state or 'real time' over some given horizon) to which the question applies. Answers take the form of a financing mode-contingent sequence of dynamic multipliers.

The open economy versions of the Keynesian budget constraint literature (see, for example, Branson, 1975; 1976; and Jones and Kenen, 1985) added much of interest, but for our purposes the essentials of debt dynamics in Keynesian models are represented adequately by the closed economy models. Rather than spending any time on old-fashioned classical long-run crowding out (see, for example, Buiter, 1979; and Tobin and Buiter, 1976), the important insights of the classical perspective will be discussed within a rational expectations setting.

3.5.5 Portfolio crowding out

Tobin (1961; 1969) extended the Keynesian two-asset (money–bonds) model, with its implicit assumption of perfect substitutability in private portfolios between bonds and claims on capital, to a general three-asset (money–bonds–capital) model. The effect on investment of an increase in the stock of debt will depend on the relative degrees of substitutability of bonds *vis-à-vis* money and bonds *vis-à-vis* capital. When bonds and capital are closer substitutes, an increase in debt will raise the required rate of return on capital along with the interest rate. When bonds and money are closer substitutes, an increase in debt will lower the required rate of return on capital although the interest rate will still rise. Friedman (1985) and Frenkel (1983) have provided empirical evidence, using US data and a capital-asset pricing version of the money–bonds model, of the effect of changes in the stock of debt on the yield differentials between bonds and capital. In general, these will be a function of asset supplies, the degree of risk aversion, and the perceived correlation of asset returns. Frenkel finds negligible effects of relative asset supplies on yield premiums. Friedman finds statistically significant and small but non-negligible effects. Their evidence, however, relates to the *relative* required rates of return on bonds and capital. The effect of debt on the overall *level* of rates of return is not analyzed. A zero effect of relative asset supplies on the bonds–capital return differential (the traditional Keynesian perfect-substitutes case) is, of course, quite consistent with a strong crowding out effect of debt through the level of common required rate of return on bonds and capital. (See also Friedman, 1984; and Roley, 1983.)

3.5.6 Rational expectations-augmented Keynesian crowding out

Within the Keynesian tradition, the incorporation of forward-looking rational expectations of endogenous variables has made an important contribution to our understanding of the effects of fiscal policy on aggregate demand. Intertemporal speculation or arbitrage enters Keynesian models in two ways: first, in closed economy models, through an arbitrage condition linking short and long interest rates (or short interest rates and a stock market-index); and second, in open economy models, through an arbitrage condition linking the exchange rate and domestic–foreign interest differentials. Not only must the financing mode and the term be specified before an answer to any question concerning the effects of tax or spending changes can be given, but the manner in which information about the policy instruments (and about all other exogenous 'fundamentals') accrues to and is absorbed by private agents must be detailed. In order to make meaningful use of the model one must specify whether the exogenous variables are: (a) unanticipated or anticipated (and if the latter, when); and (b) perceived as permanent, transitory, or reversible. The structure of the model and the current, past and expected future values of the exogenous variables determine the current behavior of the economy. It is impossible to study the short-run behavior of the model without at the same time (and as part of the same exercise) solving for the entire future (expected) behavior of the model, including its long-run steady-state properties.

The easiest way to see what this implies for the crowding-out debate is to assume that investment depends inversely on the long interest rate rather than the short interest rate as in the conventional *IS–LM* model introduced above (Blanchard, 1981). Long and short rates are linked through the 'expectations' hypothesis of the term structure: the short rate equals the expected return on long debt (yield plus expected capital gains or losses). This makes today's long rate a forward-looking moving average of current and future expected short rates. In this modified model the effect of an

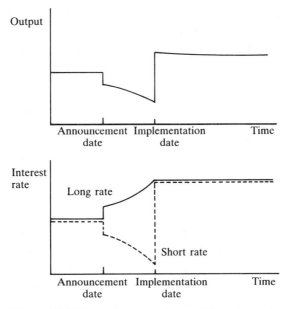

Figure 3.7 Effects of an anticipated future tax cut

unanticipated, immediate and permanent cut in taxes (or increase in spending) is the same as in the simple Keynesian model. What is different is that the impact effect of the unexpected announcement of a *future* expansionary fiscal policy move (a cut in taxes or increase in spending) is contractionary. The intuition is clear. Between the *announcement date* and the *implementation date* there is not yet any stimulus to demand from higher spending or lower taxes. Investors in financial markets do, however, take into account the future increase in demand. Short-term interest rates are therefore expected to be higher after implementation, when the fiscal boost gets under way. At the announcement date, therefore, the long rate increases in line with the higher expected future short rates, thus lowering investment, current output, and the current short rate of interest. (In terms of Figure 3.6 the *IS* schedule shifts leftwards.) The behavior of output, and of long and short rates over time, is sketched in Figure 3.7. The main point is that the announcement effect of an anticipated future fiscal expansion will result in a negative impact multiplier. When the fiscal stimulus finally occurs, output will, of course, rise in the manner indicated by the traditional short-run *IS–LM* model.

A role very similar to that played by the long rate of interest in the closed economy model is played by the (real) exchange rate in the rational-expectations version of the open economy model with perfect capital mobility and a freely floating exchange rate. Arbitrage between domestic and foreign assets implies that, on the assumption of risk neutrality, any interest differential in favor of the home country must be offset by expected depreciation of the domestic currency. The deviation of the nominal (real) exchange rate from its underlying equilibrium value is then given as a forward-looking moving average of the domestic–foreign nominal (real) interest differential. A fiscal expansion which is immediate, permanent, and unanticipated raises all current and expected future domestic interest rates; given foreign interest rates, the nominal exchange rate will therefore 'jump'-appreciate. Given foreign interest rates and the domestic and foreign price levels, the real exchange rate also jump-appreciates. In this case, it is easily checked that there will be full crowding out: output does not increase as the fiscal stimulus is negated by a loss of competitiveness. An *anticipated* future fiscal expansion will be contractionary as the exchange rate appreciates, because of the expectation of future higher domestic interest rates, before the demand stimulus from the fiscal expansion occurs.

Both these examples of negative fiscal announcement impact multipliers have nothing to do with deficits *per se*. They would occur even if the fiscal stimulus were of the balanced-budget variety and indeed as a result of any anticipated private or public, domestic or foreign shock that shifts future *IS* curves to the right. To highlight the role of deficits in a rational expectations setting, we need to marry our modified closed-economy short-run Keynesian model, in which investment depends inversely on long rather than short real interest rates, with the asset accumulation implied by the government budget identity that underlies the discussion in Subsection 3.5.4. In Appendix 3B I show how such a model can yield a negative impact multiplier from an immediately implemented 'expansionary' fiscal policy such as a permanent tax cut. Essentially this comes about because anticipated future deficits and a bias towards bond rather than money finance raise future short real interest rates and, through the expectations hypothesis of the term structure, also raise the current long real interest rate. If the effect of long real interest rates on investment is sufficiently powerful the reduction in investment could more than offset the immediate expansionary effect on the tax cut *per se*. There is thus more than 100 per cent crowding out in the short term. If capacity is endogenous the reduction in investment may gradually reduce the capital stock and thus induce more than 100 per cent crowding out even in the long term when full employment is restored.

I have discussed the possibility of negative impact effects of tax cuts at some length both because some of these models are relatively recent, and perhaps unfamiliar, and because in the policy debate opponents of fiscal expansion sometimes rely explicitly or implicitly on such effects. Thus, while I am happy to acknowledge their theoretical possibility, I should make very clear that I do not believe there is much evidence to support their relevance in the circumstances currently faced by most of the industrial nations. Such considerations should not stand in the way of an appropriate (temporary) fiscal expansion when countries face a Keynesian recession.

3.5.7 Rational expectations — augmented classical crowding-out and the impossibility of cutting taxes

This is a suitable point to bring out one of the consequences of the government's having to satisfy its intertemporal budget constraint. Given the real exhaustive spending program, and given the revenues from future seigniorage, a tax cut today requires, on average, a tax increase tomorrow if the government is to satisfy its solvency constraint. We should therefore talk of an intertemporal reallocation or redistribution of taxes and transfer payments. Consider the government solvency constraint presented in Equations (3.4) and (3.4a). The present value of government spending is not automatically given when the entire current and future path of spending is given, because current and expected future real interest rates need not be invariant under the changes in fiscal policy that are being considered. The simplest case is the small open economy whose external terms of trade are exogenous and constant and whose internal rate of interest is determined exclusively by the exogenously given world rate of interest. This makes the present value of government spending independent of any changes in the policy mix. The authorities merely reshuffle a given present discounted value of taxes over time. A current tax cut must imply a future tax increase of equal present value. That is not to say that such a reallocation of taxes towards the future will have no effects. In a classical, rational expectations model such as that of Blanchard (1985), uncertain lifetimes cause private individuals to discount future income and taxes at a rate higher than the government's discount rate. A sequence of early tax cuts followed by a later tax increase of equal present value when discounted at the government's discount rate will represent a net reduction in the present value of current and future taxes when discounted at the higher discount rate used by private individuals. This boost in private sector human capital will have the familiar result of boosting consumption, lowering private saving in the short run, reducing the current account surplus, and reducing private non-human wealth in the long run. In the small open economy, the capital–output ratio is held in place by the world interest rate, and long-run crowding out takes the form of a reduction in the country's financial claims on the rest of the world.

In a closed economy or an open economy large enough to influence the terms of trade or the world interest rate, the path of the discount rate will be a function of the government's financing policy. In Blanchard (1984;

1985) and Buiter (1984b) it is shown that it is still true that an early tax cut requires a later tax increase (if the public spending program is held constant) or a later exhaustive spending cut (if the tax-transfer program is held constant except for the early cuts). The real interest rate rises immediately and stays high even when in due course the tax cuts are reversed. The reason is that, in the meantime, a sequence of government budget deficits has added to the total outstanding stock of debt, which keeps interest rates high at home and abroad. Investment declines at home and abroad in the short run, and in the long run the capital intensity of production is lowered. Domestic public debt thus crowds out capital formation at home and abroad. It also results in a domestic current account deficit and a long-run reduction in the home country's net external asset position. Tanzi (1985) discusses in more detail the international consequences of fiscal deficits in the United States.

For some purposes it is convenient to think about the steady state, the long run in which all real variables are constant. However, such analysis requires some care, and logical pitfalls must be avoided. To illustrate, consider a steady state in which spending and taxes are constant and real output growth is zero. The steady-state government budget identity implies that the surplus of taxes over exhaustive spending must equal interest payments for debt service.

This appears to suggest that the way to reduce the outstanding stock of government debt in the long run is to cut taxes or raise public spending! This, of course, is nonsense. A tax cut implies higher borrowing in the short run and therefore higher debt and increased debt service and yet higher borrowing in the long run. The process is explosive. The correct interpretation of the steady-state government budget identity is that if a country wishes to have lower taxes (or higher exhaustive public spending) in the long run, it will have to reduce its debt service burden. For given levels of exhaustive spending and real interest rates, this requires an initial period of high taxes, budget surpluses, and debt repurchase. Only then will a lower long-run debt stock allow lower taxes in the long run.

The same caution in interpreting steady-state multipliers is required when one considers the long-run net foreign asset position of a country. The analogue of the government budget identity is that net acquisition of foreign assets is identical to the excess of national income (including interest receipts on foreign asset holdings) over domestic spending (absorption). Thus, in the steady state, when no accumulation or decumulation of foreign assets is taking place, (net) interest from abroad is exactly equal to the excess of domestic spending over domestic income. This could be misinterpreted as saying that in order to increase a country's holdings of foreign assets one should boost absorption relative to domestic income. What it means instead is that if a country wishes to increase its long-run absorption relative to its domestic income, it must first have acquired foreign assets which will generate the income stream to make good the difference. To build up such foreign assets, domestic absorption must initially be held below domestic income.

There are two qualifications to these results concerning the intertemporal reallocation of taxes (or primary surpluses more generally). First, all of the analysis has been carried out assuming continuous full employment — all of the models by Blanchard (1984; 1985), Buiter (1984) and Frenkel and Razin (1984), assume markets clear. The cost–benefit analysis of an intertemporal tax reallocation program may be very different if the initial situation is one of Keynesian unemployment; then it is possible to boost private investment or net foreign investment. With spare capacity, additional demand may simply call forth additional output.

Second, real world taxes are not lump-sum but typically take the form of a tax rate (or schedule of rates) applied to a tax base such as value added, wages, profits, or sales revenue. Consider the simplest case where tax receipts are a linear function of income. While it is still true that (given spending) a cut in total taxes now requires an increase in total taxes later, it is not necessarily the case that a cut now in either thresholds or the tax rate will require a future increase in either thresholds or the tax rate. The tax *base* could increase sufficiently as a result of the early tax rate cut (or increase in thresholds) to permit the higher required future taxes to be raised at an unchanged (or conceivably lower) tax rate and an unchanged (or higher) threshold. The contributions of Blinder and Solow (1973), and Tobin and Buiter (1976), discussed earlier, analyzed this possibility in a Keynesian fixed-price setting, and, in the case of Tobin and Buiter, in a full-employment, flexible-price setting. No stable Keynesian model that I know, however, has the property that a cut in threshold or tax rates will boost output on impact to such an extent that total tax receipts actually increase and deficits fall in the short run. That feat, as we saw, can only be achieved in the long run if the positive wealth effect on consumption demand of a larger stock of public debt outweighs the effect on money demand by enough to generate an increase in taxable income that is sufficient to service the increase in debt at the lower tax rates.

The classical version of the Keynesian super-multiplier is the Laffer effect; lower tax rates lead to a reduction in distortions and misallocations and boost incentives to work, save, invest and innovate to such an extent that 'full employment' output increases by enough to generate increased tax revenues at a lower tax rate. I know of no empirical evidence to support the proposition that (the absolute value of) the elasticity of the tax base with respect to the tax rate is greater than unity. It goes without saying that even without the extreme versions of the Keynesian demand multiplier and Laffer's supply multiplier being relevant, careful attention to both the demand-(de)stabilizing properties and the (mis)allocative effects of tax changes is essential for economic policy design.

3.6 MEASURES OF FISCAL STANCE

The discussion of Section 3.5 should have made it clear that in order to obtain a measure of the effect of the stance of fiscal policy on aggregate demand, one needs a *model* of the economy, and a *bench-mark* or *reference specification* for policy. As regards the former, I can only restate the conclusion reached by Blinder and Solow (1974) that there are no 'model-free' measures of fiscal impact on aggregate demand. Different views on how the economy works will give rise to conclusions about the demand effect of fiscal policy measures (whether they be isolated changes in the values of certain instruments or changes in the parameters describing fiscal and financial decision rules) that may differ not only in magnitude but even in direction. The need for a bench-mark or reference path is equally obvious. 'Expansionary (or contractionary) relative to what?' should be the immediate response to the question whether the stance of fiscal policy is expansionary or contractionary. If total tax receipts increase, is this a discretionary move to tighten fiscal policy (the reference point is the pre-existing level of taxes) or the automatic response of tax receipts to endogenous fluctuations in economic activity, given the existing tax rates and thresholds (the bench-mark is the original tax rates and thresholds)? As long as one is explicit about the bench-mark reference path or 'origin' for one's comparison, there should be no confusion on this account.

Certain conclusions about much-abused fiscal indicators are worth stating explicitly.

1. There is no existing model of the economy that yields the public sector deficit, the change in the public sector deficit, its share in GDP or the change in its share in GDP as a measure of fiscal impact on demand, short-run, long-run, or real-time.
2. There is no existing model of the economy that yields the cyclically corrected (full-employment) deficit, the change in this deficit, its share in GDP or the change in its share in GDP as a measure of fiscal impact on aggregate demand in any run.
3. There is no existing model of the economy that yields the cyclically and inflation-corrected deficit (its change, share in GDP or change in its share in GDP) as a measure of fiscal impact on aggregate demand in any run.
4. There is no existing model of the economy that yields the level or change in the debt–GDP ratio as a measure of fiscal impact on aggregate demand in any run.

From (2) and (3) it follows, for example, that both the OECD's and the IMF's fiscal measures are uninformative as measures of fiscal impact on demand (see IMF, 1985; and OECD, 1985).

What would a proper measure of fiscal impact on aggregate demand look like? Basically, it involves a comparison of two simulations (or two sets of stochastic simulations) of an economic model with different sets of parameter values in certain fiscal and financial decision rules. Sometimes, with very simple models, this can be done analytically.

In Appendix 3C, I derive an explicit solution for the impact effect on aggregate demand of fiscal policy in the simple static expectations, closed-economy Keynesian model. It is constructed by weighting together changes in government spending and taxes, where the weights are the usual Keynesian impact multipliers. These multiplier weights are evaluated at the actual (not necessarily the cyclically-corrected) level of output and will be smaller when monetary policy is non-accommodating than when it is accommodating (because a fiscal expansion leads to a rise in interest rates and some crowding out of investment when monetary policy is non-accommodating).

In the same appendix, I present a rather different measure of fiscal impact derived from Blanchard's (1985) classical model with rational expectations and uncertain lifetimes. Here consumers correctly anticipate the increase in future taxes associated with any current increase in government spending or reduction in taxes but, because of their uncertain longevity, these are discounted more heavily than if the discounting were carried out at market interest rates. The explicitly forward looking nature of this measure of fiscal stance contrasts strongly with the simple Keynesian measure. Expectations of future spending, taxes, and interest rates must be modeled to obtain the current demand effect of fiscal and financial policy. Spending on goods and services by the government only boosts demand if current spending exceeds its 'permanent' or average expected future value. Government debt has an effect on demand only to the extent that consumers discount the future more heavily than the (infinitely lived) government.

While these two illustrative fiscal stance measures are at opposite ends of the spectrum, they do convey the right flavor of the range of views on the fiscal stance that different economists (or even the same economist at different times) can hold.

It is informative to look at some of the indices that have been (ab)used as measures of fiscal stance. Figure 3.8 graphs five measures of fiscal stance for the United States and Figure 3.9 does the same for the United Kingdom. For both countries we show the change in the actual general government financial deficit as a percentage of GDP and two measures of the change in the cyclically-corrected (full-employment or structural) deficit as a percentage of GDP, one constructed and published by the IMF and one by the OECD. Also for both countries we have the change in the inflation-corrected and cyclically-adjusted general government financial deficit as a percentage of GDP. Finally, for the United States there is a short run of figures giving an estimate of the change in Blanchard's measure of fiscal

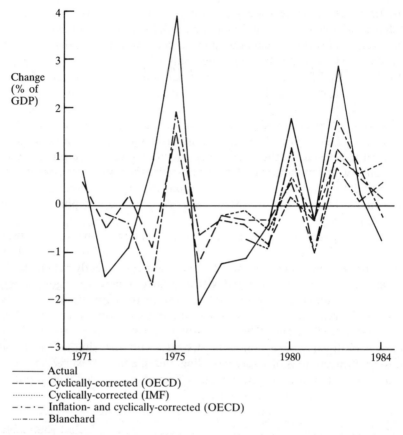

Actual
----- Cyclically-corrected (OECD)
············ Cyclically-corrected (IMF)
– · – · – Inflation- and cyclically-corrected (OECD)
····–···– Blanchard

Figure 3.8 Five general government fiscal impulse measures, United States

stance, and for the United Kingdom there is a set of National Institute of Economic and Social Research (NIESR) estimates of the change in 'demand-weighted', cyclically-corrected deficit measure. The latter represents an attempt to estimate the impact effect of discretionary fiscal changes on the demand for currently produced domestic output in a simple Keynesian world.

The summary statistics provided in Tables 3.6–3.8 show that the different indices tell quite different stories. For the United States, over the brief period for which all five measures are available (1978–84), the divergence between the various indices is smallest. Even here, the mean change in the deficit as a percentage of GDP lies between 0.36 for the actual deficit and 0.00 for Blanchard's measure. The standard deviation of the actual deficit change is about twice that of the other measures. The measures are all positively correlated, but the correlation ranges from a

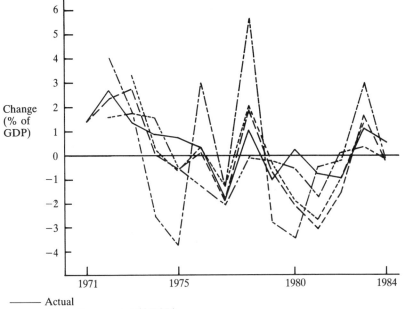

——— Actual
----- Cyclically-corrected (OECD)
············ Cyclically-corrected (IMF)
– · – · – Inflation- and cyclically-corrected (OECD)
····–····– Demand-weighted, cyclically-corrected (NIESR)

Figure 3.9 Five general government fiscal impulse measures, United Kingdom

Table 3.6 Behavior of five indices of fiscal stance, United States, 1978–84*

Variables	Mean	Standard deviation
Actual	0.36	1.46
Cyclically-corrected (OECD)	0.14	0.70
Cyclically-corrected (IMF)	0.33	0.61
Inflation- and cyclically- corrected (OECD)	0.16	0.88
Blanchard	0.00	0.88

* Change in (corrected) deficit as a percentage of actual or potential GNP.

Correlation matrix

	Actual	OECD	IMF	Infl-OECD	Blanchard
Actual	1.00				
Cyclically-corrected (OECD)	0.78	1.00			
Cyclically-corrected (IMF)	0.58	0.86	1.00		
Inflation- and cyclically- corrected (OECD)	0.83	0.86	0.76	1.00	
Blanchard	0.72	0.84	0.88	0.64	1.00

Table 3.7 Behavior of three indices of fiscal stance, United States, 1972–84

Variable	Mean	Standard deviation
Actual	0.12	1.79
Cyclically-corrected (OECD)	−0.008	0.81
Inflation- and cyclically-corrected (OECD)	−0.02	1.00

Correction matrix

Actual	1.00		
Cyclically-corrected (OECD)	0.78	1.00	
Inflation- and cyclically-corrected (OECD)	0.70	0.87	1.00

Table 3.8 Behavior of five indices of fiscal stance, United Kingdom, 1973–84*

Variable	Mean	Standard deviation
Actual	0.18	1.03
Cyclically-corrected (OECD)	−0.23	1.74
Cyclically-corrected (IMF)	−0.01	1.61
Inflation- and cyclically-corrected (OECD)	−0.05	2.93
Demand-weighted, cyclically-corrected (NIESR)	−0.21	1.15

* Change in (corrected) deficit as a percentage of actual or potential GNP.

Correlation matrix

Actual	1.00				
Cyclically-corrected (OECD)	0.75	1.00			
Cyclically-corrected (IMF)	0.69	0.99	1.00		
Inflation- and cyclically-corrected (OECD)	0.39	0.65	0.64	1.00	
Demand-weighted, cyclically-corrected (NIESR)	0.64	0.65	0.69	0.09	1.00

high of 0.88 (between Blanchard's measure and the IMF's cyclically-corrected measure) to a low of 0.58 between the IMF's cyclically-corrected deficit measure and the actual deficit. Similar conclusions emerge when the sample period includes 1972–5, when the IMF and Blanchard's measure are unavailable (see Table 3.7).

For the United Kingdom (Table 3.8), the five measures behave very differently over the period 1973–84. The mean change in the deficit as a percentage of GDP ranges from 0.18 for the actual deficit to −0.23 for the OECD's cyclically-corrected measure. The change in the actual deficit is the least volatile of the five measures, while for the United States it was the most volatile. The wildest swings are exhibited by the inflation and cyclically-corrected deficit measure of the OECD because of the great volatility of *ex post* UK annual inflation rates over the period. The IMF's and the OECD's cyclically-corrected measures are almost perfectly positively correlated. Very low correlations are recorded for the actual deficit and the inflation- and cyclically-corrected deficit (0.39) and for the demand-weighted cyclically-corrected deficit and the inflation- and cyclically-corrected deficit (0.09).

Incorrect measures may sometimes give the right answer: the man who always insists it is 12 o'clock will be correct twice a day. Blanchard's measure and the NIESR's measure have the virtue of being model-based. Those who like the model must like the measure; those who disagree can be explicit and precise about the nature of the disagreement and so arrive at their own preferred model-based measure. None of the other measures have interpretations as indices of the impact of fiscal policy on aggregate demand. Some (such as a superior version of the inflation- and cyclically-corrected deficit) may be crude approximations to one of the 'permanent deficit' or solvency measures.

In general, the information required to obtain a measure of fiscal impact on demand consists of the following:

1. A model of the economy (one hopes for one that respects stock-flow identities and treats expectations seriously).
2. A specification of the length of the period over which one wishes to measure the impact of fiscal policy.
3. A full specification of the bench-mark and the alternative policies. This includes the following:
   (a) How fiscal policy is parameterized (the tax and spending functions).
   (b) How monetary and financial policy are parameterized. (Is monetary policy fully accommodating, non-accommodating, or something in between? What is the exchange rate rule? etc.)
4. A full specification of how information about the changes in fiscal and financial policy actions or rules is disseminated to and processed by the private sector. This includes at least a characterization of the unanticipated/anticipated, current/future, and permanent/transitory aspects of the policy change.

All this is hard work. It is also essential for informed policy debate. It is possible that there are reasonable shortcuts, but we will not know this until we have first obtained the results from following the correct procedures, which can then be compared with the answers suggested by seat-of-the-pants methods.

3.7 CONCLUSIONS

Probably more uninformed statements have been made on the issue of public sector debt and deficits than on any other topic in macroeconomics. Proof by repeated assertion has frequently appeared to be an acceptable substitute for the more conventional methods of proof by deduction or by induction. The public debt in the long run, and (except under some rather special parameterizations of fiscal and financial policy) the public sector deficit in the long run and in the short run, are endogenously determined by the interaction of the economic system and the government's policy rules. As with all predetermined or endogenous variables, observations on public sector debt and deficits contain information about the current state and future evolution of the economy; they are signals from which the careful practitioner can extract information. The practical problem is that (changes in) debt and deficits can signal almost anything, depending on the nature of the exogenous shocks perturbing the system and on the structure of the rest of the transmission mechanism. A larger deficit may signal a loosening of fiscal policy or a tightening of fiscal policy (without which the deficit would have been even larger) in response to a fall in export demand or a collapse in domestic confidence. A larger deficit could also reflect a tightening of monetary policy with an unchanged fiscal stance. It may signal increased eventual future monetization, higher expected future taxes, lower expected future spending, or a greater probability of debt-repudiation. It may also signal none of the above. To determine the significance of the behavior of public debt and deficits, we must get away from the dangerous shortcuts of 'model-free' single-figure indices of fiscal stance. The way to deal with a complex issue is not by pretending that it is really quite simple. The fiscal and financial policy choices that codetermine the behavior of public debt and deficits are too serious a matter for them to be left either to fiscal quacks or to purveyors of conventional wisdom.

3.8 NOTES

1. See Buiter (1983) for an extended discussion of the real interest rate which is most appropriate for such calculations.
2. Models such as that of Sidrauski (1967), with infinitely-lived households characterized by a constant pure rate of time preference, show no long-run effect of anticipated money growth or inflation on the real interest rate. Money–capital models in the spirit of Tobin (1965) have a negative long-run effect of higher inflation on the marginal product of capital and thus on the real interest rate, as portfolio holders switch from money to real capital in response to a higher rate of inflation. Carmichael and Stebbing (1983) found that the data supported a negative relationship between the real rate of interest and the rate of inflation. The proposition that the nominal interest rate was invariant

under the rate of inflation could not be rejected. See also the papers collected in Tanzi (1984).

3. Formally, if real money demand $m = l(i, \pi, y)$ such that $l_i, l_\pi \leq 0 \leq l_y$ then $d(\mu m)/d\mu = m + \mu(l_i + l_\pi) > 0$ if $(l_i + l_\pi)\mu/m > -1$ (where i, π, y, and μ respectively denote nominal interest rate, inflation rate, real output, and nominal money growth). Note that this condition relates to the elasticity of real money demand with respect to money growth μ. The elasticity condition with respect to the inflation rate π will be identical only when real output growth is negligible relative to inflation and money growth.

4. When the inflation rate was included as a regressor, neither the short nor either of the two long interest rates was significant. The estimated long-run income elasticity of 2.89 is implausibly high, but may reflect the inclusion of the time trend which implies an annual trend decline of 7.66 per cent per annum in base money demand. Ideally, the trend should capture institutional changes in financial, monetary, and payments mechanisms which were responsible for the secular rise in velocity over the period. It seems likely that the current income term mainly captures the cyclical effects and that longer-run income effects are partly reflected in the trend term. More general lag structures, additional regressors (such as private consumption as a proxy for permanent income), and a respecification of the equation in per capita terms all failed to yield more plausible results. Re-estimation of Equation (3.1) by instrumental variables (using public spending on goods and services, the volume of world trade, a measure of the world price level, and the US Treasury Bill rate as instruments for output and inflation) did not lead to significantly different results but worsened the residual autocorrelation properties.

5. If a government can borrow abroad by issuing debt denominated in its own currency, the foreign exchange value of debt and debt service will vary with the exchange rate, and may tempt debtor governments to devalue. This may explain why most major debtor countries have to issue debt denominated in a foreign currency, usually US dollars. It will be interesting to see for how long the United States itself will be able to borrow abroad through debt denominated in US dollars. Already [1985] the United States is a net external debtor, and on current trend it could become a major one within a couple of years.

6. The data are not ideal for our purposes. They reflect par values rather than actual values and thus seriously overstate the current value of long debt issued in the past when inflation expectations were low. The maturity classification is very coarse and conceals within-class changes. Index-linked debt, which has risen from 0.9 per cent of UK national debt in 1981 to 5.4 per cent in 1984, should also be removed for our purposes.

7. I am indebted to Patrick Minford for this point.

8. I am grateful to Stanley Fischer for this point.

9. 'Residual' because it omits certain taxes and transfers whose capitalized value was included in Hills's balance sheet.

10. See Eaton and Gersovitz (1981a; 1981b); Sachs (1984); Sachs and Cooper (1984); and Ghosh (1985). An interesting and as yet open question is under what conditions a policy of 'honest' debt service is time-consistent, i.e. compatible with future incentives not to renege.

11. Disposable income is scarcely more satisfactory as a transactions proxy than the usual gross income measure. Both ignore intermediate transactions (which exceed value added) and transactions in existing assets (which dwarf both). Money is also needed to pay taxes.

3.9 REFERENCES

Barro, Robert J. (1974) 'Are government bonds net wealth?', *Journal of Political Economy*, 82, November–December, pp. 1095–117.

Barro, Robert J. (1979) 'On the determination of the public debt', *Journal of Political Economy*, 87, October, pp. 940–71.

Barro, Robert J. and D. Gordon (1983) 'Rules, discretion and reputation in a model of monetary policy', *Journal of Monetary Economics*, 12, pp. 101–21.

Basevi, G. and F. Giavazzi (1983) 'Stabilization policies in an explosive economy: announcements and expectations', unpublished manuscript, University of Bologna.

Blanchard, O.J. (1981) 'Output, the stock market, and interest rates', *American Economic Review*, March.

Blanchard, O.J. (1984) 'Current and anticipated deficits, interest rates, and economic activity', *European Economic Review*, 71, pp. 132–43.

Blanchard, O.J. (1985) 'Debt, deficits, and finite horizons', *Journal of Political Economy*, 93, April, pp. 233–47.

Blanchard, O.J., W. Buiter and R. Dornbusch (1985) 'Public debt and fiscal responsibility', paper prepared for the Centre for European Policy Studies, Brussels, Belgium.

Blinder, A.S. and R.M. Solow (1973) 'Does fiscal policy matter?', *Journal of Public Economics*, 2, pp. 319–37.

Blinder A.S. and R.M. Solow (1974) *The Economics of Public Finance*, The Brookings Institution, Washington, DC.

Branson, W.H. (1974) 'Stocks and flows in international monetary analysis' in A. Ando, R. Herring and R. Marston (eds), *International Aspects of Stabilization Policies*, International Seminar in Public Economics, Federal Reserve Bank of Boston, Boston.

Branson, W.H. (1976) 'The dual roles of the government budget and the balance of payments in the movement from short-run to long-run equilibrium', *Quarterly Journal of Economics*, 90, pp. 345–68.

Buiter, Willem H. (1977) ' "Crowding out" and the effectiveness of fiscal policy', *Journal of Public Economics*, 7, pp. 309–28 (also Chapter 6, this volume).

Buiter, Willem H. (1979) *Temporary and Long-run Equilibrium*, Garland Publishing, New York.

Buiter, Willem H. (1980) ' "Crowding out" of private capital formation by government borrowing in the presence of intergenerational gifts and bequests', *Greek Economic Review*, 2, August, pp. 111–42.

Buiter, Willem H. (1982) 'Deficits, crowding out and inflation: the simple analytics', Centre for Labour Economics, London School of Economics, Discussion Paper no. 143.

Buiter, Willem H. (1983) 'The theory of optimum deficits and debt' in *The Economics of Large Government Deficits*, Federal Reserve Bank of Boston, Boston.

Buiter, Willem H. (1984a) 'Measuring aspects of fiscal and financial policy', Centre for Labour Economics, London School of Economics, Discussion Paper no. 193.

Buiter, Willem H. (1984b) 'Fiscal policy in open, interdependent economies', *NBER Working Paper*, no. 1429.

Calvo, C. (1978) 'On the time-consistency of optimal policy in a monetary economy', *Econometrica*, 46, pp. 1411–28.

Carmichael, J. and P.W. Stebbing (1983) 'Fischer's paradox and the theory of interest', *American Economic Review*, 83, pp. 619–30.

Chamley, C. (1985) 'On a simple rule for the optimal inflation rate in second-best taxation', *Journal of Public Economics*, 26, pp. 35–50.

Christ, C. (1968) 'A simple macroeconomic model with a government budget restraint', *Journal of Political Economy*.

Committee on National Debt and Taxation (1927) Cmnd 2800, XI.371, HMSO, London.

Diamond, P. (1965) 'National debt in a neo-classical growth model', *American Economic Review*, 55, December, pp. 1126–50.

Drazen, A. (1985) 'Tight money and inflation: further results', *Journal of Monetary Economics*, 15, pp. 113–20.

Eaton, J. and M. Gersovitz (1981a) 'Debt with potential repudiation: theoretical and empirical analysis', *Review of Economic Studies*, 48, pp. 289–309.

Eaton, J. and M. Gersovitz (1981b) 'Poor-country borrowing in private financial markets and the repudiation issue', *Princeton Studies in International Finance*, no. 4.

Feldstein, M. (1984) 'Can an increased budget deficit be contractionary?', *NBER Working Paper*, no. 1434.

Frankel, J. (1983) 'Tests of portfolio crowding out and related issues in finance', *NBER Working Paper*, no. 1205.

Frenkel, J.A. and A. Razin (1984) 'Budget deficits, and rates of interest in the world economy', *NBER Working Paper*, no. 1354.

Friedman, B. (1984) 'Implications of government deficits for interest-rates, equity returns, and corporate financing', *NBER Working Paper*, no. 1520.

Friedman, B. (1985) 'Crowding out or crowding in? Evidence on debt-equity substitutability', *NBER Working Paper*, no. 1565.

Ghosh, A.R. (1985) 'Dynamic reputational equilibrium in international capital markets', mimeo, Harvard University.

Greenwald, B. and J.E. Stiglitz (1984) 'Pecuniary and market-mediated externalities: towards a general theory of the welfare economics of economies with incomplete information and incomplete markets', *NBER Working Paper*, no. 1304.

Grossman, S.J. and O.D. Hart (1983) 'Implicit contracts made under asymmetric information', *Quarterly Journal of Economics* (Supplement).

Hills, J. (1984) 'Public assets and liabilities and the presentation of budgetary policy', in *Public Finance in Perspective*, Institute for Fiscal Studies, London.

International Monetary Fund (1985) *World Economic Outlook*, Washington, DC.

Jones, R.W. and P.B. Kenen (eds) (1985) *Handbook of International Economics*, Vol. 2, North-Holland, Amsterdam.

Kindleberger, C.P. (1984) *A Financial History of Western Europe*, George Allen & Unwin, London.

Kydland, Finn and Edward C. Prescott (1977) 'Rules rather than discretion: the inconsistency of optimal plans', *Journal of Political Economy*.

Laffont, J.J. (1985) 'On the welfare analysis of rational expectations equilibria with asymmetric information', *Econometrica*, 53, pp. 1–29.

Layard, R., G. Basevi, O. Blanchard, W. Buiter and R. Dornbusch (1984) 'Europe, the case for unsustainable growth', Centre for European Policy Studies, Paper no. 8/9.

Lucas, Robert E. and Nancy L. Stokey (1983) 'Optimal fiscal and monetary policy in an economy without capital', *Journal of Monetary Economics*, 12, pp. 55–93.

Mankiw, N.G. and L.H. Summers (1984) 'Are tax cuts really expansionary?', *NBER Working Paper*, no. 1443.

Miller, M. (1983) 'Inflation-adjusting the public sector financial deficit' in J. Kay (ed.), *The 1982 Budget*, Basil Blackwell, London.

Miller, M. and S. Babbs (1983) 'The true cost of debt service and the public sector

94   *Setting the scene*

financial deficit', mimeo, University of Warwick.
Mitchell, B.R. and P. Deane (1962) *Abstract of British Historical Statistics*, Cambridge University Press, Cambridge.
Mitchell, B.R. and H.G. Jones (1971) *Second Abstract of British Historical Statistics*, Cambridge University Press, Cambridge.
Modigliani, F. and R.A. Cohn (1979) 'Inflation, rational valuation and the market', *Financial Analysts Journal*, 37, March/April, pp. 24–44.
Persson, M., T. Persson and L. Svensson (1985) 'Time consistency of fiscal and monetary policy', mimeo, Institute for International Economic Studies, Stockholm.
Phelps, E.S. (1973) 'Inflation in the theory of public finance', *Swedish Journal of Economics*, 75, pp. 76–82.
Price, W.R. and P. Muller (1984) 'Structural budget indicators and the interpretation of fiscal policy stance in OECD economies', *OECD Economic Studies*, no. 3.
Roley, V.V. (1983) 'Asset substitutability and the impact of federal deficits', *NBER Working Paper*, no. 1082.
Sachs, J. (1984) 'Theoretical issues in international borrowing', *Princeton Studies in International Finance*.
Sachs, J. and R. Cooper (1984) 'Borrowing abroad: the debtor's perspective', mimeo, Harvard University.
Sargent, T.J. (1983) 'Stopping moderate inflation: the methods of Poincaré and Thatcher' in R. Dornbusch and M.H. Simonson (eds), *Inflation, Debt, and Indexation*, MIT Press, Cambridge, MA.
Sargent, T.J. and N. Wallace (1981) 'Some unpleasant monetarist arithmetic', *Federal Reserve Board of Minneapolis Quarterly Review*, 5, Fall.
Sidrauski, M. (1967) 'Rational choice and patterns of growth in a monetary economy', *American Economic Review*, 57, May, pp. 534–44.
Stiglitz, J. and A. Weiss (1981) 'Credit rationing in markets with imperfect information', *American Economic Review*, 71, June, pp. 393–410.
Tanzi, V. (ed.) (1984) *Taxation, Inflation, and Interest Rates*, International Monetary Fund, Washington, DC.
Tanzi, V. (1985) *The Economy in Deficit*, AEI essays in contemporary economic problems, edited by P. Cagan.
Tobin, J. (1961) 'Money, capital, and other stores of value', *American Economic Review*, 51, pp. 26–37.
Tobin, J. (1965) 'Money and economic growth', *Econometrica*, 33, October, pp. 671–84.
Tobin, J. (1969) 'A general equilibrium approach to monetary theory', *Journal of Money, Credit, and Banking*, 1, February, pp. 15–29.
Tobin, J. and W.H. Buiter (1976) 'Long-run effects of fiscal and monetary policy on aggregate demand' in J. Stein (ed.), *Monetarism*, North-Holland, Amsterdam, pp. 273–309 (also Chapter 10, this volume).
Tobin J. and W.H. Buiter (1980) 'Fiscal and monetary policies, capital formation, and economic activity' in G. von Furstenberg (ed.), *The Government and Capital Formation*, Ballinger, Cambridge, MA, pp. 73–151.
Turnovsky, S. and W. Brock (1980) 'Time-consistency and optimal government policies in perfect foresight equilibrium', *Journal of Public Economics*, 13, pp. 183–212.
Webb, D. (1980) 'The net wealth effect of government bonds when credit markets are imperfect', *Economic Journal*, 91, June, pp. 405–14.
Williamson, S.D. (1984) 'Costly monetary loan contracts and equilibrium credit rationing', Queens University, Institute for Economic Research Discussion Paper no. 572.

APPENDIX 3A: ARITHMETIC OF THE GOVERNMENT BUDGET CONSTRAINT

In formal terms the government budget identity (3.3) can be written:

$$p^{-1}[\dot{M} + \dot{B}^s + p^L\dot{B}^L - p_N\dot{N}^G]$$

$$\equiv c^G + \delta K^G + \dot{K}^G - T + \frac{iB^s + cB^L}{p} - \varrho_K K^G - \varrho_N N^G \qquad (3A.1)$$

Total government exhaustive spending is broken down into consumption spending, c^G; replacement investment δK^G (where δ is the rate of depreciation, and K^G is the public sector capital stock), and net investment $\dot{K}^G$. $\varrho_K K^G$ is the income from public sector capital and $\varrho_N N^G$ is the income accruing from natural resource property rights. ϱ_K and ϱ_N are the rates of return in each case. Deficits may be financed by creating base money (M), selling short bonds (nominal value B^s paying interest rate i) or perpetuities (quantity B^L paying coupon c and selling at a price p^L). In addition the left-hand side recognizes that deficits can also be financed by the sale of assets, specifically of natural resource property rights. Properly speaking, the sale of productive assets, such as British Telecom, also belongs on the left-hand side but to keep things simple Equation (3A.1) does not distinguish between net investment spending on currency produced capital goods and sales and purchases of existing assets. Foreign assets and liabilities are also omitted for simplicity.

The government's intertemporal budget constraint is the integral of Equation (3A.1):

$$PV(c^G, t, r) \equiv p_K(t)K^G(t) + p_N(t)N^G(t)$$

$$- \left(\frac{B^s(t) + p^L(t)B^L(t)}{p(t)}\right) + PV(T, t, r) + PV\left(\frac{\dot{M}}{p}, t, r\right)$$

$$+ PV((p_K - 1)\dot{K}, t, r) + \Omega(t) \qquad (3A.2)$$

where

$$PV(X, t, r) \equiv E_t \int_t^\infty X(z)\exp\left(-\int_t^z r(u)\,du\right)dz;$$

$$X = c^G, T, \dot{M}/p, (p_K - 1)\dot{K}.$$

$$\Omega(t) \equiv \lim_{z \to \infty} E_t\left[\frac{M(z) + B^s(z) + p^L(z)B^L(z)}{p(z)}\right.$$

$$\left. - p_K(z)K^G(z) - p_N(z)N^G(z)\right] \exp\left(-\int_t^z r(u)\,du\right).$$

Hence $PV(c^G, t, r)$ denotes the present value, at time t, of the government's planned or expected real consumption spending programme, when

r is the instantaneous real discount rate. Similarly $PV(T, t, r)$ is the present value of the government's real tax-transfer program and $PV(\dot{M}/p, t, r)$ is the present value of real seigniorage. The stock of publicly owned capital is valued by the present value of the future quasi-rents accruing to the public sector, $p_K(t) \equiv PV(\varrho_K, t, r)$, and natural resource property rights are valued by the present value of the income accruing from their exploitation, $p_N(t) \equiv PV(\varrho_N, t, r)$. Note that $p_K(t)$ or $p_N(t)$ could be negative if the public sector capital stock (natural resource endowment) is operated at a loss. Note also that public sector capital formation only affects government net worth to the extent that the shadow price of public sector capital (p_K) differs from its opportunity cost (unity).

To turn Equation (3A.2) into a solvency constraint we assume that $\Omega(t) = 0$. If $r > n$ then this is implied by the requirement that the ratio of net marketable public sector debt to trend output remains bounded. If $r < n$ the condition is somewhat arbitrary. Consequently we obtain:

$$\frac{B^s(t) + p^L(t)B^L(t)}{p(t)} - p_K(t)K^G(t) - p_N(t)N^G(t)$$
$$\equiv PV[T - c^G + (p_K - 1)\dot{K}, t, r] + PV\left(\frac{\dot{M}}{p}, t, r\right) \qquad (3A.3)$$

Equation (3A.3) states that the market value of the government's net non-monetary debt has to be matched by the present value of the expected future primary *current* surpluses and the present value of expected future seigniorage. It can be rewritten as:

$$\frac{B^s(t) + p^L(t)B^L(t)}{p(t)Y(t)} - p_K(t)\frac{K^G(t)}{Y(t)} - p_N(t)\frac{N^G(t)}{Y(t)}$$
$$\equiv PV\left(\frac{T - c^G + (p_K - 1)\dot{K}}{Y}, t, r - n\right) + PV\left(\frac{\dot{M}}{pY}, t, r - n\right) \quad (3A.4)$$

Equation (3A.4) expresses the same relationship in terms of net debt–output ratios, future primary current surpluses as a share of GNP and seigniorage as a proportion of GNP. The relevant discount rate is the real interest rate minus the natural rate of growth. Note that the appropriate primary deficit is the government's *current account* deficit.

The eventual monetization implied by a given fiscal-financial program (Equation (3.5)) is, holding $\dot{M}/M$ and $pY/M = v$ constant:

$$\frac{\dot{M}}{M} \equiv [R(t) - n]\left[PV\left(\frac{c^G - T + (1 - p_K)\dot{K}}{Y}, t, r - n\right)\right.$$
$$\left. + \frac{B^s(t) + p^L(t)B^L(t)}{p(t)Y(t)} - \frac{p_K(t)K^G(t)}{Y(t)} - \frac{p_N(t)N^G(t)}{Y(t)}\right] \qquad (3A.5)$$

where $R(t)$ is the real long rate of interest.

APPENDIX 3B: NEGATIVE IMPACT MULTIPLIERS FROM BUDGET DEFICITS IN A KEYNESIAN MODEL WITH RATIONAL EXPECTATIONS

We assume that long real interest rates rather than short real interest rates affect investment. Otherwise the structure is that of a conventional *IS–LM*-aggregate supply model augmented by the government budget constraint.

$$C\left(y + i\frac{B}{p} - T, \frac{M + B}{p}\right) + I(R) + G = y \tag{3B.1}$$

$$l\left(i, y, \frac{M + B}{p}\right) = \frac{M}{p} \tag{3B.2}$$

$$i - E_t\frac{\dot{p}}{p} = R - E_t\frac{\dot{R}}{R} \tag{3B.3}$$

$$\frac{\dot{M} + \dot{B}}{p} = G + i\frac{B}{p} - T \tag{3B.4}$$

$$\frac{\dot{p}}{p} = \psi(y - \bar{y}) + \mu \tag{3B.5}$$

where i is the short nominal interest rate, r is the short real interest rate, R is the long real interest rate, $\bar{y}$ is capacity output, μ the rate of core inflation, and the other nomenclature is standard. Equation (3B.1) is the *IS* schedule, Equation (3B.2) is the demand for money, Equation (3B.3) is an arbitrage relation between short and long debt, Equation (3B.4) is the government budget constraint, and Equation (3B.5) is a price-expectations-augmented Phillips curve. The price level is predetermined. To keep the dynamic analysis simple, I assume that the government uses a combination of money and bond finance that keeps the share of money and bonds in total government debt constant:

$$M = \alpha W \tag{3B.6a}$$

$$B = (1 - \alpha)W \tag{3B.6b}$$

$$W = M + B \tag{3B.6c}$$

The augmentation term in the price-Phillips curve μ is the policy-determined proportional rate of growth of total nominal government liabilities.

$$\mu = \dot{W}/W \tag{3B.7}$$

The specification of the monetary–fiscal–financial decision rules in this example is: exogenous G, α and μ. Taxes are therefore endogenously determined. An increase in μ, given G, can only be brought about by a tax cut. Let $w = W/p$, the real stock of money plus bonds. $i = H(R, w; G, \mu, \alpha)$ and $y = F(R, w; G, \mu, \alpha)$ are the *IS–LM* solutions for i and y from Equations (3B.1) and (3B.2).

In the neighbourhood of a steady-state equilibrium $\bar{R}$, $\bar{w}$, the behavior of this economy can be described by Equation (3B.8):

$$\begin{bmatrix} \dot{R} \\ \dot{w} \end{bmatrix} = \begin{bmatrix} \bar{R}(1 - H_R + \psi F_R) - \bar{R}(H_w - \psi F_w) \\ -\psi F_R \quad\quad -\psi F_w \end{bmatrix} \begin{bmatrix} R - \bar{R} \\ w - \bar{w} \end{bmatrix}$$

$$+ \begin{bmatrix} -\bar{R}(H_G - \psi F_G) & \bar{R}(1 - H_\mu + \psi F_\mu) & -\bar{R}(H_\alpha - \psi F_\alpha) \\ -\psi F_G & -\psi F_\mu & -\psi F_\alpha \end{bmatrix} \begin{bmatrix} G - \bar{G} \\ \mu - \bar{\mu} \\ \alpha - \bar{\alpha} \end{bmatrix}$$

$$\tag{3B.8}$$

If government debt is net wealth, the *IS* curve shifts to the right in i–y space when w increases. An increase in w increases the demand for money (if $l_w > 0$) which tends to shift the *LM* curve to the left. A proportion α of the increase in the government's liabilities is in the form of money issues. This tends to shift the *LM* curve to the right. Thus, while $F_w > 0$, an increase in w will raise the short interest rate, i, if α is small (in a high-debt economy) but lowers it if α is sufficiently large (a low-debt economy). Specifically:

$$H_w = \frac{(1 - C_y)(\alpha - l_w) - l_y(C_w + C_y\mu)}{(1 - C_y)l_i} \tag{3B.9}$$

For reasons of space, only the high-debt economy is considered in what follows. The system described in Equation (3B.8) has one predetermined state variable w and one non-predetermined one, R. For there to exist a unique convergent saddle-point equilibrium, it is necessary and sufficient that $F_w(1 - H_R) + F_R H_w > 0$. In the low-debt economy (which behaves more or less like an economy under pure money-financed deficits) this condition is always satisfied. In the high-debt, low-α economy, which behaves approximately like an economy under pure bond financing, explosive behavior cannot be ruled out a priori. If there exists a convergent saddle-point equilibrium, it is likely to have the configuration shown in Figure 3B.1 with an upward-sloping saddle-path $S_0 S_0$.

The long-run effect of an increase in μ is a larger real volume of total government debt (w increases) and a higher R (and i):

$$\frac{d\bar{w}}{dG} = \frac{(C_y - 1)l_i}{\Omega} \tag{3B.10a}$$

$$\frac{d\bar{R}}{dG} = \frac{(\alpha - l_w)(C_y - 1)}{\Omega} \tag{3B.10b}$$

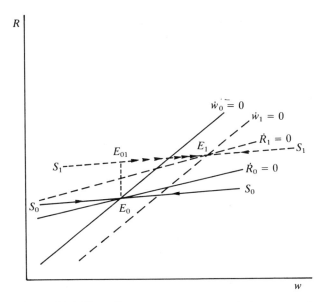

Figure 3B.1 The adjustment to an unexpected permanent tax cut in the rational-expectations-augmented Keynesian model with gradual price adjustment: an example of super-crowding out

$$\frac{d\bar{w}}{d\mu} = \frac{l_i(I' - C_y w)}{\Omega} \tag{3B.10c}$$

$$\frac{d\bar{R}}{d\mu} = \frac{-(C_y \mu + C_w)l_i + (l_w - a)C_y w}{\Omega} \tag{3B.10d}$$

where $\Omega = l_i(C_y \mu + C_w) - I'(l_w - a)$.

An unexpected, immediate and permanent increase in μ (which implies a short-run and long-run tax cut) causes the long real interest rate to jump immediately from E_0 to E_{01}, onto $S_1 S_1$, the convergent saddle-path through the new long-run equilibrium at E_1. There will, however, be a recession during the entire adjustment process. We know this because the real stock of government liabilities rises throughout the adjustment process. This can only happen if the rate of inflation is below the nominal rate of growth of these liabilities μ. From the Phillips curve it is clear that this requires $y < \bar{y}$. It is therefore not impossible to come up with examples in which even immediately implemented 'expansionary' fiscal policy (e.g., a permanent tax cut) will have a depressing effect on real economic activity because the anticipated future deficits and the bias towards bond financing (low a) raise the long real interest rate by enough to induce more than 100 per cent crowding out of private interest-sensitive spending in the short run and throughout the adjustment process.

APPENDIX 3C MEASURES OF FISCAL STANCE

Keynesian measures

Consider the following standard $IS-LM$ model:

$$C(y_d, w) + I(i) + G = y \qquad 0 < C_{y_d} < 1; \; C_w > 0 \qquad I' < 0 \quad (IS)$$
$$\tag{3C.1}$$

$$l(i, y, w) = \frac{M}{p} \qquad l_i < 0; \; l_y > 0; \; 1 > l_w > 0 \quad (LM) \tag{3C.2}$$

$$y_d \equiv y + i\frac{B}{p} - T \tag{3C.3}$$

$$w \equiv \frac{M + B}{p} \tag{3C.4}$$

$$T = \theta_0 + \theta_1 y \qquad 0 < \theta_1 < 1 \tag{3C.5}$$

With the specific bench-mark policy $G = \bar{G}$ and the tax function (3C.5), the impact effect on aggregate demand of fiscal policy given an accommodating monetary policy (i constant) is:

$$dy = \psi[dG - C_{y_d}d\theta_0 - C_{y_d}y\,d\theta_1] \tag{3C.6a}$$

$$\psi = \frac{1}{1 - C_{y_d}(1 - \theta_1)} \tag{3C.6b}$$

The impact effect of fiscal policy on aggregate demand under a non-accommodating monetary policy (M constant) for this model is:

$$dy = \psi'[dG - C_{y_d}d\theta_0 - C_{y_d}y\,d\theta_1] \tag{3C.7a}$$

$$\psi' = [(1 - C_{y_d})(1 - \theta_1)l_i + l_y(I' + C_{y_d}B)]^{-1} \tag{3C.7b}$$

Notice that the fiscal parameters dG, $d\theta_0$, and $d\theta_1$ are multiplier-weighted and that these weights are evaluated at the actual (not necessarily the cyclically-corrected) level of output.

Blanchard's measure

In Blanchard's (1985) model consumers face an instantaneous probability of death λ. Then a measure of the effect of public spending on goods and services and (lump-sum) taxes on consumption demand (at given current and expected future interest rates) denoted $f(t)$ is given by:

$$f(t) = G(t) - (\lambda + \varrho)E_t \int_t^\infty G(z)\exp\left(-\int_t^s (r(u) + \lambda)\,du\right)ds$$

$$+ (\lambda + \varrho) \left[B(t) + E_t \int_t^\infty (G(s) - T(s)) \exp\left(-\int_t^s (r(u) + \lambda) \, du \right) ds \right]$$

$$(3C.8)$$

where ϱ is the private sector's rate of time preference and $B(t)$ the outstanding real stock of interest-bearing debt. The first two terms on the right-hand side of Equation (3C.8) give the effect of balanced-budget (tax-financed) exhaustive spending. Spending on goods and services by the government only boosts demand if current spending exceeds its 'permanent' or average future expected value. When $\varrho = r$, for example, a constant level of spending has no effect on demand. The third term on the right-hand side of Equation (3C.8) is zero if private decision horizons are infinite ($\lambda = 0$). It is positive if horizons are finite ($\lambda > 0$). This presents the effect of debt-financing. Bonds are 'wealth' if $\lambda > 0$ and consumption demand is an increasing function of the outstanding stock of bonds. Note how in Equation (3C.8), unlike in Equation (3C.6a) and (3C.7a), expectations of future spending, taxes, and interest rates must be modeled to obtain the current demand effect of fiscal and financial policy.

PART II

ISSUES OF MEASUREMENT

4 · MEASUREMENT OF THE PUBLIC SECTOR DEFICIT AND ITS IMPLICATIONS FOR POLICY EVALUATION AND DESIGN

This paper studies budgetary, financial, and monetary policy evaluation and design in a framework of comprehensive wealth and income accounting. Although the focus is on the public sector accounts, inevitably some attention is paid to the private and overseas sectors. Construction of stylized comprehensive balance sheets for the public sector and for its 'flow' counterpart (the change in real public sector net worth) forms the basis for a comparison of these balance sheets with the conventionally measured balance sheet and the flow of funds accounts. The conventionally measured public sector balance sheet typically contains only marketable financial assets and liabilities. On the asset side, it omits such items as the value of the stock of social overhead capital, the value of government-owned land and mineral rights, and the present value of planned future tax revenues. On the liability side, it omits the present value of social insurance and other entitlement programs.

The conventionally measured financial surplus of the public sector, even when evaluated at constant prices, presents a potentially misleading picture of the change in the real net worth of the public sector. One reason is that capital gains and losses on outstanding stocks of government assets and liabilities are not included in the flow of funds. For example, the following are omitted: capital gains or losses that are due to changes in relative prices (e.g., changes in the real value of mineral rights); changes in the real value of nominally-denominated public sector debt that are due to inflation; and changes in the real value of foreign-currency-denominated assets and liabilities that are caused by changes in exchange rates.

A second reason is that changes in tax and entitlement programs, in the

---

This paper was originally published in *International Monetary Fund Staff Papers*, 30, June 1983, pp. 306–49.

future revenue base, and in discount rates, etc., may significantly alter the planned or expected future streams of taxes and benefits and their present value. Capital gains and losses on such implicit non-marketable assets and liabilities are part of the Hicks–Simon concept of income, but they are excluded from the flow of funds accounts.

The differences between the conventionally measured accounts and the comprehensive accounts can be very large. In inflationary periods, large public sector deficits (conventionally measured) may be more than offset by the inflation-induced reduction in the real value of the government's nominal liabilities. Changes in the current account deficit of the balance of payments (conventionally measured) may be offset or enhanced by changes in the value of external assets and liabilities associated with exchange rate changes. Changes in social security legislation may alter the future flows of benefits and contributions. With efficient forward-looking financial markets, such policy changes will not merely alter *future* rates of return when the financial implications of current legislation become visible and directly measurable — for example, through changes in the amount of public sector borrowing. They will have an effect on *current* financial asset prices and rates of return; larger anticipated future deficits may raise current interest rates.

After presenting the comprehensive and conventionally measured accounts for the public sector, the private sector, and the overseas sector, I propose some general rules for policy design. These rules derive from a reasonable policy norm or objective and from rather minimal and uncontroversial assumptions about private sector behavior. To translate these general (and, indeed, perhaps rather vague) rules into concrete policies is a task that is well beyond the scope of this paper because a wealth of country-specific knowledge would be required in each case.

The essence of the argument is that, in a first-best world, private agents, governments, and international organizations would decide on spending, saving, lending, production, and portfolio allocation programs, constrained only by comprehensive wealth or permanent income. Single-period or other short-run 'budget constraints' would not represent further effective or binding constraints on economic behavior. The perfect internal and external capital markets required to implement the first-best solution, however, do not exist. Private agents are constrained by the illiquidity and non-marketability of certain assets (e.g., pension rights, human capital, and expected future tax cuts). Dearth of suitable collateral often renders infeasible the borrowing required to spend in line with permanent income. These cash flow constraints, illiquidity, credit rationing, lack of collateral, non-marketability of certain assets and liabilities, and a host of other capital market imperfections force the actions of private agents and national governments to depart from the behavior that would be optimal if comprehensive net worth or permanent income constraints alone had to be taken into account.

Flow-of-funds accounting on a cash or transactions basis and the analysis of balance sheets consisting only of marketable claims are useful precisely because they will help to identify the conditions under which the behavior of economic agents is likely to be constrained by factors other than comprehensive net worth.

Within a national economy, conventional accounting helps to decide when and how the national authorities, through appropriate fiscal, financial, and monetary measures, can help private agents to avoid or overcome obstacles to spending and saving in line with permanent income (for households) and impediments to production in pursuit of long-run profit or social net benefit (for enterprises). Within the international economy, conventional accounting serves to identify the conditions under which international organizations should extend or restrict credit to national governments to enable them to develop in line with their long-run potential..Exercises in financial evaluation, such as the IMF's financial programming, should, therefore, start from two sets of accounts. The first set contains the conventional cash-based flow-of-funds accounts, the income expenditure accounts of the United Nations System of National Accounts (SNA), and the conventional balance sheets of marketable assets and liabilities. The second set contains the comprehensive balance sheets or wealth accounts outlined in the paper and their flow counterparts, describing the changes in real sectoral net worth over time and thus permanent income — that is, the ultimate accrual-based accounts.

Both national governments and international agencies should design fiscal, financial, and monetary policies so as to induce an evolution of the conventionally measured balance sheet and flow-of-funds accounts that permits private agents and national economies, respectively, to approximate the behavior that would be adopted if either comprehensive wealth or permanent income were the only binding constraint on economic behavior.

The approach developed in this paper implies that conventional financial planning is an essential input into optimal (or even merely sensible) policy design. It also suggests that a set of comprehensive wealth and permanent income accounts (or the best practicable approximation to them) should complement the conventional data base. Without the conventional accounts, of course, analyses based just on the comprehensive wealth and permanent income accounts will fail to take into account many of the actual binding constraints on economic behavior.

'Stabilization policy', as viewed in this paper, is potentially useful and effective even if goods and factor markets clear continuously. The existence of capital market imperfections that prevent private agents from spending in line with permanent private disposable income and nations from spending in line with national permanent income is necessary before there can be scope for stabilization policy — that is, policy actions or rules designed to permit smoothing of consumption over time by removing or neutralizing constraints on spending other than permanent income. Successful stabilization policy keeps disposable income in line with permanent income and ensures and adequate share of disposable financial wealth in comprehensive wealth. Another necessary condition for potentially desirable stabilization policy is that governments have access to capital markets on terms that are more favorable than those faced by private agents, or, more generally, it is necessary for governments to have financial options that are not available to private agents. *Mutatis mutandis*, the same condition applies in an international setting to certain international agencies *vis-à-vis* national governments. The existence of Keynesian effective demand failures that are due to disequilibria in goods and factor markets would, of course, strengthen the case for stabilization policy.

This view of stabilization policy implies that the government's financing policies (changes in its tax, transfer, borrowing, and money creation mix) should be used for stabilization rather than for variations in its spending program on goods and services. The spending program should aim to achieve the best feasible public–private consumption mix based on national permanent income.

4.1 A STYLIZED SET OF PUBLIC SECTOR ACCOUNTS

Table 4.1 presents a stylized and simplified 'comprehensive' balance sheet for the public sector. Many definitional problems are ignored; for example, throughout this paper the terms 'government' and 'public sector' are used interchangeably (see Boskin, 1982). It is assumed that an extremely heterogeneous set of assets and liabilities can somehow be expressed in common value terms, despite the fact that some of the assets are not marketable (stock of social overhead capital, K^{soc}) or, even if potentially marketable, may lack a current observable market price (stock of public enterprise capital, K^G). Some assets and liabilities are neither marketable nor tangible and merely represent implicit non-contractual (and reversible) political commitments (present value of tax programs, T, and present value of entitlement programs, N).

Referring to T, N and the net value of government's cash monopoly, A^M, as present discounted values of future streams of payments or receipts involves a rather cavalier use of certainty equivalence; the conditional mathematical expectations of the uncertain future revenues or outlays are discounted by using 'risk-adjusted' discount rates. If, for example, future tax revenues are highly uncertain, T would be correspondingly small. The relevant horizon is, in principle, infinite.

Table 4.1 Comprehensive consolidated public sector balance sheet

	Assets		Liabilities
$p_{K^{soc}}K^{soc}$	Social overhead capital (non-marketable)	B^H	Net interest-bearing debt denominated in domestic currency, held by residents
$p_G K^G$	Equity in public enterprises (partly potentially marketable)	B^F	Net interest-bearing debt denominated in domestic currency, held by nonresidents
$p_R R^G$	Land and mineral assets (marketable)	eB^{*H}	Net interest-bearing debt denominated in foreign currency, held by residents
eE^*	Net foreign exchange reserves	eB^{*F}	Net interest-bearing debt denominated in foreign currency, held by nonresidents
T	Present value of future tax program, including social security contributions, tariff revenue, etc. (implicit asset)	$p\bar{B}^H$	Net interest-bearing index-linked debt, held by residents
		$p\bar{B}^F$	Net interest-bearing index-linked debt, held by nonresidents
pA^M	Imputed net value of government's cash monopoly	H	Stock of high-powered money
		N	Present value of social insurance and other entitlement programs (implicit liability)
		W^G	Public sector net worth

For many purposes, it is better not to attempt to reduce marketable and non-marketable, implicit and explicit, claims to a common balance sheet measure of value. Instead, each of the items in the balance sheet would be modeled as having potentially distinct behavioral effects. The proper way of handling this will depend on the specifics of the model and the application under consideration. For a preliminary examination of the problem of comprehensive wealth and income accounting in the public sector, the balance sheet in Table 4.1 is, however, useful.

Most of the items in the balance sheet are self-explanatory. Denoting the price, rate of return on and government consumption of services of social overhead capital by $p_{K_{soc}}$, r^{soc} and G^{soc}, and the general price level by p, public sector overhead capital is assumed to yield an implicit rental $r^{soc}p_{K_{soc}}K^{soc}$, which corresponds to the item pG^{soc} (public sector consumption of social overhead capital services). If p_G is the price of public enterprise capital, then $p_G K^G$ represents the balance sheet counterpart of the operating surplus of the public enterprise sector in the public sector current account. This may well be a negative item for some of the secular public enterprise loss-makers, in which case it should be moved to the liability side of the balance sheet. The present value of current and capital grants is not entered separately; it can be viewed as subsumed under N or T. Net foreign exchange reserves (E^*) are entered separately as an asset rather than netting them out against foreign-held foreign-currency-denominated bonds (B^{*F}) or $B^{*F} + \dfrac{B^F}{e} + \bar{B}^F\dfrac{p}{e}$, where B^F represents foreign-held nominal government bonds, $\bar{B}^F$ foreign-held index-linked government bonds, and e is the nominal exchange rate (domestic-currency price of foreign exchange). For simplicity, only nominal capital-certain bonds and real capital-certain bonds are considered (see Miller, 1982).

The treatment of money in this exposition of the comprehensive wealth accounting framework is somewhat unusual. The reason for adopting this approach is that it represents the simplest way of introducing a non-trivial role for money. Specifically, it keeps the economy from becoming isomorphic to a barter economy when, in Section 4.5, the accounts of the public and private sectors are consolidated in the investigation of debt neutrality. Money, as a social asset that produces liquidity and convenience services, does not disappear when private and public sector assets and liabilities are netted out. The usefulness of the framework of comprehensive wealth accounting does not depend on the acceptability of this approach to modeling money.

Money has value to the private sector because it yields a flow of imputed non-pecuniary liquidity and convenience services. Let ϱ^M be the non-pecuniary rate of return on money. The value to the private sector of its money holdings is given by V^M in Equation (4.1):

$$V^M(t) = \frac{1}{p(t)} \int\limits_{t}^{\infty} H(t)\hat{\varrho}^M(u,t)\exp\left(-\int\limits_{t}^{u} \hat{\imath}(s,t)\mathrm{d}s\right)\mathrm{d}u, \tag{4.1}$$ [1]

where H is the stock of high-powered money, i is the nominal interest rate on bonds denominated in domestic currency, and the expression $\hat{x}(s,t)$ denotes the value of x expected at time t to prevail at time s.

The assumption that the pecuniary and non-pecuniary yields on money and bonds are equalized at the margin yields

$$\varrho^M = i = r + \frac{\hat{\dot{p}}}{p}, \tag{4.2}$$

where r is the domestic real interest rate and $\dot{p}$ is just $\mathrm{d}p/\mathrm{d}t$.

Equations (4.1) and (4.2) imply that

$$V^M = \frac{H}{p}. \tag{4.3}$$

Let Π^M be the present discounted value of the expected future flow of profits to the government from operating the printing presses. Assuming that cash can be produced without cost, the result is

$$\Pi^M(t) = \frac{1}{p(t)} \int_t^\infty \hat{H}(u,t) \exp\left(-\int_t^u \hat{i}(s,t)ds\right)du.[2] \tag{4.4}$$

Integrating Equation (4.4) by parts produces

$$\Pi^M(T) = -\frac{H(t)}{p(t)} + A^M(t),[3] \tag{4.4a}$$

where

$$A^M(t) = \frac{1}{p(t)} \int_t^\infty \hat{i}(u,t)\hat{H}(u,t)e\left(-\int_t^u \hat{i}(s,t)ds\right)du. \tag{4.5}$$

Thus, $A^M(t)$, the net value of the government's cash monopoly, can be interpreted as the present discounted value of the interest income that the central bank expects to earn at each future date on a portfolio of government bonds that is equal in value to the stock of high-powered money at that date.

The conventionally measured public sector balance sheet typically omits from Table 4.1 all non-marketable and non-financial assets and liabilities — that is, K^{soc}, K^G, government-owned land and rights to natural resources (R^G), T, N and A^M.

The current and capital accounts of the public sector whose balance sheet is given in Table 4.1 are represented in Table 4.2 (see Ott and Yoo, 1980). They are stylized SNA accounts and have a number of significant shortcomings when used uncritically as a guide to the changes over time in the balance sheet — especially as regards the evolution of the *real* comprehensive net worth of the public sector and its components.

For simplicity, it is assumed that government consumption (G^c) and the imputed rental services from social overhead capital have the same price (p).[4] A uniform depreciation rate (δ) for different types of capital is also imposed. Foreign exchange reserves are assumed to pay the same interest rate as other foreign-currency-denominated financial claims. All of these assumptions serve only illustrative purposes.

The 'public sector budget constraint', which was rediscovered by macroeconomic theorists in the early 1970s, is obtained by consolidating the current and capital accounts of Table 4.2. Imputed income and consumption are netted out. Deflating by the general price level yields the conventionally measured public sector financial surplus (at constant prices) given in Equation (4.6):

$$\frac{\tau}{p} - \frac{n}{p} - G^c - \frac{p_{K^{soc}}}{p}\delta K^{soc} - \frac{p_G}{p}\delta K^G - i\left(\frac{B^H + B^F}{p}\right)$$

$$-\frac{e}{p}i^*(B^{*H} + B^{*F} - E^*) - r(\bar{B}^H + \bar{B}^F) + r^G\frac{p_G}{p}K^G$$

Table 4.2 Public sector income and expenditure and capital finance accounts

Debit		Credit	
Current account			
Government consumption including imputed rental from social overhead capital	$p(G^c + G^{soc})$	Tax receipts (including social security contributions)	τ
Capital consumption	$\delta(p_{K^{soc}}K^{soc} + p_G K^G)$	Profits from public enterprises and ownership of natural resources	$r^G p_G K^G + r^R p_R R^G$
Transfer and benefit payments	n		
Interest paid	$i(B^H + B^F) + ei^*(B^{*H} + B^{*F})$ $+ rp(\bar{B}^H + \bar{B}^F)$	Interest received	$ei^* E^*$
		Imputed return from social overhead capital	$r^{soc} p_{K^{soc}} K^{soc}$
Surplus on current account	S^G		
Capital account			
Gross investment in structures	$p_{K^{soc}}(\dot{K}^{soc} + \delta K^{soc})$ $+ p_G(\dot{K}^G + \delta K^G)$	Surplus on current account	S^G
Net financial investment	$-[\dot{B}^H + \dot{B}^F + e(\dot{B}^{*H} + \dot{B}^{*F} - \dot{E}^*)$ $+ p(\dot{\bar{B}} + \dot{\bar{B}}^F) + H]$	Capital consumption	$\delta(p_{K^{soc}}K^{soc} + p_G K^G)$
Net purchases of existing assets	$p_R \dot{R}^G$		

$$+ r^R \frac{p_R}{p} R^G \equiv \frac{p_{K^{soc}}}{p} \dot{K}^{soc} + \frac{p_G}{p} \dot{K}^G + \frac{p_R}{p} \dot{R}^G - \frac{1}{p}(\dot{B}^H + \dot{B}^F)$$

$$- \frac{e}{p}(\dot{B}^{*H} + \dot{B}^{*F} - \dot{E}^*) - (\dot{\tilde{B}}^H + \dot{\tilde{B}}^F) - \frac{\dot{H}}{p} \tag{4.6}$$

where B^H, B^{*H} and $\tilde{B}^H$ represent domestically-held nominal, domestically-held foreign-currency-denominated and domestically-held index-linked government bonds, respectively; i^* is the nominal interest rate on foreign-currency-denominated bonds; E^* is the stock of foreign exchange reserves; r^G and r^R represent the rates of return on public enterprise capital and on ownership of land and natural resources, respectively; and p_G and p_R are the prices of public enterprise capital and of land and property rights to natural resources, respectively; τ and n are defined in Table 4.2.

Even this 'real' surplus, however, is likely to be a poor indicator of the change in the real net worth of the public sector, as defined from the balance sheet in Table 4.1. This change in the real net worth of the government is given in Equation (4.7):

$$\frac{d}{dt}\left(\frac{W^G}{p}\right) \equiv \frac{p_{K^{soc}}}{p} \dot{K}^{soc} + \frac{p_G}{p} \dot{K}^G + \frac{p_R}{p} \dot{R}^G$$

$$- \frac{1}{p}(\dot{B}^H + \dot{B}^F) - \frac{e}{p}(\dot{B}^{*H} + \dot{B}^{*F} - \dot{E}^*)$$

$$- (\dot{\tilde{B}}^H + \dot{\tilde{B}}^F) - \frac{\dot{H}}{p} + \frac{1}{p}(\dot{T} - \dot{N}) + \dot{A}^M$$

$$+ \left(\frac{\dot{p}_{K^{soc}}}{p_{K^{soc}}} - \frac{\dot{p}}{p}\right)\frac{p_{K^{soc}}}{p}K^{soc} + \left(\frac{\dot{p}_G}{p_G} - \frac{\dot{p}}{p}\right)\frac{p_G}{p}K^G$$

$$+ \left(\frac{\dot{p}_R}{p_R} - \frac{\dot{p}}{p}\right)\frac{p_R}{p}R^G + \frac{\dot{p}}{p}\left(\frac{B^H + B^F + H}{p}\right)$$

$$- \left(\frac{\dot{e}}{e} - \frac{\dot{p}}{p}\right)\frac{e}{p}(B^{*H} + B^{*F} - E^*)$$

$$- \frac{\dot{p}}{p}(T - N),^5 \tag{4.7}$$

where W^G is public sector net worth. A comparison of the right-hand sides of Equations (4.6) and (4.7) reveals that the difference between the 'real', or constant price surplus and the change in real net worth is due to capital gains and losses (Ω) and to changes in the value of the implicit assets and liabilities (Δ) where

$$\Omega = \left(\frac{\dot{p}_{K^{soc}}}{p_{K^{soc}}} - \frac{\dot{p}}{p}\right)\frac{p_{K^{soc}}}{p}K^{soc} + \left(\frac{\dot{p}_G}{p_G} - \frac{\dot{p}}{p}\right)\frac{p_G}{p}K^G + \left(\frac{\dot{p}_R}{p_R} - \frac{\dot{p}}{p}\right)\frac{p_R}{p}R^G$$

$$+ \frac{\dot{p}}{p}\left(\frac{B^H + B^F + H}{p}\right) - \left(\frac{\dot{e}}{e} - \frac{\dot{p}}{p}\right)\frac{e}{p}(R^{*H} + R^{*F} - F_i^*)$$

$$- \frac{\dot{p}}{p}(T - N) \tag{4.8a}$$

and

$$\Delta = \frac{1}{p}(\dot{T} - \dot{N}) + \dot{A}^M \tag{4.8b}$$

As regards Ω, the statement that the change in wealth or net worth equals saving *plus* capital gains is not surprising. The importance of fully accounting for capital gains and losses on existing government assets and liabilities to obtain a correct understanding of the short-run and long-run implications of past, present, and prospective budgetary, monetary, and financial policies has not, however, been appreciated universally.

Considerable interest attaches to behavior by an economic agent, sector, or group of sectors that leaves real comprehensive net worth unchanged. Such agents or sectors consume their permanent income, and their behavior is *ex ante* permanently sustainable. For policy design, policies aimed at keeping total national (public *plus* private) consumption in line with national permanent income — that is, policies focusing on the con-solidated public and private sector comprehensive balance sheet accounts — are of special relevance. These are considered in Section 4.5. While there are certainly valid reasons for optimal consumption to depart from permanent income, such divergences must necessarily be temporary, with overshooting and undershooting of the permanent income bench-mark canceling each other in terms of present value. The focus on spending behavior that is consistent with constant real comprehensive net worth should, therefore, come naturally in policy evaluation and design. It is noted that Equations (4.7), (4.8a), and (4.8b) represent *ex post* or realized measures only. For planning, including consumption planning, the *ex ante* measures are relevant. They are obtained by replacing actual changes in prices with anticipated changes in prices in Equations (4.7) and (4.8a), and by substituting anticipated changes in the value of implicit assets and liabilities for actual changes in Equations (4.7) and (4.8b). In what follows, *anticipated* capital gains and losses replace the *ex post* measures whenever planned private or public sector behavior is discussed.

4.2 AMORTIZATION OF PUBLIC DEBT THROUGH INFLATION AND CURRENCY APPRECIATION

Let us consider, first, changes in the public sector balance sheet that are due to 'pure' or general inflation, which is defined as a situation in which all money prices (including the prices of real capital assets) change at the same rate — that is,

$$\frac{\dot{p}_{K^{soc}}}{p_{K^{soc}}} = \frac{\dot{p}_G}{p_G} = \frac{\dot{p}_R}{p_R} = \frac{\dot{p}}{p}.$$

For reasons of space, we ignore capital gains or losses on the implicit assets and liabilities T and N that are caused by inflation.

Inflation-induced changes in real public sector net worth (Ω') are given by

$$\Omega' = \frac{\dot{p}}{p}\left(\frac{B^H + B^F + H}{p}\right) + \left(\frac{\dot{p}}{p} - \frac{\dot{e}}{e}\right)(B^{*H} + B^{*F} - E^*)\frac{e}{p} \qquad (4.9a)$$

4.2.1 The closed economy

In a closed economy, the last term on the right-hand side of Equation 4.9a) can be ignored, $B^F = 0$ and the reduction in the real value of the outstanding stock of nominally denominated government liabilities is given by

$$\Omega'' = \frac{\dot{p}}{p}\left(\frac{B^H + H}{p}\right) \qquad (4.9b)$$

Proper wealth accounting requires that the amortization of public debt through inflation should be put 'below the line' in measuring the financing of the government's net 'real' borrowing.[6] Above the line, a higher rate of inflation will (if interest rates are free) swell the measured deficit as nominal interest rates rise with the rate of inflation. If the Fisher hypothesis holds and real interest rates are invariant with respect to the rate of inflation, the increased nominal interest payments associated with a higher rate of inflation will be exactly matched by the reduction in the real value of the government's stock of nominally denominated interest-bearing debt (Ω'''), defined by

$$\Omega''' = \frac{\dot{p}}{p}\frac{B^H}{p} \qquad (4.9c)$$

Subtraction of Ω''' from the conventionally measured deficit yields the deficit 'at real interest rates' — what the conventionally measured deficit would have been if all interest-bearing debt had been index linked. In models that do not exhibit 'non-Ricardian' debt neutrality, changes in the real value of the stock of government interest-bearing debt are the major proximate determinant of 'financial crowding out' — the displacement of private capital formation by government borrowing, holding constant the size and composition of the government's real spending program. The exact nature (degree, scope, and time pattern) of financial crowding out will, of course, be 'model-specific'. A number of simple examples are analyzed in a sequel to this paper (see Buiter, 1982c). The central (and obvious) point is that, *ceteris paribus*, private agents (whose portfolio demands are for real stocks of assets if agents are free from money illusion) will absorb additional issues of nominal government bonds equal to the erosion in the real value of their existing holdings caused by (anticipated) inflation, without requiring any increase in the real rate of interest. Such government borrowing, therefore, does not raise the degree to which the public sector competes with the private sector for real investible resources.

The *ceteris paribus* clause of the preceding paragraph includes a given stock of real money balances. Additional monetary financing equal to the inflation tax on existing money balances, $\left(\dfrac{\dot{p}}{p}\dfrac{H}{p}\right)$, leaves real money balances unchanged. A conventionally measured deficit equal to Ω'', financed by borrowing an amount, $\dfrac{\dot{p}}{p}\dfrac{B^H}{p}$, and by money creation equal to $\dfrac{\dot{p}}{p}\dfrac{H}{p}$ is, therefore, consistent with constant real interest rates and a constant degree of aggregate financial crowding-out pressure.[7] Note that subtracting Ω'' from the conventionally measured deficit yields a somewhat wider concept of the deficit at real interest rates, since the real rate of return (ignoring non-pecuniary liquidity and convenience services) on high-powered money bearing a zero nominal interest rate is *minus* the rate of inflation.[8]

The argument for public sector inflation accounting in the closed economy can be summarized succinctly by using a simplified version of equations (4.1) and (4.2). Ignoring G^{soc}, K^{soc}, and R^G, let us assume that $p_G = p$ and define $G^I = \dot{K}^G$ (net investment by public sector enterprises) and $\bar{\tau} = \dfrac{\tau - n}{p}$ (real taxes net of transfers and other benefits). If it is assumed, in addition, that $r = i - \dfrac{\dot{p}}{p}$, then the conventionally measured government budget constraint is given by

$$\frac{\dot{H} + \dot{B}^H}{p} + \dot{B}^H \equiv G^c + G^I + \delta K^G - \bar{\tau} + \left(r + \frac{\dot{p}}{p}\right)\frac{B^H}{p}$$
$$+ r\bar{B}^H - r^G K^G. \tag{4.10}$$

The change in the real value of the stock of interest-bearing debt is given by

$$\frac{\mathrm{d}}{\mathrm{d}t}\left(\frac{B^H}{p} + \tilde{B}^H\right) \equiv G^c + G^I + \delta K^G - \tilde{\tau} + r\left(\frac{B^H}{p} + \tilde{B}^H\right)$$
$$- r^G K^G - \frac{\dot{H}}{p}. \tag{4.11}$$

The deficit measure that is relevant for aggregate financial crowding-out pressure on private capital formation, given in Equation (4.11), will depend on the amount of monetary financing permitted by the authorities. Useful bench-marks are (a) monetary financing sufficient to keep the real money stock constant: $\dfrac{\dot{H}}{p} = \dfrac{\dot{p}}{p}\dfrac{H}{p}$; and (b) monetary financing consistent with a zero trend rate of inflation: $\dfrac{\dot{H}}{p} = \gamma\dfrac{H}{p}$, where γ is the natural rate of growth.[9]

Equation (4.11) answers the questions as to whether the fiscal stance (defined by G^c, G^I, and $\tilde{\tau}$) and the monetary target $\left(\text{defined by } \dfrac{\dot{H}}{p}\right)$ imply aggregate financial crowding-out pressure $\left(\dfrac{\mathrm{d}}{\mathrm{d}t}\left(\dfrac{B^H}{p} + \tilde{B}^H\right) > 0\right)$ or crowding-in pressure $\left(\dfrac{\mathrm{d}}{\mathrm{d}t}\left(\dfrac{B^H}{p} + \tilde{B}^H\right) < 0\right)$. This issue can be addressed in the short run (for a single period), in the medium term (by applying Equation (4.11) sequentially for as many periods as one is interested in), or in the steady state. Note that inflation-induced capital gains or losses on non-indexed bonds cancel the inflation premium in the nominal interest payments; in Equation (4.11), all debt service is evaluated at real rates of interest.[10]

For aggregate crowding-out pressure on total national (private *plus* public sector) capital formation, a useful simple measure (noting that $G^I = \dot{K}^G$) is

$$\frac{\mathrm{d}}{\mathrm{d}t}\left(\frac{B^H}{p} + \tilde{B}^H - K^G\right) = G^c - \tilde{\tau} + r\left(\frac{B^H}{p} + \tilde{B}^H - K^G\right)$$
$$+ (r - (r^G - \delta))K^G - \frac{\dot{H}}{p}. \tag{4.12}$$

The conventional deficit measure is further modified in Equation (4.12) by subtracting net investment by public sector enterprises. Interest payments on net non-monetary liabilities $(B^H + \tilde{B}^H - K^G)$ are evaluated at the real interest rate, r. If the net rate of return on public enterprise capital $(r^G - \delta)$ exceeds the opportunity cost of borrowing (r), the 'corrected' deficit is further reduced. If the opposite prevails, the corrected deficit is larger by an amount $(r - (r^G - \delta))K^G$.

The decline in the real value of total tangible net worth of the public sector is given by

$$\frac{d}{dt}\left(\frac{H + B^H}{p} + \tilde{B}^H - K^G\right) = G^c - \tilde{\tau} + r\left(\frac{B^H}{p} + \tilde{B}^H - K^G\right)$$

$$+ (r - (r^G - \delta))K^G - \frac{\dot{p}}{p}\frac{H}{p}. \qquad (4.13)$$

This could be called the inflation-corrected government current account deficit. Debt service payments and receipts on all assets and liabilities (including money) are evaluated at real rates of return.[11]

Some idea of the magnitude of the overstatement of the government's true borrowing by the conventionally measured deficit under inflationary circumstances is provided by Table 4.3 for the United Kingdom and Table 4.4 for the United States.

In 1981 the public sector borrowing requirement in the United Kingdom was £10.6 billion, and the public sector financial deficit rose to £7.5 billion. The inflation correction in that year amounted to about £11 billion, using a variety of estimates. The inflation-corrected deficit was actually a surplus. If it is noted that during 1981 the UK economy was also experiencing the worst recession since the 1930s, there can be no doubt that the inflation-corrected and cyclically adjusted (trend or permanent) deficit was actually a sizeable surplus. It is a matter of some practical importance whether that constitutes wise countercyclical fiscal policy. The United States during the period 1979–81 also had an inflation-corrected balanced Federal budget. Any reasonable cyclical correction for 1981 produces a large inflation-corrected cyclically adjusted surplus. High US real interest rates in 1981 can be explained by the fiscal stance only if large anticipated future inflation-corrected cyclically-adjusted deficits are postulated.

4.2.2 The open economy

In an open economy, governments can borrow and lend domestically or abroad. Their financial assets and liabilities can be denominated in foreign or domestic currency or can be index-linked. Consider Equation (4.9a). The real value of public sector debt denominated in domestic currency is reduced by domestic inflation whether this debt is owned by the private sector or the rest of the world. While, *ceteris paribus*, inflation also reduces the real value of foreign-currency-denominated financial claims, exchange rate depreciation increases it. If purchasing power parity holds $\left(\frac{\dot{p}}{p} - \frac{\dot{e}}{e} = \frac{\dot{p}^*}{p^*}\right)$, where p^* is the foreign general price level, and through choice of units, $ep^* = p\right)$, Equation (4.9a) becomes

Table 4.3 Correcting the public sector deficit for inflation, United Kingdom, 1967–81

Year	Public sector debt (market value) (% of GDP)*	Public sector borrowing requirement (£ billions)	(% of GDP)	Public sector financial deficit (£ billions)	(% of GDP)	Inflation correction (£ billions) (1)**	(2)†	(3)‡
1967	81	1.9	4.6	1.5	3.8	0.5	0.6	1.0
1968	77	1.3	3.0	0.9	2.0	1.4	2.0	1.2
1969	70	−0.4	−1.0	−0.5	−1.1	1.2	2.0	1.3
1970	67	0.0	0.0	−0.7	−1.3	2.1	2.7	1.4
1971	59	1.4	2.4	0.3	0.53	3.0	3.2	1.5
1972	58	2.1	3.2	1.5	2.4	3.3	3.2	1.7
1973	49	4.2	5.8	2.8	3.8	3.0	4.0	2.3
1974	43	6.4	7.7	4.7	5.7	7.0	9.3	3.3
1975	41	10.5	9.9	7.7	7.3	10.3	11.9	3.9
1976	43	9.1	7.3	8.3	6.6	7.5	7.4	5.0
1977	47	6.0	4.2	5.9	4.1	10.1	9.3	5.8
1978	44	8.4	5.1	8.1	4.9	6.2	6.4	6.5
1979	42	12.6	6.6	8.1	4.2	12.3	13.8	8.2
1980	36	12.2	5.4	9.7	4.3	9.6	12.1	10.5
1981	38	10.6	4.1	7.5	2.9	10.8	11.7	11.8

Source: Miller (1982).

* GDP = gross domestic product.

** Inflation correction (1) = annual rate of inflation *times* market value of public sector debt (mid-year).

† Inflation correction (2) = annual rate of inflation *times* nominal value of public sector debt.

‡ Inflation correction (3) is based on the assumption of a long-run real interest rate of 2 per cent.

120   *Issues of measurement*

Table 4.4 Federal deficits and debt, United States, 1967–81
(cols. 1–4 in US $ billions)

Fiscal year	Total federal budget and offbudget deficit for fiscal year (1)	Par value of public debt securities held by private investors, end of fiscal year (2)	Par value of public debt securities held by private investors, end of fiscal year (in 1967 prices) (3)*	Inflation correction (4)**	Public debt–GNP ratio (5)
1967	8.7	204.4	204.4	5.9	0.26
1968	25.2	217.0	208.3	9.1	0.25
1969	−3.2	214.0	194.9	11.6	0.23
1970	2.8	217.2	186.8	12.8	0.22
1971	23.0	228.9	188.7	9.8	0.21
1972	23.4	243.6	194.4	8.0	0.21
1973	14.9	258.9	194.5	16.1	0.20
1974	6.1	255.6	173.1	28.1	0.18
1975	53.2	303.2	188.1	27.6	0.20
1976	73.7	376.4	220.8	21.8	0.22
1977	53.6	438.6	241.7	28.5	0.23
1978	59.2	488.3	249.9	37.6	0.23
1979	40.2	523.4	240.8	59.1	0.22
1980	73.8	589.2	238.7	79.5	0.22
1981	78.9	665.4	244.3	69.2	0.23

Source: *Economic Report of the President* (Washington, DC, February 1982).
* Col. (3) = col. (2) deflated by consumer price index.
** Col. (4) = col. (2) *times* proportional rate of change of consumer price index.

$$\Omega' = \frac{\dot{p}}{p}\left(\frac{B^H + B^F + H}{p}\right) + \frac{\dot{p}^*}{p^*}\left(\frac{B^{*H} + B^{*F} - E^*}{p^*}\right) \tag{4.14}$$

With purchasing power parity, reductions in the real value of foreign-currency-denominated public sector debt can be calculated by multiplying the foreign rate of inflation by the real value of net foreign-currency-denominated liabilities.

Consider the following stylized representation of the position of a number of small, open developing countries that lack a significant domestic capital market. Government debt is largely placed abroad and tends to be denominated in foreign currency (typically US dollars). In such countries, $B^H = B^F = \tilde{B}^H = \tilde{B}^F = B^{*H} = 0$. The conventionally measured public sector deficit is[12]

$$\frac{\dot{H}}{p} + \frac{e}{p}(\dot{B}^{*F} - \dot{E}^*) = G^c + G^l + \delta K^G - \bar{\tau}$$

$$+ \frac{e}{p} i^*(B^{*F} - E^*) - r^G K^G. \tag{4.15}$$

If, in addition, only the government borrows overseas, $\frac{d}{dt}(B^{*F} - E^*)$ equals the current account deficit (in terms of foreign currency) of the balance of payments, as shown in Equation (4.16):

$$\frac{e}{p}(\dot{B}^{*F} - \dot{E}^*) = -X + \frac{e}{p} i^*(B^{*F} - E^*). \tag{4.16}$$

Here, X denotes real net exports of goods and services (excluding debt service) *plus* net transfers and grants from abroad.

Compare the current account balances of two countries, identical in real terms but facing different rates of world inflation. If r^* is the world real rate of interest, $i^* = r^* + \frac{\dot{p}^*}{p^*}$, or

$$\frac{e}{p}(\dot{B}^{*F} - \dot{E}^*) = -X + \frac{e}{p}\left(r^* + \frac{\dot{p}^*}{p^*}\right)(B^{*F} - E^*). \tag{4.16a}$$

If the world real rate of interest is independent of the inflation rate and if purchasing power parity prevails, the current account deficit of the country facing the higher rate of world inflation $\left(\frac{\dot{p}^*}{p^*}\right)_1$ will exceed that of the country facing the lower rate of world inflation $\left(\frac{\dot{p}^*}{p^*}\right)_2$ by an amount $\left(\left(\frac{\dot{p}^*}{p^*}\right)_1 - \left(\frac{\dot{p}^*}{p^*}\right)_2\right) e \left(\frac{B^{*F} - E^*}{p}\right)$ equal to the difference in external debt service payments. This difference in current account balances should, however, have no real consequences, since the higher debt service item above the line is matched below the line by the larger reduction in the real value of its external liabilities; higher world inflation means faster amortization of external indebtedness. Thus, $\frac{d}{dt}\left(\frac{e}{p}(B^{*F} - E^*)\right)$, or the change in net real external liabilities, is the same in the two economies. The country facing the larger current account deficit owing to higher world inflation should be able to borrow to finance its higher external interest payments (see Sachs, 1981).

What has occurred in recent years is an increase in world real interest rates (r^*). This increase does require adjustment rather than, or in addition to, mere financing, with the relative weights on adjustment versus financing depending on the extent to which the increase in world real interest rates is perceived as permanent rather than transitory. Also, to the extent that countries have borrowed on a long-term rather than a short-term basis (or at variable interest rates), unanticipated changes in interest rates will result in once-and-for-all real capital gains or losses on external debt. Finally, significant departures from purchasing power parity have been the rule, especially since the breakdown of the Bretton Woods system of par values. Thus, even with a given world real interest rate (r^*), a country's real external indebtedness will increase whenever $\dfrac{\dot{p}^*}{p^*} - \left(\dfrac{\dot{p}}{p} - \dfrac{\dot{e}}{e} \right)$ — the excess of the world rate of inflation over the domestic rate of inflation *minus* the percentage depreciation of the exchange rate — increases.

Many other kinds of open economy can be analyzed, starting from the general framework of Equations (4.6), (4.7), and (4.9a), but the general principles should be clear from the simple example that was just analyzed.

4.3 BUDGETARY POLICY AND MONETARY GROWTH: EVENTUAL MONETIZATION OF DEFICITS

If bond financing of deficits causes concern about the crowding out of private capital formation and, in the open economy, about possible adverse consequences for external indebtedness, monetization of deficits is a source of concern because of its inflationary implications. It has been seen that it was necessary to correct the conventionally measured budget deficit for the effects of inflation and exchange rate appreciation on the real value of outstanding stocks of public sector financial assets and liabilities in order to assess changes in the extent to which the public sector competes with the private and overseas sectors for investible resources.

Similar adjustments are required to understand the monetary implications of the deficit, as is shown in this section.

4.3.1 The closed economy

From the simplified government budget constraint in Equation (4.10), the following expression is derived for the proportional rate of growth of the nominal money stock.[13]

$$
\frac{\dot{H}}{H} = V \left[\frac{G^c + G^I + \delta K^G - \bar{\tau}}{Y} + \left(r + \frac{\dot{p}}{p} \right) \frac{B^H}{pY} + r \frac{\dot{B}^H}{Y} - r^G \frac{K^G}{Y} \right.
$$
$$
\left. - \frac{\dot{B}^H}{pY} - \frac{\dot{B}^H}{Y} \right]
\tag{4.17}
$$

$V \equiv \dfrac{pY}{H}$ is the income velocity of circulation of money. To evaluate the implications of the fiscal stance for monetary growth, it is necessary to specify paths both for public spending and taxation and for non-money financing. A particularly useful bench-mark for financing policy is one that keeps constant the real values of all government assets and liabilities (other than money) per unit of output. This policy would be one of constant crowding-out pressure per unit of output. These constant liability–output (or asset–output) ratios need not be the historically inherited ones. The exercise can be applied to evaluating the longer-run implications for monetary growth after the debt–output ratios have acquired some desired long-run (or even steady-state) values. Given this rule,

$$\frac{G^I}{K^G} = \frac{\dot{B}^H}{\bar{B}^H} = \gamma$$

and

$$\frac{\dot{B}^H}{B^H} = \gamma + \frac{\dot{p}}{p}$$

Equation (4.17) then becomes

$$\frac{\dot{H}}{H} \equiv V\left[\frac{G^c - \bar{\tau}}{Y} + (r - \gamma)\left[\frac{B^H}{pY} + \frac{\bar{B}^H}{Y} - \frac{K^G}{Y}\right]\right.$$
$$\left. + (r - (r^G - \delta))\frac{K^G}{Y}\right] \tag{4.18}$$

Defining the longer-run fiscal stance by given constant values of $\dfrac{B^H}{pY}, \dfrac{\bar{B}^H}{Y}$, and $\dfrac{K^G}{Y}$ and by given, but not necessarily constant, paths of $\dfrac{G^c}{Y}$ and $\dfrac{\bar{\tau}}{Y}$, it can be seen from Equation (4.18) that longer-run monetary growth is governed by a deficit concept that differs from the conventionally measured deficit in a number of ways. First, the reduction in the real value of the stock of nominal government bonds owing to inflation is subtracted from the conventional measure. Second, in a growing economy the real stocks of government assets and liabilities can increase at the natural rate γ while leaving the asset–output or debt–output ratios constant. The net debt service term in Equation (4.18), therefore, involves the real growth-adjusted interest rate $(r - \gamma)$. Under inflationary conditions, this rate can be significantly less than $i = r + \dfrac{\dot{p}}{p}$ — the nominal interest rate. To infer the long-term implications for monetary growth (and thus for inflation) of the fiscal stance, a correction for inflation is applied only to the interest-bearing component of the government's nominal liabilities. The conventionally measured deficit should not also be reduced by the erosion of the real value of the nominal stock of high-powered money balances $\left(\dfrac{\dot{p}}{p}\dfrac{H}{p}\right)$ because constancy of the real value of all (monetary and non-monetary) government debt per unit of output is consistent with any deficit and any rate of inflation.

Large conventionally measured deficits (even if cyclically adjusted) that correspond to small inflation-corrected deficits (or even surpluses)[14] reflect *current* high inflation. They do not indicate the inevitability of high crowding-out pressure or high rates of monetary growth in the future. Even without correction for real growth, an inflation-corrected or 'trend' surplus means that (a) with zero money financing, there would be (aggregate) crowding in, and (b) with a bond-financing policy of zero (aggregate) crowding in, there would be negative monetary base growth.

Equation (4.18) alone does not lead to conclusions about the effects of, say, changes in fiscal stance on monetary growth. It is necessary to use positive economic models to incorporate the effect of any parameter changes on endogenous variables, such as velocity (V), real rates of interest (r and r^G), and even the natural rate of growth (γ). Such an analysis is simplest in classical monetarist models, such as that of Sargent and Wallace (1981), in which velocity, the real interest rate, and the natural rate of growth are constants, but Equation (4.18) can be incorporated in models of any type (see also Buiter, 1982a; 1982b).

4.3.2 The open economy

From the budget constraint of the simplified open economy, the expression for the percentage growth rate of the nominal money stock given in Equation (4.19) can be obtained, as follows:

$$
\begin{aligned}
\frac{\dot{H}}{H} = V\Bigg[& \frac{G^c + \delta K^G - \tilde{\tau}}{Y} + \left(r + \frac{\dot{p}}{p}\right)\left(\frac{B^H + B^F}{pY}\right) + r\left(\frac{\tilde{B}^H + \tilde{B}^F}{Y}\right) \\
& + \frac{i^* e}{pY}(B^{*H} + B^{*F} - E^*) - r^G \frac{K^G}{Y} + \frac{\dot{K}^G}{Y} - \frac{1}{p}\left(\frac{\dot{B}^H + \dot{B}^F}{Y}\right) \\
& - \left(\frac{\dot{\tilde{B}}^H + \dot{\tilde{B}}^F}{Y}\right) - \frac{e}{p}\left(\frac{\dot{B}^{*H} + \dot{B}^{*F} - \dot{E}^*}{Y}\right)\Bigg].
\end{aligned}
\tag{4.19}
$$

To evaluate the longer-run monetary implications of the fiscal stance, it is again assumed that all stock–flow ratios on the right-hand side of Equation (4.19) are kept constant. Equation (4.19) then reduces to

$$
\frac{\dot{H}}{H} = V\left[\frac{G^c - \tilde{\tau}}{Y} + (r - \gamma)\left(\frac{B^H + B^F}{pY} + \frac{\tilde{B}^H + \tilde{B}^F}{Y} - \frac{K^G}{Y}\right)\right.
$$

$$+ \left(i^* - \left(\frac{\dot{p}}{p} - \frac{\dot{e}}{e} \right) - \gamma \right) \left(\frac{B^{*H} + B^{*F} - E^*}{pY} \right) e$$

$$+ (r - (r^G - \delta)) \frac{K^G}{Y} \Bigg]. \tag{4.20}$$

With purchasing power parity, this simplifies to

$$\frac{\dot{H}}{H} = V \Bigg[\frac{G^c - \bar{\tau}}{Y} + (r - \gamma) \left(\frac{B^H + B^F}{pY} + \frac{\dot{B}^H + \dot{B}^F}{Y} - \frac{K^G}{Y} \right)$$

$$+ (r^* - \gamma) \left(\frac{B^{*H} + B^{*F} - E^*}{p^* Y} \right) e$$

$$+ (r - (r^G - \delta)) \frac{K^G}{Y} \Bigg]. \tag{4.20a}$$

The evaluation of the long-term monetization implied by the fiscal stance requires the consideration of a deficit measure that has nominal debt service payments 'corrected' for the effects of domestic inflation, exchange rate appreciation, and real growth.

In any particular period, the economy may well be far removed from the long-run trend captured in Equations (4.18) and (4.20) or (4.20a). Actual monetary growth in the short run will be given by Equations (4.17) or (4.19). If current inflation is a function only of current monetary growth, as would be true, for example, if velocity were constant, the price level were perfectly flexible, and output grew at its exogenously given trend rate γ,

then $\frac{\dot{p}}{p} = \frac{\dot{H}}{H} - \gamma$. Authorities concerned with inflation in the short run may not be gratified to know that the long-run rate of inflation implied by their fiscal stance is low, if current monetary growth and inflation are high. If, as seems more likely, current inflation is a function of current and past monetary growth, and a fortiori if current inflation depends also on anticipated future monetary growth (as it does in models with forward-looking rational expectations), then the long-run monetary growth expressions in Equations (4.18), (4.20) and (4.20a) become relevant even for short-term and medium-term policy.

4.4 ROLE OF IMPLICIT ASSETS AND LIABILITIES

On the asset side of the public sector balance sheet, there are T, the present value of planned or anticipated future tax revenues, and A^M, the imputed value of the government's cash monopoly. On the liability side is N, the present value of future transfers and benefits under various entitlement programs. This section considers how the value of these implicit assets and liabilities changes over time, with the focus on N. The treatment of T, A^M, and private sector human wealth (in Section 4.5) is analytically identical. The symbol N is defined as[15]

$$N(t) \equiv \int_t^\infty \left(\exp\left[-\int_t^u \hat{\imath}(s,t)\mathrm{d}s \right] \right) \hat{n}(u,t)\mathrm{d}u. \tag{4.21}$$

The change in the present discounted value of expected future benefits is given by

$$\frac{\mathrm{d}}{\mathrm{d}t}N(t) = i(t)N(t) - n(t) + \int_t^\infty \left(\exp\left[-\int_t^u \hat{\imath}(s,t)\mathrm{d}s \right] \right) \left(\frac{\partial}{\partial}\hat{n}(u,t) \right.$$
$$\left. - \hat{n}(u,t)\int_t^u \frac{\partial}{\partial t}\hat{\imath}(s,t)\mathrm{d}s \right)\mathrm{d}u. \tag{4.22}$$

The first two terms on the right-hand side of Equation (4.22) show how the present value of future benefits changes if all expectations concerning the future flow of benefits and future interest rates remain the same. The last term shows the effect of changes (at time t) in expectations concerning future benefits $\left(\frac{\partial}{\partial t}\hat{n}(u,t) \right)$ and future interest rates $\left(\frac{\partial}{\partial t}\hat{\imath}(s,t) \right)$. As expected, upward revisions in future benefit entitlements raise the value of N, while higher future expected interest rates lower its value.

The only item on the right-hand side of Equation (4.22) that appears in the cash-based public sector deficit or flow of funds accounts is $n(t)$, current benefit payments; $i(t)N(t)$ does not appear because future entitlements are not a marketable interest-bearing liability of the authorities. Changes in planned or expected future benefit entitlements appear in the accounts only if and when they actually become payable in the future, yet such 'revaluations' of N are of considerable policy interest. Even if financial markets are not forward-looking — even if government borrowing affects market rates of return only when it actually occurs — increases in N unmatched by increases in T (or by cuts in other spending programs) imply increased future borrowing or money issues and thus mean trouble for the future. Financial markets, furthermore, appear to be linked intertemporally (as formalized, for example, by models of efficient asset market equilibrium that incorporate forward-looking rational expectations). A larger anticipated future borrowing requirement therefore affects asset prices and rates of return today. An unanticipated increase in future expected (inflation corrected) deficits crowds out private spending today. The intangible items in the public sector balance sheet must be taken into account.

Table 4.5 Private sector balance sheet

	Assets		Liabilities
B^H	Net interest-bearing government debt denominated in domestic currency, held by residents	T	Present value of future taxes
		W^P	Private sector net worth
eB^{*H}	Net interest-bearing government debt denominated in foreign currency, held by residents		
$p\bar{B}^H$	Net interest-bearing index-linked government debt, held by residents		
H	Stock of high-powered money		
N	Present value of social insurance and other entitlement programs		
F^H	Net interest-bearing claims on foreign sector denominated in domestic currency		
eF^{*H}	Net interest-bearing claims on foreign sector denominated in foreign currency		
$p_{K^P}K^P$	Value of claims on real reproducible capital (including inventories)		
$p_R(\bar{R} - R^G)$	Land and mineral assets		
L	Present value of expected future labor income		

4.5 PUBLIC SECTOR ACCOUNTS AND PRIVATE BEHAVIOR

4.5.1 The private and overseas sectors' accounts

Comprehensive balance sheets analogous to the public sector balance sheet of Table 4.1 are drawn up for the private sector and the overseas sector (see Table 4.5 and 4.6). For reasons of space, the private sector balance sheet consolidates the household sector, the corporate sector, and the private financial sector. For practical applications, further sectoral disaggregation is often required. The balance sheets need little further explanation. Consumer durables and private residential housing can be viewed as included in the stock of private capital, K^P, and their imputed service flows are subsumed under private income and consumption in the budget constraint.

For simplicity, it is assumed that all claims on, or debts to, the rest of the world take the form of interest-bearing financial claims. Direct foreign ownership of domestic real capital or of domestic resources is not considered but could be added without difficulty. Human wealth (L), the present discounted value of expected future labor income, is a non-marketable asset in the household balance sheet. The total national stock of land and mineral rights is assumed to be given by $\bar{R}$.[16]

The conventionally measured financial surplus of the private sector (at constant prices) and the change in real private net worth are given in Equations (4.23) and (4.24), respectively:

$$\frac{\ell}{p} + r^P \frac{p_{K^P}}{p} K^P + r^R \frac{p_R}{p} R^P + \left(r + \frac{\dot{p}}{p} \right) \left(\frac{B^H}{p} + \frac{F^H}{p} \right)$$

$$+ \frac{ei^*}{p} (B^{*H} + F^{*H}) + r\bar{B}^H + \frac{n}{p} - \frac{\tau}{p} - C - \delta K^P \equiv \left(\frac{\dot{B}^H + \dot{F}^H}{p} \right)$$

$$+ \dot{B}^H + \frac{e}{p} (\dot{B}^{*H} + \dot{F}^{*H}) + \frac{\dot{H}}{p} + \frac{p_{K^P}}{p} \dot{K}^P - \frac{p_R}{p} \dot{R}^G \qquad (4.23)$$

$$\frac{d}{dt} \left(\frac{W^P}{p} \right) \equiv \left(\frac{\dot{B}^H + \dot{F}^H}{p} \right) + \dot{B}^H + \frac{e}{p} (\dot{B}^{*H} + \dot{F}^{*H}) + \frac{\dot{H}}{p} + \frac{p_{K^P}}{p} \dot{K}^P$$

$$- \frac{p_R}{p} \dot{R}^G + \frac{1}{p} (\dot{L} + \dot{N} - \dot{T}) + \left(\frac{\dot{p}_{K^P}}{p_{K_p}} - \frac{\dot{p}}{p} \right) \frac{p_{K^P}}{p} K^P$$

$$+ \left(\frac{\dot{p}_R}{p_R} - \frac{\dot{p}}{p} \right) \frac{p_R}{p} (\bar{R} - R^G) - \frac{\dot{p}}{p} \left(\frac{B^H + F^H + H}{p} \right)$$

$$+ \left(\frac{\dot{e}}{e} - \frac{\dot{p}}{p} \right) \frac{e}{p} (B^{*H} + F^{*H}) - \frac{\dot{p}}{p} (L + N - T) \qquad (4.24)$$

where p_{K^P} and r^P are the price of and rate of return on private capital, respectively; R^P represents privately-owned land and rights to natural resources; C is private consumption; ℓ is current labor income; F^H and F^{*H} are the domestic and foreign-currency-denominated private claims on the overseas sector; and W^P is defined in Table 4.5. The conventionally measured financial surplus of the overseas sector (at constant prices) and the change in the real net worth of the overseas sector are given in Equations (4.25) and (4.26), respectively:

$$-X + \frac{e}{p} i^* (B^{*F} - F^{*H} - E^*) + \left(r + \frac{\dot{p}}{p} \right) \left(\frac{B^F - F^H}{p} \right) + r\bar{B}^F$$

Table 4.6 Overseas sector balance sheet

Assets		Liabilities	
B^F	Overseas holdings of nominal government bonds denominated in domestic currency	eE^*	Net foreign exchange reserves of government
		F^H	Net interest-bearing debt to domestic private sector denominated in domestic currency
eB^{*F}	Overseas holdings of government bonds denominated in foreign currency		
		eF^{*H}	Net interest-bearing debt to domestic private sector denominated in foreign currency
$p\bar{B}^F$	Overseas holdings of index-linked government debt	W^F	Overseas sector net worth

$$\equiv \frac{e}{p}(\dot{B}^{*F} - \dot{F}^{*H} - \dot{E}^*) + \left(\frac{\dot{B}^F - \dot{F}^H}{p}\right) + \dot{B}^F \tag{4.25}$$

$$\frac{\mathrm{d}}{\mathrm{d}t}\left(\frac{W^F}{p}\right) \equiv \frac{e}{p}(\dot{B}^{*F} - \dot{F}^{*H} - \dot{E}^*) + \left(\frac{\dot{B}^F - \dot{F}^H}{p}\right) + \dot{B}^F$$

$$- \frac{\dot{p}}{p}\left(\frac{B^F - F^H}{p}\right) + \left(\frac{\dot{e}}{p} - \frac{\dot{p}}{p}\right)\frac{e}{p}(B^{*F} - F^{*H} - E^*),$$

$$\tag{4.26}$$

where W^F is defined in Table 4.6. These equations require little explanation. For the private sector, the difference between the financial surplus (at constant prices) and the change in real net worth reflects capital gains and losses on existing marketable assets and liabilities (including capital gains and losses that are due to inflation and exchange rate changes) and changes in the value of the intangible and non-marketable items L, N, and T. On the left-hand side of Equation (4.23), because only cash transactions are included, the implicit liquidity and convenience yield on money balances $\left(\varrho^M \frac{H}{p} = i\frac{H}{p}\right)$ as an item of private consumption and of private income is omitted.

4.5.2 Positive irrelevance and normative relevance of debt neutrality

The simplest theory of the interaction of the private and public sectors is based on the so-called non-Ricardian debt-neutrality hypothesis (see Barro, 1974; Carmichael, 1979; Buiter and Tobin, 1979; Buiter, 1980; and Tobin and Buiter, 1980). This hypothesis holds that, given the level and composition of the public sector's real spending on goods and services, private sector behavior is invariant with respect to changes in the taxation/ borrowing mix that finances this spending. Most of the formal models dealing with this issue concern closed barter economies, and the formal invariance propositions tend to be stated in terms of borrowing versus taxing without explicit consideration of monetary financing. For all three financing modes, the informal literature on the subject does, however, assert the irrelevance for real outcomes of the way in which governments finance their spending. The argument underlying this Modigliani–Miller theorem for the public sector *vis-à-vis* the private sector runs as follows. Spending must be financed (in a closed economy) by taxation, by borrowing, or by printing money. Borrowing is merely deferred taxation. A switch between taxation and borrowing should, therefore, not affect the permanent income and consumption behavior of rational well-informed private agents. Monetary financing implies the imposition of an inflation tax, which under restrictive conditions has the same effect on permanent income as explicit taxes.[17]

With debt neutrality, private sector spending behavior (for a given program of public spending on goods and services) is constrained only by the consolidated national balance sheet, as shown in Table 4.7. The distribution of the ownership of the nation's resources between the public and private sectors is irrelevant. The national flow of funds account, including non-marketable imputed income and consumption streams, is given by

$$
\frac{1}{p} \{ \ell + r^{soc} p_{K^{soc}} K^{soc} + r^G p_G K^G + r^P p_{K^P} K^P + r^R p_R \bar{R}
$$

$$
+ i^* e(E^* + F^{*H} - B^{*F})
$$

$$
+ i(F^H - B^F) - rp\bar{B}^F + iH\} - \left[G^c + G^{soc} + C \right.
$$

$$
+ \frac{\delta}{p} (p_{K^{soc}} K^{soc} + p_G K^G + p_{K^P} K^P) + \varrho^M \frac{H}{p} \right] \equiv \frac{1}{p} \{ p_{K^{soc}} \dot{K}^{soc}
$$

$$
+ p_G \dot{K}^G + p_{K^P} \dot{K}^P + e(\dot{E}^* + \dot{F}^{*H} - \dot{B}^{*F})
$$

$$
+ \dot{F}^H - \dot{B}^F - p\dot{\bar{B}}^F\} \equiv \frac{S}{p} \tag{4.27}
$$

S being total national saving. The first bracketed term on the left-hand side of Equation (4.27) contains current income, including the imputed return from the government's cash monopoly $i\frac{H}{p}$. This item is matched in the second bracketed term, containing current consumption, by $\varrho^M \frac{H}{p}$, the imputed value of the non-pecuniary services of money consumed by the private sector. It is possible to omit both items if desired. The change in real national comprehensive net worth is given by

Table 4.7 Consolidated public and private sector balance sheet

Assets	Liabilities
$p_{K^{soc}}K^{soc}$ $p_G K^G$ $p_{K^p}K^p$ $p_R\bar{R}$ $e(E^* + F^{*H} - B^{*F})$ $+ F^H - B^F - p\bar{B}^F$ L pA^M	$W^p + W^G$

$$\frac{\mathrm{d}}{\mathrm{d}t}\left(\frac{W}{p}\right) \equiv \frac{\mathrm{d}}{\mathrm{d}t}\left(\frac{W^p + W^G}{p}\right) \equiv \frac{S}{p} + \left(\frac{\dot{p}_{K^{soc}}}{p_{K^{soc}}} - \frac{\dot{p}}{p}\right)\frac{p_{K^{soc}}K^{soc}}{p}$$

$$+ \left(\frac{\dot{p}_G}{p_G} - \frac{\dot{p}}{p}\right)\frac{p_G}{p}K^G$$

$$+ \left(\frac{\dot{p}_{K^p}}{p_{K^p}} - \frac{\dot{p}}{p}\right)\frac{p_{K^p}}{p}K^p + \left(\frac{\dot{p}_R}{p_R} - \frac{\dot{p}}{p}\right)\frac{p_R}{p}\bar{R}$$

$$+ \left(\frac{\dot{e}}{e} - \frac{\dot{p}}{p}\right)\frac{e}{p}(E^* + F^{*H} - B^{*F})$$

$$- \frac{\dot{p}}{p}\{F^H - B^F\} + (\dot{L}/p) + \dot{A}^M. \tag{4.28}$$

The change in real net worth equals saving $\left(\frac{S}{p}\right)$ *plus* capital gains on marketable assets *plus* changes in the imputed or implicit value of non-marketable items of wealth. A program of total national consumption in line with permanent national income means a choice of the value of the second bracketed terms in Equation (4.27) such that the expected value of $\frac{\mathrm{d}}{\mathrm{d}t}\left(\frac{W}{p}\right) = 0$. Such a consumption program is *ex ante* indefinitely sustainable and serves as a useful bench-mark for consumption planning in this debt-neutral economy.

Debt neutrality is bad positive economics. It requires private agents to be infinite-lived or to have operative intergenerational bequest and child-to-parent gift motives in every generation. Perfect capital markets are another necessary condition: future labor income is a source of current spending power on a par with current disposable income and current holdings of government debt.[18]

The economic behavior that would be generated under debt neutrality is, however, a useful guide to what the aims of policy should be in a world in which a variety of capital market imperfections prevent the 'unaided' private sector from acting according to permanent income principles.

It is, for example, well known that, in the absence of operative private intergenerational transfer motives, changes in the borrowing/taxation mix can redistribute the burden of financing a given government spending program between generations, even without the existence of capital market imperfections. If government is motivated by a concern for the utility (lifetime consumption patterns) of future generations as well as of the current generation, it can use the budgetary and financial mechanism to induce the current generation to act as if it were constrained by permanent private sector income rather than merely by the present value of its own lifetime resources.

The endowments listed on the asset side of Table 4.7, the nation's technology (broadly defined) and the international trading and lending or borrowing conditions that it faces, represent the unavoidable constraints on the nation's intertemporal transformation of resources.[19] The purpose of financing policy — that is, the choice of the tax, transfer, borrowing, and money creation mix for a given real public spending program on goods and services — should be to keep additional constraints, such as cash flow short-falls, inadequate liquidity, insufficient collateral, non-marketability of assets, and credit rationing, from becoming binding or, failing that, to minimize their incidence and consequences.[20]

Through their budgetary and financing policies, governments (within a national economy) and international organizations (within the international economic system) can act as superior financial intermediaries in changing the composition of private sector portfolios and nation-state portfolios, respectively. Well-designed policy interventions of this kind can minimize the extent to which disposable income, current cash flow, and the portfolio of liquid marketable financial assets become binding constraints on consumption, investment, production, and portfolio allocation, enforcing undesirable departures from behavior according to permanent income principles. Governments, through their unique ability to impose taxes, through their monopoly of legal tender, and through the superior quality of their debts, have a 'comparative advantage' over the private sector in borrowing to smooth out income streams.[21] The same holds, although perhaps to a lesser extent, for certain international organizations *vis-à-vis* nation-states.

In what follows, a few examples are given to illustrate this role of the government as the natural borrower and the unique ability of the government to restructure the conventionally measured sectoral balance sheets, flow of funds accounts, and income expenditure accounts so as to permit the economy as a whole to approximate more closely behavior that is constrained only by comprehensive wealth or permanent income.

Fiscal aspects of discovery of a natural resource
Consider the effects of an oil discovery on public sector and private sector balance sheets. This discovery can be represented by an unexpected increase in p_R, the value of property rights in land and mineral assets by, say, $dp_R > 0$. To the extent that these property rights are privately owned and marketable, disposable private net worth increases by $(\bar{R} - R^G)dp_R$. Following permanent income principles, private agents would consume the perpetuity equivalent of this capital gain in each period. If spending were constrained by a dearth of marketable financial wealth to begin with, a temporarily larger increase in private consumption spending would result. The value of public sector assets increases by $R^G dp_R$. The government could choose to increase its own consumption spending in line with the permanent income equivalent of this capital gain. If it chooses not to do so, it faces the problem of enabling the private sector to raise its spending by the perpetuity equivalent of $R^G dp_R$.

One way to approach this situation would be to distribute to the private sector (in the form of tax cuts or increased transfer payments) the stream of actual additional oil revenues as and when they accrue. The present value of such anticipated future tax cuts or increases in transfer payments is, however, a non-marketable highly illiquid asset that is singularly poor collateral for private borrowing. If there is a gestation period before the new oil comes on stream and a fortiori if development costs have to be incurred before the oil starts to flow, the additional cash flow to the government, and thus to the private sector, may well be negative for several years.

Private agents whose current spending is constrained by current disposable income or other forms of illiquidity will therefore be unable to raise their spending in line with their permanent income. A superior fiscal option is for the government, as soon as the new oil wealth is discovered, to cut taxes or raise transfers by an amount equal to the perpetuity equivalent or annuity value of the discovery (see Flemming, 1982). This option will require additional government borrowing until the moment when actual revenues exceed their permanent value, at which time the authorities will be able to retire the temporary debt issues, whose function is merely to relax the spending limits on cash-flow-constrained households. With this transformation of future tax cuts into present tax cuts, the nation can consume in line with its new and higher permanent income; the government has transformed future tax cuts into disposable income.

An alternative proposal to handle the same problem has been made by Samuel Brittan of the *Financial Times*. His proposal amounts to a capital gift to the private sector by the public sector — the equity in the newly discovered oil riches is transferred to the private sector. If this newly privatized wealth takes the form of marketable financial claims, private spending in line with permanent income is again likely to be encouraged, relative to a policy of cutting taxes in line with current oil revenues —

the government has transformed future tax cuts into disposable financial wealth.

In this paper, the same symbol T is used both for the present value to households of expected future tax payments and for the present value to the government of expected future tax receipts. Similarly, N represents both the household asset and the government liability corresponding to the stream of future benefits (n).

The presence of an impact on private spending of offsetting changes in, say, T, N, and B^H that would prima facie appear to leave household net worth unchanged is then attributed, in a rather *ad hoc* manner, to differences in the liquidity, marketability, and usefulness as collateral of T, N, and B^H. An alternative (but still *ad hoc*) way of avoiding the debt-neutrality conundrum is to assume that households discount future taxes and benefits at a higher rate than the market rate of return on bonds (and at a higher rate than the government discounts its tax revenues and benefit payments). To avoid the use of even more symbols and notation, this approach was not adopted here. A truly satisfactory treatment of these issues requires the tools of the new microeconomics of credit rationing, collateral, and other capital market imperfections, whose beginnings can be found, for example, in the work of Jaffee and Russell (1976), Benjamin (1978), Stiglitz and Weiss (1981), and Webb (1981; 1982).

'Cyclical' corrections to public sector deficits

Consider an economy in which the level of economic activity — as measured, for example, by output and employment — cycles around a trend. It is not assumed at this stage that these cycles represent Keynesian departures from full employment and normal capacity utilization. They could be regular swings in the natural rate of unemployment.

If the economy represented by Equation (4.10) is simplified even further by ignoring public sector capital and index-linked bonds, the government budget constraint becomes

$$\frac{\dot{H} + \dot{B}^H}{p} \equiv G^c - \bar{\tau} + \left(r + \frac{\dot{p}}{p}\right)\frac{B^H}{p}. \tag{4.29}$$

$\bar{Y}$, the trend level of output, grows at a proportional rate, γ. Actual output (Y) cycles steadily around this trend. If the demand for debt is a demand for real debt per capita and if population (in efficiency units) and $\bar{Y}$ grow at the same rate, then government financing tends to exercise upward pressure on the real interest rate when $\frac{d}{dt}\left(\frac{B^H}{pY}\right) > 0$ at the given real interest rate and the given real per capita stock of money balances. From Equation (4.29), it can be seen that

$$\frac{d}{dt}\left(\frac{B^H}{p\bar{Y}}\right) = \frac{G^c - \bar{\tau}}{\bar{Y}} + (r - \gamma)\frac{B^H}{p\bar{Y}} - \frac{\dot{H}}{p\bar{Y}}. \tag{4.30}$$

It is a stylized empirical fact that, while exhaustive public spending (G^c) tends to grow in line with trend output, taxes net of transfers ($\bar{\tau}$) tend to vary positively with the current level of economic activity. These two relationships can be summarized by

$$G^c = g^c \bar{Y} \qquad 1 > g^c > 0 \qquad\qquad (4.31a)$$

$$\bar{\tau} = \theta Y \qquad 1 > \theta > 0. \qquad\qquad (4.31b)$$

Substituting Equations (4.31a) and (4.31b) into Equation (4.30) yields

$$\frac{d}{dt}\left(\frac{B^H}{p\bar{Y}}\right) = g^c - \frac{\theta Y}{\bar{Y}} + (r - \delta)\frac{B^H}{p\bar{Y}} - \frac{\dot{H}}{p\bar{Y}}. \qquad\qquad (4.32)$$

Similarly, the proportional rate of growth of the money stock, assuming that the authorities keep constant the stock of real bonds per capita or per unit of trend output, is given by

$$\frac{\dot{H}}{H} = V\left[g^c\frac{\bar{Y}}{Y} - \theta + (r - \delta)\frac{B^H}{p\bar{Y}}\right]. \qquad\qquad (4.33)$$

Thus, the current change in $\dfrac{B^H}{p\bar{Y}}$ overstates (understates) its trend or long-run average rate of change, and the current rate of growth of the nominal money stock overstates (understates) its trend or long-run average rate of growth whenever output is below (above) its trend value.

Even if it is only the current values of $\dfrac{d}{dt}\left(\dfrac{B^H}{p\bar{Y}}\right)$ and $\dfrac{\dot{H}}{H}$ that matter for current crowding out and current inflation, respectively, the trend or long-run behavior of $\dfrac{d}{dt}\left(\dfrac{B^H}{p\bar{Y}}\right)$ and $\dfrac{\dot{H}}{H}$, obtained by evaluating Equations (4.32) and (4.33) with output at its trend value $\bar{Y}$, will still be of interest to all but the most short-sighted governments.

Furthermore, if current crowding out is a function of anticipated future changes in $\dfrac{B^H}{p\bar{Y}}$ and current inflation depends on anticipated future monetary growth (as well as possibly on past monetary growth), current $\dfrac{d}{dt}\left(\dfrac{B}{p\bar{Y}}\right)$ and $\dfrac{\dot{H}}{H}$ will be a poor proxy for future developments if there are transitory swings in the deficit. From this perspective, cyclical corrections are a simple, if *ad hoc*, way of approximating the long-run implications of the fiscal stance for crowding out and monetary growth — that is, a quick method for calculating the permanent deficit.

Evaluation of Y and $\bar{Y}$ in Equations (4.32) and (4.33) yields a reasonable approximation to the long-run averages only if the positive and negative deviations of Y from $\bar{Y}$ cancel each other out in the long run, as would be true, for example, if output followed a regular sinusoidal motion about trend, such as $\dfrac{Y(t)}{\bar{Y}(t)} = 1 + A\cos(\omega t + \epsilon)$. If positive and negative deviations of Y from $\bar{Y}$ do not balance on average, the simple cyclical correction gives a biased estimate of the long-run crowding-out pressure and monetary growth implications of the deficit. Such estimates will have to be replaced by an explicit averaging of Equations (4.32) and (4.33) over long periods.

There are good reasons for letting taxes net of transfers vary with the current level of economic activity rather than making them functions of long-run or permanent income. It is assumed, as seems reasonable, that during the downswing a significant number of private agents are constrained in their spending by current disposable income.[22] By reducing taxes and increasing borrowing during the downswing, public spending during that period will be financed to a larger extent by private agents who are not constrained by current disposable income (the purchasers of the bonds). Total consumption, therefore, declines by less than it would decline if taxes (which are assumed to fall equally on disposable-income-constrained and permanent-income-constrained private agents) had been kept constant. In the upswing, the additional debt incurred during the downswing can be repaid out of higher than normal taxes.[23] The net result is that consumption is smoothed out over the cycle — a desirable result on grounds of intertemporal allocative efficiency even if product and factor markets cleared continuously. If wage or price stickiness exists, Keynesian problems of failure of effective demand can also occur. Exogenous shocks to demand can set in motion contractionary or expansionary multiplier processes if private agents are constrained in their spending by current disposable income. The usefulness of automatic stabilizers and of counter-cyclical budget deficits derives from private spending that is constrained by current disposable income and from other capital market imperfections. It is reinforced by output and labor market disequilibrium.

Constraints of current disposable income on private consumption need not be absolute. Regular anticipated cycles in real income do not, of course, imply corresponding cycles in consumption, even for individuals who can borrow only on very unfavorable terms in order to consume in excess of their current disposable income. They have the option of accumulating a stock of liquid savings that can be run down and built up again cyclically. Even with uncertain stochastic swings in the level of economic activity, a buffer stock of liquid financial assets may permit a measure of income smoothing. Such private saving strategies are, however, likely to be inferior substitutes for access to borrowing on the terms available to the government.

A further option available to the government is to choose partial money financing of increases in cyclical deficits rather than borrowing. This option is more attractive the smaller the number and the less the wealth of private agents that are not constrained by current disposable income and liquidity. The more inelastic the demand for government bonds, the larger the increase in interest rates that is required to unload additional bond issues on the private sector. (Access to international capital markets may make the total demand for domestic government bonds considerably more interest-elastic than private domestic demand alone.) Such countercyclical money issues and withdrawals need not imply any increase in the trend rate of growth of the money stock.

It is to be noted that this view of stabilization policy suggests that taxes and transfers, rather than 'exhaustive' public spending on goods and services, should be used to dampen fluctuations in economic activity. Public consumption spending, like all consumption spending, should be smoothed over time in line with permanent income. Public sector capital formation should have its time profile determined largely by the optimal public sector consumption program. Public works and other public spending on goods and services can be effective in regulating the overall level of demand and of economic activity, but they are likely to distort the optimal private sector/public sector consumption mix, unlike well-designed changes in the taxation, borrowing, and money financing mix.

Sales of public sector assets and cosmetic changes in PSBR
Sales of existing public sector financial assets do not appear in the SNA public sector financial surplus, but they do appear in the public sector borrowing requirement (PSBR) and similar transactions records. A 'stock-shift' sale of government-owned rights to natural resources $(-dR^G)$ or of claims to public enterprise capital $(-dK^G)$ to the private sector would not in itself alter public sector or private sector net worth. If it is assumed that the government wishes neither to reduce the level of the money stock nor to acquire private sector capital, the counterpart of a reduction in R^G or in K^G would be a reduction in B^H, B^{*H}, or $\bar{B}^H$ with $P_R dR^G + p_K{}^G dK^G = dB^H + edB^{*H} + pd\bar{B}^H$.

Nationalizing or denationalizing may, of course, be desirable for reasons of efficiency. Total national net worth is altered by such transfers of ownership if the efficiency with which the resources are managed differs between sectors. The financial consequences, however, are virtually nil, because bonds in private portfolios are replaced by other financial claims. If the government gradually sells its assets to finance a flow of spending $\left(p_R \dfrac{\mathrm{d}}{\mathrm{d}t} R^G\right.$

$\left. + p_G \dfrac{\mathrm{d}}{\mathrm{d}t} K^G < 0\right)$, the difference between this policy and one of conventional financing by borrowing is also largely cosmetic.[24] When it borrows, the government incurs an obligation to service the additional debt. When it sells assets, it loses the future income from the assets that it sells. It makes little sense, therefore, to attribute economic significance to the distinction between sales of public debt (below the line) and sales of government financial assets (above the line) as is done with the PSBR in the United Kingdom.

4.6 CONCLUSION

The general conclusions have been stated in the introductory paragraphs. This section contains some more specific and practical remarks.

Comprehensive wealth and permanent income accounting requires explicit judgements concerning expectations about the future because of the need to evaluate non-marketable, often intangible, and merely implicit assets and liabilities, such as future tax and benefit streams. This requirement is considered to be a salutary aspect of comprehensive wealth accounting. It brings out the distinction between mechanistic bookkeeping and recording of transactions, on the one hand, and accounting for economic policy evaluation and design, on the other hand.

Inflation accounting in the public sector is long overdue. Money illusion in the public sector should cease to be an obstacle to sensible budgetary policy. Taken alone, the public sector financial deficit and the PSBR (at current or constant prices or as a proportion of gross national product) are not very informative statistics. They must be corrected for the change in the real value of the outstanding stocks of interest-bearing public debt to evaluate either the implications of the deficit for financial crowding out or the 'eventual monetization' implied by the government's fiscal stance. Analogous corrections should be made to the conventionally measured external current account deficit or surplus; it is necessary to allow for changes in the real value of external assets and liabilities owing to changes in the price level and the nominal exchange rate.

Omission of government-owned capital and public sector property rights in land and natural resources from the public sector balance sheet can give a misleading picture of the net worth of the public sector and of its present and future fiscal and financial options. This holds true especially for countries where the government owns significant mineral rights (such as Norway, the United Kingdom, the United States, and many of the oil producing nations) and countries in which the nationalized sector accounts for a large share of economic activity (such as the United Kingdom and many developing countries). The *sign* of the effect on public sector net worth of including publicly owned capital is not self-evident; virtually open-ended commitments to subsidize loss-making public enterprises depress net worth.

The implicit assets and liabilities of the public sector represented by the streams of future tax revenues and of future benefits and transfer payments may well dwarf the marketable financial assets and liabilities in the government balance sheet.

Transitory (e.g., cyclical) deficits and surpluses are mechanisms that enable private agents who are constrained by current disposable income to smooth out consumption and to keep it more closely in line with permanent income. By permitting consumption to be maintained in the face of a transitory decline in income, they also mitigate unemployment and excess capacity if price and wage rigidities prevent an instantaneous market-clearing response to demand shocks. It is sound fiscal management for governments to borrow in the downswing 'on behalf of' private agents with less favored access to capital markets and to retire these counter-cyclical debt increases during the upswing, regardless of the rate of inflation. Alternatively, cyclical increases in the deficit could be partly or wholly financed by money creation, to be reversed during the upswing. The optimal financing mix of cyclical (or transitory and reversible) deficits need not be the same as that of permanent deficits. A consideration of this important issue would require the analysis of specific detailed models, which are well beyond the scope of this paper. The focus here is on general propositions that rely on as few detailed model-specific properties as possible.

4.7 NOTES

1. Or equivalently, by

$$V^M(t) = \int_t^\infty \frac{H(t)}{\hat{p}(u, t)} \hat{\varrho}^M(u, t) \exp\left(-\int_t^u \hat{r}(s, t)\,ds\right) du.$$

2. Or equivalently, by

$$\Pi^M(t) = \int_t^\infty \frac{\mathring{H}(u, t)}{\hat{p}(u, t)} \exp\left(-\int_t^u \hat{r}(s, t)\,ds\right) du.$$

3. It is assumed that for any variable x, $\hat{x}(t_1, t_2) = x(t_1)$ for $t_1 \leq t_2$: the past and present are assumed to be known.
4. Consumption of the imputed services from social overhead capital can be viewed as a transfer (in kind) from the public sector to the private sector rather than as an item of public sector consumption. Alternatively, the services from the stock of public sector overhead capital could be an input into private production.
5. No behavioral significance should be attached to the specification of T and N in nominal terms.
6. Clear statements of this proposition can be found in Siegel (1979) and in Taylor and Threadgold (1979). See also Buiter and Miller (1981) and Buiter (1982b).
7. It is assumed that borrowing and money creation, *per se*, do not affect determinants of the demand for public debt other than expected real rates of return.

8. This is the *ex post* measure. The *ex ante* real yields are defined in terms of the expected rate of inflation.
9. Money demand is assumed to be unit-elastic in income and wealth.
10. The accounting framework does not indicate whether or not the real interest rate varies with the inflation rate.
11. For certain purposes, crowding-out pressure per unit of capacity output or crowding-out pressure per unit of efficiency labor is of interest (see, for example, Sargent and Wallace, 1981). This would involve replacing Equation (4.11) by the following:

$$\frac{d}{dt}\left(\frac{\bar{B} + B^H p^{-1}}{Y}\right) = \frac{G^c + G^I + \delta K^G - \bar{\tau}}{Y} + (r - \gamma)\left(\frac{B^H}{pY} + \frac{\bar{B}^H}{Y}\right)$$
$$- \frac{r^G K^G}{Y} - \frac{\dot{H}}{pY},$$

   where Y represents real output.
12. Simplifying assumptions about the public sector accounts made earlier in this section are maintained.
13. Throughout this paper, the money stock is the high-powered money stock. Addition of a private banking sector will, in general, be required for practical applications but does not significantly alter the conceptual framework outlined here.
14. That is, deficits corrected for the reduction due to inflation in the real value of the stock of nominal government bonds.
15. The appropriate discount rate may include a risk premium.
16. If Table 4.5 represents the balance sheet of those private agents currently alive, the horizons involved in N, T, and L would be finite if operative intergenerational bequest motives are absent. The values of N and T in the private balance sheet could, therefore, be different from the corresponding items in the public sector balance sheet, even if public sector and private sector discount rates were identical. If there are operative intergenerational bequest motives, or if the private sector is viewed abstractly as containing both current and future generations, an infinite horizon for T, N, and L in Table 4.5 is appropriate. Even with common horizons, different discount rates for the public and private sectors could lead to changes in private net worth resulting from changes in the public sector balance sheet that leave public sector net worth unchanged. These issues are discussed later in this section.
17. The Modigliani–Miller theorem for money financing has been established formally for models in which money serves only as a store of value. Such 'money' has only the name in common with what economists have always meant by money — that is, a means of payment or a medium of exchange (see Wallace, 1981).
18. Debt neutrality — that is, invariance of the solution trajectories of real economic variables under changes in the borrowing/taxation mix of the government — also requires lump-sum taxes. With non-lump-sum (or distortionary) taxes, transfers, and subsidies, public sector claims on the private sector and private sector claims on the public sector still are netted out in the balance sheet. Real behavior is altered when the borrowing/taxation mix changes because the familiar allocative effects of non-lump-sum taxes, etc., will alter equilibrium prices and rates of return.
19. While it might, for example, be possible for an individual to consume today by borrowing against the present value of future labor income, a closed economic

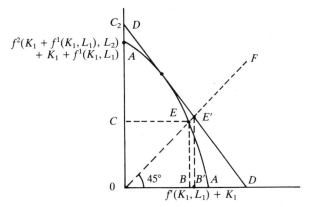

Figure 4.1 The intertemporal consumption possibility frontier

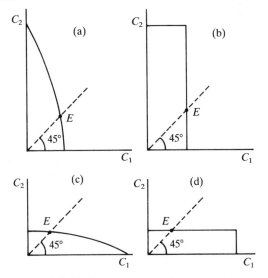

Figure 4.2 Limits to consumption smoothing

system cannot effect intertemporal shifts of future labor endowments. In an ideal market economy, these and other technological constraints are reflected in the sequence of demands and supplies over time and thus in equilibrium prices (including the asset prices that enter the balance sheets) at each point in time. In an ideal planned economy, the programming of material balances and the use of shadow prices would ensure the same outcomes.

Consider, for example, a simple two-period economy. The trade-off along the intertemporal consumption possibility frontier of c_1 (consumption in period 1) for c_2 (consumption in period 2) is given by AA in Figure 4.1. It is defined by the initial endowment of capital (K_1), the labor endowments in periods 1 and 2 (L_1 and L_2), the well-behaved production functions in the two periods

$[f^1(K_1, L_1)$ and $f^2(K_2, L_2)]$ and the constraint $[0 \leqslant c_1 \leqslant f^1 + K_1, 0 \leqslant c_2 \leqslant f^2 + K^2, c_1 = f^1(K_1, L_1) + K_1 - K_2]$ (see Figure 4.1).

The permanent income in this closed system is given by $OB = OC$, determined by the intersection of the consumption possibility frontier with the 45° line OF. The opportunity for international lending and borrowing at a rate r would raise the permanent income of this system unless the slope of the international capital market constraint DD (given by $-(1 + r)$) equals the slope of the closed economy locus at E. For the figure, it is shown how a low external interest rate raises permanent income to OB'. Figure 4.2 shows when a closed economy should not consume its permanent income in each period. Very favorable intertemporal transformation possibilities (Figure 4.2(a) and 4.2(b)) suggest consumption in excess of permanent income in period 2; the opposite applies in Figure 4.2(c) and 4.2(d). It is still the comprehensive balance sheet that matters for consumption, but constant net worth is unlikely to be optimal. Even with international lending and borrowing, the presence of non-traded goods, whose production can be augmented only slowly and at considerable cost, can make a program of consumption equal to permanent income infeasible or suboptimal.

20. The most desirable policy — eliminating capital market imperfections as far as possible — should be pursued to the full. Budgetary policies should aim to neutralize the imperfections that cannot be eliminated.

21. Because governments have the unique power to impose taxes (unrequited transfers to itself) and because of their ability to declare certain of their liabilities legal tender, the risk of default on government bonds is less than that on private debt. Total current and future natural income is in a sense the collateral for government borrowing. National income tends to be much less variable and uncertain than the income of individual private agents.

    Governments effectively pool individual risks and thus eliminate diversifiable risk. An obvious question is why this risk-sharing cannot be done equally well through private insurance markets. One answer is that, even if this were possible, it would be more costly than making minor alterations to a tax structure that is required in any case. A second answer relies on familiar problems of moral hazard in insurance markets. It may be possible to devise efficient private insurance schemes for 'bad luck' default. Private insurance markets will operate inefficiently (or may not exist at all) if there is frequent 'voluntary' or 'dishonest' default and if lenders and insurers cannot differentiate between honest and dishonest borrowers. If it is easier and less costly for the government to levy taxes on reluctant taxpayers than it is for private lenders and insurers to compel performance by dishonest borrowers, then governments have a role as financial intermediaries and government debt is not 'neutral' (see Webb, 1981; 1982).

22. It may be desirable to replace the phrase 'spending constrained by current disposable income' by the following: the effect of current disposable income on spending exceeds that of permanent income multiplied by the share of current disposable income in permanent income (allowing for the effect of changes in current income on expectations about future income streams).

23. These higher taxes during the upswing fall on a population that, on average, is likely to be less constrained by current disposable income than it was during the downswing.

24. The earlier caveat about differences in the efficiency with which the assets are managed also applies here.

4.8 REFERENCES

Barro, Robert J. (1974) 'Are government bonds net wealth?', *Journal of Political Economy*, 82, November–December, pp. 1095–117.

Benjamin, Daniel K. (1978) 'The use of collateral to enforce debt contracts', *Economic Inquiry*, 16, July, pp. 333–59.

Boskin, Michael J. (1982) 'Federal government deficits: some myths and realities', *American Economic Review, Papers and Proceedings*, 72, May, pp. 296–303.

Buiter, Willem H. (1980) 'Crowding out of private capital formation by government borrowing in the presence of intergenerational gifts and bequests', *Greek Economic Review*, 2, August, pp. 111–42.

Buiter, Willem H. (1982a) 'Comment on T.J. Sargent and N. Wallace: Some unpleasant monetarist arithmetic', *NBER Working Paper* no. 867, March.

Buiter, Willem H. (1982b) 'Money, deficits, crowding out, and inflation: the economic foundations of the MTFS', paper presented at the Conference on Monetary Policy, Financial Markets, and the Real Economy, International Center for Monetary and Banking Studies, Geneva, June.

Buiter, Willem H. (1982c) 'Deficits, crowding out, and inflation', unpublished, September.

Buiter, Willem H. and Marcus Miller (1981) 'The Thatcher experiment: the first two years', *Brookings Papers on Economic Activity*, 2, pp. 315–67.

Buiter, Willem H. and James Tobin (1979) 'Debt neutrality: a brief review of doctrine and evidence' in G.M. von Furstenberg (ed.), *Social Security versus Private Saving*, Ballinger, Cambridge, MA, pp. 39–63 (see Chapter 9, this volume).

Carmichael, J. (1979) 'The role of government financial policy in economic growth', Princeton University.

Flemming, John S. (1982) 'U.K. macro-policy response to oil price shocks of 1974–75 and 1979–80', *European Economic Review*, 18, May–June, pp. 223–34.

Jaffee, Dwight M. and Thomas Russell (1976) 'Imperfect information, uncertainty, and credit rationing', *Quarterly Journal of Economics*, 90, November, pp. 651–66.

Miller, Marcus (1982) 'Inflation-adjusting the public sector financial deficit: measurement and implications for policy' in J. Kay (ed.), *The 1982 Budget*, Basil Blackwell, London.

Ott, Attiat F. and Jang H. Yoo (1980) 'The measurement of government saving' in G.M. von Furstenberg (ed.), *The Government and Capital Formation*, Ballinger, Cambridge, MA, pp. 117–241.

Sachs, Jeffrey D. (1981) 'The current account and macroeconomic adjustment in the 1970s', *Brookings Papers on Economic Activity*, 1, pp. 201–68.

Sargent, T.J. and N. Wallace (1981) 'Some unpleasant monetarist arithmetic', *Federal Reserve Board of Minneapolis Quarterly Review*, 5, Fall.

Siegel, Jeremy J. (1979) 'Inflation-induced distortions in government and private saving statistics', *Review of Economics and Statistics*, 61, February, pp. 83–90.

Stiglitz, J. and A. Weiss (1981) 'Credit rationing in markets with imperfect information', *American Economic Review*, 71, June, pp. 393–410.

Taylor, C.T. and A.R. Threadgold (1979) ' "Real" national saving and its sectoral composition', Bank of England Discussion Paper no. 6, October.

Tobin, James and Willem H. Buiter (1980) 'Fiscal and monetary policies, capital formation, and economic activity' in G.M. von Furstenberg (ed.), *The*

Government and Capital Formation, Ballinger, Cambridge, MA, pp. 73–151 (also Chapter 11, this volume).

Wallace, N. (1981) 'A Modigliani–Miller theorem for open-market operations', *American Economic Review*, 71, June, pp. 267–74.

Webb, D. (1981) 'The net wealth effect of government bonds when credit markets are imperfect', *Economic Journal*, 91, June, pp. 405–14.

Webb, D. (1982) 'Default risk in a model of corporate and government finance', *Journal of Public Economics*, 17, April, pp. 289–306.

5 · THE ARITHMETIC OF SOLVENCY

5.1 DEBT, DEFICITS AND SOLVENCY

How is the solvency of the public sector to be evaluated, and, more specifically, is the threat of government insolvency in the main industrial countries an obstacle to expansionary fiscal policy actions in some, many or all of them? The issue of government solvency is quite clear in principle, although the data required for any practical evaluation still tend to be beyond what is available. Consider the stylized consolidated budget identity of the general government and the central bank:

$$\frac{\Delta H - E\Delta F^* + \Delta B}{PY} \equiv g - t + \frac{\Delta K}{Y} + \frac{iB}{PY} - \frac{i^*EF^*}{PY} - \varrho\frac{K}{Y} \quad (5.1)$$

H is the nominal stock of high-powered money; B the stock of interest-bearing government debt (assumed to be denominated in terms of domestic currency and to have a fixed nominal value); F^* the stock of official foreign exchange reserves; K the public sector capital stock; g government final consumption as a proportion of GDP; t taxes net of transfers and subsidies as a proportion of GDP; Y real GDP; P the GDP deflator; E the nominal spot exchange rate; i the nominal interest rate on public debt; i^* the interest rate on reserves; and ϱ the rate of return on the public sector capital stock accruing to the government (net of depreciation). Let lower-case quantities denote upper-case quantities as a proportion of GDP, i.e.

$h \equiv \dfrac{H}{PY}, f^* \equiv \dfrac{F^*E}{PY}, b \equiv \dfrac{B}{PY}$ and $k \equiv \dfrac{K}{Y}$. Let $\pi \equiv \dfrac{\Delta P}{P}$ denote the rate of

inflation; $n \equiv \dfrac{\Delta Y}{Y}$ the growth rate of real GDP; $r \equiv i - \pi$ the short real interest rate; and $\epsilon \equiv \dfrac{\Delta E}{E}$ the proportional rate of depreciation of the nominal exchange rate. Finally, let the net non-monetary debt of the public sector be defined by:

$$D \equiv B - EF^* - K, \tag{5.2}$$

and $d \equiv \dfrac{D}{PY}$.

The budget identity (5.1) can be rewritten as:

$$\Delta d \equiv g - t + (r - n)d + \ell - s \tag{5.3a}$$

$$\ell \equiv (r - \varrho)k + (i - (i^* + \epsilon))f^* \tag{5.3b}$$

$$s \equiv \dfrac{\Delta H}{PY} = \Delta h + (\pi + n)h. \tag{5.3c}$$

where ℓ represents losses due to the cash rate of return on public sector capital $(\varrho + \pi)$ and the rate of return on international reserves $(i^* + \epsilon)$ falling short of the opportunity cost of borrowing (i); and s represents seigniorage or the real resources appropriated by printing money. The net debt–GDP ratio of government will be rising if $\Delta d > 0$, that is, if the primary (non-interest) current deficit $(g - t)$, *plus* interest paid on the (net) debt corrected for inflation and real GDP growth and imputing a common nominal rate of return i to all assets and liabilities $((r - n)d)$, plus $\ell - s$, is positive. A government is solvent at time t_0 if

$$
\begin{aligned}
d(t_0) = {} & PDV(t - g; r - n; t_0) - PDV(\ell; r - n; t_0) \\
& + PDV(s; r - n; t_0);^{1}
\end{aligned}
\tag{5.4}
$$

that is, if the value of the existing stock of debt at t_0 is equal to the present discounted value of future primary current surpluses as a proportion of GDP (using real interest rates net of real growth rates, $r - n$, to discount future surpluses), *minus* the present discounted value of future losses on capital and international reserves, *plus* the present discounted value of future seigniorage.

The solvency constraint or intertemporal budget constraint (5.4) is obtained from the current flow budget identity (5.3a) by imposing the 'terminal' or transversality condition that the present discounted value, at t_0, of government debt very far (strictly speaking infinitely far) into the future will be equal to zero.[2] This means that ultimately the debt–GDP ratio will have to grow at a rate below the real interest rate minus the growth rate of GDP, or equivalently that ultimately the real debt must grow at a rate below the real interest rate or again that the nominal debt will ultimately have to grow at a rate below the nominal interest rate. This rules out everlasting 'Ponzi games': the government cannot forever pay the interest on its outstanding debt simply by borrowing more. At some stage the debt must be serviced either by running primary surpluses or through seigniorage, i.e. by recourse to the inflation tax.

Before attempting to apply this intertemporal consistency check to the fiscal, financial and monetary strategies of the main industrial countries, four brief remarks are in order.

First, the accounting framework can conceptually be extended quite easily to include other assets and liabilities. Public sector natural resource property rights, the stream of income from them and the proceeds from their sale through privatization are important for a number of countries such as the United Kingdom. Contingent public sector liabilities such as formally or informally publicly guaranteed private debt can be allowed for (in a certainty-equivalent manner) by including on the liability side the full value of these liabilities multiplied by the probability that the guarantee will be called upon.

Second, the interest rates used in the present-value calculations should be after-tax interest rates. Whose tax rate corresponds to the appropriate marginal rate is by no means obvious.

Third, the solvency constraint should be viewed as a consistency check on a specific set of plans for future taxation, spending and monetization. Only if there exists no economically and politically feasible set of tax, spending, and seigniorage plans that permits the existing stock of debt to be serviced, can one truly speak of insolvency. If, say, extrapolation of current values of $t - g$, ℓ and s violates Equation (5.4) we cannot infer that (part of) the debt will be defaulted on. Instead alternative tax, spending, and monetization policies are likely to be adopted that will ensure that Equation (5.4) holds.

Fourth, seigniorage $\dfrac{\Delta H}{PY}$ can be decomposed into two components, as shown in Equation (5.3c). Higher real growth and higher inflation mean, *ceteris paribus*, that the demand for nominal money balances will grow more rapidly and that the authorities can appropriate a higher volume of real resources through the inflation tax. This is the $(\pi + n)h$ component. Higher inflation however, and the higher nominal interest rates associated with it, will tend to reduce the demand for real money balances (i.e. to raise the velocity of circulation of high-powered money). The Δh component will be negative in that case. Another way of looking at this is to note that seigniorage can be rewritten as

$$s = \frac{\mu}{V} \tag{5.5}$$

where $\mu \equiv \dfrac{\Delta H}{H}$ is the proportional growth rate of the nominal stock of high-powered money, and $V = \dfrac{Y}{PH}$ is its income velocity of circulation.

A higher value of μ can be viewed as an increase in the seigniorage *tax rate*. Given the seigniorage *tax base*, it will raise seigniorage revenue. V is the reciprocal of the seigniorage tax base. If higher monetary growth rates sooner or later imply higher inflation, V will rise, i.e. the seigniorage tax base will fall. A higher value of μ will only raise seigniorage revenue if the elasticity of velocity with respect to the inflation rate is less than unity.

The available data on industrial countries' debt and deficits in recent years are given in Tables 5.1 and 5.2.

The general government and central government deficits shown in Table 5.1 perhaps contain one or two surprises. First, the US general government deficit (as a proportion of GDP) has been below the OECD average for every year since 1981. Italy and the smaller European countries contributed significantly to the high OECD average. The European countries as a group had a general government deficit well above that of the United States for the entire 1981–7 period. It is, of course, true that the United States' general government deficit increased sharply from 1981 on while Japan sharply reduced its general government deficit and the European countries, after a small increase, were back in 1986 where they had been in 1981. The increase in the US general government deficit is more than accounted for by the increase in its federal deficit. State and local government maintained and even increased slightly its surplus.

It may be the case that the state and local government surplus in the United States is to a certain extent spurious, say because contributions to effectively funded pension schemes are counted as current receipts. While this would raise the true general government deficit in the United States, it is not obvious that it would raise it relative to the deficits in the rest of the industrial world if similar corrections were made there. Even if just the central government deficits are considered, the US deficit relative to GDP is very similar (since 1982) to the Japanese and European deficits.

To single out the US deficit for special concern and opprobrium therefore requires one to go beyond the recorded deficit shares by relating the government deficits to the perceived existing real slack in the economy (in the case of Europe) and to differences in private savings propensities (in the case of Japan).

The 1987 (estimated) US general government deficit of 2.7 per cent of GDP and (estimated) Federal deficit of 4.0 per cent are very close to being 'full-employment deficits'. If the high European unemployment rates reflect to a significant extent cyclical or demand-deficient rather than structural (real-wage-constrained, etc.) unemployment, then the longer-term implications for the growth of the public debt are more serious in the United States than in Europe on the assumption, underlying cyclical corrections, that a 'normal' cyclical recovery will occur in Europe in the absence of further 'discretionary' fiscal actions.

As regards the United States–Japan comparison, similar public sector deficits may have very different macroeconomic implications in the United States with a gross private saving ratio of 16.2 per cent in 1986 (and a gross private investment ratio of 16.3 per cent) and in Japan with a private saving

Table 5.1 General and central government financial balance (Surplus or deficit as a percentage of GNP/GDP)

		1978	1979	1980	1981	1982	1983	1984	1985	1986	1987
United States	G	0.2	0.6	−1.2	−1.0	−3.5	−3.8	−2.7	−3.4	−3.3	−2.7
	C	−2.0	−1.1	−2.3	−2.4	−4.1	−5.6	−4.9	−5.1	−5.0	−4.0
Japan	G	−5.5	−4.8	−4.5	−3.8	−3.6	−3.7	−2.1	−0.8	−0.9	−0.9
	C	−5.2	−6.1	−6.2	−5.9	−5.9	−5.6	−4.9	−4.1	−4.3	−4.7
Germany	G	−2.5	−2.6	−2.9	−3.7	−3.3	−2.4	−1.9	−1.1	−1.2	−1.5
	C	−2.1	−1.8	−1.6	−2.1	−2.1	−2.0	−1.8	−1.1	−0.7	−0.8
France	G	−1.9	−0.7	0.2	−1.8	−2.7	−3.1	−2.9	−2.6	−2.9	−2.7
	C	−1.6	−1.5	−1.1	−2.6	−2.8	−3.3	−3.4	−3.3	−2.9	−2.5
United Kingdom	G	−4.2	−3.5	−3.5	−2.8	−2.3	−3.6	−3.9	−2.7	−2.9	−2.7
	C	−3.3	−2.3	−2.5	−2.9	−2.7	−3.1	−3.2	−2.4	−2.6	−2.4
Italy	G	−9.7	−9.5	−8.0	−11.9	−12.6	−11.7	−13.0	−14.0	−12.6	−12.6
	C	−13.1	−10.8	−10.8	−12.8	−15.1	−16.4	−15.5	−16.3	−14.2	−13.1
17 OECD countries	G	−2.2	−1.8	−2.5	−2.7	−4.0	−4.2	−3.4	−3.4	−3.3	−3.0
European countries	G				−4.5	−4.9	−4.7	−4.5	−4.2	−4.1	−4.0
Seven major countries excl. United States	C	−4.4	−4.1	−4.1	−4.5	−5.0	−5.3	−5.1	−4.7	−4.3	−4.2

Sources: OECD, *Economic Outlook*, June 1987 (general government). IMF, *World Economic Outlook*, April 1987 (central government).

Table 5.2 Net debt of general government (percentage of GNP/GDP)

	1973	1978	1979	1980	1981	1982	1983	1984	1985	1986	1987
United States	22.9	21.0	19.4	19.5	18.8	21.4	24.0	25.1	26.8	28.8	29.9
Japan	−6.1	11.3	14.9	17.3	20.7	23.2	26.2	26.9	26.5	26.2	26.6
West Germany	−6.7	9.4	11.5	14.3	17.4	19.8	21.4	21.7	22.1	22.2	23.0
France	8.3	10.2	9.8	9.1	9.9	11.3	13.4	15.2	16.7	18.5	20.4
United Kingdom	57.5	53.3	48.6	48.0	47.2	46.4	47.1	48.5	46.9	46.9	46.1
Italy	52.1	63.9	63.7	61.8	66.8	73.4	80.6	87.8	96.3	99.2	103.9
Canada	2.7	10.6	10.7	11.5	10.7	16.9	20.4	24.7	30.3	34.0	36.7
Total of the above countries	17.2	21.6	21.2	21.8	22.5	25.1	27.8	29.3	30.8	32.2	33.3

Source: OECD, *Economic Outlook*, June 1987.

ratio in 1986 of 28.7 per cent (and a gross private investment ratio of 23.2 per cent).

On balance, the case that general government or central government fiscal deficits in the United States are larger and less sustainable than those in Europe appears to be much less straightforward than it is often made out to be. The same holds, as regards central government deficits, also when comparing the United States and Japan.

The same ambiguous message is carried by the public debt–GDP ratios reported in Table 5.2. The United States ratio, while rising, is still below the average for the seven main industrial countries. Omitting Italy brings the United States up to the average of the remaining six main industrial countries. A little arithmetic shows that with nominal income growth of 7.5 per cent in 1987 and a debt–GDP ratio of 30 per cent, the US debt–GDP ratio will rise only if the deficit–GDP ratio exceeds 2.25 per cent (ignoring seigniorage). The current deficit projections are above this threshold level, but not by very much.[3] The increase in the US high-powered money stock was $5.2 billion in 1986, $8.4 billion in 1985 and $1.1 billion in 1984 (0.12 per cent, 0.21 per cent, and 0.03 per cent of GDP, respectively).

With no more than 0.1–0.2 per cent of GDP extracted through seigniorage, the threshold US general government deficit that just stabilizes the debt–GDP ratio would go up to 2.35–2.45 per cent of GDP.

To evaluate the sustainability of current fiscal, financial and monetary policy in the main industrial countries we need, from Equation (5.4), the current net stock of debt, current and prospective future primary current deficits, current and prospective future interest losses on international reserves and public sector capital, current and prospective future seigniorage and interest rate projections. Most of these can be disposed of quite easily.

Seigniorage has in recent years been a negligible source of revenue in all the main industrial countries except Italy. For example, recent US figures hovered between 0 per cent and 0.2 per cent of GDP and the UK average for 1981–3 was 0.21 per cent of GDP. In Italy the shares were 2.8 per cent in 1985, 2.2 per cent in 1984, and 2.3 per cent in both 1983 and 1982. Recent changes in central bank policy in Italy are likely to have lowered these percentages sharply. An estimate in Buiter (1985) of the maximal amount of seigniorage that could have been extracted in the United Kingdom over the period since 1948 is 2.74 per cent of GDP (at an annual inflation rate of 67 per cent). Except in the case of Italy, it seems safe to put the likely contribution of seigniorage to government financing at no more than 0.2 per cent of GDP.

Interest losses on international gold and foreign exchange reserves are negligible in the industrial countries, especially now that foreign exchange reserves earn (close to) market rates of interests. In what follows, foreign exchange reserves will be omitted altogether.

As regards income from the general government capital stock, no usable data are available but two informative bench-marks can be calculated. The first assumes that there is no gross cash return from the capital stock, i.e. that the net return is minus public sector capital consumption: $\varrho = -\delta$. Letting a denote gross public sector capital formation as a proportion of GDP, the budget identity can (ignoring international reserves) in this case be rewritten as:

$$\Delta b \equiv g + a - t + (r - n)b - s. \tag{5.6a}$$

The solvency constraint in this case is:

$$b(t_0) = PDV(t - (g + a); r - n; t_0) + PDV(s; r - n; t_0). \tag{5.7a}$$

In the second bench-mark case, the net cash rate of return on the general government capital stock equals the opportunity cost of borrowing, i.e. $\varrho = i - \pi$. In that case the budget identity (again ignoring international reserves) can be rewritten as:

$$\Delta d \equiv g - t + (r - n)d - s, \tag{5.6b}$$

where $d \equiv b - k$. The solvency constraint becomes:

$$d(t_0) = PDV(t - g; r - n; t_0) + PDV(s; r - n; t_0). \tag{5.7b}$$

While we cannot confidently predict the future course of the primary current government deficit (crucial for Equation (5.7b)) or of the primary current government deficit plus gross public sector capital formation (crucial for Equation (5.7a)), we can evaluate the implications of extrapolating recent values of these deficits (as proportions of GDP).

For the United States reasonable *net* debt interest figures are available, both for the general government and for the Federal government, given in Table 5.3.

The recent US general government primary surpluses are given in Table 5.4. The first line shows the surplus on the pessimistic assumption that the net cash return on the general government capital stock is negative (and equal to the depreciation of the capital stock). It shows a small surplus in 1980 and 1981, a deficit of 1.6 per cent in 1982 and 1.8 per cent in 1983, and a smaller deficit of less than 1 per cent of GDP in 1985 and 1986. The second line shows the surplus on the optimistic assumption that the net cash rate of return on general government capital equals the opportunity cost of borrowing. It shows a large surplus in 1980 and 1981 which almost vanishes in 1983 and settles at just over 1.5 per cent of GDP in 1984, 1985 and 1986.

necessary to service the outstanding public debt of the United States in the pessimistic case ($\varrho = -\delta$)? Assuming $r - n$ and s to be constant at $\overline{r - n}$ and $\bar{s}$ respectively, the answer is, from Equation (5.7a), given by:

Table 5.3 United States Federal government net interest paid and primary surplus (percentage of GDP)

	1978	1979	1980	1981	1982	1983	1984	1985	1986	1987
Net interest paid	1.6	1.7	1.9	2.2	2.6	2.7	3.0	3.2	3.3	
Primary surplus ($\varrho = -\delta$)	-0.4	0.6	-0.4	-0.2	-1.5	-2.9	-1.9	-1.9	-1.7	

Source: Economic Report of the President, 1987; and OECD, Economic Outlook, June 1987.

Table 5.4 Primary general government surplus, United States (percentage of GDP)

	1978	1979	1980	1981	1982	1983	1984	1985	1986	1987
$\varrho = -\delta$	1.5	1.8	0.2	0.7	−1.6	−1.8	−0.4	−0.8	−0.7	
$\varrho = i - \pi$	3.2	3.5	1.9	2.2	−0.1	−0.3	1.0	0.8	n.a.	

Source: OECD, *Economic Outlook*, June 1987; and *Economic Report of the President*, 1987.

$$\overline{t - (g + a)} = \overline{(r - n)}\, b(t_0) - \overline{s}.^4 \tag{5.8}$$

With $\overline{s} = 0.002$ and $b(t_0) = 0.3$, we can calculate the debt burden stabilizing permanent primary surplus for different values of $\overline{r - n}$ as follows:[5]

$$
\begin{aligned}
\overline{t - (g + a)} &= 0.1\% & (\overline{r - n} = 0.01)\\
&= 0.4\% & (\overline{r - n} = 0.02)\\
&= 0.7\% & (\overline{r - n} = 0.03)\\
&= 1.0\% & (\overline{r - n} = 0.04)
\end{aligned}
\tag{5.9}
$$

Even when the long run (after-tax) real interest rate exceeds the long-run real growth rate by much as four percentage points, the required primary surplus is only 1 per cent of GDP. More plausible values of $\overline{r - n}$ of 0.02 or 0.03 yield required primary surpluses of 0.4 per cent and 0.7 per cent of GDP, respectively. Compared to recent actual general government primary surpluses in the pessimistic case of −0.8 per cent in 1985 and −0.7 per cent in 1986, a permanent reduction in the primary deficit of between 1.0 per cent and 1.5 per cent of GDP would be sufficient to restore solvency.

In the optimistic case ($\varrho = i - \pi$), solvency is already assured and there is indeed room for a reduction in the permanent general government primary surplus. From Equation (5.7b) the permanent primary current surplus $\overline{t - g}$ required to stabilize the current net debt ratio is:

$$\overline{t - g} = \overline{(r - n)}\, d(t_0) - \overline{s} \tag{5.10}$$

Since $d(t_0) = b(t_0) - k(t_0)$, $\overline{t - g}$ is strictly less than $\overline{t - (g + a)}$ for the same values of $\overline{r - n}$ and $\overline{s}$. The actual recent values of the primary current surplus of the general government in the optimistic case are equal to the largest value given in Equation (5.9). Indeed, with $\overline{r - n} = 0.02$ or 0.03, the primary surpluses reported in the second line of Table 5.4 indicate that the US government would be on course for paying off the national debt if the optimistic case were correct.

For the US Federal government I could not find information on gross fixed capital formation. Table 5.3 therefore gives only the pessimistic case calculation of the Federal primary deficit. Net Federal government debt in the second quarter of 1986 was about 36 per cent of GDP (*Economic Report of the President*, 1987). The Federal debt share stabilizing per-

Table 5.5 Interest payments and receipts of general government (percentage of GDP)

	1960	1970	1980	1981	1982	1983	1984	1985	1986
United States									
Payments	2.0	2.2	3.1	3.6	4.1	4.3	4.7	4.9	5.0
Receipts	0.7	1.0	1.7	1.9	2.2	2.3	2.4	2.3	2.4
Net payments	1.3	1.2	1.4	1.7	1.9	2.0	2.3	2.6	2.6
Japan									
Payments			3.1	3.6	3.8	4.2	4.4	4.5	
Receipts			1.9	2.2	2.3	2.4	2.4	2.6	
Net payments			1.2	1.4	1.5	1.8	1.9	1.8	
West Germany									
Payments			1.9	2.2	2.7	2.9	3.0	2.9	
Receipts			1.1	1.3	1.8	1.8	1.8	1.8	
Net payments			0.8	1.0	0.9	1.2	1.2	1.1	
United Kingdom									
Payments		4.0	4.7	5.0	5.1	4.7	4.9	5.0	4.9
Receipts		1.8	1.6	1.7	1.9	1.6	1.6	1.8	
Net payments		2.2	3.1	3.3	3.1	3.1	3.3	3.2	

Source: National Income Accounts.

manent primary surplus in the United States for the pessimistic case is in that case given by:

$$\overline{t - (g + a)} = 0.16\% \qquad (\overline{r - n} = 0.01)$$
$$= 0.52\% \qquad (\overline{r - n} = 0.02)$$
$$= 0.88\% \qquad (\overline{r - n} = 0.03)$$
$$= 1.24\% \qquad (\overline{r - n} = 0.04) \qquad (5.11)$$

This would imply the need for a reduction in the primary Federal deficit of between 2.0 and 2.5 per cent of GDP if the Federal debt–GDP ratio is to be stabilized.

For the other industrial countries, the interest on the national debt reported in the national accounts is gross of any general government interest receipts, which are often quite sizeable. Table 5.5 shows interest payments, receipts and net interest payments for the United States, Japan, West Germany, and the United Kingdom.

In order to have an indirect check on the reported net interest payments figures, I have constructed an alternative estimate by multiplying the net debt figures of Table 5.2 by the nominal interest rates on long government debt. As these are before-tax interest rates, they are likely to overstate the net debt payments, a problem I also believe to affect even the 'net' US interest payment figures. The method is very crude, as it ignores the maturity structure of the existing debt, but may at least give some idea of orders of magnitude. The net interest payments estimates are in Table 5.6

Table 5.6 Estimated net interest payments of general government
(percentage of GDP)

	1978	1979	1980	1981	1982	1983	1984	1985	1986	1987
United States	1.8	1.8	2.2	2.6	2.8	2.7	3.1	2.8	2.2	
Japan	0.7	1.1	1.5	1.7	1.9	2.0	2.0	1.7	1.4	
West Germany	0.5	0.9	1.2	1.8	1.8	1.8	1.7	1.5	1.3	
France	0.9	0.9	1.2	1.6	1.6	1.7	1.9	1.8	1.6	
United Kingdom	6.7	6.3	6.6	6.9	6.0	5.1	5.2	5.0	4.6	
Italy	8.8	9.0	9.9	13.8	15.3	14.5	13.0	12.5	10.3	
Canada	1.0	1.1	1.4	1.6	2.4	2.4	3.2	3.3	3.2	

Source: Net debt of general government as a percentage of GDP: Table 5.2. Long-term
interest rates on public debt: IMF, *World Economic Outlook*, April 1987.

and estimates of the general government primary surpluses are in Table
5.7. As the United Kingdom estimates in Table 5.6 are about the same as
the official gross data reported in Table 5.5, either the estimates in Table
5.6 still overstate true net interest payments for the United Kingdom or the
interest receipts entry for the United Kingdom in Table 5.5 is suspect.

5.2 DEBT, DEFICITS AND MONETIZATION

The analysis of the previous subsection can be turned on its head by
treating debt and the primary deficit as exogenous and considering the
implications for seigniorage and inflation. If the real debt burden is to be
kept constant at some given level $\bar{b}$ (not necessarily the current debt–GDP
ratio) and if the primary deficit is a fixed share of GDP, $\overline{g + a - t}$, the
implied seigniorage is given, for the pessimistic case, by:

$$s = \overline{g + a - t} + (r - n)\bar{b}. \tag{5.12}$$

From Equation (5.5), the proportional rate of growth of the nominal high-
powered money stock is:

$$\mu = V(\overline{g - t} + (r - n)\bar{d}). \tag{5.13}$$

A higher value of $\overline{g + a - t} + (r - n)\bar{b}$, the long-run inflation-and-real-
growth-corrected deficit as a proportion of GDP, implies a need for more
seigniorage to satisfy the government budget identity. At a given velocity,
V, more seigniorage means higher inflation. Lower inflation, however,
means lower velocity and therefore, given μ, more seigniorage. Many
standard money demand functions (e.g. the linear and the log-linear ones)
have the property that any given amount of real seigniorage can be extracted both with a low rate of inflation and a low velocity (on the nice side
of the 'seigniorage Laffer curve') and with a high rate of inflation and a

Table 5.7 General government primary surpluses in the main industrial countries (percentage of GDP)

		1978	1979	1980	1981	1982	1983	1984	1985	1986
United States*	$\varrho = -\delta$	1.5	1.8	0.2	0.7	-1.6	-1.8	-0.4	-0.8	-0.7
	$\varrho = i - \pi$	3.2	3.5	1.9	2.2	-0.1	-0.3	1.0	0.8	n.a.
United States**	$\varrho = -\delta$	2.0	2.4	1.0	1.6	-0.7	-1.1	0.4	-0.6	-1.1
	$\varrho = i - \pi$	3.7	4.1	2.8	3.1	0.8	0.4	1.8	1.0	n.a.
Japan*	$\varrho = -\delta$	-4.8	-3.9	-3.3	-2.4	-2.1	-1.9	-0.1	n.a.	n.a.
	$\varrho = i - \pi$	1.3	2.4	2.8	3.7	4.0	3.9	5.4	n.a.	n.a.
Japan**	$\varrho = -\delta$	-4.8	-3.7	-3.0	-2.1	-1.7	-1.7	-0.1	0.9	0.5
	$\varrho = i - \pi$	1.3	2.6	3.1	4.0	4.1	3.8	5.0	5.7	n.a.
West Germany*	$\varrho = -\delta$	-1.8	-2.0	-2.1	-2.7	-2.4	-1.2	-0.7	0.0	n.a.
	$\varrho = i - \pi$	1.5	1.4	1.5	0.5	0.4	1.3	1.7	2.3	n.a.
West Germany**	$\varrho = -\delta$	-2.0	-1.7	-1.7	-1.9	-1.5	-0.6	-0.2	0.4	0.1
	$\varrho = i - \pi$	1.3	1.7	1.9	1.3	1.3	1.9	2.2	2.7	n.a.
United Kingdom*	$\varrho = -\delta$			-0.4	0.5	0.8	-0.5	-0.7	0.5	n.a.
	$\varrho = i - \pi$			2.0	2.3	2.3	1.4	1.3	2.4	n.a.
United Kingdom**	$\varrho = -\delta$	2.5	2.8	3.1	4.1	3.7	1.5	1.3	2.3	1.7
	$\varrho = i - \pi$				5.9	5.2	3.4	3.3	4.2	n.a.
France**	$\varrho = -\delta$	-1.0	0.2	1.4	-0.2	-1.1	-1.4	-1.0	-0.8	-1.3
Italy**	$\varrho = -\delta$	-0.9	-0.5	1.9	1.9	2.7	1.5	0.0	-1.5	-2.6

* Using net interest payments from Table 5.5.
** Using estimated interest payments from Table 5.6.

high velocity (on the unpleasant side of the seigniorage Laffer curve). For this reason alone, the use of Equation (5.13) to infer the 'eventual monetization' implied by the fiscal program is problematic (see Sargent and Wallace, 1981; and Buiter, 1987). With velocity rising with inflation there may be more than one solution to Equation (5.13).

Quite apart from the theoretical considerations, seigniorage seems to have disappeared as a serious source of government revenue in the main industrial countries (except Italy). Very minor increases in t or cuts in g would allow the authorities to dispense altogether with the 0.1–0.2 per cent of GDP brought in through seigniorage.

The data in Table 5.7 suggest that, even in the pessimistic case ($\varrho = -\delta$), Japan and West Germany now are running small primary surpluses while the United Kingdom even has a sizeable primary surplus. The United States and France have primary deficits of just under and just over 1 per cent of GDP, respectively. Italy has a rapidly growing primary deficit which reached 2.6 per cent of GDP in 1986 (note that seigniorage was 2.8 per cent of GDP in Italy during 1985). In the optimistic case ($\varrho = i - \pi$) all industrial countries, with the possible exception of Italy, would be running primary surpluses, several of them quite large. Except in the case of Italy, the analysis does not suggest that great fiscal stringency is required in order to avoid either threats to solvency or the need for much increased recourse to the inflation tax.

5.3 NOTES

1. Instead of discounting future flows as a proportion of GDP using $r - n$ we could equivalently discount future real flows using r or future nominal flows using i. In the last case, Equation (5.4) could be rewritten as:

$$D(t_0) = PDV(P(T - G); i; t_0) - PDV(PY\ell; i; t_0) + PDV(\Delta H; i; t_0).$$

2. Technically, the condition is $\lim_{\tau \to \infty} d(\tau) \exp\left(-\int_{t_0}^{\tau} [r(u) - n(u)] du\right) = 0$.

3. The actual US general government deficit turned out to be 2.4 per cent of GDP for 1987. Nominal GDP growth for 1987 was only 6 per cent. The debt–GDP ratio therefore increased by just over half a percentage point.
4. Note that this primary surplus would keep b constant.
5. The final results are multiplied by 100 to give percentages of GDP.

5.4 REFERENCES

Buiter, Willem H. (1985) 'A guide to public sector debt and deficits', *Economic Policy*, vol. 1, no. 1, November, pp. 14–79 (also Chapter 3, this volume).

Buiter, Willem H. (1987) 'A fiscal theory of hyperdeflations? Some surprising monetarist arithmetic', *Oxford Economic Papers*, 39, March, pp. 111–18 (also Chapter 12, this volume).
Sargent, T.J. and N. Wallace (1981) 'Some unpleasant monetarist arithmetic', *Federal Reserve Board of Minneapolis Quarterly Review*, 5, Fall.

PART III

CROWDING OUT

6 · 'CROWDING OUT' AND THE EFFECTIVENESS OF FISCAL POLICY

6.1 INTRODUCTION

'Crowding out' refers to the displacement of private economic activity by public economic activity. Known as 'diversion' to Keynes (see Keynes and Henderson, 1929), the subject has a long history in macroeconomic theory and policy debate. In recent years the dangers of public borrowing crowding out private borrowing and of public spending crowding out private spending have again been emphasized in the financial press and by government officials.[1] At the same time papers by Barro (1974; 1976), Feldstein (1976), David and Scadding (1974), Kochin (1974) and Peltzman (1973) have analyzed some of the implications of 'ultrarationality' in the relation between the private sector and the public sector.

In Section 6.2 an attempt is made to bring some order into this frequently confused debate by developing a comprehensive taxonomy. Crowding out is shown to be a multi-dimensional concept.[2] The different notions of crowding out are related to the existing literature and their implications for the effectiveness of fiscal policy are evaluated in some familiar simple macroeconomic models. Section 6.3 uses a simple closed-economy full-employment model to study the short-run and long-run implications of 'direct crowding out', one of the major categories in the taxonomy developed in Section 6.2. Section 6.4 touches on three special problem areas.

This paper is based on Chapter 3 of my Ph.D. dissertation 'Temporary equilibrium and long-run equilibrium', Yale, 1975. Comments, criticism and advice from James Tobin, Gary Smith, Katsuhito Iwai, Alan Blinder, A.B. Atkinson and an anonymous referee are gratefully acknowledged. This paper was originally published in the *Journal of Public Economics*, 7, 1977, pp. 309–28.

6.2   A TAXONOMY OF CROWDING OUT

6.2.1 Short run and long run

The short-run–long-run dichotomy contrasts the impact effect of changes in government activity — for given values of the short-run exogenous but long-run endogenous (or predetermined) variables such as asset stocks and expectations about the future — with the long-run, steady-state effect of such changes when stocks and expectations have adjusted fully to the change in government policy. Until fairly recently the neo-Keynesian literature dealt mainly with short-run crowding out.[3] A number of more recent papers investigate various aspects of long-run crowding out (e.g., Mundell, 1965; Christ, 1968; Blinder and Solow, 1973; Friedman, 1972; Tobin and Buiter, 1976. The slightly older crop of monetary growth models can also be considered to fall into the long-run crowding-out category (e.g., Tobin, 1955; 1965; Stein, 1966; Johnson, 1967; Levhari and Patinkin, 1968; Foley and Sidrauski, 1971).

Often neither the impact effect nor the long-run, steady-state effect correspond to the 'run' one is most interested in for policy purposes. For policy, the real (i.e. calendar) time effects of policy changes over a period of, say, a few years tend to be most pertinent. In principle this represents no great problems. The method of comparative dynamics — solving the dynamic system and comparing trajectories under different assumptions about initial conditions, other parameter values or the behavior of policy control variables — permits one to find the degree of crowding out for any time interval. In practice explicit analytical solutions of non-linear dynamic economic systems tend to be difficult to obtain. Numerical solutions through computer simulations are required to derive the interim multipliers (see, for example, Chow, 1975).

It is important to realize that the degree of crowding out is not necessarily greater in the long run than in the short run. Tobin and Buiter (1976) analyze an extreme case in which complete crowding out of real private spending by public spending in the short run, because of full employment of all resources and a fixed capital stock, is contrasted with a positive long-run effect of government spending on real output because of capital deepening.

6.2.2 Direct crowding out[4]

The degree of direct crowding out or ultrarationality is the extent to which the government sector can be subsumed under the private sector in specifying the structural behavioral relationships of the economy. Direct crowding out is a multi-dimensional concept, the dimensions being characterized by the government activities that are crowding out (the denominator of the multiplier) and the private activities that are being crowded out (the numerator of the multiplier).[5] If every action undertaken by the government is neutralized by a corresponding action in the opposite direction by the private sector, the government is but another veil waiting to be removed by probing economists.[6] In the textbook *IS–LM* model direct crowding out would be reflected in the inability of fiscal policy actions to shift the *IS* curve.

The most important dimensions are the following:

1. *Income.* What is regarded as income by the private sector? Is government spending on final goods and services regarded as part of private income? Free school milk, school lunches, housing subsidies and food stamps are examples of public expenditure constituting private income in kind. Are government deficits excluded, i.e. are current deficits (surpluses) viewed as equivalent to current taxes (transfers) and is public saving a perfect substitute for private saving? Certain kinds of taxes are directly competitive with discretionary private saving: social security contributions and state-run compulsory retirement or health insurance schemes are substitutes for voluntary private saving for old age and sickness (see, for example, Katona, 1965; Cagan, 1965; Juster and Lipsey, 1967; Taylor, 1971).

2. *Wealth.* What is regarded as wealth by the private sector? This is the capital account counterpart to the current account question asked above. If the private sector regards current deficits as equivalent to current taxes because the financing of the deficit is regarded as equivalent to taxation — no matter what combination of high-powered money creation, new borrowing and taxation is actually used to finance the deficit — government interest-bearing debt will not be counted as part of private sector net worth.[7]

3. *Consumption.* What is regarded as consumption by the private sector, i.e. to what extent is public consumption a substitute for private consumption? Certain types of public consumption expenditure that are directly competitive with private consumption spending are public spending on education, law and order, health care and care for the elderly (Peltzman, 1973).

4. *Investment.* What is regarded as investment by the private sector, i.e. to what extent is public investment a substitute for private investment?[8]

5. *Borrowing.* How close substitutes are government bonds for corporate bonds and other private bonds in private portfolios?[9]

Ultimately questions about the presence and strength of various forms of ultrarationality can only be answered by looking at the facts.[10] All I shall attempt here is to indicate the range of theoretical possibilities and the logical implications of certain assumptions. Some casual empirical remarks about the importance of various forms of ultrarationality will occasionally be ventured.

The implications of completely subsuming public sector behavior under private sector behavior can be far-reaching. The simple model presented in Section 6.3 shows how in a full-employment economy with complete crowding out in all dimensions, fiscal policy is completely powerless if all taxes are lump-sum. The public sector has effectively been worked out of the model altogether.

6.2.3 Indirect crowding out

Indirect or system-wide crowding out refers to the substitution of public economic activity for private economic activity (e.g., the substitution of public spending for private spending or of public saving for private saving) that comes out of the working of the entire model of the economy without there being any 'ultrarationality' at the level of the individual structural relationships. There is indirect crowding out, in other words, when the reduced-form derivatives (or multipliers) of the model show that increased government taxation reduces private spending or increased government spending reduces private spending even if the private and public consumption functions cannot be consolidated into a single 'social' consumption function with government economic decision-making subsumed entirely under private economic activity. Indirect crowding out is induced by changes in prices and interest rates resulting from changes in the value of some government policy instrument.

An example of 100 per cent short-run indirect crowding out of private spending by public spending in the simple fixed-price, closed-economy, unemployment version of the $IS-LM$ model is the absence of any effect on real income of changes in public spending when the LM curve is vertical or the IS curve is horizontal. (No empirical support exists for these two theoretical possibilities.) In general, if the government spending multiplier is positive but less than unity, there is partial short-run crowding out of private investment and/or consumption spending. With a downward-sloping IS curve and an upward-sloping LM curve a rise in the interest rate accompanies an increase in real income due to a higher level of government spending. While this reduces the magnitude of the equilibrium increase in real income below the magnitude of the rightward shift of the IS curve (which gives the multiplier at a given rate of interest), the equilibrium change in real income is nevertheless positive. The multiplier is reduced by a scarcity not of real resources (labor and capital) but of money, which pushes up interest rates when the economy begins to expand. This situation could, therefore, be better described as the crowding out of private spending by restrictive monetary policy than by public spending.

In the open-economy version of the same model under a flexible exchange rate regime with perfect capital mobility, changes in government spending will have no (short-run) effect on real income (Mundell, 1962; Fleming, 1962). Government spending crowds out export demand (and 'crowds in' import demand) dollar for dollar.

In the closed-economy, full-employment version of the IS–LM model with a classical labor market there will be 100 per cent crowding out of private spending by public spending in the short run. With real output fixed, each unit of output appropriated by the government means one less unit of output available for private consumption and investment. When the cause of 'spending' crowding out is competition for limited funds in an economy with unemployed real resources, expansionary monetary policy can help bring the economy to its production possibility frontier where the real scarcities set in. No such easy way of obtaining something for nothing exists when the economy is already operating on its efficient boundary: the allocation of scarce resources among alternative uses applies to the allocation of resources between the public and private sector as much as to the allocation of resources within the private sector (Ott and Korb, 1973). Expansionary monetary policy has only inflationary consequences in an economy operating at or near full employment.[11]

Competition between the public and the private sector is not limited to the demand side of the market for final goods and services. In a fully employed economy, a government wishing to engage in productive activity of its own will compete with the private sector in factor markets and intermediate product markets for labor and other resources. Many other examples of indirect crowding out could be given, but the small sample offered here is sufficient to illustrate the point that short-run indirect crowding out has been a mainstream macroeconomic theory and policy issue for at least four decades.

The taxonomy developed here is summarized in Table 6.1, together with some of the contributions to each of the categories.

In Section 6.3 the short-run and long-run effects of direct crowding out will be discussed in greater detail using a simple closed-economy full-employment model.

6.3   SOME EXAMPLES OF DIRECT CROWDING OUT IN A FULL-EMPLOYMENT MODEL AND THEIR IMPLICATIONS FOR FISCAL POLICY

A full-employment IS–LM model will be used in this section to analyze some of the forms of direct crowding out discussed in Section 6.2. Labor force growth, technical change and depreciation are ignored. The long-run equilibrium of the model will therefore be a stationary state. In a stationary

Table 6.1 Short-run and long-run effects of an increase in public consumption

	Direct	Indirect
Short run	Spencer and Yohe (1970)	
	Bailey (1971)	Hicks (1937)
	Peltzman (1973)	Keynes and Henderson
	David and Scadding (1974)	(1929); Keynes (1936)
	Kochin (1974)	Friedman (1970)
	Miller and Upton (1974)	Blinder and Solow (1973)
	Carlson and Spencer (1975)	
Long run		Christ (1968)
		Johnson (1967)
	Barro (1974; 1976)	Foley and Sidrauski (1971)
	Feldstein (1976)	Friedman (1972)
		Blinder and Solow (1974)
		Tobin and Buiter (1976)

state real asset stocks are constant and expectations are realized (or at least no longer revised).

The notation is as follows:

M = nominal quantity of money,
B = nominal quantity of bonds,
K = stock of real reproducible capital; $K = K^P + K^G$,
K^P = privately owned capital stock,
K^G = publicly owned capital stock,
P = money price level,
x = expected rate of inflation,
C^P = private consumption,
C^G = public consumption,
I^P = private investment,
I^G = public investment,
T = real taxes,
R = nominal rate of return on bonds.

For concreteness I shall assume that an adaptive expectations mechanism characterizes the formation of price expectations and that expectations about capital gains on claims to real reproducible capital are static. The constant labor force is scaled to unity. Taxes are lump-sum. The production function is a constant returns-to-scale neoclassical production function $f(K); f' > 0, f'' < 0$. Private consumption (C^P) depends on income (Y), with a marginal propensity to consume between zero and one, and on (non-human) net worth (W), with $C_W^P > 0$. The demand for real money balances (L) depends on the after-tax real rate of return differential between money and other assets. It is essential, for bond financing of government spending to be equivalent to tax financing, that the public sector interest-bearing financial liability be a perfect substitute in private sector portfolios for some private sector claim. Thus, in our model with only one private sector asset, government bonds and claims to the earnings of existing capital are assumed to be perfect substitutes in private portfolios. If, in the eyes of private economic agents, government bonds were qualitatively different from claims to private capital (e.g., because of different risk properties) the real trajectory of the economy will not be invariant under different choices of bond and tax financing policies. Private economic agents could then not, in general, 'undo' changes in government financing policies by borrowing or lending on personal account (see Barro, 1974). The nominal rate of return on money balances is institutionally fixed at zero. Bonds are fixed nominal face value, variable interest rate claims. The demand for real balances also depends on wealth,

$$L = L(R, W), \qquad L_R < 0, \quad 0 < L_W < 1.$$

The momentary equilibrium is given by the IS curve and the LM curve

$$C^P + C^G + I^P + I^G = f(K), \qquad (IS) \tag{6.1}$$

$$L = \frac{M}{P}. \qquad (LM) \tag{6.2}$$

Denoting $\dfrac{du}{dt}$ as $\dot{u}$, the dynamic equations are

$$\dot{K} = I^P, \tag{6.3}$$

$$\dot{K}^G = I^G, \tag{6.4}$$

$$\frac{d}{dt}\left(\frac{B}{P}\right) = \gamma\left(C^G + I^G + \frac{RB}{P} - T - f'(K)K^G\right) - \frac{\dot{P}}{P}\frac{B}{P}, \tag{6.5}$$

$$\frac{d}{dt}\left(\frac{M}{P}\right) = (1 - \gamma)\left(C^G + I^G + \frac{RB}{P} - T - f'(K)K^G\right) - \frac{\dot{P}}{P}\frac{M}{P}, \tag{6.6}$$

$$\dot{x} = \beta\left(\frac{\dot{P}}{P} - x\right), \qquad \beta > 0, \tag{5.7}$$

Equations (6.5) and (6.6) are derived from the government budget identity. γ is the share of the deficit financed by borrowing. The change in the real value of private sector holdings of a government debt instrument is the real value of current changes in the nominal stock of the instrument plus capital gains on existing holdings. Pure fiscal policy is commonly defined as changes in some parameter(s) of public spending or taxation with any resulting deficit (or surplus) financed by borrowing (or retiring bonds), i.e. $\gamma = 1$. Equations (6.3) and (6.4) reflect the simplifying assumptions that there are no sales of capital between the public and the private sectors and no depreciation.

Without direct crowding out of investment, we assume private investment to be an increasing function of q, the ratio of the market value of claims on the existing stock of capital to the value of the stock of capital at current reproduction costs, or equivalently, the ratio of the rate of return obtainable by investing a dollar in the production of new capital goods to the rate of return obtainable by investing a dollar in existing capital goods,

$$q = \frac{f'(K)}{R - x}.$$

Thus without direct crowding out along the investment dimension,

$$I^P = I(f'(K)/(R - x)], \qquad I' > 0, \quad I(1) = 0. \tag{6.8}$$

If public investment is a substitute for private investment we can specify private investment as follows:

$$I^P = I^P(I^G, f'(K)/(R - x)), \qquad -1 \leq I_1^P \leq 0. \tag{6.8a}$$

Perfect substitutes would be characterized by $I_1^P = -1$. Another way of representing the perfect substitutes case would be to use Equation (6.8b):

$$I^P = I[f'(K)/(R - x)] - I^G. \tag{6.8b}$$

If complementarity relations exist between private and public investment the private investment function is given by Equation (6.8a) with $I_1^P \geq 0$.

The private consumption function without direct crowding out along the consumption dimension can be written as:

$$C^P = C(Y, W), \qquad 0 \leq C_1 \leq 1, \quad C_2 > 0. \tag{6.9}$$

Direct substitutability or complementarity relations between public and private consumption can be represented by:

$$C^P = C^P(C^G, Y, W), \qquad C_1^P \lesseqgtr 0. \tag{6.9a}$$

The perfect substitutes case is $C_1^P = -1$. This could also be written as:

$$C^P = C(Y, W) - C^G. \tag{6.9b}$$

Two other forms of direct crowding out that can be conveniently analyzed in this simple model are direct crowding out along the income and wealth dimensions. Y and W are arguments in the private consumption function and the money demand function. Y and W go through a sequence of transformations as different forms and degrees of direct crowding out are assumed.

In models that ignore all forms of direct crowding out, real private income (including expected capital gains due to inflation) is given by:

$$Y = f(K) + \frac{RB}{P} - x\left(\frac{M+B}{P}\right) - T - f'(K)K^G. \tag{6.10}$$

Let $1 - \alpha$ denote the proportion of the private sector's holdings of public sector interest-bearing debt that is offset by the present discounted value of the future taxes 'required' to service that debt: after the future taxes implied by current deficits are taken into account, only a fraction α of private sector holdings of public sector bonds will be part of private sector net worth and therefore subject to capital gains or losses due to expected inflation. On the income side a fraction $(1 - \alpha)$ of the bond-financed part of the deficit will be subtracted from the initial concept of real private income in Equation (6.10),

$$Y' = f(K) + \frac{RB}{P} - x\frac{(M + \alpha B)}{P} - T - f'(K)K^G$$

$$- (1 - \alpha)\gamma\left(C^G + I^G + \frac{RB}{P} - T - f'(K)K^G\right). \tag{6.10a}$$

If, in addition, government spending is counted as an addition to private income to the extent indicated by proportions $0 \leq \varepsilon_1$, $\varepsilon_2 \leq 1$, multiplying C^G and I^G respectively, real private income becomes

$$Y'' = f(K) + \frac{RB}{P} - x\frac{(M + \alpha B)}{P} - T - f'(K)K^G$$

$$- (1 - \alpha)\gamma\left(C^G + I^G + \frac{RB}{P} - T - f'(K)K^G\right) + \varepsilon_1 C^G + \varepsilon_2 I^G. \tag{6.10b}$$

Complete crowding along the income dimensions requires $\alpha = 0$ and $\varepsilon_1 = \varepsilon_2 = 1$. The final private real income concept, perhaps better labeled real social income, is $f(K) + (1 - \gamma)[C^G + I^G + (RB/P) - T - f'(K)K^G] - x(M/P)$, or

$$Y''' = f(K) + \frac{\dot{M}}{P} - x\frac{M}{P}. \tag{6.10c}$$

Private sector non-human marketable wealth, W, goes through an analogous sequence of transformations. In the absence of any ultra-rationality, we have

$$W = \frac{M + B}{P} + qK^P. \tag{6.11}$$

When the future taxes 'required' to service the debt are taken into account, this becomes

$$W' = \frac{M + \alpha B}{P} + qK^P. \tag{6.11a}$$

When, in addition, a proportion ε_2 of public investment is counted as part of private income, we get

$$W'' = \frac{M + \alpha B}{P} + qK^P + q\,\varepsilon_2 K^G. \qquad (6.11\text{b})$$

Complete crowding out ($\alpha = 0$, $\varepsilon_2 = 1$) gives

$$W''' = \frac{M}{P} + qK. \qquad (6.11\text{c})$$

It could be argued that with the consolidation of the private and the public sectors having gone this far, the distinction between inside and outside assets has become blurred. There appears to be little rationale left for counting expected capital gains or losses on the stock of outside money as part of net worth. Carrying the consolidation to its logical conclusion would reduce real income to real output and net worth to the value of the stock of capital.

The ultrarational version of the *IS–LM* model with bond-financed deficits or surpluses (complete direct crowding out along the investment, consumption, income and net worth dimensions, given by Equations (6.1)–(6.4), (6.5) and (6.6) with $\gamma = 1$, and (6.7), (6.8b), (6.9b), (6.10c) and (6.11c), can be summarized as follows:

$$C\!\left(f(K) - x\frac{M}{P}, \frac{f'(K)}{R - x} K + \frac{M}{P}\right) + I\!\left(f'(K)/(R - x)\right) = f(K), \quad (IS)$$
$$\qquad (6.12\text{a})$$

$$L\!\left(R, \frac{f'(K)}{R - x} K + \frac{M}{P}\right) = \frac{M}{P}, \quad (LM) \qquad (6.12\text{b})$$

$$\dot{K} = I(f'(K)/R - x), \qquad (6.12\text{c})$$

$$\frac{d}{dt}\left(\frac{M}{P}\right) = -\frac{\dot{P}}{P}\frac{M}{P}, \qquad (6.12\text{d})$$

$$\dot{x} = \beta\!\left(\frac{\dot{P}}{P} - x\right). \qquad (6.12\text{e})$$

The distinction between publicly owned capital and privately owned capital has disappeared. Government deficits and surpluses are bond-financed but the bond debt of the public sector has effectively disappeared from the model. It is irrelevant whether or not the budget balances, since neither private income nor private portfolios are affected by the government's financing policy. The equation giving the change in the real value of the stock of bonds is irrelevant for the rest of the model and has been omitted. The private sector is indifferent about the amount of bonds the government wishes to issue, because with every bond that is issued a perfectly equivalent tax liability is imposed. The net effect is equivalent to the complete absence of government bonds from the economy.[12] The government as an independent spending and revenue-raising agent has been consolidated out of the model. In this model there is, trivially, complete crowding out of private spending by government spending and of private saving by lump-sum taxation both in the short run, given by the IS and LM curves for given values of stocks and expectations, and in the long run, given by the IS and LM curves and the values of K, M/P and x obtained by setting $\dot{K} = d/dt(M/P) = \dot{x} = 0$. The government can influence neither real nor nominal magnitudes by operating on C^G, I^G and T.

Two points should be made about this result. First, it depends on the tax being a lump-sum tax. If there were, say, a tax at a rate θ on factor incomes and debt service, $R(1 - \theta)$ rather than R would be an argument in the money demand function and the government could influence the real economy by varying the tax *rate*.[13]

Second, 100 per cent direct crowding out of private consumption by public consumption (or of private investment by public investment) is not sufficient to guarantee the absence of long-run effects of changes in public consumption (or public investment). In addition, government bonds should not appear as an argument in any private sector behavioural relationship.

Consider the general model Equations (6.1)–(6.4), (6.5) and (6.6) with $\gamma = 1$, (6.7), (6.8a), (6.9a), (6.10b) and (6.11b). When $C^P = -1$ there is complete direct crowding out of private consumption by public consumption: in the short run an increase in C^G will merely displace an equal amount of C^P. Even if there were no direct crowding out of C^P by C^G, the full-employment assumption would ensure complete short-run indirect crowding out of private spending by public spending through increases in the price level and the rate of interest. With complete direct crowding out even the price level and the interest rate are unaffected in the short run. If, however, government bonds constitute private net worth to any extent ($\alpha \neq 0$), financing the deficit or surplus resulting from the change in public spending by issuing or retiring debt will gradually change private net worth; Equation (6.5), describing the rate of change of the stock of real government debt, again becomes an integral part of the dynamics of the model, and the balanced budget condition is again a relevant steady-state condition. Thus, even if ultrarationality prevails in all dimensions except for private sector behavior not being invariant under different amounts of government interest-bearing debt held in private portfolios, changes in government spending or taxing behavior will have real long-run effects when bonds are used to finance the resulting budget imbalance.

If the government deficit or surplus is exclusively money-financed, the ultrarational version of the model is given by Equations (6.1)–(6.4), (6.5) and (6.6) with $\gamma = 0$, (6.7), (6.8b), (6.9b), (6.10b) and (6.11c).

$$C\left(f(K) + C^G + I^G + \frac{RB}{P} - T - f'(K)K^G - x\frac{M}{P}, \frac{f'(K)}{R - x}K + \frac{M}{P}\right)$$
$$+ I[f'(K)/(R - x)] = f(K), \quad (IS) \tag{6.13a}$$

$$L\left(R, \frac{f'(K)}{R - x}K + \frac{M}{P}\right) = \frac{M}{P}, \quad (LM) \tag{6.13b}$$

$$\dot{K} = I[f'(K)/R - x)], \tag{6.13c}$$

$$\frac{d}{dt}\left(\frac{B}{P}\right) = -\frac{\dot{P}}{P}\frac{\dot{B}}{P}, \tag{6.13d}$$

$$\frac{d}{dt}\left(\frac{M}{P}\right) = C^G + I^G + \frac{RB}{P} - T - f'(K)K^G - \frac{\dot{P}}{P}\frac{M}{P}, \tag{6.13e}$$

$$\dot{x} = \beta\left(\frac{\dot{P}}{P} - x\right). \tag{6.13f}$$

Even though bonds are not part of private sector net worth, the volume of bonds affects the size of the government deficit and therefore the rate of change of M. Equation (6.13d) can therefore not be ignored. For simplicity, take $I^G = K^G = 0$. The long-run equilibrium (IS and LM with $\dot{K} = d/dt(B/P)$ $= d/dt(M/P) = \dot{x} = 0$) is again a zero-rate-of-inflation equilibrium if $B \neq 0$. Changes in C^G and T will have short-run effects on the price level and the rate of interest. Across steady states an increase in C^G or a decrease in T will cause equiproportionate increases in the nominal stock of money and the price level. K and R are unaffected. If there were no bonds in the model ($B = 0$) the rate of inflation could be non-zero in long-run equilibrium. In that case changes in C^G and T will cause changes in the steady-state rate of inflation. There would be long-run real effects of such fiscal policy changes because the nominal rate of return on money balances is institutionally fixed. The real rate-of-return differential between money and capital would therefore be altered.

The analysis developed so far can be applied to a variety of issues. In what follows I shall use it to develop a possible interpretation of the *Newsweek* statement by Milton Friedman (1975) that the true cost of government is measured by government spending, not by explicit taxes. My interpretation of this statement is that real private income consists of net national product plus capital gains minus government spending on goods and services. (Alternatively — but not in the context in which it was written — one could interpret the statement as simply referring to the indirect crowding out of private spending by public spending in the short run in a fully employed economy.) In our notation

$$Y = f(K) - x\frac{M}{P} - (C^G + I^G). \tag{6.14}$$

This is the real private income concept one obtains when the entire government budget deficit is subtracted from the conventional measure of real private income (and government bonds do not constitute private net worth to any extent). For simplicity, public investment and capital are again ignored in what follows.

The *Newsweek* model is a special case of our general model (Equations (6.1)–(6.9), (6.10a) and (6.11a) with $\alpha = I^G = K^G = 0$, under bond-financed deficits ($\gamma = 1$)). It can be summarized as follows:

$$C^G + C^P \left(f(K) - x \frac{M}{P} - C^G, \frac{M}{P} + \frac{f'(K)}{R - x} K \right)$$
$$+ I[f'(K)/(R - x)] = f(K) \tag{6.15a}$$

$$L\left(R, \frac{M}{P} + \frac{f'(K)}{R - x} K \right) = \frac{M}{P}, \tag{6.15b}$$

$$\dot{K} = I[f'(K)/R - x)], \tag{6.15c}$$

$$\frac{d}{dt}\left(\frac{M}{P}\right) = -\frac{\dot{P}}{P}\frac{M}{P}, \tag{6.15d}$$

$$\frac{d}{dt}\left(\frac{B}{P}\right) = C^G + \frac{RB}{P} - T - \frac{\dot{P}}{P}\frac{B}{P}, \tag{6.15e}$$

$$\dot{x} = \beta\left(\frac{\dot{P}}{P} - x\right). \tag{6.15f}$$

The long-run equilibrium values of R, P, K and B are determined by

$$C^G + C^P \left(f(K) - C^G, \frac{M}{P} + K \right) = f(K), \tag{6.16a}$$

$$L\left(R, \frac{M}{P} + K \right) = \frac{M}{P}, \tag{6.16b}$$

$$f'(K) = R, \tag{6.16c}$$

$$C^G + \frac{RB}{P} - T = 0. \tag{6.16d}$$

The stock of bonds only enters Equations (6.15e) and (6.16d), and does not affect the behavior of R, P and K.

The impact effect of an increase in C^G is to shift the *IS* curve to the right in R–P space, raising R and P and crowding out private consumption and investment to the extent required to make room for the larger amount of government consumption. Solving Equation (6.16c) for K as a function of R, $K = g(R)$, $g' = 1/f'' < 0$ and substituting this into Equations (6.16a) and (6.16b) we can represent the long-run equilibrium in R–P space as

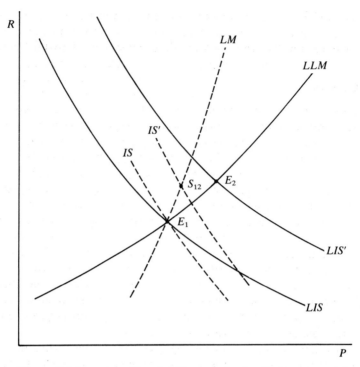

Figure 6.1 Long-run *IS* and *LM* curves in the *Newsweek* model

$$C^G + C^P \left(f(g(R)) - C^G, \frac{M}{P} + g(R) \right) = f(g(R)). \quad (LIS \text{ curve})$$
$$(6.16a)$$

$$L \left(R, \frac{M}{P} + g(R) \right) = \frac{M}{P}. \qquad\qquad (LLM \text{ curve})$$
$$(6.16b)$$

Short-run *IS* and *LM* curves corresponding to the long-run equilibrium E_1 and the long-run *LIS* and *LLM* curves are drawn in Figure 6.1 (the *LLM* curve could be steeper than the *LM* curve). The short-run result of an increase in C^G is to create a new momentary equilibrium at S_{12}. In the long run, an increase in government consumption spending will reduce real output (raise R and P) as drawn in Figure 6.1, if the *LIS* curve is downward-sloping or if it is upward-sloping and steeper than the *LLM* curve, and raise real output otherwise.[14]

Thus, even if the full government deficit is viewed as equivalent to current taxation and government interest-bearing debt is not counted as private sector net worth to any extent, changes in public consumption spending will have real long-run effects unless there also happens to be complete direct crowding out along the consumption dimension.

6.4 CAVEATS

The results established so far are subject to three broad qualifications.

6.4.1 Corners

Consider the case of complete direct crowding out of private consumption of some commodity by public consumption — a change in the level of public consumption causing merely a change in the *composition* of total (private *plus* public) consumption of that commodity without changing its level. For this crowding out of private spending to be possible, it has to be assumed that no individual consumer is 'at a corner' beyond which consumption cannot be reduced for technical or physiological reasons. As an example, with the consumption of private education constrained to lie in the non-negative orthant, no dollar-for-dollar offset of an increase in public spending on education is possible with private spending already at the origin. *Mutatis mutandis*, the same applies to the other forms of direct crowding out. As another example, private portfolio reshuffles and changes in borrowing and lending behavior can only negate an increase in the volume of public debt if private agents hold sufficient amounts of government bonds to begin with (Barro, 1974).

In an overlapping generations model, changes in the volume of public debt will have no real effect only if current generations are connected to future generations by a chain of operative intergenerational transfers. An increase in forced intergenerational transfers can only be offset by a reduction in voluntary intergenerational transfers, if voluntary intergenerational transfers are not zero initially (Barro, 1974).

The importance of corner solutions for economic activities in which crowding out is potentially important is an empirical issue on which little hard evidence is available.

6.4.2 Substitutes and complements

A specific commodity or service supplied (competitively or otherwise) by the government may be a substitute for a privately supplied commodity or service. At the level of theoretical possibilities with some empirical plausibility, complementarity relations between certain categories of public and private spending also ought to be considered. Public investment, for example, may be competitive with private investment in certain instances (as in public housing construction) but complementarity relations between certain categories of investment in social overhead capital and private investment are certainly possible. Public investment in projects with increasing returns or massive overheads such as the construction of a dam come to mind.

6.4.3 Effective demand and notional demand

Even when there is complete direct crowding out of, say, private consumption by public consumption in terms of *notional* private demand, there need not be complete crowding out of *effective* private demand. In a Clower–Barro–Grossman world with households unable to execute their notional consumption plans because they are quantity-constrained in the labor market and firms unwilling to execute their notional labor-hiring plans because they are quantity-constrained in the output market, an increase in public consumption might well cause a smaller reduction in effective private consumption demand than in notional private consumption demand (Clower, 1965; Barro and Grossman, 1971).

The same fundamental problem arises with indirect crowding out of private spending by public spending in the presence of involuntary unemployment of labor and idle capital. The textbook neo-Keynesian model with unemployment permits, at least temporarily, the existence of insufficient private effective demand at current (non-market-clearing) prices and interest rates and given the current state of expectations. This can then be remedied by increasing public spending or reducing taxation. Two fundamental issues are whether such a state of affairs requires private behavior to be irrational and whether the information available to the public sector is assumed to be superior to that available to the private sector. It is beyond the scope of this paper to deal with these problems[15] (see Gordon, 1976).

6.5 CONCLUSION

The model developed in Section 6.3 offers considerable scope for further analysis of alternative combinations of types and degrees of direct crowding out. More useful, at this stage, would be careful empirical analysis of the existence and importance of the many types of direct crowding out. The analysis of Section 6.3 was conducted using a full-employment model. The important issues associated with indirect crowding out under conditions of involuntary unemployment of labor and idle capital were only mentioned in passing.

The conditions under which changes in public spending have no long-run effect on real variables are very stringent indeed. Complete direct crowding out of private spending by public spending and full equivalence between taxes and public sector deficits are required. The fact that even complete direct crowding out along any one dimension does not prevent fiscal policy from having real long-run effects does not imply that direct crowding out is unimportant for policy purposes. Some degree of direct (and indirect) crowding out is definitely a theoretical and a practical possibility — along each of the many dimensions. A number of examples were given in Section 6.2 and others can undoubtedly be thought of. The degree of crowding out along each dimension is an empirical matter that will have to be settled if accurate policy-oriented models are to be constructed. It is important to beware of jumping from accepting the plausibility of some degree of direct (or indirect) crowding out to presenting the (on a priori and empirical grounds) implausible case of 100 per cent crowding out as the only relevant one.

6.6 NOTES

1. See, for example, the *Economic Report of the President* (1975, pp. 4, 25).
2. Crowding out is not, of course, an all-or-nothing phenomenon. The degree of crowding out can be defined as the ratio of the induced change in the scale of some private activity to the change in the scale of the public economic activity that brought it about. The crowding out debate, in other words, is about the signs and magnitudes of public policy multipliers.
3. The theoretical and empirical literature on this subject is surveyed comprehensively in Blinder and Solow (1974); see also Friedman (1970).
4. Alternative descriptions would be 'structural' or *ex ante* crowding out for direct crowding out and 'reduced form' or *ex post* crowding out for indirect crowding out. The *ex ante–ex post* nomenclature is found in David and Scadding (1974).
5. The best single reference on direct crowding out is the 'textbook' by Bailey (1971), esp. pp. 152–64. Another recent textbook that deals with some aspects of ultrarationality is Miller and Upton (1974).
6. An analogous issue within the private sector is the relationship between households and corporations. Is the corporation merely an extension of the households that own it, i.e. can its actions be entirely subsumed under household decision-making or is the corporate veil not quite as easily removed?
7. This argument has a long history. See, for example, Tobin (1952), Patinkin (1965), Meyer (1974) and Barro (1974). A recent exchange between Barro (1976), Feldstein (1976) and Buchanan (1976) has brought out the importance of population growth and intertemporal inefficiency. There has not yet been a systematic investigation of the intuitively plausible proposition that, with imperfect capital markets and binding cash-flow or liquidity constraints on spending and borrowing for some private economic agents, the composition of income flows and wealth portfolios will affect behavior and the mix of financing instruments chosen by the government will affect real economic activity.
8. The crowding out of consumption and investment can, of course, be disaggregated by type of consumption good and capital good.
9. An alternative classification scheme would distinguish forms of direct crowding out that depend on the specific *content* of government spending programs from those that depend on the *financing* of government spending programs, irrespective of their specific content. The consumption and investment dimensions fall into the former category. The inclusion of government spending on final goods and services in private income will depend on the specific content of the spending program. The wealth dimension and the government budget deficit are financing issues. The borrowing dimension fits neatly into neither category.
10. Some (inconclusive) empirical evidence is already available on various aspects

180   *Crowding out*

of 'ultrarationality' (e.g., Denison, 1958; David and Scadding, 1974; Kochin, 1974; and Peltzman, 1973).

11. Note that the public spending on final goods and services considered under indirect crowding out was assumed not to affect private consumption and investment directly. This does not require us to assume that governments purchase goods and services and proceed to throw them into the sea, although that would be a possible rationalization. Government spending that directly affects private utility functions or opportunity sets was considered under direct crowding out.

12. It is unfortunate that there is no convenient analytical way of differentiating between the effect of financial intermediation in saving real resources and facilitating saving and accumulation and the effect of increasing the quantity of some financial claim, given a financial system of a given degree of sophistication.

13. The point that changes in non-lump-sum taxes will virtually always affect behavior in a way that will not be canceled out is, of course, a more general one. The effect of changes in wage tax rates on labor supply and demand is another example.

14.

$$\left.\frac{dR}{dp}\right|_{LIS} = \frac{C_W^P \frac{M}{P^2}}{[(C_Y^P - 1)f' + C_W^P]/f''} < 0 \quad \text{if} \quad (C_Y^P - 1)f' + C_W^P > 0,$$

$$\left.\frac{dR}{dp}\right|_{IS} = \frac{-C_W^P \frac{MR}{P^2}}{KC_W^P + I'} < 0, \quad \text{(at the long-run equilibrium)},$$

$$\left.\frac{dR}{dp}\right|_{LLM} = \frac{(L_W - 1)\frac{M}{P^2}}{L_R + L_W/f''} > 0,$$

$$\left.\frac{dR}{dp}\right|_{LM} = \frac{(L_W - 1)\frac{M}{P^2}}{L_R - L_W \frac{K}{R}} > 0.$$

15. A complete solution will, in our opinion, have to incorporate the following two elements. First, the assumption that prices clear labor and output markets continuously — or in each market period — must be abandoned. (This is not the same as assuming permanent price rigidity.) Second, the unique position of the government as the 'spender of last resort' — not subject to the same budget constraints as private agents because of its monopoly in the issue of legal tender, its ability to tax and its resulting lower risk of default — must be recognized.

6.7 REFERENCES

Bailey, M.J. (1971) *National Income and the Price Level: A Study in Macroeconomic Theory*, 2nd edn, McGraw-Hill, New York.
Barro, Robert J. (1974) 'Are government bonds net wealth?', *Journal of Political Economy*, 82, November–December, pp. 1095–117.

Barro, Robert J. (1976) 'Reply to Feldstein and Buchanan', *Journal of Political Economy*, 84, pp. 343–9.

Barro, Robert J. and H.I. Grossman (1971) 'A general disequilibrium model of income and employment', *American Economic Review*, 61, pp. 82–93.

Blinder, A.S. and R.M. Solow (1973) 'Does fiscal policy matter?', *Journal of Public Economics*, 2, pp. 319–37.

Blinder, A.S. and R.M. Solow (1974) 'Analytical foundations of fiscal policy' in A.S. Blinder and R.M. Solow, *The Economics of Public Finance*, The Brookings Institution, Washington, DC, pp. 3–19.

Buchanan, J.M. (1976) 'Barro on the Ricardian equivalence theorem', *Journal of Political Economy*, 84, pp. 337–42.

Cagan, P. (1965) 'The effect of pension plans on aggregate saving', *NBER Occasional Paper*, no. 95.

Carlson, K.M. and R.W. Spencer (1975) 'Crowding out and its critics', *Federal Reserve Bank of St. Louis Review*, 47, pp. 2–17.

Christ, C. (1968) 'A simple macroeconomic model with a government budget restraint', *Journal of Political Economy*, 76, pp. 53–67.

Chow, G. (1975) *Analysis and Control of Dynamic Economic Systems*, John Wiley, New York.

Clower, R.W. (1965) 'The Keynesian counter revolution: A theoretical appraisal' in F.H. Hahn and F.P.R. Brechling (eds.), *The Theory of Interest Rates*, Macmillan, London, pp. 103–25.

David, P.A. and J.L. Scadding (1974) 'Private savings: "Ultrarationality", aggregation and Denison's Law', *Journal of Political Economy*, 82, pp. 225–49.

Denison, E.F. (1958) 'A note on private saving', *Review of Economics and Statistics*, 40, pp. 261–7.

Feldstein, M. (1976) 'Perceived wealth in bonds and social security: A comment', *Journal of Political Economy*, 84, pp. 331–6.

Fleming, J.M. (1962) 'Domestic financial policies under fixed and floating exchange rates', *IMF Staff Papers*, 9, pp. 369–79.

Foley, D.K. and M. Sidrauski (1971) *Monetary and Fiscal Policy in a Growing Economy*, Macmillan, London.

Friedman, M. (1970) 'A theoretical framework for monetary analysis' in Friedman et al. (1974).

Friedman, M. (1972) 'Comments on the critics', *Journal of Political Economy*, 80, pp. 906–50.

Friedman, M. et al. (1974) *Milton Friedman's Monetary Framework: A Debate with his Critics*, University of Chicago Press, Chicago.

Friedman, M. (1975) 'Wonderland scheme', *Newsweek*, 27 January, pp. 24–5.

Gordon, R.J. (1976) 'Recent developments in the theory of inflation and unemployment', *Journal of Monetary Economics*, 2, pp. 185–221.

Hicks, J.R. (1937) 'Mr. Keynes and the classics', *Econometrica*, 5, pp. 147–59.

Johnson, H.G. (1967) 'Money in a neo-classical one-sector growth model' in H.G. Johnson, *Essays in Monetary Economics*, Allen & Unwin, London, pp. 143–78.

Juster, T.F. and R.E. Lipsey (1967) 'A note on consumer asset formation in the U.S.', *Economic Journal*, 77, pp. 834–47.

Katona, G. (1965) *Private Pensions and Individual Saving*, University of Michigan Survey Research Center, Monograph 40, Ann Arbor, MI.

Keynes, J.M. and H.D. Henderson (1929) 'Can Lloyd George do it?' in J.M. Keynes, *Essays in Persuasion*, Macmillan, London, pp. 118–34.

182   *Crowding out*

Keynes, J.M. (1936) *The General Theory of Employment, Interest and Money*, Macmillan, London.

Kochin, L.A. (1974) 'Are future taxes anticipated by consumers?', *Journal of Money, Credit and Banking*, 6, pp. 385–94.

Levhari, D. and D. Patinkin (1968) 'The role of money in a simple growth model', *American Economic Review*, 68, pp. 713–53.

Meyer, L.H. (1974) 'Wealth effects and the effectiveness of monetary and fiscal policy', *Journal of Money, Credit and Banking*, 6, pp. 481–503.

Miller, M.H. and C.W. Upton (1974) *Macroeconomics: A Neoclassical Introduction*, Richard D. Irwin, Homewood, IL.

Mundell, R.A. (1962) 'The appropriate use of monetary and fiscal policy for internal and external stability', *IMF Staff Papers*, 9, pp. 70–9.

Mundell, R.A. (1965) 'A fallacy in the interpretation of macroeconomic equilibrium', *Journal of Political Economy*, 73, pp. 61–5.

Ott, D.J. and L.J. Korb (1973) *Public Claims on U.S. Output*, American Enterprise Institute for Public Policy Research, Washington, DC.

Patinkin, D. (1965) *Money, Interest and Prices*, 2nd edn, Harper and Row, New York.

Peltzman, S. (1973) 'The effect of public subsidies-in-kind on private expenditures: The case of higher education', *Journal of Political Economy*, 81, pp. 1–27.

Spencer, R.W. and W.P. Yohe (1970) 'The "crowding out" of private expenditures by fiscal policy actions', *Federal Reserve Bank of St. Louis Review*, 52, pp. 12–24.

Stein, J.L. (1966) 'Money and capacity growth', *Journal of Political Economy*, 74, pp. 451–65.

Taylor, L.D. (1971) 'Saving out of different types of income', *Brookings Institution Papers on Economic Activity*, 2, pp. 283–407.

Tobin, J. (1952) 'Asset holdings and spending decisions', *American Economic Review, Papers and Proceedings*, 42, pp. 109–26.

Tobin, J. (1955) 'A dynamic aggregative model', *Journal of Political Economy*, 63, pp. 103–15.

Tobin, J. (1965) 'Money and economic growth', *Econometrica*, 33, pp. 671–84.

Tobin, J. and W.H. Buiter (1976) 'Long-run effects of fiscal and monetary policy on aggregate demand' in J.L. Stein (ed.), *Monetarism*, North-Holland, Amsterdam, pp. 273–309 (also Chapter 10, this volume).

7 · DEBT NEUTRALITY, REDISTRIBUTION AND CONSUMER HETEROGENEITY: A SURVEY AND SOME EXTENSIONS

7.1 INTRODUCTION

The teacher–pupil relationship between Jim Tobin and me by no means came to an end after I obtained my Ph.D. in 1975. Like so many who experienced his influence, I have tried to internalize his insistence that we practice economics as if it mattered beyond the narrow confines of the profession. No matter how formal and abstract our analyses may have to be in order to answer certain complex substantive questions, our subject is not an intellectual game or a branch of pure logic. It is a potentially powerful tool for understanding and influencing the real world and the lives of many who may not even be aware of the existence of an academic discipline called economics and its practitioners.

At the methodological level, I have become convinced more and more of the correctness of his view that representative agent models make for uninteresting economics. Robinson Crusoe did not need much economic theory before Friday arrived. After that he needed game theory. No economic policy issue of any significance can be addressed satisfactorily without introducing some measure of heterogeneity among (depending on the issue) consumers, producers, workers, employers or investors. This poses a serious problem for macroeconomics, which approaches economic policy issues using highly aggregative sequential general equilibrium models. How much disaggregation and heterogeneity is possible before the virtues of simplicity, transparency and analytical tractability are lost completely?

Many potentially important kinds of heterogeneity come to mind. Con-

This paper was written for *Macroeconomics, Finance and Economic Policy*; *Essays in Honor of James Tobin*, W. Brainard, W. Nordhaus, and H. Watts (eds), MIT Press, Cambridge, MA, forthcoming 1990.

sumers and workers can have heterogeneous endowments (including abilities), opportunities (including market environment), ages, life expectancies, tastes (risk aversion, impatience, etc.), habits, norms, views on fairness, group or class identification and association, information sets and perceptions of reality. Producers can have different technologies, tastes, information sets, market environments, etc. In this paper I shall consider the consequences of four kinds of consumer heterogeneity for debt neutrality. An economic system exhibits debt neutrality if, given a program for public spending on goods and services over time, the equilibrium of the economy is not affected by a change in the pattern over time of lump-sum taxes. This means that debt neutrality, e.g. the substitution of government borrowing today for lump-sum taxation today (followed by such further changes in the path of future lump-sum taxes as may be required to maintain the solvency of the public sector), does not affect current and future private consumption, capital formation and interest rates. The four kinds of consumer heterogeneity are age, life expectancy, time preference and elasticity of intertemporal substitution. The overlapping generations (OLG) model is the natural vehicle for this kind of modeling as it is designed specifically to handle the 'entry' and 'exit' of consumers.

The issue of debt neutrality is central to an understanding both of the short-run cyclical stabilization role of fiscal policy and of the long-run effect of fiscal and financial policy on the path of the capital stock. (See, for example, the contributions in Ferguson, 1964; and Modigliani, 1961). It therefore comes as no surprise that Jim Tobin studied this subject early in his career (Tobin, 1952) and returned to it time and again (e.g., Tobin, 1976; 1979; 1980). I was fortunate to be involved in two collaborations with him on this subject matter (Buiter and Tobin, 1979; Tobin and Buiter, 1980).

There is no better way to introduce the key issue than by quoting from one of Jim's key writings on the subject:

> How is it possible that society merely by the device of incurring a debt to itself can deceive itself into believing that it is wealthier? Do not the additional taxes which are necessary to carry the interest charges reduce the value of other components of private wealth? There certainly must be effects in this direction (Tobin, 1952, p. 117).

The central issue can be phrased as follows: when does (at given prices and interest rates) postponing lump-sum taxation, while maintaining public sector[1] solvency, change binding constraints faced by consumers[1] alive today in such a way that aggregate consumption changes? The answer is that postponing lump-sum taxation must achieve one or both of the following. First, it redistributes (lifetime) resources among 'isolated' heterogeneous survivors, i.e. among households alive in the period when the taxes are cut. Second, it redistributes (lifetime) resources between survivors (who may be homogeneous) and overlapping new entrants from whom they are 'isolated' (and who may also be homogeneous), i.e. households that are born after the period during which taxes are cut but whose life-span overlaps with that of households alive when the taxes are cut. 'Isolation' here means a situation without interior solutions for gifts or bequests, intertemporal or atemporal. This can either be the result of egoistic utility functions (only own lifetime consumption yields utility) or of zero gift or bequest corner solutions despite altruistic utility functions.

Absence of debt neutrality therefore requires that postponing lump-sum taxation causes *redistribution* among *heterogeneous* households.

The plan of the remainder of the paper is as follows. Section 7.2 reviews some important features of the two-period OLG model with intergenerational gift and bequest motives. It draws heavily on the recent work of Kimball (1987a; 1987b), which contains the first (to my knowledge) complete solution of the two-sided intergenerational caring problem with population growth and parthogenesis. This model has a positive birth rate (the representative household born in any given period is assumed to have at least one child) and a finite (in this case a two-period) lifetime, i.e. a zero probability of death at the end of the first period and a 100 per cent probability of death at the end of the second period. Debt neutrality occurs for (small) changes in the pattern of borrowing and lump-sum taxation when the equilibrium is one with an operative intergenerational gift or bequest motive (i.e. with positive bequest or child-to-parent gift). If the intergenerational gift and bequest motives are non-operative there is no debt neutrality as long as there is a positive birth rate. If there is a zero birth rate, we are, of course, back in the representative consumer model. The representative consumer has a finite horizon, but this does not mean that she will benefit from postponing taxes as there are no 'new entrants' (succeeding generations) to whom (part of) the tax burden can be shifted.

If there is a positive birth rate, the presence of debt neutrality despite heterogeneity when there is an operative intergenerational gift or bequest motive can be attributed to the failure to achieve intergenerational redistribution by postponing lump-sum taxes. Changes in official involuntary intergenerational transfers are offset by changes in private voluntary intergenerational transfers in the opposite direction, as long as the legal constraints that gifts and bequests cannot go negative do not become binding. Alternatively, the sequence of altruistically linked successive generations can be interpreted as a single dynastic representative consumer. Absence of heterogeneity is the reason for debt neutrality in this view.

The key references for this section are Barro (1974): Carmichael (1979; 1982); Buiter (1979; 1980); Buiter and Carmichael (1984); Burbridge (1983); Abel (1985); Weil (1987); and especially Kimball (1987a; 1987b).

Section 7.3 considers an OLG model without intergenerational gift and bequest motives but with potentially infinite-lived consumers. The birth rate is non-negative and there is a common age- and time-independent probability of death which can be zero. When there is a positive probability of death, an efficient competitive life insurance or annuities market is assumed to exist. When the utility function is time-additive and the single-period utility function has constant elasticity of marginal utility, it can be shown that a positive birth rate is necessary and sufficient for absence of debt neutrality. Uncertain lifetimes (or productivity growth) do not destroy debt neutrality when there is zero birth rate. Note that in this model with its uniform death rate, and productivity growth rate,[2] age is the only form of household heterogeneity. A zero birth rate destroys this one form of heterogeneity. This section draws on the work of Yaari (1965); Blanchard (1985); Weil (1985); Frenkel and Razin (1986); Abel (1987); and Buiter (1988a; 1988b).

In Section 7.4 the perfect capital market assumption is relaxed. I first consider the case of a complete absence of life insurance markets. As long as there is no consumer heterogeneity, however, this capital market imperfection is no independent source of absence of debt neutrality. (In quite a different context a similar point has been made by Yotsuzuka, 1987.)

When there is heterogeneity in death rates, there will be absence of debt neutrality even with a zero birth rate and perfect annuities markets. Postponing taxes will redistribute lifetime resources towards the households with the highest death rate (assuming the current tax cuts and later tax increases fall equally on all households alive at the time, independently of their death rates). These households have a higher marginal propensity to spend out of lifetime resources. Postponing lump-sum taxes therefore redistributes wealth from high savers to low savers, boosting aggregate consumption. Note that heterogeneity through different time preference rates does not cause absence of debt neutrality when there is a common death rate and a zero birth rate. The reason is, of course, that postponing uniform lump-sum taxes (i.e. taxes falling equally on all alive, regardless of time preference rates) does not redistribute income between high and low time preference households as both kinds have the same life expectancy. Redistribution and heterogeneity are both necessary for absence of debt neutrality.

7.2 AN OLG MODEL WITH FINITE LIFETIMES AND INTERGENERATIONAL GIFT AND BEQUEST MOTIVES

7.2.1 The consumer's problem

The utility function of a representative member of the generation born in period t is given by Equation (7.1). Utility is additively separable intergenerationally.

$$W_t = u(c_t^1, c_t^2) + (1 + \varrho)^{-1}W_{t-1} + (1 + \delta)^{-1}W_{t+1} \qquad \delta, \varrho > 0 \qquad (7.1)$$

A member of generation t derives utility directly from his own lifetime consumption. This is captured by $u_{0,0}^t = u(c_t^1, c_t^2)$. I shall refer to $u_{0,0}^t$ as the egoistic utility of a member of generation t and to W_t as her total utility. Where there is no ambiguity the superscript and subscripts will be omitted. Each consumer lives for two periods. Labor–leisure choice is omitted.[3] u is strictly concave, increasing, and twice continuously differentiable. It satisfies the Inada conditions. Note that Equation (7.1) exhibits *direct* two-sided intergenerational altruism: a member of generation t cares directly both about his parent[4] and about his $1 + n$ children. For most of this section we consider the case of one or more children, i.e. $n \geqslant 0$. ϱ is the discount rate applied to parental utility and δ that applied to the utility of one's children. There are no crucial modifications to the model if the consumer lives for $N > 2$ periods and cares directly about the $2(N - 1)$ generations with whom he overlaps.[5] All members of all generations have identical egoistic and total utility functions.

In the case of one-sided intergenerational caring, $\delta > 0$ is required for boundedness of the utility functional when the parent-to-child bequest motive is the only one $((1 + \varrho)^{-1} = 0)$ and there is no 'last generation' in finite time; $\varrho > 0$ is required for boundedness of the utility functional when the child-to-parent gift motive is the only one $((1 + \delta)^{-1} = 0)$ and there is no 'first generation' a finite number of periods in the past. As shown in Carmichael (1979) and Buiter (1980) and recently in Kimball (1987a; 1987b), stronger conditions that $\varrho > 0$ and $\delta > 0$ are required to obtain a sensible objective functional with two-sided caring.

W_{t+1} is to be interpreted as the average total utility of the $n + 1$ children of the member of generation t, i.e.

$$W_{t+1} = \frac{1}{1 + n} \sum_{i=1}^{1+n} W_{t+1,i},$$

where i indexes the children of the member of generation t. Equation (7.1) is, however, consistent with a 'the more, the merrier' view of intergenerational caring by reinterpreting $1 + \delta$ in the way suggested below:

$$1 + \delta = \frac{1 + \delta'}{1 + n}.$$

Here δ' is the true discount rate applied to the sum of the utilities of the $1 + n$ children each of which is weighted equally in the parent's objective functional. We continue to express our algebra in terms of δ rather than δ'.

A member of generation t is assumed not to care directly about her n siblings. She will, of course, care indirectly about her siblings (and about more distant relatives of the same generation) to the extent that her parent (and through her more remote ancestors) do.

Kimball (1987a, Appendix D), in an argument that is both ingenious and involved, shows, for the case of more than one child ($n > 0$), how the total utility of a member of generation t, W_t, can be expressed as a function of the egoistic utilities of all relatives (contemporaries, ancestors and descendants). $u^t_{j,k,i}$ is the egoistic utility of the ith relative of type (j,k) of a member of generation t. The index j measures 'vertical' or generational distance and the index k measures 'horizontal' or lateral distance. $\gamma_{j,k}$ is the weight attached to the egoistic utility of any relative of type j,k,[6] i.e.

$$W_t = \sum_{j,k,i} \gamma_{j,k} u^t_{j,k,i}. \tag{7.2}$$

j ranges from $-\infty$ to $+\infty$; k ranges from 0 to $+\infty$, i ranges from 1 to $N(j,k)$, the number of relatives of type (j,k).

Tedious calculation shows that

$$N(j,k) = \begin{cases} 1 & j \leqslant 0, \ k = 0 \\ (1 + n)^j & j \geqslant 0, \ k = 0 \\ n(1 + n)^{k-1} & j \leqslant 0, \ k \geqslant 1 \\ n(1 + n)^{k-1}(1 + n)^j & j \geqslant 0, \ k \geqslant 1. \end{cases} \tag{7.3}$$

Let $u^t_{j,k}$ be the average egoistic utility of all relatives of type j,k, i.e.

$$u^t_{j,k} \equiv \frac{1}{N(j,k)} \sum_{i=1}^{N(j,k)} u^t_{j,k,i}.$$

This permits us to rewrite Equation (7.2) as:

$$W_t = \sum_{j,k} N(j,k) \gamma_{j,k} u^t_{j,k}. \tag{7.4}$$

Kimball imposes the following reasonable restrictions on the $\gamma_{j,k}$.

(a) $\gamma_{j,k} \geqslant 0$ for all j,k (i.e. there is no ill-will towards relatives and no self-hatred);
(b) for $j < 0$, $\gamma_{j,k}$ is a geometric series in j for every k;
(c) $\gamma_{j,0}$ is a geometric series in j for $j \geqslant 0$;
(d) $\lim_{j \to -\infty} \gamma_{j,k} = 0$ \quad for all k;
(e) $\lim_{j \to +\infty} (1 + n)^j \gamma_{j,0} = 0$.

Restriction (c) is a necessary condition for dynamic consistency of choice across generations. Restriction (b) is necessary, for example to rule out forms of dynamic inconsistency in models with more than two overlapping generations in which grandparents overlap with their grandchildren. Restrictions (d) and (e) assert that the indirect concern for very distant ancestors and descendants should vanish.

These restrictions imply that

$$\frac{1}{1 + \delta} + \frac{1}{1 + \varrho} < 1 \tag{7.5}$$

If $\delta = \varrho$, this implies the need for an intergenerational discount rate of over 100 per cent! Equation (7.5) is equivalent to $\delta\varrho > 1$, the condition given in Buiter (1980) for well-behaved steady-state utility.

Given the five restrictions (a)–(e), Kimball (1987a) shows that the weights $\gamma_{j,k}$ are given by:

$$\gamma_{0,0} = \frac{1}{\sqrt{1 - 4(1 + \delta)^{-1}(1 + \varrho)^{-1}} + \dfrac{n}{1 + n}\mu(1 + \varrho)^{-1}} \tag{7.6a}$$

$$\gamma_{j,k} = \begin{cases} \gamma_{0,0}\left(\dfrac{\mu}{1 + n}\right)^{j}\left(\dfrac{\mu}{(1 + n)\lambda}\right)^{k} & j \geq 0 \quad k \geq 0 \\[2.5ex] \gamma_{0,0}\lambda^{j}\left(\dfrac{\mu}{(1 + n)\lambda}\right)^{k} & j \leq 0 \quad k \geq 0 \end{cases} \tag{7.6b}$$

$$\mu = \left(\frac{1 + \varrho}{2}\right)[1 - \sqrt{1 - 4(1 + \delta)^{-1}(1 + \varrho)^{-1}}] \qquad 0 < \mu < 1 \tag{7.6c}$$

$$\lambda = \left(\frac{1 + \varrho}{2}\right)[1 + \sqrt{1 - 4(1 + \delta)^{-1}(1 + \varrho^{-1})}] \qquad \lambda > 1. \tag{7.6d}$$

Substituting Equations (7.3) and (7.6) into (7.4) and rearranging yields:

$$W_t = \gamma_{0,0}\left\{\left[u_{0,0}^t + \frac{n}{1 + n}\sum_{k=1}^{\infty}\left(\frac{\mu}{\lambda}\right)^{k}u_{0,k}^t\right]\right.$$

$$+ \sum_{j=-\infty}^{-1}\lambda^{j}\left[u_{j,0}^t + \frac{n}{1 + n}\sum_{k=1}^{\infty}\left(\frac{\mu}{\lambda}\right)^{k}u_{j,k}^t\right]$$

$$+ \left.\sum_{j=1}^{\infty}\mu^{j}\left[u_{j,0}^t + \frac{n}{1 + n}\sum_{k=1}^{\infty}\left(\frac{\mu}{\lambda}\right)^{k}u_{j,k}^t\right]\right\}. \tag{7.7}$$

Having expressed the utility function (7.1) in terms of Equation (7.7), with $\gamma_{0,0}$, μ and λ given by Equations (7.6a) and (7.6c, d), I now turn to the lifetime budget constraint of the representative *i*th member of generation *t*: where there is no ambiguity, the superscript *i* is omitted.

$$\left(\frac{B_{t-1}}{1 + n} - G_t^i + w_t - c_t^1 - \tau_t^1\right)(1 + r_{t+1}) \geq c_t^2 + B_t - \sum_{j=1}^{1+n}G_{t+1}^j + \tau_t^2 \tag{7.8}$$

B_t is the total bequest left in the second period of her life by the *i*th member of generation *t* to her $1 + n$ children. The bequest is assumed to be shared equally among the children. G_{t+1}^j is the gift given by the *j*th child ($j = 0, 1, \ldots, 1 + n$) born in period $t + 1$ to his parent. w_t is the real wage earned while young. Each worker-consumer only works during the first period of his life and supplies labor inelastically during that period. A lump sum per capita tax or transfer is paid (received) during one's youth, τ_t^1, and during old age, τ_t^2. r_{t+1} is the one-period real interest rate established in period t. Equation (7.8) will hold as a strict equality.

Note that Equation (7.8) does not include gifts to siblings, to more distant lateral relatives (cousins, etc.) or to more distant (non-lineal) relatives in generations $t - 1$ and $t + 1$. Kimball (1987a) shows (see Equation (7.6b)) that while with $n > 1$ one will always care *indirectly* for one's siblings, etc. (because one's parent does) one will always (when all agents of a given generation have the same egoistic utility levels) care less about a sibling than about oneself. Similarly, siblings will carry more weight than more distant lateral relatives and non-lineal relatives will carry less weight than linear relatives of the same age cohort. No one will, when all agents of a given generation have the same egoistic utility, ever give anything to a sibling or to a non-lineal relative.

The consumer maximizes Equation (7.1) by optimally choosing c_t^1, c_t^2, B_t and G_t, subject to constraint (7.8) and

$$c_t^1, c_t^2 \geq 0 \tag{7.9a}$$

$$B_t \geq 0 \tag{7.9b}$$

$$G_t \geq 0. \tag{7.9c}$$

The Inada conditions ensure that condition (7.9c) is satisfied as long as the consumer has positive lifetime resources. Conditions (7.9b) and (7.9c) reflect legal restrictions that rule out the possibility of a private individual 'taxing' her parents or children.

The consumer is competitive in the labor and capital markets and takes taxes to be exogenous. It is also assumed that all relatives of a given type (j,k) have the same egoistic utilities and behave in the same manner.

To obtain a well-defined unique solution, many further restrictions must be imposed on the 'games' the household plays with members of other generations. The following assumptions are made.

Intergenerational Nash behavior
A member of generation t takes B_{t-1} and G_{t+1}^j, $j = 0, 1, \ldots, 1 + n$, as given (i.e. as independent of her choices of c_t^1, c_t^2, B_t and G_t). Note that this is not trivial, as the bequest B_{t-1} is left in period t simultaneously with c_t^1 and G_t, while the gifts G_{t+1}^j, $j = 0, \ldots, 1 + n$, are given in period $t + 1$ after c_t^1 and G_t and simultaneously with c_t^2 and B_t. This intergenerational Nash assumption is by no means overwhelmingly plausible, but simplifies the analysis greatly.

Further strategic conjectures are required as regards the behavior of one's siblings, if there is more than one child (see Abel, 1985; and Kimball, 1987a; 1987b), ($n \geq 0$). I will consider the following two.

Sibling Nash gift behavior
This means that the siblings of the ith child born in generation t are assumed not to change their gift behavior when the ith child changes its consumption, gift or bequest behavior:

$$\frac{\partial G_t^j}{\partial G_t^i} = \frac{\partial G_t^j}{\partial c_t^1} = \frac{\partial G_t^j}{\partial c_t^2} = \frac{\partial G_t^j}{\partial B_t} = 0; j = 1, \ldots, 1 + n, j \neq i.^7$$

Abel (1985) favors this assumption.

Co-operative sibling gift behavior
Kimball (1987b, p. 316) proposes a co-operative solution among siblings in which each sibling agrees to give exactly the same amount that each of the others gives while one of them decides the total amount to be given. The agent who decides the total amount to be given to the common parent simply maximizes her own *total* utility and therefore effectively values the egoistic utility loss of each of her n siblings only $\mu/[(1 + n)\lambda]$ as much as her own egoistic utility loss (see Equation (7.6b) with $j = 0$ and $k = 0$ (own utility) versus $j = 0$ and $k = 1$ (sibling utility)). This kind of behavior is probably better characterized as *imitative* rather than as *co-operative*.

Let i be the 'leader', then:

$$\frac{\partial G_t^j}{\partial c_t^1} = \frac{\partial G_t^j}{\partial c_t^2} = \frac{\partial G_t^j}{\partial B_t} = 0; j = 1, \ldots, 1 + n, j \neq i$$

and

$$\frac{\partial G_t^j}{\partial G_t^i} = 1; j = 1, \ldots, 1 + n; j \neq i.$$

Extended Nash behavior
The consumption choices of relatives of type (j, k) other than siblings are affected by the choices of the current generation only if the latter directly affect their budget constraints. Formally we assume that:

$$\frac{\partial u_{j,k}^t}{\partial c_t^1} = \frac{\partial u_{j,k}^t}{\partial c_t^2} = 0; \quad \begin{array}{l} j \leq -1 \text{ and } k \geq 0; \quad j \geq 1 \text{ and } k \geq 0; \\ k \geq 1 \text{ and } j = 0. \end{array} \tag{7.10a}$$

$$\frac{\partial u_{j,k}^t}{\partial B_t} = 0; \quad \begin{array}{l} j \leq -1 \text{ and } k \geq 0; \quad j > 1 \text{ and } k \geq 0; \\ k \geq 1 \text{ and } j = 0; \quad k > 1 \text{ and } j = 1. \end{array} \tag{7.10b}$$

$$\frac{\partial u_{j,k}^t}{\partial G_t} = 0; \quad \begin{array}{l} j < -1 \text{ and } k \geq 0; \quad j \geq 1 \text{ and } k \geq 0; \\ k \geq 1 \text{ and } j = 0; \quad k > 1 \text{ and } j = -1. \end{array} \tag{7.10c}$$

This assumption that changes in c_t^1, c_t^2, B_t and G_t only affect the consumption of relatives (other than siblings) if these relatives' lifetime budget constraints are directly affected[8] is implicit in Kimball (1987a; 1987b). It is discussed at greater length in Carmichael (1979) and Buiter (1980).

Given all this, the maximization of Equation (7.7) subject to Equation (7.8) (holding as a strict equality) and Equation (7.9) yields:

$$\frac{\partial}{\partial c_t^1} [u_{0,0}^t(c_t^1, c_t^2)] = (1 + r_{t+1})\frac{\partial}{\partial c_t^2} [u_{0,0}^t(c_t^1, c_t^2)] \tag{7.11a}$$

$$\frac{\partial}{\partial c_t^2} [u_{0,0}^t(c_t^1, c_t^2)] \geq \frac{\mu}{1 + n} \frac{\partial}{\partial c_t^1} [u_{1,0}^t(c_{t+1}^1, c_{t+1}^2)]. \tag{7.11b}$$

If $B_t > 0$ then Equation (7.11b) holds with equality. If Equation (7.11b) holds as a strict inequality, then $B_t = 0$.

With Nash sibling gift behavior we also have

$$\frac{\partial}{\partial c_t^1} [u_{0,0}^t(c_t^1, c_t^2)] \geq \lambda^{-1} \frac{\partial}{\partial c_{t-1}^2} [u_{-1,0}^t(c_{t+1}^1, c_{t+1}^2)]. \tag{7.11c}$$

If $G_t > 0$ then Equation (7.11c) holds with equality. If Equation (7.11c) holds as a strict inequality, then $G_t = 0$.

With co-operative sibling gift behavior we have instead (see Kimball, 1987a; 1987b):

$$\frac{\partial}{\partial c_t^1} [u_{0,0}^t(c_t^1, c_t^2)] + \frac{n}{1 + n} \frac{\mu}{\lambda} \frac{\partial}{\partial c_t^1} [u_{0,1}^t(c_t^1, c_t^2)]$$

$$\geq (1 + n)\lambda^{-1} \frac{\partial}{\partial c_{t-1}^2} [u_{-1,0}^t(c_{t-1}^1, c_{t-1}^2)]. \tag{7.11d}$$

If $G_t > 0$ then Equation (7.11d) holds with equality. If Equation (7.11d) holds as a strict inequality, then $G_t = 0$.

Using Equation (7.11a), Equation (7.11b) can be rewritten as:

$$\frac{\partial}{\partial c_t^2} [u_{0,0}^t(c_t^1, c_t^2)] \geq \frac{\mu}{1 + n} (1 + r_{t+2})\frac{\partial}{\partial c_t^2} [u_{1,0}^t(c_{t+1}^1, c_{t+1}^2)]. \tag{7.12a}$$

Equality holds if $B_t > 0$; if strict inequality holds, then $B_t = 0$. Equations (7.11c) and (7.11d) can be rewritten as:

$$\frac{\partial}{\partial c_t^1} [u_{0,0}^t(c_t^1, c_t^2)] \geq \frac{\lambda^{-1}}{1 + r_t} \frac{\partial}{\partial c_{t-1}^1} [u_{-1,0}^t(c_{t-1}^1, c_{t-1}^2)] \quad \text{(Nash)} \tag{7.12b}$$

$$\frac{\partial}{\partial c_t^1} [u_{0,0}^t(c_t^1, c_t^2)] + \frac{n}{1 + n} \frac{\mu}{\lambda} \frac{\partial}{\partial c_t^1} [u_{0,1}^t(c_t^1, c_t^2)]$$

$$\geq (1 + n)\frac{\lambda^{-1}}{1 + r_t}\frac{\partial}{\partial c_{t-1}^1} [u_{-1,0}^t(c_{t-1}^1, c_{t-1}^2)] \quad \text{(Co-operative)}. \tag{7.12c}$$

Again, equality holds if $G_t > 0$; if strict inequality holds, then $G_t = 0$.

In a stationary equilibrium with an operative intergenerational bequest motive ($B > 0$) Equation (7.13) must hold:

$$\frac{1 + r}{1 + n} = \frac{1}{\mu} \tag{7.13}$$

Since $0 < \mu < 1$, this means that Proposition 1 holds, as shown in Carmichael (1979), Buiter (1980) and Kimball (1987a; 1987b):

Proposition 1. Any stationary state in which a bequest motive is operative is dynamically efficient, i.e. the interest rate, r, exceeds the population growth rate, n.

Note that if there is only the bequest motive $((1 + \varrho)^{-1} = 0)$, Equation (7.13) reduces to $(1 + r)/(1 + n) = 1 + \delta$.

Weil (1987) shows that dynamic inefficiency of the economy without bequest motive is sufficient to rule out operative bequests in the economy with a bequest motive[9] both for an endowment economy and in the Diamond (1965) production economy.

Similarly, in a stationary equilibrium with an operative intergenerational gift motive $(G > 0)$, Equation (7.14a) must hold in the case of Nash sibling gift behavior and Equation (7.14b) must hold in the case of cooperative sibling gift behavior

$$1 + r = \frac{1}{\lambda} \qquad \text{(Nash)} \qquad (7.14a)$$

$$\frac{1 + r}{1 + n} = \frac{1}{\lambda \left(1 + \dfrac{n}{1 + n} \dfrac{\mu}{\lambda}\right)}. \qquad \text{(Cooperative)} \qquad (7.14b)$$

Since $\lambda > 1$, $\mu > 0$ and $n \geq 0$, it follows that Proposition 2, holds as shown in Carmichael (1979), Buiter (1980) and Kimball (1987a; 1987b):

Proposition 2. Any steady state in which a child-to-parent gift motive is operative is dynamically inefficient (r < n).

Note that if there is only the gift motive $((1 + \delta)^{-1} = 0)$, Equation (7.14a) becomes $1 + r = (1 + \varrho)^{-1}$, and Equation (7.14b) becomes

$$\frac{1 + r}{1 + n} = (1 + \varrho)^{-1}$$

As shown in Kimball (1987a; 1987b), a constant proportional rate of growth of steady-state per capita income π can be incorporated easily into the analysis if the egoistic utility function assumes the constant elasticity of marginal utility form given in Equation (7.15)

$$u(c_t^1, c_t^2) = \frac{1}{1 - \alpha}(c_t^1)^{1-\alpha} + \frac{\beta}{1 - \alpha}(c_t^2)^{1-\alpha} \qquad \alpha > 0; \quad \beta > 0. \tag{7.15}$$

In steady state, consumption will grow at the constant rate π, i.e. $c_t^1 =$

$(1 + \pi)c^1_{t-1}$ and $c^2_t = (1 + \pi)c^2_{t-1}$. Equation (7.12a) becomes, with $B > 0$,

$$\frac{1 + r}{(1 + n)(1 + \pi)} = \frac{1}{\mu}\left(\frac{1}{1 + \pi}\right)^{(1-\alpha)}. \tag{7.16a}$$

With $G > 0$, Equations (7.12b) and (7.12c) become respectively (in steady state):

$$\frac{1 + r}{(1 + n)(1 + \pi)} = \frac{1}{\lambda(1 + n)}\left(\frac{1}{1 + \pi}\right)^{(1-\alpha)} \quad \text{(Nash)} \tag{7.16b}$$

$$\frac{1 + r}{(1 + n)(1 + \pi)} = \frac{1}{\lambda\left(1 + \dfrac{n}{1 + n}\dfrac{\mu}{\lambda}\right)}\left(\frac{1}{1 + \pi}\right)^{(1-\alpha)} \text{(Cooperative)}. \tag{7.16c}$$

Note that with α, the elasticity of marginal utility, greater than 1, a sufficiently large per capita income growth rate (high value of π) will ensure dynamic efficiency $(1 + r > (1 + n)(1 + \pi))$ in a steady state with operative gifts. $\alpha \leq 1$ will ensure inefficiency of a steady state with operative gifts if $\pi > 0$.

It might appear from Equation (7.16a) that with $\pi > 0$ and $\alpha < 1$ we might get dynamic inefficiency $(1 + r < (1 + n)(1 + \pi))$ with an operative bequest motive. As pointed out in Kimball (1987a; 1987b), this is not in fact the case, since Equation (7.16a) no longer characterizes a privately optimal plan if $1 + r < (1 + n)(1 + \pi)$. The total utility functional no longer converges and even the overtaking criterion cannot be used to rank feasible paths.

7.2.2 Production and market equilibrium

The production technology is identical to that in Diamond (1965). A single homogeneous durable commodity is produced by a well-behaved neoclassical production function which is linear homogeneous in capital and labor. Productivity growth is omitted for simplicity.

$$Y_t = F(K_t, L_t). \tag{7.17}$$

F is increasing, strictly concave, twice continuously differentiable and satisfies the Inada conditions. L_t is the size of the labor force in period t, i.e. the number of (young) members of the generation born in period t; $L_t = (1 + n)L_{t-1}$. Let $y_t \equiv Y_t/L_t$ and $k_t \equiv K_t/L_t$. Equation (7.17) can be rewritten in intensive form as follows:

$$y_t = f(k_t) \quad f' > 0; f'' < 0; f(0) = 0; \lim_{k\to 0} f'(k) = +\infty; \lim_{k\to\infty} f'(k) = 0. \tag{7.17a}$$

The labor market and the capital rental market clear and are competitive:

$$w_t = f(k_t) - k_t f'(k_t) \tag{7.18}$$

$$r_t = f'(k_t). \tag{7.19}$$

Output market equilibrium is given by

$$c_t^1 L_t + c_{t-1}^2 L_{t-1} + E_t + K_{t+1} - K_t = Y_t \tag{7.20}$$

where E_t denotes total public consumption expenditure in period t. From the public sector budget identity given in Equation (7.21) it follows that Equation (7.20) can be replaced by the equivalent Equation (7.22). D_t denotes the stock of public debt outstanding at the end of period $t - 1$. Debt has a fixed face value of unity and a maturity of one period.

$$E_t + r_t D_t - \tau_t^1 L_t - \tau_{t-1}^2 L_{t-1} = D_{t+1} - D_t \tag{7.21}$$

$$\left(w - c_t^1 - \tau_t^1 + \frac{B_{t-1}}{1+n} - G_t \right) L_t = D_{t+1} + K_{t+1}. \tag{7.22}$$

Equation (7.22) states that the savings of the young in period t have to equal the sum of the capital stock and the public debt stock in period $t + 1$. Letting $d_t \equiv D_t/L_t$ and $e_t \equiv E_t/L_t$, Equations (7.21) and (7.22) can be rewritten as:

$$e_t + r_t d_t - \tau_t^1 - \underbrace{\tau_{t-1}^2}_{1+n} = (1+n)d_{t+1} - d_t \tag{7.21a}$$

$$w_t - c_t^1 - \tau_t^1 + \underbrace{B_{t-1}}_{1+n} - G_t = (d_{t+1} + k_{t+1})(1+n). \tag{7.22a}$$

7.2.3 Stationary equilibrium

A stationary equilibrium is characterized by equations 7.23–7.28. In Equation (7.25) co-operative sibling gift behavior is assumed.

$$u_1(c^1, c^2) = (1 + f'(k))u_2(c^1, c^2) \tag{7.23}$$

$$\frac{1 + f'(k)}{1 + n} \leq \frac{1}{\mu} \tag{7.24}$$

Equation 7.24 holds with equality if $B > 0$; if it holds with strict inequality then $B = 0$.

$$\frac{1 + f'(k)}{1 + n} \geq \frac{1}{\lambda \left(1 + \dfrac{n}{1+n} \dfrac{\mu}{\lambda} \right)} \tag{7.25}$$

Equation 7.25 holds with equality if $G > 0$; if it holds with strict inequality then $G = 0$.

$$(f(k) - kf'(k) - c^1)(1 + f'(k)) =$$

$$c^2 + \tau^1(1 + f'(k)) + \tau^2 + (n - f'(k))\left[\frac{B}{1+n} - G\right] \quad (7.26)$$

$$w - c^1 - \tau^1 + \frac{B}{1+n} - G = (d + k)(1 + n) \quad (7.27)$$

$$e - \tau^1 - \frac{\tau^2}{1+n} = (n - f'(k))d. \quad (7.28)$$

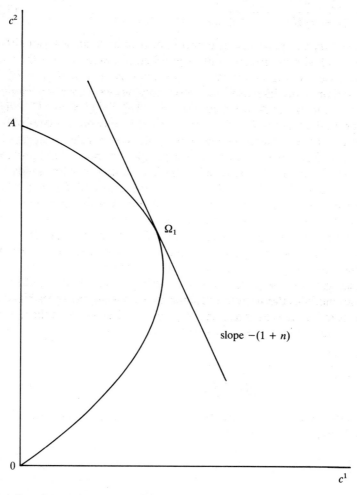

Figure 7.1 Stationary competitive possibility locus without gifts and bequests and without government

When there is no gift or bequest motive $((1 + \delta)^{-1} = (1 + \varrho)^{-1} = 0$ and $B = G = 0)$ nor a public sector $(\tau^1 = \tau^2 = e = d = 0)$, Equations (7.26) and (7.27) can be solved for c^2 as a function of c^1 as in Equation (7.29):

$$c^2 = \psi(c^1), \tag{7.29}$$

with

$$\psi' = -(1 + f')\left[1 + \frac{k(n - f')}{1 + f'}f''(1 + n + kf'')^{-1}\right]. \tag{7.30a}$$

In the case of a Cobb–Douglas production function with $f(k) = k^{\bar{a}}, 0 < \bar{a} < 1$,

$$\psi' = \frac{(1 + n)(1 + \bar{a}^2 k^{(\bar{a}-1)})}{(1 - \bar{a})\bar{a}k^{\bar{a}-1} - (1 + n)}. \tag{7.30b}$$

The stationary competitive consumption possibility locus without gifts and bequests and without government, is graphed in Figure 7.1 for the Cobb–Douglas case. At the origin $(k = 0)$ its slope is $(1 + n)\bar{a}/(1 - \bar{a})$. The capital–labor ratio increases monotonically as we move up along the locus from 0 to A. At A, when $c_1 = 0$ again, $1 + r = (1 + \bar{a}n)/(1 - \bar{a})$ and the slope of the locus is $\bar{a} - 1 - \bar{a}^2(1 + n) < 0$. For small values of $\bar{a}$, the interest rate at A is therefore below the golden rule value n (if $n > 0$). If $\bar{a} > n/(1 + 2n)$, then even the lowest possible stationary interest rate is always above the golden rule value. It is assumed in what follows that $\bar{a} < n/(1 + 2n)$. The golden rule capital–labor ratio k^* defined by $f'(k^*) = n$ therefore defines a point somewhere on the downward portion of the locus, such as Ω_1. The locus is strictly concave towards the origin. For more general constant returns to scale production functions than the Cobb–Douglas, ψ' can become positive again for large k. Such a backward and downward-bending locus represents a case of extreme overaccumulation.[10]

Adding gifts and bequests but still omitting government spending, debt and taxes modifies the stationary competitive consumption possibility locus as in Figure 7.2. It is assumed that $\bar{a} < n/(1 + 2n)$ and that there exists a feasible value of k, k^G say, such that

$$\frac{1 + f'(k^G)}{1 + n} = \frac{1}{\lambda\left(1 + \dfrac{n}{1 + n}\dfrac{\mu}{\lambda}\right)}$$

(the condition for $G > 0$). In that case there certainly exists a feasible value of k, k^B say, such that $B > 0$, i.e.

$$\frac{1 + f'(k^B)}{1 + n} = \frac{1}{\mu}.$$

Note that bequests and child-to-parent gifts cannot be positive simultaneously in steady state.

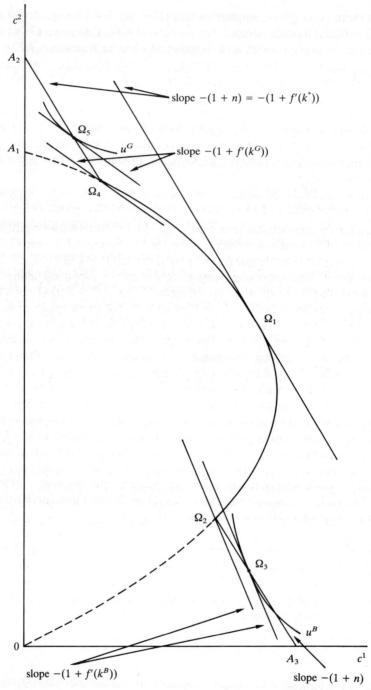

Figure 7.2 Stationary competitive possibility locus with gifts and bequests but without government

The stationary competitive consumption possibility locus with bequests and gifts is obtained by deleting from the stationary competitive consumption possibility locus without bequests and gifts the segment corresponding to capital–labor ratios above k^B (i.e. the dotted segment $O\Omega_2$) and the segment corresponding to capital–labor ratios above k^G (i.e. the dotted segment $\Omega_4 A_2$).

From Ω_2 to A_3 the straight line segment with slope $-(1 + n)$ gives the locus where bequests are positive. With k given, $\partial c^1/\partial B = 1/(1 + n)$ and $\partial c^2/\partial B = -1$. Along the positive bequest locus therefore, $dc^2/dc^1 = -(1 + n)$. Larger bequests correspond to movements towards the southeast along $\Omega_2 A_3$.

From Ω_4 to A_2 the straight line segment with slope $-(1 + n)$ gives the locus where child-to-parent gifts are positive. With k given, $\partial c^1/\partial G = -1$ and $dc^2/dG = 1 + n$ so again $\partial c^2/\partial c^1 = -(1 + n)$. Larger gifts correspond to movement to the north-west along $\Omega_4 A_2$.

The complete stationary competitive consumption possibility locus with gifts and bequests is therefore given by the curve $A_3\Omega_2\Omega_4 A_2$ and consists of three segments: the positive bequest locus $A_3\Omega_2$ where $(1 + f'(k^B)) = (1 + n)/\mu$; the locus with zero bequest and zero gift, $\Omega_2\Omega_4$, corresponding to the segment of the original no gift or bequest locus with $k^B > k > k^G$; and the positive gift locus $\Omega_4 A_2$, where

$$(1 + f'(k^G)) = \frac{1 + n}{\lambda\left(1 + \dfrac{n}{1 + n}\dfrac{\mu}{\lambda}\right)}.$$

A typical steady state with positive bequest has been drawn at Ω_3 where the indifference curve u^B has a tangent to an intertemporal budget constraint with slope $-(1 + f'(k^B))$.[11] A typical steady state with positive gift has been drawn at Ω_5 where the indifference curve u^G has a tangent to an intertemporal budget constraint with slope $-(1 + f'(k^G))$.[12] Stationary equilibria with zero gift and zero bequest on the segment $\Omega_2\Omega_4$ could either have the interest rate above the golden rule level (on $\Omega_2\Omega_1$) or below it (on $\Omega_1\Omega_4$).

For reasons of space, the analysis of fiscal policy will be focused on the consideration of steady states, with but a brief excursion into non-steady-state behavior. τ^2, e and d will be treated as steady-state policy parameters. τ^1 adjusts endogenously to satisfy the steady-state government budget identity given in Equation (7.31):

$$\tau^1 = e - \frac{\tau^2}{1 + n} + (f'(k) - n)d. \tag{7.31}$$

The substitution of Equation (7.31) into the steady-state private lifetime budget constraint and capital market equilibrium condition yields Equations (7.32) and (7.33):

$$f(k) - kf'(k) - c^1 - e$$

$$= k(1 + n) - \left[\frac{\tau^2}{1 + n} + \frac{B}{1 + n} - G - (1 + f'(k))d\right] \qquad (7.32)$$

$$f(k) - kf'(k) - c^1 - e = (1 + f'(k))^{-1}\left[c^2 + (n - f'(k))\left(\frac{\tau^2}{1 + n}\right.\right.$$

$$\left.\left. + \frac{B}{1 + n} - G - (1 + f'(k))d\right)\right]. \qquad (7.33)$$

Outside the steady state, the fiscal policy parameters τ^2, d and e can be governed by any rules that are consistent with convergence to the steady state. We consider three policy experiments: (1) an increase in the debt stock, financial with taxes on the young or on the young and the old; (2) a balanced budget increase in unfunded social security payments to the old financed by higher taxes on the young; (3) an increase in exhaustive public spending financed by a tax on the young. The last experiment is not concerned with debt neutrality, as exhaustive public spending is varied, but is interesting in its own right.

7.2.4 Steady-state comparative statics of debt neutrality

From Equations (7.32) and (7.33), note that, holding k constant, $\partial c^1/\partial d = -(1 + f')$ and $\partial c^2/\partial d = (1 + f')(1 + n)$. Again, therefore, $\partial c^2/\partial c^1 = -(1 + n)$. A larger stock of public debt financed with taxes on the young (with τ^1 increasing if $f' > n$ and decreasing if $f' < n$) acts just like a reduction in benefits (when $B > 0$) or an increase in child-to-parent gifts (when $G > 0$). In general, it shifts the stationary competitive consumption possibility locus in Figure 7.3 from $A_3\Omega_2\Omega_1\Omega_4A_2$ up and to the left to $A_3\Omega_2'\Omega_1\Omega_4'A_2$.

A larger stock of public debt financed in steady state with higher taxes on the old, has, at given k, the following effects on consumption while young and while old on the locus: $\partial c^1/\partial d = -(1 + n)$; $\partial c^2/\partial d^2/(1 + n)^2$, so again $\partial c^2/\partial c^1 = -(1 + n)$.

A balanced budget increase in τ^1 and reduction in τ^2, i.e. an increase in the scale of an unfunded social security retirement scheme, has the following effect on the locus at given k: $-\partial c^1/\partial \tau^2 = -1/(1 + n)$ and $-\partial c^2/\partial \tau^2 = 1$. Like a larger stock of debt, it therefore shifts the locus to the northwest.

At given k, an increase in public consumption financed with taxes on the young simply shifts the consumption possibility locus to the left one-for-one: $\partial c^1/\partial e = -1$ and $\partial c^2/\partial e = 0$.

The following results are immediately apparent. For public debt increases financed by taxing the young, Propositions 3a, 3b and 3c hold:

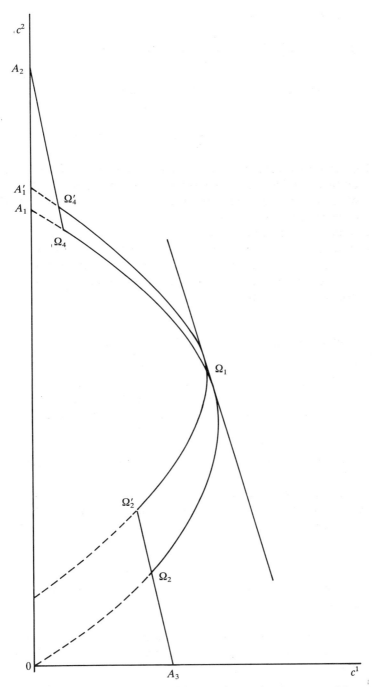

Figure 7.3 Effect of public debt on the stationary competitive consumption possibility locus

Proposition 3a. When the bequest motive is operative (B > 0 and r > n) a larger stock of public debt financed with higher taxes on the young will be offset by larger bequests: $\Delta B = ((1 + r)/(1 + n))\Delta d$; c^1, c^2, and k will be unaffected. A smaller stock of public debt financed with lower taxes on the young will be offset by smaller bequests as long as $-((1 + r)/(1 + n))\Delta d$ does not exceed the initial bequest and the B ≥ 0 constraint does not become binding.

Proposition 3b. When the gift motive is operative (G > 0 and r < n), a larger stock of public debt 'financed' with higher transfer payments to the young[13] will be offset by reduced child-to-parent gifts as long as $(1 + r)\Delta d$ does not exceed the initial child-to-parent gift and the G ≥ 0 constraint does not become binding; $\Delta G = -(1 + r)\Delta d$. *A smaller stock of public debt financed with higher taxes on the young will be offset by increased child-to-parent gifts.*

If neither the bequest motive nor the gift motive is operative ($B = 0$ and $G = 0$), if we are in the interior of the no gift and no bequest region initially, in the new steady state and during the adjustment process consumption is the same as in the Diamond (1965) model and can be written as:

$$c_t^1 = c^1(w_t - \tau_t^1, \tau_t^2, r_{t+1}) \tag{7.34a}$$

$$c_t^2 = (1 + r_{t+1})(w_t - c_t^1 - \tau_t^1) - \tau_t^2. \tag{7.34b}$$

Proposition 3c (Diamond, 1965). When neither the bequest motive nor the gift motive is operative, the long-run effect of a higher public debt stock (financed with taxes on the young) on the capital–labour ratio is given by

$$\frac{\partial k}{\partial d} = \frac{[1 + c_w^1 n + (1 - c_w^1)r](1 + n)^{-1}}{(c_w^1 - 1)f''(k + d) - (1 + n + f''c_r^1)}. \tag{7.35}$$

If the model is locally stable when d is kept constant throughout, with τ_t^1 varying endogenously to keep the budget balanced, if both goods are normal ($0 < c_w^1 < 1$) and if a higher interest rate does not raise consumption in period 1 ($c_r^1 \leq 0$), then the denominator of Equation (7.35) is negative, and if $r, n > 0$, $\partial k/\partial d < 0$, public debt crowds out private capital.

For public debt increases financed by taxing the old, Propositions 4a, 4b and 4c hold:

Proposition 4a. When the bequest motive is operative (B > 0 and r > n) a larger stock of public debt financed with higher taxes on the old will be offset by larger bequests $\Delta B = (1 + n)^2 \Delta d$. *A smaller stock of public debt 'financed' with lower taxes on the old will be offset by smaller bequests as long as* $-(1 + n)^2 \Delta d$ *does not exceed the initial bequest.*

Proposition 4b. When the child-to-parent gift motive is operative (G > 0 and r < n) a larger stock of public debt financed with higher transfer payments to the old will be offset by reduced child-to-parent gifts; $\Delta G = -(1 + n)\Delta d$ as long as $(1 + n)\Delta d$ does not exceed the initial child-to-parent gift.

A smaller stock of public debt financed with higher taxes on the old will be offset by increased child-to-parent gifts.

Proposition 4c. When neither the bequest motive nor the gift motive are operative, the effect on the long-run capital–labor ratio of an increase in public debt financed with taxes on the old is given by:

$$\frac{\partial k}{\partial d} = \frac{(1 + n)(1 + c_w^1 n + (1 - c_w^1)r)(1 + r)^{-1}}{\left[(c_w^1 - 1)k + \dfrac{c_w^1}{1 + r}(1 + n)d\right]f'' - (1 + n + c_r^1 f'')};^{14} \quad (7.36)$$

Local stability when d is constant implies

$$\left|\left[(c_w^1 - 1)k + \frac{c_w^1}{1 + r}(1 + n)d\right]f''(1 + n + c_r^1 f'')^{-1}\right| < 1.$$

Even with $0 < c_w^1 < 1$ and $c_r^1 \leq 0$, this does not suffice to ensure that the denominator of Equation (7.36) is negative as $(c_w^1 - 1)k + (c_w^1/((1 + r)^{-1}(1 + n)d))$ could be positive. It is clear that the smaller c_w^1 and the smaller d, the more likely it is that $\partial k/\partial d < 0$, but the opposite outcome cannot be ruled out in the present case.

When equal taxes are levied on the old and the young ($\tau^1 = \tau^2$) a higher level of public debt when the bequest motive is operative leads to an increase in bequests given by $\Delta B = ((2 + r)/(2 + n))\Delta d$. When the gift motive is operative gifts are cut (if they are large enough initially) by $\Delta G = -(1 + n)(2 + r)/(2 + n)\Delta d$. When neither altruistic motive is operative, crowding out of private capital by public debt again follows under conditions that are more restrictive than when only the young were taxed and less restrictive than when only the old were taxed.

An increase in taxes on the young (τ^1) with τ^2 lowered to maintain budget balance continuously acts exactly like an increase in public debt with τ^1 endogenously maintaining budget balance. When the bequest motive is operative, bequests are increased by $\Delta B = (1 + n)\Delta\tau^1$. When the gift motive is operative, gifts are cut (assuming they are sufficiently large initially) by $\Delta G = -\Delta\tau^1$. When neither motive is operative, the effect of the increase in the scale of the unfunded social security retirement scheme (assuming for simplicity that $d = 0$) is

$$\frac{\partial k}{\partial \tau^1} = \frac{[1 + c_w^1 n + (1 - c_w^1)r](1 + r)^{-1}}{(c_w^1 - 1)kf'' - [1 + n + c_r^1 f'']}. \quad (7.37)$$

Again local stability, a non-positive effect of r on c^1, normality of c^1 and r, $n > 0$ are sufficient to guarantee a lower capital–labor ratio as a result of higher social security taxes and retirement benefits.

7.2.5 Debt neutrality outside the steady state

It is easily checked that all the neutrality propositions (such as Propositions 3 and 4 that apply to stationary equilibria extend to non-steady-state responses as long as the policy action or other exogenous shock does not alter the 'regimes' (the gift or bequest constraints that are binding and which may vary from generation to generation), for current and future generations. Consider an unexpected immediate permanent change in d (financed with an increase in τ^1) in period t. The intertemporal consistency of child-to-parent gift and bequest behavior (see Burbridge, 1983; and Buiter and Carmichael, 1984) rules out the possibility of any two generations simultaneously wishing to make voluntary transfers to each other, i.e. $G_t > 0 \Rightarrow B_{t-1} = 0$; $B_{t-1} > 0 \Rightarrow G_t = 0$; $B_t > 0 \Rightarrow G_{t+1} = 0$ and $G_{t+1} > 0 \Rightarrow B_t = 0$. Any given generation, t say, may of course wish both to make a gift to its parent and to leave a bequest to its children if, absent the gift and bequest, the welfare of parent and children would be very different from its own (reflecting, say, differences in endowments, taxes or factor prices). That is, $G_t > 0$ may be consistent with $B_t > 0$. In a stationary equilibrium this is ruled out; Equations (7.13) and (7.14a) or (7.14b) cannot hold simultaneously.

When, in any given period t, the gift and bequest motives of generation t, the bequest motive of generation $t - 1$ and the gift motive of generation $t + 1$ are non-operative (before and after a policy change or shock) the dynamic analysis of the Diamond (1965) model is applicable for that period. For example, when d is raised in period t (financed with a tax on the young), the response of the capital stock is given by

$$\frac{\partial k_{t+1}}{\partial d} = \frac{[1 + c_w^1 n + (1 - c_w^1)r](1 + n)^{-1}}{-(1 + n + c_r^1 f'')}.$$

This is negative if $0 < c_w^1 < 1, c_r^1 \leq 0$ and $r, n > 0$, so public debt crowds out the private capital stock in the short run as well.

7.2.6 Debt neutrality and exhaustive public spending

The presence or absence of debt neutrality has implications for the analysis of fiscal policy experiments other than those involving public debt and lump-sum taxes.

In steady state, when the bequest motive is operative, the successive generations of consumers are in many respects equivalent to the standard model of a single representative infinite-lived consumer with an exogenous pure rate of time preference who discounts his future utility of consumption. One of the key similarities is that the long-run real interest rate is fixed by policy-invariant parameters: $1 + r = (1 + n)(1/(1 + \pi))^{-\alpha}1/\mu$ in the OLG model with an operative bequest motive; $1 + r = (1 + \delta^1)$ $(1/(1 + \pi))^{-\alpha}$ in the representative agent model with a pure rate of time preference δ^1.

If in steady state the gift motive is operative, the aggregate behavior of the successive generations is equivalent to that of a single representative infinite-lived consumer with an exogenous rate of negative time preference, i.e. one who *discounts* his past utility of consumption. For the positive analysis of changes in exhaustive public spending it is immaterial that with $G > 0$ we have the equivalent of the standard representative consumer standing on his head. All that matters is that the real interest rate is again fixed by policy-invariant parameters when sibling gift behavior is operative, i.e.:

$$1 + r = (1 + n) \left(\frac{1}{1 + \pi} \right)^{-\alpha} \frac{1}{\lambda \left(1 + \frac{n}{1 + n} \frac{\mu}{\lambda} \right)}.$$

When neither the gift motive nor the bequest motive is operative, a higher level of exhaustive public spending (financed, say, with taxes on the young) will lead to a lower long-run capital stock and a higher real interest rate if the model is locally stable.

$$\frac{\partial k}{\partial e} = \frac{1 - c_w^1}{(c_w^1 - 1)f''k - (1 + n + c_r^1 f'')} < 0 \qquad \text{if } 0 < c_w^1 < 1 \text{ and } c_r^1 \leq 0.^{15}$$

(7.38)

c^1 will fall (since w is down, τ^1 is up and r is up) but the effect on c^2 is ambiguous[16] because of the increase in r.

When either the gift or the bequest motive is operative, changes in exhaustive government spending that leave the gift or bequest motive operative do not alter the long-run real interest rate and capital–labor ratio.

In Figure 7.4, higher exhaustive public spending financed with taxes on the young shifts the stationary competitive consumption possibility locus horizontally to the left by the amount of the increase in e and in τ^1. The old locus is $A_1A_2A_3A_4$. The new locus is $A_1'A_2'A_3'A_4'$. If the initial equilibrium has positive bequests (as at Ω_1 on the private budget constraint B_1B_1) the corresponding point on the new locus with the same bequest is Ω_2 on the private budget constraint B_2B_2. If consumption in both periods is a normal good, Ω_2 cannot be an equilibrium since at an unchanged intertemporal relative price the lower after-tax income is reflected only in lower period 1 consumption. Bequests will increase and move the private budget con-

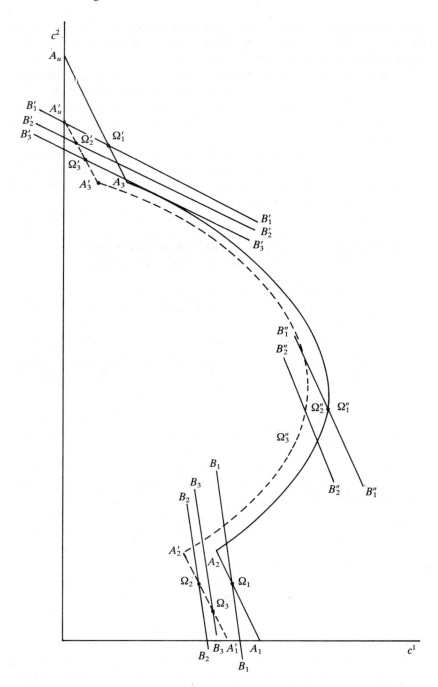

Figure 7.4 An increase in exhaustive public spending financed by taxes on the young

straint to the right. The new equilibrium is at a position such as Ω_3 on the private budget constraint B_3B_3 with both c^1 and c^2 reduced and $u_1(c^1, c^2) = u_2(c^1, c^2)(1 + r)$ in Ω_1 and Ω_3.

When the gift motive is operative as at Ω_1' on the private budget line $B_1'B_1'$, higher exhaustive public spending will, following the same reasoning, lead to a new equilibrium such as Ω_3' on the private budget line $B_3'B_3'$ with both c^1 and c^2 lower than at Ω_1'. Child-to-parent gifts will be lower in Ω_3' than in Ω_1'.

When neither the gift motive nor the bequest motive is operative as at Ω_1'' on $B_1''B_1''$, the new long-run equilibrium following an increase in exhaustive public spending has a higher real interest rate. Ω_2'' on $B_2''B_2''$ is an example of such an equilibrium.

7.3 THE IRRELEVANCE OF FINITE HORIZONS AND UNCERTAIN LIFETIMES FOR DEBT NEUTRALITY

To evaluate the role of finite horizons and uncertain lifetimes for debt neutrality, the OLG model of Section 7.2 is modified in two ways. First, gift and bequest motives are omitted $((1 + \delta)^{-1} = (1 + \varrho)^{-1} = 0)$. Gift and bequest motives could be added to the model to be considered, in which case the analysis that follows can be interpreted as applying only to those equilibria in which gift or bequest motives are non-operative. Second, instead of living for an exogenously given number of periods, N, with certain death at the end of the Nth period, each agent currently alive is given an age- and time-independent probability γ of surviving to the next period. We consider the range $0 < \gamma \leq 1$ so the infinite-lived consumer ($\gamma = 1$) is included in our specification. This OLG model was developed by Blanchard (1985) from a model of consumer behavior with uncertain lifetimes due to Yaari (1965). The individual consumer's discrete time version is from Frenkel and Razin (1986).

7.3.1 The individual consumer

Each individual consumer born at time $t - s$, $s \geq 0$ and alive at time $t \geq s$ maximizes the time-additive objective functional given in Equation (7.39). All consumers of all ages have identical objective functionals.

$$\Omega(t - s, t) = E_t \sum_{i=t}^{\infty} \left(\frac{1}{1 + \theta}\right)^{i-t} u(\bar{c}(t - s, i)) \qquad s \geq 0. \tag{7.39}$$

$\theta > 0$ is the pure rate of time preference. E_t is the expectation operator conditional on information at time t. $\bar{c}$ is individual private consumption, $\bar{a}$ individual non-human wealth, $\bar{w}$ the individual wage rate and $\bar{\tau}$ individual lump-sum taxes on labor income.

Assuming that the uncertainty concerning time of death is the only form of uncertainty, Equation (7.39) can be rewritten as:

$$\Omega(t - s, t) = \sum_{i=t}^{\infty} \left(\frac{1}{1 + \theta}\right)^{i-t} \gamma^{i-t} u(\bar{c}(t - s, i)). \tag{7.39a}$$

The single period utility function is of the constant elasticity of marginal utility class:

$$u(\bar{c}) = \begin{cases} \dfrac{1}{1 - \alpha}\bar{c}^{1-\alpha} & \alpha > 0,\ \alpha \neq 1 \\ \ln \bar{c} & (\alpha = 1). \end{cases} \tag{7.40}$$

The individual's budget identity is given by:

$$\bar{a}(t - s, t + 1) \equiv (1 + r(t + 1))\gamma^{-1}[\bar{a}(t - s, t) + \bar{w}(t - s, t) \\ - \bar{\tau}(t - s, t) - \bar{c}(t - s, t)] \qquad s \geq 0. \tag{7.41}$$

Equation (7.41) reflects the assumption of the existence of an efficient competitive annuity or life insurance market. r is the risk-free single-period real rate of interest. Each agent alive today contracts with a life insurance company to receive a gross rate of return $(1 + r(t + 1))\psi$ on his non-human wealth $\bar{a}$ as long as he survives. If he dies all of $\bar{a}$ accrues to the insurance company. If $\bar{a}$ is negative, the consumer pays a gross premium rate ψ as long as he survives with the debt canceled when he dies. The insurance market is competitive with risk-neutral firms and free entry. Each age cohort is assumed to consist of a large number of identical agents. γ is not only the individual's probability of surviving for one period but also the fraction of each cohort (and therefore of the total population) which survives each period. It follows that $\psi = 1/\gamma$.

We define the market present value factor R as:

$$R(t) \equiv \prod_{i=0}^{t} (1 + r(i))$$

with $R(0) = 1$. Note that $1 + r(t + 1) = \dfrac{R(t + 1)}{R(t)}$.

Solving Equation (7.41) forward in time and imposing the transversality condition in Equation (7.42) we obtain the present value budget constraint (7.43):

$$\lim_{j \to \infty} \gamma^{j-t} \frac{R(t)}{R(j)} \bar{a}(t - s, j) = 0 \tag{7.42}$$

$$\bar{a}(t - s, t) + \bar{h}(t - s, t) \equiv \sum_{i=t}^{\infty} \bar{c}(t - s, i) \gamma^{i-t} \frac{R(t)}{R(i)}. \tag{7.43}$$

Human capital, $\bar{h}$, the present value of after-tax labor income, is given by

$$\bar{h}(t - s, t) \equiv \sum_{i=t}^{\infty} [\bar{w}(t - s, i) - \bar{\tau}(t - s, i)]\gamma^{i-t}\frac{R(t)}{R(i)},\tag{7.44}$$

or, in difference form,

$$\bar{h}(t - s, t + 1) = \frac{R(t + 1)}{R(t)}\gamma^{-1}\{\bar{h}(t - s, t) - [\bar{w}(t - s, t) - \bar{\tau}(t - s, t)]\}.\tag{7.44a}$$

Maximizing Equation (7.39a) with respect to current and future choices of consumption yields the familiar linear consumption function.

$$\bar{c}(t - s, t) = \eta(t)[\bar{a}(t - s, t) + \bar{h}(t - s, t)]\tag{7.45}$$

$$\eta(t) = \begin{cases} \left[\sum_{i=t}^{\infty}\left(\frac{R(t)}{R(i)}\gamma^{i-t}\right)^{\frac{a-1}{a}}\left(\frac{\gamma}{1+\theta}\right)^{(i-t)\frac{1}{a}}\right]^{-1} & \alpha \neq 1 \\ 1 - \dfrac{\gamma}{1+\theta} & \alpha = 1. \end{cases}\tag{7.46}$$

7.3.2 Aggregation

Without loss of generality, let population size at time 0 be $L(0) = 1$. To every person alive in period t, $\beta \geq 0$ identical children are born. I shall refer to β as the birth rate. The size of the surviving cohort at time t which was born at time $t - s$, $s \geq 0$ is $\beta L(t - s)\gamma^s = \beta(1 + \beta)^{t-s}\gamma^t$ as $L(t + 1) = (1 + \beta)\gamma L(t)$.

Note that total population can, if $\beta > 0$, be expressed as the sum of all survivors of all past cohorts:

$$L(t) = (1 + \beta)^t\gamma^t = \begin{cases} \sum_{s=1}^{\infty}\beta(1 - \beta)^{t-s}\gamma^t & \beta > 0 \\ \gamma^t & \beta = 0. \end{cases}$$

Corresponding to any individual agent's stock or flow variable $\bar{v}(t - s, t)$ we define the population aggregate, $V(t)$, by:

$$V(t) \equiv \begin{cases} \sum_{s=1}^{\infty}\beta(1 + \beta)^{t-s}\gamma^t\bar{v}(t - s, t) & \beta > 0 \\ \bar{v}(0, t)\gamma^t & \beta = 0.^{17} \end{cases}\tag{7.47}$$

Each surviving agent, regardless of age, earns the same wage income and pays the same taxes, i.e.

$$\bar{w}(t - s, t) = \bar{w}(t)\qquad s \geq 0$$

$$\bar{\tau}(t - s, t) = \bar{\tau}(t) \qquad s \geqslant 0.$$

It follows that each surviving agent has the same human capital:

$$\bar{h}(t - s, t) = \bar{h}(t) \qquad s \geqslant 0.$$

Noting that $\bar{a}(t, t + 1) = 0$ (people are born with just their human capital) and using the notational convention given in Equation (7.47), aggregate consumption is, by direct consumption, determined by Equations (7.48a)–(7.48c),

$$C(t) = \eta(t)[A(t) + H(t)] \tag{7.48a}$$

$$A(t + 1) = (1 + r(t + 1))[A(t) + W(t) - T(t) - C(t)] \tag{7.48b}$$

$$H(t) = \sum_{i=t}^{\infty} [W(i) - T(i)] \left(\frac{1}{1 + \beta}\right)^{i-t} \frac{R(t)}{R(i)} \tag{7.48c}$$

$$H(t + 1) = (1 + \beta)(1 + r(t + 1))[H(t) - W(t) + T(t)]. \tag{7.48d}$$

Comparing Equations (7.41) and (7.48b) we notice that the intra-private sector payments associated with the insurance scheme from the point of view of the individual cancel out when the behavior of aggregate non-human wealth is concerned: in the aggregate, non-financial wealth earns the riskless rate. Comparing Equations (7.44) or (7.44a) and (7.48c) or (7.48d), we notice that $H(t)$ is the human capital of those currently alive. It excludes the present discounted value of the future after-tax labor income of the 'new entrants', i.e. those born in period t and later. The practical consequence is that the effective single-period discount factors applied by those currently alive to the *aggregate* future expected after-tax labor income stream (which includes the disposable wage income of the 'new entrants'), is raised from $1/(1 + r(t + i))$ to $1/[1 + r(t + i)][1 + \beta]$.

Let there be labor-augmenting productivity growth at a constant proportional rate π. The level of productivity at $t = 0$ equals unity by choice of units. For each population aggregate stock or flow variable V the corresponding quantity 'per unit of labor measured in efficiency units', v, is defined as:

$$v(t) \equiv V(t)[(1 + \pi)(1 + \beta)\gamma]^{-t}. \tag{7.49}$$

Consumption per unit of efficiency labor is therefore governed by:

$$c(t) = \eta(t)[a(t) + h(t)] \tag{7.50a}$$

$$a(t + 1) = \frac{(1 + r(t + 1))}{(1 + \pi)(1 + \beta)\gamma} [a(t) + w(t) - \tau(t) - c(t)] \tag{7.50b}$$

$$h(t) = \sum_{i=t}^{\infty} [w(i) - \tau(i)] \frac{R(t)}{R(i)} [(1 + \pi)\gamma]^{i-t} \tag{7.50c}$$

or

$$h(t + 1) = \frac{(1 + r(t + 1))}{(1 + \pi)\gamma} [h(t) - w(t) + \tau(t)]. \tag{7.50d}$$

Note that aggregate consumption behavior is the same as the behavior of a representative consumer who discounts his future expected labor income using a discount rate in excess of the rate of return on his non-human assets, the excess being equal to the birth rate, β.

7.3.3 The government

As before, $E(t)$ denotes total government consumption spending, T_t total lump-sum taxes net of transfers, and D_t the stock of public debt outstanding at the end of period $t - 1$. The government budget identity is:

$$D(t + 1) = [1 + r(t + 1)][D(t) + E(t) - T(t)].$$

Letting d, e and τ denote public debt, public spending and taxes per unit of efficiency labor, respectively, we have

$$d(t + 1) = \frac{(1 + r(t + 1))}{(1 + \pi)(1 + \beta)\gamma} [d(t) + e(t) - \tau(t)]. \tag{7.51}$$

With the terminal condition

$$\lim_{v \to \infty} d(t + v) \frac{R(t)}{R(v)} [(1 + \pi)(1 + \beta)\gamma]^{v-t} = 0,$$

the budget identity generates the government's present value budget constraint or solvency constraint:

$$d(t) = \sum_{i=t}^{\infty} [\tau(i) - e(i)] \frac{R(t)}{R(i)} [(1 + \pi)(1 + \beta)\gamma]^{i-t}. \tag{7.52}$$

The government's future tax revenue stream consists of taxes levied not only on the survivors among those currently alive, but also on the survivors among cohorts yet to be born.

Debt neutrality in the Yaari–Blanchard–Weil model
There will be no debt neutrality if, holding constant the path of exhaustive public spending, varying the future time path of lump-sum taxes (subject to the constraint that the government remains solvent) will alter private consumption at given current and future wages and interest rates and given the stock of private non-human assets other than government debt. Equivalently (subject to the same conditions) if a change in the initial stock of public debt (with future changes in lump-sum taxes to satisfy Equation (7.52) alters private consumption, there is no debt neutrality.

For simplicity, let non-human wealth consist of the real capital stock and government debt.

$$a \equiv k + d \tag{7.53}$$

k denotes the capital stock per unit of efficiency labor. Substitute for $a(t)$ and $h(t)$ in the consumption function (7.50a) using Equations (7.53) and (7.50c), respectively. Then add and subtract the term

$$\eta(t) \sum_{i=t}^{\infty} e(i) \frac{R(t)}{R(i)} [(1 + \pi)\gamma]^{i-t}$$

and rearrange. This yields

$$c(t) = \eta(t) \left[k(t) + \sum_{i=t}^{\infty} [w(i) - e(i)] \frac{R(t)}{R(i)} [(1 + \pi)\gamma]^{i-t} \right]$$

$$+ \eta(t) \left[d(t) + \sum_{i=t}^{\infty} [\tau(i) - e(i)] \frac{R(t)}{R(i)} [(1 + \pi)\gamma]^{i-t} \right]. \tag{7.54}$$

The first term on the right-hand side of Equation (7.54) represents what consumption would be, given debt neutrality. Current consumption is affected by fiscal policy only through current and anticipated future exhaustive public consumption spending,

$$\left[[-\eta(t) \sum_{i=t}^{\infty} e(i)] \frac{R(t)}{R(i)} [(1 + \pi)\gamma]^{i-t} \right].$$

The second term represents the influence of debt and lump-sum taxes. It is identically zero if and only if the birth rate is zero, i.e. $\beta = 0$, in which case

$$d(t) = \sum_{i=t}^{\infty} [\tau(i) - e(i)] \frac{R(t)}{R(i)} [(1 + \pi)\gamma]^{i-t} \Big],$$

from the government solvency constraint (7.52).

How does consumption differ when $\eta(t)$, $k(t)$, $R(t)$, $R(i)$, $w(i)$ and $e(i)$ ($i \geq t$) are the same and only debt and current and future lump-sum taxes differ (say $d^I(t)$ and $\tau^I(i)$, $i \geq t$, in the first case and $d^{II}(t)$ and $\tau^{II}(i)$, $i \geq t$, in the second)? It is easily checked that

$$c^I(t) - c^{II}(t) = \eta(t) \left[\sum_{i=t}^{\infty} [\tau^I(i) - \tau^{II}(i)] \frac{R(t)}{R(i)} [(1 + \pi)\gamma]^{i-t} \right.$$

$$((1 + \beta)^{i-t} - 1) \Big]. \tag{7.55}$$

$c^I(t) = c^{II}(t)$ for all possible $\tau^I(i)$ and $\tau^{II}(i)$ ($i \geq t$) if and only if the birth rate, β, equals zero. Weil (1985) showed that a positive birth rate was *sufficient* for absence of debt neutrality in OLG models without an operative bequest motive. Buiter (1988a) shows that in the Yaari–Blanchard–Weil OLG model a positive birth rate is *necessary* for absence of debt neutrality as well. In the original Blanchard model, a constant population was assumed, i.e. $(1 + \beta) = \gamma^{-1}$. Only the death rate appeared explicitly in the model, doing 'double duty'. When the birth rate and death rate are disentangled, it is clear that a positive probability of death in a Yaari–Blanchard model with a zero birth rate does not cause absence of debt neutrality. With $\beta = 0$, all surviving agents are identical. Postponing lump-sum taxes, therefore, does not redistribute income or wealth between heterogeneous consumers. While the probability of surviving to pay the future taxes declines exponentially as γ^{i-t}, $i > t$; the per capita tax burden of the survivors increases exponentially as γ^{t-i}, $i > t$. The two effects cancel each other out exactly.

This suggests the following proposition:

Proposition 5. In the Yaari–Blanchard–Weil model, a zero birth rate is both necessary and sufficient for debt neutrality.
Corollary 1: When the birth rate is zero, uncertain lifetimes or productivity growth do not generate absence of debt neutrality.
Corollary 2: When the birth rate is positive, infinite individual lifetimes do not generate debt neutrality.

It is easy, once we specify the initial value of the public debt and the behavior of taxes, to be more precise about the nature of the non-neutrality. In the example discussed earlier, let $d^{\mathrm{I}}(t) > d^{\mathrm{II}}(t)$. From the government's solvency constraint (7.52) it is apparent that the higher initial debt in scenario I could be serviced by a strictly higher path of future taxes in scenario I, i.e. $\tau^{\mathrm{I}}(i) \geq \tau^{\mathrm{II}}(i)$ for all $i \geq t$ and $\tau^{\mathrm{I}}(i) > \tau^{\mathrm{II}}(i)$ for some $i \geq t$. From Equation (7.55) this implies that $c^{\mathrm{I}}(t) > c^{\mathrm{II}}(t)$: higher government debt 'crowds out' private saving.

Note that in the OLG model of Section 7.2 a zero birth rate gives us a representative consumer model with a finite (two-period horizon). Debt neutrality obviously prevails again.

7.4 DEBT NEUTRALITY AND CAPITAL MARKET IMPERFECTIONS, HETEROGENEOUS SURVIVAL RATES AND DISCOUNT RATES

7.4.1 The complete absence of life insurance or annuity markets

Now consider the case where there are no markets for insuring against the risks associated with an unexpected death. The individual's budget constraint (7.41) is affected in two ways. First he now earns the riskless rate $1 + r(t + 1)$ rather than $[1 + r(t + 1)]\gamma^{-1}$ on his savings. Second, he receives (or pays) an amount $\bar{\lambda}(t - s, t)$, reflecting the fact that other consumers will be dying (unexpectedly) in debt or with positive non-human assets. Without bequest or gift motive, these 'involuntary bequests' are assumed to accrue to the state and to be returned by it to the surviving agents. For the moment all that matters is that the individual agent takes $\bar{\lambda}(t - s, t)$ as exogenous. Specifically, he does not see it as an additional return on his non-human assets $\bar{a}(t - s, t)$.

The individual consumer's budget identity now is:

$$\bar{a}(t - s, t + 1) \equiv (1 + r(t + 1))[\bar{a}(t - s, t) + \bar{w}(t - s, t) - \bar{\tau}(t - s, t)$$
$$+ \bar{\lambda}(t - s, t) - \bar{c}(t - s, t)]. \tag{7.56}$$

$\bar{\tau}(t - s, t)$ is lump-sum taxes net of transfers excluding payments or receipts associated with involuntary bequests. The terminal condition is

$$\lim_{j \to \infty} \frac{R(t)}{R(j)} \bar{a}(t - s, j) = 0.$$

Optimal consumption is given by:

$$\bar{c}(t - s, t) = \hat{\eta}(t)[\bar{a}(t - s, t) + \bar{h}(t - s, t)] \tag{7.57a}$$

where

$$\bar{h}(t - s, t + 1) = (1 + r(t + 1))[\bar{h}(t - s, t) - \bar{w}(t - s, t)$$
$$+ \bar{\tau}(t - s, t) - \bar{\lambda}(t - s, t)] \tag{7.57b}$$

or

$$\bar{h}(t - s, t) = \sum_{i=t}^{\infty} [\bar{w}(t - s, i) - \bar{\tau}(t - s, i) + \bar{\lambda}(t - s, i)] \frac{R(t)}{R(i)} \tag{7.57c}$$

$$\hat{\eta}(t) = \begin{cases} \left[\sum_{i=t}^{\infty} \left(\frac{R(t)}{R(i)} \right)^{\frac{a-1}{a}} \left(\frac{\gamma}{1 + \theta} \right)^{(i - t)\frac{1}{a}} \right]^{-1} & a \neq 1 \\ 1 - \frac{\gamma}{1 + \theta} & a = 1. \end{cases} \tag{7.57d}$$

If we assume that not only $\bar{w}$ and $\bar{\tau}$ but also $\bar{\lambda}$ are independent of age we have the following aggregate consumption function

$$C(t) = \hat{\eta}(t)[A(t) + H(t)]$$

where

$$A(t + 1) = [1 + r(t + 1)]\gamma[A(t) + W(t) - T(t) + \Lambda(t) - C(t)]$$

and

$$H(t + 1) = [1 + r(t + 1)]\gamma(1 + \beta)[H(t) - W(t) + T(t) - \Lambda(t)].$$

Per unit of efficiency labor, aggregate consumption is given by

$$c(t) = \hat{\eta}(t)[a(t) + h(t)] \tag{7.58a}$$

$$a(t + 1) = \frac{(1 + r(t + 1))}{(1 + \pi)(1 + \beta)} [a(t) + w(t) - \tau(t) + \lambda(t) - c(t)] \quad (7.58b)$$

$$h(t + 1) = \frac{(1 + r(t + 1))}{(1 + \pi)} [h(t) - w(t) + \tau(t) - \lambda(t)]. \quad (7.58c)$$

$\lambda(t)$ is the sum of the involuntary bequests per consumer measured in efficiency units. It follows that:

$$\lambda(t) = \left(\frac{1 - \gamma}{\gamma}\right) [a(t) + w(t) - \tau(t) - c(t)]. \quad (7.59)$$

Note that we have assumed that $\bar{\lambda}(s, t) = \lambda(t)(1 + \pi)^t$ for all s, i.e. each consumer gets the same share of the aggregate involuntary bequests.

Aggregate non-human wealth evolves in the same way as with perfect life insurance markets

$$a(t + 1) = \frac{(1 + r(t + 1))}{(1 + \pi)(1 + \beta)\gamma} [a(t) + w(t) - \tau(t) - c(t)] \quad (7.60a)$$

$$h(t + 1) = \frac{(1 + r(t + 1))}{(1 + \pi)} \left[h(t) - \frac{1}{\gamma}[w(t) - \tau(t)] + \left(\frac{\gamma - 1}{\gamma}\right)[a(t) - c(t)] \right]. \quad (7.60b)$$

While optimal individual consumption satisfies the simple autoregressive process in Equation (7.61), aggregate consumption cannot be written as a function of lagged aggregate consumption only, but depends on non-human wealth as well, as shown in Equation (7.62):

$$\bar{c}(t - s, t + 1) = \begin{cases} \dfrac{[1 + r(t + 1) - \hat{\eta}(t)]}{\hat{\eta}(t)} \hat{\eta}(t + 1)\bar{c}(t - s, t) & \alpha \neq 1 \\[4mm] \left(r(t + 1) + \dfrac{\gamma}{1 + \theta}\right)\bar{c}(t - s, t) & \alpha = 1,^{18} \end{cases}$$
$$(7.61)$$

$$c(t + 1) = \begin{cases} \left(\dfrac{1}{1 + \pi}\right)\dfrac{[1 + r(t + 1) - \hat{\eta}(t)]}{\hat{\eta}(t)} \hat{\eta}(t + 1)c(t) \\[4mm] - \hat{\eta}(t + 1)\beta a(t + 1) & \alpha \neq 1 \\[4mm] \left(\dfrac{1}{1 + \pi}\right)\left(r(t + 1) + \dfrac{\gamma}{1 + \theta}\right)c(t) - \left(\dfrac{\theta + 1 - \gamma}{1 + \theta}\right)\beta a(t + 1) \\[4mm] \hspace{6cm} \alpha = 1. \quad (7.62) \end{cases}$$

Clearly, there is absence of debt neutrality if $\beta > 0$, as the authorities can, by varying lump-sum taxation over time, influence $a(t + 1)$. Solving Equation (7.60a) forward in time, imposing the usual terminal condition,[19] substituting in the government's solvency constraint (7.52), and using the definition $a(t) \equiv k(t) + b(t)$, we obtain

$$k(t) + \sum_{i=t}^{\infty} \frac{R(t)}{R(i)} \left[(1 + \pi)\gamma(1 + \beta) \right]^{i-t} [w(i) - e(i)]$$

$$= \sum_{i=t}^{\infty} \frac{R(t)}{R(i)} \left[(1 + \pi)\gamma(1 + \beta) \right]^{i-t} c(i). \tag{7.63}$$

When the birth rate equals zero ($\beta = 0$), the 'Euler equation' for aggregate consumption (Equation (7.62)) is independent of government debt and lump-sum taxes. So is the aggregate private sector solvency constraint (Equation (7.63)).

This means there is debt neutrality when $\beta = 0$, even if there are uncertain lifetimes ($\gamma < 1$).[20] The complete absence of annuities or life insurance markets does not in itself constitute another sufficient condition for absence of debt neutrality. When all surviving agents are identical (except in non-human wealth) and when the involuntary bequests are distributed in lump-sum fashion to the survivors,[21] the non-existence of life insurance markets does not mean that postponing lump-sum taxation permits the government to redistribute income between heterogeneous agents. If every agent alive today or tomorrow is affected in the same manner by a capital market imperfection, the imperfection does not generate absence of debt neutrality. We summarize this as Proposition 6:

Proposition 6. In the Yaari–Blanchard–Weil model with uncertain lifetimes and no life insurance markets, a zero birth rate remains necessary and sufficient for debt neutrality if involuntary bequests are distributed in a lump-sum manner among the survivors.

Corollary: Under the conditions of Proposition 8, when the birth rate is zero, the absence of life insurance markets does not cause absence of debt neutrality.

7.4.2 Heterogeneous survival rates, time preference rates and elasticities of marginal utility

Since a zero birth rate is necessary and sufficient for debt neutrality in the Yaari–Blanchard–Weil model with identical agents (except for age), we only consider the zero birth rate ($\beta = 0$) case when other kinds of heterogeneity are introduced. For simplicity (and because nothing hinges on it) productivity growth, π, will also be set equal to zero.

There are two kinds of consumer, labeled with subscripts 1 and 2, who may have different survival rates, γ_1 and γ_2, different time preference rates, θ_1 and θ_2, and different elasticities of marginal utility α_1 and α_2. The number of consumers of type i in period t is γ_i^t, $i = 1, 2$. Total population is $\gamma_1^t + \gamma_2^t$.

Perfect life insurance markets are again assumed. A consumer of type j earns a gross rate of return $(1 + r(t + 1))\gamma_j^{-1}$ on his non-human assets, i.e. the insurance company can identify the survival probability of each consumer. Each consumer of both types earns the same wage w and pays the same lump-sum tax τ.

Aggregate consumption is given by Equation (7.64). d_j is per capita real capital government debt for consumers of type j, k_j is per capita real capital for consumers of type j, etc.

$$
C(t) = \gamma_1^t \eta_1(t) \left[k_1(t) + \sum_{i=t}^{\infty} \frac{R(t)}{R(i)} \gamma_1^{(i-t)} w(i) \right]
$$

$$
+ \gamma_2^t \eta_2(t) \left[k_2(t) + \sum_{i=t}^{\infty} \frac{R(t)}{R(i)} \gamma_2^{(i-t)} w(i) \right]
$$

$$
+ \eta_1(t) \gamma_1^t \left[d_1(t) - \sum_{i=t}^{\infty} \frac{R(t)}{R(i)} \gamma_1^{(i-t)} \tau(i) \right]
$$

$$
+ \eta_2(t) \gamma_2^t \left[d_2(t) - \sum_{i=t}^{\infty} \frac{R(t)}{R(i)} \gamma_2^{(i-t)} \tau(i) \right] \tag{7.64}
$$

$$
\eta_j(t) = \left[\sum_{i=t}^{\infty} \left(\frac{R(t)}{R(i)} \right)^{\left(\frac{a_j - 1}{a_j}\right)} \left(\frac{1}{1 + \theta_j} \right)^{(i-t)\frac{1}{a_j}} \gamma_j^{(i-t)} \right]^{-1} \qquad a_j \neq 1, j = 1, 2
$$

$$
= 1 - \frac{\gamma_j}{1 + \theta_j} \qquad\qquad a_j = 1. \tag{7.65}
$$

The government's solvency constraint is:

$$
d(t) = \frac{\gamma_1^t d_1(t) + \gamma_2^t d_2(t)}{\gamma_1^t + \gamma_2^t} = \sum_{i=t}^{\infty} \frac{R(t)}{R(i)} \frac{(\gamma_1^i + \gamma_2^i)}{(\gamma_1^t + \gamma_2^t)} [\tau(i) - e(i)]. \tag{7.66}
$$

Substituting Equation (7.66) into (7.64) and rearranging yields:

$$
C(t) = \gamma_1^t \eta_1(t) \left[k_1(t) + \sum_{i=t}^{\infty} \frac{R(t)}{R(i)} \gamma_1^{(i-t)} [w(i) - e(i)] \right]
$$

$$
+ \gamma_2^t \eta_2(t) \left[k_2(t) + \sum_{i=t}^{\infty} \frac{R(t)}{R(i)} \gamma_2^{(i-t)} [w(i) - e(i)] \right]
$$

$$
+ [\eta_2(t) - \eta_1(t)] \gamma_2^t \left[d_2(t) - \sum_{i=t}^{\infty} \frac{R(t)}{R(i)} \gamma_2^{(i-t)} [\tau(i) - e(i)] \right]. \tag{7.67}
$$

For there to be debt neutrality, the third term on the right-hand side of Equation (7.67) should be identically equal to zero. This requires either

$$
\eta_2(t) = \eta_1(t) \tag{7.68a}
$$

(identical marginal propensities to consume out of comprehensive wealth) or

$$d_j(t) = \sum_{i=t}^{\infty} \frac{R(t)}{R(i)} \gamma_j^{i-t}[\tau(i) - e(i)] \qquad \begin{matrix} j = 1, 2 \\ t \geq 0 \end{matrix} \tag{7.68b}$$

(no redistribution). Note that the 'marginal consumption propensities out of comprehensive wealth', η_1 and η_2 will in general be different when $\gamma_1 \neq \gamma_2$, $\theta_1 \neq \theta_2$ or $\alpha_1 \neq \alpha_2$ since, as can be checked easily,

$$\frac{\partial \eta_j(t)}{\partial \gamma_j} < 0$$

$$\frac{\partial \eta_j(t)}{\partial \theta_j} > 0$$

and $\dfrac{\partial \eta_j(t)}{\partial \alpha_j} > 0; \quad j = 1, 2.$

A redistribution of comprehensive wealth between the two types of consumers will, if $\eta_1 \neq \eta_2$, affect aggregate consumption. Postponing lump-sum taxation will redistribute wealth when survival probabilities differ unless Equation (7.68b) holds.

From the government solvency constraint (7.66) it follows that, without the ability to levy different per capita taxes on the different types of consumer, Equation (7.68b) will hold only if $\gamma_1 = \gamma_2$. In that case Equations (7.66) and (7.68b) can both hold if $d_1(t) = d_2(t)$.

Consider a one-period postponement of one unit of lump-sum taxation per capita in period t. From the government solvency constraint,

$$\Delta\tau(t + 1) = -\frac{(\gamma_1^t + \gamma_2^t)}{\gamma_1^{t+1} + \gamma_2^{t+1}} (1 + r(t + 1))\Delta\tau(t) \tag{7.69}$$

with $\Delta\tau(t) = -1$. From Equation (7.67), the effect on aggregate consumption is:

$$\Delta C(t) = [\eta_2(t) - \eta_1(t)]\gamma_2^t\gamma_1^t \frac{(\gamma_2 - \gamma_1)}{\gamma_2^{t+1} + \gamma_1^{t+1}} \Delta\tau(t). \tag{7.70}$$

Let $\theta_1 = \theta_2$ and $\alpha_1 = \alpha_2$. It follows that $\gamma_2 < \gamma_1$ implies $\eta_2 > \eta_1$ and $\gamma_2 > \gamma_1$ implies $\eta_2 < \eta_1$. Postponing lump-sum taxes ($\Delta\tau(t) = -1$) therefore raises aggregate consumption whenever $\gamma_1 \neq \gamma_2$. It redistributes income from those with a low death rate (high probability of survival) to those with a high death rate (low probability of survival). The higher-death-rate consumers have the higher marginal propensity to consume out of wealth.

This suggests the following proposition:

Proposition 7. Heterogeneous survival probabilities cause absence of debt neutrality even with perfect life insurance markets. Ceteris paribus, *postponing lump-sum taxation will raise aggregate consumption.*

Proposition 8 follows immediately from Equation (7.70):

Proposition 8. When survival probabilities are the same, heterogeneous time preference rates or heterogeneous elasticities of marginal utility do not cause absence of debt neutrality.

The intuition behind Proposition 8 is that while $\theta_1 \neq \theta_2$ or $\alpha_1 \neq \alpha_2$ imply (*ceteris paribus*) $\eta_1 \neq \eta_2$, postponing lump-sum taxation does not redistribute income when $\gamma_1 = \gamma_2$.

Finally, a little tedious algebra establishes the following.

Proposition 9. Propositions 7 and 8 also hold when there is a complete absence of life insurance markets.

It can be shown that Propositions 7 and 8 hold even when the following more realistic insurance market imperfection exists. The insurance companies cannot identify the survival probability of individual agents but know the two possible values of γ_j and their frequency in the population. In a pooling equilibrium they consequently charge the same insurance premium (pay the same annuity rate of return) to all consumers. The competitive gross rate of return on non-human assets is therefore

$$\frac{1 + r(t + 1)}{\gamma_1 \sigma_1 + \gamma_2 (1 - \sigma_1)},$$

where σ_1 is the fraction of consumers with survival probability γ_1. The length of this paper is, however, adequately excessive without working through this example.

7.5 CONCLUSION

Heterogeneity and *redistribution* are necessary and sufficient for absence of debt neutrality. Capital market imperfections are neither necessary nor sufficient, although differential incidence of capital market imperfections may well, empirically, be an important source of heterogeneity and a further reason why intertemporal redistributions of lump-sum taxes may not be neutral.

The analysis of the consequences of 'deficit financing', i.e. of the intertemporal redistribution of lump-sum taxes by the government, requires the abandonment of the representative consumer model if it is not to beg all the important questions. More generally, virtually every important issue in fiscal, financial and monetary policy involves government actions that alter binding constraints faced by heterogeneous consumers, investors, workers or firms. In order to be policy-relevant, the profession will have to invest in macroeconomics without a representative agent.

7.6 NOTES

1. Or by producers. The latter possibility is not considered here.
2. And with age-independent wage income and taxes.
3. The exogenous labor endowment when young is scaled to unity. The labor endowment when old is zero.
4. Each consumer is assumed to have a single parent. Parthogenesis (asexual reproduction) is a key simplifying assumption.
5. The analysis goes through also if the consumer cares directly about generations with whom he does not overlap.
6. For example, $\gamma_{0,0}$ is the weight attached to my own egoistic utility; $\gamma_{0,1}$ is the weight attached to each of my n siblings; $\gamma_{-2,0}$ is the weight attached to my grandmother's egoistic utility $\gamma_{2,1}$ is the weight attached to my sibling's grandchildren, etc.
7. $\dfrac{\partial G_t^j}{\partial c_t^2} = \dfrac{\partial G_t^j}{\partial B_t} = 0$ are plausible as c_t^2 and B_t are chosen in period $t + 1$.
8. Obvious modifications would be required if there were more than two overlapping generations.
9. He only considers the one-sided altruism case with $(1 + \varrho)^{-1} = 0$.
10. With the Cobb–Douglas production function, as $k \to \infty$ (in the infeasible region beyond A) the slope of the locus tends to -1.
11. U^B is $[1 - (1 + \varrho)^{-1} + (1 + \delta)^{-1}]^{-1}$ times the representative egoistic utility function.
12. U^G is $[1 - (1 + \varrho)^{-1} + (1 + \delta)^{-1}]^{-1}$ times the representative egoistic utility function.
13. Since $r < n$.
14. Note that $c_w^1 = -(1 + r)c_r^1 2$.
15. For simplicity it is assumed that $d = 0$.
16. $\dfrac{dc^2}{de} = \dfrac{(1 - c_w^1)[f''c^2/(1 + r) + (1 + r)(1 + n)]}{(c_w^1 - 1)f''k - (1 + n + c_r^1 f'')}$.
17. When the birth rate is zero we assume, without loss of generality, that the initial population arrived in one batch out of the blue at $t = 0$.
18. Note that: $[\hat{\eta}(t + 1)]^{-1} = [(\hat{\eta}(t))^{-1} - 1][1 + r(t + 1)]^{\left(\frac{a-1}{a}\right)}\left(\dfrac{\gamma}{1 + \theta}\right)^{-\frac{1}{a}}$.
19. $\lim\limits_{i \to \infty} a(i)\, \dfrac{R(t)}{R(i)}[(1 + \pi)(1 + \beta)\gamma]^{i-t} = 0$.
20. Equations (7.61) and (7.63), together with the government solvency constraint (7.52), imply that, when $\beta = \pi = 0$,

$$c(t) = \Omega(t)\left[k(t) + \sum_{i=t}^{\infty}\frac{R(t)}{R(i)}\gamma^{(i-t)}[w(i) - e(i)]\right]$$

$$\Omega(t) = \left[\sum_{i=t}^{\infty}\frac{R(t)}{R(i)}\gamma^{(i-t)}\prod_{\ell=0}^{i-t-1}\left(\frac{1 + r(i - \ell) - \hat{\eta}(i - 1 - \ell)}{\hat{\eta}(i - 1 - \ell)}\right)\hat{\eta}(i - \ell)\right]^{-1}.$$

21. If all individuals have identical $\hat{\eta}$s (i.e. identical θs, αs and γs) as we assume, the involuntary bequests need not even be distributed equally among the

survivors for debt neutrality to hold despite the absence of life insurance markets.

7.7 REFERENCES

Abel, A. (1985) 'Gifts and bequests: comments and extensions', mimeo, Harvard University.

Abel, A. (1987) 'Birth, death and taxes', mimeo, Wharton School, University of Pennsylvania, March.

Barro, Robert J. (1974) 'Are government bonds net wealth?', *Journal of Political Economy*, vol. 82, November–December, pp. 1095–117.

Blanchard, O. (1985) 'Debt, deficits and finite horizons', *Journal of Political Economy*, vol. 93, pp. 223–47.

Buiter, Willem H. (1979) 'Government finance in an overlapping generations model with gift and bequests' in G.M. von Furstenberg (ed.), *Social Security versus Private Saving*, Ballinger, Cambridge, MA.

Buiter, Willem H. (1980) 'Crowding out of private capital formation by government borrowing in the presence of intergenerational gifts and bequests', *Greek Economic Review*, vol. 2, August, pp. 111–42.

Buiter, Willem H. (1988a) 'Death, birth, productivity growth and debt neutrality', *Economic Journal*, June.

Buiter, Willem H. (1988b) 'Structural and stabilization aspects of fiscal and financial policy in the dependent economy', *Oxford Economic Papers*.

Buiter, Willem H. and J. Carmichael (1984) 'Government debt: comment', *American Economic Review*, vol. 74, pp. 762–5.

Buiter, Willem H. and J. Tobin (1979) 'Debt neutrality: a brief review of doctrine and evidence' in G.M. von Furstenberg (ed.), *Social Security versus Private Saving*, Ballinger, Cambridge, MA (also Chapter 9, this volume).

Burbridge, J. (1983) 'Government debt in an overlapping generations model with bequests and gifts', *American Economic Review*, vol. 73, pp. 222–7.

Carmichael, J. (1979) 'The role of government financial policy in economic growth', Ph.D. thesis, Princeton University.

Carmichael, J. (1982) 'On Barro's theorem of debt neutrality: the irrelevance of net wealth', *American Economic Review*, vol. 72, pp. 202–13.

Diamond, Peter (1965) 'National debt in a neoclassical growth model', *American Economic Review*, vol. 55, pp. 1126–50.

Ferguson, J. (1964) *Public Debt and Future Generations*, University of North Carolina Press, Chapel Hill.

Frenkel, J. and A. Razin (1986) 'Fiscal policies in the world economy', *Journal of Political Economy*, vol. 94, no. 3, pp. 564–94.

Kimball, M. (1987a) 'Making sense of two-sided altruism' in M. Kimball, 'Essays on intertemporal household choice', Ph.D. thesis, Harvard University, Chapter 2.

Kimball, M. (1987b) 'Making sense of two-sided altruism', *Journal of Monetary Economics*, vol. 20, September, pp. 301–26.

Modigliani, F. (1961) 'Long-run implications of alternative fiscal policies and the burden of the national debt', *Economic Journal*, December.

Tobin, J. (1952) 'Asset holdings and spending decisions', *American Economic Review*, vol. 42, no. 3, May, pp. 109–23.

Tobin, J. (1976) 'Discussion' in *Funding Pensions: Issues and Implications for Financial Markets*, Federal Reserve Bank of Boston.

Tobin, J. (1979) 'Deficit spending and crowding out in shorter and longer runs' in

H.I. Greenfield *et al.* (eds), *Economic Theory for Economic Efficiency: Essays in Honor of Abba P. Lerner*, MIT Press, Cambridge, MA.

Tobin, J. (1980) *Asset Accumulation and Economic Activity*, Basil Blackwell, Oxford.

Tobin, J. and W. Buiter (1980) 'Fiscal and monetary policies, capital formation and economic activity' in G.M. von Furstenberg (ed.), *The Government and Capital Formation*, Ballinger, Cambridge, MA (also Chapter 11, this volume).

Weil, P. (1985) 'Essays on the valuation of unbacked assets', Ph.D. thesis, Harvard University.

Weil, P. (1987) 'Love thy children: reflections on the Barro debt neutrality theorem', *Journal of Monetary Economics*, vol. 19, pp. 377–91.

Yaari, M. (1965) 'The uncertain lifetime, life insurance and the theory of the consumer', *Review of Economic Studies*, vol. 32, April, pp. 137–50.

Yotsuzuka, T. (1987) 'Ricardian equivalence in the presence of capital market imperfections', *Journal of Monetary Economics*, vol. 20, September, pp. 411–36.

8 · DEBT NEUTRALITY, PROFESSOR VICKREY AND HENRY GEORGE'S 'SINGLE TAX'

8.1 INTRODUCTION

In the overlapping generations model without operative intergenerational gift and bequest motives due to Blanchard (1985) (based on Yaari, 1965), a positive birth rate has been shown to be sufficient (Weil, 1985) and necessary (Buiter, 1988a; 1988b) for absence of debt neutrality. Debt neutrality prevails when equilibrium prices and quantities are independent of the mix of government borrowing and lump-sum taxation, holding constant current and future exhaustive public spending.

Professor W. Vickrey recently[1] pointed out to me that even with a positive birth rate, debt neutrality would still prevail if the tax in question were a tax on land. This note simply demonstrates that Professor Vickrey is correct. Models in the Blanchard tradition assume (implicitly) that the lump-sum tax is a tax on the income from *human* capital. Postponing the tax means that some of it will be paid by the 'new entrants', i.e. by new generations not yet alive when the tax was postponed. (This holds true even if each agent lives for ever; finite or uncertain lifetimes are irrelevant; only the positive birth rate matters (see Buiter, 1988a; 1988b)). Postponing taxes will make those currently alive better off and, *ceteris paribus*, this will boost current consumption.

If instead the tax is paid on the income from (or on the capital value of) a fixed factor of production ('land' in what follows), if all land that is or ever will be is owned by those currently alive and if the land market is efficient, then postponing land taxes will (assuming the government satisfies its solvency constraint) leave the value of land and aggregate consumption unchanged.

With a tax on human capital income, debt neutrality would prevail only

This paper was originally published in *Economics Letters*, 29, 1989, pp. 43–7.

if those currently alive possessed ownership claims on the after-tax wage income of all future generations, i.e. if future generations were, effectively, the slaves of the generations currently alive. Operative intergenerational gift and bequest motives effectively (at the margin) give those alive today command over the human capital of future generations, and debt neutrality results.

8.2 THE MODEL

All the ingredients of the model are familiar, so little time will be spent in motivating it (see, for example, Buiter, 1988a; 1988b).

$$c(t) = \mu(t)\, w(t) \tag{8.1}$$

$$\mu(t) = \left\{ \int_t^\infty \exp\left(-\left[\left[\frac{\gamma}{\gamma-1}\right] \int_t^s r(u)\,du + (s-t)\left(\lambda + \left[\frac{1}{1-\gamma}\right]\delta\right)\right]\right) ds \right\}^{-1} \tag{8.2}$$

$$w(t) = a(t) + h(t) \tag{8.3}$$

$$\dot{a} = (r - n)a + v - \tau - c \tag{8.4}$$

$$h(t) = \int_t^\infty \exp\left(-\int_t^s (r(u) + \lambda)\,du\right) [v(s) - \tau(s)]\,ds \tag{8.5}$$

$$n \equiv \beta - \lambda \tag{8.6}$$

$$a = qz + b \tag{8.7}$$

$$r(t) = \frac{f'(\ell(t))\, L(t)(1 - \theta(t))}{q(t)\bar{Z}} + \frac{\dot{q}(t)}{q(t)} \tag{8.8}$$

$$z(t) = \bar{Z}\exp(-nt) \tag{8.9a}$$

$$\ell(t) = L(t)\exp(-nt), \qquad L(t) \text{ exogenous.} \tag{8.9b}$$

$$v = f(\ell) - \ell f'(\ell) = v(\ell) \tag{8.10}$$

$$\dot{b} \equiv (r - n)b + g - \tau - \theta \ell f'(\ell) \tag{8.11}$$

$$(\gamma < 1; \delta > 0; \lambda \geqslant 0; \beta \geqslant 0)$$

All stocks and flows are (real) per capita quantities. c is private consumption, v the real wage, τ the lump-sum tax on wage income, g exhaustive public spending, θ the tax rate on land rental income, w total private wealth, the sum of non-human wealth (a) and human wealth (h). Human capital is the present discounted value of future after-tax labor income. The stock of government interest-bearing debt is denoted b, the fixed stock of ownership claims to current and future land rentals is $\bar{Z} > 0$. Land ownership claims per capita are denoted z. The physical stock of land at time t is $L(t)$ and land per worker is $\ell(t)$. Note that a 'share' of land, with price q, is an entitlement to one-$\bar{Z}$th part of the future income stream from all physical land. The physical stock of land may vary over time. β is the constant instantaneous birth rate and λ the constant instantaneous probability of death; $n \equiv \beta - \lambda$ is the instantaneous growth rate of population and labor force. The size of population at time zero is scaled to unity.

Each household maximizes a time additive objective functional over an infinite horizon. The instantaneous pure rate of time preference is δ and the risk-of-death adjusted subjective discount rate is $\delta + \lambda$. Each surviving agent, regardless of age, has the same expected streams of future labor income and of future taxes on labor income and therefore possesses the same stock of human capital.

Instantaneous utility is given by the constant elasticity of marginal utility function $(1/\lambda)\bar{c}^{\lambda}$ where $\bar{c}$ denotes individual consumption.[2] Competitive life insurance or annuities markets exist (with free entry and exit).

The economy produces a single non-storable commodity which can be used either for private or for public consumption. There is a constant returns to land and labor production function, strictly concave with positive marginal products and satisfying the Inada conditions. Output per capita is denoted $f(\ell)$. The labor market is competitive (Equation (8.10)).

Financial wealth consists of claims on land (with unit price q) and government debt. These two claims are perfect substitutes in private portfolios, as shown in Equation (8.8). The riskless instantaneous real interest rate is r. The government spends on goods and services, pays interest on its debt, raises revenue through lump-sum taxes on labor income and a land tax and borrows to cover any shortfall of current revenue from current outlays. Imposing the terminal condition:

$$\lim_{s \to \infty} \exp\left(-\int_t^s (r(u) - n)\,\mathrm{d}u\right) b(s) = 0,$$

the government budget identity (8.11) implies the government solvency constraint (8.12):

$$b(t) = \int_t^{\infty} [r(s) + \theta(s)\ell(s)f'(\ell(s)) - g(s)] \exp\left(-\int_t^s (r(u) - n)\,\mathrm{d}u\right)\mathrm{d}s \tag{8.12}$$

Substitute for w in Equation (8.1) using (8.3) and use the right-hand side of Equation (8.5) to substitute for $h(t)$. Substitute $qz + b$ for a and note that, solving Equation (8.8) forward for q, imposing the terminal condition

$$\lim_{s \to \infty} \exp\left(-\int_t^s r(u)du\right) q(s) = 0,$$

we get:

$$q(t)\bar{Z} = \int_t^\infty \left[\exp\left(-\int_t^s r(u)du\right)\right] f'(\ell(s)) L(s) (1 - \theta(s)) ds. \qquad (8.13)$$

Substituting for ℓ using Equation (8.9b) and for b using the government's solvency constraint (8.12) and rearranging, we get:

$$c(t) = \mu(t) \left\{ \int_t^\infty [f'(L(s) \exp(-ns)) L(s) \exp(-ns) - g(s)] \right.$$

$$\exp\left(-\int_t^s (r(u) - n)du\right) ds$$

$$+ \int_t^\infty v(L(s) \exp(-ns)) \exp\left(-\int_t^s [r(u) + \lambda]du\right) ds$$

$$\left. + \int_t^\infty \tau(s) \exp\left(-\int_t^s (r(u) + \lambda)du\right) (\exp(\beta(s - t)) - 1) ds \right\}.$$

$$(8.14)$$

From the last term inside the brackets on the right-hand side of Equation (8.14), it is apparent that, unless $\beta = 0$, there will not be debt neutrality for intertemporal redistributions of lump-sum taxes on human capital τ. Note, however, that the tax on land, which is, of course, also a lump-sum tax, 'disappears' when the valuation equation for land (Equation (8.13)) and the government solvency constraint (8.12) are substituted into the consumption function. Holding constant the paths of exhaustive public spending and of lump-sum taxes on human capital income, changes in the path of the land tax rate and associated changes in government deficits or surpluses do not alter private consumption. (In the model under consideration, where $c(t) = f(\ell(t)) - g(t)$ and $\ell(t)$ and $g(t)$ are exogenous, debt neutrality shows up in equilibrium through the absence of changes in the path of interest rates). Since land is supplied inelastically ($L(t)$ is exogenous), the tax on land rental income will not alter equilibrium allocations through familiar incentive or allocative effects.

The price of land, $q(t)$, is independent of intertemporal redistributions of land taxes that satisfy the government's solvency constraint. It is, of course, not only for inelastically supplied factors such as land that the equality in Equation (8.15) (whose left-hand side comes from the land valuation equation and whose right-hand side comes from the government solvency constraint) holds. It holds for all non-human factors of production, fixed or variable, already in existence or still to emerge (or to be produced), for which ownership claims exist today (and are priced efficiently).

$$\exp(-nt) \int_t^\infty \exp\left(-\int_t^s r(u)\,du\right) f'\left(L(s)\exp(-ns)\right) L(s)\theta(s)\,ds$$

$$= \int_t^\infty \exp\left(-\int_t^\infty (r(u) - n)\,du\right) f'\left(L(s)\exp(-ns)\right) L(s)\exp(-ns)\theta(s)\,ds.$$

$$(8.15)$$

Other 'fully owned' non-human assets that are supplied elastically (in the short run and/or the long run) will share with land the property that current owners cannot, by postponing taxes, shift (part of) the tax burden to future owners of new assets that will become available in the future but are not currently owned by anyone. In the case of elastically supplied factors, a proportional tax such as the land tax considered here is distortionary and will have the usual allocative and welfare effects. Debt neutrality therefore prevails only (assuming a positive birth rate and no operative intergenerational gift and bequest motive) for changes in non-distortionary taxes on the income from non-human factors of production.

Note again that debt neutrality will hold if the fixed factor grows or shrinks in an exogenously given manner (e.g., through exogenous quality improvement or deterioration or even through (exogenous) land reclamation[3]). What matters for debt neutrality to prevail is that agents alive today possess ownership claims to the current and future after-tax income from *all* land, both that physically present today and any land 'emerging' in the future. In this way, the ownership claims to the land will, if the market for these claims is efficient, fully reflect all current and future land taxes.

8.3 CONCLUSION

Henry George had a solution to the US budget deficit problem: scrap all existing taxes and replace them by taxes on fixed factors. His 'single tax' on (unimproved) land values is one example. Any tax on the productive contribution of 'nature' would do equally well. A suitable compensation scheme could take care of one unpleasant distributional implication of this proposal: large-scale redundancy among specialists on deficit financing. Since the imposition of such a tax would (in spite of this note) come as a complete surprise to everyone, the associated compensation scheme would also be lump-sum and would not distort the process of investment in (redundant) knowledge.

8.4 NOTES

1. At the Conference in Honour of James Tobin, 6–7 May 1988, at Yale University.
2. When $\gamma = 0$, the instantaneous utility function is ln c.
3. A matter of some interest to the Netherlands!

8.5 REFERENCES

Blanchard, O.J. (1985) 'Debt, deficits and finite horizons', *Journal of Political Economy*, 93, April, pp. 233–47.
Buiter, Willem H. (1988a) 'Death, birth, productivity growth and debt neutrality', *Economic Journal*, 98, June, pp. 279–93.
Buiter, Willem H. (1988b) 'Debt neutrality, redistribution and consumer hetero-geneity: a survey and some extensions', mimeo, March (also Chapter 7, this volume).
Weil, P. (1985) 'Essays on the valuation of unbacked assets'. Ph. D. thesis, Harvard University.
Yaari, M.E. (1965) 'Uncertain lifetime, life insurance and the theory of the consumer', *Review of Economic Studies*, 32, April, pp. 137–50.

9 · DEBT NEUTRALITY: A BRIEF REVIEW OF DOCTRINE AND EVIDENCE

(with James Tobin)

The macroeconomic theory of public debt has become increasingly controversial in recent years. The debate concerns not only the explicit interest-bearing financial obligations of the government but also its implicit deferred liabilities for social insurance benefits. This paper provides some historical background for the current theoretical debate. It also reviews some empirical tests of the proposition that government debt is neutral in real macroeconomic effects, and offers some additional tests. The conclusions are generally against the neutrality thesis. The evidence is that tax and debt finance of government expenditure are not equivalent in their effects on private saving and consumption. Debt issue does absorb private saving. That is why it is more of a stimulus to the economy in the short run than tax finance, and why it may diminish private capital formation in the long run. This paper indicates that concern expressed over the effects of unfunded social security programs on capital formation[1] is well founded.

9.1 HISTORICAL PERSPECTIVES

The influence on the consumption–investment mix of alternative methods of financing a given volume of government spending has been the subject of debate since Adam Smith's *Wealth of Nations* (see also Cannan, 1937) and David Ricardo's 'Principles of Political Economy and Taxation' (see McCulloch, 1871) and 'Funding System' (see Sraffa, 1951). In recent years, under the rubrics of 'debt neutrality' and 'ultrarationality', the issues have been restated as 'Are government bonds net wealth?' (Barro, 1974), and 'Are future taxes anticipated by consumers?' (David and Scadding, 1974;

This paper was originally published in G. M. von Furstenberg (ed.) (1979) *Social Security Versus Private Saving*, Ballinger, Cambridge, MA pp. 39–63.

Kochin, 1974; Carlson and Spencer, 1975; Barro, 1976; 1977; Buchanan, 1976; Feldstein, 1976a; Buiter, 1977).

The 'new classical macroeconomics' gives some dramatic answers to these questions. The effect of government, it says, is fully measured by the size and content of real government spending, regardless of how this spending is financed. Thus the Modigliani–Miller theorem for corporate finance (Modigliani and Miller, 1958; Stiglitz, 1969; 1974) is extended from the household sector *vis-à-vis* the corporate sector to the private sector as a whole *vis-à-vis* the public sector. An important recent statement of this theorem for public sector financing has been made by Barro (1974). Less formal statements can be found in the popular writings of Milton Friedman (1978, p. 59):

> The total tax burden on the American people is what the government spends, not those receipts called taxes. Any deficit is borne by the public in the form of hidden taxes — either inflation or the even more effectively hidden tax corresponding to borrowing from the public.

Buchanan (1976) has referred to the alleged neutrality of public sector financing as the 'Ricardian equivalence theorem'.

It is true that Ricardo stated the argument with characteristic clarity. He also added important qualifications, however, and concluded, almost passionately, that deferment of taxes by internal borrowing is bad fiscal policy. Ricardo, like Adam Smith before him, argued that given the volume and composition of what would today be called 'exhaustive' public spending (government purchases), taxes reduce mainly current consumption while internal borrowing results in reduced saving and private capital formation. He thus refuted rather than upheld the notion that the form of financing is irrelevant.[2] In fact, after giving a clear statement in his *Principles* of the 'Ricardian equivalence theorem', Ricardo proceeds to deny emphatically its validity. His grounds were partly what is now called 'public debt illusion' (Vickrey, 1961), and partly his fear that expectations of future taxes would induce evasive behavior, even including emigration. Here are the master's own words, first stating the equivalence theorem:

> When, for the expenses of a year's war, twenty millions are raised by means of a loan, it is the twenty millions which are withdrawn from the productive capital of the nation. The million per annum which is raised by taxes to pay the interest of this loan, is merely transferred from those who pay it to those who receive it, from the contributor to the tax, to the national creditor. The real expense is the twenty millions, and not the interest which must be paid for it. Whether the interest be or not be paid, the country will be neither richer nor poorer. Government might at once have required the twenty millions in shape of taxes, in which case it would not have been necessary to raise annual taxes to the amount of a million (McCulloch, 1871, pp. 146–7).

In 'Funding System', Ricardo also makes the point, since reformulated by Barro (1974), that the intergenerational redistribution of income associated with a switch from tax financing to borrowing could be neutralized by offsetting changes in voluntary intergenerational gifts and bequests:

> It would be difficult to convince a man possessed of 20,000 £ or any other sum, that a perpetual payment of 50 £ per annum was equally burdensome with a single tax of 1,000 £. He would have some vague notion that the 50 £ per annum would be paid by posterity, and would not be paid by him; but if he leaves his fortune to his son, and leaves it charged with this perpetual tax, where is the difference whether he leaves him 20,000 £, with the tax, or 19,000 £ without it? (Sraffa, 1951, p. 187).

Having thus stated the equivalence theorem, Ricardo quickly proceeds to deny its validity: 'That an annual tax of 50 £ is not deemed the same in amount as 1,000 £ ready money, must have been observed by everybody' (Sraffa, 1951, p. 187). One of the reasons given is public debt illusion:

> it must not be inferred that I consider the system of borrowing as the best calculated to defray the extraordinary expenses of the state. It is a system which tends to make us less thrifty — to blind us to our real situation. If the expenses of a war be 40 millions per annum, and the share which a man would have to contribute towards that annual expense were 100 pounds, he would endeavor, on being at once called upon for this portion, to save speedily the 100 pounds from his income. By the system of loans, he is called upon to pay only the interest of this 100 pounds, or 5 pounds per annum, and considers that he does enough by saving this 5 pounds from his expenditure, and then deludes himself with the belief that he is as rich as before. The whole nation, by reasoning and acting in this manner, save only the interest of 40 millions, or two millions (McCulloch, 1871, p. 148).

Evasive behavior, to the point of emigrating in order to avoid the continuing stream of taxes is given as another argument against borrowing in the same place:

> it becomes the interest of every contributor to withdraw his shoulder from the burthen and to shift this payment from himself to another; and the temptation to remove himself and his capital to another country, where he will exempted from such burthens, becomes at last irresistible, and overcomes the natural reluctance which every man feels to quit the place of his birth, and the scene of his early associations (p. 148).

Finally, to leave no room for any doubt about his feelings on the subject, he concludes:

> It must, however, be admitted, that during peace, our unceasing efforts should be directed towards paying off that part of the debt which has been contracted during war; and that no temptation of relief, no desire of escape from present, and I hope temporary distresses, should induce us to relax in our attention to that great object.

This excursion into the early history of economic thought leads us to conclude that the 'neo-Ricardian equivalence theorem' should be relabeled the 'non-Ricardian equivalence theorem' and Ricardo's doctrine relabeled the 'Ricardian nonequivalence theorem'.

In the last 30 years, the issue of the differential incidence of tax financing and borrowing has resurfaced a number of times. Until the burden-of-the-debt controversy which followed the publication of James Buchanan's *Public Principles of Public Debt* (1958), post-war economists generally agreed with the 'equivalence theorem'. At least they agreed to it as applied to fully employed economies. A country fights and pays for a war with current resources. This burden cannot be postponed by borrowing internally. This went along with a clear distinction between internal debt — 'we owe it to ourselves' — and external debt.

There never has been any serious argument about the burden of the external debt in an economy with full employment. In the short run, the ability to borrow abroad, that is, to run a current account deficit, enables a country to absorb more resources than it currently produces. Such borrowed real resources can be used to boost current consumption, public or private, or can be devoted to public or private capital formation. In the case of a consumption loan a real burden is placed on the future, when current account surpluses will have to be generated in order to service and repay the overseas debt. If the current account deficit is devoted to domestic capital formation, future generations will be better off if the social rate of return on the additional domestic investment exceeds the marginal cost of foreign borrowing, and worse off if the opposite holds. To the extent that, in long-run equilibrium, rates of return are equalized between countries joined by well-functioning financial markets, foreign borrowing cannot enhance future consumption possibilities.

But, as regards internally held debt, popular concern about the debt burden on future generations was considered a naive fallacy. This classical doctrine was conveniently married to Keynesianism. The 'functional finance' doctrine associated with Abba Lerner (1943; 1946) downgraded the debt burden. The only purpose of taxation — and one which it was deemed capable of achieving — was to control private spending, mainly consumption spending, so as to achieve the right amount of aggregate demand and to avoid inflation at full employment. The marriage produced somewhat inconsistent views of the long-run and the short-run effects of borrowing. Lerner and others seemed to say that the debt stock did not substitute for the capital stock in the long run, but that saving was absorbed in the short run by public sector deficits financed by bond issue.

Also during the 1940s a debate began about the proper base for the real balance effect proposed by Gottfried Haberler (1941) and Arthur Pigou (1943; 1947) and elaborated upon by James Tobin (1947; 1952), Don Patinkin (1948; 1956), and John Gurley and Edward Shaw (1960). Exactly the same issue was involved as in the debt neutrality debate: Does the base for the wealth effect include only base money? all nominal public debt? any nominal debt? nothing? Patinkin (1948, pp. 550–1) argued that the base 'clearly consists of the net obligation of the government to the private sector of the economy. That is, it consists primarily of the total interest- and non-interest-bearing government debt held outside the treasury and central bank.'[3] Shortly afterwards, in a discussion of the wealth effect in private consumption, Tobin (1952, p. 117) questioned the full inclusion of interest-bearing public debt in net private wealth.

> How is it possible that society merely by the device of incurring a debt to itself can deceive itself into believing that it is wealthier? Do not the additional taxes which are necessary to carry the interest charges reduce the value of other components of private wealth? There certainly must be effects in this direction.

Reasons mentioned for the incompleteness of the offset included the government's option of paying the interest on its debt not by taxes but by incurring further debt and the effect of the creation of public debt on the *distribution* and *composition* of private wealth, especially with regard to liquidity.

The burden-of-the-debt controversy of the late 1950s and 1960s concerned the long-run effects of substitution of borrowing for tax financing, the same issue that Ricardo had addressed. Does public debt diminish private demand for private financial claims and for stocks of real reproducible capital? Can the burden of current exhaustive government spending be shifted to future generations? The major protagonists were Buchanan (1958; 1964), Meade (1958), Bowen, Davis and Kopf (1960), Vickrey (1961), Modigliani (1961), Mishan (1963), Ferguson (1964) and Thompson (1967). In this debate Buchanan and some others objected both to classical neutrality doctrine and to functional finance in any form. But they seemed to define burden as compulsory payment — debt purchases are voluntary, tax payments are not — and thus their claim that the burden was postponable was almost tautological. The main area of controversy was clarified by the 'neoclassical synthesis' (see Samuelson, 1951; 1955), applied to the debt controversy most notably by Modigliani (1961). It focused attention on the central issue, whether and how public debt absorbs saving permanently and thus reduces the long-run capital stock.

Diamond (1965) first applied the overlapping generations model developed by Samuelson (1958) to the analysis of the longer-run effects of public debt on capital formation. He also considered the consequences of overseas borrowing by the public sector. His model did not permit private domestic agents access to international capital markets. This part of this analysis therefore has limited applicability to developed market economies integrated into an international financial system. Less-developed countries where the government is the sole agent with international creditworthiness are more closely approximated by the open economy Diamond model. This is an area that deserves further research.

A considerable amount of further theoretical work has built on the closed overlapping generations growth model (e.g., Cass and Yaari, 1967; Feldstein, 1974; 1976a; 1976b; Barro, 1974; 1976; Buiter, 1979; Tobin and Buiter, 1980).

Empirical work on debt neutrality has been scant; some recent contributions are reviewed in the next section. One area that has long attracted interest and continues to be investigated in depth is the effect of social security on private and national saving (Feldstein, 1974; Munnell, 1974; 1976; Barro, 1978). An unfunded, 'pay-as-you-go' social security scheme is a tax-transfer scheme that redistributes income between working and retired people. Its effect on saving and the long-run capital stock is governed by the same considerations as the effect of a change in the government's borrowing/taxation mix. On these issues the new classical macroeconomics, as exemplified by Barro (1974) and by Miller and Upton (1974), has a striking and extreme view: voluntary private intergenerational transfers can and will offset the involuntary public intergenerational transfers associated with public borrowing and social security. The private transfers negate any effects of public debt and social security on aggregate saving and the long-run capital stock. The most vocal opponent of this view is Buchanan and Wagner (1977). Unfortunately their sweeping condemnation of deficit finance — which they represent as the major source of most our current economic ills — is not complemented by a tightly reasoned economic analysis of the sources of nonequivalence.

Elsewhere, Buiter (1979) and Tobin and Buiter (1980) seek to make clear again what seemed obvious to Ricardo 150 years ago. Here we turn to empirical findings adduced by proponents of 'Ricardian' equivalence. We find that empirical evidence better supports Ricardo's final judgment.

9.2 EMPIRICAL FINDINGS RELEVANT TO THE DEBT-NEUTRALITY ISSUE

Very little empirical research has been addressed directly to the debt-neutrality issue. In a paper by Kochin (1974) some simple consumption functions are estimated that include the Federal budget deficit as one of the explanatory variables. A paper by David and Scadding (1974) analyzes 'Denison's Law' (Denison, 1958), the proposition that the gross private savings ratio (GPSR) has been very stable in the United States. While this phenomenon is different from debt-neutrality, the authors' interpretation of GPSR stability as reflecting 'ultrarational' behavior is germane to the debt-neutrality issue.

Finally, a fairly sizeable volume of research, while not addressed directly to the debt-neutrality issue, nevertheless has important implications for it. Work in the 1970s by Feldstein (1974; 1976b), Munnell (1974), and Barro

(1978) on the relation between social security and private saving extends earlier research in this area by Katona (1960; 1965), Cagan (1965), Taylor (1971), and Juster and Wachtel (1972). These three bodies of empirical research will be discussed in turn.

9.2.1 Are government deficits equivalent to current taxes?

To test the hypothesis that government deficits are equivalent to explicit current taxes, Kochin (1974, p. 391) estimated the equations given below:

$$CND = 5.56 + 0.283\ YD - 0.224\ FDEF + 0.643\ CND_{-1}$$
$$\quad\ (1.81)\quad (3.79)\qquad\quad (2.56)\qquad\qquad (5.12)\qquad\qquad (9.1)$$

$R^2 = 0.9989$; $SE = 2.23$; DW $= 0.680$; annual data 1952–71.

$$\Delta CND = 2.88 + 0.392\ \Delta YD - 0.109\ \Delta FDEF + 0.218\ \Delta CND_{-1}$$
$$\qquad (3.44)\quad (7.86)\qquad\qquad (2.95)\qquad\qquad\quad (2.42)\qquad\qquad (9.2)$$

$R^2 = 0.892$; $SE = 1.26$; DW $= 1.79$; annual data 1952–71.

CND denotes consumer expenditures on nondurables and services, *YD* is personal disposable income, and *FDEF* the Federal deficit. Each variable is deflated by the implicit price index for consumption expenditures.

Kochin finds that the negative significant coefficient on *FDEF* supports the debt-neutrality thesis. However, it does not support its strict and strong form, because it is smaller in absolute value than the coefficient of *YD* (markedly so in the second equation). In any case, a number of econometric and economic objections can be made to Kochin's regressions.

1. First, there are familiar problems of simultaneity and identification. In cyclical fluctuations, consumer spending, disposable income, and the Federal surplus all move together. History seldom performs the critical experiment of raising disposable income and reducing the Federal surplus by equal amounts. So it is difficult to estimate the separate *YD* and *FDEF* effects. Moreover, a high propensity to spend means a buoyant economy and a low deficit, reverse causation which Kochin's regressions do not screen out. Kochin attempts to solve this problem by using the full-employment deficit, in equations not reported here. But this is, for other reasons, quite inappropriate. Except at full employment, the full-employment deficit does not provide a measure of the present value of the future taxes required to service the debt issued.
2. Why is only the *Federal* deficit considered equivalent to current taxes? The claim that households internalize public debts is surely more credible for state and local governments. They are subject to legal and economic debt limits; they cannot print money; there are

fairly direct links between their outlays, including debt service, and their tax levies.

3. If the household sector subsumes the public sector under its own behavior, we can surely expect it to do the same for the corporate sector. *Private* disposable income, inclusive of corporate retained earnings, rather than *personal* disposable income, should be entered as an argument in Equations (9.1) and (9.2).

4. Kochin apparently views spending on consumer durables as a form of saving; this accounts for his choice of *CND* rather than personal consumption expenditures as the dependent variables in his regressions. Conceptually the proper dependent variable is consumption, including imputed services from durables. The excess of the value of these services over depreciation of the stock should be imputed as income and added to the National Income Accounts calculation of disposable income.

5. It is probably better to specify the consumption function in per capita terms.

6. The two regressions differ in economic substance as well as in their assumptions about the serial dependence of errors. The second implies a time trend in *CND*, absent in the first.

Kochin's investigation was motivated by his observation that unusually high saving rates occurred in the late 1960s and early 1970s when the Federal deficit was high. His results, whatever their econometric merits, are dramatically altered when the years 1972–6 are added to the sample. Personal saving definitely did not adjust to offset the Federal budget deficits run in 1975 and 1976.

Probably owing to data revisions for his sample period, we were unable to duplicate exactly the results obtained by Kochin. Our Equations (9.1a) and (9.2a) are Kochin's specifications[4] using the data provided in the 1978 *Economic Report of the President:*

$$CND = 4.504 + 0.2498\ YD - 0.1781\ FDEF + 0.6981\ CND_{-1}$$
$$(1.26)\quad (3.45)\qquad\quad (2.43)\qquad\qquad (6.94)\qquad\quad (9.1a)$$

$\bar{R}^2 = 0.999$; $SE = 2.66$; DW = 1.21; annual data 1952–71.

$$\Delta CND = 4.069 + 0.355\ \Delta YD - 0.086\ \Delta FDEF + 0.268\ \Delta CND_{-1}$$
$$(2.55)\quad (5.20)\qquad\quad (1.85)\qquad\qquad (2.10)\qquad\quad (9.2a)$$

$\bar{R}^2 = 0.790$; $SE = 2.28$; DW = 2.17; annual data 1952–71.

Adding the years 1972–76 to the sample has the result, hardly surprising in the light of the high spending propensities and deficits of recent years, of depriving the Federal deficit of all explanatory power, as shown in Equations (9.1b) and (9.2b).[5]

$$CND = \underset{(1.97)}{7.503} + \underset{(5.41)}{0.381} \; YD + \underset{(0.26)}{0.018} \; FDEF + \underset{(5.25)}{0.516} \; CND_{-1} \qquad \text{(9.1b)}$$

$\bar{R}^2 = 0.999$; $SE = 3.97$; DW $= 1.41$; annual data 1949–76.

$$\Delta CND = \underset{(2.13)}{4.639} + \underset{(5.98)}{0.406} \; \Delta YD - \underset{(0.60)}{0.035} \; \Delta FDEF + \underset{(1.54)}{0.195} \; \Delta CND_{-1} \qquad \text{(9.2b)}$$

$\bar{R}^2 = 0.657$; $SE = 4.18$; DW $= 1.83$; annual data 1950–76.

To correct the specifications and statistical procedures, we modified Kochin's original equation in three ways. First, the equation was specified in per capita terms.[6] Second, the total public sector deficit rather than just the Federal deficit was used. Third, the business sector was subsumed under the household sector. Let y denote per capita real national income, g per capita purchases of goods and services by governments (Federal, state, and local), $gdef$ the real per capita public sector deficit, and t real per capita taxes net of transfers $(gdef \equiv g - t)$. The appropriate per capita real income concept is $y - t - gdef = y - g$, if, from the point of view of the private sector, public sector deficits are equivalent to current taxes. We test the hypothesis that y, t, and $gdef$ have the same coefficients. Both real per capita consumption spending on nondurables and services, cnd, and total real per capita consumer expenditures, c, are used as dependent variables. The results are presented in Equations (9.3)–(9.8), using annual data for 1949–76.

$$cnd = \underset{(1.57)}{-133.139} + \underset{(4.43)}{0.224} \; y - \underset{(1.30)}{0.337} \; t - \underset{(1.04)}{0.254} \; gdef + \underset{(13.46)}{0.798} \; cnd_{-1} \qquad \text{(9.3)}$$

$\bar{R}^2 = 0.998$; $SE = 19.34$; $SSR = 8{,}604$; DW $= 1.73$.

$$cnd = \underset{(1.38)}{-114.730} + \underset{(4.64)}{0.192} \; y - \underset{(0.98)}{0.239} \; g + \underset{(14.81)}{0.821} \; cnd_{-1} \qquad \text{(9.4)}$$

$\bar{R}^2 = 0.998$; $SE = 19.42$; $SSR = 9{,}050$; DW $= 1.78$.

$$cnd = \underset{(4.48)}{-97.002} + \underset{(6.11)}{0.186} \; (y - g) + \underset{(20.68)}{0.813} \; cnd_{-1} \qquad \text{(9.5)}$$

$\bar{R}^2 = 0.998$; $SE = 19.05$; $SSR = 9{,}068$; DW $= 1.75$.

$$c = \underset{(1.26)}{-218.806} + \underset{(4.05)}{0.424} \; y - \underset{(1.26)}{0.682} \; t - \underset{(0.99)}{0.496} \; gdef + \underset{(6.24)}{0.652} \; c_{-1} \qquad \text{(9.6)}$$

$\bar{R}^2 = 0.994$; $SE = 40.23$; $SSR = 37{,}218$; DW $= 1.44$.

$$c = \underset{(0.932)}{-156.242} + \underset{(4.03)}{0.352} \; y - \underset{(0.82)}{0.408} \; g + \underset{(6.63)}{0.682} \; c_{-1} \qquad \text{(9.7)}$$

$\bar{R}^2 = 0.994$; $SE = 40.63$; $SSR = 39{,}621$; DW $= 1.51$.

$$c = -135.697 + 0.345 \, (y - g) + 0.673 \, c_{-1}$$
$$\quad\quad (2.97) \quad (5.08) \quad\quad\quad (9.04) \quad\quad\quad\quad\quad (9.8)$$

$$\bar{R}^2 = 0.994; \; SE = 39.82; \; SSR = 39{,}648; \; DW = 1.50.$$

Equations (9.3)–(9.8) indicate that the debt-neutrality hypothesis is not supported for either consumption spending on nondurables and services or for total consumer spending. In Equations (9.4) and (9.7), the coefficient on g has the 'right' sign but is insignificantly different from zero. In Equations (9.3) and (9.6) both t and $gdef$ have the right signs but are statistically insignificant. Accurate estimation of the coefficients on y, t, $gdef$, and g is complicated by considerable collinearity among these variables in annual data for 1948–76 as shown by the matrix of zero-order correlation coefficients below:

	y	t	$gdef$
t	0.91		
$gdef$	0.38	−0.03	
g	0.99	0.88	0.44

The lack of statistical significance of the variables that should reflect the presence or absence of debt neutrality (g and $gdef$) is reflected in our inability to reject the hypothesis that the coefficients on y, t, and $-gdef$ are the same, at the 5% level of significance. This holds both when cnd is the dependent variable (Equation (9.3) versus (9.5)) and when c is the dependent variable (Equation (9.6) versus (9.8)). The hypotheses that t and $gdef$ have the same coefficients (Equation (9.3) versus (9.4) or Equation (9.6) versus (9.7)) and that y and g have the same coefficients (Equation (9.4) versus (9.5) or Equation (9.7) versus (9.8)) similarly cannot be rejected. This gives scant comfort to proponents of debt neutrality, however; the coefficients of g and $gdef$ are statistically insignificantly different from zero, and therefore also differ insignificantly from values close to zero.

Success, as measured by high $\bar{R}^2$, significant t-statistics, and an acceptable Durbin–Watson statistic, is cheap in aggregate time series analysis. This should be kept in mind when evaluating the significance of the 'successful' Equations (9.5) and (9.8). The simplest Keynesian consumption function is estimated in Equation (9.9), in which yd denotes real per capita personal disposable income.

$$c = 123.431 + 0.875 \, yd \quad\quad\quad\quad\quad\quad\quad\quad (9.9)$$
$$\quad\quad (4.53) \quad (100.44)$$

$$\bar{R}^2 = 0.997; \; SE = 27.01; \; SSR = 18{,}970; \; DW = 1.47;[7]$$
$$\text{annual data 1949–76}$$

In terms of conventional statistical criteria, Equation (9.9) (and its first-order autocorrelation-corrected version) is preferable to Equation (9.8). For nondurables and services, permanent disposable income[8] in Equation (9.10) also performs as well as the corresponding debt-neutral specification (9.5).

$$cnd = 31.747 + 0.369\ yd + 0.528\ cnd_{-1} \qquad (9.10)$$
$$\quad\ (1.28)\quad\ (6.39)\qquad (6.46)$$

$\bar{R}^2 = 0.998;\ SE = 18.52;\ SSR = 8{,}577;\ DW = 1.51;$
annual data 1949–76.

9.2.2 The stability of the private saving rate

David and Scadding (1974) draw attention to the historical stability in the United States of the ratio, GPSR, of gross private saving to GNP. The explanation, they say, is what they call 'ultrarationality'. However, their 'ultrarationality' is by no means the same rationality invoked by proponents of public debt neutrality. The debt-neutrality proposition relates to the stability of *social saving* (private plus public) as a function of social wealth or permanent social real income. A stable private saving ratio, in conjunction with significant variation in the public saving ratio, is inconsistent with the debt-neutrality proposition. David and Scadding (1974, p. 236) impute to private savers quite a different interpretation of the meaning of shifts between taxes and debt in the financing of public expenditure:

> [The] regularity in the GPSR ... is not the result of constant sectoral savings propensities, of a stable distribution of output between the public and the private sectors, and, within the latter, of a stable division of income between the corporate and household sectors ... First there has been a shift in the composition of private saving away from personal saving to corporate saving and expenditure on consumer durables. Second, the total of private saving has been almost totally insensitive to the share of output absorbed by the public sector, given the level of output ... [The second point] implies a high degree of substitutability ... between private consumption and taxes and between private investment and government dissaving.

This reasoning is an exercise in arithmetic dressed up as theory. Assume, for the sake of argument, that personal saving, corporate saving, and the accumulation of consumer durables are perfect substitutes. Let S denote gross private saving, C private consumption, T taxes net of transfers, Y gross national product, I gross domestic capital formation, G government spending on goods and services, and X the international current account surplus. From the national income accounting identities we have

$$\frac{S}{Y} \equiv \frac{Y - (C + T)}{Y} \equiv \frac{I + X + G - T}{Y}. \qquad (9.11)$$

Constancy of S/Y means that, for given Y, C and T are perfect substitutes and also that $I + X$ and $G - T$ are perfect substitutes. Going straight from these *ex post* accounting identities to *ex ante* structural behavioral relationships, David and Scadding (1974, p. 243) come up with a startling proposition: 'An extra dollar of government deficit will displace a dollar of private investment expenditure because households autonomously treat deficits as public investment and regard the public and private sector's investment projects as interchangeable.' Applied literally to year-to-year variations in budget outcomes, this would impute to private savers belief that the public sector increased its investment between 1974 and 1975 by $60 billion and cut it the next year by $30 billion! This could only be described as ultra*ir*rationality. Some of the evidence presented by David and Scadding (1974, pp. 236–8) can be interpreted as suggesting that their proposition does not apply to short-run cyclical variations of public sector deficits and surpluses, which result from fluctuations in the tax base and from discretionary countercyclical fiscal policies; instead they intend it, like the 'Denison's Law' which inspired their article, to apply only to longer-run variations as reflected in deficits averaged across business cycles. This restriction would deprive their 'ultrarationality' of its most striking policy implications; their proposition could not be used to argue that deficit spending is ineffective for short-run stabilization because it displaces private investment. The policy conclusions drawn by David and Scadding (1974, p. 245), however, are that 'fiscal policy would be useless for stabilization purposes'. This requires their form of ultrarationality to be operative in the short run and not merely 'on average' over the cycle. While this interpretation of David and Scadding's findings is in agreement with their emphasis on the smallness of the *year-to-year variability* in the GPSR (in addition to the absence of a trend in this ratio), it requires the rather unusual view of public sector deficits and public sector investment referred to earlier.

The GPSR is quite stable, as shown in Table 9.1, which presents summary statistics for it and eight other saving ratios. The most important features of Table 9.1 are the following. First, the gross private saving ratio is much more stable (as measured by range, standard deviation, or coefficient of variation) than either the personal saving ratio (PSR) or the gross national saving ratio (GSSR).[9] Second, the net saving ratios, whether private or public, are much less stable than the gross saving ratios. The reasons for this disquieting result are not clear.[10] In principle, rational or ultrarational behavior should lead to greater stability in net saving ratios.[11]

Further investigating the phenomena reported in Table 9.1, we estimated a large number of simple saving functions with alternative dependent and independent variables. The measure of saving used as dependent variable included all combinations of net and gross, private and social, and saving with and without purchases of consumer durables.

Table 9.1 Stability of saving rates, United States, 1948–76

	Mean	Range	Standard deviation	Coefficient of variation
GPSR	0.167	0.147–0.179	0.006	0.036
GPSR'	0.256	0.238–0.274	0.009	0.035
NPSR	0.084	0.064–0.100	0.010	0.119
NPSR'	0.182	0.160–0.208	0.012	0.066
GSSR	0.163	0.137–0.202	0.015	0.092
GSSR'	0.252	0.224–0.302	0.018	0.071
NSSR	0.080	0.034–0.134	0.021	0.263
NSSR'	0.178	0.132–0.239	0.024	0.135
PSR	0.082	0.048–0.102	0.012	0.146

Annual data 1948–76; *source: Economic Report of the President*, 1978. GPSR = gross private saving ratio; GPSR' = (gross private saving + gross purchases of consumer durables)/GNP; NPSR = net private saving ratio; NPSR' = (net private saving + gross purchases of consumer durables)/NNP; GSSR = gross national saving (private + public)/GNP; NSSR = net national saving/NNP; NSSR' = (net national saving + gross purchases of consumer durables)/NNP; PSR = personal saving/personal disposable income.

Explanatory variables were appropriately matched to the saving concept. They included GNP, NNP, GNP or NNP minus public sector purchases of goods and services, and personal income. Some regressions also included lagged dependent variables. None of these equations performed as well as the simple traditional consumption functions given in Equations (9.9) and (9.10), or as the restricted debt-neutrality equations (9.5) and (9.8). The saving functions that incorporated the debt-neutrality assumption, that is, those with national saving as the dependent variable, were dominated by those that had private saving as the dependent variable.[12]

The stability of the GPSR is an interesting phenomenon deserving a credible explanation. Perhaps the answer should be sought on the right-hand side of Equation (9.11) as well as on the left-hand side, in the offsets to private saving as well as in private saving behavior. In cyclical fluctuations, I/Y tends to be positively correlated with Y, while endogenous components of X/Y and $(G - T)/Y$ are negatively correlated. If fluctuations in Y are driven by autonomous variations of I, X, and $G - T$, including those engineered by deliberate compensatory policy, the sum of the ratios could be fairly stable. In the longer run, the explanation of Denison's Law may be different before and after the Great Depression and Second World War. In the earlier period, there were strong economic and political constraints holding X/Y and $(G - T)/Y$ constant and close to zero. As Kuznets (1952; 1961a; 1961b) observed, gross domestic private investment was a fairly constant share of national product over the decades since the Civil War. This stylized fact of economic growth can be attributed to technology and to the long-term stability of the real interest rate. Since the Second World War the constraints on X/Y and $(G - T)/Y$ have been relaxed. But the national commitment to full employment and the 'fiscal revolution' have meant that, secularly as well as cyclically, $(G - T)/Y$ bends to adapt in compensation for variation in I/Y and X/Y.

None of these suggestions is inconsistent with one of the implications of David–Scadding 'ultrarationality'. This is that, in the long run, anyway, households pay attention to the increments of wealth they acquire via equity appreciation reflecting the retention and reinvestment of corporate profits. Non-human wealth, in one form or another, is a significant variable in most modern empirical consumption functions (see, for example, Arena, 1964; 1965; Bosworth, 1975; Mishkin, 1977). These equations generally imply that retained earnings fully reflected in stock values will eventually increase consumption and displace other forms of wealth accumulation. They also imply that the effects of retained earnings on consumption and personal saving are much slower than those of dividend distributions. But for the long run this component of 'ultrarationality' is much more credible, and much more consistent with evidence, than the second component, the notion that private savers regard a public deficit as the counterpart of public investment and as equivalent to private capital formation.

9.2.3 Saving out of different types of income

Social insurance and other public and private programs compelling saving for retirement and other contingencies have grown spectacularly since the Second World War. What effect has their growth had on other, discretionary private saving? What is the net effect on funds available for capital formation?

Recently a number of observers have sounded the alarm that social insurance (OASI) and other government pension plans are significantly diminishing national saving and investment. Feldstein (1974) estimates that social security depresses personal saving by as much as 30–50 per cent. Munnell (1976) concludes that personal saving has been reduced by private pension plans. The negative effects alleged by these critics arise from the unfunded 'pay-as-you-go' nature of some of these programs. For example, the social security taxes or contributions paid by or for workers are not invested to provide for the benefits to which these workers will be entitled on retirement. They do not suffice for that. They are used to pay contemporary beneficiaries. In effect the government is engaging in deficit finance. The debt is not explicitly evidenced by bills, notes, or bonds; it is the implicit commitment to pay benefits to current participants when they later become eligible. In other words, the taxes (or contributions) to pay these commitments have been postponed; they will be levied on the generation at work when the currently contributing participants have retired. In the view of Feldstein and other critics, participants reduce their discretionary saving because their compulsory saving and the associated prospect of benefits fulfil the same purpose.

Clearly those who worry about unfunded retirement plans are not believers in the neo- (or non-)Ricardian equivalence theorem.[13] They do not regard the net debt to future beneficiaries as innocuous. If they are analytically and empirically correct, then the protagonists of debt neutrality are wrong. Barro (1974; 1976; 1978) says that Feldstein and others forgot that the public, knowing full well that future social security taxes will have to be higher to pay for benefits already committed, will save enough to pay the extra future taxes. This additional saving may be done by the future beneficiaries themselves, to make up by gifts or bequests the taxes the younger generation will have to pay. Or it may be done by the future taxpayers themselves. The critics of unfunded pension plans tend to use the life cycle model of saving behavior, or at any rate a model that imputes finite horizons to savers. The advocates of debt neutrality assume infinite horizons, or the equivalent obtained via endless linkage of generations through operative bequest or gift motives.

From this perspective we can review some of the evidence on the substitutability between compulsory or contractual saving and discretionary saving.

Taylor (1971) concludes from his time-series analysis of personal saving that households consider contributions to social insurance a form of saving. He finds a very large (-2) negative marginal propensity to save in other forms with respect to social security. This estimate is consistent with one form of 'ultrarationality': worker-consumers appear to take into account their employers' contributions as well as their own. His basic equation (Taylor, 1971, p. 391) is:

$$S_t = \underset{(43.79)}{0.955\ S_{t-1}} + \underset{(4.21)}{0.449\ \Delta L} - \underset{(0.86)}{0.277\ \Delta p} + \underset{(2.86)}{0.893\ \Delta TR} - \underset{(3.30)}{2.16\ \Delta SI}$$

$$\underset{(4.87)}{-\ 0.901\ \Delta T} + \underset{(2.08)}{3.65\ \Delta r} \tag{9.12}$$

$\bar{R}^2 = 0.899$; $SE = 2.01$; DW: missing; data: 1953 I–1969 IV.

S denotes saving, ΔL the change in labor income, Δp the change in income from property, ΔTR the change in transfer income, ΔSI the change in personal contributions to social security, ΔT the change in personal tax payments, and Δr the change in the nominal yield on Baa bonds. All variables except the interest rate are in billions of current dollars.

The interpretation of these coefficients is not straightforward. The several income components differ in their positions in the transitory–

permanent spectrum: household distributions by total income, wealth, or age differ for the various income components. Furthermore, they are imperfect substitutes because of differences in the liquidity and marketability of the assets that yield the income or taxes. The high marginal propensity to save out of transfer payments is undoubtedly due partly to the liquidity and wealth positions of the recipients and partly to the transitory, cyclical nature of some transfer increases and reductions. On the whole, the Taylor study provides strong though indirect evidence against the behavioral hypotheses underlying the debt-neutrality thesis, and provides moderate support for the worries of the critics of unfunded pensions and retirement insurance, by concluding that the various components, positive and negative, of personal disposable income are not perfect dollar-for-dollar substitutes for each other.

A similar conclusion was reached by Juster and Wachtel (1972). When they re-estimated Equation (9.12) for the period from the first quarter of 1954 through the third quarter of 1972, the only significant change was a reduction in the numerical value of the coefficient on the change in personal social security contributions (ΔSI) from -2.16 to -1.55. (From the debt-neutrality point of view this would indicate a decline in the 'degree of ultrarationality' of worker-consumers with respect to employers' contributions to only 50 per cent.)

Earlier studies by Cagan (1965) and Katona (1960; 1965) found that households do not curtail discretionary saving when they are covered by compulsory retirement plans. The studies of Taylor, Katona, and Cagan unfortunately are not comparable. Taylor uses aggregate time-series data, Katona a cross-section sample of households, and Cagan both types of data.[14] Cagan (1965, p. 43), like Taylor, found an almost dollar-for-dollar offset of discretionary saving for contractual saving when he analyzed aggregate time series. In the decade-and-a-half before 1963, the 'aggregate personal saving–income ratio declines slightly while group pension funds (including government plans but excluding social security) have increased dramatically, indicating a full offset to pension growth by reductions in other forms of saving'.

A closer look by Cagan at household saving behavior after a household has come under a pension plan, however, yields results that are the opposite of those suggested by the aggregate saving ratio: the net addition to aggregate personal saving apparently equals the full amount of employees' and employers' contributions. Katona, in his analyses of sample survey data, found that discretionary saving, if anything, increases. In another contribution he argues (Katona, 1960, p. 98) that the reason for the complementarity observed, in cross-section data, between discretionary private saving and 'collective security plans' could be a major shift in the ways financial provision is made for old age.

In former generations financial protection for old age was not generally achieved by individual saving efforts. In many socioeconomic groups this type of aid was provided by relatives, particularly grown children. Also, at the present time and probably for years to come, there is a considerable gap between the standard of living to which an employed family is accustomed and the standard of living provided by social security benefits and private pension plans. It is conceivable, therefore, that the minimal protection afforded by collective insurance plans may even stimulate people to save in order to achieve more adequate protection. Without these plans, economic insecurity would be inescapable for many lower- and middle-income families. With these plans people may be feeling closer to their goal and highly motivated to attain it.

While the attitude toward risk attributed, in this quotation, to a representative household may be somewhat perplexing, the point about the major shift in the ways financial provision is made for old age is important. It is consistent with the view that in Western society a combination of factors — affluence, mobility and independence, lengthened life — has weakened the lineal and extended family and the responsibility felt by and expected of children for taking care of aged parents. Social security and the proliferation of private pension plans are a collective response to this phenomenon. During the transition to the new system, these institutions brought financial independence in old age within reach for the first time for many people, and consequently did not lead them to reduce other provisions but perhaps even encouraged them. After the transition, however, substitution — though not necessarily perfect substitution — between one form of saving and the other would become the likely pattern.

The only conclusive evidence on the extent to which voluntary intra-family intergenerational transfers offset the effects of social security would be panel data on intrafamily transfers combined with accurate measures of the social security wealth 'owned' by each family member. Unfortunately it seems unlikely that some of the required data on intrafamily transfers, especially the in-kind ones, will ever be available. A recent attempt by Barro (1978) to evaluate the effect of social security on private saving therefore resorted to estimating the net response of aggregate private saving to social security using time-series data. The specifications he considered were very similar to those adopted by Feldstein (1974). A social security wealth variable is added as an argument to a (rather unconventional) permanent-income type consumption function which has as its arguments current and lagged personal disposable income, net corporate retained earnings, the total public sector surplus, the unemployment rate, a measure of non-human wealth, and the stock of consumer durables. The social security wealth variable is supposed to measure the perceived net increase in permanent income — given current disposable income and the other arguments — that is implied by the expected future benefit payments and the expected future social security taxes. The calculation of such a measure is a heroic task. In spite of the considerable care Feldstein (1974, Part III) devoted to coverage, life expectancy and age structure, benefit and tax rates, growth of real per capita income, and the discount rate, the final product retains many arbitrary features. Feldstein assumed, for example, that the anticipated ratio of benefits to disposable income since the beginnings of the social security system was constant at its average value over the period the program has been in existence. Barro retained this assumption in some of his regressions. In others he made the equally arbitrary assumption that anticipated future benefits and anticipated future coverage (both relative to disposable income) correspond to their current values. This is an area where the use of more sophisticated expectations mechanisms (including rational expectations) can be expected to yield interesting results. Feldstein's (1974) findings that social security depresses private saving are confirmed in two[15] of Barro's regressions. In both of these the unemployment rate is omitted as an argument. The remaining regressions yield insignificant or even perverse coefficients for the social security wealth variable. In view of the shortcomings of the social security wealth variable and the rather *ad hoc* selection of other arguments for his consumption functions, Barro's results cannot be regarded as conclusive evidence either in favor of or against the existence of a depressing effect of social security on private saving.

9.3 CONCLUSION

The debt-neutrality issue is important for a number of reasons. To the historian of economic thought it is of interest as one of the most ancient areas of professional inquiry and argument, spanning the two centuries since *The Wealth of Nations*.

To the economic theorist debt neutrality raises fundamental issues about the interrelationship of private and public economic activity. The subjects of public finance, macroeconomics, monetary theory, corporate finance, and international finance each contribute their varied perspectives to our understanding of the issues involved.

To the applied economist and the economic policy-maker the debt neutrality debate is of the utmost importance. From a long-run perspective it concerns the consequences of alternative public sector financing rules for the growth of the domestic capital stock. From a short- and medium-term point of view the usefulness of deficit financing as a stabilization instrument is at stake.

On the basis of currently available theoretical models and empirical evidence our provisional conclusion is that the case for debt neutrality is not well established. Further empirical work is urgently required, however, before any conclusion can be more than tentative.

9.4 NOTES

1. See von Furstenberg (1979), in which the present paper first appeared.
2. Both Smith and Ricardo were, of course, assuming a fully employed economy.
3. Patinkin's later views on this subject were less sanguine. A compromise solution adopted by him was to define $M_0/p + k\,V_0/rp$ as the proper base for the operation of the real balance effect. (M_0 is the initial stock of government money, V_0 the number of government bonds, where each bond is a perpetuity with a coupon of \$1, r is the nominal rate of interest, and p the price level.) The constant k is between zero and one, measuring the degree to which individuals do not discount the future tax liabilities connected with government bonds (Patinkin, 1965, p. 289). The debate about the proper base for the real balance effect has been continued in the inside-money–outside-money controversy (Pesek and Saving, 1967; Saving, 1970; 1971; Patinkin, 1969; 1971; Johnson, 1969) about the role of private bank money as a component of net (private) wealth.
4. As it was not clear from Kochin's paper whether data points had been lost because of the lagged dependent variable in Equation (9.1) and the difference operator in Equation (9.2), we also estimated Equation (9.1a) for the period 1953–71 and Equation (9.2a) for the period 1954–71. The discrepancies were greater in each case.
5. We start our sample in 1948, but the results for the period 1952–76 are not significantly different from those reported here.
6. The population series is from the *Economic Report of the President*, 1978, Table B. 22.
7. Correcting for first-order autocorrelation yielded the following equation:

$$c = 122.91 + 0.876\,yd$$
$$(4.04)\ (89.99)$$

$\bar{R}^2 = 0.997$; $SE = 26.90$; $SSR = 18,809$; $DW = 1.59$; $\varrho = 0.121$.
8. Permanent disposable income is defined here as the infinite sum of current and past values of disposable income, with declining geometric weights.
9. GPSR', NPSR', GSSR', and NSSR' include gross purchases of consumer durables in the numerator but do not include the imputed rental income from the ownership of durables in the denominator. No guess was ventured as to the magnitude of depreciation of consumer durables.
10. The unreliability of the capital consumption data may be part of the explanation.
11. Some of the same points are made by Boskin (1978).
12. These results can be obtained from the authors on request.
13. Since the way in which the social security benefit formula is designed penalizes late retirement, individuals may choose to shorten their working life. This distortionary effect of social security would be a source of concern even to those who accept all other propositions required for debt neutrality.
14. Katona's definition of saving is very narrow and amounts to the change in net liquid assets, disregarding nonliquid assets (such as houses, equity in life insurance and pension funds) and liabilities.

15. If we are willing to accept a *t*-statistic of 1.8, one more equation shows a positive significant effect of one of the social security wealth variables on consumption.

9.5 REFERENCES

Arena, John J. (1964) 'Capital gains and the "life cycle" hypothesis of saving', *American Economic Review*, 54, March, pp. 107–11.

Arena, John J. (1965) 'Postwar stock market changes and consumer spending', *Review of Economics and Statistics*, 47, November, pp. 375–91.

Barro, Robert J. (1974), 'Are government bonds net wealth?', *Journal of Political Economy*, 82, November–December, pp. 1095–117.

Barro, Robert J. (1976), 'Reply to Feldstein and Buchanan', *Journal of Political Economy*, 84, April, pp. 343–9.

Barro, Robert J. (1978) *The Impact of Social Security on Private Saving, Evidence from U.S. Time Series*, American Enterprise Institute, Washington, DC.

Boskin, Michael J. (1978) 'Taxation, saving and the rate of interest', *Journal of Political Economy*, 86, April, pp. S3–S27.

Bosworth, Barry (1975) 'The stock market and the economy', *Brookings Papers on Economic Activity*, 2, pp. 257–90.

Bowen, William G., Richard G. Davis and David H. Kopf (1960) 'The public debt: a burden on future generations', *American Economic Review*, 50, September, pp. 701–6.

Buchanan, James M. (1958) *Public Principles of Public Debt*, Irwin, Homewood, IL.

Buchanan, James M. (1964) 'Public debt, cost theory and the fiscal illusion' in James E. Ferguson (ed.), *Public Debt and Future Generations*, University of North Carolina Press, Chapel Hill.

Buchanan, James M. (1976) 'Barro on the Ricardian equivalence theorem', *Journal of Political Economy*, 84, April, pp. 337–42.

Buchanan, James M. and Richard E. Wagner (1977) *Democracy in Deficit: The Political Legacy of Lord Keynes*, Academic Press, New York.

Buiter, Willem H. (1977) '"Crowding out" and the effectiveness of fiscal policy', *Journal of Public Economics*, 7, June, pp. 309–28 (also Chapter 6, this volume).

Buiter, Willem H. (1979) 'Government finance in an overlapping generations model with gifts and bequests' in G. M. von Furstenberg (ed.), *Social Security versus Private Saving*, Ballinger, Cambridge, MA.

Cagan, Phillip (1965) 'The effect of pension plans on aggregate saving', *NBER Occasional Paper*, no. 95.

Cannan, Edwin (ed.) (1937) *An Inquiry into the Nature and Causes of the Wealth of Nations, by Adam Smith*, The Modern Library, New York.

Carlson, Keith M. and Roger W. Spencer (1975) 'Crowding out and its critics', *Federal Reserve Bank of St Louis Review*, 57, December, pp. 2–17.

Cass, David and Menahem E. Yaari (1967) 'Individual saving, aggregate capital accumulation and efficient growth' in Karl Shell (ed.), *Essays on the Theory of Optimal Economic Growth*, Maple Press, New York.

David, Paul A. and John L. Scadding (1974) 'Private savings: "ultrarationality", aggregation and Denison's Law', *Journal of Political Economy*, 82, March–April, pp. 225–49.

Dension, Edward F. (1958) 'A note on private saving', *Review of Economics and

Statistics, 40, August, pp. 261–7.

Diamond, Peter A. (1965) 'National debt in a neo-classical growth model', *American Economic Review*, 55, December, pp. 1126–50.

Feldstein, Martin S. (1974) 'Social security, induced retirement and aggregrate capital accumulation', *Journal of Political Economy*, 82, September–October, pp. 905–26.

Feldstein, Martin S. (1976a) 'Perceived wealth in bonds and social security: a comment', *Journal of Political Economy*, 84, April, pp. 331–6.

Feldstein, Martin S. (1976b) 'Social security and saving: the extended life cycle theory', *American Economic Review*, 66, May, pp. 77–86.

Ferguson, James M. (ed.) (1964) *Public Debt and Future Generations*, University of North Carolina Press, Chapel Hill.

Friedman, Milton (1978), 'The Kemp–Roth free lunch', *Newsweek*, 7 August, p. 59.

Gurley, John G. and Edward S. Shaw (1960) *Money in a Theory of Finance*, The Brookings Institution, Washington, DC.

Haberler, Gottfried (1941) *Prosperity and Depression*, 3rd edn, League of Nations, Geneva.

Johnson, Harry G. (1969) 'Inside money, outside money, income, wealth and welfare in monetary theory', *Journal of Money, Credit and Banking*, 1, February, pp. 30–45.

Juster, Thomas F. and Paul Wachtel (1972), 'A note on inflation and the saving rate', *Brookings Papers on Economic Activity*, 3, pp. 765–78.

Katona, George (1960) *The Powerful Consumer*, McGraw-Hill, New York.

Katona, George (1965) *Private Pensions and Individual Saving*, University of Michigan Survey Research Center, Monograph 40.

Kochin, Lewis A. (1974) 'Are future taxes anticipated by consumers?', *Journal of Money, Credit and Banking*, 6, August, pp. 385–94.

Kuznets, Simon (1952) 'Long-term changes in the national product of the United States of America since 1870' in International Association for Research in Income and Wealth, *Income and Wealth in the United States: Trends and Structure*, Bowes and Bowes, Cambridge.

Kuznets, Simon (1961a) *Capital in the American Economy: Its Formation and Financing*, National Bureau of Economic Research, New York.

Kuznets, Simon (1961b) 'Quantitative aspects of the economic growth of nations, IV: Long term trends in capital formation proportions', *Economic Development and Cultural Change*, 9, July.

Lerner, Abba P. (1943) 'Functional finance and the Federal debt', Social Research, 10, February, pp. 38–51.

Lerner, Abba P. (1946) *The Economics of Control*, Macmillan, New York.

McCulloch, J. R. (ed.) (1871) *The Works of David Ricardo*, John Murray, London.

Meade, James A. (1958) 'Is the national debt a burden?', *Oxford Economic Papers*, 10, June, pp. 163–83.

Miller, Merton H. and Charles W. Upton (1974) *Macroeconomics, A Neoclassical Introduction*, Irwin, Homewood, IL.

Mishan, Ezra J. (1963) 'How to make a burden of the public debt', *Journal of Political Economy*, 71, December, pp. 529–42.

Mishkin, Frederic S. (1977) 'What depressed the consumer? The household balance sheet and the 1973–75 recession', *Brookings Papers on Economic Activity*, 1, pp. 123–64.

Modigliani, Franco (1961) 'Long-run implications of alternative fiscal policies and the burden of the national debt', *Economic Journal*, 71, December, pp. 730–55.

Modigliani, Franco and Merton H. Miller (1958) 'The cost of capital, corporation finance, and the theory of investment', *American Economic Review*, 48, June, pp. 261–97.

Munnell, Alicia H. (1974) *The Effect of Social Security on Personal Saving*, Ballinger, Cambridge, MA.

Munnell, Alicia H. (1970) 'Private pensions and saving: new evidence' *Journal of Political Economy*, 84, October, pp. 1013–32.

Patinkin, Don (1948) 'Price flexibility and full employment', *American Economic Reveiw*, 38, September, pp. 543–64.

Patinkin, Don (1956) *Money, Interest and Prices*, Row, Peterson, Evanston, IL.

Patinkin, Don (1965) *Money, Interest and Prices*, 2nd edn, Harper and Row, New York.

Patinkin, Don (1969) 'Money and wealth: a review article', *Journal of Economic Literature*, 7, December, pp. 1140–60.

Patinkin, Don (1971) 'Inside money, monopoly bank profits and the real balance effect', *Journal of Money, Credit and Banking*, 3 May, pp. 271–5.

Pesek, Boris and Thomas R. Saving (1967) *Money, Wealth and Economic Theory*, Macmillan, New York.

Pigou, Arthur C. (1943) 'The classical stationary state', *Economic Journal*, 53, December, pp. 343–51.

Pigou, Arthur C. (1947) 'Economic progress in a stable environment', *Economica*, 14(55), August, pp. 180–8.

Samuelson, Paul A. (1951) 'Principles and rules in modern fiscal policy: a neo-classical reformulation' in *Money, Trade and Economic Growth: Essays in Honor of Henry Williams*, Macmillan, New York.

Samuelson, Paul A. (1955) 'The new look in tax and fiscal policy', Joint Committee on the Economic Report, 84th Congress, 1st Session, Federal Tax Policy for Economic Growth and Stability, 9 November 1955, United States Government Printing Office, Washington, DC.

Samuelson, Paul A. (1958) 'An exact consumption loan model of interest with or without the social contrivance of money', *Journal of Political Economy*, 66, December, pp. 467–82.

Saving, Thomas R. (1970) 'Outside money, inside money and the real balance effect', *Journal of Money, Credit and Banking*, 2, February, pp. 83–99.

Saving, Thomas R. (1971) 'Inside money, short-run rents and the real-balance effect', *Journal of Money, Credit and Banking*, 3, May, pp. 276–80.

Sraffa, Piero (1951) *The Works and Correspondence of David Ricardo*, Vol. IV, Cambridge University Press, Cambridge.

Stiglitz, Joseph E. (1969) 'A re-examination of the Modigliani–Miller theorem', *American Economic Review*, 59, December, pp. 784–93.

Stiglitz, Joseph E. (1974) 'On the irrelevance of corporate financial policy', *American Economic Review*, 64, December, pp. 851–66.

Taylor, Lester D. (1971) 'Saving out of different types of income', *Brookings Papers on Economic Activity*, 2, pp. 383–407.

Thompson, Earl A. (1967) 'Debt instruments in both macroeconomic theory and capital theory', *American Economic Review*, 57, December, pp. 1196–210.

Tobin, James (1947) 'Money wage rates and employment' in Seymour E. Harris (ed.) *The New Economics*, Knopf, New York.

Tobin James (1952) 'Asset holdings and spending decisions', *American Economic Review*, 42, May, pp. 109–23.

Tobin, James and Willem H. Buiter (1980) 'Fiscal and monetary policies, capital formation and economic activity' in G.M. von Furstenberg (ed.), *The*

Government and Capital Formation, Ballinger, Cambridge, MA (also Chapter 11, this volume).

Vickrey, William (1961) 'The burden of the public debt: comment', *American Economic Review*, 51, March, pp. 132–7.

von Furstenberg, G.M. (ed.) (1979) *Social Security versus Private Saving*, Ballinger, Cambridge, MA.

10 · LONG-RUN EFFECTS OF FISCAL AND MONETARY POLICY ON AGGREGATE DEMAND

(with James Tobin)

10.1 INTRODUCTION: THE SETTING OF THE PROBLEM

This paper is a theoretical exercise addressed to a rather esoteric and artificial question in the logic of aggregate demand. Does expansionary fiscal policy raise aggregate demand permanently or at best only temporarily? The controversy is reminiscent of the Pigou–Keynes–Lerner controversy on the efficacy of reduction of money wages and prices in expanding aggregate demand, where also much was made of the distinction between short-run impacts and ultimate cumulative effects. The trouble with such discussions, including this one, is that a long run constructed to track the ultimate consequences of anything is a never-never land. For that abstraction we apologize in advance.

A characteristic monetarist proposition is that pure fiscal policy does not matter for aggregate real demand, nominal income, and the price level. The course of aggregate nominal demand, stochastic influences aside, depends solely on the path of the quantity of money somehow defined. Although increases in this monetary aggregate may frequently in practice be associated with budget deficits, the central bank always can break this link and very often does. The fiscal policies alleged not to matter are variations of government expenditure, transfer payments, and taxes while the quantity of money or its path over time remain unchanged.

We have stated this monetarist proposition baldly for the purpose of theoretical discussion. We realize that monetarists, Professor Friedman in particular, usually soften their assertions with qualifying adjectives and adverbs — 'minor', 'almost', etc. After all, no one would wish to have his

This paper was originally published in J. Stein (ed.) *Monetarism*, North Holland, Amsterdam, pp. 273–309.

salvation depend on the literally complete independence of any two variables in a complex interdependent economy. Hedges of this order really do not alter the monetarist message for theory and policy, and they are not intended to. Therefore, let us hope that we can discuss the strong proposition without semantic and textual quarrel about the strength and purity with which it has been asserted.

Non-monetarists have argued on numerous occasions that a necessary condition for the proposition is zero elasticity of demand for money with respect to interest rates, and we have offered against the proposition the theoretical reasons and empirical evidence for believing this elasticity is not zero. In the comparative statics of short-run macroequilibrium this condition appears as a vertical *LM* curve. When the condition is not met, the analysis indicates that a shift in the *IS* curve — which could be brought about by an increase in the rate of government expenditures or transfers or by reduction in the flow of tax revenues — will raise aggregate real demand.

The extent to which this expansion evokes an increase in supply depends on how close the economy is to its productive capacity. Perhaps we should stress the point that no one is contending that fiscal policy can increase output when production is supply-constrained. Neither can monetary policy. Moreover, this particular debate is not about the existence or size of the natural rate of unemployment. Logically the natural rate proposition is distinct from the monetarist propositions about fiscal policy; one could accept either one without the other.

Even when output is supply-constrained issues concerning aggregate demand remain. The monetarist proposition then is that expansionary fiscal policy — purged of incidental and extrinsic monetary expansion — does not affect the price level. Basically the assertion is that government cannot change, by its own spending behavior or by measures designed to affect that of taxpayers and other citizens, the income velocity of money.

On its face this is a very surprising assertion. If a few individuals were to decide to lower their average cash holdings while maintaining their spending, national income velocity would obviously rise, though the change would hardly be detectable by our measuring devices. If the Fortune 100 did likewise, it would be detectable. Why not when the Federal government does so — especially considering that the measure of velocity includes its spending in the numerator but excludes its cash from the denominator?

Monetarists argue that their proposition holds whether or not the *LM* curve is vertical. Friedman (1972, pp. 915–17) reaffirmed this view in his rejoinder to Tobin's comments on his 'theoretical framework' articles. He says that fiscal effects are 'certain to be temporary and likely to be minor', and that our difference of opinion is 'mostly, whether one considers only the impact effect of a change or the cumulative effect'. He agrees that the impact effect of a rise in government expenditure or reduction in taxes is expansionary; there is a once-for-all shift of '*IS*' and this pulls up income and interest rate along a non-vertical *LM* locus. By labeling this effect on income not only 'minor' but 'temporary' he seems to be saying that non-monetary financing of the accompanying budget deficits moves LM to the left, canceling the expansionary shift of *IS*. But he does not say this explicitly, stressing instead that monetary financing of the same fiscal program would be more and longer expansionary than the issue of interest-bearing debt.

Anyway, the issue we wish to discuss is whether and when the impact effects typified by *IS–LM* statics are reversed, modified, or amplified by shifts in those curves. But we have a few more general observations in prelude.

First, how relevant is this issue to the policy controversy which generated the theoretical debate in the first place? The policy controversy concerns such practical matters as the effects of the 1964 tax cut; the anti-inflationary content of the 1968 tax surcharge; the role of the escalation of war spending in escalating inflation in 1966; and the importance of budget economy in fighting inflation or accentuating recession in 1974. In cases like these, advocates of fiscal measures were looking for short-term effects on aggregate demand, without committing themselves to changes of expenditures and taxes never to be repeated or reversed. They were certainly not contemplating that the stock of money should remain forever constant while the stocks of other assets grew. When Walter Heller argued that the tax cut of 1964 would increase demand and reduce unemployment he was talking about what would happen in 1965. He was not talking about what would happen in 1970 or 1980 if the tax cut were even then the only change from pre-1964 monetary and fiscal policies. In this context it was no answer to say that years of accumulation of debt in exclusively non-monetary form would be contractionary. It *was* an answer, right or wrong, to say that demand for money is interest-inelastic.

Second, the claim that growth of non-monetary government debt has the same qualitative effects as reduction of money supply depends on a particular view about asset preferences — roughly that non-monetary debt is a closer substitute in portfolios for capital than for money. This is the traditional view, shared by Keynes. Tobin (1971) distinguished between fiscal or flow effects of government budgets and deficits and the monetary or stock effects of the accumulated debt. He pointed out that, for a one-time change of budgetary program, the flow effect is one-shot while the stock effect cumulates. A corollary is that the flow effect is reversed when the budgetary change is reversed, while the stock effect persists. But at the same time Tobin entertained the possibility that the stock effect of non-monetary debt may be expansionary, that such assets are in investors' eyes closer to money than to capital. If so, the growth of non-monetary debt would shift the *LM* curve to the right rather than to the left. (The relevant interest rate on the Hicks diagram would be in this case the true Modigliani –Miller cost of equity capital, which would diverge from the rates on government securities.) We mention this here because we shall not pursue the matter in this paper, where we shall acquiesce in an extreme version of the traditional assumption, namely that government securities and capital are perfect substitutes in portfolios.

Third, there is some tendency to couple the monetarist proposition with a general attack on the use of equilibrium analysis and comparative statics, particularly the *IS–LM* apparatus, in short-run macroeconomics. The attack has some justification, because it is generally true that the *incomplete* stock–flow equilibrium determined in such models implies changes in some stocks whose assumed constancy was a condition of the flow equilibrium itself. What is not true is that recognition of the temporary nature of the 'equilibrium' invalidates all the propositions of such analysis or validates contrary propositions.

Keynes explicitly restricted his *General Theory* to a time period in which the stock of capital is for practical purposes constant. Yet a Keynesian equilibrium generally involves non-zero net investment, implying changes in capital stock and thus quite possibly in the investment function and other behavioral equations of his model. The same short-run assumption applies to other stocks and flows, including government debt and deficit: the analysis does not apply to a 'run' long enough for the flow to make a significant change in the stock. Careful teachers of *IS–LM* have never allowed their students to use the apparatus on questions like 'the effects of an increase in government spending financed by printing money' because they knew that the change in money stock was indeterminate and time-dependent. Unfortunately they seldom get around to dynamic models in which the question makes sense.

10.2 THE ORGANIZATION OF THE PAPER

In a pioneering paper, Blinder and Solow (1973), inspired by the same questions which concern us, presented a model of long-run equilibrium similar to the one we shall discuss below.[1] Our reasons for offering another version are two. First, we wish to consider some additional ways of modeling fiscal and monetary policy. Second, we wish to structure the long-run demands for wealth, capital, and money somewhat more definitely and explicitly than Blinder and Solow did, especially in their original article. We shall discuss the differences in some detail in Section 10.3.

Like Blinder and Solow, we shall consider a Pigovian stationary state. The advantage of this abstraction is that it allows in a simple manner for adjustments of stocks of capital and other assets. It avoids the possible flow stock inconsistencies of the short-run equilibrium models. It therefore permits us to consider the monetarist claim that the apparent power of fiscal policy in those models depends wholly on such inconsistencies. Yet the model is artificial in several respects. To be relevant to the issue at hand, the model must permit unemployment even in long-run stationary equilibrium: and this requires the implausible indefinite persistence of wage and price rigidities. We shall also, however, consider the effects of fiscal policy on the price level in a long-run equilibrium with full employment and flexible prices.

The plan of the rest of the paper is as follows. Section 10.3 discusses briefly the Blinder–Solow contributions. Section 10.4 discusses the long-run comparative statics and stability properties of pure fiscal measures in economies with unemployed labor. In Model I the instrument of fiscal policy is G', government purchases of goods and services plus debt interest net of taxes on such interest. We trace the effects of once-for-all changes of G', while both the money stock and the proportional tax rate remain constant. As net debt interest changes, government purchases are adjusted dollar for dollar in the opposite direction to hold G' at its policy-determined level.

In Model II, the parameter of fiscal policy is G, government expenditure, excluding net debt interest, as it is in the Blinder–Solow model. This means that the fiscal stimulus varies endogenously as the volume of debt and the interest rate change.

Finally, Section 10.4 analyzes briefly the use of the tax rate, θ, as an instrument of fiscal policy.

Section 10.5 takes up, still in the context of long-run unemployment, the effects of changing the quantity of money. Two kinds of monetary change are considered. One is a change in the quantity of money via open market operations, while fiscal instruments, θ and G or G', are held constant. The second is monetary change linked to fiscal policy: budget deficits consequent to a change in G or G' are financed by printing money while the non-monetary public debt is fixed.

Section 10.6 shifts from the Keynesian world of long-run unemployment to the neo-classical long run of full employment and flexible prices. Once again the questions are how variation of G' affects the long-run equilibrium and whether the equilibrium is stable.

In the unemployment models of Sections 10.4 and 10.5, employment, N, is always less than labor force, $\bar{N}$, the price level, p, is assumed constant, and the expected rate of inflation, x, is zero. In the full employment model of Section 10.6, N is equal to $\bar{N}$, and both p and x are endogenous.

Non-monetary debt is modeled like bills of short maturity, indeed strictly like interest-bearing deposits. It is always valued at par although its yield is market-determined and varies. The only convenient alternative, the one adopted by Blinder and Solow, is to go to the opposite extreme and to assume that all government debts are perpetuities with constant coupons but variable prices. The difference is not consequential for the questions of interest. More realistic specifications, with debts of finite maturity, enmesh dynamic analysis in a morass of complex bookkeeping which is not worth the trouble.

It is assumed throughout that real net national product, Y, obeys a constant-returns-to-scale function of capital, K, and labor, N, with the usual neoclassical properties. In equilibrium the marginal product of capital derived from the production function, is equal to the real before-tax rate of return on debt (R in Sections 10.4 and 10.5, $R - x$ in Section 10.6). As previously stated, we follow — without endorsing — the Keynesian assumption that debt and capital are perfect substitutes in portfolios. At times of disequilibrium the marginal product of capital may differ from the return on debt. Their divergence is the signal and incentive for net investment or disinvestment in capital.

10.3 THE BLINDER – SOLOW MODELS OF FISCAL EFFECTS

Blinder and Solow present first a 'long-run' model with a fixed capital stock but variable government debt, and then a model in which both stocks are endogenous. The first has at best expository relevance, since it is unrealistic and potentially misleading to assume that over a horizon in which wealth and government debt change no capital accumulation can occur. For that reason, we will confine our comments and comparison to their variable-capital model. Using our own notation, we can write their model as follows:

$$Y = C[Y + B - T(Y + B), M + (B/R) + K]$$
$$+ I(R, K) + G; \qquad 0 < C_Y < 1, C_W > 0, \qquad (10.1)$$

$$M = L[R, Y, M + (B/R) + K]: 0 < T' < 1, \qquad (10.2)$$

$$\dot{K} = I(R, K); \qquad I_R < 0, I_K < 0, \qquad (10.3)$$

$$\dot{B} = [G + B - T(Y + B)]R, \qquad L_R < 0, L_Y > 0,$$
$$0 < L_W < 1, \qquad (10.4)$$

where B denotes the number of bonds and the money value of current debt service (bonds being consols with a coupon of one unit of money); C and T are consumption and tax functions, respectively; $Y = F(B, K)$ and $R = H(B, K)$ are the *IS–LM* solutions for income and interest rate, respectively; M is the nominal stock of money, K the capital stock, C private consumption, I private investment, G public spending on goods and services, Y real output, R the long rate of interest, L money demand and W private financial wealth. Subscripts denote partial derivatives; primes denote derivatives of functions with a single argument; a dot over a variable denotes its instantaneous rate of change.

The main differences between this model and ours are in the specification and in policy options considered:[2]

1. We have opted to put more explicit structure on the stationary-state demand functions for stocks of wealth and capital. Our short-run saving and investment functions are derived from these demand functions via mechanisms of adjusting actual to desired stocks. In the Blinder–Solow model, in contrast, the long-run desired stocks are implicit in the consumption and investment equations (by setting $C + G = Y$ and $I = 0$ in Equations (10.1) and (10.3)).
2. The investment function (10.3), in the original Blinder–Solow model, is poorly motivated. They argue that the function 'is in line with modern investment theory, which envisions an equilibrium demand for capital stock and a disequilibrium demand for investment' (Blinder and Solow 1973, p. 330). Yet the omission of Y from the function vitiates this rationalization for a model in which Y is endogenous. The omission is corrected in their second exposition (Blinder and Solow, 1974, p. 55). The investment function here is $\dot{K} = I(R, Y, K)$, presumably with $I_Y > 0$. However, the stability conditions repeated in the second version are those derived for the model with the misspecified investment equation.

   In their original model, sufficient conditions for stability are $F_B > (1 - T')/T'$, and $I_K + C_W < 0$ (F_B is the reduced-form impact multiplier of an increase in the number of bonds held by the private sector). It can be shown that in this model stability implies $dB/dG > 0$ and vice versa (if $F_B > (1 - T')/T'$) — the new equilibrium number of bonds after an increase in government spending on goods and services is larger than the old equilibrium number of bonds if, and only if, the equilibrium is stable.

   In the model with the amended investment function, two things happen. First, the stability conditions become very much more stringent – the linearized system is now

$$\begin{bmatrix} \dot{B} \\ \dot{K} \end{bmatrix} = \begin{bmatrix} R(1 - T' - T'F_B) & R(-T'F_K) \\ I_R H_B + I_Y F_B & I_K + H_K I_R + F_K I_Y \end{bmatrix} \begin{bmatrix} (B - B^*) \\ (K - K^*) \end{bmatrix}.$$

$(1 - T')/T' < F_B$ and $F_K < 0$ (that is, $C_W + I_K < 0$) are no longer sufficient for stability, since the determinant condition is no longer necessarily satisfied.

Second, stability of the system now is not sufficient to guarantee $dB/dG > 0$, or vice versa. If $dB/dG < 0$, the long-run multiplier for bond-financed deficit spending no longer exceeds that for money-financed deficit spending (Blinder and Solow, 1973, p. 327). It is even possible that dB/dG is negative and so large numerically that it causes

$$\frac{dY}{dG} = \left(1 + (1 - T') \frac{dB}{dG}\right) \bigg/ T'$$

to become negative. This comparative-static result can obtain whether or not the equilibrium is stable.

In the stable case, this intuitively implausible result would require the government to run more surpluses than deficits along the adjustment path, even though the initial impact of higher government spending may be to create deficits. This problem arises because Blinder and Solow do not restrict, by their consumption function, the long-run equilibrium relationship of wealth to income. It may turn out that, when the public is content with the fixed money stock and has adjusted both capital and wealth to desired magnitudes, there is less, not more, room in portfolios for debt. This possibility is evaded by their original investment function, which implies an equilibrium capital stock independent of Y, but it can occur when desired K rises with Y.

3. As regards the fiscal policy options considered, Blinder and Solow deal exclusively with our Model II. The possibility that the long-run government spending multiplier is negative under bond-financed deficits arises only in that regime. In our Model I the multiplier for G' is always positive.

10.4 ANALYSIS OF EFFECTS OF DEBT-FINANCED GOVERNMENT EXPENDITURES

Variations of fiscal policy are characterized by changes in government outlays, with the tax rate, θ, and the money stock, M, held constant. In Model I the parameter of policy is G'; in Model II it is G. The former is simpler analytically and in a sense more plausible in examining the long-run consequences of a one-step change of the parameter. Model I assumes that if debt interest increases purchases are curtailed correspondingly.[3] Model II, as in the Blinder–Solow model, credits a given fiscal policy with expansionary effect just because interest rate increases or deficits raise outlays for debt interest. Some might regard this procedure not as a constant fiscal policy but as an ever more expansionary policy.

10.4.1 Comparative statics in the two models

In this subsection, we present the long-run equilibrium equations for Models I and II. The condition for zero private saving is given by

$$W = \mu(Y - RK)(1 - \theta) = \mu(1 - \theta)(1 - \alpha)Y = \hat{\mu}Y, \qquad (10.5)$$

where W is real private wealth, μ is $\mu > 0$ and α is capital's share in income. On life-cycle principles, wealth is a multiple of disposable labor income. For simplicity, μ and α, and thus $\hat{\mu}$, are taken to be constants, but they could be made functions of R.

The condition for zero government saving — a balanced budget — is given by

(I) $G' - \theta Y = 0,$
(II) $G + R(1 - \theta)D - \theta Y = 0,$ \qquad (10.6)

where D is nominal government interest-bearing debt. The tax rate, θ, applies to wages, capital income, and debt interest.

Since debt and capital are perfect substitutes, a complete description of portfolio allocation is given by

$$M = L(r, Y/W)W = L(r, 1/\hat{\mu})\hat{\mu}Y, \qquad L_1 < 0, \hat{\mu}L > L_2 > 0, \qquad (10.7)$$

where $r = R(1 - \theta)$ is the after-tax rate of return.

The fraction of wealth held in money is inversely related to the after-tax return on alternative assets and positively related to the income–wealth ratio, which is constant in equilibrium.

Capital stock, K, may be expressed as

$$K = F(R)Y$$
$$= (\alpha/R)Y. \qquad (10.8)$$

Technologically, the capital–output ratio is inversely related to the rate of return on capital.

Finally, we define private wealth as

$$W = K + D + M. \qquad (10.9)$$

The stationary-state equilibrium of this model has the following properties. At the equilibrium value of Y, the public has the desired amount of wealth W. Some of it is in money, the amount of which is the constant M. The interest rate r is such that the public is willing to hold the fraction M/W of its wealth in monetary form. Some of the public's wealth is in capital, K, namely an amount such that the return on capital is R. The rest of the public's wealth is in non-monetary government debt, D. These conditions can be met for any Y. But the budget-balance equation for the government is necessary to keep D fixed, and the addition of this requirement determines the equilibrium Y.

The models can be condensed into two relations of Y and R, taking as given G' or G, M, and θ. The long-run 'LM' curve, which we shall denote LLM, is given by

$$L(r, 1/\hat{\mu})\hat{\mu}Y = M. \tag{10.10}$$

The long-run budget-balance equation, denoted GT, is expressed as

(I) $G' - \theta Y = \dot{D} = 0,$

(II) $r(\hat{\mu}Y - M - F(R)Y) + G - \theta Y = \dot{D} = 0.$ (10.11)

It also takes into account full adjustment of W and K to Y and R, which with M given implies a value for D. But this D does not meet portfolio preferences unless Equation (10.10) is also satisfied.

The slope of LLM is given by

$$\left(\frac{\partial R}{\partial Y}\right)_{LLM} = -\frac{M/Y}{L_1\hat{\mu}Y(1 - \theta)} > 0. \tag{10.12}$$

The slope of GT is

(I) $\left(\dfrac{\partial R}{\partial Y}\right)_{GT} = \infty,$

(II) $\left(\dfrac{\partial R}{\partial Y}\right)_{GT} = \dfrac{(G - rM)/Y}{(1 - \theta)(D - RF'(R)Y)}.$ (10.13)

For non-negative D, the denominator of the slope for Model II is certainly positive. The numerator is also positive if G exceeds the hypothetical after-tax interest on the money stock, negative otherwise. $(G - rM)/Y$ is equal to $\theta - \hat{\mu}r + \alpha(1 - \theta)$, and is the rate at which an increase of Y raises the budget surplus with R constant, starting from a position of budget balance.

We are interested in the shift of GT for an increase of G' or G.

(I) $\left(\dfrac{\partial Y}{\partial G'}\right)_{GT} = \dfrac{1}{\theta},$

(II) $\left(\dfrac{\partial Y}{\partial G}\right)_{GT} = \dfrac{1}{(G - rM)/Y}.$ (10.14)

In Model I the long-run 'multiplier' is simply the reciprocal of the tax rate. In Model II the multiplier is positive if GT is upward sloping, but GT shifts left if it is downward sloping. With non-negative D, GT always shifts downward; when G increases. R must decrease in order to lower debt interest and keep the budget balanced.

Model I is pictured in Figure 10.1. To the right of GT, the budget deficit $\dot{D}$ is negative: to the left, it is positive. Above LLM — given M and assuming that W and K are fully adjusted to R and Y — the stock of debt,

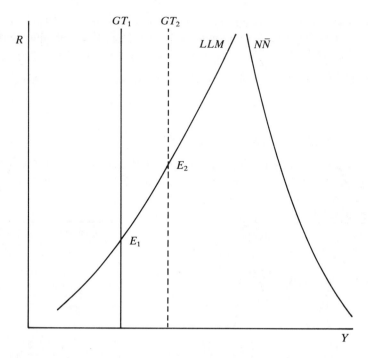

Figure 10.1 Long-run equilibria in Model I

D, is too small; the public would like to exchange money for debt. Below *LLM*, D is too large. As the shift of *GT* illustrates, an increase of G' leads to higher equilibrium values for both Y and R.

Model II is pictured in the three panels of Figure 10.2. Case IIa is little different from Model I. In case IIb, the *LLM* curve is the steeper. The comparative statics suggests that fiscal expansion diminishes Y and R, but perverse results of this type make one doubt the stability of the equilibria. In case IIc, *GT* is negatively sloped, the comparative static result is again 'perverse' and there is reason to doubt stability.

These comparative statics apply, of course, only for $N \leqslant \bar{N}$. Equilibrium demand for labor depends directly not only on Y but also on R, because higher R means use of labor-intensive technique. The full-employment ceiling to Y is shown in Figures 10.1 and 10.2, as $N\bar{N}$. A demand equilibrium on the far side of $N\bar{N}$ means an inflationary gap. One way it can be eliminated is reduction of the real stock of money by inflation; we discuss this case in Section 10.6.

10.4.2 Temporary solutions and dynamics: stability in Model I

Our dynamic story is the familiar *IS–LM* tale. We postulate conventional *IS* and *LM* loci for the Keynesian short run, i.e. for given stocks of wealth,

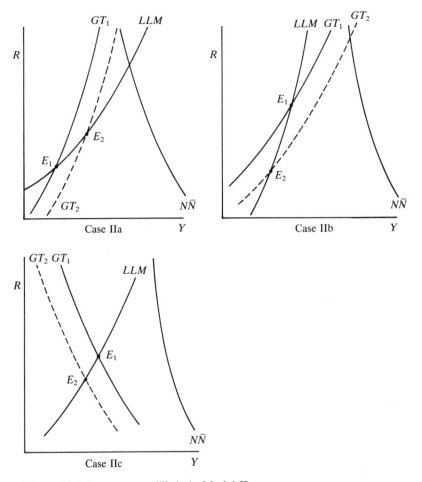

Figure 10.2 Long-run equilibria in Model II

debt, capital, and money. The solution of this system determines the momentary values of Y and R. As the stocks change, the solution changes. The question is whether this process leads to the stationary equilibrium.

The short-run LM relation is implicit in the equation $L(r, Y/W)W = M$, holding W constant. Its short-run slope, $-L_2/\{L_1(1 - \theta)W\}$, is less steep than its long-run slope, $\{-L(r, 1/\hat{\mu})\hat{\mu}\}/\{L_1(r, 1/\hat{\mu})(1 - \theta)W\}$, on the usual assumption, empirically supported, that the short-run income elasticity of demand for money, L_2Y/LW is less than unity. It is convenient to put the LM curve in explicit form (suppressing θ so long as it is being held constant),

$$R = R(Y, W, M); \quad R_1, R_2, > 0; \quad R_3 < 0. \tag{10.15}$$

The short-run slope is R_1; the long-run slope is $R_1 + \hat{\mu}R_2$.

The short-run *IS* locus is derived from the usual identity that capital accumulation equals the sum of private and public saving. Since asset revaluations have been assumed away, private saving is equal to $\dot{W}$. The identity differs between Models I and II:

(I) $\dot{K} + G' = \dot{W} + \theta Y,$
(II) $\dot{K} + G = \dot{W} + \theta Y - rD.$ (10.16)

We assume investment and saving functions of the stock-adjustment type,

$$\dot{K} = i(F(R)Y - K),$$
$$\dot{W} = s(\hat{\mu}Y - W). \tag{10.17}$$

The *IS* curves are combinations of Equations (10.16) and (10.17).

(I) $Y(s\hat{\mu} + \theta - iF(R)) = G' + sW - iK,$
(II) $Y(s\hat{\mu} + \theta - iF(R)) - Dr = G + sW - iK.$ (10.18)

The coefficient of Y in Equation (10.18) is the reciprocal of the conventional multiplier m. We assume throughout that $\hat{\mu}$ exceeds $F(R)$ in the range of relevant values: the desired wealth–income ratio exceeds the desired capital–output ratio. Indeed we shall assume that $1/m$ is positive even if $i > s$. We wish to bypass questions of short-short-run dynamics and instability. Nevertheless, in Model II the *IS* curve may become upward-sloping for high stocks of debt. This can be seen from

(I) $\left(\dfrac{\partial R}{\partial Y}\right)_{IS} = \dfrac{1/m}{YiF'(R)} < 0,$

(II) $\left(\dfrac{\partial R}{\partial Y}\right)_{IS} = \dfrac{1/m}{YiF'(R) + D(1 - \theta)}.$ (10.19)

Consider first the dynamics of Model I. Figure 10.3 duplicates Figure 10.1 for *LLM* and *GT* curves, and in addition shows the short-run LM_1 and IS_1 curves corresponding to the initial equilibrium at E_1, i.e. corresponding to the equilibrium stocks W, K, D, M at E_1 and to the initial value of G'. The short-run loci naturally intersect at E_1. Now suppose that G' is increased in one step, shifting the *GT* locus and indicating a new long-run equilibrium E_2. The immediate impact is to shift the *IS* curve to IS_2, producing a short-run solution S_{12}. This is evanescent, of course, because stocks do not remain at their initial E_1 values. The question now is whether the configuration of Figure 10.1 is stable.

At the new equilibrium E_2, with higher Y and R, the public will hold more wealth, but smaller fractions of wealth in money and in capital ($\partial L/\partial R$ and dF/dR are both negative). Consequently the volume of debt will be higher, both absolutely and as a proportion of wealth and income.

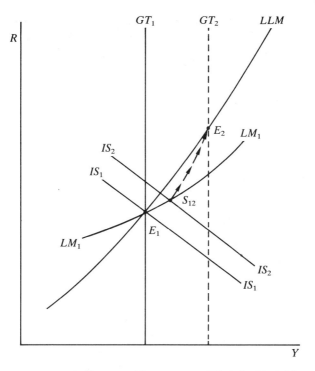

Figure 10.3 Short- and long-run equilibria in Model I

A dynamic path from E_1 to S_{12} to E_2 must involve deficits which achieve this accumulation of debt.

As Figure 10.3 is drawn, IS_2 is shifted horizontally from E_1 by less than the shift of GT. This means that the short-run multiplier m is less than the long-run multiplier $1/\theta$, and it guarantees that at S_{12} the budget is in deficit. It is conceivable that m exceeds $1/\theta$, if the short-run marginal propensity to invest $iF(R)$ is high. But m would have to exceed $1/\theta$ by some margin to place S_{12} in the budget surplus region to the right of GT_2.

Taking $m < 1/\theta$ as pictured, at S_{12} both W and D are increasing. LM will be shifting up. The growth of wealth also tends to shift IS up (via the sW term). We cannot be sure whether $\dot{K}$ is positive or negative at S_{12}. Compared with E_1, the increase in Y raises the demand for capital but the increase in R lowers it.

A path from S_{12} to E_2 in Figure 10.3 seems plausible. On such a path stocks of assets other than M are increasing and shifting upward both IS and LM. But the dynamics are not easy to display graphically, and the pictured path is not the only possibility. We turn to formal stability analysis.

The system consists of four equations in (K, D, Y, R):

$$\dot{K} = i(F(R)Y - K)$$
$$\dot{D} = G' - \theta Y$$
$$0 = Y(s\hat{\mu} + \theta - iF(R)) - sM - sD - (s - i)K - G'$$
$$0 = R - R(Y, M + D + K, M).$$

(10.20)

The local stability of the system can be analyzed from the following characteristic quadratic equation in λ:

$$\begin{vmatrix} -i - \lambda & 0 & iF(R) & iYF'(R) \\ 0 & -\lambda & -\theta & 0 \\ -(s - i) & -s & 1/m & -iYF'(R) \\ -R_2 & -R_2 & -R_1 & 1 \end{vmatrix} = 0.$$

(10.21)

Here $1/m$ is, as before, shorthand for the coefficient of Y in the third equation of system (10.20).

Considering Equation (10.21) as $a\lambda^2 + b\lambda + c = 0$, sufficient and necessary conditions for local stability — the real parts of both roots negative — are that both b/a and c/a exceed zero. Both conditions are met on assumptions already made, that the multiplier m is positive, that $\hat{\mu} > F(R)$ (so that there is room in portfolios for assets other than capital), that $F'(R) \leqslant 0$, and that R_1 and R_2 are both positive. It turns out that

$$a = (1/m) - R_1 iYF'(R) > 0,$$

$$c = \theta i s > 0,$$

(10.22)

$$b = \theta s + \theta i + is(\hat{\mu} - F(R)) - isF'(R)Y(R_1 + \hat{\mu}R_2).$$

All the terms of b are positive under the assumptions. Note that, in contrast to the Blinder–Solow conditions, no restriction on the relative sizes of s and i, other than the one required to keep the multiplier positive, is part of the sufficient conditions for stability.

10.4.3 Stability in Model II

The system of four equations is

$$\dot{K} = i(F(R)Y - K)$$
$$\dot{D} = G + rD - \theta Y$$
$$0 = Y(1/m) - sM - (s + r)D - (s - i)K - G$$
$$0 = R - R(Y, M + K + D, M).$$

(10.23)

The characteristic equation is

$$\begin{vmatrix} -i - \lambda & 0 & iF(R) & iYF'(R) \\ 0 & r - \lambda & -\theta & D(1 - \theta) \\ -(s - i) & -(s + r) & 1/m & -iYF'(R) - D(1 - \theta) \\ -R_2 & -R_2 & -R_1 & 1 \end{vmatrix} = 0.$$

(10.24)

Calling this equation $a'\lambda^2 + b'\lambda + c'$,

$$a' = a - R_1 D(1 - \theta) = (1/m) - R_1(iYF'(R) + D(1 - \theta)),$$
$$b' = b + r(s\hat{\mu} - iF(R)) + rR_1 iYF'(R) - D(1 - \theta)(s\hat{\mu}R_2 + (s + i)R_1),$$
$$c' = is(\theta - r\hat{\mu} + rF(R)\} - is(R_1 + \hat{\mu}R_2)(D(1 - \theta) - rYF'(R)).$$
$$(10.25)$$

For interpretation, we recall the slopes of GT and LLM given above in Equations (10.12) and (10.13) and restate them in the symbols of this section of the paper:

$$\left(\frac{\partial R}{\partial Y}\right)_{LLM} = R_1 + R_2\hat{\mu}, \tag{10.12a}$$

$$\left(\frac{\partial R}{\partial Y}\right)_{GT} = \frac{\theta - \hat{\mu}r + rF(R)}{D(1 - \theta) - rF'(R)Y}. \tag{10.13a}$$

Given the non-negativity of the denominator in Equation (10.13a) and the expression for c' in Equation (10.25),

$$\left(\frac{\partial R}{\partial Y}\right)_{GT} \gtreqqless \left(\frac{\partial R}{\partial Y}\right)_{LLM}$$

as

$$(\theta - \hat{\mu}r + F(R)) - (R_1 + \hat{\mu}R_2)(D(1 - \theta) - rF'(R)Y) \gtreqqless 0,$$

i.e. as $c' \gtreqqless 0$. Hence in case IIa, c' is positive, while in cases IIb and IIc, c' is negative.

The value of a' is the effect of G on the short-run solution Y, specifically $\partial Y/\partial G$ calculated from the third equation of system (10.23). The normal expectation is that it is positive; indeed the issue under discussion is whether this positive effect is temporary or not. With positive a', we know that in cases IIb and IIc one of the roots λ is positive. With normal short-run effects, therefore, the stationary equilibrium is unstable in those cases, as previously conjectured.

As for case IIa, with a' positive the equilibrium will be stable if b' is positive, unstable otherwise. Now even with D low enough to make a' positive, b' may be negative. Thus IIa may be either stable or unstable.

A negative value of a' seems at first glance to reverse these stability findings, making IIb and IIc possibly stable. Then one might conclude that fiscal expansion is contractionary both in the short and long run! But this conclusion is illusory. The $IS-LM$ solution itself is unstable under usual assumptions about short-run dynamics. This may be seen as follows. Let the IS slope (Equation (10.19), Model II) be $(1/m)/z$. Then $a' = 1/m - R_1 z$. R_1 is the LM slope. The possibilities are presented in Table 10.1. (i) is

268   *Crowding out*

Table 10.1 *LM* slope in Model II for different *IS* slopes

	$m > 0$	$m < 0$
$z < 0$	(i) $a' > 0$	(iii) if $a' < 0$ $(1/m)/z \gtrless R_1 \gtrless 0$
$z > 0$	(ii) if $a' < 0$ $0 < (1/m)/z < R_1$	(iv) $a' < 0$ $(1/m)/z < 0 < R_1$

the normal case already discussed. In case (ii) an increase in G shifts the *IS* curve right; it is upward-sloping but flatter than *LM*. In cases (iii) and (iv) an increase in G shifts the *IS* curve left. In (iii) it is upward-sloping but steeper than *LM*. In (iv) it is downward sloping. The four cases are pictured in Figure 10.4. The short-run dynamics indicated by the arrows follow the usual assumption that R always moves towards *LM*, while Y moves towards *IS* if $m > 0$ and away from it if $m < 0$. On this assumption, case (i) is the only stable configuration. (Cases not shown, which are also stable, involve $a' > 0$, $z < 0$.)

10.4.4 Variation in tax rate

We briefly consider the long-run effects in Model I of a third type of pure fiscal policy: changing the tax rate θ, keeping G' constant and financing temporary deficits by debt issue.

A reduction in θ shifts the vertical GT line of Model I to the right. The long-run multiplier $\partial Y/\partial \theta$ is $-Y/\theta$. But the LLM curve is not invariant to this type of fiscal action. It may shift either way. On the one hand, a tax reduction increases, for given R and Y, the opportunity cost of holding money; this effect moves LLM right. On the other hand, tax reduction increases after-tax human wealth and therefore, other things equal, raises $\hat{\mu}$. This effect moves LLM left. The net effect is uncertain, and so we cannot exclude the possibility that equilibrium R will be lower with lower θ. The stability analysis is the same as in Section 10.4.2.

10.5 MONETARY POLICY IN THE LONG RUN

Of the several possible meanings of monetary policy in this framework, we shall consider two. The first is a one-shot open market purchase. The second is a combination of fiscal and monetary expansion, a once-for-all increase in government expenditure with deficits financed by printing money instead of issuing interest-bearing debt.

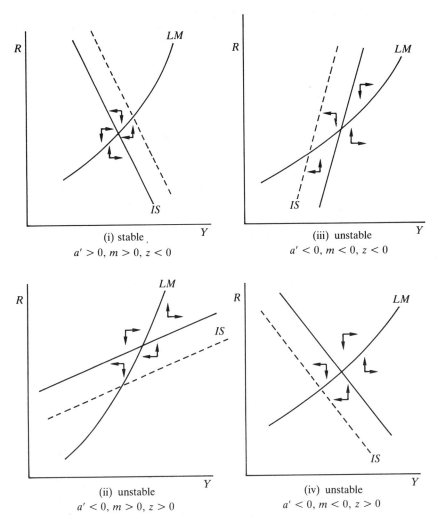

Figure 10.4 Stability or instability of short-run *IS–LM* solution

10.5.1 Open market purchase of bonds

The story of the open market purchase is pictured in Figure 10.5. The framework is Model I, in which $G' = G + rD$ is the parameter of budget policy. The economy starts in long-run equilibrium E_1, with the associated short-run curves LM_1 and IS_1. The new long-run curve LLM_2 implies a new equilibrium E_2, with unchanged Y and lower R. The new stock equilibrium involves the same wealth $W = \hat{\mu}Y$, but a different portfolio. At E_2 the public will hold more money, and less debt-cum-capital, than at

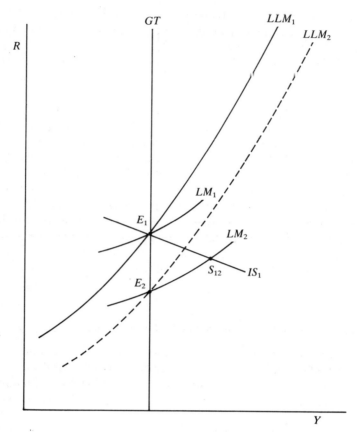

Figure 10.5 Short- and long-run effects of open market purchase in Model I

E_1. But they will also hold more capital, because the desired capital–output ratio $F(R)$ is increased by the reduction in R. Thus ultimately there are two substitutions against debt, one of money in the initial open market operation and one of capital during the process of adjustment.

The shift of short-run LM accomplished by the open market purchase reflects only a money-for-debt substitution. The subsequent capital-for-debt substitution does not affect the LM curves. That is why LM_2 and LLM_2 cross the vertical GT line at the same point. The IS curve is unaffected by the initial operation. (If capital gains on bonds were taken into account, as in the Blinder–Solow model. IS would shift up because of the increase in wealth.) The first impact of the monetary expansion is the short-run solution S_{12}. But the increase in income is temporary. The government is now running a surplus, and, as we have already seen, the contraction of debt brings income down. Meanwhile the public is also saving more (wealth is below $\hat{\mu}Y$) and investing more (capital is less than

$F(R)Y$). The temporary increase in wealth retards the decline of R, and is reversed once capital and wealth catch up with income, which is on its way down.

In Model II, higher interest rates and debt accumulation have an expansionary fiscal effect because they enlarge the budget deficit. The story for case IIa is essentially the same as for Model I, except that the open market purchase shifts the *LIS* curve up. E_2 represents a *smaller* output than E_1. It may seem paradoxical that monetary expansion is, in the long run, contractionary. We do not think the result should be taken seriously, given that it depends on the assumption that monetary expansion entails a fiscal contraction via reduction of debt interest transfers.

In case IIb, E_2 is at higher levels of Y and R than E_1. But there is no way to get there. The open market purchase shifts down the short-run LM curve, increases Y, and decreases R. But from this point the dynamic previously described moves the temporary solution down and to the left.

In case IIc it is quite possible that the dynamics lead to the new equilibrium E_2 with lower R and possibly higher Y.

10.5.2 Fiscal expansion with money-financed deficits

We turn briefly to the monetary financing of deficits combined with expansionary fiscal policy. The previous discussion of fiscal policy is now altered by holding D constant instead of M. In Model I, the long-run GT locus is unchanged, still vertical. But the LM locus becomes

$$\hat{\mu}Y - L(r, 1/\hat{\mu})\hat{\mu}Y - F(R)Y = D, \tag{10.26}$$

$$\left(\frac{\partial R}{\partial Y}\right)_{LLM} = \frac{D/Y}{L_1(1 - \theta)\hat{\mu}Y + F'(R)Y} < 0. \tag{10.27}$$

Thus we see that the long-run LLM locus is negatively sloped. A rightward shift of $\overline{GT}$, as shown in Figure 10.6, is bound to raise equilibrium income Y and lower equilibrium R. The conclusion is not altered in Model II. There the GT locus has an upward slope due to the term rD in the budget-balance equation, even though D is constant. But it is still true that a rightward shift in GT raises equilibrium Y and lowers R.

The dynamics are as follows. The short-run LM locus is

$$W - L(R(1 - \theta), Y/W)W - K = D. \tag{10.28}$$

It is upward-sloping, because M does not increase until a budget deficit actually appears.

$$\left(\frac{\partial R}{\partial Y}\right)_{LM} = -\frac{L_2}{L_1(1 - \theta)W} > 0. \tag{10.29}$$

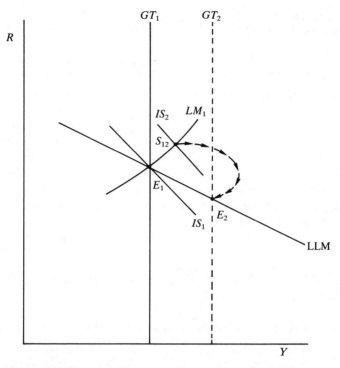

Figure 10.6 Short- and long-run effects of monetized deficit
spending in Model I

The short-run *IS* curve, defined as before, shifts to the right with the increase
of G', but on usual assumptions not as far as the *GT* line. The temporary
solution is at S_{12}. But now there is a budget deficit: M increases, W increases,
IS moves up, *LM* moves down. When the solution crosses GT_2 budget
surpluses appear and arrest the expansion.

For formal analysis of the dynamics of this case, it is convenient to
express the short-run model in terms of the four variables K, W, Y, and R,

$$
\begin{aligned}
\dot{K} &= i(F(R)Y - K) \\
\dot{W} &= s(\hat{\mu}Y - W) \\
0 &= Y(s\hat{\mu} + \theta - iF(R)) - sW + iK - G' \\
0 &= R - R(K, W, Y).
\end{aligned}
\tag{10.30}
$$

Here the function $R(K, W, Y)$ is implicit in Equation (10.28), and its
partial derivatives are

$$
R_1 = \frac{-1}{L_1(1 - \theta)W} > 0
$$

$$R_2 = \frac{1 - L + L_2(Y/W)}{L_1(1 - \theta)W} < 0 \tag{10.31}$$

$$R_3 = \frac{-L_2}{L_1(1 - \theta)W} > 0.$$

The characteristic equation is

$$\begin{vmatrix} -i-\lambda & 0 & iF(R) & iF'(R)Y \\ 0 & -s-\lambda & s & 0 \\ i & -s & 1/m & -iF'(R)Y \\ -R_1 & -R_2 & -R_3 & 1 \end{vmatrix} = 0. \tag{10.32}$$

In the quadratic equation $a\lambda^2 + b\lambda + c$ all three coefficients a, b, c are unambiguously positive, confirming that the comparative static story of Figure 10.6 makes sense.

10.6 EFFECTS OF FISCAL POLICY WITH FULL EMPLOYMENT AND FLEXIBLE PRICES

The standard short-run *IS–LM* analysis applies to situations of full employment as well as unemployment, and in this section we extend our long-run analysis to conditions of full employment and flexible prices and wages. In the short run, output is fixed by the full-employment labor supply. The standard short-run comparative statics is familiar: expansionary fiscal policy, with constant nominal money stock, always raises the interest rate. Unless the demand for money is interest-inelastic and the *LM* curve vertical, it also raises the velocity of money and the price level. Increased real government expenditure 'crowds out' private investment, and possibly also private consumption, to the extent necessary to equate total real demand to fixed real supply. But the short-run analysis does not trace the further effects of these changes on the rates of growth of capital and government debt.

Our long-run full-employment model resembles as closely as possible both the long-run models of the previous sections and the standard short-run full-employment version of *IS–LM* analysis. But differences necessarily arise. Once the price level is made endogenous in a long-run model, we must explicitly consider price expectations and distinguish real and nominal rates of return. Moreover, in a long-run full-employment model the capital stock is endogenous. Output is not fixed, as it is in the short run, by labor supply; output per worker varies with the capital–output ratio and the real interest rate, as illustrated by the $N\bar{N}$ curves of Figures 10.1 and 10.2.

Capital and bonds are, as before, perfect substitutes in portfolios. The portfolio choice of money versus bonds-and-capital depends on the real after-tax rate of return differential between money and bonds. The nominal rate of return on money balances is institutionally fixed at zero. If x is the expected instantaneous proportional rate of change of the price level p, and R the nominal rate of return on bonds, the real rate of return on bonds is $R - x$, and the real after-tax rate of return differential is $R(1 - \theta)$. Portfolio balance is therefore given by

$$L\left(R(1 - \theta),\ Y\middle/\frac{M + D}{P} + K\right)\left(\frac{M + D}{P} + K\right) = \frac{M}{P}.$$ (10.33)

The production function is, as throughout the paper, a well-behaved constant returns to scale neoclassical production function in capital and labor, N,

$$Y = Nf(K/N); \qquad f' > 0, \qquad f'' < 0.$$ (10.34)

Labor is supplied inelastically and is always fully employed. Since we are only considering stationary states we choose units such that $N = 1$.

Rather than specifying the investment function as $I = i[F(R - x)f(K) - K]$, we shall now find it convenient to write it as

$$I = I(f'(K) - (R - x)), \qquad I(0) = 0,\ I' > 0.$$ (10.35)

This function makes the rate of investment an increasing function of the difference between the rate of return obtainable from investing a dollar in the production of new capital goods and the rate of return on existing assets.

We shall consider three simple mechanisms for generating price expectations:

Static expectations: $x(t) = 0,$ (10.36a)

Myopic perfect foresight: $x(t) = \dot{p}(t)/p(t),$ (10.36b)

Adaptive expectations: $\dot{x}(t) = \beta[(\dot{p}/p) - x(t)]; \beta > 0.$ (10.36c)

Government consumption expenditure is fixed in real terms. With bond-financed deficits, the government budget restraint is therefore given by

(I) $\dot{D}/p = G' - \theta f(K),$ (10.37a)
(II) $\dot{D}/p = G + (1 - \theta)R(D/p) - \theta f(K).$ (10.37b)

For reasons of space we shall consider only Model I.

10.6.1 The long-run equilibrium

The complete dynamic model is

$$(IS)\quad I[f'(K) - R + x] + G' - \theta f(K) - s\left[\hat{\mu}f(K) - \left(\frac{M + D}{p}\right) - K\right]$$

$$-x\left(\frac{M + D}{p}\right) = 0. \tag{10.38}$$

The last term in Equation (10.38) represents expected additions, positive or negative, to wealth, due to changes in the real values of nominal stocks of money and debt. It is assumed that current saving from income is adjusted correspondingly.

$$(LM) \quad L\left[R(1 - \theta), \frac{pf(K)}{M + D + pK}\right]\left[\frac{M + D}{p} + K\right] = \frac{M}{p}, \tag{10.39}$$

$$\left(\frac{\dot{D}}{p}\right) = G' - \theta f(K) - \frac{\dot{p}}{p}\frac{D}{p}, \tag{10.40}$$

$$\left(\frac{\dot{M}}{p}\right) = -\frac{\dot{p}}{p}\frac{M}{p}, \tag{10.41}$$

$$\dot{K} = I[f'(K) - R + x], \tag{10.42}$$

$$x = 0, \tag{10.43a}$$

$$x = \frac{\dot{p}}{p}, \tag{10.43b}$$

$$\dot{x} = \beta\left[\frac{\dot{p}}{p} - x\right]. \tag{10.43c}$$

In a stationary long-run equilibrium, expectations are realized, momentary equilibrium holds at each point of time, and real stocks and flows remain constant. Since we are considering only fiscal policies with a constant nominal quantity of money, actual and expected rates of inflation must be zero in long-run equilibrium. In summary,

$$\dot{p}/p = x = \dot{x} = \dot{D} = \dot{K} = 0.$$

The choice of expectations function is irrelevant for the comparative static results of the model, although it crucially affects the dynamics. The stationary-state equilibrium is completely described by the following four equations, which as it happens are recursive, in K, R, p and D.

$$(GT) \quad G' = \theta f(K), \tag{10.44}$$

$$R = f'(K), \tag{10.45}$$

$$(LLM) \quad L\left[R(1 - \theta), \frac{1}{\hat{\mu}}\right]\hat{\mu}f(K) = \frac{M}{p}, \tag{10.46}$$

$$\hat{\mu}f(K) = \frac{M + D}{p} + K. \tag{10.47}$$

Equation (10.45) gives a stationary state relationship between K and R,

$$K = g(R), \qquad g'(R) = 1/f'' < 0.$$

We can therefore represent the long-run equilibrium in $R - p$ space by the GT and LLM curves.

$$G' = \theta f(g(R)),$$

$$L\left[R(1 - \theta), \frac{1}{\hat{\mu}} \right] \hat{\mu} f(g(R)) = \frac{M}{p}.$$

These are illustrated in Figure 10.7.

The slope of the LLM curve is

$$\left(\frac{dR}{dp} \right)_{LLM} = \frac{-Mf''(K)}{[\hat{\mu}f(K)L_1(1 - \theta)f''(K) + L\hat{\mu}f'(K)]p^2} > 0.$$

The slope of the GT curve is

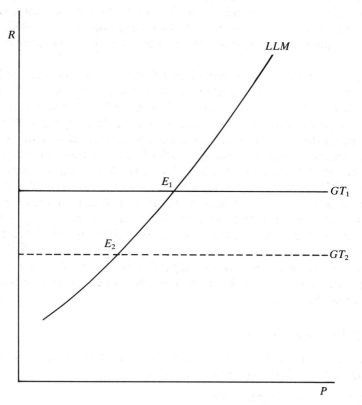

Figure 10.7 Long-run equilibria in the full-employment model

$$\left(\frac{dR}{dp}\right)_{GT} = 0.$$

An increase in G' from G'_1 to G'_2 shifts the GT curve down along the LLM curve in Figure 10.7, lowering equilibrium R and p. Algebraically,

(a) $\dfrac{\partial R}{\partial G'} = \dfrac{f''}{\theta f'} < 0,$

(b) $\dfrac{\partial p}{\partial G'} = -\dfrac{L_1 \hat{\mu} f''(1 - \theta) + L_{\hat{\mu}} \hat{\mu} f'}{\theta f'(K)(M/p^2)} < 0.$

(10.48)

Note that even in the full employment model $\partial Y/\partial G' > 0$; the reason here, however, is capital deepening rather than the elimination of unemployment of labor.

Note also that the effectiveness of fiscal policy here is not at all dependent on the fact that government interest-bearing debt has been counted as part of private sector net worth. Even if the capitalized value of future taxes 'required' to service the debt were exactly equal to the value of these bonds — and there are many sound economic reasons for arguing against such a complete offset — the balanced-budget condition, $G' = \theta f(K)$, will guarantee the long-run effectiveness of fiscal policy, in a comparative-static sense.

The intuitive story behind Equations (10.16) is simple: an increase in G' requires, given θ, a higher level of income to balance the budget. With full employment and a fixed labor force, this means a larger capital stock. This in turn requires a lower R and a higher stationary-state level of wealth. The LLM curve shows that both these effects will increase the demand for real money balances. Since the nominal stock of money is fixed, the price level must be lower to increase the real value of the fixed nominal quantity of money. Prima facie these results would seem to be unstable. As we observed at the outset of this section, the impact effect of an increase in G' is to shift the short-run IS curve to the right and to raise R and p. For the long-run equilibrium to be stable, these impact effects have to be reversed, implying that the economy 'overshoots' in the short run. Nevertheless, under certain conditions, which depend crucially on the expectations mechanism and on the precise numerical values of certain coefficients, the model may be stable.

10.6.2 The impact effects

Figure 10.8 shows the impact effect of an increase in government expenditure G'. The slope of the IS curve is

$$\left(\frac{dR}{dp}\right)_{IS} = -\frac{(s - x)(M + D)}{I' p^2}.$$

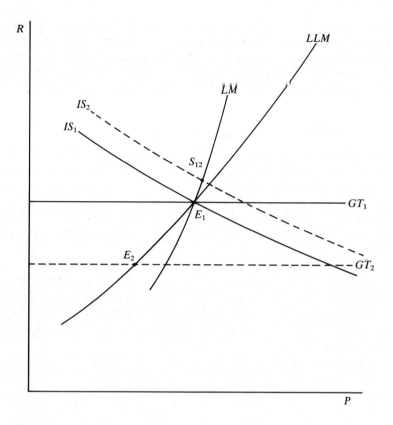

Figure 10.8 Short- and long-run effects of expansionary fiscal policy in the full-employment model

When we are considering the *IS* curve that goes through the long-run equilibrium, $x = 0$ and

$$\left(\frac{dR}{dp}\right)_{IS} = -\frac{s(M + D)}{I'p^2} < 0.$$

The impact effect of an increase in G' will be to shift the *IS* curve to the right.

$$\left(\frac{\partial R}{\partial G'}\right)_{IS} = \frac{1}{I'} > 0.$$

The slope of the *LM* curve is

$$\left(\frac{dR}{dp}\right)_{LM} = \left(-L_2\frac{f(K)}{p}\left[1 - \frac{K}{W}\right] - \frac{MK}{Wp^2}\right)\Big/ WL_1(1 - \theta) > 0.$$

The impact effect of an increase in G' — given M, D, K, x, θ, and the new higher level of G' — is a new temporary equilibrium, as shown in Figure 10.8 (before stocks and expectations have had time to change), at S_{12} with higher p and R. At S_{12}, D will be increasing and K will be decreasing. Except in the case of static expectations, $\dot{x}$ will be positive. The new long-run equilibrium, however, is at E_2, with lower R and p than at E_1.

10.6.3 Stability

The tedious mathematics of the local stability conditions for the full-employment model are relegated to Appendix 10A. To summarize, the long-run equilibrium is unstable in case of static expectations (Equation (10.43a)) and potentially but not necessarily stable in cases of myopic perfect foresight (Equation (10.43b)). In the intermediate case of adaptive expectations (Equation (10.43c)), stability requires but is not guaranteed by a finite minimum speed of adaptation.

These results may seem paradoxical. Usually static expectations are considered stabilizing, while quick translation of actual price experience into expectations is considered destabilizing. The opposite conclusion here is related to the difference in direction between short- and long-run effects, as exhibited in Figure 10.8. This means that some overshooting is necessary for the long-run equilibrium to be stable.

The apparent paradox arises from the endogeneity of K and Y, and the related endogeneity of $\dot{D}$ and D. At a position like S_{12} in Figure 10.8, the Pigou effect is pulling consumption down, and the increase in $R - x$ is unfavorable to investment. On the other hand, the real deficit is positive and D is growing, an effect accentuated as real tax revenues decline along with the capital stock K and real income Y. The latter effect, which is the source of instability, is absent from the short-run story. The expected rate of inflation itself has two effects on short-run aggregate demand along the adjustment path. One is to raise investment by lowering the real rate of interest, and the other is to increase saving to make up for expected real capital losses on money and debt. A necessary, but not sufficient, condition for stability is that the investment effect is the stronger. This means that if the rate of inflation slows down and if the slowdown is translated fairly promptly into expectations, aggregate demand and the income-related demand for money will weaken. A weakening of aggregate demand leads, in an economy with flexible prices, to a reduction in the price level and the real interest rate and to an increase in capital stock and real income. Unfortunately, the issue of stability turns on relatively minor details of specification and on small differences in values of coefficients. It is possible that fiscal expansion sets off an unstable spiral of inflation, deficits, rising interest rates, and dwindling capital stock and output. It is also possible that it is the start of an oscillation that converges to an equilibrium with lower price level, lower interest rate, higher capital stock and income.

10.7 CONCLUSION

Nothing in the analysis of this paper supports the claim that expansionary fiscal effects on aggregate demand are only transitory. To investigate the question, the main section of this paper focused on the pure logic of aggregate demand. Supply constraints were assumed away — there is always labor available to produce the output demanded. In this situation, an increase in government expenditure either leads to a new long-run equilibrium with higher real income or, in unstable cases, to an explosive increase in income and interest rate. We do not stress the latter possibility, since it depends on built-in fiscal expansion via debt interest payments and since the economy would sooner or later hit a full-employment ceiling.

Interest-inelasticity of demand for money seems to be crucial for the strong monetarist proposition after all. A fiscally driven expansion could, of course, occur but vanish if the short-run *LM* curve is not vertical while the long-run *LLM* curve is vertical. We are not aware that this argument has been made.

In future work on this subject, not motivated by any particular propositions, monetarist or otherwise, we would embed the moving short-run equilibria in a growth model rather than a stationary state. (The growth model is more confining. A stationary-state equilibrium just requires zero changes of stocks, and there are lots of configurations of stocks consistent with that condition. An equilibrium growth path requires that flows stand in the same relation to each other as the corresponding stocks.) Moreover, we would find more congenial a model which allows debt and capital to be imperfect substitutes with distinct rates of return. Clearly a more satisfactory model would also recognize that even when the economy is not at full employment nominally denominated stocks change in real value from price movements as well as from fiscal and monetary policies.

In Section 10.6 we considered the long-run effects of fiscal expansion in an economy with full employment and flexible prices. Here there is a striking difference between impact and ultimate effects. The new long-run equilibrium, after a permanent increase of government expenditure, has larger real income and capital stock but lower price level and interest rate. But such equilibria are stable, if at all, only if price expectations adapt fairly quickly to price experience.

Finally, we observe again that it is disturbing that the qualitative properties of models — the signs of important system-wide multipliers, the stability of equilibria — can turn on relatively small changes of specification or on small differences in values of coefficients. We do not feel entitled to use the 'correspondence principle' assumption of stability to derive restrictions on structural equations and parameters. There is no divine guarantee that the economic system is stable.

10.8 NOTES

1. A summary, with an important amendment, is given by the same authors in Blinder and Solow (1974, pp. 45–58). The amendment is to include income, Y, in the investment function: we discuss its significance in Section 10.3. Blinder and Solow appear to have contributed the first systematic treatment of long-run effects of fiscal policy in an economy without binding labor constraints on output. Of course, growth theory has treated the long-run effects of fiscal and monetary policies in economies with full employment and flexible prices. Even there, fiscal and monetary measures are generally so intertwined that 'money-growth' models shed little light on the issues concerning 'pure' fiscal and monetary effects.

2. An inessential difference, the modelling of government debt as perpetuities, has already been mentioned.

3. An alternative which would be more plausible would be to aim fiscal policy for budget balance at a target income level, Y^*, fixing the level of government exhaustive expenditures at G, and letting θ vary with debt interest so as to maintain budget balance at Y^*. We investigated such a model, but the analysis is too messy to report.

10.9 REFERENCES

Blinder, A.S. and R.M. Solow (1973) 'Does fiscal policy matter?', *Journal of Public Economics*, 2, pp. 319–37.

Blinder, A.S. and R.M. Solow (1974) *The Economics of Public Finance*, Brookings Institution, Washington, DC.

Friedman, M. (1972) 'Comments on the critics', *Journal of Political Economy*, September.

Tobin, J. (1971) *Essays in Economics, Vol. I: Macroeconomics*, North-Holland, Amsterdam, pp. 378–455.

APPENDIX 10A: STABILITY IN THE FULL EMPLOYMENT MODEL

We solve the short-run *LM* and *IS* equations for R and P as functions of D, K and x, given M, G' and θ, and evaluate these solutions at the long-run equilibrium $(D^*, K^*, 0)$,

$$R = h^1(D, K, x; M, G', \theta), \tag{10A.1a}$$

$$P = h^2(D, K, x; M, G', \theta). \tag{10A.1b}$$

The reduced-form impact multipliers are solved for from

$$
\begin{bmatrix}
-I' & \dfrac{-s(M + D)}{p^2} \\[2ex]
WL_1(1 - \theta) & \dfrac{L_2 f(K)}{p}\left(1 - \dfrac{K}{W}\right) + \dfrac{MK}{Wp^2}
\end{bmatrix}
\begin{bmatrix}
\mathrm{d}R \\[2ex]
\mathrm{d}P
\end{bmatrix}
$$

$$
= \left[
\begin{array}{c}
\dfrac{-s}{p}\mathrm{d}D + \left((\theta + s\hat{\mu})f'(K) - I'f''(K) - s\right)\mathrm{d}K - \left(I' - \dfrac{(M+D)}{p}\right)\mathrm{d}x \\[12pt]
\left(\dfrac{L_2 f(K)}{pW} \quad \dfrac{L}{p}\right)\mathrm{d}D + \left(\; L_2 f'(K) + \dfrac{L_2 f(K)}{W} \quad L \right)\mathrm{d}K
\end{array}
\right]
$$

The signs of these derivatives are not all determined, given the a priori restrictions we have imposed so far:

$h_D^1 > 0$,
h_K^1 is undetermined; if $(\theta + s\hat{\mu})f' - I'f'' - s < 0$, $h_K^1 > 0$,
h_D^2 is undetermined,
h_K^2 is undetermined; if $(\theta + s\hat{\mu})f' - I'f'' - s > 0$, $h_K^2 < 0$,
h_x^1 is undetermined; $h_x^1 > 0$ if and only if $I' - (M + D)/p > 0$,
h_x^2 is undetermined; $h_x^2 > 0$ if and only if $I' - (M + D)/p > 0$.

We now consider stability for the three mechanisms for generating expectations:

Static expectations: $x = 0$

The dynamic equations are

$$\dot{D} = p[G' - \theta f(K)], \tag{10A.2a}$$

$$\dot{K} = I[f'(K) - R]. \tag{10A.2b}$$

Substituting Equations (10A.1a) and (10A.1b) into these equations, and taking the linear approximation at the long-run equilibrium (D^*, K^*) we get

$$
\begin{bmatrix} \dot{D} \\ \dot{K} \end{bmatrix} =
\begin{bmatrix} 0 & -p\theta f' \\ -I'h_D^1 & I'[f'' - h_K^1] \end{bmatrix}
\begin{bmatrix} D - D^* \\ K - K^* \end{bmatrix}. \tag{10A.3}
$$

Necessary and sufficient conditions for stability are

$$I'(f'' - h_K^1) < 0, \tag{10A.4a}$$

$$-I'h_D^1 p\theta f' > 0. \tag{10A.4b}$$

Equation (10A.4a) may be satisfied, Equation (10A.4b) never is; the long-run equilibrium is unstable under static expectations. Figure 10A.1 illustrates this instability with the familiar phase diagram in $D-K$ space.

Myopic perfect foresight: $\dot{p}/p = x$

The complete dynamic system can in this case be written as

$$I\left[f'(K) - R + \frac{\dot{p}}{p}\right] + G' - \theta f(K)$$

$$-s\left[\hat{\mu}f(K) - \frac{M + D}{p} - K\right] - \frac{\dot{p}}{p}\frac{M + D}{p} = 0, \tag{10A.5a}$$

$$L\left[R(1 - \theta), \frac{pf(K)}{M + D + pK}\right]\left[\frac{M + D}{p} + K\right] = \frac{M}{p}, \tag{10A.5b}$$

$$\dot{D} = p[G' - \theta f(K)], \tag{10A.5c}$$

$$\dot{K} = I\left[f'(K) - R + \frac{\dot{p}}{p}\right]. \tag{10A.5d}$$

We solve Equation (10A.5b) for R as a function of p, K and D, given M and θ,

$$R = R(p, D, K), \tag{10A.5e}$$

$$R_p = \left(\frac{-L_2 f(K)}{p}\left[1 - \frac{K}{W}\right] - \frac{MK}{Wp^2}\right)\bigg/ WL_1(1 - \theta) > 0, \tag{10A.6a}$$

$$R_D = \left(\frac{L_2 f(K)}{pW} - \frac{L}{p}\right)\bigg/ WL_1(1 - \theta) > 0, \tag{10A.6b}$$

$$R_K = \left(-L_2 f'(K) + \frac{L_2 f(K)}{W} - L\right)\bigg/ WL_1(1 - \theta) > 0. \tag{10A.6c}$$

Substituting Equation (10A.5e) into Equations (10A.5a), (10A.5c) and (10A.5d) and linearizing at the equilibrium (K^*, D^*, p^*) gives

$$\begin{bmatrix} \dot{p} \\ \\ \dot{D} \\ \\ \dot{K} \end{bmatrix} = \begin{bmatrix} \dfrac{\left[I'R_p + s\dfrac{(M + D)}{p^2}\right]p}{I' - \dfrac{M + D}{p}} & \dfrac{\left[-\dfrac{s}{p} + I'R_D\right]p}{I' - \dfrac{M + D}{p}} \\ \\ 0 & 0 \\ \\ \dfrac{I'\dfrac{M + D}{p}\left[R_p + \dfrac{s}{p}\right]}{I' - \dfrac{M + D}{p}} & \dfrac{\dfrac{I'}{p}[R_D(M + D) - s]}{I' - \dfrac{M + D}{p}} \end{bmatrix}$$

$$\begin{bmatrix} \dfrac{[-I'f''(K) + I'R_K + \theta f'(K) + s\hat{u}f'(K) - s]p}{I' - \dfrac{M + D}{p}} \\[2em] -p\theta f'(K) \\[1em] \dfrac{I'\left[-f''(K)\dfrac{M + D}{p} + R_K\dfrac{M + D}{p} + \theta f'(K) + s\hat{u}f'(K) - s\right]}{I' - \dfrac{M + D}{p}} \end{bmatrix} \begin{bmatrix} p - p^* \\[1em] D - D^* \\[1em] K - K^* \end{bmatrix}$$

$$(10A.7)$$

The characteristic equation of the coefficient matrix can be written as

$$a_0\lambda^3 + a_1\lambda^2 + a_2\lambda + a_3 = 0; \qquad a_0 > 0.$$

Necessary and sufficient for all characteristic roots to have negative real parts are

$$a_1 > 0,$$

$$a_2 > 0,$$

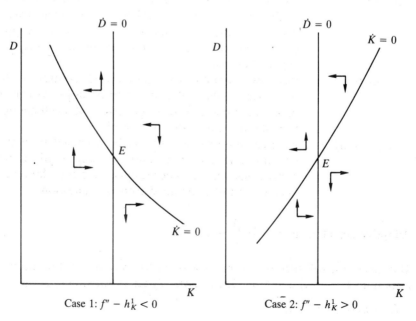

Case 1: $f'' - h_K^1 < 0$ Case 2: $f'' - h_K^1 > 0$

Figure 10A.1 Stability in the full-employment model under static expectations

$a_3 > 0,$

$a_1 a_2 - a_0 a_3 > 0,$

One of the first two inequalities can be eliminated since it is implied by the remaining three.

The characteristic equation of the system is

$$\lambda^3 + \left(\frac{-I'\left[\dfrac{(M+D)}{p}(R_K - f'') + f'(\theta + s\hat{\mu}) - s\right] - \left[I'R_p + s\dfrac{(M+D)}{p^2}\right]p}{I' - \dfrac{M+D}{p}} \right)\lambda^2$$

$$+ I'\left(\frac{\theta f'[R_D(M+D) - s] + R_p[f'(\theta + s\hat{\mu}) - s]p + \dfrac{s}{p}(M+D)(f'' - R_K)}{I' - \dfrac{M+D}{p}} \right)\lambda$$

$$+ \frac{s\theta I' f'[pR_p + (M+D)R_D]}{I' - \dfrac{M+D}{p}} = 0.$$

A detailed analysis of the necessary and sufficient conditions for stability would require a lot of space for rather little additional insight; some brief remarks will suffice:

$a_3 > 0,$ requires $I' - (M + D)/p > 0$: the effect of an increase in the expected rate of inflation is to create excess demand in the goods market. As we shall see, this condition is also necessary for stability in the adaptive expectations case.

$a_1, a_2 > 0,$ these two conditions set rather strict bounds on the permissible values of s; it has to be large enough to make the numerator of a_1 positive, but small enough to make the numerator of a_2 positive.

$a_1 a_2 - a_0 a_3 > 0,$ no great intuitive insight can be obtained from this condition; it does not contradict any a priori sign restrictions on the coefficients; stability, however, becomes a rather detailed empirical question.

Adaptive expectations: $\dot{x} = \beta\left(\dfrac{\dot{p}}{p} - x\right)$

This case too, will turn out to be at least potentially stable. Substituting Equations (10A.1a) and (10A.1b) into the dynamic equations, we get

$$\dot{D} = p(G' - \theta f(K)),$$

$$\dot{K} = I[f'(K) - h^1(D, K, x) + x],$$

$$\dot{x} = \left(\beta \frac{\dot{h}^2(D, K, x)}{h^2(D, K, x)} - x \right).$$

A linear approximation at the equilibrium $(D^*, K^*, 0)$ gives

$$
\begin{bmatrix} \dot{D} \\ \\ \dot{K} \\ \\ \dot{x} \end{bmatrix}
=
\begin{bmatrix}
0 & -p\theta f' \\
-I'h_D^1 & I'(f'' - h_K^1) \\
\dfrac{-\beta h_K^2 I'h_D^1}{p - \beta h_x^2} \quad \dfrac{p\beta}{p - \beta h_x^2}\left[-h_D^2\theta f' + \dfrac{h_K^2}{p}I'(f'' - h_K^1) \right]
\end{bmatrix}
$$

$$
\begin{bmatrix}
0 \\
I'(1 - h_x^1) \\
\dfrac{p\beta}{p - \beta h_x^2}\left[\dfrac{h_K^2}{p}I'(1 - h_x^1) - 1 \right]
\end{bmatrix}
\begin{bmatrix}
D - D^* \\
K - K^* \\
x - 0
\end{bmatrix}.
$$

$$(10A.8)$$

The characteristic equation is

$$
\lambda^3 - \left\{ I'(f'' - h_K^1) + \frac{p\beta}{p - \beta h_x^2}\left[\frac{h_K^2}{p}I'(1 - h_x^1) - 1 \right] \right\}\lambda^2
$$

$$
- \left\{ I'(f'' - h_K^1)\frac{p\beta}{p - \beta h_x^2} - I'(1 - h_x^1)\frac{p\beta}{p - \beta h_x^2}h_D^2\theta f' + I'h_D^1 p\theta f' \right\}\lambda
$$

$$
- I'h_D^1 p\theta f' \frac{p\beta}{p - \beta h_x^2} = 0.
$$

The linearized version of the static expectations model (10A.3) is found back as the upper left 2×2 submatrix in the linearized version of the adaptive expectations model (10A.8). The static expectations model can therefore be regarded as a limiting case of the adaptive expectations model, when $\beta = 0$ (and terms like h_x^1 and h_x^2 are irrelevant because $x \equiv 0$),

$$
a_3 = -I'h_D^1 p\theta f' \frac{p\beta}{p - \beta h_x^2} > 0
$$

is necessary for stability. Since $h_D^1 > 0$, $a_3 > 0$ if and only if $p - \beta h_x^2 < 0$, i.e. only if $h_x^2 > 0$; the impact effect of a rise in inflationary expectations is to increase the price level. $h_x^2 > 0$ if and only if $I' - [(M + D)/p] > 0$, which is the condition we derived for myopic perfect foresight. It is clear that with $\beta = 0$ (the static expectations case) $a_3 = 0$ and the system will not be stable.

11 · FISCAL AND MONETARY POLICIES, CAPITAL FORMATION, AND ECONOMIC ACTIVITY

(with James Tobin)

Large econometric models assign to fiscal and monetary policies considerable influence on the paths of output, employment, investment, and other real economic variables, and through them on wages, prices, and inflation. These models are generally Keynesian in structure. They attribute short-run fluctuations in economic activity primarily to variation of aggregate demand. They explain aggregate demand for goods and services from its components — consumption, domestic investment, government purchases, foreign investment. Among the determinants of these expenditures and their subcomponents are macroeconomic policies, or variables more or less directly dependent on these policies. Empirical models of this genre are widely used for forecasting and for comparing alternative policies.

Yet their theoretical foundations are under strenuous attack. The attacks differ, but they converge on a single point: fiscal and monetary policies have little or no influence on real economic outcomes, short or long run. Active use of these instruments to stabilize and steer the economy will not succeed and may have adverse side effects. These views have gained a substantial following among economists, policy-makers, and influential laymen. If they are correct, most econometric models are wrong, and so are similar but less elaborate and less formal accounts of the way macroeconomic policies work.

This paper will review major theoretical issues concerning the effects of fiscal and monetary policies, with particular stress on their effects on capital formation. We will consider challenges to the modern Keynesian paradigm. The lively theoretical controversies of recent years have sharpened understanding of macroeconomic structure and of the complexities of policy-making. We conclude that the essential messages of the paradigm

This paper was originally published in G.M. von Furstenberg (ed.) (1980) *The Government and Capital Formation*, Ballinger, Cambridge, MA, pp. 73–151.

remain relevant: macroeconomic policies have important and durable real effects, for better or worse.

Readers who wish to avoid the technicalities of formal analysis of theoretical models will be able to find our central message in the text. However, Appendix 11A sets forth a model of asset and commodity markets in which the effects of government fiscal and financial policies are rigorously analyzed.

11.1   CROWDING-OUT AND NEUTRALITY: THEORETICAL ISSUES

The government policies to be discussed are of three main types: purchases of goods and services; financing of purchases by taxation, debt issue, and monetary issue; and other monetary and financial policies. The first refers principally to variations in the aggregate real amount of goods and services purchased for government use. The content of these purchases — for example, the mix of public investment, collective consumption, and 're- grettable necessities' like defense and internal security — is also relevant to some issues. The second refers to the mixture of sources of financing of a given expenditure program. Taxation is to be reckoned net of transfer payments or 'negative taxes', government payments to economic agents for which no goods or services are currently rendered in return. The kinds of taxes and transfers used — whether lump-sum, direct, or indirect — are important for some issues. Debt issue means sale of interest-bearing obligations to non-governmental buyers, typically at market-determined prices. Public debt obligations are predominantly promises to pay the national currency at specified dates in the future. Price-indexed bonds are seldom issued, and we shall not consider them in this paper.

A national government can also finance outlays by issuing its own currency, which bears no interest at all. With modern banking institutions, the printing press is largely supplanted by a more sophisticated process. Central bank purchases of its government's securities augment, directly or indirectly, the government's demand deposit account in the central bank. As the Treasury draws on the account to pay its bills, this convenient equivalent of currency is transferred to private ownership. In the United States deposits in Federal Reserve Banks are reserves for member com- mercial banks. The supply of base money, or what we call 'high-powered' money, is also augmented when the central bank buys foreign currency assets, gold, or other international reserves. Monetary financing of current government expenditure is operationally the same as monetization of pre- existing debt by central bank open market purchases. But it is useful to maintain a conceptual distinction between monetary issue for financing the current budget deficit and other open market operations. The third category of policies could include central bank manipulation of other instruments including its lending rate, reserve requirements, and ceiling rates on bank deposits. But we shall not discuss them in this paper.

The effects of these policies are likely to depend on the economic environment in which they are applied and to differ with the length of time during which the economy adapts to them. With respect to economic environment, the important distinction is between situations with unemployed resources which can be productively employed by expansion of aggregate demand, and situations in which output is limited by supplies of productive resources. By supply limits we do not mean the technological and physical maxima applicable to wartime mobilizations. We refer rather to market-clearing equilibria in which product and factor prices have successfully balanced supplies and demands throughout the economy. Output is not supply-constrained in disequilibria in which excess supplies of labor, capital services, and other resources persist at prevailing prices, disequilibria to which price and wage levels and trends adjust slowly and sluggishly. Some theorists — the protagonists of the 'new classical macro-economics' — contend that underemployment disequilibria are infrequent and transient. They describe the economy as a sequence of market-clearing equilibria. This viewpoint naturally colors their view of macroeconomic policy interventions.[1] We shall not debate this empirical proposition here, but simply record our belief that underemployment of labor and capital is sufficiently frequent and persistent to justify analysis of policy interventions in both environments.

As for time horizons, we shall consider short runs of both environments, and long runs with full utilization, meaning by 'short run' a period in which the economy has not reached a stationary or steady growth equilibrium, and, in particular, has not adapted completely to prevailing policies. Full adaptation has several dimensions. One is that expectations about policy and other variables are realized: agents have no reason in experience to revise the expectations on which they act. Another is that stocks of assets and debts are stationary or growing at a common steady rate; otherwise behavior will change as a result of uneven stock accumulation. But, unlike Keynes's short run, ours are not so short that asset accumulation is altogether ignored. We wish to allow current saving and financial flows to affect supplies and demands in asset markets, saving to augment wealth, investment to increase the capital stock, government deficits to raise the public debt. The model specified in Appendix 11A enables us to examine both stock and flow effects of government financial policies.

We shall also analyze the effects of policies in long-run stationary or steady-growth equilibrium, where expectations are fulfilled and asset supplies have adjusted to permanent long-run demands. In both 'runs', one of our interests is the effect of policy on capital formation. In the short run the variable of interest is real investment; in the long run it is the stock of capital per worker or per unit of output.

11.1.1 Government purchases of goods and services

The proposition that government purchases have macroeconomic effects is scarcely controversial. In buying goods and services for public use, the government is clearly doing something real, which will almost inevitably have real consequences. Neutrality has been claimed for government financial policies, but rarely for exhaustive (resource-using) public expenditures. Indeed those who argue that finance does not matter stress that the true measure of fiscal burden is always the share of national product used by government.

In a fully employed closed economy, public purchases always displace other uses of resources. The only question is which ones. The answer may depend partly on the nature of public expenditures. Perhaps they provide goods or services which are close substitutes for current private consumption. Perhaps they are capital projects which will yield future consumption or augment the productivity of the nation's resources, whether employed privately or publicly. Perhaps they are expenditures for war or defense or internal security, which substitute for neither present nor future consumption. Rarely are government purchases perceived to provide citizens with such close duplicates of what they are already doing for themselves that citizens cut their private purchases and automatically cede the economic room. As a rule, less direct mechanisms of 'crowding out' are needed: increases in prices or interest rates.[2]

In underemployment situations, 'crowding-out' is not arithmetically inevitable. The question is then the degree to which government purchases increase aggregate demand. If the government provides goods that are by nature substitutes for private consumption or investment, direct 'crowding out' may occur. Otherwise, government purchases add to aggregate demand at prevailing prices and interest rates. Private agents have no incentive to make offsetting reductions in their spending, and no tightening of their budget constraints forces them to do so. According to the famous 'balanced budget multiplier theorem', this is true even if the incremental government expenditures are matched by taxes: the multiplier is one. It is *at least* equally true if they are financed by borrowing or by printing money. Keynesians would expect the multiplier to exceed one in those cases; presumably the 'neo-Ricardians' who argue that finance does not matter would keep it at one if the spending increase is temporary.

11.1.2 Monetary crowding-out versus monetary accommodation

However, monetary policy may not *accommodate* an increase in national product as large as the increase in government purchases. In this case, the multiplier will be less than one, perhaps zero. Private expenditures for goods and services will decline, perhaps by as much as government purchases rise. Monetary crowding-out is a third mechanism, to be distinguished from crowding-out forced by supply constraints and from displacement by individual agents' substitution of public for private goods.

Accommodation means that the central bank provides an additional supply of money equal to the additional demand for money generated by the new government purchases, enough to keep constant the interest rates relevant for private spending decisions. The additional demand for money arises from the extra private transactions involved; agents receive incomes from selling goods and services to government, and return the funds to government in taxes or purchases of securities. To manage the extra transactions, they may need on average somewhat higher cash balances. (The government does, too, but its cash balances are not conventionally counted in the money stock under any definition. For this reason, the extra transactions demand for money is smaller when GNP rises from government purchases than when it rises by the same amount from private purchases.) If the central bank does not provide the extra money, the attempts of households and businesses to obtain it by borrowing or selling securities will raise interest rates; monetary crowding-out will occur.

The most common scenario is that interest rates rise, inducing some economy in cash management and reduction in money demand but also inducing some reduction in investment, and possibly in consumption. Complete crowding-out would occur if the money stock were maintained unchanged and if the rise in interest rates induced no economy of money demand.[3]

Analyses of this kind assume a monetary policy, expressed in terms of money stock or interest rates or some combination, which remains the same regardless of the government budget and its consequences for aggregate demand. Normally, though not invariably, the monetary authority has discretion. The central bank can accommodate or not, as it chooses. Thus the central bank can oppose and offset a fiscal stimulus by restricting the money stock and its growth as necessary. Or the central bank can accommodate the fiscal stimulus by whatever money supply is needed to validate its multiplier. In this sense, whatever crowding-out occurs is either accidental and unintentional or is the deliberate consequence of monetary policy.[4] Leaving aside transient errors of policy, it is possible to attribute decline in investment to an increase in government purchases if and only if one takes for granted the path of total national product the central bank is willing to accommodate. The monetary constraint on output then has the same effect as a resource or supply constraint.

In interpreting and appraising monetary crowding-out, several possible cases should be distinguished.

1. The central bank and the fiscal authorities — Congress and president in the United States — agree on the desirable path of GNP. The increase in government purchases is not intended to stimulate the economy but only to carry out the government's substantive programs. Here it is quite appropriate that the needed resources be obtained from other uses of GNP. Individual economists and citizens may, of course, disagree either with the macroeconomic policy or with the allocation of resources. But the policies are consistent. The policy-makers may regard a GNP path with unemployed resources as desirable because the government desires to diminish the prevailing inflation rate or to avoid risks of accelerating inflation by a more rapid growth in aggregate demand. Or the government may be unwilling to accept the external consequences, current account deficit, loss of international reserves or exchange depreciation, of a higher GNP path.

2. The central bank and the fiscal authorities differ in their GNP targets, and the central bank has independent power. The government would welcome a higher GNP path, but cannot persuade the central bank to bring it about. The government tries to reach its objective by fiscal stimulus, or at least welcomes the expansionary by-products of budget expenditures adopted on their own merits. The central bank's refusal to accommodate thwarts the fiscal stimulus, and crowding-out is a symptom and consequence of this unresolved conflict over macroeconomic policy. Here it is almost inevitable that the composition of output, along whatever aggregate path results from the policy tug-of-war, is less than optimal from the viewpoint of either side. For example, the path will contain less private investment and more government purchases than either would have desired had they compromised in advance on the actually realized GNP path. Even though the central bank has the last word, the realized path is not necessarily its original target. Apart from the inevitable errors of monetary marksmanship, the central bank probably modifies its GNP target in the government's direction, for obvious political reasons but also for economic reasons. One reason to give a little on GNP is to avoid large increases in interest rates and to limit the crowding-out of investment.

3. The central bank and the fiscal authority agree that more rapid expansion of aggregate demand is desirable. But the monetary managers are, or feel they are, unable to bring it about. Consequently fiscal stimulus is welcomed by both sets of policy-makers, and the central bank is happy to accommodate. Why is monetary stimulus impossible? One case is the 'liquidity trap', the nominal interest rate floor Keynes detected in the Great Depression. The floor is no problem today, but the economy may be highly liquid even when

nominal interest rates are well above zero. In such circumstances expansionary monetary policy may work but only weakly and slowly; as the central bankers say, 'You can't push on a string.' Another case is that external financial objectives establish a floor for interest rates. In the early 1960s, for example, exchange rates were pegged and US payments deficits threatened losses of gold reserves and of foreign confidence in the dollar. The Federal Reserve and Treasury were committed to hold short-term interest rates competitive with those abroad. Fiscal stimulus was the only tool available for the 1961–5 recovery.

4. The central bank is making policy by reference to its instruments or to intermediate targets, as well as or instead of macroeconomic results. The result of fiscal stimulus then depends on what this policy is. During most of the 1950s and 1960s Federal Reserve policy was 'leaning against the wind'. The Treasury–Federal Reserve Accord of 1951 released the Fed from its wartime commitment to peg interest rates on government securities. Thereafter the central bank supplied only partially the bank reserves required to meet the demands for credit and deposits generated by cyclical expansion of economic activity, and withdrew only partially the reserves released in cyclical contractions. As a result, interest rates moved procyclically. In effect, the policy introduced a short-run positive interest elasticity to money supply, reinforcing whatever negative interest elasticity there is in money demand. In this monetary environment, expansionary fiscal policy — like any other autonomous increase in demand — has a positive multiplier but crowds out some interest-sensitive private expenditure. In the 1970s the Fed has shifted toward money stock targets, specifically to ranges of growth rates for monetary aggregates. They have not gone so far in this direction as to adopt the strict monetarist rule advocated by Milton Friedman, namely growth of money stock at a constant rate invariant to interest rates and other economic events. The result of this policy shift is to increase the procyclical variability of interest rates, to make the short-run *LM* curve steeper, to diminish fiscal policy multipliers, and to increase the degree of crowding-out attributable to government expenditures.

11.1.3 The financing of government expenditure

We turn now to the financing of government expenditures for goods and services. Given the volume and composition of government expenditures, does it matter whether they are financed by taxes, debt issues, or printing money? Does it make any difference to aggregate demand? Do tax reductions or increased transfer payments stimulate business activity? Do they increase employment and output when there is slack in the economy? Are they inflationary when resources are fully employed? Do government deficits absorb saving that would otherwise either disappear in unemployment or finance private capital formation?

'Yes' is the traditional Keynesian answer to all these questions. 'No' is the new classical answer: only government purchases are a burden or stimulus, and their effect is independent of their financing.

The issue is whether or not households internalize government saving or dissaving and adjust private saving dollar for dollar to realize a desired amount of total national saving. Keynes argues that they do not. In his discussion of the national propensity to save he included the government budget as an independent determinant (Keynes, 1936, Chapter 8, especially pp. 94–5, 98). In subsequent theoretical and empirical work, this view was rationalized and simplified by relating personal consumption and saving to *disposable income*, income after taxes and transfer payments (and excluding retained corporate profits). This specification implies that a dollar of tax reduction, for example, increases personal saving from a given pre-tax income only by a fraction of a dollar, the marginal propensity to save.

Real disposable income 'explained' extraordinarily well both variations of annual real consumption in the United States between the two world wars and variations across households in cross-section surveys. Consequently many theorists, statistical model-builders, and textbook writers embraced this simple consumption function too uncritically. Abba Lerner's (1946, Chapter 24) doctrine of *functional finance*, for example, relied on the premise that consumer spending could be closely controlled by adjusting taxes and transfers.

This position emphasized, if only tacitly, consumers' dependence on income receipts for the cash needed to make purchases. This emphasis is suggested by the very word 'disposable'. It surely exaggerates the dependence of consumers on contemporaneous receipts as a source of liquid cash. Moreover, disposable income as computed omits some cash inflows and contains some illiquid accruals, for example, deductions and employer contributions for pensions and other fringe benefits which appear as 'other labor income' in US national income accounts. Keynes himself, in expounding the consumption function as a 'psychological law', did not regard it as a liquidity-constrained relation between cash inflow and cash outflow.

Over the post-war years the theory and statistical practice of consumption and saving relations have moved toward a longer-run perspective on household behavior. Most households do not live hand-to-mouth, but consciously or unconsciously base consumption outlays on calculation of the standard of living they can afford over a horizon of months or years or decades. They are able to free consumption from slavish conformity to receipts by reducing their current saving, by borrowing, or by drawing down liquid assets. Their budget constraints allow considerable choice between consumption now and at various future dates. From this perspective, wealth — the sum over the horizon of current net worth and the present value of future after-tax earnings from household labor and of future transfers — becomes the effective constraint. This modification increases the estimated marginal propensity to save from current disposable income and lowers the tax-cut or transfer multiplier.

According to the *permanent income hypothesis* of Milton Friedman (1957), current consumption is related to average expected disposable income, *permanent income*, rather than to contemporaneous disposable income alone. His theoretical development of the hypothesis refers to horizons of expectation varying from infinite to two periods. In empirical applications he seems to have in mind horizons of only three to five years. The claim that the marginal propensity to consume from transient deviations of current from permanent income, is zero does not apply strictly to finite horizons. But the hypothesis explains why consumption is less variable than income and why saving is more volatile than either consumption or income. And it predicts that temporary tax reductions or transfers will have much less effect on consumption than permanent changes of equal annual amount.

In similar spirit the *life cycle* model assumes a lifetime horizon and relates consumption and saving to the present value of lifetime consumable resources. This model also downgrades the effect of temporary tax cuts or transfers. Current consumption and saving are simply one decision variable in a household's multi-period plan designed to spread existing and expected resources over a lifetime in a pattern that maximizes expected utility.

Household horizons can be extended to allow for utility enjoyed by descendants and for intergenerational bequests and gifts. In the extreme, these linkages make the household's horizon infinite. Just as utility allows directly or indirectly for the consumption of descendants, so the effective budget constraint includes their expected earnings discounted to the present. Individuals' concern for the well-being of their parents and grandparents, and gifts from younger to older contemporaries, can also be modeled. The longer the horizon the weaker the connection between consumption and contemporary income, and the greater the influence of remote events on current behavior.

In application of these models to government financial policy, a great deal depends on what expectations current policies generate about future real incomes after taxes. For example, conventional analysis of the effects of temporary tax cuts or transfers assigns them some stimulative power, though less than permanent changes, on the assumption that taxes and transfers will revert to the levels previously anticipated. The multi-period budget constraint faced by a typical household is relaxed; the present value of current and future tax liabilities net of transfers is diminished.

A stronger assumption is that the current fiscal stimulus will be offset by subsequent increases in taxes above the reference path, to pay the interest and/or principal of the currently incurred government debt. Assuming households perceive those liabilities and discount them at the interest rate at which the government borrows, their multi-period budget constraint has not changed, and neither will their behavior. Current fiscal deficits are perceived simply as deferred tax levies, as certain as death and taxes are proverbially reputed to be. This is the new classical or 'Ricardian' theory of public debt, supporting the proposition that government finance has no effect on either aggregate demand or its composition.[5]

The proposition, in its strongest form, is applied both to debt finance and to money finance. When the government shifts from taxes to interest-bearing debt, expectations of additional future taxes of equal present value offset the current tax reduction. When the shift is to money, free of nominal interest, there is no implication that taxes will be higher in the future. What losses, currently incurred or expected, offset the public's increased holdings of money? The losses are losses of purchasing power because of changes in commodity prices, current or expected. To assimilate those losses to explicit taxes, they are metaphorically described as inflation taxes.

These strong assertions of neutrality deserve serious consideration. We shall discuss first the case of debt finance, examining critically the Ricardian theory. This is followed by discussion of monetary finance and by critique of monetarist propositions that real economic outcomes are invariant to changes in the stock of money or its rate of growth. Section 11.4 reports the implicationis of our model, formally described in Appendix 11A, concerning the effects of government fiscal and financial policies. Section 11.5 offers some concluding remarks.

11.2 DEBT NEUTRALITY: CRITIQUE OF RICARDIAN THEORY

The Ricardian doctrine has strong implications for the short-run effects of government finance, both in unemployment and full-employment situations, and for its long-run effects: in short-run underemployment disequilibrium, a shift from tax finance to debt finance is not expansionary. It does not increase consumption demand, or aggregate demand, at prevailing prices; therefore it will not increase realized output, real income, and employment. In short-run full-employment equilibrium, debt finance is not inflationary. Since it leaves aggregate demand unchanged, supply and demand will still balance without any increase in prices or any rise of interest rates. In long-run steady states, debt finance does not reduce the capital intensity of the economy.

The common thread of these propositions is that substitution of government debt for taxation absorbs no saving. That is why it is not expansionary or inflationary. That is why it does not crowd out investment in the short run or displace capital in the long run. That is why the present generation cannot shift the burden of its public expenditures to future generations. If as voters they try to do so by lowering their own taxes and issuing bonds, they will as individuals buy the bonds to enable their heirs to pay the deferred taxes.

As expounded by Robert Barro (1974), the modern Ricardian theory relies on a number of simplifying assumptions: households so linked to subsequent and past generations by bequests and gifts that their horizons are effectively infinite; correct beliefs that current deficits imply future taxes of equal present value; lump-sum taxes, no liquidity constraints; and homogeneity of households, allowing their behavior in aggregate to be represented as that of a single representative household.

Buiter (1979) presents a model of overlapping generations which shows that decentralized competitive behavior will not necessarily produce outcomes invariant to government financial policy, even when intergenerational bequests and gifts are taken into account. Here we consider plausible ways in which Barro's assumptions may be violated and argue that realistic departures from his assumptions support modern Keynesian views of the short-run and long-run effects of debt finance.

11.2.1 The endless chain of intergenerational gifts and bequests

Clearly voters always have some incentive to shift the burden of public expenditure to other taxpayers whose welfare is of no concern. Any citizen with no heirs, or none he cares about, would be glad to defer taxes beyond his own lifetime; and he would consume his gains today. Ricardian theory depends on complete effective intergenerational chains of bequests and gifts. How plausible are they? A chain is broken in any lineal family if any generation is childless or indifferent to the utility of its successor. Though parents may care about their own children, their bequests will be smaller if they know that their great-grandchildren will have no children they care about. In particular, they will not adjust their bequests to provide for any increase in taxes to be levied after the break in the chain.

For the neutrality theorem to be valid, bequest and gift motives have to be operative for each and every economic agent affected by the public-sector financing policies. Some households in each generation are childless or do not care about their children's well-being. They consume more as their taxes are shifted to future generations. The remaining households, who have children and care about them, cannot maintain both their own lifetime consumption and that of their children, because the latter will also be liable for the taxes shifted from the childless members of the older generation. The net result for the households who care will be an increase in bequests, to be sure, but not enough to pay their children's taxes. Aggregating both kinds of households, the substitution of debt finance for tax finance increases current consumption.

Parents' utility may well depend in some degree on the size of their bequests to their children, independently of the utility or earning potential of the children. The convention of equal division among children, who may differ widely in wealth from other sources, suggests this motivation. To the extent that giving is for the gratification of the giver rather than the welfare of the receiver, bequests are related to the wealth of the parents rather than to the well-being of the child. There is then no presumption that bequests will be increased enough to keep children at the same utility level when taxes are shifted on to the children.

Utility optima at zero bequest 'corners' can occur even for households that are concerned with their children's utility. The parents would choose negative bequests if these were an available option. Accordingly, they will not bequeath more but consume more if taxes are shifted to their heirs. Corner solutions are more likely if households' utility functions place small weight on the future utility of their heirs, if they place large probability weights on the possibilities that the chain will somehow be broken, and if the economy is experiencing productivity growth leading parents to expect their descendants to be much better off than they are.

11.2.2 Dependence of future taxes on current deficits, and expectations about their relationship

It is an empirical question how individuals' expectations of future real incomes are altered by their perceptions of current fiscal policy. What inferences do taxpayers draw from reading about large budget deficits? These probably differ from time to time and from one individual to another. Future tax policy is rarely announced in advance; and even when tax surcharges or tax credits have been legislated as temporary, everyone knows that expiration dates can be changed and frequently are. It is not obvious that citizens will always assume that a current deficit carries with it future tax liabilities of equal present value. Nor is it necessarily irrational 'public debt illusion' if they assume and behave otherwise.

The government's net worth may be considered as the present value of its stream of net revenues less its stream of purchases of goods and services. Suppose that to every dollar of currently outstanding public debt corresponds a dollar of discounted value — at the government's interest rate — of future tax receipts to pay coupons and principal. Then the dollar of debt subtracts nothing from the government's net worth. And if purchases are also balanced, in present value, with taxes the net worth of government is zero. But there is no reason that this should always be so or that taxpayers should always believe it to be so. Perhaps the debt will grow with the interest rate, new debt always being issued to service existing debt. Then the net worth of the government is negative, and private citizens would be correct so to estimate it. They could also be correct to expect that current government deficits do not foreshadow future taxes of equivalent present value. It is very likely, and very fortunate, that Americans did not scale their tax expectations up to the debt inherited from the Second World War.

The sole condition on collective rationality is that basic economy-wide constraints on current and future capacities to produce be respected. The combined present values of government and private consumption cannot exceed the existing capital stock and the present value of future resource endowments. It would be irrational for society to behave, as voters, taxpayers, and private consumers and investors, on expectations which violate these constraints. But it is quite possible for the government to have negative net worth, and for the private sector to have correspondingly a net worth exceeding the national wealth, without their joint consumption plans exceeding productive capacity. A well-known example occurs in long-run growth models, where some private saving is diverted from capital formation into acquisition of public debt. In certain circumstances, such diversion is not only feasible but optimal.

Consider, as another example, a deficit incurred in recession either as passive result of revenue shortfall or as active countercyclical policy. It is not 'public debt illusion' to observe that the economy is operating inside its production possibilities, long-run as well as short-run. If so, taxpayers can rationally believe that the deficits represent a permanent increase in public debt with no implications of higher taxes later — that is, a downward adjustment of government's net worth. The public can rationally believe that the adjustment will yield for them higher real incomes, produced by resources otherwise underutilized. Acting on that belief, they can consume more today and help to confirm their own expectations. It is hard to see how this self-consistent scenario can be ruled out, except by those who deny a priori, indeed tautologically, the possibility that the economy can ever be operating short of capacity. In the present context, they would be saying that prices always adjust to clear markets so that the public buys all the potential output the government does not take, regardless of present and expected taxes, or however large or small the government's net worth.

11.2.3 Lump-sum and conditional taxes

Ricardian doctrine assumes that all taxes are lump-sum. Our vast array of non-lump-sum indirect and direct taxes, transfers and subsidies, will alter the shapes of private opportunity sets. Such sources of non-neutrality are no less important for being so obvious. The nature of real world tax systems creates a presumption that debt finance of government spending increases current consumption.

First, taxes induce tax-reducing behavior. Consider, for example, current lump-sum transfer payments financed by debt issues to be serviced by future taxes on wealth or on income from wealth. The combination will surely encourage substitution against saving and capital formation. Wage taxes will have qualitatively similar effects to the extent that they tax the proceeds of human capital investments. They will also induce substitution in favor of leisure and other untaxed uses of time. Anticipating this kind of behavior by his heirs, a Ricardian parent will know that in order to maintain his heirs' utilities it is unnecessary to maintain their real incomes against an expected increase in wage taxes. Labor and leisure substitution will do part of the job, and the parent can consume some of his tax reduction without reducing his heirs' utility.

Second, the positive correlation of tax liability with wealth and income means that higher future tax rates reduce the variance of the present value of future consumable resources. At the same time, the current tax cut or transfer maintains the mean. Household saving is in some degree motivated by risk aversion, designed to limit losses of future consumption if earnings are disappointing. To the extent that the tax and transfer system insures this risk, current consumption can be increased at the expense of future consumption without loss of utility.

An individual's expectation of his future tax liabilities depends on his expectations of his tax base, and the taxes are at least as uncertain as the base. If there is no uncertainty about tax incidence, he will discount the future taxes at the same rate at which he discounts the base. For many reasons, some of which will be discussed below, this rate is higher than the interest rate applicable to government securities.

11.2.4 Liquidity constraints

The crude Keynesian function relating consumption to disposable income exaggerated the importance of liquidity constraints, but that is no license for ignoring them altogether. Financial markets do not in fact provide unlimited opportunities for consuming future incomes today; they certainly do not provide these opportunities for intertemporal substitution at the interest rates at which governments borrow. Consequently many households may be at 'corners'. They cannot dissave, or dissave on attractive terms, when the government taxes them even if they perceive the current taxes as substitutes for future taxes on themselves or their heirs. By the same token, they will not save more on their own when tax cuts or transfers increase their current disposable income; they will take advantage of an opportunity, which capital markets do not provide them, for consuming now resources that they or their descendants will have at their disposition later. The government is in effect lending to them at its borrowing rate of interest, an option not available to these households in the private credit markets.

The liquidity effects of deficit finance have considerable importance for countercyclical stabilization policy. Consider a stochastic economy subject to regular cycles in real economic activity. Capital markets are imperfect and the fraction of economic agents that are constrained in their current spending by current cash flow varies countercyclically. The government does not have enough information to single out the cash-flow-constrained agents from those that are constrained only by net worth. A lump-sum transfer payment to everyone during the slump, financed by borrowing, will expand real demand during the slump, even if the government announces that it will use tax revenues to service and redeem the bonds during the next boom. During the slump the bonds are bought by those economic agents that are not cash-flow-constrained. The transfers go at least in part to economic agents with marginal spending propensities of unity because of binding cash flow constraints. The future taxes required to service the debt will be levied during the boom on a population that is, on average, less cash-flow-constrained than it was during the slump. To a liquidity-constrained individual, the value of the transfer payments in the slump exceeds the value of the future tax payment of equal actuarial value. The implicit discount rate is higher than the market rate of interest.

11.2.5 Heterogeneity of households, portfolio, and distributional effects

A number of important dimensions in which households differ in circumstances, tastes, and behavior have been discussed in the preceding four subsections. In this subsection we look at the role of government securities in private portfolios, in combination with private securities and expected future tax liabilities. The neutrality proposition assumes that government securities are a perfect hedge against tax liabilities, so that the introduction of both into a portfolio would change neither its expected return nor its risk. Given the uncertainties about when, how, and on whom future taxes will be levied, and about future issues of debt to refund maturing issues or finance new deficits, it is hard to see how so perfect a hedge against all contingencies could be constructed. In any case we observe some holders of government securities with little or no taxes to pay in future, and some future taxpayers with no government securities.

The Ricardian theory, however, also assumes that government interest-bearing debt and private debt are perfect substitutes. On this assumption private debt can also be used to hedge tax liabilities. Thus any private economic agent can, by borrowing or lending on personal account (via home-made leverage), construct a portfolio that is equivalent to a portfolio containing any amount of public debt. The menu of assets from which the individual can choose has not been enlarged by the introduction of government debt.

The assumption that households can lend and borrow on the same terms as governments is strictly for classroom use only. The Modigliani–Miller theorem is an unrealistically simplistic description of the relationship between households and corporations, and it is unlikely to apply any better to households *vis-à-vis* government. The power of the government to tax and to declare its liabilities legal tender is unique. The risk and liquidity properties of central government debt cannot be duplicated by private debtors.

Barro (1974) correctly points out that the effect of government borrowing on the risk composition of private portfolios requires an analysis of both the asset and the liability side of these portfolios. Future tax liabilities, whether they are associated with current public debt or not, should be included in the risk–return analysis of the entire private portfolio. To argue that the effect of public sector borrowing and associated tax expectations on the 'total risk' contained in private portfolios might go either way does not warrant an appeal to the principle of insufficient reason to support his neutrality conclusion.

An interesting area for future research is to investigate to what extent or under what circumstances it is possible to represent the effects of uncertainty by applying different subjective discount rates to anticipated future streams of interest income and tax payments. The traditional Keynesian position, as already noted, has been to argue that the discount rate for future taxes is the one appropriate for the streams of income on which the taxes are levied. Given the uncertainties in those streams (but ignoring additional uncertainty caused by uncertain incidence), that rate is higher than the discount rate for government obligations. The differential means that government bond issue does indeed raise effective net wealth even if taxpayers correctly expect that higher future taxes will match the increased income from the debt.

11.3 MONETARY FINANCE: NEUTRALITY AND SUPERNEUTRALITY

Monetary finance, unlike debt finance, entails no explicit obligations to pay interest or principal. Consequently, it induces no expectations of future explicit taxes to meet such obligations. The argument that substitution of deficit spending for taxation, in the finance of a given government expenditure program, has no real effect, takes different shapes for money and for debt. One difference concerns the role of commodity prices and inflation. The new Ricardian argument for debt neutrality implies that at prevailing prices of commodities and assets, current and expected, aggregate demand for goods and services is unchanged by shifting from tax to debt finance. In short, bond-financed deficits are neither expansionary nor inflationary. This argument does not apply to money finance. Rather the alleged neutrality depends on the argument that price increases, current or expected, deprive monetary issue of any real effects. Unlike bonds, money is inflationary.

11.3.1 Open market operations

The two neutrality arguments, for debt and for money, are logically bound together. The Ricardian story of interest-bearing debt is a necessary premise of monetarism. To see their connection, it is convenient and instructive to analyze open-market operations by which the central bank buys publicly held government debt with money. The reverse operation, selling debt for money, would be symmetrical. Substitution of money financing for taxation can be viewed in two steps: substitution of debt issue for taxes, and open market purchases of the debt issue. This is in fact how it occurs in the United States.

Here is the Ricardian-monetarist description of an open market purchase. Replacing interest-bearing public debt in the public's hands with non-interest-bearing money, the central bank wipes the corresponding tax expectations from the minds of taxpayers. The public's net worth is increased by the amount of the operation, just as if the same amount of currency had been dropped by helicopter. At existing prices, households will wish to consume some of these gains. But if the economy was already in equilibrium, additional demand cannot be accommodated by supply. To maintain supply–demand equilibrium, both current and expected prices rise in proportion to the increase in the quantity of money. Real (and nominal) interest rates and other relative prices are unchanged. Portfolios contain the same asset mixtures as before. True, the real stock of bonds is smaller, but equally so is the real stock of future tax liabilities. These are equivalent but opposite in sign in wealth-owners' portfolios; together they constitute a composite asset whose supply is zero both before and after the open market purchase.

If the initial situation were one of deficient aggregate demand, with excess supplies of labor and other productive resources, the open market purchase would not necessarily be neutral even if the Ricardian theory of public debt holds. Additional demand at prevailing prices could result in additional output and employment, with sticky current prices rising less than the proportionate increase of money stock and possibly less than expected future prices. The monetarist story is still a consistent one: a full price increase would leave the economy in the same real situation — with the same excess supplies — as before. The actual outcome depends on the mechanism by which product and factor prices are determined in disequilibrium. Appeal to market-clearing cannot provide the answer; by assumption, the disequilibrium signifies that markets are not clearing.

Here is another critical split in contemporary macroeconomics. Keynesians, econometric model-builders, and students of wage and price determination in imperfectly competitive markets would not expect money wages and prices to jump on the news of central bank open market purchases. They rely on Phillips curves and full cost pricing equations which give great weight to historical trends in wages and prices and some weight to the tightness of labor and product markets. Monetarists tend to think of the commodity price level as the reciprocal of the price of the asset money and as being determined, both in short run and in long run, in the money 'market', along with other assets, rather than in the markets for the commodities being priced. That is, they think of the price level, rather than other arguments in the demand-for-money function, as the variable that immediately adjusts to equate demand for and supply of money.

More fundamental objections to the monetarist scenario apply if for any or all of the reasons advanced above the Ricardian propositions on neutrality of debt fail. It will not be true that tax expectations match debt holdings in aggregate, or that government securities are found in portfolios just as hedges against future tax liabilities. It will not be true that open market purchases annihilate an equal amount of present value of tax obligation. It will not be true that the open market purchase is the equivalent of a helicopter drop of money; the purchase will increase private wealth but by less than 100 per cent of the amount. A proportionate increase in prices will not by itself restore portfolio equilibrium, keep interest rates constant, and avoid changes in real variables. Should a proportionate rise in prices occur and interest rates remain constant, real money balances would be unchanged, but the real value of outstanding government bonds would be smaller relative both to money and to involuntarily held tax debt. Therefore, private net wealth would be less than before the operation, and aggregate real demand would be smaller, too. Hence that scenario is inconsistent. To sustain a full-employment equilibrium takes a lesser price increase; thus the real stock of money increases while that of bonds falls. To sustain portfolio balance then requires that the yields on bonds and on real capital fall relative to that on money. The open market purchase alters the composition of output in favor of investment. With full employment, consumption must decline; this requires a net reduction of wealth, engineered by the combination of higher price level and lower nominal bond supply. If there are unemployed resources, part of the adjustment will occur by increase in output and real income. These short-run fiscal and monetary effects are formally analyzed below with the help of the model in Appendix 11A.

11.3.2 Money, government debt, and other assets as imperfect substitutes

Some insight as to why open market operations work can be obtained by reflecting on the nature of money, government debt, and other portfolio assets, and on the reasons why money is held at a lower explicit yield than competing assets. The characteristics of government-issued money are imparted in some degree to the government's debt issues, time obligations to pay its own money. The same reflections, therefore, explain also why government debts provide services which enable them to be held at lower explicit yields than private debts, and accordingly why increasing their supply adds to private wealth and liquidity.

Why do wealth-owners hold money at zero nominal interest when they can earn a positive rate on government bonds? The answer, of course, is that money yields services worth the difference. Large average cash balances mean that people wait a long time, as cash receipts build up, before converting cash into interest-earning assets, and convert those assets into cash long in advance of the payments for which the cash is needed. Conversions cost resources, if only the time and trouble of the investor. Given the volume and pattern of cash transactions, the larger are average money holdings the lower are conversion costs. Marginal saving of conversion costs is one of the services of money that compensates for loss of interest, and it declines with the size of real money holdings. Another service is avoidance of risk: as cash receipts and desired cash outlays are uncertain, holding money lowers the probability of making costly conversions, conversions at unfavorable asset prices, or costly postponements of outlays. The marginal gain from precautionary balances also declines with the size of real money holdings.

The government has a monopoly of issue of legal tender currency generally acceptable throughout its jurisdiction. Additions to the stock of currency, measured in purchasing power equivalent, provide the social gains — economizing resources and reducing risk — just mentioned. Holders of currency pay for those gains by accepting a lower interest rate than they would get on government debt or other assets. Taxpayers escape taxes to pay debt interest; their government earns 'seigniorage' as currency monopolist. This situation prevails so long as the real supply of money falls short of the amount that would drive to zero the *net* marginal value of its services, that is, the difference between the non-pecuniary return from holding an additional dollar of currency and that from holding an extra dollar's worth of an alternative asset. If this implicit advantage of money were zero, the explicit yield of money would have to be equal to that of other assets. In particular, nominal interest rates on the government's time obligations would have to be zero if the nominal zero rate on its demand obligations, money, were maintained.

From this standpoint the bite of monetary policy may be seen to depend on two related facts. First, the public is generally not, save in the exceptional circumstances of the Great Depression described by Keynes as 'liquidity trap', saturated with money. Second, other portfolio assets are substitutes, albeit imperfect ones, for money; central bank operations that lower the net marginal advantage of money will lower the explicit yield differentials of substitute assets, including real capital as well as government securities. By open market purchases of securities with money the central bank can, at least in the first instance, lower interest rates on securities and increase the public's wealth. At unchanged commodity prices, this operation increases consumption demand, by increasing wealth and possibly by lowering interest rates. It also increases investment demand; wealth-owners shift from money and bonds, with lower yields but increased joint supply, to real capital. If goods and labor markets are already in equilibrium, these new demands are excess and generate price increases that in part nullify the central bank's attempt to augment the real value of the public's money holdings. But only in part — as we have seen in the previous subsection, the open market operation is not (except in a Ricardian world) neutral in its effects even in full-employment environments. It alters the total real wealth of the public, the real supplies of assets available to wealth-owners, the structure of asset yields, and the composition of output.

Why not saturate the economy with cash balances, providing the public the extra services and wealth? It is not easy to do unless the economy is also saturated with capital. So long as capital investment offers a marginal return above the explicit real return on money (its nominal yield of zero less the expected inflation rate), the real stock of money must be consistent with a positive net marginal service value. Open market purchases increasing the nominal money stock can hardly go so far as to saturate the economy with real cash balances; the demand-increasing and price-increasing consequences of such purchases make this an unrealistic option.

A possible way to bring the public closer to saturation would be to move in the opposite direction, progressively diminishing the nominal money stock relative to GNP and generating deflation. But practical consequences, given the slowness of downward price adjustments in modern industrial economies, would be unfavorable to output, employment, and capital formation. The important institutional fact is that the nominal interest rate on money is fixed — not that it is fixed at zero, although it would take awkward practical arrangements to set it at any other level on circulating currency. The way to increase the public's holdings of nominal and real cash balances simultaneously is to raise the nominal yield of money at the same time as the nominal stock of money balances is increased.

The explanation of the expansionary and inflationary content of monetary finance applies also — with less force, to be sure — to debt finance of government purchases. An analogous argument can be made for government securities which are close substitutes for money, even though the interest on them may burden future government budgets. The government's securities are promises to pay its own currency at specified future dates — tomorrow, next month, next year, ten or 20 years from now. The government's currency monopoly extends to these future currency contracts as well; no private debtor can print the wherewithal to pay his own debts. Within the class of nominal assets, all of which share risks of changes in commodity prices and market interest rates, government time obligations have advantages in liquidity, marketability, and security against default. Individual citizens choose voluntarily how much, if any, and what kinds of the government's monetary and non-monetary debts to hold. Like holders of money, citizens holding government obligations are willing to pay in interest forgone for liquidity and for risk reduction. Others are as taxpayers in effect borrowing through the government more cheaply than they lend or invest. The government is an efficient financial intermediary connecting the two groups. As in the case of money, the government is gaining seigniorage on its debt obligations and increasing the outstanding stock adds to public wealth. This is the basic logic underlying the model described below, which shows that debt-financed increases in government purchases and tax reductions expand aggregate demand, raising output in situations of underemployment and raising prices in situations of full employment.

11.3.3 Inflation expectations and monetary financing: short-run effects

So far we have argued, contrary to the Ricardian-monetarist position, that government finance is not neutral in its macroeconomic effects. In particular, substitution of debt finance for taxation raises aggregate demand, and increases output or prices depending on the state of the economy; substitution of money finance for taxes or debt finance is likewise expansionary or inflationary, and changes the composition of output in favor of investment; and the consequences of a one-shot increase in money stock, by open market purchase of outstanding debt, are not confined to price increases; the real state of the economy is altered.

We have not yet considered the effects of fiscal and monetary policies that alter expected and realized rates of price inflation. Those who argue that the financing of public expenditure does not matter have cited inflation as an anticipated cost of money holding which will induce saving in advance.[6] Anticipation of the 'inflation tax', it is argued, deprives money finance of demand effects in the same way that anticipation of explicit taxes neutralizes debt finance. We now turn to this question.

The analogy is faulty in several respects. First, the inflation tax falls on those who hold the money the government has printed to finance deficits. Explicit taxes fall on bondholders only to the extent that those who expect to pay additional taxes voluntarily hold bonds. Second, any individual can diminish his inflation tax by holding less money. It is clearly not a lump-sum tax. Neither are the explicit taxes that might be levied to service interest-bearing debt, but these are harder and costlier to dodge. Third, a one-shot increase in debt carries with it, in the Ricardian scenario, expectations of future taxes. A one-shot increase in money carries with it, in a classical world, the expectation of an immediate equal proportional increase in the general price level. This is analogous to a capital levy, reducing the value of previously acquired money. It is not *per se* a source of expectations of higher inflation. Those expectations, as monetarists usually tell us, are aroused by anticipations of a *sustained* increase in growth rates of money stock.

Expectation of higher inflation, however generated, is certainly not neutral in its short-run macroeconomic effects. The basic source of non-neutrality is the institutional fact that the nominal interest rate on currency and other government-issued money (reserve balances in the central bank) is fixed. In the US system, bank deposits and other inside money also have legally or conventionally fixed nominal rates. The expected real return on these dollar-denominated assets declines whenever the expected inflation rate rises. This is a real effect, lowering the demand for real money balances in favor of other stores of value. Other real rates will move to balance asset demands and supplies. In general an increase in the expected rate of inflation will lower real rates of interest and encourage capital investment.[7] While an inflation premium will be added to nominal interest rates, it is less than one point per point of expected inflation.

For this reason, a financial policy that involves more rapid increase of money stock is not neutral. In an underemployment environment, where wage and price trends are dominated by historical inertia, the policy will clearly be expansionary. Its wealth and interest rate effects increase aggregate demand even without any revision of inflationary expectations. If the expectation of higher monetary growth also raises inflationary expectations, the expansionary effect is reinforced. For the reasons given above, real interest rates decline with inflationary expectations, even though nominal rates rise. However, a one-for-one translation of monetary growth rates into expected inflation will not be confirmed by events if actual wage and price trends are sticky and output responds to increased demand. Of course, if an easier monetary policy breeds expectations of its own reversal, fears of future recession may deprive the policy of its normal expansionary effects. But in that case it can scarcely be inflationary, either.

In a short-run full-employment environment, expectation of more rapid monetary growth will raise both inflationary expectations and the current price level. A one-shot jump in the price level is necessary to restrain aggregate demand, to offset the increase in demand due to higher expected inflation. This does not mean that the policy is neutral. The composition of output will be altered; it is not possible to generalize about the nature of the change. Substitution of money for taxes in financing government deficits has, on impact, consumption effects in both directions. The reduction of taxes increases consumption, as does any accompanying increase in the expected rate of inflation, but the rise in the price level works the other way.

11.3.4 Long-run effects of monetary growth and steady inflation: superneutrality?

Superneutrality is the monetarist proposition that long-run equilibria are the same in the magnitudes of real variables, whatever the inflation rate. This means that they are invariant with respect to the *rate of growth* of the nominal money stock. Whether government financial policies engineer a monetary growth trend of 10 per cent per year, or 0 per cent, or −10 per cent, steady-state capital stock, real output, real wage, consumption, and real interest rates will all be the same. (This is a stronger proposition than simple neutrality, which says merely that one-shot variation of the *level* of the nominal money stock will not alter real economic outcomes. We discussed simple neutrality in the previous section.)

Superneutrality seems dubious on its face. As we already observed, a change in the expected rate of inflation alters the real interest rate on monetary assets with fixed nominal rates. This is a real variable, and in general one would not expect the long-run equilibrium values of other real variables to be unaffected (Tobin, 1965).

However, one theoretical recipe for long-run superneutrality which appears in various guises in the literature merits comment (see, for example, Sidrauski, 1967; Fischer, 1978). The argument is essentially that asset stocks are not direct substitutes for each other in the long run. Rather, each asset will be independently accumulated until its marginal advantage to the representative consumer just compensates him for postponing consumption. Consumer-savers will hold each asset in whatever quantity provides acceptable payoff in future consumption for refraining from additional consumption today. Capital, in particular, will be held in whatever amount yields a return that compensates consumers for their subjective discount of future consumption. If another asset, money, for example, is also available and can also yield such a return, households will simply expand their total wealth holdings to include it. Money, too, will be held in such quantity, in real terms, that its marginal return compensates consumers for their discount of future consumption. The marginal return on money includes the subjective value of its implicit services in facilitating transactions, providing liquidity, and limiting risk, as well as its objective or explicit yield, positive or negative, from price deflation or inflation. The same argument applies to government debt and other financial assets, except that their explicit returns include nominal interest. The implication is that variations in explicit returns on financial assets, including the rate of inflation, will be absorbed wholly by changes in the real quantities of these assets held, changes that alter their implicit returns just enough to keep their total returns intact. Consequently the equilibrium capital stock is independent of the stocks of other assets and their explicit returns.

To state the argument more precisely, suppose that the total return to each asset j can be decomposed into an explicit return r_j and an implicit service return s_j. In long-run equilibrium assets are held in such amounts that the total returns $r_j + s_j$ are all equal to ϱ, the consumers' rate of discount of future consumption. Differences in the s_j make up for the commonly observed differences in r_j. Now suppose, first, that each s_j depends only on its own real stock X_j relative to income or consumption, and not on any other stock; and second, that the common intertemporal consumption discount, ϱ, does not vary with total wealth or its composition. These assumptions are necessary and sufficient for the independence and additivity of asset demands described in the previous paragraph. Their necessity makes clear how special and restrictive is the case for superneutrality. We consider the two assumptions in turn.

Implicit service returns s_j are to be viewed relative to one another; they are just interest rate differentials by another name. The marginal implicit advantage of bonds over equity, for example, can be expected to decline when the stock of bonds rises; but the same reasons apply when the equity stock falls. If cross-effects are allowed, the demand for capital will not be independent of alternative asset supplies and of the explicit returns on them.

One source of interdependence is that financial stocks — money, in particular — may be substitutes for capital and labor in the handling of transactions. The larger the real money stock the less resources are diverted to managing conversions between money and other assets, thus the higher may be the consumption path corresponding to a given capital intensity. However, the corresponding rate of return to capital is not altered if transactions technology uses capital and labor in the same proportions as commodity production. We do not pursue this line of analysis here. A complete story would require not only specification of transactions technology but also consideration of the fiscal alternatives to the 'inflation tax' and the deadweight losses they entail.

The second assumption implies that savers' long-run demands for wealth in aggregate and for individual assets are infinitely elastic at the constant rate of return ϱ. Savers will hold whatever quantities of assets yield them that total return, implicit plus explicit. Suppose instead that wealth demand is finite at any rate of return, possibly inelastic or possibly following a schedule along which the required return is greater as wealth is larger. Then imagine, for example, a variation of policy, or some other exogenous change, that lowers the inflation rate and adds to the demand for real money balances. It may thus add to the total demand for wealth. But if the public will hold more wealth only when its general intertemporal consumption return is higher, other assets — including capital — will have to clear a higher hurdle. Therefore their stocks will be cut back to make room for at least some of the additional money desired.

The difference between perfectly and imperfectly elastic wealth demand can be associated with the difference between infinite and finite horizons in household saving behavior. We noted above that infinite horizons are essential for the Ricardian equivalence theorem, and it is not surprising they are also crucial for superneutrality. Consider steady growth equilibrium of a money-capital model with immortal consumers. Along every possible path the rate of growth of per capita consumption is the same, namely the exogenous rate of labor-augmenting technological progress. There will be some intertemporal discount rate, some terms on which present consumption can be exchanged for future, that will make the typical consumer content with the path, content not to make any intertemporal exchanges that deviate from it. This discount rate ϱ is formally $\delta + \lambda\varepsilon$, where δ is the pure rate of time preference, λ the rate of growth of per capita consumption, and $-\varepsilon$ the elasticity of the marginal utility of consumption with respect to consumption.[8] The term δ allows for the postponement of consumption and the term $\lambda\varepsilon$ for its declining marginal utility. Both time preference δ and the elasticity $-\varepsilon$ must be constants, independent of time and consumption level, for a steady state to be possible at all. This condition also implies that ϱ is the same in every steady stare, for the steady states differ in level of consumption path and not in λ. The equilibrium steady state is the one for which the marginal productivity of capital, net of the rate of population growth n, is equal to ϱ. Immortal consumers, in the form of households who anticipate the number of their descendants and the utilities of each, internalize the capital requirements of population growth.

On the other hand, a life-cycle or finite horizon model of saving and wealth demand is also consistent with steady-state growth equilibrium. We argued above that for many reasons it is the more realistic model. The life-cycle model implies that the aggregate desired wealth–consumption ratio is a finite constant along any path of steady growth. Its value depends on the age distribution of the population and thus on its rate of growth; the typical age-earnings profile, which depends in turn on the rate of technological progress; and the age-consumption profile chosen by the typical household, which will in general vary with the returns to saving. There is a definite age sequence of wealth holdings for each household, and by summation over households of various ages a finite aggregate wealth demand at each date. The desired ratio of wealth to labor income or to consumption may be greater when returns to capital and other assets are higher. In any case capital must compete with other assets in the portfolios of life-cycle savers. If they decide to hold more money, it will be at least partly at the expense of capital.

Asset interdependence and finite interest-sensitive wealth demand are assumed in our formal model in Appendix 11A, discussed in Section 11.4. We impose some further restrictions on asset and wealth demand functions. The demand for each asset, in relation to income, depends on the entire list of explicit rates of return. So also does the demand for wealth in total. Assets are assumed to be gross substitutes: an increase in the return on any asset, other things equal, raises the demand for that asset and diminishes, or anyway does not increase, the demand for any other. The net effect on demand for wealth is assumed to be positive or zero. Thus expectation of higher inflation may be, as often warned, a disincentive to saving. But it is mainly a disincentive to saving in the form of money and actually a positive incentive to save in other assets, particularly goods and equities in goods. The net effect on total saving might well be negative, but — other things equal — it seems likely that a reduction in the real rate of return on money will make savers wish to accumulate more of those assets which have become relatively more attractive. This is why our model implies that higher steady inflation rates, expected and realized, are generally associated with greater capital formation.

It may seem paradoxical that the long-run capital intensity of the economy can be greater under policies that diminish the total private propensity to save. Total saving is (in a closed economy) necessarily equal to capital investment plus the government deficit, all in real terms. Likewise, total private real wealth is equal to the sum of the capital stock and the real value of government debt, bonds plus money. Investment and capital stock can be larger, while private saving and wealth are smaller, if and only if the government's deficit and debt are even smaller in real terms. Now in long-run steady states the real magnitudes of the deficit and debt are not determined by the government alone, but also by the willingness of savers to acquire and hold government liabilities. These liabilities are expressed in nominal terms, that is, in dollars, and the price *level* is free to adjust the real values of the stocks to the amounts desired by savers and wealth-holders. Policies that lead to more inflation diminish those desired holdings, and by our assumptions about asset choice diminish them by more than they reduce total private saving. This is why those policies allow more room for capital formation.

Things are not always what they seem, and policy variations sometimes have consequences the reverse of normal intuition and the reverse of their short-run effects. The rate of growth of government liabilities, of money or of promises to pay money, is not itself a policy parameter. It is the endogenous outcome of basic policy parameters: government expenditure, taxation, the composition of deficits and debt. An increase in spending or reduction in taxation appears to be a deficit-increasing policy. But such a policy does not necessarily increase the steady-state *real* deficit or debt relative to national output. By leading to more inflation it may make government liabilities less attractive, and the price level will then be high enough to diminish the real quantities of those liabilities to the amounts that savers desire. Thus a fiscal or financial policy that looks expansionary, and is inflationary, may in the final analysis absorb less saving rather than more, and divert saving into capital formation.

To illustrate the mechanism we compare tax finance and money finance in a steadily growing economy with only two assets, money and capital. In this example interest-bearing public debt is ignored for simplicity. The natural growth rate is g, and a constant fraction z of real national output Y is purchased by government. Taxes, net of transfers, are a proportion t of Y. Let H/p be the real stock of government-issued high-powered money held by the public. Let i be the actual and expected rate of inflation $\dot{p}/p$, and h be the rate of growth of the nominal money stock $\dot{H}/H$. In a steady state we know that $h = g + i$. The government's budget equation is

$$\dot{H}/p = h(H/p) = (z - t)Y = (g + i)(H/p)$$

or

$$z = (g + i)(H/pY) + t.$$

Now if $h = g$ and $i = 0$, t must be $z - gH/pY$. Compare a more inflationary policy: $h' > g$, yielding $i' > 0$. Now t' must be $z - h'H/pY$, equal to $t - i'H/pY$ if H/pY is the same. The inflation tax $i'H/pY$ is substituted for part of the explicit tax t. But it does not make sense to assume that H/pY remains the same. Presumably it will be smaller, because a reduction in the real return on money — possibly also an increase in the after-tax return on capital — shifts saving and wealth from money to capital. Capital stock is higher relative to labor force and output, and its before-tax return is accordingly lower.

If the asset substitution elasticity is very high, an inflation tax cannot be substituted for explicit taxation. Indeed, a more inflationary policy might be associated with a *higher* tax rate t. To state the matter the other way round, the only way to have a low real deficit might be to have such a high inflation rate that people are reconciled to the small quantity of money the tight fiscal policy supplies. It would require a value exceeding unity for the total (that is, not holding other rates of return constant but allowing them to adjust as necessary to restore equilibrium) elasticity of demand for high-powered money with respect to the sum of the inflation rate and the growth rate, E_h. Note that this condition could be met, for positive inflation rates, even if the absolute value of the elasticity of money demand with respect to the inflation rate, E_i, is smaller than unity, as conventionally believed, since $E_h = [1 + (g/i)]E_i$.

Notice that we are here comparing two steady states, one with a higher tax take t than the other, and asking which has the higher inflation rate. In theory the answer can go either way. It depends on the relationship of the product $h(H/pY)$ to h. The higher the tax rate the lower the tax base will be. If a reduction in the inflation rate i lowers the product — as will be the case if the H/pY desired by the public is not very sensitive to i — then i will be lower in a steady state with a higher t. If an increase in the inflation rate i lowers the product — the H/pY desired by the public is very sensitive to i — then i will be higher in a steady state with higher t. These comparisons say nothing about the stability of steady-state equilibria. We may well suspect that the second possibility — higher t associated with higher i — is unstable. After all, in the short run we expect an increase in tax rate, a tightening of fiscal policy, to slow down inflation. The range of possible outcomes becomes even wider when government interest-bearing debt is included as a third asset.

11.4 A MODEL OF ASSET MARKETS AND MACROECONOMIC POLICIES

Here we summarize the results of a formal analysis of short-run and long-run effects of government fiscal and financial policies. The mathematical model and analysis are presented in Appendix 11A.

11.4.1 Structure of the model

The model focuses on the balance of supply and demand in three-asset markets: high-powered money, government bonds, and claims to productive capital. In an extension of the model to apply to an open economy, a fourth asset — securities of foreign issue denominated in foreign currency — is added.

In the short run, the public begins with initial holdings of the several assets and decides how much to accumulate of each one during a period of time. These decisions are saving and portfolio choices combined. They depend on the rates of return expected on the assets, on income and taxes, and on the initial holdings. On the supply side, the increments of money and government debt depend on the government's budget deficit and on how it is financed. Also, the central bank can, during any period, engage in open market transactions in money and government securities, and in foreign assets in the open-economy model. The incremental supply of capital during the period results from real investment decisions, which are taken to depend on the difference between the expected rate of profit on the commodity cost of capital goods and the market yield on equity claims. The increment to the nation's stock of foreign assets is the surplus in international current-account transactions.

In the long-run steady state, asset stocks are stationary in real terms, or are growing at a common constant rate, the natural rate of growth of the economy, that is, the sum of the rate of growth of the labor force and the rate of labor-augmenting technical progress. The asset demand–supply equations of the model then refer to stocks that meet the steady-state condition. Stocks are adjustable to savers' preferences in the long run, unconstrained by initial holdings. The parameters of fiscal and financial policy determine the available supplies of money and government debt per unit of output or per efficiency unit of labor. For capital the long-run supply function is the technological relation between capital intensity — the capital–output ratio or ratio of capital to efficiency labor — and the rate of return to capital. In an open economy the current account payments surplus must keep the stock of foreign assets, measured in purchasing power over domestic goods, constant relative to output. Long-run asset demands depend on real rates of return including the real return on money, the negative of the inflation rate.

Note that balance of the government budget is not a requirement of long-run equilibrium, even if the natural rate of growth is zero.[9] A constant real steady-state deficit per unit of output provides for the required growth in the nominal stocks of money and government bonds. The inflation rate is endogenous and can adjust to reconcile a large variety of deficit outcomes to the steady-state conditions of the previous paragraph. In long-run equilibrium the nominal stocks of money and government bonds must grow at the natural rate of growth plus the rate of inflation. Of course, if the deficit is endogenous its equilibrium value might happen to be zero. Or a balanced budget might be a deliberate policy choice. In these cases the stocks of government-issued assets would be constant in nominal amounts in long-run equilibrium, and their real growth at the natural rate would be accomplished by steady deflation. Steady-state budget surpluses would mean dwindling nominal stocks accompanied by price deflation faster than the natural rate.

Applied to the short run, the three asset equations of the closed-economy model determine three variables in each period. Two of these within-period endogenous variables are rates of return, on government bonds and capital equity. The third real rate of return, that on money, is not endogenously determined within a period. The expected rate of inflation is taken to be predetermined from past history; it varies, but only as periods go by and history accumulates. Thus the system of three equations is free to determine a third variable each period. Two obvious choices are real income and price level. These correspond to the two short-run environments discussed throughout this paper: an underemployment case, in which output is demand-determined at historically predetermined prices, and a full-employment situation in which output is supply-constrained and the price level adjusts flexibly within the period. An intermediate case would involve adding a within-period price adjustment equation and solving for both price and output. The open-economy model adds one equation. The corresponding endogenous variable is either the foreign exchange rate or, for a regime of fixed parities, the quantity of foreign assets purchased or sold by the central bank and government.

In the long run the inflation rate is endogenous, along with the real rates of return on capital and government bonds. The inflation rate, moreover, affects both asset demands and asset supplies, in ways discussed in Section 11.3. No equation is needed for output or the price level. The capital–output ratio follows immediately from the solution value of the return on capital; given this ratio and an initial condition the path of real income is determined. Likewise, once the solution of the system gives the permanent inflation rate, an initial value for any nominal variable suffices to pin down the path of prices.

The short-run system can be viewed as a generalized Keynesian *IS–LM* model. (The *IS* equation is actually the sum of the asset demand–supply equations, and we do not use it explicitly in our analysis in Appendix 11A. The same results could be obtained by dropping one of the asset equations instead and keeping the *IS* relation.) The major generalization is on the portfolio side. Keynes's assumption of perfect substitutability between long-term bonds and equity is dropped. Instead all the three or four assets are assumed to be gross substitutes, both in short-run saving decisions and in long-run portfolio choice. For the purposes of this paper we retained the simplifying assumption of aggregation, that the economy produces one homogeneous commodity, usable either in consumption or in investment or as exports. It is not, however, the same as the commodity imported from abroad. Conversion of current output into capital is subject to diminishing returns; rapid additions to the capital stock entail adjustment costs. This is why the rate of investment is a finite increasing function of the difference between the marginal efficiency of capital at normal replacement cost and the market yield of equity. Finally, for the purposes of this paper it was not necessary to model the labor market separately.

We deliberately chose to model time in discrete periods, within which variables assume one value and one value only. At each hypothetical set of values of endogenous variables the agents in asset markets formulate demands and supplies related to positions desired at the end of the period. The clearing of the markets determines an 'end-of-period' equilibrium (Foley, 1975; Buiter, 1975). This means that the saving decision and the portfolio allocation decision cannot be separated.[10] In addition, government deficits have time within the period to add to supplies of money or bonds or both, business investment increases the supply of equities in the same period, and current account surpluses immediately augment the supply of foreign assets. The continuous-time *IS–LM* snapshot has been charged with failure to take account of the stock-increasing effects of the flows its solution generates. These could be handled by dynamic analysis that tracks stocks. Otherwise the *IS–LM* account of the effects of a deficit-increasing fiscal policy omits the financial consequences of the additions to stocks of money or debt that will occur with the passage of time. Some critics have contended that such neglect of the 'government budget constraint' is responsible for misleading conclusions about the effects of fiscal policy. The short run of our model, which does not neglect the government budget identity or any other mechanical flow–stock relationships, does not substantiate this complaint. It shows that standard Keynesian conclusions survive explicit recognition of these phenomena.

11.4.2 Short-run policy effects

In the short run an increase in public spending or a cut in taxes will stimulate output in the unemployment model or raise the price level in the full-employment model. Investment varies positively with current profits per unit of capital and negatively with the rate of return on equity, the required rate of return on capital. In the short run, profits per unit of capital increase with the level of output. The positive effect on output of expansionary fiscal policy in the unemployment model will therefore encourage investment. There will be 'crowding-in'.

In the full-employment model this effect is absent. The effect of changes in public spending and taxation on the required rate of return on capital depends crucially on the manner in which the government finances its budget deficits or surpluses. If money financing is chosen, the required rate of return on capital is lowered by an increase in public spending or a tax cut, both in the full-employment model and in the unemployment model. In both cases expansionary fiscal policy, combined with accommodative monetary policy, 'crowds in' investment. If mixed financing or bond financing is chosen, the effect on the required rate of return on capital, r_K, is ambiguous. With bond financed deficits, r_K is more likely to increase if bonds and equity are close substitutes. If r_K increases, expansionary fiscal policy definitely 'crowds out' private investment in the full-employment model. In the unemployment model the negative effect on investment of a higher r_K will be offset at least partly by higher output and profits.

An open market sale of bonds raises the real rate of return on bonds. It lowers output in the unemployment model and the price level in the full-employment model. The rate of return on equity is likely to be increased if government bonds and equity are close substitutes, lowered if bonds and money are close substitutes.

There is a widely held view that the combination of contractionary fiscal policy and expansionary monetary policy favors investment. We evaluate this proposition by considering the effect on investment of different combinations of fiscal and financial policy parameters that keep constant real output or the price level. For example, raise taxes or reduce public spending and compensate for the contractionary effect by raising the share of money in financing the deficit. The traditional veiw is confirmed for a reduction in public spending combined with an increase in the share of money. A tax increase, however, may, by its direct effect on disposable income, have such a strong negative effect on the demand for equity, that r_K increases, discouraging investment.

It is sometimes argued that an increase in public spending, or a tax cut, raises inflation expectations, especially if financed by printing money. The model shows that a rise in inflation expectations will give a boost to investment by encouraging a portfolio shift toward real assets. This conclusion might not hold if the higher expected rate of inflation were systematically accompanied by increased uncertainty about the future. It would not hold if households and businesses have learned to expect severely restrictive monetary and fiscal measures whenever the expected rate of inflation increases.

11.4.3 Long-run policy effects

Analysis of the long-run effects of fiscal and financial policies proceeds by comparison of balanced growth paths. All real stocks and flows grow at the natural rate of growth, the sum of the rate of growth of the labor force and the rate of labor-augmenting technical change. Expectations are realized. The economy is fully adjusted to the values assumed by the policy instruments.

In Section 11.3 above a number of long-run policy issues have already been discussed, especially those concerned with superneutrality. The propositions advanced there are formally substantiated in Appendix 11A. In the three-asset model, the long-run effects of fiscal policy changes on variables like the capital–output ratio and the rate of inflation are complicated and frequently ambiguous without further quantitative information. A number of propositions emerge clearly, however.

Long-run crowding-out of private capital by public spending or by a shift from tax financing to bond or money financing is a possibility, but not a necessity. The proximate effect of an increase in public spending or a cut in taxes — for a given rate of inflation and given values of the real rates of return on bonds and capital — is to increase the steady-state stocks of bonds and money. *Ceteris paribus*, this will stimulate the demand for capital without affecting the supply. There will therefore be a tendency for the required rate of return on capital to go down and for the capital–output ratio to increase. Of course, this is not the complete story. The proximate effect of these same policy changes on the bond market and the money market is to create excess supply. If bonds and equity are close substitutes, this will create upward pressure on r_K. When we allow for these further substitution and wealth effects, the final outcome can go either way. Neither 'crowding-out' nor 'crowding-in' can be ruled out on a priori grounds.

11.4.4 Implications of the analysis for open economies

The analysis is extended to an economy that is open to international commodity trade and financial transactions. The home country is large in the market for its exports and small in the market for its imports. The terms of trade are therefore endogenous. The asset menu is enlarged by adding an internationally traded financial claim, denominated in foreign currency. Domestic government bonds, money, and equity are not internationally traded, and the internationally traded asset is a gross substitute, but not a perfect substitute, for the domestic assets. Therefore, both the quantity of money and either the exchange rate or the official settlements deficit in international payments can be controlled by domestic policy.

In both fixed and floating exchange rate regimes, the short-run effects of fiscal and financial policy on output, the required rate of return on capital and the rate of investment are very similar to those in the closed economy. The open-economy model, of course, explains a wider set of endogenous variables, including the current account, the capital account, and either the official settlements balance or the exchange rate, depending on the regime. It also includes an additional instrument of financial policy: either the exchange rate or the volume of open market transactions in the internationally traded asset by the monetary authority.

The possibility of long-run 'crowing-in' of capital by expansionary fiscal policy, discussed above for the closed-economy model, also applies to the open economy. Perhaps more important than the sign of these long-run multipliers is the conclusion that changes in fiscal, monetary and financial instruments will have real effects, short-run and long-run. Properly specified econometric models will not be policy-neutral. In general, *both* fiscal and monetary instruments have domestic macroeconomic consequences in the expected directions in both exchange rate regimes, fixed and floating. It is also true that floating exchange rates will not insulate the economy from foreign shocks, for example changes in export demand.

11.5 CONCLUDING REMARKS

The economic performance of the United States and other capitalist democracies in the 1970s has been disappointing in many respects. The non-Communist world has suffered the deepest recession, the highest general inflation, and the highest unemployment of the three decades since the Second World War. Until the late 1960s the post-war record had been remarkably good, with 20 years of unparalleled stability, prosperity, and growth. Many observers, economists and others, assigned much credit to the active use of government fiscal and financial policies for management of aggregate demand. But with the reverses of the 1970s, disillusion and reaction have replaced earlier euphoria, and the same government policies receive much of the blame. Within the economics profession and beyond, intellectual challenges to the neo-Keynesian foundations of macroeconomic policy are increasingly influential.

One dimension of recent economic performance that has evoked widespread concern, particularly in the United States, is the low rate of private non-residential capital formation. The share of potential GNP devoted to this purpose, always low in this country compared to other more rapidly growing economies, has fallen in this decade. A future capital shortage, inhibiting growth in output and employment, is predicted and feared. One aspect of the disenchantment with government policies is the charge that they inhibit capital formation, overtaxing the earnings of capital, channeling an excessive share of the nation's resources to the public sector, diverting into finance of budget deficits private saving that would otherwise finance private investment. The growth of the Federal budget in the last decade and the large deficits realized in recent years of recession and slow recovery have accentuated the charges of 'crowding out'. At the same time, the inflation of the 1970s has been attributed to government financial policies.

In the economics profession the reaction against neo-Keynesian macro-economic theory and policy has taken two distinct shapes. Both find the theory mistaken and the policies unsuccessful. One school, following traditional conservative lines, also finds the policies harmful and dangerous, distorting the allocation of resources, crowding out private investment, and causing debilitating inflation. The other school, the *new* classical macro-economics, finds the policies ineffectual, harmless except that the public has to go to the trouble of figuring them out and bypassing them.

In this setting, our paper has re-examined the theory of the macro-economic effects of fiscal and financial policies. Our conclusions are intel-lectually conservative, in the sense that we confirm the general thrust of the neo-Keynesian paradigm. But we hope that our analysis contains some novel features. We reject the neutrality propositions of the new Ricardian theorists who contend that the financing of government expenditure — whether by taxation, bond issue, or printing money — makes no difference to real economic outcomes. The conditions required for these neutrality propositions are so special and so unrealistic that it would be foolish and foolhardy to base policy upon them. Thus we agree with the more traditional critics of demand management policies that they are capable of doing harm as well as good. We do not agree that they have done nothing but harm, or all the harm attributed to them.

We share the concerns about the inadequacy of capital formation in the United States in recent years. The Federal government should be concerned about it, too. The neutrality doctrines that we have criticized in this paper imply that the government need not worry about the nation's economic future because citizens as individuals will take care of it on their own. This is bad advice, whether applied to the conservation of natural resources or to the overall management of the economy. Government is an essential part of the mechanism by which societies provide for their continuity and survival; one big reason for its institution is to make collective provisions for future generations supplementing the provisions individuals make for their own descendants.

It is important to be clear when and how government finance crowds out capital investment and when and how it encourages it, crowds it *in*. One of the more misguided episodes of recent public economic discussion was the flurry of anxiety about 'crowding-out' when the government was running large deficits in 1975 and 1976. The economy had barely begun to recover from the severe recession of 1974–5. The deficits were largely the result of the depressed level of business activity, which lowered taxable income and raised entitlements to unemployment insurance and other transfers. They were partly the result of modest tax rebates and reductions voted by the Congress to stimulate recovery. High unemployment and excess capacity indicated that the economy was operating nowhere near its productive potential. Capital investment was low, not because saving and finance were in short supply, but because excess capacity, low equity prices, and dim prospects of future sales made it unattractive. In these circumstances it was absurd to complain that Federal deficits were displacing private investment. Additional government spending or tax reduction probably would have stimulated — crowded in — investment. Resources were adequate to increase consumption, government purchases, and investment all at the same time. Certainly the opposite policies, had they been adopted in an effort to trim the deficit, would have slowed the recovery or prolonged the recession and made investment even weaker. As we stressed in previous sections, it is important to distinguish situations in which output is limited by resources and investment is limited by potentially available saving from cases in which output and investment are both limited by demand.

In underemployment situations any crowding-out that occurs through financial stringency is the work of the central bank. If the monetary authority refuses to accommodate increases in output in response to fiscal stimulus, then rising interest rates and declining share prices will indeed deter some investment. Only if the central bank's view of the desirable path of total output is accepted can fiscal policy be blamed for substituting consumption, private and public, for investment. In Section 11.1 we discussed the importance of co-ordinating fiscal and monetary policy. Unfortunately, the repeated use of fiscal measures for stimulus and of monetary measures for restraint results in a policy mix unfavorable to capital formation in the long run. A mix favorable to investment would involve an easier monetary stance offset by taxes bearing particularly on consumption.

Economists have long debated the optimal trend of prices — rising, stable, or falling. An advantage of a steadily rising price level is the incentive it gives for investment in real productive capital, by making the holding of wealth in liquid form unrewarding. We examine and formalize this idea in the body of the paper, and we investigate the fiscal and financial implications of policies aimed at high long-run capital–labor ratios. Deficit finance provides the growing nominal stocks of money and debt that sustain steady inflation and, somewhat paradoxically, reduce the *real* stocks desired by savers. So it is quite possible that deficit finance, especially if an adequate share of it takes monetary form, 'crowds in' capital formation. If so, this effect is purchased at the cost of depriving the society of the services that larger stocks of money and debt, with higher explicit returns, could provide.

A theoretical finding that steady inflation is favorable to capital investment no doubt seems bizarre in the 1970s, when the opposite view has become an unquestioned article of faith in business and financial circles. The reason is that the central bank, government, and public are committed to bringing down a rate of inflation generally regarded as intolerable. The only weapons at their command are restrictive financial policies that slow the economy down, causing recessions, or interventions in private price decisions and wage bargains. These weapons all seem to threaten profitability, and that is why inflation news is discouraging to investors. By the same token disinflation would be a good sign, but only if the authorities took advantage of it to aim for higher aggregate output and faster growth.

Is there a long-run investment-oriented strategy that does not rely on deficits and inflation to diminish savers' preferences for liquid forms of wealth? The government could serve more directly and explicitly as a financial intermediary, investing in private sector financial claims the proceeds of issuing its unique monetary and non-monetary obligations. Then the public could enjoy the services these assets provide without tying up in them any net saving at the expense of capital formation. There is no reason that the assets of Federal Reserve Banks cannot include private debts and even equities, as well as Treasury obligations.

The economic malaise of the 1970s relates at bottom to the intractable inflation/unemployment dilemma, a problem outside the scope of this paper. Government financial policy is the scapegoat for the frustrations bred by stubborn stagflation. No doubt some policy errors, notably the deficit financing of the Vietnam war, contributed to our present plight. But inflationary bias seems to be endemic in the political and economic institutions of modern capitalist democracies. It is naive whistling in the dark to think that the problem will disappear if only central banks and legislatures follow different monetary and fiscal rules. The combinations of inflation and unemployment feasible with existing policy instruments are just not acceptable to the society. Unless we find new instruments to make acceptable combinations feasible, or until we wearily decide that some feasible combination is acceptable, macroeconomic performance will continue to be disappointing and frustrating, and capital formation and other provisions for the future will continue to be inadequate.

11.6 NOTES

1. The view that the economic system is always at the natural rate of unemployment or the natural level of capacity utilization, except for transient disturbances due to errors in private economic agents' price or wage forecasts, was first formalized by Milton Friedman (1968) and Edmund Phelps (1970). The proposition that the only source of departures from the natural rate are expectational errors has recently been combined with the 'rational expectations' assumption that forecast errors are completely random and cannot be affected by deterministic policy behavior. Jointly, the two hypotheses of the short-run natural rate and rational expectations formation imply that stabilization policy, or at any rate monetary policy, will be powerless (Lucas, 1976; Sargent and Wallace, 1976; Barro, 1976). For an opposing view see Tobin (1972); Fischer (1977); Phelps and Taylor (1977); and Bailey (1978). The separate roles of the rational expectations assumption and the market clearing assumption can be brought out with a simple example: p_t denotes the actual price level in period t, p_t^* the equilibrium price level, and $\hat{p}_{t-1,t}$ the price level anticipated, in period $t - 1$, for period t (all in logs); Y_t is actual output, and $\bar{Y}_t$ full capacity output. Consider the 'Lucas supply function'

$$p_t^* = \alpha(Y_t - \bar{Y}_t) + \hat{p}_{t-1,t} \qquad \alpha > 0.$$

The actual price level adjusts sluggishly toward the equilibrium price level, according to

$$\Delta p_t \equiv p_t - p_{t-1} = \beta(p_t^* - p_{t-1}) \qquad 0 \leqslant \beta \leqslant 1.$$

Such a partial adjustment function is not implausible for an economic system with no underlying inflationary or deflationary trend. If such trends occurred, the disequilibrium price adjustment mechanism would be likely to involve first or higher differences of p_t and p_t^*. Note that instantaneous equilibrium is the special case of our lagged price adjustment equation when $\beta = 1$. In that case $p_t^* \equiv p_t$. Combining the equilibrium price equation and the disequilibrium price adjustment equation, we obtain

$$\Delta p_t = \alpha\beta(Y_t - \bar{Y}_t) + \beta(\hat{p}_{t-1,t} - p_{t-1}).$$

Rational expectations, or perfect foresight in this deterministic model, imply $\hat{p}_{t-1,t} = p_t$. Thus rational expectations rule out systematic deviations of actual from capacity output if and only if $\beta = 1$. If we are not always in temporary Walrasian equilibrium, policy can affect price behavior through the market disequilibrium channel even if price forecasts are rational.

2. For a discussion of the distinction between direct and indirect crowding-out, see Buiter (1977a).
3. This is the vertical *LM* 'curve' of textbook fame. A less plausible extreme scenario is that private real spending is perfectly elastic with respect to the prevailing interest rate; national product is limited by the volume of transactions the money supply will finance at that rate. This means that the *IS* 'curve' is a horizontal line. It is not the only case that can be so described in the Hicksian diagram. Another case applies to an open economy with perfect international capital mobility, facing a fixed foreign interest rate. If the foreign exchange rate is market-determined without official interventions, the economy's foreign investment, equal to its current account surplus, is perfectly elastic at the fixed interest rate. Given that rate and the domestic money stock, additional government purchases crowd out foreign investment 100 per cent, simply by appreciating the home currency and reducing net exports. Another case of horizontal *IS* can occur when expenditure on national product is less than infinitely elastic with respect to interest rate. Suppose the marginal propensity to spend with respect to national product itself, including investment as well as consumption, happens to be exactly unity. The *IS* curve is horizontal, but the interest rate level at which it is horizontal will be raised by government purchases or by any other increase in autonomous expenditure. Here complete crowding out will not occur if the higher interest rate will reduce money demand or increase money supply. If the *IS* locus is given by $Y = E(Y, r) + G$, its slope is $(1 - E_Y)/E_r$, and is zero if $E_Y = 1$, $E_r < 0$. However, at any given Y, $dr/dg = -1/E_r$. It is important not to confuse this case with either of the first two.
4. In a recent paper Fair (1978) demonstrates, via simulation experiments with his econometric model, that fiscal policy effects are very sensitive to the behavior of the Federal Reserve.
5. In 'Debt Neutrality: A Brief Review of Doctrine and Evidence', Chapter 9 of this volume, we point out that while Ricardo clearly stated the proposition that taxation and government borrowing are equivalent in their economic effects, he also refuted this 'equivalence theorem'. In spite of the injustice to Ricardo, we shall for convenience conform to prevalent usage and refer to the modern revival of neutrality doctrine as Ricardian.
6. For a discussion of inflation effects, see Wachtel (1980).
7. If this theoretical proposition seems surprisingly unrealistic in the light of the economic history of the 1970s, there are several explanations. The inflation that erupted in 1973–4 was associated with several events and policies discouraging to investment. This definitely does not mean that inflation *per se* is bad for investment. A dramatic increase in the price of energy relative to product prices reduced estimates of profitability in many industries. It also brought about a severe though temporary inflationary bulge. Anti-inflationary monetary policy engineered a sharp rise in the cost of financial capital and a severe recession. Extrapolating from this history, businessmen and other economic agents now believe that increases in inflation rates will induce similar restrictive policies in future.
8. If real money balances are added as an argument in the direct utility function — a very questionable practice — as in Sidrauski (1967) and Fischer (1978), the expression for ε is somewhat different. c denotes real per capita consumption, m the stock of real per capita money balances, a real per capita household wealth, $\bar{k}$ the stock of capital per unit of efficiency labor, L the size of the natural labor force, $\bar{L}$ the size of the labor force in efficiency units, p the price

level, T lump-sum transfers, and M the nominal stock of money. $\dot{L}/L = n$ and $\dot{L}/\bar{L} = n + \lambda$. The model involves maximizing

$$\int_0^\infty u(c, m)e^{-\delta t}dt,$$

Subject to

$$m + \frac{\bar{L}}{L}\bar{k} = a$$

$$\dot{a} = \frac{\bar{L}}{L}f(\bar{k}) + \frac{T}{pL} - c - \frac{\dot{p}}{p}m - na$$

$$\dot{\bar{k}} = f(\bar{k}) - \frac{L}{\bar{L}}c - (n + \lambda)\bar{k}$$

$$\dot{M} = T.$$

The first two constraints are individual balance sheet and budget constraints; the last two are economy-wide constraints. An interior solution to this problem is given by the four constraints and by

$$u_c(f' + \frac{\dot{p}}{p}) - u_m = 0$$

$$u_c(f' - n - \delta) + u_{cc}\dot{c} + u_{cm}\dot{m} = 0.$$

In long-run equilibrium the last equation becomes $f' = n + \delta + \varepsilon\lambda$,

where $-\varepsilon = c\dfrac{u_{cc}}{u_c} + m\dfrac{u_{cm}}{u_c}$, the sum of the elasticities of the marginal utility of consumption with respect to consumption and to real money balances. For a steady state to exist if $\lambda > 0$ we require not only that ε be constant but that $\dfrac{u_m}{u_c}$ be constant, that is, that

$$c\frac{u_{mc}}{u_m} + m\frac{u_{mm}}{u_m} + \varepsilon \text{ be constant.}$$

9. Some earlier contributions (Christ, 1968; Blinder and Solow, 1973; Tobin and Buiter 1976) may have fostered the opposite view. See, however, Phelps and Shell (1969); Buiter (1977b); Christ (1978); and Currie (1978a; 1978b). It is true that budget balance is an equilibrium condition for stationary economies with fixed price level, as discussed in Blinder and Solow (1973) and Tobin and Buiter (1976). But in general this is not true, and therefore one cannot derive long-run effects of policy measures from a balanced budget equation. All steady-state relations, including long-run portfolio balance equations, enter into determination of the long-run policy multipliers.

10. This approach is therefore different from the continuous time portfolio balance approach. The latter permits separate treatment of the saving decision — adding to existing wealth — and the portfolio allocation decision — the reshuffling of existing net worth (Tobin, 1969).

11.7 REFERENCES

Baily, Martin. N. (1978) 'Stabilization policy and private economic behavior', *Brookings Papers on Economic Activity*, 1, pp. 11–50.

Barro, Robert J. (1974) 'Are government bonds net wealth?' *Journal of Political Economy*, 82, November–December, pp. 1095–117.

Barro, Robert J. (1976) 'Rational expectations and the role of monetary policy', *Journal of Monetary Economics*, 2, January, pp. 1–32.

Blinder, Alan S. and Robert M. Solow (1973) 'Does fiscal policy matter?' *Journal of Public Economics*, 2, November, pp. 319–37.

Buiter, Willem H. (1975), 'Temporary equilibrium and long-run equilibrium', Ph.D. thesis, Yale University, Garland Publishing Inc. (1979), New York.

Buiter, Willem H. (1977a) 'Crowding out and the effectiveness of fiscal policy', *Journal of Public Economics*, 7 June, pp. 309–28 (also Chapter 6, this volume).

Buiter, Willem H. (1977b) "An integration of short run neo-Keynesian analysis and growth theory', *De Economist*, 125(3), pp. 340–59.

Buiter, Willem H. (1978) 'Short-run and long-run effects of external disturbances under a floating exchange rate', *Economica*, 45, August, pp. 251–72.

Buiter, Willem H. (1979) 'Government finance in an overlapping generations model with gifts and bequests' in G.M. von Furstenberg (ed.), *Social Security versus Private Saving in Post-industrial Democracies*, Ballinger, Cambridge, MA.

Buiter, Willem H. and James Tobin (1979) 'Debt neutrality: a brief review of doctrine and evidence' in G.M. von Furstenberg (ed.), *Social Security versus Private Saving*, Ballinger, Cambridge, MA (also Chapter 9, this volume).

Christ, Carl F. (1968) 'A simple macroeconomic model with a government budget restraint', *Journal of Political Economy*, 76, January, pp. 53–67.

Christ, Carl. F. (1978) 'Some dynamic theory of macroeconomic policy effects on income and prices under the government budget restraint', *Journal of Monetary Economics*, 4, January, pp. 45–70.

Currie, David (1978a) 'Macroeconomic policy and the government financing requirement: a survey of recent developments' in Michael Artis and R. Nobay (eds), *Studies in Contemporary Economic Analysis*, vol. 1, Croom Helm, London.

Currie, David (1978b) 'Monetary and fiscal policy and the crowding-out issue', mimeo, January.

Fair, Ray C. (1978) 'The sensitivity of fiscal-policy effects to assumptions about the behavior of the Federal Reserve', *Econometrica*, 46, September, pp. 1165–78.

Fischer, Stanley (1977) 'Long-term contracts, rational expectations, and the optimal money supply rule', *Journal of Political Economy*, 85, February, pp. 191–206.

Fischer, Stanley (1978) 'Capital accumulation and the transition path in a monetary optimizing model', mimeo, February.

Foley, Duncan K. (1975) 'On two specifications of asset equilibrium in macroeconomic models', *Journal of Political Economy*, 83, April, pp. 303–24.

Friedman, Milton (1957) *A Theory of the Consumption Function*, Princeton University Press, Princeton, NJ.

Friedman, Milton (1968) 'The role of monetary policy', *American Economic Review*, 58, March, pp. 1–17.

Keynes, John Maynard (1936) *The General Theory of Employment, Interest and Money*, Macmillan, London.

Lerner, Abba P. (1946) *The Economics of Control*, Macmillan, New York.

Lucas, Robert E. (1976) 'Econometric policy evaluation: a critique' in Karl Brunner and Allan H. Meltzer (eds) *The Phillips Curve and Labor Markets*, North-Holland, Amsterdam.

Phelps, Edmund S. and Karl Shell (1969) 'Public debt, taxation, and capital intensiveness', *Journal of Economic Theory*, 1, October, pp. 330–46.

Phelps, Edmund S. and John B. Taylor (1977) 'Stabilizing powers of monetary policy under rational expectations', *Journal of Political Economy*, 85, February, pp. 163–90.

Phelps, Edmund S. et al. (1970) *Microeconomic Foundations of Employment and Inflation Theory*, W. W. Norton, New York.

Sargent, Thomas J. and N. Wallace (1976), 'Rational expectations and the theory of economic policy', *Journal of Monetary Economics*, 84 April, pp. 207–37.

Sidrauski, Miguel (1967) 'Rational choice and patterns of growth in a monetary economy', *American Economic Review*, 57, May, pp. 534–44.

Tobin, James (1965) 'Money and economic growth', *Econometrica*, 33, October, pp. 671–84.

Tobin, James (1969) 'A general equilibrium approach to monetary theory', *Journal of Money, Credit, and Banking*, 1, February, pp. 15–29.

Tobin, James (1972) 'Inflation and unemployment', *American Economic Review*, 62, March, pp. 1–19.

Tobin, James and Willem H. Buiter (1976) 'Long-run effects of fiscal and monetary policy on aggregate demand' in Jerome Stein (ed.), *Monetarism*, North-Holland, Amsterdam (also Chapter 10, this volume).

Wachtel, Paul (1980) 'Inflation and the saving behavior of households: A survey', in G.M. von Furstenberg (ed.), *The Government and Capital Formation*, Ballinger, Cambridge, MA, pp. 153–74.

APPENDIX 11A

A formal model of short- and long-run effects of fiscal and financial policies

Notation

r_K	real one-period after-tax return on capital.
r_B	real one-period rate of return on government bonds.
r_H	real one-period rate of return on money balances.
r_A	real one-period rate of return on foreign assets.
r_A^*	rate of return on foreign assets in terms of foreign currency.
p	price of domestic output.
p_f^*	price of imports in terms of foreign currency.
w	unit labor cost.
q_K	price of installed capital in terms of current output.
q_B	price of government bonds in dollars.
e	foreign exchange rate (number of dollars per unit of foreign exchange).
b	coupon on the government bond in dollars per period.
$x(p)$	expected one-period proportional rate of change in p.
$x(q_K)$	expected one-period proportional rate of change in q_K.
$x(q_B)$	expected one-period proportional rate of change in q_B.
$x(e)$	expected one-period proportional rate of change in e.
H	nominal stock of money balances per unit of efficiency labor.

B number of government bonds per unit of efficiency labor.

K capital per unit of efficiency labor.

A value, in foreign exchange, of foreign bonds held by the private sector, per unit of efficiency labor.

$\hat{A}$ value, in foreign exchange, of foreign bonds held by the public sector, per unit of efficiency labor.

Y real output per unit of efficiency labor.

I resources devoted to investment per unit of efficiency labor.

G government spending on goods and services per unit of efficiency labor.

X trade balance surplus per unit of efficiency labor.

R real profits before taxes per unit of capital.

D real value of public sector deficit per unit of efficiency labor.

T real taxes net of transfers per unit of efficiency labor.

t proportional tax rate on factor income.

γ_B share of the public sector deficit or surplus financed by bonds.

γ_H share of the public sector deficit or surplus financed by money.

Z_B dollar value of total net government bond sales, per unit of efficiency labor, minus the value of bond sales associated with the financing of the public sector deficit through the deficit-financing rule of our model; a negative value of Z_B means government purchases of bonds.

Z_H dollar value of total net money issues by the government, per unit of efficiency labor, minus the value of money issues associated with the financing of the public sector deficit through the deficit financing rule of our model; a negative value of Z_H means government purchases of money.

Z_A dollar value of total net sales of foreign bonds by the government, per unit of efficiency labor; a negative value of Z_A means government purchases of foreign bonds.

n proportional rate of growth of the labor force.

λ proportional rate of labor augmenting technical change.

$g = n + \lambda$

$i = \Delta p / p$

Δ forward difference operator $\Delta Z(\tau) \equiv Z(\tau + 1) - Z(\tau)$, where τ designates period.

$\bar{Q}$ Q per unit of output.

The closed economy model

The model is essentially a representation of asset demands and supplies, both stocks and flows. Three assets are available to wealth-owners: government fiat money, perpetual government bonds paying a coupon of b dollars per period, and equity claims to real capital.

One share of equity represents ownership of one unit of physical capital. One good is produced and can either be used as a private or public consumption good or can be converted, at some cost, into durable productive capital. The real price of a unit of installed capital and the real value of a share of equity, q_K, is equal to the marginal cost of producing goods and converting them into capital. This cost depends each period on the amount of new investment relative to the existing stock.

Equity in our model stands for all claims on the productive capital assets of business enterprises and on the earnings from those assets. In actuality, of course, such claims take a variety of forms, including debts denominated in dollars as well as shares. We do not model those business financial decisions that determine the supplies of the several types of claims or the separate demands of savers for them. Our 'equity' stands for the whole package of shares and debts of business. The reader should not identify it with shares alone. Thus the q_K to which real investment is related below would be empirically approximated by summing the market values of all financial claims on business firms, debts as well as shares, netting out financial assets of firms, and comparing the resulting net market value to the replacement cost of the real capital stock at commodity prices. Likewise the real-world counterpart of the return to 'equity', r_K, would not be the one-period yield of shares alone but a properly weighted average of the yields of the several claims on capital stock and earnings. Interest and appreciation on bonds would enter this calculation, along with dividends and appreciation on stocks.

While our framework could easily handle a larger menu of assets, for example, splitting 'equity' into shares and business debts, the simpler three-asset model is capable of handling the issues addressed in this paper. The Modigliani–Miller theorem justifies aggregation of financial claims on a business firm into a single asset by showing that, under certain conditions, the value and yield of the aggregate are independent of its composition. The conditions are unrealistically restrictive, and disaggregation would be important and interesting for a number of problems. But for our present purposes, all we need is that the package of claims we call 'equity' be a gross substitute for the two government-issued assets in our model. Our treatment implies that corporate bonds and government bonds are not perfect substitutes for each other. If they were, corporations could finance virtually all their capital investment at the government bond rate. Our three-asset model respects the essential distinction between interest-bearing claims on government and claims, of whatever financial form, on private business. But most of our results would stand even if we adopted the frequent convention of macroeconomic models of requiring government bonds to bear the same real return as 'equity'.

Asset demands are for end-of-period stocks to be carried over to the next period. Market supplies consist of stocks carried over from the previous period and new 'production' of assets during the period. Thus current period flows of financial claims — generated by public sector deficits or private sector investment — have immediate effects in asset markets. Equations (11A.1), (11A.2), and (11A.3) represent demand/supply equilibrium for one period for the three assets:

$$F^K - q_K K = I(q_K, K) \tag{11A.1}$$

$$F^B - q_B \frac{B}{p} = \gamma_B \left(G + \frac{b}{p} B - T \right) + \frac{Z_B}{p} \tag{11A.2}$$

$$F^H - \frac{H}{p} = \gamma_H \left(G + \frac{b}{p} B - T \right) + \frac{Z_H}{p}. \tag{11A.3}$$

The left-hand sides represent savers' demand for acquisition of the several assets during the period. They are in each case the difference between the market value of the stock desired at the end of the period (F^K, F^B, F^H), each expressed in real terms, and the real value of the beginning-of-period stock (K, B, H). The end-of-period stock demands F^K, F^B, F^H are all functions of the same list of variables: the three rates of return r_K, r_B, r_H; the values of the initial stocks $q_K K$, $q_B B/p$, H/p; real output, Y, and taxes, T. We impose the following restrictions on these demand functions. With respect to rates of return, the assets are gross substitutes. An increase in any rate of return increases total asset demand $F^K + F^B + F^H$. An increase in the value of beginning-of-period asset holdings or current income is allocated over all three assets. An increase in the aggregate value of any initial holding increases total asset demand but by less than the increment in the initial holding; it increases consumption, too.

A fourth equilibrium condition, the *IS* curve, is implied by the other three. Let S denote real saving:

$$S \equiv F^K + F^B + F^H - \left(q_K K + q_B \frac{B}{p} + \frac{H}{p} \right) = I + G + \frac{bB}{p} - T. \tag{11A.4}$$

The investment function is given by

$$I = I(q_K, K) \qquad (I(1, K) = (n + \lambda)K; I_{q_K} > 0; I_K < 0). \tag{11A.5}$$

Taxes, net of transfers, are simply proportional to output:

$$T = tY \, (0 < t < 1). \tag{11A.6}$$

Coupons on government bonds are free of tax. Capital gains are not taxed. Earnings of capital are taxed before distribution to share-owners.

The government deficit $G + (bB)/p - T$ is financed either by printing money or by issuing bonds, in proportions γ_H and γ_B, respectively. Open market operations are swaps of money for bonds of equal value. Thus

$$\gamma_B + \gamma_H = 1 \qquad (\gamma_B, \gamma_H \geqslant 0) \tag{11A.7a}$$

$$Z_B + Z_H = 0. \tag{11A.7b}$$

Real one-period rates of return are related to current and expected asset prices as follows:

$$r_B \approx \frac{b}{q_B} + x(q_B) - x(p) \tag{11A.8a}$$

$$r_K \approx \frac{R(1 - t)}{q_K} + x(q_K) \tag{11A.8b}$$

$$r_H \approx -x(p). \tag{11A.8c}$$

Profits per unit of capital vary positively with real output and inversely with the capital stock:

$$R = R(K/Y) \qquad R' < 0. \tag{11A.9}$$

For the short-run analysis of the model, we consider two versions: one with price p predetermined for the period and, thanks to unemployment of labor and capital, with output in infinitely elastic supply at the prevailing price; the other with full employment and a price level completely flexible. In the full-employment version the capacity constraint is

$$Y = f(K) \qquad (f' > 0; f'' < 0). \tag{11A.10a}$$

In the unemployment version price is set for the period by past history. But events of the period determine the next period price, via an augmented price Philips curve:

$$\frac{\Delta p}{p} = \psi(Y - f(K)) + x(p) \qquad \psi' > 0; \psi(0) = 0. \tag{11A.10b}$$

$x(p)$ could be interpreted as the expectation of inflation. If so, Equation (11A.10b) implies that actual output can differ from full capacity output if and only if there are errors in the inflation forecast. Another interpretation is that $x(p)$ depends on the past history of prices and stands for all the factors in the economy that give inertia to built-in trends in wages and prices. In either case the first term of Equation (11A.10b) could differ systematically and for many periods from zero. With the first interpretation this will be the case if there is gradual adjustment of inflation expectations, as exemplified, for example, by an adaptive expectation mechanism. With the second interpretation, anticipated stabilization policy can have systematic effects on real output even if rational expectations or perfect foresight prevail (see note 1). The dynamics of the model are provided by changes of assets stocks and of expectations, and by the Phillips curve in the unemployment version.

For most of the analysis, we assume that the expected rates of change of q_B, q_K, and p are predetermined each period. As time passes, they are revised in response to forecast errors.

$$\Delta x(q_B) = \alpha_1(\Delta q_B/q_B - x(q_B)) \tag{11A.11a}$$

$$\Delta x(q_K) = \alpha_2(\Delta q_K/q_K - x(q_K)) \quad (\alpha_1, \alpha_2, \alpha_3 \geqslant 0) \tag{11A.11b}$$

$$\Delta x(p) = \alpha_3(\Delta p/p - x(p)) = \alpha_3(i - x(p)). \tag{11A.11c}$$

The changes of real asset stocks (per unit of efficiency labor) are given by

$$\Delta K = \frac{I}{q_K} - gK \tag{11A.12}$$

$$\Delta \frac{q_B B}{p} \approx \gamma_B\left(G + \frac{bB}{p} - T\right) + \frac{Z_B}{p} - \left(i + g - \frac{\Delta q_B}{q_B}\right)\frac{q_B B}{p} \tag{11A.13}$$

$$\Delta \frac{H}{p} \approx (1 - \gamma_B)\left(G + \frac{bB}{p} - T\right) - \frac{Z_B}{p} - (i + g)\frac{H}{p}. \tag{11A.14}$$

The only approximation in Equations (11A.13) and (11A.14) involves our ignoring capital gains or losses on current-period additions to stocks of money and bonds.

Short-run effects of fiscal and financial policies in the unemployment model
The basic equations (11A.1), (11A.2), and (11A.3) can be solved for r_K, r_B, and Y after using Equations (11A.6), (11A.8), and (11A.9) to eliminate q_K, q_B, and T. The system expresses the three endogenous variables as implicit functions of predetermined variables (stocks, expectations, price level) and of policies. There are four parameters of policy. Fiscal policy is described by G and t, financial policy by γ_B ($\gamma_H = 1 - \gamma_B$), and monetary policy by Z_B ($Z_H = -Z_B$).

The equations for the 12 multipliers with respect to policy parameters are tedious to print and read but, along with other mathematical details not presented here, are available from the authors on request. The structure of these equations is as follows:

$$\begin{bmatrix} + & - & +(?) \\ - & + & + \\ - & - & + \\ + & + & + \end{bmatrix}\begin{bmatrix} dr_K \\ dr_B \\ dY \end{bmatrix} = \begin{bmatrix} 0 & 0 & 0 & -(?) \\ \gamma_B & D & \frac{1}{p} & -(?) \\ 1 - \gamma_B & -D & -\frac{1}{p} & -(?) \\ 1 & 0 & 0 & - \end{bmatrix}\begin{bmatrix} dG \\ d\gamma_B \\ dZ_B \\ dt \end{bmatrix} \tag{11A.15}$$

$$D \equiv G + \frac{bB}{p} - tY.$$

Our a priori restrictions on the sum of the elements of each column are given below the columns. An increase in the required rate of return on capital stimulates saving and reduces investment. An increase in the rate of return on bonds stimulates saving. Expansion of real output is assumed to have a stronger effect on saving than on investment (the analogy of the assumption that the *IS* curve is downward-sloping in the simple *IS–LM* model). If an increase in output creates excess demand in the market for equity, the last column of the Jacobian on the left-hand side of Equation (11A.15) is positive and its determinant is also positive. Even if an increase in output were to create excess supply in the equity market, the determinant of the Jacobian will be positive if the excess demand created in the money market by an increase in Y is larger.

Another ambiguity is the effect of an increase in the tax rate t on excess demand in the three asset markets. In aggregate, increasing t creates excess demand for assets. The deficit declines, and the new government supply of money-cum-bonds is diminished more than the reduction in private saving induced by the decline of disposable income. This is indicated by the negative sign for the sum of the last right-hand side column in Equation (11A.15). But this effect may not prevail for every asset individually. For example, if γ_B is close or equal to zero, the deficit reduction does little or nothing to the supply of bonds, and the general saving-reducing effect of the decline of disposable income may dominate. In the case of equity, the tax effects on demand and supply are somewhat different. Lowering the deficit does not directly diminish the new supply of equity; however, the higher tax rate deters private investment. On the asset flow demand side, the decline in disposable income and the reduction in after-tax returns have negative effects, offset only by the capital loss on equity inflicted by the tax increase.

Table 11A.1 shows the results for the 12 multipliers, so far as definite signs follow from our assumptions. The final t column assumes that the excess demand effects dominate in all three assets (negative signs throughout the dt column of Equation (11A.15)). The signs shown in Table 11A.1 for γ_B, the share of the deficit that is bond-financed, assume a positive deficit.

Table 11A.1 Signs of one-period policy multipliers, unemployment model

Policy Variable	G					t
	$\gamma_B = 0$	$0 < \gamma_B < 1$	$\gamma_B = 1$	γ_B	Z_B	
r_K	−	?	?	?	?	?
r_B	−	?	+	+	+	?
Y	+	+	+	−	−	−

If the budget is initially in surplus, an increase in γ_B would have the opposite effects. Of course, a change in γ_B would have no effect if the budget was balanced. An increase in Z_B, like an increase in γ_B with an initial deficit, involves the sale of bonds for money by the central bank. They both raise the real rate of return on bonds and reduce aggregate demand and output. The after-tax rate of return on equity, r_K, is likely to be higher if bonds and equity are close substitutes, lower if bonds and money are close substitutes. If r_K increases, q_K will be lower because Y also declines. Private capital formation is 'crowded out'. If r_K declines, the net effect on q_K is ambiguous.

An increase in public spending, G, will raise output. Its effect on r_K is uncertain. If deficits are exclusively money-financed, $\gamma_B = 0$, an increase in G will lower r_K and stimulate investment. In that case the stimulating effect on investment of higher current profits is reinforced by a lower required rate of return. Both raise q_K. With money-financed budget deficits and surpluses, an increase in G will also lower r_B. Thus, given idle resources, an increase in public spending, coupled with accommodating monetary policy, will 'crowd in' private investment. This may happen even if γ_B exceeds zero. The monetary share of deficit finance does not have to be 100 per cent to prevent r_B from rising. Furthermore, r_B can rise — as will certainly happen if $\gamma_B = 1$ — while r_K falls. This would occur if bonds are in some sense closer to money than to capital in the chain of asset substitution.

Short-run effects of fiscal and financial policies in the full-employment model

The solution for the full-employment version is obtained by reversing the roles of Y and p. Output Y is predetermined by the capital stock previously accumulated, given, of course, the exogenous supply of efficiency labor. The price level p is endogenous within the period. As in the previous section, the system consists of the three basic Equations (11A.1), (11A.2), and (11A.3) with extra variables eliminated by use of subsequent equations. In our comparative static analysis of this version of the model we add a fifth exogenous variable, $x(p)$, to the four policy parameters. The structure of the equations for the 15 multipliers in given in Equation (11A.16), and the results are summarized in Table 11A.2.

Table 11A.2 Signs of one-period multipliers, full-employment model

Policy Variable	G			γ_B	Z_B	t	$x(p)$
	$\gamma_B = 0$	$0 < \gamma_B < 1$	$\gamma_B = 1$				
r_K	−	?	?	?	?	?	−
r_B	−	?	+	+	+	?	−
p	+	+	+	−	−	−	+

$$
\begin{bmatrix}
+ & - & ? \\
- & + & + \\
- & - & + \\
+ & + & +
\end{bmatrix}
\begin{bmatrix}
dr_K \\
dr_B \\
dp
\end{bmatrix}
=
\begin{bmatrix}
0 & 0 & 0 & -(?) & - \\
\gamma_B & D & \dfrac{1}{p} & -(?) & - \\
1-\gamma_B & -D & -\dfrac{1}{p} & -(?) & + \\
+1 & 0 & 0 & - & +
\end{bmatrix}
\begin{bmatrix}
dG \\
d\gamma_B \\
dZ \\
dt \\
dx(p)
\end{bmatrix}
$$

$$(11A.16)$$

The Jacobian matrix, on the left-hand side of Equation (11A.16), differs from that of Equation (11A.15) for the unemployment case only by having a question mark in the third column. In general, an increase in the price level stimulates saving via the 'real balance effect'. This is the only effect at work; our assumption that $x(p)$ is given eliminates any possible substitution effect from a rise in the current price level relative to the future price level. The reduction in the real value of existing holdings of bonds and money is the reason for the plus signs in the second and third entries of the column and in the sum for total saving at the bottom. Does this loss of wealth spill over into more saving in the form of equity, too? This is the uncertainty indicated in the first row. But even if the answer is negative, it is likely that the positive effect on saving in the form of money is absolutely larger than the negative effect on equity saving. This is sufficient, but not necessary, to ensure that the Jacobian still has a positive determinant, as is assumed in Table 11A.2. The other assumptions of Table 11A.2 are the same as for Table 11A.1.

The policy effects on p are straightforward. An increase in public spending, G, raises the price level and a substitution of bonds for money lowers it. As in the unemployment version, the effect of an increase in the income tax rate is complicated by the non-lump-sum nature of the tax which directly affects the rate of return on investment and the required rate of return on equity. The tax column of Table 11A.2 assumes again that an increase in t causes excess demand for all three assets. To obtain the result that a substitution of bonds for money raises r_B, it is sufficient (but not necessary) that the effect of an increase in the price level on the bond market is larger, in absolute value, than the effect in the equity market. With that assumption, we can determine the signs of a few more multipliers. First, the substitution of bonds for money will raise r_K when bonds and equity are close substitutes, lower r_K if money and bonds are close substitutes. Second, with money financing ($\gamma_B = 0$) an increase in G lowers r_K and r_B.

Note that whenever real output increases in the unemployment model, the price level rises in the full-employment model. In the latter version, private spending is crowded out by public spending dollar for dollar. Resources appropriated by the government may come partially or wholly from private consumption rather than private investment, however. With sufficient money-financing, investment may even be 'crowded in' by deficit finance. This is particularly likely if the source of increased deficit is tax reduction rather than exhaustive government purchases.

An autonomous rise in expected inflation is a decline in the real return on money, and by our standard assumption will generate excess supply of money and excess demand for the other two assets. This is reflected in the last column of the matrix on the right-hand side of Equation (11A.16). The last column of Table 11A.2 shows the implications: an increase in p and declines in the other real rates of return r_K and r_B. Along with the decline in r_K goes an increase in capital investment. Room in the economy is made by a decrease in consumption, in response to the wealth losses arising from the price level increase which more than offsets the stimulating effect on consumption of the general reduction in rates of return.

The fiscal–monetary policy mix and capital formation
The analysis can be simplified in a number of ways by assuming that the tax is a lump-sum tax, T_0, rather than a proportional tax on labor and capital income. This simplification will be used to consider the validity of a common proposition about the monetary–fiscal policy mix most likely to favor investment. It is widely held that a combination of expansionary monetary policy and restrictive fiscal policy favors capital formation by keeping interest rates low while taxes discourage private consumption.

In the unemployment version of the model, we shall evaluate this proposition for the short run by investigating what combinations of the tax, T_0, and of the share of money in the deficit, $\gamma_H = 1 - \gamma_B$, keep Y constant. The analysis is repeated for combinations of G and γ_H. We then consider the effect of such changes in policy mix on r_K, and thus on q_K and I. In the full-employment version of the model we shall consider, by analogy, which combinations of T_0 or G and γ_H sustain a given price level, and how capital formation varies when the policy mix is altered in a way that preserves the price level. We continue to assume the government budget to be in deficit initially.

We summarize the results verbally. Mathematical details of the analysis are available from the authors.

An increase in G, with an offsetting change in γ_H that just keeps Y at its original level, raises r_K. With Y constant by assumption, q_K will fall and investment is crowded out. As one would expect, a downward compensating change in γ_H is needed to keep Y constant when G increases. This result supports the view that a combination of expansionary fiscal policy and restrictive financial policy deters investment. The reverse policy, a fall in G and a rise in γ_H, will favor capital formation.

The case of tax increases and monetary expansion is not completely straightforward, however, Granted that an increase in taxes raises the sum of private and public saving, this policy can, and in our model will, initially reduce saving in the specific form of equity. If this effect is very strong, the excess supply pressure in the equity market could raise r_K, and thus lower q_K and investment when taxes increase. This is less likely to happen the smaller is the income effect on the demand for equity. If this effect is zero, an increase in T_0, with a compensating change in γ_H to keep Y constant, unambiguously lowers r_K and stimulates investment; r_B is also lower. The direction of the compensating change in γ_H is unambiguously positive when there is no income effect on the demand for equity because we assume throughout that the mix of bond and money financing is such that, *ceteris paribus*, an increase in taxes would create excess demand in both the bond market and the 'money market'. With both r_K and r_B lowered, the demand for money will increase further. To preserve equilibrium, γ_H will have to increase.

The counterintuitive phenomenon — an increase in taxes reduces the demand for equity to such an extent that the required rate of return on capital is increased — cannot occur in the traditional Keynesian *IS–LM* model. The reason is that bonds and claims to real reproducible capital are in that model perfect substitutes in private portfolios. The more general portfolio-theoretic structure of our model includes the Keynesian model as a special case but can also generate the non-traditional results just mentioned.

In the full-employment version, the relevant fiscal–monetary policy trade-offs are those that keep the price level constant. The analysis is exactly the same as for the unemployment model. In both cases both p and Y are formally exogenous, one by policy manipulation and one by assumption regarding the economic environment. The financial parameter γ_B, or γ_H, is formally endogenous. The results just presented apply to either environment.

Tax cuts, deficits, inflation expectations, and investment
In the short-run analysis of our model, we have so far treated expectations as parametric. The expected proportional rates of change of the price of capital, the price of bonds and the general price level are given for any single period. In the long-run steady state of the model, expectations are always realized. To extend this perfect foresight assumption to the short run is fashionable but probably not very useful in many cases. Instead we shall analyze the impact of a specific combination of tax and financing policies under the assumption that economic agents (or at any rate the portfolio holders whose behavior is modeled in our asset-demand functions) have 'crude monetarist' expectations. A cut in taxes will, when deficits are financed mainly or entirely by increased money creation, lead to an increase in the expected rate of inflation. The full-employment version of the model

will be used to analyze the impact of a tax cut on capital formation under these circumstances. Taxes are again taken to be lump-sum.

An increase in the expected rate of inflation will induce substitution out of money balances. With the nominal interest rate on money fixed, the real rate of return declines by the full amount of the increase in the expected rate of inflation. Bonds, too, are nominally denominated. We would, therefore, expect substitution out of bonds as well. The portfolio reshuffling consequent on an increase in the expected rate of inflation, however, results in changes in the nominal interest rate on bonds which compensate, although in all likelihood only partly, for the increase in expected inflation. The higher expected rate of inflation will correspondingly lower q_B, the nominal price of the bonds.

As we have seen above, an increase in the expected rate of inflation will by itself reduce both r_K and r_B. (The positive effect on investment implied by this analysis needs to be qualified in real-world application, as we suggested in the text, by allowing for the increased uncertainty, and increased likelihood of subsequent restrictive policy, possibly engendered by higher inflation.) As we also observed above, a tax reduction by itself normally will 'crowd in' investment, especially if the resulting deficit is financed by money; the only reservation is that the resulting rise in the price *level* and decrease in wealth might tend to diminish saving in equity. Thus if inflationary expectations are enhanced by tax reduction, there is a double reason for expecting favorable effects on capital formation. It is not inflation *per se*, but the future policy responses associated with inflation (monetary contraction, tax increases, and so on) that might discourage investment.

Steady-state equilibrium

We now describe the steady-state characteristics of the model. In long-run equilibrium, all real stocks and flows grow at the natural rate of growth, $g = n + \lambda$, and expectations are realized. The open market operations parameter, Z_B, is set to zero. Unless we state otherwise, the government is assumed to pursue mixed deficit financing policies ($0 < \gamma_B < 1$). Certain steady-state conditions are set out in Equations (11A.17).

$$x(q_B) = \frac{\Delta q_B}{q_B} = 0; x(q_K) = \frac{\Delta q_K}{q_K} = 0; x(p) = i \qquad (11A.17a)$$

$$q_K = 1 \qquad (11A.17b)$$

$$Y = f(K) \qquad (11A.17c)$$

$$\frac{H}{p} = \frac{(1 - \gamma_B)}{\gamma_B} \frac{q_B B}{p} \qquad (11A.17d)$$

$$\frac{H}{p} + \frac{q_B B}{p} = \left(G + \frac{bB}{p} - tY\right)\Big/(g + i) \tag{11A.17e}$$

$$r_K = R(K/Y)(1 - t) \tag{11A.17f}$$

$$r_B = \frac{b}{q_B} - i \tag{11A.17g}$$

$$r_H = -i. \tag{11A.17h}$$

Equation (11A.17a) states that expectations are realized. Since the nominal coupon on government bonds, b, is constant, the nominal price of bonds, q_B, is constant even in an inflationary or deflationary steady state. There are no real capital gains on equity. Equation (11A.17b) implies that net investment is at its steady-state value: $I = gK$. From Equation (11A.17c) we see that output is at the full-employment level. The ratio of the value of the money stock to the value of the bond stock is given by $(1 - \gamma_B)/\gamma_B$, the ratio of the shares of money and bonds in the financing of budget deficits or surpluses (Equation (11A.17d)). The real value of the public sector deficit has to be sufficient to maintain the real value of total government debt per unit of efficiency labor, in the face of price level changes, labor force growth and technical change (Equation (11A.17e)). Equations (11A.17f)–(11A.17h) define real rates of return, all constant in a steady state.

Steady states cannot exist at all unless the behavioral and technological relations of the economy satisfy certain homogeneity properties. The production function must be homogeneous in capital and efficiency labor, as already assumed in Equations (11A.17c) and (11A.17f). Thus each possible steady state is characterized by a capital–output ratio constant over time. Policies also must be consistent with growth of all real variables at the common natural growth rate of the economy. Thus both G and T must be proportional to output Y. Finally, asset portfolio demands must allow all real stocks to grow at the same rate, g, as Y and other aggregate real variables. We exploit these homogeneity properties by expressing the steady-state equations in terms of stocks and flows per unit of output, as follows (stocks and flows per unit of output are distinguishable by bars):

$$\bar{K} = \bar{K}(R) \qquad \bar{K}' < 0. \tag{11A.18a}$$

This is just the inverse of the R function in Equation (11A.17f).

Likewise, the steady-state supplies $\bar{H}$ and $\bar{B}$ depend on fiscal and financial policies and on rates of return. Using Equations (11A.17d), (11A.17e) and (11A.17g) we obtain

$$\frac{q_B \bar{B}}{p} = \frac{\gamma_B(\bar{G} - t)}{g - (\gamma_B r_B - (1 - \gamma_B)i)} \tag{11A.18b}$$

$$\frac{\bar{H}}{p} = \frac{(1 - \gamma_B)(\bar{G} - t)}{g - (\gamma_B r_B - (1 - \gamma_B)i)}. \tag{11A.18c}$$

Note that the denominator in these two expressions could be written as $g - r_D$, where r_D is the weighted average of the real rates r_D and r_H on government debt, with the weights corresponding to the shares of the two kinds of debt in the total.

We write steady state demands for asset stocks proportional to output Y as $F^{\bar{K}}$, $F^{\bar{B}}$, and $F^{\bar{H}}$. Each is a function of the three rates of return and of the tax rate $(R(1 - t), r_B, -i, t)$. Thus the basic equations are

$$F^{\bar{K}} = \bar{K} \tag{11A.19a}$$

$$F^{\bar{B}} = \frac{q_B \bar{B}}{p} \tag{11A.19b}$$

$$F^{\bar{H}} = \frac{\bar{H}}{p}, \tag{11A.19c}$$

where the right-hand-side variables can be eliminated by use of Equations (11A.18). The three Equations (11A.19) determine the three rates of return $(R, r_B, -i)$ as functions of the policy parameters $(\bar{G}, t, \gamma_B)$. Once the rates of return are determined, Equations (11A.18) can be used to find the steady state stocks. In particular, Equation (11A.18a) gives steady-state capital intensity.

Before looking at some special cases, we make some general observations about the steady-state solutions and the long-run policy multipliers.

Budget balance, asset growth, and steady-state inflation

First, the steady state is not in general characterized by a balanced public sector budget (Currie, 1978b; Christ, 1978). The long-run balanced budget emerges only under very special circumstances. One trivial circumstance, related to the algebra of steady states, occurs when both nominally-denominated debt instruments of the government are demanded by the private sector in non-zero amounts, while the government finances by only a single instrument ($\gamma_B = 0$ or $\gamma_B = 1$). If the nominal quantity of one government-issued asset is kept constant at a non-zero level, the nominal quantity of the other liability must be constant in the steady state, so that *all* real stocks and flows may grow at the common natural rate of growth. In that case the growth of real holdings of nominal public debt is generated exclusively by a steady proportional rate of price level deflation equal to g (Tobin and Buiter, 1976; Buiter, 1977b). A second circumstance occurs when the government pursues mixed financing policies ($0 < \gamma_B < 1$). Either by design — the policy authority fixes the common steady-state rate of growth of H and B at zero by appropriately adjusting one or both of its fiscal controls ($\bar{G}, t$) — or by coincidence, the endogenous steady-state budget deficit assumes the value zero. Finally, the steady-state budget will have to be balanced if the price level is fixed even in the long run in a model without growth (Blinder and Solow, 1973; Tobin and Buiter, 1976).

Second, it is easily seen from Equations (11A.17d) and (11A.17e) that the steady-state rate of inflation equals the excess of the common steady-state rate of growth of the two nominally-denominated public sector debt instruments over the natural rate of growth.

$$\frac{\Delta H}{H} - g = \frac{\Delta B}{B} - g = i \tag{11A.20}$$

Third, we stress that the role of money is quite different in the long run from the short run. The reason is that its real rate of return is in the long run endogenous. In our short runs, it was exogenous: we took the nominal return on money as constant at zero and the expected rate of inflation as temporarily predetermined. In the long run the nominal rate on money is still fixed, but the assumed flexibilities of prices and their rates of change plus the requirement that expected and actual inflation rates coincide make the real return endogenous. This removes money from its special position and makes it like other assets. If its real supply is to be increased, one way the public can be persuaded to accept it is by an increase in its real rate of return, a decline in inflation. This means that some of the effects customarily associated with money, as compared to government bonds, need not show up in comparison of long-run steady states. For example, steady states with larger deficits or larger monetary shares of deficits need not be more inflationary; wealth-owners may instead be led to accept the larger monetary issues because inflation rates are lower.

Crowding out and crowding in

In analyzing the long-run effects of government fiscal and financial policies, we will be comparing the steady-state equilibria associated with different values of policy parameters. 'Crowding out' in this context means that the steady state associated with a changed value of a policy parameter, say a higher value of $\bar{G}$, has a smaller capital intensity $\bar{K}$ than a reference steady-state path associated with another parameter value, say a lower value of $\bar{G}$. 'Crowding in' means that the variation of the policy parameter is associated with an increase in capital intensity.

Clearly crowding out means that steady-state private saving, relative to national product Y, in the specific form of equity capital is decreased, while crowding in means that it is increased. There are several ways in which the private rate of equity saving may vary. One mechanism is that total private saving is higher relative to output in one steady state than in another and that at least part of the increment goes into equity. Another mechanism is that private saving is diverted from government liabilities into equity even though total private saving is not increased. A policy variation may tend to crowd in via the first mechanism if it generally fosters private saving; this is in our model, for example, one effect of tax reduction. A policy variation may tend to crowd in via the second mechanism if it lowers the real return on government bonds and money and induces savers to shift to equity, even though total private saving is deterred; this is also a possible effect of tax reduction, though as we shall see it could work the other way.

Things are not always what they seem, and policy variations sometimes have long-run consequences that are the reverse of normal intuition and the reverse of their short-run effects. In our model the nominal rate of growth of government liabilities is not itself a policy parameter. It is the endogenous outcome of more basic policy parameters $\bar{G}$, t, and γ_B. Another way to state the point is that the rate of inflation, i, is an endogenous outcome of the whole system, and the nominal growth of both government bonds and money is necessarily $g + i$. It is important to remember also that there is a presumption of generally negative relationship between the nominal growth of these government liabilities and their real stocks. This arises because a high rate of inflation means a low real return on money, and usually on the substitute asset, government bonds, as well. This shifts savers to capital, as discussed in the previous paragraph. The level of prices adjusts to make the high nominal stocks of debt and money the low real stocks that savers wish to hold.

An increase in $\bar{G} - t$ appears to be a deficit-increasing policy. But it does not necessarily increase the steady-state real deficit or debt as a percentage of national product. As shown by Equations (11A.18b) and (11A.18c), the debt–income ratio is $(\bar{G} - t)/(g - r_D)$. An increase in $\bar{G} - t$ may or may not increase this ratio. It may so lower r_D, by raising the rate of inflation, that the ratio actually declines. Then the fiscal policy looks expansionary, and is inflationary, but it absorbs less rather than more saving. Private saving and wealth are shifted into the more attractive asset, equity, whose rate declines, too. Thus there can be 'crowding in' by asset substitution and reduction — *ex post* — of the real public sector deficit per unit of output, even though total private saving is smaller. The opposite is also possible: an increase in $\bar{G} - t$ may crowd out capital and be counterinflationary. The outcomes depend on the system as a whole. That is the reason why the analysis is sometimes complex and why the results sometimes cannot be determined, even in sign, without empirical knowledge of the asset demand and supply functions.

Neutrality, superneutrality, and other long-run policy neutrality
From the short-run equilibrium equations of the full-employment model, we can conclude that money is not neutral, but that money and bonds together are neutral. A once-and-for-all increase in H accompanied by an equal proportional increase in p — and, as $x(p)$ is assumed constant, an equal proportional increase in the future expected price level — will not

restore the original real equilibrium. The real quantity of bonds would be reduced, necessitating further real adjustments. A hypothetical once-for-all equal proportional increase in H, B, and p will, however, leave the real equilibrium unchanged.

Shifting from level changes to *rate of growth* changes, we notice from the long-run model that a given percentage point increase in the rate of growth of H alone will not be consistent with an equal percentage point increase in the steady-state rate of inflation. Both nominally denominated assets must grow at the same rate in a steady state, and then the rate of inflation will be associated point-for-point with their common growth rate. However, the consequences of changing the common steady-state rate of change of H and B are not limited to an equal change in the steady-state rate of inflation. Money and bonds are in general not 'superneutral'. Changes in the steady-state rate of inflation alter the steady-state real rate of return on money balances. The reason for this is the fact that the nominal interest rate on the monetary base is institutionally fixed (realistically at zero, as assumed in this model). A higher rate of inflation will, *ceteris paribus*, induce portfolio holders to shift out of money into other assets. These other assets can be real-valued financial claims such as equity, or nominally-denominated claims with market-determined rates of return. The portfolio shift out of money into capital and bonds will tend to reduce their real rates of return. This rather informal argument suggests that a steady state characterized by a higher rate of inflation will also have higher capital–labor and capital–output ratios. The formal analysis below demonstrates that this is indeed a possible configuration, but not the only one.

As explained in the text, *superneutrality* means formally that real long-run outcomes are independent of the rate of growth of the money supply. We can generalize this to general, long-run *policy neutrality*, the property that real long-run outcomes are independent of any government fiscal and financial policies. In the context of our model, it means specifically that R and $\bar{K}$ are unaffected by the government policies. Taken together, Equations (11A.18) and (11A.19) — and, in particular, the combination of Equations (11A.18a) and (11A.19a) to give $F^{\bar{K}} = \bar{K}(R)$ — reveal what policy neutrality necessitates. This equation of equity demand and capital supply must give the same steady-state solution for R, the pre-tax return on capital, whatever the settings of policy instruments.

Now the only policy parameter directly involved in the equation is t, the tax rate. So one requirement of superneutrality is that these direct tax effects on demand for equity be zero. There are two such effects. One is the wedge that taxation of profit income enters between the marginal productivity of capital, R, and the after-tax return to savers, r_K. We observed in the text that neutrality propositions evidently assume lump-sum taxation. The other direct tax effect on equity saving, which would apply even to lump-sum taxes, is the disposable income effect on saving and demand for wealth. Assuming it to be zero means that savers will aim at the same ratio of wealth to consumption regardless of the level of consumption. In the text, a rationalization of this assumption is sketched: consumers with infinite horizons make intertemporal choices in accordance with time discounts invariant across steady states.

The other requirement of policy-neutrality, in terms of our model, is that there be no cross-effects of r_B and r_H $(= -i)$, the rates of return on bonds and money, on demand for capital equity, $F^{\bar{K}}$. This makes the equity-capital equation by itself sufficient to determine R and thus $\bar{K}$. Policy parameters $(\bar{G}, t, \gamma_B)$ obviously affect r_B and $-i$ in the two other equations, and would indirectly affect R if the values of the other rates of return make a difference to $F^{\bar{K}}$. Assuming those cross-effects to be zero says that any additional demands for bonds and money induced by increases in their yields do not come even partially by diversion of saving from equity but represent wholly additional saving. The special assumptions involved in this zero-substitution theory of saving are examined in the text.

A money-capital model: balanced budget
We now turn to formal analysis of the effect of changes in the policy instruments on the steady-state endogenous variables, with special emphasis on R. It is instructive to consider first a simplified version of the model that includes only money and capital as assets. The steady-state equations of this simplified model are obtained by setting $\gamma_B = 0$ in the full model and omitting r_B, B, and the bond market equation. The condensed model is as follows:

$$F^{\bar{K}} = \bar{K}(R) \tag{11A.21a}$$

$$F^{\bar{H}} = \bar{H}/p. \tag{11A.21b}$$

Equation (11A.18c) becomes, with $\gamma_B = 0$,

$$\frac{\bar{H}}{p} = \frac{\bar{G} - t}{g + i}. \tag{11A.18d}$$

It is instructive to consider first a balanced budget policy: $\bar{G} = t$. Imagine, to begin, that no stock of government-issued money is available to the public; capital is the only vehicle for saving and for holding wealth. The equity market equation (11A.21a) says that an increase in t — to finance an increase in $\bar{G}$ — will increase R and diminish $\bar{K}$. The reasons are straightforward and familiar. The reduction in disposable income diminishes savers' desired wealth relative to pre-tax income Y. In addition to this income effect, higher taxation of earnings from capital deters equity saving and favors present consumption. This is a very orthodox story. Increasing government consumption and taxation crowds out capital.

An economy without government-issued money is hard to imagine. Suppose there is a fixed nominal stock of such money, inherited from the distant past, the same throughout every possible steady-state path. Suppose that the government budget is balanced as above, and consider how steady states vary with the size of the budget. All steady states must have the same real rate of return on money, namely g; this is accomplished by price deflation at the natural growth rate. Given g, Equations (11A.21) determine the two variables R and $\bar{H}/p$. The latter is the ratio $\bar{H}/pY$, where $\bar{H}$ is the fixed nominal stock. The price level p is in any steady state falling at rate g, but the *level* of this path can adjust to reconcile $\bar{H}$ to any $\bar{H}/p$ that wealth-owners desire. Clearly the outcome is the same as in the previous paragraph. With the deflation rate invariant at g, the capital equation is independent of the second equation, and, for the reasons already given, an increase in t raises R and lowers $\bar{K}$. Formally, the structure of this system is

$$
\begin{bmatrix} + & 0 \\ - & -1 \\ + & - \end{bmatrix}
\begin{bmatrix} dR \\ d\left(\dfrac{\bar{H}}{p}\right) \end{bmatrix}
=
\begin{bmatrix} + & + \\ ? & - \\ + & - \end{bmatrix}
\begin{bmatrix} dt \\ dg \end{bmatrix}
\qquad (11A.22)
$$

The question mark in Equation (11A.22) indicates ambiguity about the tax effect on demand for money. The disposable income effect is in the same direction as for capital, but the substitution effect goes the other way, encouraging accumulation of the asset whose yield is untaxed. However, our assumption that the cross-effects of a rate of return will never exceed the own-effect means, in this case, that the overall effect of a tax increase on wealth demand is negative (so that the dt column on the right-hand side has a positive sum). Consequently the increase in t (and $\bar{G}$) will lower $\bar{H}/p$ as well as $\bar{K}$; in other words, a larger budget spells a generally higher price path.

   The natural growth rate g is not a policy variable, at least within the spectrum of fiscal and financial policies here examined. But it is of some interest to note that, because g here is also the real rate of return on money, an increase in it will raise R and $\bar{H}/p$, lower p and $\bar{K}$. This conclusion abstracts from any direct effects an increase in the economy's real growth rate might have on desired wealth relative to income.

   There is another way in which a long-run balanced budget policy could be reconciled with the need of the economy for governmental money. This is for the government to serve as an intermediary, issuing money and buying private sector assets with the proceeds. In our primitive two-asset model, the government can only buy equities; a more likely mechanism would involve government loans to private borrowers, negative public debt. In the two-asset model this simply means that the supply of capital, relative to Y, available for private ownership is reduced from $\bar{K}(R)$ to $\bar{K}(R) - \bar{H}/p$, where $\bar{H}/p$ is now a parameter of government policy, the volume of its equity holdings relative to national product. Equity purchases are not counted in $\bar{G}$, purchases for government consumption. The rate of inflation is now endogenous. The formal structure is as follows:

$$
\begin{bmatrix} + & - \\ - & + \end{bmatrix} \begin{bmatrix} dR \\ d(-i) \end{bmatrix} = \begin{bmatrix} + & -1 \\ ? & +1 \end{bmatrix} \begin{bmatrix} dt \\ d\bar{H}/p \end{bmatrix} \qquad (11A.23)
$$

$$
\begin{array}{cccc} + & + & & + \quad 0 \end{array}
$$

Analysis easily shows that a balanced-budget increase in t once again raises R and lowers $\bar{K}$. The effect on the inflation rate is definitely negative if the disposable income effect on demand for money dominates (the question mark in Equation (11A.23) is $+$), and may be negative in the other case. An increase in H/p, providing private portfolio owners with more real money balances and less capital, naturally lowers the real return on capital R and raises that of money $(-i)$. Such a policy is both counterinflationary and favorable to capital formation.

However, practical implementation of the intermediary strategy just described would be difficult. The steady-state equilibria of system (11A.23) may well be unstable. The short-run impact of purchases of equities — or, in general, other privately owned assets — with new money is to raise the price level. Only if this leads to a reduction in inflationary expectations can the public be induced to hold larger real money balances. A more reliable way to increase the real return on money, while channeling the public's money holdings into the equity market, would be to raise the nominal yield on money.

A money-capital model: deficit budget
The government's normal method of providing its money to the economy is to issue money to finance budget deficits. We now consider cases where $\bar{G}$ exceeds t, and $\bar{H}/p$ is determined by Equation (11A.18d). Since $\bar{H}/p$ is by nature non-negative, we are also assuming that $g + i$ is positive, that is, that the real rate of return on money is smaller than the economy's growth rate g. This does not mean that either R or r_K, before- and after-tax returns to capital, are less than the growth rate. In general, we expect r_K, and, a fortiori, R, to exceed the return on money for familiar reasons of risk and liquidity.

The equations for the multipliers now have the following structure:

$$
\begin{bmatrix} + & - \\ - & ? \end{bmatrix} \begin{bmatrix} dr \\ d(-i) \end{bmatrix} = \begin{bmatrix} 0 & + \\ \dfrac{1}{g+i} & - \end{bmatrix} \begin{bmatrix} d\bar{G} \\ dt \end{bmatrix} \qquad (11A.24)
$$

$$
\begin{array}{cccc} + & ? & & \dfrac{1}{g+i} \quad - \end{array}
$$

The ambiguity in the Jacobian arises from the double role of the inflation rate. A lowering of i increases the demand for money, but it also — as inspection of the right-hand side of Equation (11A.18d) shows — increases the supply. We assume that an increase in the tax rate lowers the sum of $F^{\bar{K}}$ and $F^{\bar{H}}$ for given rates of return, but lowers the deficit even more. The previous ambiguity about the effect of a tax increase on the excess demand for money is thus removed; the decline in supply of money reinforces the increase in demand due to substitution of money for capital.

The ambiguity in the Jacobian leaves us with two cases to consider. In what we shall call the standard case, the Jacobian determinant is negative. Demand for money is relatively insensitive to its own real rate of return. The implications of system (11A.24) are, first, that an increase in $\bar{G}$ lowers R and raises $\bar{K}$, 'crowding in' capital. It also raises the rate of inflation i. Although an increase in government purchases takes resources that might be used for capital formation, its financial consequence is to increase the deficit and thus to accelerate the growth of the nominal money supply. The inflationary result makes money a less attractive asset and induces wealth-owners to place savings in equity instead. Second, an increase in t lowers the rate of inflation and increases R. Capital intensity is diminished. As might be expected, these results are just the opposite of those for an increase in $\bar{G}$. The after-tax return on capital, r_K, may move either way. It would rise if taxes were lump-sum and did not alter the marginal return on capital. But if the tax is a disincentive to equity investment, r_K may decline. This does not, however, mean that capital intensity is increased; it will be diminished because the before-tax return R is higher. Third, an equal increase in $\bar{G}$ and t, keeping the real deficit unchanged, can be analyzed by adding the two columns in the matrix on the right-hand side of system (11A.24), so that both entries are positive. The result of the marginally balanced budget operation is to raise the rate of inflation. It may or may not crowd out capital. The decline in both after-tax rates of return is discouraging to accumulation of wealth and capital, but if the direct tax effects on equity investment are weak, the inflation effect — substitution of equity for money — may prevail.

The non-standard case arises if the Jacobian determinant is positive. This means that the elasticity of demand for money with respect to its own real return is high. Or it could occur if the deficit was small. As discussed in the text, the implications reverse the standard case. Higher $\bar{G}$ is associated with lower i, higher R, lower $\bar{K}$. Higher t is associated with higher i; the effects on R, r_K, and $\bar{K}$ are not clear. As for a balanced increase in $\bar{G}$ and t, both i and $\bar{K}$ are reduced.

Figure 11A.1 illustrates the money-capital model. The horizontal axis measures the real rate of return on money, the negative of the inflation rate. Reading right to left from the vertical line at g, the horizontal axis shows $g + i$, positive values only. The vertical axis measures $\bar{H}/p$, the amount of money held relative to income. The hyperbola $S_0 S_0'$ gives $(\bar{G}_0 - t)/(g + i)$. Clearly an increase in $\bar{G}$ from $\bar{G}_0$ to $\bar{G}_1$ (or a reduction of t) shifts this, the money supply curve, upwards to $S_1 S_1'$. Now for each value of i — and for given t — solve the capital Equation (11A.21a) for R, and add to $S_0 S_0'$ the corresponding amount $\bar{K}(R)$. This operation yields the locus WW'. Along it as r_H increases from left to right R is rising, too, and $\bar{K}$ is falling. The curve DD' shows the demand for money for each value of r_H and the associated value of R. DD' must be steeper than WW', but it can be either steeper or flatter than $S_0 S_0'$. In the standard case, depicted in Figure 11A.1, it is flatter. As the figure shows, an increase in $\bar{G}$ leads to higher inflation and larger $\bar{K}$. The reverse would be true if DD' crossed $S_0 S_0'$ from below. Graphical analysis of a tax cut is more difficult, because DD' and WW' are shifted upward, too.

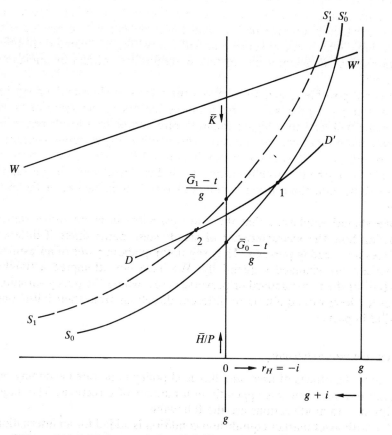

Figure 11A.1 Money-capital model: illustration of effect of fiscal expansion on steady-state inflation and capital stock

Policy effects in the three-asset model

The reintroduction of government bonds as a third asset, providing the government with a third instrument, γ_B, widens the range of possible steady-state effects of policy variations. Adding Equations (11A.18b) and (11A.18c), and recalling the definition of r_D as the weighted average rate of return on total debt, we note that total debt may be written as $(\bar{G} - t)/(g - r_D)$. The analogy to Equation (11A.18d) suggests that it might be possible to apply the above analysis of the money-capital model to the three-asset model, making it in effect a two-asset, debt-capital, economy. This could be misleading, however. The composition of the portfolio as between capital and total debt is not independent of the composition of debt between bonds and money.

Analysis of the three-asset model disclosed ambiguities of the same nature as those of the money-capital model but greater in number. Once again, a standard case implies that expansionary fiscal policies will be inflationary and 'crowd in' capital investment. But there are also 'perverse' cases in which restrictive policies and lower deficits are associated with more inflationary steady states and with 'crowding in'. Numerical information about behavioral parameters is required to obtain unambiguous answers.

It is not possible to generalize about the effects of altering the financing parameter γ_B. Under some circumstances increasing the share of bond-financing will lead to a higher inflation rate and/or to a lower return on capital and greater capital intensity. This is not really as counter-intuitive as it sounds, or as it would be in the short run. When all rates of return are flexible, it may be that wealth-owners are induced to absorb a larger supply of bonds by reductions in competing rates as well as an increase in the own-rate.

We should emphasize that these are exercises in comparative statics, showing how the characteristics of steady-state paths differ if different policies are steadily pursued. They say nothing about paths of adjustment if policies are changed sequentially. We have not attempted a stability analysis of the non-standard or perverse cases, where the policy variations push the long-run equilibria in different directions from their initial one-period impacts.

Open economy extension

To study the effects of fiscal and financial policy in an open economy, we extend the model of this appendix in a number of directions. The major additions and modifications are the following.

A fourth asset market equilibrium condition is added for an internationally traded private bond. This bond has a fixed market value and a fixed rate of return r_A^* in terms of foreign currency. Domestic supply of the foreign bond consists of private domestic holdings at the end of the previous period, A, eA in home currency value, plus the private capital account deficit of the current period. The private capital account deficit is the sum of the current account surplus and the net sales of foreign assets by the government (the official settlements deficit on the balance of payments). The current account surplus is the trade surplus, X, plus net interest income (private and public) from abroad. Official holdings of foreign bonds are denoted $\hat{A}$.

The exchange rate, e, is the domestic currency price of foreign currency. A rise in e is depreciation, a fall is appreciation, of the home currency. There are two channels connecting the exchange rate and the domestic economy: capital account and current account. In the capital account, exchange rate depreciation increases, appreciation decreases, the domestic currency value of net holdings of foreign bonds, the only internationally traded financial claim. Expectations of depreciation increase the return on foreign bonds to domestic holders, and expectations of appreciation lower the return. Domestic money, government bonds and equity are not held by foreigners. To the home country, small in the international financial market, r_A^* is given; any amount of foreign bonds can be traded at that interest rate. But domestic and foreign bonds are not assumed to be perfect substitutes in private portfolios. Instead the gross substitutes assumption is extended to all four assets.

In the current account, the trade surplus is assumed to vary positively with the ratio of the price of imports to the price of domestic output — the Marshall–Lerner conditions are satisfied — and negatively with domestic output Y. To the home country, the foreign price of imports p_f^* is parametric. Likewise, to foreign export markets the price of domestic output, p, is parametric.

$$X = X(ep_f^*/p, Y) \qquad X_{ep_f^*/p} > 0 \qquad X_Y < 0. \tag{11A.25}$$

The domestic price level, p, is influenced directly by the cost of imports. We use the simple specification (Buiter, 1978)

$$p = w^\beta (ep_f^*)^{1-\beta} \qquad 0 < \beta < 1. \tag{11A.26}$$

Here w is the domestic component of unit costs of production. It consists mainly of labor costs. In the unemployment version of the model, w is treated as parametric in the short run. Its behavior over time can then be determined by the expectations-augmented Phillips curve $\dfrac{\Delta w}{w} = \psi(Y - f(K)) + x(w)$, or $\dfrac{\Delta w}{w} = \psi(Y - f(K)) + x(p)$. In the full-employment version, w is modeled as a short-run endogenous variable and actual and capacity output are assumed equal: $Y = f(K)$. Interest on private and official foreign asset holdings is, in real terms, $er_f^*(A + \hat{A})/p$. Government budget receipts now include the interest income on official holdings of foreign bonds. Open market operations now include sales of foreign assets Z_A as well as domestic bonds and money:

$$Z_H + Z_B + Z_A = 0. \tag{11A.27}$$

The real rate of return on foreign assets equals the foreign interest return plus the expected rate of depreciation of the domestic currency minus the expected rate of change of the domestic general price level.

$$r_A = r_A^* + x(e) - x(p). \tag{11A.28}$$

Short-run effects of fiscal and financial policy
The short-run equilibrium conditions are summarized in Equations (11A.29).

$$F^K - q_K K = I \tag{11A.29a}$$

$$F^B - q_B \frac{B}{p} = \gamma_B D + \frac{Z_B}{p} \tag{11A.29b}$$

$$F^A - \frac{eA}{p} = X\left(\frac{ep_f^*}{p}, Y\right) + er_A^*\left(\frac{A}{p} + \frac{\hat{A}}{p}\right) + \frac{Z_A}{p} \tag{11A.29c}$$

$$F^H - \frac{H}{p} = (1 - \gamma_B)D - \left(\frac{Z_B + Z_A}{p}\right). \tag{11A.29d}$$

The list of variables in the asset demand functions includes those in the closed economy model, and in addition r_A and eA/p. The real deficit, D, is $G + \dfrac{bB}{p} - tY - \dfrac{er_A^* \hat{A}}{p}$. These four asset market equations can be summed to yield the open economy *IS* curve.

$$S = I + G + \frac{bB}{p} - tY + X + er_A^* \frac{A}{p}. \tag{11A.29e}$$

In the unemployment version of the model, the four market-clearing conditions determine the temporary equilibrium values of Y, r_B, r_K and one foreign exchange variable. This could be the exchange rate e if policy fixes Z_A, or Z_A if policy holds e at a predetermined rate. Intermediate regimes could be modeled, but we shall concentrate on the freely floating exchange rate ($Z_A = 0$) and the fixed exchange rate. Under both exchange rate regimes H, B, A, $\hat{A}$, K, $x(q_K)$, $x(q_B)$, $x(p)$, and $x(e)$ are short-run predetermined variables. The unemployment model has w as an additional predetermined variable, while the full-employment model has Y instead.

In addition to extending the gross substitutes assumption to all four assets, we also extend two other assumptions. First, an increase in the rate of return on any asset increases total saving. Second, an increase in the value of existing holdings of any asset increases the values demanded for all assets and for current consumption.

To save space we present only the analysis of the unemployment model. Subject to minor qualifications, the results again carry over to the full-employment model, with the price level taking qualitatively the place of real output. A few of the short-run effects of changes in G, t, γ_B, and Z_B on r_K, r_B, and Y are considered both for fixed and floating exchange rate regimes. When considering a fixed exchange rate we shall, in addition, derive the impact effect of a devaluation. With a market-determined exchange rate the effect of open market sales of foreign bonds by the government can also be considered.

Policy effects with a fixed exchange rate

The impact multipliers for the unemployment model under a fixed exchange rate can be found from equations with the structure shown in system (11A.30). The rows correspond to the asset demand–supply equations for equity, domestic bonds, foreign bonds, and money in that order. It is assumed that the domestic counterpart of official sales or purchases of foreign bonds is always money, that is, that there is no 'sterilization'. It is also assumed that the government budget is initially in deficit and that private holdings of foreign bonds are positive.

$$\begin{bmatrix} + & - & 0 & +(?) \\ - & + & 0 & + \\ - & - & + & + \\ - & - & - & + \\ + & + & 0 & + \end{bmatrix} \begin{bmatrix} dr_K \\ dr_B \\ d(-Z_A) \\ dY \end{bmatrix} = \begin{bmatrix} 0 & ? & 0 & 0 & +(?) \\ + & -(?) & D & \frac{1}{p} & -(?) \\ 0 & + & 0 & 0 & +(?) \\ + & -(?) & -D & -\frac{1}{p} & -(?) \\ 1 & -(?) & 0 & 0 & ? \end{bmatrix} \begin{bmatrix} dG \\ dt \\ d\gamma_B \\ dZ_B \\ de \end{bmatrix}$$

$$(11A.30)$$

The Jacobian matrix of system (11A.30) has a dominant diagonal and positive determinant. We shall consider the effects of changes in G, γ_B, and e on the short-run endogenous variables. A cut in t will, subject to the qualifications mentioned for the closed economy, have effects of the same signs as those of an increase in G. An increase in Z_B has the same impact effects as an increase in γ_B.

An increase in G will raise Y however it is financed. It will lower the returns on capital and bonds r_K and r_B if public sector deficits are wholly money-financed. With mixed financing or exclusively bond-financing, the effect on r_K is ambiguous. The trade balance and the current account deteriorate as Y increases, the relative price of imports and exports remaining unchanged. If budget deficits are exclusively money-financed, the official settlements deficit Z_A on the balance of payments increases. The lowering of r_K and r_B induces portfolio substitution toward domestic money and foreign assets. The deterioration in the trade balance is therefore compounded by an increased deficit on the private capital account. If budget deficits are not exclusively money-financed, either r_K or r_B, or both, may be higher when G is increased. In that case improvement in the private capital account may accompany and even overcome the deterioration in the current account.

An increase in γ_B or in Z_B lowers Y and raises r_B, as in the closed economy model. Since the rate of return on the foreign asset is fixed, the effect on r_K depends only on the relative degrees of substitutability among money, domestic bonds and capital. The closer substitutes are bonds and equity, compared to bonds and money, the more likely is r_K to increase. The decline in Y improves the trade account. Lower Y and higher r_B both reduce demand for foreign bonds. If r_K also increases, this shift out of foreign assets will be reinforced and the capital account will definitely improve. The official settlements balance will then reflect improvements in both current and capital accounts.

Devaluation will operate through a number of channels. With the foreign currency price of imports determined exogenously and with w predetermined in the short run, devaluation shifts the terms of trade against the home country. By assumption this will improve the trade balance and thereby stimulate domestic output. This 'elasticities effect' will be countered by a 'monetary effect,' however. Exchange rate depreciation increases the domestic general price level, p, and reduces the real value of given nominal stocks of money and domestic bonds. This will tend to depress domestic consumption demand for domestic output. As the country is assumed to be a net creditor to the rest of the world, devaluation will increase the domestic currency value and the real value of foreign-currency-denominated assets. This will generate a positive wealth effect on domestic consumption demand. (If the country were a net foreign debtor, the opposite outcome would prevail.) If the column sum corresponding to de in system (11A.30) is negative, devaluation is on balance contractionary as regards aggregate demand for domestic goods and services, a result consistent with the monetary approach to the balance of payments. A positive column sum favors the elasticities approach. The general scenario suggested by the monetary approach pictures a devaluation increasing r_K and r_B, reducing Y, and improving the official settlements balance. In our model that is a possible scenario, but not the only possible one.

Policy effects with a floating exchange rate

The structure of the matrix equation from which impact multipliers can be derived for the floating exchange rate regime is given in Equations (11A.31). We shall make the Keynesian, 'elasticities approach', assumption that, *ceteris paribus*, exchange rate depreciation is expansionary in the domestic output market. The column sum of the third column of the Jacobian of system (11A.31) is therefore negative. The d*e* column of system (11A.30) for the fixed rate regime had a positive sum under the same assumption, but now that column is on the left-hand side. We also assume that exchange rate depreciation, augmenting the value of existing holdings of foreign bonds, creates excess supply in that market. This spills over into excess demands for domestic assets, reinforced in the case of bonds and money by the reduction in the real value of existing stocks because of the import component of the domestic price level. We assume the net wealth effect to be non-negative for equity demand as well. A small negative effect on equity demand would not alter our conclusions.

$$
\begin{bmatrix}
+ & - & + & +(?) \\
- & + & + & + \\
- & - & - & + \\
- & - & + & + \\
+ & + & - & +
\end{bmatrix}
\begin{bmatrix} dr_K \\ dr_B \\ de \\ dY \end{bmatrix}
=
\begin{bmatrix}
0 & (?) & 0 & 0 & 0 \\
+ & -(?) & D & \dfrac{1}{p} & 0 \\
0 & + & 0 & 0 & \dfrac{1}{p} \\
+ & -(?) & -D & -\dfrac{1}{p} & -\dfrac{1}{p} \\
1 & -(?) & 0 & 0 & 0
\end{bmatrix}
\begin{bmatrix} dG \\ dt \\ d\gamma_B \\ dZ_B \\ dZ_A \end{bmatrix}
\quad (11A.31)
$$

The determinant of the Jacobian matrix of system (11A.31) is negative. (If the signs of the d*e* column were reversed, the matrix would have the familiar standard sign pattern.) We have seen that most of the results derived for the closed economy remain valid in the open economy when the exchange rate was fixed. With a floating exchange rate, there is one new complication: the general price level, p, becomes a short-run endogenous variable even in the unemployment model. Domestic costs are sticky; import prices in domestic currency are not.

As in all other cases, an increase in public spending will boost real income. If the public sector deficit is financed by money creation ($\gamma_B = 0$), the rate of return on capital equity and the real rate of return on domestic bonds will fall and the exchange rate will depreciate. Domestic capital formation will be stimulated. With mixed public sector deficit-financing policies, real rates of return on domestic bonds and/or equity may rise and the exchange rate may appreciate.

An open market sale of foreign assets by the government ($dZ_A > 0$) will cause the exchange rate to appreciate and will depress real output. Remember that domestic bonds and foreign bonds are not perfect substitutes in private portfolios and that the rate of return on domestic bonds is not determined in international markets.

Steady-state equilibrium

As in the closed economy case, a long-run steady-state equilibrium requires that all asset stocks grow in real value at the natural growth rate of the economy. For foreign assets, this means that some combination of exchange depreciation, current account surplus and inflation must keep the real stock in constant ratio to national output. This ratio, like those for other asset stocks, will be endogenously determined, partly by portfolio and saving demands that are functions of the several real rates of return.

In a fixed exchange rate regime, two of the four rates of return are exogenously determined. The domestic inflation rate must equal the foreign inflation rate, uninfluenced by events in the small open economy. Otherwise the terms of trade will be continuously changing. The real rate on foreign assets is likewise exogenous. What, then, are the two endogenous variables besides R and r_B? One is the ratio of domestic price to foreign price. This must be such that the trade surplus, X, is consistent with growth of foreign assets at the natural rate. The other is one of the policy parameters; the government must adjust one endogenously in order to make the nominal stocks of its bonds and money grow at the predetermined rate, $g + i$, while meeting savers' demands. Among the policy instruments which might be endogenous in this sense is the ratio of official reserves of foreign assets, in real value, to national output. Alternatively, the government might set a target for its foreign exchange reserves, and let one of its domestic fiscal or financial instruments adjust as necessary to achieve this target.

Under a floating exchange rate regime, domestic inflation can differ from the world inflation rate, with steady exchange depreciation or appreciation equal to the difference. The real rate of return on foreign assets is still exogenous, equal to the real rate on such assets abroad. The four basic equations determine the other three rates of return, among them the domestic rate of inflation. As in the fixed exchange rate regime, the terms of trade provide another endogenous variable. Choice of exchange rate regimes is much less momentous in the long run than in the short run. By assumption prices are flexible in the long run, unlike the short run. Price flexibility can accomplish the same adjustments in terms of trade as exchange rate flexibility. The government has no more free policy instruments in one regime than the other; under floating rates official reserve stocks and interventions are constrained to be zero. The opportunity to have a divergent inflation rate may none the less, be useful. Conceivably some objectives — regarding the composition of output and the capital intensity of the economy — might be unattainable if the domestic rate of inflation and thus the real return on money were constrained to equal the international rate of inflation.

We have already seen that, even with three assets and a closed economy, it is impossible to generalize about the effects of steady-state policies on equilibrium capital intensity and inflation rates. Naturally the number of possible cases is multiplied by opening the economy and enlarging the asset menu. For example, whether the nation is a creditor or debtor to the rest of the world will make an important difference. The relevance of steady-state exercises is, in any event, more doubtful for open than closed economies. The trade surplus, for instance, will not have the homogeneity property needed for steady growth equilibrium unless foreign export demand is, for given terms of trade, expanding at the natural rate of growth of the domestic economy. It would also be desirable, of course, to model two or more interacting economies rather than a small economy in a big world. The United States is not powerless to influence inflation rates and interest rates overseas.

We can conclude, anyway, that the major policy issues cannot be solved by theoretical analysis alone but require empirical estimates of economic structure and behavior. No shortcuts are available in sweeping a priori claims of neutrality.

PART IV

THE FISCAL ROOTS OF INFLATION

12 · A FISCAL THEORY OF HYPERDEFLATIONS? SOME SURPRISING MONETARIST ARITHMETIC

In a paper that has already become a classic, Sargent and Wallace (1981; 1984) explored some unfamiliar implications of the government budget constraint and proposed a 'fiscal theory of inflation'. Once the real per capita stock of non-monetary, interest-bearing government debt stabilizes (say, because it reaches some upper limit reflecting real resource constraints), and with the primary deficit (the public sector deficit net of interest payments) treated as exogenous, monetary growth is endogenously or residually determined by the requirement that the real value of seigniorage (the real value of nominal money-stock increases) should satisfy the government budget constraint. Their paper then goes on to analyze the consequences for inflation, in the short and long run, of short-run changes in monetary growth not accompanied by changes in the primary deficit. Elsewhere I have commented at length on that issue (Buiter, 1983; 1984). This short note focuses on a neglected aspect of the Sargent–Wallace model: its implications for the nascent theory of hyperdeflations. It is shown how, according to the equation of motion alone, a sufficiently large fiscal deficit will result in unstable, explosive behavior of the money growth rate, the inflation rate, and the stock of real money balances. This explosive process, however, is not a hyperinflation but a hyperdeflation: the rates of money growth and inflation decline and the per capita real money stock increases without bound. Such behavior obviously is not sustainable, and the model's side-conditions make this clear. In the Sargent–Wallace two-period, two-class overlapping generations model, the real stock of money balances equals the saving out of period 1 income (and the purchases of consumption goods in the second period of their lives) by the poor. Income and the supply of consumer goods are bounded; an unbounded real money stock

This paper was originally published in *Oxford Economics Papers*, 39, 1987, pp. 111–18.

therefore cannot characterize an equilibrium. That notwithstanding, I will suggest that the Sargent–Wallace model may temporarily generate a bit of hyperdeflation, before the unsustainability of their trajectory dawns on the inhabitants of the Sargent–Wallace universe and the model disappears off the page.

In any case, whatever the merit of hyperdeflations, in the Sargent–Wallace model deficits can never generate hyperinflations. In spite of this, the spirit, although not the letter (or the formal structure) of this model underlies Sargent's (1982) well known empirical study of four hyper-inflations. Dornbusch and Fischer (1986), in their study of four hyper-inflations, note the possibility that if the deficit is too high no stationary equilibrium may exist in the Sargent–Wallace model. They infer that 'Hyperinflation would be a strong possibility' (Dornbusch and Fischer, 1986, p. 5). This note shows that, with rational expectations, hyperinflation is impossible but hyperdeflation may get under way. The paucity of em-pirical data on hyperdeflations (indeed their absence) should not be a deterrent to a thorough theoretical analysis of the phenomenon. After all, a large fraction of the profession has worked and is now working on the theory of general competitive equilibrium.

I shall present the model in continuous time, rather than in the original discrete-time format, because of the presentational usefulness of continuous time phase-diagrams. The exact same points can, however, be made using the discrete time model. m denotes the real per capita stock of money balances; b the real per capita stock of interest-bearing public debt; δ the real per capita primary deficit; r the exogenous real interest rate; n the exogenous proportional growth rate of the population; and π the rate of inflation. The real per capita stock of debt is kept constant at a given value $b = \bar{b}$. Nominal bond issues, $\dot{B}$ are therefore just sufficient to offset the erosion in the real per capita stock of bonds due to population growth and inflation: $\dot{B} = (n + \pi)B$. The government budget constraint then implies that

$$\dot{m} = \delta + (r - n)\bar{b} - (\pi + n)m. \tag{12.1}$$

It is assumed until further notice, that $\delta + (r - n)\bar{b} > 0$. The per capita demand for real money balances depends inversely on the expected rate of inflation. Rational inflation expectations prevail:

$$m = \gamma_1 - \gamma_2\pi \qquad \gamma_1, \gamma_2 > 0 \tag{12.2a}$$

$$0 \leqslant m \leqslant \bar{m}, \tag{12.2b}$$

where $\bar{m}$ is the upper bound on the real per capita money stock referred to earlier. Substituting Equation (12.2a) into Equation (12.1), we obtain

$$\dot{m} = \delta + (r - n)\bar{b} - (\gamma_2^{-1}\gamma_1 + n)m + \gamma_2^{-1}m^2. \tag{12.3}$$

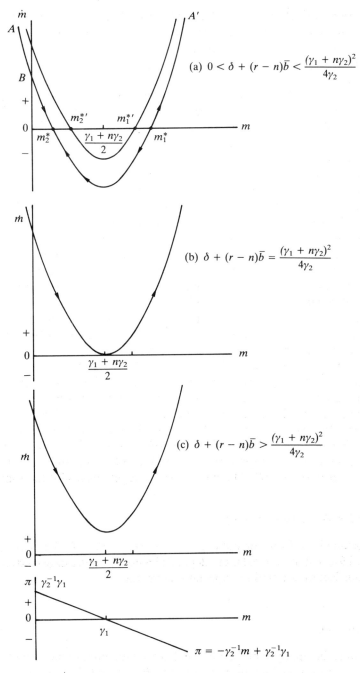

Figure 12.1 Alternative configurations of the 'unpleasant monetarist arithmetic' model

This differential equation either has two, one or zero stationary equilibria. The three cases are illustrated in Figure 12.1. In Figure 12.1a m_1^* is the locally unstable low inflation stationary equilibrium; m_2^* is the locally stable high inflation stationary equilibrium. It is easily checked that

$$m_{1,2}^* = \frac{\gamma_1 + n\gamma_2 \pm [(\gamma_1 + n\gamma_2)^2 - 4\gamma_2(\delta + (r - n)\bar{b})]^{\frac{1}{2}}}{2}. \tag{12.4}$$

The case with two stationary equilibria corresponds to 'small' deficits $\left(\delta + (r - n)\bar{b} < \dfrac{(\gamma_1 + n\gamma_2)^2}{4\gamma_2} \right)$. The case with no stationary equilibrium corresponds to 'large' deficits $\left(\delta + (r - n)\bar{b} > \dfrac{(\gamma_1 + n\gamma_2)^2}{4\gamma_2} \right)$.

Sargent and Wallace (1981) considered only the small deficit case depicted in Figure (12.1a). They also opted for the locally unstable low-inflation steady state m_1^*. Presumably, this choice was prompted by analogy with the common practice, in linear rational espectations models, of associating non-predetermined state variables with unstable eigenvalues. The general price level in this classical, flexible price model is non-predetermined and so therefore is m.

The transversality or terminal boundary condition that the system should converge continuously (except possibly at moments when 'news' arrives) to a steady state, for constant values of the forcing variables, only suffices to determine a unique initial value for m if the steady state equilibrium in question is m_1^*. If the terminal boundary condition required convergence to m_2^*, any initial value of m on AA' to the left of m_1^* and to the right of B would be eligible. There would seem to be no economic rationale for choosing m_1^* rather than m_2^*. If m_1^* is a feasible stationary solution ($m_1^* \leqslant \bar{m}$) then so is m_2^*. No economic or physical constraints will impede solutions moving toward m_2^* from anywhere between B and m_1^*.

The issue as to whether there exist, for the small deficit case depicted in Figure 12.1a, reasonable economic restrictions that allow one to choose a unique convergent solution from among the continuum of solutions that converge to m_2^*, is not resolved here. Instead, I propose to focus on the two diagrams in Figure 12.1c which depict the explosive, non-stationary behavior that will be exhibited when this economy has large deficits $(\delta + (r - n)\bar{b} > \dfrac{(\gamma_1 + n\gamma_2)^2}{4\gamma_2}$.

When the real per capita debt stock is constant, larger deficits (strictly speaking larger inflation-and-real-growth-corrected government full-employment current account deficits) require more seigniorage revenue, that is, a greater yield of the inflation tax. Let μ denote the proportional rate of growth of the nominal money stock and σ real per capita seigniorage:

$\sigma \equiv \mu m$. In a steady state, $\sigma = \gamma_2^{-1} m^2 - (\gamma_2^{-1} \gamma_1 + n)m$. The value of m, $\hat{m}$ say, that maximizes steady-state seigniorage is given by

$$\hat{m} = \frac{\gamma_1 + n\gamma_2}{2}. \tag{12.5a}$$

The maximum steady-state value of seigniorage is

$$\hat{\sigma} = \frac{(\gamma_1 + n\gamma_2)^2}{4\gamma_2}. \tag{12.5b}$$

The steady-state seigniorage-maximizing rate of inflation is

$$\hat{\pi} = \tfrac{1}{2}(\gamma_1 \gamma_2^{-1} - n). \tag{12.5c}$$

Not surprisingly, the large deficit case depicted in Figure 12.1c is the one for which it is not possible to find a steady state in which the inflation tax is sufficient to close the budget gap $(\delta + (r - n)\bar{b} > \hat{\sigma})$. It is possible, however, (at least until $m > \bar{m}$) to generate the necessary seigniorage revenue in a non-steady-state manner. While the high-deficit economy depicted in Figure 12.1c cannot raise the necessary seigniorage at a constant rate of inflation and a constant value of m, it can generate the required inflation tax revenue with a steadily rising stock of real per capita money balances and steadily falling rates of inflation and nominal money stock growth.

A lower rate of nominal money growth will be associated with an increase in real per capita seigniorage if the elasticity of money demand with respect to the rate of monetary growth exceeds unity $\left(\eta_{m\mu} = \dfrac{-\mu \, \mathrm{d}m}{m \, \mathrm{d}\mu} > 1 \right)$. From the money demand function (12.2a) we see that the effect on real seigniorage of a reduction in money growth is given by

$$\gamma_1 - \gamma_2\pi - \mu\gamma_2 \frac{\mathrm{d}\pi}{\mathrm{d}\mu}.$$

In steady states, $\pi = \mu - n$ and the steady-state effect on real seigniorage of a permanent reduction in the rate of growth of nominal money is positive if $\mu > \tfrac{1}{2}(\gamma_1\gamma_2^{-1} + n)$, the steady-state real seigniorage-maximizing rate of money growth. This will occur, for example, if in Figure (12.1a) the initial stationary equilibrium is the locally stable m_2^*. A larger deficit will in that case be associated with a new long-run equilibrium such as $m_2^{*\prime}$ with a lower rate of money growth and a lower rate of inflation. Both m_2^* and $m_2^{*\prime}$ are on the wrong side of the long-run 'seigniorage Laffer curve'. If the relevant stationary equilibrium is the locally unstable m_1^*, a lower rate of money growth will, comparing steady states, be associated with a smaller real seigniorage revenue. Larger deficits are associated with increased inflation in the long run.

For a given real per capita deficit (i.e. along a given solution parabola in Figure 12.1), constant real per capita seigniorage revenue equal to $\delta + (r - n)\bar{b}$ is generated at every instant, both when the *long-run* money demand schedule is elastic (for high π) and when it is inelastic (for low π).[1] Consider, for example, the explosive large deficit case depicted in Figure 12.1c. With m rising, $\pi = -\gamma_2^{-1}m + \gamma_2^{-1}\gamma_1$ falling, and $\mu = \dfrac{\mu + (r - n)\bar{b}}{m}$ falling, the same amount of real seigniorage is raised with a steadily falling inflation tax rate and a steadily expanding inflation tax base.[2]

Thus the price of fiscal irresponsibility appears to be hyperdeflation. Clearly, if such a process got under way it could not be sustained because of the real resource constraints that set an upper bound on m. There exists a view of rational expectations models which holds that a process that cannot be sustained would not get started. I consider such a view to be unnecessarily restrictive and would regard as admissable those solution trajectories that spend some time on an explosive, unsustainable course.

Even if one rejects the conclusion that the Sargent–Wallace model generates hyperdeflation as a result of large inflation-and-real-growth-corrected public sector current account deficits, there is no way in which that model can ever generate hyperinflation. If the hyperdeflation case (Figure 12.1c) is ruled out, then there is simply *no* solution to the large-deficit $(\delta + (r - n)\bar{b} > \hat{\sigma})$ case. There is no hyperinflation solution. If we are in the small deficit case $(0 < \delta + (r - n)\bar{b} < \hat{\sigma})$ of Figure 12.1a, an increase in the deficit can either raise the long-run rate of inflation (if we choose the locally unstable equilibrium) or lower the long-run rate of inflation (if we choose the locally stable equilibrium). Even when the long-run inflation rate increases, this increase is a finite one, not a runaway explosive hyperinflation.

Now consider the case where the inflation-and-real-growth-corrected government current account deficit is negative: $\delta + (r + n)\bar{b} < 0$. This government surplus economy is depicted in Figure 12.2. $\delta + (r - n)\bar{b}$ is measured by the intersection of the parabola with the vertical $\dot{m}$ axis at B.

Note that as long as $\gamma_1 + n\gamma_2 > 0$, there will still be one stationary equilibrium with a positive value of m, the unstable one at m_1^*. If we consider only non-negative values of m to be admissable and if we impose the 'no-bubble' transversality condition that if there exists a convergent solution, the economy will pick it, solutions will be unique. The response of the system to a reduction in the surplus then is the same as the response to an increase in the deficit in Figure 12.1a when the locally unstable stationary equilibrium m_1^* is considered to be the relevant one. The long-run effect (and also the impact effect if the reduction in the surplus is unanticipated, immediate and permanent) is a finite increase in the rate of inflation. If we admit bubbles, the system could either move north-east along m_1^*A' (the hyperdeflation case) or along m_1^*B with a falling m and a

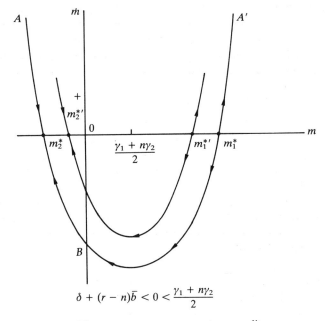

Figure 12.2 The government as monetary creditor

rising rate of inflation. Even when m hits zero, at B, the rate of inflation is only $\gamma_2^{-1}\gamma_1$. This may seem paradoxical until it is realized that m becomes equal to zero not because the price level becomes infinite with a positive nominal money stock, but because the nominal money stock declines to zero with a finite (if rising) price level as the government uses its surpluses to contract the nominal money stock. The grounds for confining the analysis (in both Figures 12.1 and 12.2) to a non-negative real money stock then become rather shaky. It is indeed simple to modify the Sargent–Wallace model in such a way as to permit the poor private agents to borrow from the government by issuing monetary liabilities. Negative values of m then simply reflect negative values of the nominal money stock, i.e. a net creditor position of the government *vis-à-vis* its poor citizens. The case of Figure 12.2 then becomes in all important respects the same as the small deficit case depicted in Figure 12.1a. Whichever way one turns it, the model cannot generate a hyperinflation.

One might be tempted to try and save the model for the analysis of hyperinflations by restricting the analysis to the range of 'small' deficits for which there are two stationary equilibria and identifying as hyperinflation the transition from the low-inflation stationary equilibrium to the high-inflation stationary equilibrium. This, however, would be a bit silly. Both stationary equilibria are just that: well-behaved long-run equilibria with

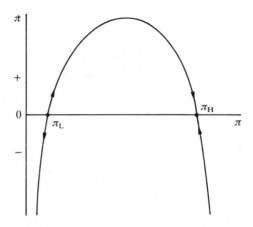

Figure 12.3 Transitions from a low inflation
equilibrium to a high inflation equilibrium

constant, finite rates of inflation. There is nothing 'runaway' or explosive
about the transition from the low to the high inflation steady state. In fact
the move from the low-inflation equilibrium to the high inflation equilibrium
involves initially an accelerating rate of inflation ($\dot{\pi}$ rises) but ultimately a
decelerating rate of inflation ($\dot{\pi}$ falls) with $\dot{\pi}$ smoothly approaching zero as
the economy eases into the high-inflation steady-state. (See the transition
from π_L to π_H in Figure 12.3). To describe the traverse from π_L to π_H as a
hyperinflation is akin to describing a mild summer breeze as a hurricane.
Unlike the adaptive expectations (Cagan, 1956) version of this model, the
Sargent and Wallace (1984) rational expectations version cannot generate
hyperinflations.

While there is a certain scarcity of empirical observations on hyperdeflations, one can take encouragement from the thought that among the many
countries now facing intractable budgetary deficits, there may well be a few
that will be compelled to monetize these deficits at ever decreasing rates of
monetary growth. The United States might even be the place where this
new chapter in monetary history is written.

NOTES

1. Obviously along any given solution parabola, the instantaneous elasticity of
   money demand with respect to the rate of money growth, $\eta_{m\mu}$, equals unity.
2. Note that, if $m > 0$ and $\delta + (r - n)\bar{b} > 0$, μ always remains positive for finite
   values of m. π is a linear decreasing function of m and will be negative for $m > \gamma_1$.
   There will be an increasing divergence between the growth rate of the nominal
   money stock and the rate of inflation, since $\dfrac{d\pi}{d\mu} = \dfrac{m^2}{(\delta + (r - n)\bar{b})\gamma_2}$ increases
   with m.

REFERENCES

Buiter, Willem H. (1983) 'Deficits, crowding out and inflation: the simple analytics', *NBER Working Paper*, no. 1078, February.
Buiter, Willem H. (1984) 'Comment on T. J. Sargent and N. Wallace: Some unpleasant monetarist arithmetic' in B. Griffiths and G. E. Wood (eds), *Monetarism in the U.K.*, Macmillan, London, pp. 42–60.
Cagan, P. (1956) 'The monetary dynamics of hyperinflation' in M. Friedman (ed.), *Studies in the Quantity Theory of Money*, University of Chicago Press, Chicago.
Dornbusch, R. and S. Fischer (1986) 'Stopping hyperinflations past and present', *NBER Working Paper*, no. 1810, January.
Sargent, T. J. (1982) 'The ends of four big inflations' in R. E. Hall (ed.), *Inflation: Causes and Effects*, University of Chicago Press, Chicago, pp. 41–97.
Sargent, T. J. and N. Wallace (1981) 'Some unpleasant monetarist arithmetic', *Federal Reserve Bank of Minneapolis Quarterly Review*, 5, Fall.
Sargent, T. J. and N. Wallace (1984) 'Some unpleasant monetarist arithmetic' in B. Griffiths and G. E. Wood (eds), *Monetarism in the U.K.*, Macmillan, London, pp. 42–60.

13 · CAN PUBLIC SPENDING CUTS BE INFLATIONARY?

13.1 INTRODUCTION

This paper studies the consequences for inflation of public expenditure cuts. The setting is that of a small open economy, but most of the analysis is applicable to closed economic systems as well. While the emphasis is on the long run, transitional dynamics will be considered briefly.

While the purpose of this paper is to develop a general theoretical framework, the question it addresses was motivated by the recent experience of the Mexican economy (see Feltenstein and Morris, 1987; Jarque, 1987; and Jung, 1987).

With but minor abuse of language we can pose the question that is the title of this paper in terms of the demand for and supply of *seigniorage revenue*. Monetary financing is viewed as the residual financing mode of the government. Specifically, real per capita public spending, current and capital, are treated as exogenous, as are real per capita lump-sum taxes and the proportional tax rate on domestic value added. Real per capita stocks of public debt, internal and external, are also taken as given. Cuts in public spending will therefore affect the demand for seigniorage revenue by changing the (inflation-and-real-growth-corrected) public sector deficit

This paper was written while the author was a consultant for the World Bank (Country Economics Department, Public Economics Division (CECEM)). The findings, interpretations, and conclusions are the results of research supported by the World Bank; they do not necessarily represent the official policy of the Bank. The Bank does not accept responsibility for the views expressed herein, which are those of the author and should not be attributed to the World Bank or to its affiliated organizations. The designations employed, the presentation of material, and any maps used in this document are solely for the convenience of the reader and do not imply the expression of any opinion whatsoever on the part of the World Bank or its affiliates concerning the legal status of any country, territory, city, area, or of its authorities, or concerning the delimitation of its boundaries, or national affiliations.

that must be financed by printing money.[1] The paper emphasizes the potentially important distinction, as regards their effect on the public sector deficit, of cuts in public sector consumption and cuts in public sector capital formation.

Real seigniorage revenue (the real value of new issues of nominal high-powered or base money) can be written as the product of a 'seigniorage tax rate' (the proportional rate of change of the high-powered nominal money stock, μ) and the 'seigniorage tax base' (the real stock of money balances or the real stock of money balances per capita, m).

Across steady states there is a one-for-one association between the seigniorage tax rate and the rate of inflation; in classical flex-price models, such a relationship may exist also in the short run, say for unanticipated, immediate and permanent changes in μ. The seigniorage tax is indeed often referred to as the inflation tax and we will follow this rather sloppy usage.

Given the seigniorage tax base, there will be a unique seigniorage tax rate that generates ('supplies') the required seigniorage revenue. However, because the velocity of circulation of high-powered money is not independent of the (expected) inflation rate, the seigniorage tax base is likely to vary (negatively) with the seigniorage tax rate, at any rate in the long run. This leads to the possibility of a 'seigniorage Laffer curve': the elasticity of the seigniorage tax base with respect to the seigniorage tax rate can become greater than unity in absolute value,[2] so higher growth rates of the nominal money stock (and sooner or later higher actual and expected inflation) will appropriate a smaller amount of real resources for the government.

If there is perfect international capital mobility and the long-run real interest rate is independent of the government's spending behavior, and if there are multiple rates of inflation yielding the same real seigniorage revenue, a cut in public consumption spending reduces the long-run rate of inflation as long as the authorities always choose the lower rate of inflation, i.e. as long as the equilibrium is on the (globally) revenue-efficient segment of the seigniorage Laffer curve.

When cuts in public sector capital formation are considered, the *expenditure effect* — which, *ceteris paribus*, reduces the budget deficit one-for-one, lowers inflation (and is the only effect in the case of public consumption cuts) — is supplemented by three further effects. The *direct revenue effect* represents any cash returns the government may receive as a direct consequence of its ownership of the public sector capital stock (including infrastructure). The *indirect revenue effect* measures the implications of a lower public sector capital stock for domestic production and thus for production- or income-related taxes. The *money demand effect* is the effect of a lower public sector capital stock on money demand (at a given real interest rate and inflation rate) through its effect on the scale variable (some measure of income or wealth) in the money demand function. While the direct revenue effect is ambiguous, the indirect revenue effect and the money demand effect will mitigate and may even reverse competely the inflation-reducing expenditure effect of cuts in public sector capital formation.

When there is limited international capital mobility (this paper considers the zero capital mobility case) the real interest rate becomes endogenous. The response of the real interest rate to public spending cuts when money is the residual financing instrument is ambiguous, however. It is quite possible that the real interest rate would rise, even in the long run.

Note that the paper studies the effect of spending cuts on the inflation rate, not on the *level* of the path of money prices. The possibility of a negative association between the volume of public spending and the general price level has been discussed by Hall (1987) and will only be reviewed here in brief. Let M be the nominal stock of high-powered or base money, V the income velocity of circulation of high-powered money, P the general price level and Y real income. The identity of exchange states that $MV \equiv PY$. Let M be given at a point in time, through policy choice in a closed economy, in an open economy through a freely floating exchange rate or, if the exchange rate is managed, through capital or exchange controls. Velocity is generally taken to be a non-decreasing function of the opportunity cost of holding outside money, which is the nominal interest rate, i, when the monetary base does not earn any interest.[3] In many macromodels (but not necessarily in the one considered in this paper), a public spending cut has a non-positive effect on the real interest rate, r. Consider the case where r actually falls. Holding constant inflationary expectations (an assumption that is not in general consistent with rational expectation formation), i falls and velocity falls with it. Nominal income therefore declines. If real income stays constant or rises, the price level falls unambiguously. Only if real income falls by more (proportionally) than the decline in velocity, will the price level rise.

A *necessary* condition for such an association is a positive effect on real output of an increase in public spending. In a Keynesian model with demand-constrained output and employment, real output does, of course, decline in response to a cut in public spending,[4] but the price level is either taken to be predetermined or assumed to decline with output along a public-spending-invariant upward-sloping aggregate supply schedule.

There are a whole range of possible direct and indirect, short-run and long-run effects of public spending on equilibrium output. These include *direct* substitutability or complementary between current public spending and current private spending (see Buiter, 1977) or between current public spending and the supply of labor. There also can be short-run real interest rate effects on the supply of labor (through the intertemporal substitution mechanism emphasized by Hall, 1987) and on the demand for labor (through working capital channels as in Blinder, 1987). This paper does not consider these effects but does allow for a long-run effect of public spending on the private capital stock.

The organization of the paper is as follows. Section 13.2 develops the model. In Section 13.2.1 we consider the public sector and its 'demand for seigniorage'. Section 13.2.2 models production and factor demand with special emphasis on the role of public sector capital. Private consumption and portfolio behavior (including money demand) are developed in Section 13.2.3. Market equilibrium and the external accounts are given in Section 13.2.4. Section 13.3 contains a brief discussion of seigniorage and the exchange rate regime. In Section 13.4 we consider the long-run effects of public spending cuts on the rate of inflation, while Section 13.5 contains a brief discussion of dynamic issues. Section 13.6 concludes.

13.2 THE MODEL

13.2.1 The public sector

Equation (13.1) gives the budget identity of the consolidated public sector, i.e. general government, state enterprises and central bank:

$$\frac{\dot{M}}{P} - \frac{E}{P}\dot{R}^* + \frac{\dot{B}}{P} + \frac{E}{P}\dot{B}^* \equiv C^G + I^G - T - J + \frac{iB}{P} + i^*\frac{E}{P}(B^* - R^*).$$

M is the nominal stock of high-powered money, base money or reserve money. It consists of coin and currency held by the public and reserves held by the commercial banking system. It bears a zero nominal interest rate. B is the stock of domestic-currency-denominated interest-bearing public debt. It has a fixed nominal market value and a variable nominal interest rate, i, and is only held domestically. B^* is foreign-currency-denominated public debt. It bears a nominal interest rate, i^*, and is only held abroad. R^* is the stock of official foreign exchange reserves, which are assumed to bear the same interest rate, i^*, as foreign-currency-denominated public debt. C^G is public consumption spending, I^G gross public sector capital formation, T taxes net of transfers and J government cash income from the public sector capital stock K^G. C^G, I^G, T, J and K^G are all measured in terms of domestic output. E is the nominal spot exchange rate, P the domestic GDP deflator and P^* the foreign GDP deflator. $\dot{X}$ denotes the rate of change of the variable X. Ignoring depreciation, gross (and net) public sector capital formation, I^G, and the public sector capital stock, K^G, are related by

$$\dot{K}^G \equiv I^G.$$

The government's *direct* gross return from the stock of public sector capital (including social overhead capital), J, is the product of the capital stock K^G and its gross cash rate of return ϱ^G, i.e.

$$J \equiv \varrho^G K^G.$$

$F^{*G} \equiv R^* - B^*$ is the government's net stock of foreign assets. We define the following ratios to the labor force (or to the population) L.

$$m \equiv \frac{M}{PL};$$

$$k^G \equiv \frac{K^G}{L};$$

$$b \equiv \frac{B}{L};$$

$$f^{*G} \equiv \frac{EF^{*G}}{PL};$$

$$\bar{R}^* \equiv \frac{ER^*}{PL};$$

$$b^{*G} \equiv \frac{EB^{*G}}{PL};$$

$$c^G \equiv \frac{C^G}{L};$$

$$i^G \equiv \frac{I^G}{L};$$

$$\tau \equiv \frac{T}{L};$$

Let $\pi \equiv \dot{P}/P$ be the domestic rate of GDP inflation, $\pi^* \equiv \dot{P}^*/P^*$ the foreign rate of GDP inflation, $\varepsilon \equiv \dot{E}/E$ the proportional rate of depreciation of the nominal exchange rate, and $n \equiv \dot{L}/L$ the proportional growth rate of the labor force and population. $\Gamma \equiv EP^*/P$ is the real exchange rate (defined here as the ratio of the foreign GDP deflator times the nominal spot exchange rate to the domestic GDP deflator) or the reciprocal of the terms of trade. γ is the proportional rate of depreciation of the real exchange rate, i.e.

$$\gamma \equiv \varepsilon + \pi^* - \pi$$

For the purposes of this paper the distinction between domestically produced goods and foreign goods and the endogeneity of the *real* exchange rate are not important. Using Occam's razor, we therefore restrict the analysis that follows Section 13.2.1 to a one-good world, i.e. $\gamma \equiv 0$.

The real interest rate on (domestically held) domestic-currency-denominated public debt, r, and the real interest rate on foreign-currency-denominated debt, r^*, are defined by

$$r \equiv i - \pi$$

$$r^* \equiv i^* - \pi^*.$$

The government's budget identity (13.1) can now be rewritten as:

$$\dot{b} - \dot{f}^{*G} - \dot{k}^G \equiv c^G - \tau + (r^* - n)(b - f^{*G} - k^G) + (r - r^*)b$$
$$- \gamma f^{*G} + (r^* - \varrho^G)k^G - \sigma. \tag{13.1a}$$

The real value of high-powered nominal money stock issues per worker or real seigniorage per capita, σ, can be written in three equivalent ways, given in Equations (13.2). $\mu \equiv \dot{M}/M$ is the proportional rate of growth of the nominal high-powered money stock;

$$\sigma \equiv \frac{\dot{M}}{PL} \tag{13.2a}$$

$$\sigma \equiv \dot{m} + (n + \pi)m \tag{13.2b}$$

$$\sigma \equiv \mu m. \tag{13.2c}$$

I shall refer to σ as 'seigniorage' or the 'inflation tax', although usage is not yet standardized here.[5]

Let $\tilde{d}$ denote the real per capita net non-monetary liabilities of the government:

$$\tilde{d} \equiv b - f^{*G} - k^G.$$

The budget identity can be rewritten more compactly as:

$$\dot{\tilde{d}} \equiv c^G - \tau + (r - n)\tilde{d} + \ell - \sigma \tag{13.3}$$

where

$$\ell \equiv (r - (r^* + \gamma))f^{*G} + (r - \varrho^G)k^G. \tag{13.4}$$

Equivalently, letting d denote the net real per capita *financial* non-monetary liabilities of the government, we have

$$d \equiv b - f^{*G}$$

and

$$\dot{d} \equiv c^G + i^G - \tau - \varrho^G k^G + (r - n)d + (r - (r^* + \gamma))f^{*G} - \sigma. \tag{13.5}$$

Total tax receipts are a linear function of GDP, i.e.

$$T = \theta Y + T_0, \qquad 0 \leqslant \theta < 1 \tag{13.6}$$

In what follows the proportional tax rate θ is interpreted as a value added tax.

The government's present value budget constraint or solvency constraint, is given in Equation (13.7) or (13.7a):

$$\int_t^\infty \exp\left(-\int_t^s (r(u) - n)\mathrm{d}u\right)[\tau(s) - c^G(s) - \ell(s)]\mathrm{d}s +$$

$$\int_t^\infty \exp\left(-\int_t^s (r(u) - n)\mathrm{d}u\right)\sigma(s)\mathrm{d}s \geqslant \tilde{d}(t) \tag{13.7}$$

$$\int_t^\infty \exp\left(-\int_t^s (r(u) - n)\mathrm{d}u\right)[\tau(s) + \varrho^G(s)k^G(s) - (c^G(s) + i^G(s))$$

$$- (r(s) - (r^*(s) + \gamma(s)))f^{*G}(s)]\mathrm{d}s$$

$$+ \int_t^\infty \exp\left(-\int_t^s (r(u) - n)\mathrm{d}u\right)\sigma(s)\mathrm{d}s \geqslant d(t) \tag{13.7a}$$

Equations (13.7) and (13.7a) are derived from Equations (13.3) and (13.5), respectively, by imposing the 'no-Ponzi-game' transversality conditions

$$\lim_{v \to \infty} \exp\left(-\int_t^v (r(u) - n)\mathrm{d}u\right)\tilde{d}(v) \leqslant 0$$

and

$$\lim_{v \to \infty} \exp\left(-\int_t^v (r(u) - n)\mathrm{d}u\right)d(v) \leqslant 0,$$

respectively.

13.2.2 Production

Domestic output is produced by N identical competitive firms. The production function of the ith firm is given by

$$Y_i = F(K_i, \zeta(K^G, N), L_i). \tag{13.8}$$

Y_i, K_i and L_i are the output, capital input and labor input of the ith firm respectively. K^G is the aggregate social overhead capital stock whose services are available free of charge to private firms. Y_i is increasing and linear homogeneous in K_i, ζ and L_i, strictly concave, twice continuously differentiable and satisfies the Inada conditions for K_i and L_i. ζ is increasing in K^G, non-increasing in N and twice continuously differentiable.

One simple special case of Equation (13.8) is given in Equation (13.9):

$$Y_i = F(K_i, K^G, L_i), \tag{13.9}$$

i.e. $\zeta(K^G, N) \equiv K^G$. In this version there is no 'congestion effect' involved in the impact of the public sector stock of capital on firm i. The effect of K^G on the output of the ith firm is independent of N, the number of firms. Even with free entry, there will in general be positive pure profits $K^G F_{K^G} > 0$. In this case we can model aggregate output as if it were produced by a representative firm as in

$$Y = F(K, K^G, L). \tag{13.9a}$$

Letting $y \equiv Y/L$, $k \equiv K/L$, and $k^G \equiv K^G/L$, Equation (13.9a) implies, through constant returns,

$$y = f(k, k^G). \tag{13.10}$$

Each individual firm takes K^G as given and optimally chooses K and L to maximize after-tax profits, given the real wage w and the real interest rate r. We therefore have the following first-order conditions for competitive factor demands:

$$(1 - \theta)f_1(k, k^G) = r \tag{13.11}$$

$$(1 - \theta)[f(k, k^G) - kf_1(k, k^G) - k^G f_2(k, k^G)] = w. \tag{13.12}$$

Equation (13.11) permits us to write the private capital–labor ratio as a function of the domestic real interest rate and the public sector capital–labor ratio:

$$k = k\left(\frac{r}{1 - \theta}, k^G\right);$$

$$k_1 = \frac{1}{f_{11}} < 0;$$

$$k_2 = \frac{-f_{12}}{f_{11}}. \tag{13.13}$$

All factors of production are assumed to be complements, i.e. $F_{LK} > 0$, $F_{LK^G} > 0$ and $F_{KK^G} > 0$. The last of these implies $f_{12} > 0$ and thus $k_2 > 0$.

The demand price for labor, w, can, from Equation (13.12), be written as:

$$w = (1 - \theta)\omega(k, k^G);$$

$$\omega_1 = -(kf_{11} + k^G f_{12}) > 0;$$

$$\omega_2 = -(kf_{12} + k^G f_{22}) > 0. [6] \tag{13.14}$$

With the marginal product of public sector capital (f_2) positive and k^G positive, there will be positive pure profits ($k^G f_2$ per capita) in the economy if capital and labor are paid their marginal products. We assume that the ownership claims to this stream of pure profits are not traded internationally and that they are perfect substitutes in domestic private portfolios for domestic interest-bearing debt. The real per capita value of these equity claims, s, given in Equation (13.15), is the present discounted value of future per capita pure profits (after tax), z.

$$s(t) = \int_t^\infty z(v) \exp\left(-\int_t^v r(u)du\right)dv. \tag{13.15}$$

After-tax pure profits per capita are given by

$$z = (1 - \theta)y - rk - w. \tag{13.16}$$

In the model under consideration this becomes:

$$z = (1 - \theta)k^G f_2. \tag{13.16a}$$

Per capita taxes can be written as in Equation (13.17) with $\tau_0 \equiv T_0/L$:

$$\tau = \theta f\left[k\left(\frac{r}{1-\theta}, k^G\right), k^G\right] + \tau_0. \tag{13.17}$$

The importance of the assumption that strong 'congestion effects' do not affect the contribution of public capital to the output of an individual firm, becomes apparent when we consider the extreme alternative given in the following equation:

$$Y_i = F\left(K_i, \frac{K^G}{N} - \bar{k}^G, L_i\right), \bar{k}^G > 0;$$

i.e. $\zeta(K^G, N) \equiv \frac{K^G}{N} - \bar{k}^G$. This is a simple special case of a general formulation of congestion effects, according to which, for any K^G, there exists a unique finite value of N, $\bar{N}(K^G)$ say, such that $\zeta(K^G, \bar{N}(K^G)) = 0$. This critical value of N is assumed to increase with K^G. With free entry, pure profits will disappear only if $N = \bar{N}$, i.e., in the special case under consideration, if $N = K^G/\bar{k}^G$.

Applying the representative firm approach to this formulation, we have, with free entry,

$$(1 - \theta)f_1(k, 0) = r$$
$$(1 - \theta)(f(k, 0) - kf_1(k, 0)) = w$$
$$N = \frac{K^G}{\bar{k}^G}.$$

Under this specification equilibrium output or output per worker is independent of the stock of public sector capital. A higher value of K^G

simply induces more entry of new firms, competing away any pure profits. Each of the larger number of firms employs labor and private capital in the same proportions as before (at given w and r). Total output, Y, and the total private capital stock are independent of K^G. For reasons of space this alternative approach to social overhead capital in the aggregate production function will not be pursued here.[7]

12.2.3 Private consumption behavior

Aggregate private consumption behavior is summarized in Equations (13.18)–(13.23):

$$q = \delta(a + h) \qquad \delta > 0 \tag{13.18}$$

$$\dot{a} = (r - n)a + w - \tau_0 - \varrho^G k^G - q \tag{13.19}$$

$$\dot{h} = rh + \tau_0 - \varrho^G k^G - w \tag{13.20}$$

or

$$h(t) = \int_t^\infty [w(s) - \tau_0(s) - \varrho^G(s)k^G(s)] \exp\left(-\int_t^s r(u)\mathrm{d}u\right)\mathrm{d}s \tag{13.20a}$$

$$a \equiv m + b + k + s + f^{*p} \tag{13.21}$$

$$c = \eta(i)q \qquad 0 < \eta < 1; \eta' \gtrless 0 \tag{13.22}$$

$$m^d = \left[\frac{1 - \eta(i)}{i}\right]q \qquad 1 - \eta + i\eta' \geq 0. \tag{13.23}$$

q denotes per capita 'comprehensive' consumption, i.e. the consumption of the single commodity plus the imputed value of the 'money services' consumed by domestic households. c is per capita consumption of the single commodity and m^d the per capita demand for real money balances. a denotes per capita financial wealth or non-human wealth, h the per capita stock of human capital. q, c, m^d, a and h are all measured in terms of domestic goods. f^{*p} is real per capita private ownership of net foreign assets, which are assumed to be denominated in terms of foreign currency.

This model of consumer behavior is based on Weil's (1985) reinterpretation of Blanchard's (1985) model (see also Buiter, 1987a). Each individual consumer lives for ever and has a time-additive utility functional with a constant pure rate of time preference, δ. Instantaneous utility is the logarithm of a homogeneous function of consumption of the one good and real money balances. Labor is supplied inelastically. This homogeneous function is increasing, strictly quasi-concave and twice continuously differentiable. It satisfies the Inada conditions. Internal capital markets are perfect. All domestic and internationally traded assets except money earn the same expected pecuniary rate of return. While each individual lives forever, there is a constant birth rate (and population growth rate) $n \geq 0$. Each individual earns the same wage and pays the same taxes. Human capital is therefore the same for all, regardless of age.

Per capita comprehensive consumption $q \equiv c + im$ is a constant multiple, δ, of the sum of non-human wealth, a, and human wealth, h, as shown in Equation (13.18).[8] Equation (13.19) is the equation of motion for per capita non-human wealth, and Equation (13.20) that for human wealth. Given a standard transversality condition, Equation (13.20) implies Equation (13.20a): human capital of those alive today equals the present discounted value of the future after-tax wage income earned by those currently alive. There is a charge $\varrho^G k^G$ for the use of public capital.

Note that aggregate consumption behavior looks as though it represents the behavior of a representative consumer who discounts his future human capital income at a higher rate, r, than the rate of return on his non-human capital, $r - n$. The excess of the human capital income discount rate over the rate of return on tangible assets is n, the birth rate. Without operative intergenerational gift and bequest motives, private agents currently alive do not have as collateral (and do not act as if they had as collateral) the future after-tax labor income of those yet to be born, the 'new entrants'. A positive birth rate ($n > 0$) therefore generates absence of *debt neutrality*: holding constant the path of current and future exhaustive public spending on goods and services, holding constant the path of current and future distortionary tax rates, and holding constant the path of current and future nominal money issues, changes in the path of lump-sum taxes (which are consistent with the government satisfying its solvency constraint) will affect the real equilibrium of the economy. With $n = 0$, debt neutrality prevails.

Equation (13.21) defines private sector non-human wealth. Note that domestic money, domestic-currency-denominated-public debt, equity and the domestic capital stock are held entirely by the domestic private sector.

Aggregate consumption of the single good, c, depends positively on comprehensive consumption, q and ambiguously on the *real* price of holding money balances, the nominal interest rate, i (Equation (13.22)). The demand for real money balances increases with q and decreases with i (Equation (13.23)).

13.2.4 Market equilibrium and the external accounts

When there is perfect international capital mobility and perfect substitutability between foreign-currency-denominated bonds and domestic-currency-denominated bonds, uncovered nominal interest parity prevails as in Equation (13.24a)

$$i = i^* + \varepsilon. \tag{13.24a}$$

Since this is a one-good world and the law of one price holds, this means that uncovered real interest parity also holds, as in Equation (13.24b)

$$r \equiv i - \pi = i^* - \pi^* \equiv r^* \tag{13.24b}$$

As the country is small it takes both i^* and π^* as given.

Let f^* denote the real per capita value of the nation's (private plus public sector) stock of net foreign assets, i.e. $f^* \equiv f^{*P} + f^{*G}$. The current account of the balance of payments can be written as in Equation (13.25) where i^P denotes real per capita private capital formation, i.e.

$$i^P \equiv \dot{k} + nk$$

$$\dot{f}^* \equiv y - c - c^G - i^P - i^G + (r^* - n)f^* \tag{13.25}$$

With zero international capital mobility, Equations (13.24a) and (13.24b) are inapplicable. Instead we have $\dot{f}^* \equiv 0$, i.e. absorption should equal national income. For simplicity we assume that in this case we also have a zero stock of net foreign assets, i.e. $f^* = 0$. With zero international capital mobility, therefore, we have

$$y = c + c^G + i^P + i^G. \tag{13.26}$$

We shall apply the zero international capital mobility restriction not only to the nation as a whole, but to each of the two domestic sectors individually, i.e.

$$\dot{f}^{*G} = f^{*G} = \dot{f}^{*P} = f^{*P} = 0.$$

The real after-tax rates of return on capital and domestic government debt are equalized, so repeating Equations (13.11) and (13.13) we have

$$(1 - \theta)f_1(k, k^G) = r \tag{13.27a}$$

or

$$k = k\left[\frac{r}{1 - \theta}, k^G\right]. \tag{13.27b}$$

Labor is supplied inelastically. The labor force grows at the exogenous constant proportional rate, n, and a flexible real wage ensures continuous full employment. Equations (13.12) and (13.14), reproduced below, can therefore be interpreted as labor-market clearing conditions:

$$(1 - \theta)(f - kf_1 - k^G f_2) = w \tag{13.28a}$$

or

$$w = (1 - \theta)\omega(k, k^G). \tag{13.28b}$$

The demand for real money balances equals the outstanding stock, i.e.

$$m^{\mathrm{d}} = m \equiv \frac{M}{PL}. \tag{13.29}$$

13.3 SEIGNIORAGE AND THE EXCHANGE RATE REGIME

For reasons of space little attention is paid in this paper to the wide range of possible (and actually existing) exchange rate regimes. Only a freely floating exchange rate and a crawling peg with a constant proportional rate of depreciation or appreciation are considered explicitly. Since we are focusing on the long-run inflation consequences of public expenditure cuts, any exchange rate regime that is considered should be viable in the long run. Viability has several dimensions. We consider two: long-run seigniorage consistency, and international reserve sufficiency.

13.3.1 Long-run seigniorage consistency

In steady-state equilibrium all real per capita assets and liabilities of the government are constant (i.e. $\dot{b} = \dot{k}^G = \dot{f}^{*G} = 0$ and $i^G = nk^G$) and the real interest rate, r, is constant. c^G, τ_0, θ, ϱ^G, n and r^* are parameters. In the one-good world of this paper, the terms of trade, Γ, are of course identically equal to unity and $\gamma = 0$. What follows holds, however, also for models with endogenous terms of trade or real exchange rate, since in steady state no real appreciation or depreciation occurs.

Real per capita steady state seigniorage is therefore given by[9]

$$\sigma \equiv (n + \pi)m \equiv c^G - \tau_0 - \theta f(k, k^G) + (r - r^*)f^{*G} + (n - \varrho^G)k^G$$
$$+ (r - n)(b - f^{*G}). \tag{13.30}$$

Through the money demand function, we can determine which rate(s) of inflation (there may be more than one) can generate the required steady-state real seigniorage given in Equation (13.30). The money demand function given in Equation (13.23), together with Equations (13.18), (13.19), (13.20), (13.27b), (13.28b) and (13.29) imply

$$m = \left[\frac{1 - \eta(r + \pi)}{r + \pi}\right] \delta \frac{n}{(n + \delta - r)r}$$
$$\left[(1 - \theta)\omega\left(k\left(\frac{r}{1 - \theta}, k^G\right), k^G\right) - \tau_0 - \varrho^G k^G\right]. \tag{13.31}$$

It should be noted that we assume throughout that $n > 0$, $n + \delta > r$ and $w - \tau_0 - \varrho^G k^G > 0$.[10]

Holding constant the other arguments of Equations (13.30) and (13.31), we can trace the *ceteris paribus* relationship between long-run real per capita seigniorage or the long-run real per capita stock of high-powered money and the (actual and expected) rate of inflation.

For a number of commonly used money demand functions including the linear one in Equation (13.32a) and the log-linear one in Equation (13.32b) the long-run relationship between the inflation rate (or the monetary growth rate) and real seigniorage has the 'Laffer curve' shape shown in Figure 13.1.

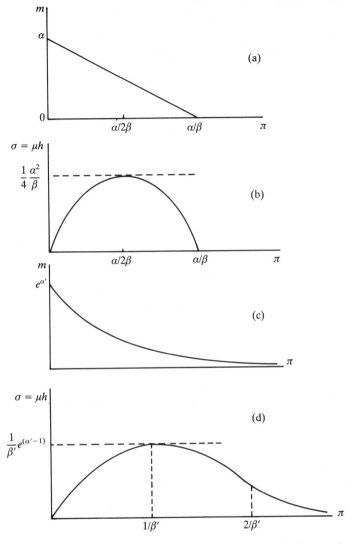

Figure 13.1 The demand for money and seigniorage in the steady state

$$m = \alpha - \beta\pi \qquad \alpha, \beta > 0; \pi < \alpha\beta^{-1} \qquad (13.32a)$$

$$\ln m = \bar{\alpha} - \bar{\beta}\pi \qquad \bar{\beta} > 0 \qquad (13.32b)$$

For the linear demand function shown in Figures 13.1a and 13.1b and for the log-linear demand function shown in Figures 13.1c and 13.1d (both drawn with $n = 0$) there is a unique finite long-run seigniorage-maximizing rate of inflation ($\hat{\pi} = (\alpha/(2\beta)) - (n/2)$) in the linear case, $\hat{\pi} = (1/\bar{\beta}) - n$

in the log-linear case). Such a unimodal long-run seigniorage Laffer curve would, of course, not exist if the money demand function were the rectangular hyperbola given in Equation (13.32c):

$$m = \frac{\bar{\bar{\alpha}}}{\bar{\bar{\beta}} + \pi} \qquad \bar{\bar{\alpha}} > 0; \bar{\bar{\beta}} > 0; \pi > -\bar{\bar{\beta}} \tag{13.32c}$$

This money demand function, which would correspond to Equation (13.31) in the Cobb–Douglas case ($\eta' = 0$) and with $r > 0$, has seigniorage increasing (decreasing) forever with π if $\bar{\bar{\beta}} > n$ (if $\bar{\bar{\beta}} < n$).

For the government's fiscal-financial-monetary strategy to be feasible if there is a seigniorage Laffer curve, the maximal amount of steady-state seigniorage $\hat{\sigma}$ should obviously be no less than the value required to satisfy the steady-state budget constraint (13.30). If there is a unimodal long-run seigniorage Laffer curve (and there are consequently two steady-state rates of inflation that generate any given feasible amount of long-run real seigniorage), it seems reasonable to assume that the lower of these two inflation rates is actually *chosen* by the policy-makers (and that we are therefore always on the revenue-efficient side of the long-run seigniorage Laffer curve) if there is a managed exchange rate regime. With somewhat less confidence the lower inflation rate may be expected to emerge endogenously under a floating exchange rate regime. No rational policy-making process would ever drive the steady-state inflation rate beyond the seigniorage-maximizing value, as in addition to the costs of higher inflation there would also be a reduction in inflation tax revenues. In what follows we assume that if there is a long-run seigniorage Laffer curve, it is unimodal.

The minimal long-run rate of inflation implied by the government's fiscal-financial-monetary strategy, $\bar{\pi}$, must be consistent with the long-run exchange rate rule. In our model, in which the law of one price holds, $\pi \equiv \varepsilon + \pi^*$ even outside the steady state. However, even if the real exchange rate is endogenous, the steady-state rate of depreciation of the nominal exchange rate, ε, must equal the excess of the minimal long-run domestic rate of inflation required to generate the required steady-state seigniorage, $\bar{\pi}$, over the exogenous world rate of inflation, π^* (assumed to be constant for simplicity), i.e.

$$\varepsilon = \bar{\pi} - \pi^*. \tag{13.33}$$

As our formal model is non-stochastic and strategic behavior is not considered, it does not matter whether we view Equation (13.33) as the steady state of an *exchange rate management rule* (i.e. a rule for E or its rate of change with the stock of international reserves and the money stock adjusting endogenously) or as the steady state of a *reserve stock* or *money stock management rule* (i.e. a rule for M or R^* with the exchange rate adjusting endogenously).

In most of what follows it is convenient to interpret exchange rate behavior as if it were generated by a crawling peg exchange rate management rule which generates the real seigniorage required to satisfy the government budget identity at each instant, given exogenously determined values of c^G, i^G, τ_0, θ, b and f^{*G} and without any 'maxi' devaluations or revaluations, i.e. without any discontinuous changes in the *level* of the nominal exchange rate. The (managed) proportional rate of change of the nominal exchange rate, ε, will in general vary over time in response to changes in c^G or i^G. Such an exchange rate management rule mimics a freely floating exchange rate except for the absence (under the exchange rate management rule) of discontinuous changes in E even at those instants when 'news' about the fundamentals reaches the private sector. With a predetermined nominal exchange rate, any stock-shift changes in the demand for real money balances (say, in response to a change in the nominal interest rate) will be reflected in changes in the stock of international reserves. As regards the behavior of *real* money balances (per capita), m, this regime is identical to a freely floating exchange rate regime. Under the latter regime, discontinuous changes in the nominal exchange rate in response to news replace discontinuous changes in official international reserves. The exchange rate management interpretation may make the selection of seigniorage revenue-efficient solutions more plausible.

13.3.2 International reserve sufficiency

Current conventional wisdom on the collapse of managed exchange rate regimes (see, for example, Krugman, 1979; Flood and Garber, 1984; and Obstfeld, 1986) implies that a collapse can occur even if there is long-run seigniorage consistency as just defined. Even if the government achieves an inflation rate and nominal exchange-rate depreciation rate that guarantee long-run seigniorage consistency (and even if the government satisfies its intertemporal solvency constraint at each instant, in or out of steady state), international foreign exchange reserves could still be declining: nominal domestic credit expansion could exceed the change in the nominal money stock demanded in equilibrium. This can occur even when c^G, τ, k^G, ϱ^G, b and f^{*G} are constant: the loss of official international reserves would be balanced in that case by a reduction in government borrowing abroad: $\dot{R}^*$ $- \dot{B}^* = (n + \pi - \varepsilon)(R^* - B^*)$ is consistent with any value of $\dot{R}^*$ (and thus, ultimately, of R^*).[11]

In the model under consideration, international reserves and foreign borrowing carry the same interest rate. The government's solvency constraint is, therefore, unaffected by equal offsetting changes in R^* and in B^*. Note that if reserves have a lower interest rate than government debt (as would be the case under a pure gold standard with a positive nominal interest rate (see Buiter, 1986, 1987), then financing a given deficit by running down reserves rather than by borrowing abroad would gradually strengthen government solvency. Similarly, a stock-shift open market sale to replenish the stock of reserves would, because the authorities incur a high interest rate liability in exchange for a low interest rate asset, weaken government solvency immediately.

As shown in Buiter (1986), when the interest rates on reserves and on government debt are the same and when a government is solvent for any rate of domestic credit expansion (however low), then the government is solvent for any other rate of domestic credit expansion (however high). There can be no 'international reserve problem' as long as there is no solvency problem.

The literature just referred to 'creates' a reserve problem by postulating some *ad hoc* lower bound on the stock of reserves (or, in the context of our model, on the real per capita stock of reserves) and by denying the government unlimited lines of credit even when solvency is guaranteed. If the actual stock of reserves falls below the critical threshold level, the current managed exchange rate regime collapses and something else takes its place. This 'something else' can be a 'free float' (possibly followed by an eventual return to another managed rate or rule), a maxi-devaluation, the imposition of capital or exchange controls or any other conceivable scheme.

I shall assume that in steady state, domestic credit expansion is such that any reserve threshold there may be is not breached. Outside the steady state, the initial stock of reserves is assumed to be sufficient to keep reserves above the exogenously imposed reserve threshold (if there is one), despite any stock-shift or gradual reserve losses incurred during the adjustment process. The focus is therefore firmly on solvency rather than on (badly understood) international liquidity problems that may occur despite solvency.[12]

13.4 LONG-RUN EFFECTS ON INFLATION OF PUBLIC SPENDING CUTS

Putting together Equations (13.30) and (13.31) we obtain:

$$(n + \pi)\left[\frac{1 - \eta(r + \pi)}{r + \pi}\right]\frac{\delta n}{(n + \delta - r)r}$$

$$\left[(1 - \theta)\omega\left(k\left(\frac{r}{1 - \theta}, k^G\right), k^G\right) - \tau_0 - \varrho^G k^G\right]$$

$$= c^G - \tau_0 - \theta f\left(k\left(\frac{r}{1 - \theta}, k^G\right), k^G\right) + (r - r^*)f^{*G} + (n - \varrho^G)k^G$$

$$+ (r - n)(b - f^{*G}). \tag{13.34}$$

Remember that n, δ, θ, τ_0, c^G, r^* and ϱ^G are taken as exogenous. The government financing rule (or an (*ad hoc*) internal debt ceiling) keeps b

constant in and out of steady state. The government financing rule (or an (*ad hoc*) external debt ceiling) keeps f^{*G} constant in and out of steady state. Since $\dot{k}^G \equiv i^G - nk^G$, the steady-state public sector capital stock is simply given by $k^G = i^G/n$. We assume $n > 0$ in what follows.

The cases of perfect capital mobility and zero capital mobility are considered in turn.

13.4.1 Perfect international capital mobility

With perfect international capital mobility ($r = r^*$), the long-run effects on inflation of changes in public consumption spending, public sector capital formation and lump-sum taxes are given by Equations (13.35). Note that, because the real interest rate is constant, the nominal interest rate varies one-for-one with the rate of inflation.

$$\frac{d\pi}{dc^G} = a_{11}^{-1} \tag{13.35a}$$

$$\frac{d\pi}{di^G} = a_{11}^{-1} b_{12} \tag{13.35b}$$

$$\frac{d\pi}{d\tau_0} = a_{11}^{-1} b_{13} \tag{13.35c}$$

where

$$a_{11} = m\left[1 - \frac{(n + \pi)}{i(1 - \eta)}(1 - \eta + i\eta')\right] \tag{13.36a}$$

and

$$b_{12} = 1 - \frac{\varrho^G}{n} - \frac{\theta}{n}\left[-f_1\frac{f_{12}}{f_{11}} + f_2\right]$$
$$+ \frac{(n + \pi)(1 - \eta)\delta}{i(n + \delta - r)r}\left[(1 - \theta)k^G\left(\frac{f_{11}f_{22} - f_{12}^2}{f_{11}}\right) + \varrho^G\right] \tag{13.36b}$$

$$b_{13} = \frac{(n + \pi)(1 - \eta)\delta n}{i(n + \delta - r)r} - 1 = \frac{\sigma}{w - \tau_0} - 1 \tag{13.36c}$$

The coefficient a_{11} is positive if we are on the revenue-efficient side of the seigniorage Laffer curve, where the elasticity of money demand with respect to the inflation rate is less than unity in absolute value.[13] A cut in public consumption spending reduces the amount of real seigniorage that needs to be extracted. In the revenue-efficient region of the Laffer curve, lower real seigniorage means lower inflation (see Equations (13.35a) and (13.36a)). Note that since money is the 'residual' mode of financing, lower public consumption spending does not imply lower explicit taxes.

The effect of higher lump-sum taxes on long-run inflation is actually ambiguous in this model. As shown in Equations (13.35c) and (13.36c), while higher lump-sum taxes reduce the amount of long-run seigniorage required to satisfy the government budget constraint, they also reduce the demand for money (at given nominal and real interest rates), which is an increasing function of *disposable* labor income. If, in the initial steady state, seigniorage is less than disposable labor income (which is likely empirically), higher lump-sum taxes will lead to lower long-run inflation (in the revenue-efficient region of the long-run seigniorage Laffer curve).

Lower public sector capital formation may (but need not) lead to higher long-run inflation (see Equations (13.35b) and (13.36b)). *Ceteris paribus*, it reduces the deficit one-for-one, thus reducing long-run required seigniorage and (in the seigniorage revenue-efficient region) long-run inflation. This we shall call the *expenditure* effect, given by the first term on the right-hand side of Equation (13.36b). However, there may be direct cash returns to the government, associated with its ownership of the public sector capital stock. If the (net) rate of return ϱ^G exceeds the real growth rate n (or equivalently if $\varrho^G k^G$ exceeds i^G) the direct effect of lower public sector capital formation on long-run seigniorage and (in the seigniorage revenue-efficient region) on inflation will be positive. Empirically, it is, of course, quite possible for ϱ^G to be negative. The permanent subsidization (for good or bad reasons) of secular public sector loss-makers would be a case in point. This *direct revenue effect* is given by the second term $-\varrho^G/n$ on the right-hand side of Equation (13.36b).

There is a further possible effect of a lower long-run stock of public sector capital on the deficit, seigniorage and inflation. Lower k^G means lower national income, both given k and by inducing a reduction in k (assuming $f_{12} > 0$). Lower national income means lower income-related tax receipts if θ is positive. This *indirect revenue effect* is captured in the third term on the right-hand side of Equation (13.36b).

Finally, there is an effect on the demand for money, captured by the last term on the right-hand side of Equation (13.36b). A lower value of k^G means a lower real wage and a lower user charge $\varrho^G k^G$. *Ceteris paribus*, a lower real wage means a lower demand for real money balances; in the revenue-efficient segment of the seigniorage Laffer curve this implies higher inflation. This will be referred to as the *money demand effect*.

In the seigniorage revenue-efficient region, the expenditure effect of a cut in public sector capital formation reduces inflation. The direct revenue effect is ambiguous even as regards its sign. The indirect revenue effect will worsen inflation as long as the marginal product of public sector capital is positive ($f_2 > 0$) or public and private capital are complements ($f_{12} > 0$). θ is likely to be quite small in many developing countries, however. The money demand effect also may raise inflation. The money demand function is likely to be adversely affected, *ceteris paribus*, by a lower social overhead capital stock as long as the marginal product of public sector capital is positive, unless the user charge effect is very strong.

13.4.2 Zero international capital mobility

When there is no international capital mobility, domestic income equals private plus public absorption, i.e. Equation (13.26) holds. Substituting for output using the production function, for private consumption using Equations (13.18), (13.19), (13.20) and (13.22), and for private investment using the steady-state condition $i^P = nk$, we obtain:

$$f\left[k\left[\frac{r}{1-\theta}, \frac{i^G}{n}\right], \frac{i^G}{n}\right] = \eta(r+\pi)\delta\frac{n}{(n+\delta-r)r}$$
$$\left[(1-\theta)\omega\left[k\left[\frac{r}{1-\theta}, \frac{i^G}{n}\right], \frac{i^G}{n}\right] - \tau_0 - \varrho^G\frac{i^G}{n}\right]$$
$$+ c^G + nk\left[\frac{r}{1-\theta}, \frac{i^G}{n}\right] + i^G. \tag{13.37}$$

Equations (13.34) (with $k^G = i^G n^{-1}$) and (13.37) can be used to solve for the long-run equilibrium values of the rate of inflation and the now endogenous real interest rate.

The long-run comparative statics of changes in c^G, i^G and τ_0 can be obtained from Equations (13.38).

$$\begin{bmatrix} a_{11} & a_{12} \\ a_{21} & a_{22} \end{bmatrix}\begin{bmatrix} d\pi \\ dr \end{bmatrix} = \begin{bmatrix} b_{11} & b_{12} & b_{13} \\ b_{21} & b_{22} & b_{23} \end{bmatrix}\begin{bmatrix} dc^G \\ di^G \\ d\tau_0 \end{bmatrix} \tag{13.38a}$$

$$a_{11} = m\left\{1 - \frac{(n+\pi)}{i(1-\eta)}(1-\eta+i\eta')\right\} \tag{13.38b}$$

$$a_{12} = \frac{(n+\pi)m}{i(1-\eta)}(1-\eta+i\eta') + \frac{(n+\pi)m(n+\delta-2r)}{(n+\delta-r)r}$$
$$+ \frac{(n+\pi)}{i}\frac{(1-\eta)\delta n}{(n+\delta-r)r}\left[k+k^G\frac{f_{12}}{f_{11}}\right] - \left[\frac{\theta}{1-\theta}\right]\frac{f_1}{f_{11}} + b \tag{13.38c}$$

$$a_{21} = \frac{\eta'c}{\eta} \tag{13.38d}$$

$$a_{22} = \frac{\eta'c}{\eta} - \frac{c(n+\delta-2r)}{(n+\delta-r)r} - \frac{\eta\delta n}{(n+\delta-r)r}\left[k+k^G\frac{f_{12}}{f_{11}}\right] + \frac{n-f_1}{f_{11}(1-\theta)} \tag{13.38e}$$

$$b_{11} = 1 \tag{13.38f}$$

$$b_{12} = 1 - \frac{\varrho^G}{n} - \frac{\theta}{n}\left[\frac{f_2 f_{11} - f_1 f_{12}}{f_{11}}\right]$$
$$+ \frac{(n+\pi)(1-\eta)\delta}{i(n+\delta-r)r}\left[(1-\theta)k^G\left(\frac{f_{11}f_{22}-f_{12}^2}{f_{11}}\right) + \varrho^G\right] \tag{13.38g}$$

$$b_{13} = \frac{\sigma}{w - \tau_0 - \varrho^G k^G} - 1 \tag{13.38h}$$

$$b_{21} = -1 \tag{13.38i}$$

$$b_{22} = \frac{1}{n}\left[f_2 - \frac{f_1 f_{12}}{f_{11}} \right] - \frac{(1 - \theta)\eta \delta k^U}{(n - \delta - r)r}\left[\frac{f_{12} - f_{11} f_{22}}{f_{11}} \right] + \frac{f_{12}}{f_{11}} - 1 \tag{13.38j}$$

$$\frac{+ \eta \delta n \varrho^G}{(n + \delta - r)rn} \tag{13.38k}$$

$$b_{23} = \frac{\eta \delta n}{(n + \delta - r)r}.$$

Equation (13.34) defines the long-run equilibrium seigniorage schedule AA_0 or AA_1 in Figure 13.2. The long-run income-absorption equilibrium schedule corresponding to Equation (13.37) is drawn as BB in Figure 13.2. The slope of the AA schedule in $\pi - r$ space is given by

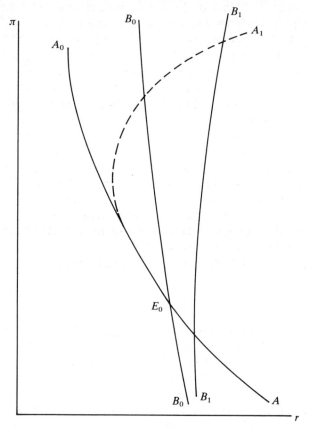

Figure 13.2 The real interest rate and inflation in the long run

$$\left.\frac{\mathrm{d}\pi}{\mathrm{d}r}\right|_{AA} = \frac{-a_{12}}{a_{11}}.$$

The coefficient a_{12} given in Equation (13.38c) measures the effect of a higher real interest rate (*ceteris paribus*) on the 'demand for seigniorage', i.e. on the inflation-and-growth-corrected government deficit on the right-hand side of Equation (13.34), relative to its effect on the 'supply of seigniorage', $(n + \pi)m$, on the left-hand side of Equation (13.34). A higher value of r raises the deficit both by raising the interest to be paid on the debt and by generating a lower private capital stock, output and income-related tax receipts. These two effects are captured by the terms b and $-(\theta/(1 - \theta))f_1/f_{11}$, respectively, in Equation (13.38c). *Ceteris paribus*, a higher real interest rate also represents a higher nominal interest rate. This nominal interest rate effect will tend to reduce m, the seigniorage tax base, since $1 - \eta + i\eta' > 0$. A higher real interest rate will, however, also raise the long-run ratio of non-human wealth to disposable wage income. It will also, provided $r > (n + \delta)/2$, raise the long-run ratio of comprehensive consumption, q, to disposable wage income and thus raise m.[14]

Finally, a higher real interest rate will tend to be associated (through a lower value of k) with a lower real wage. This effect, measured by the third term on the right-hand side of Equation (13.38c), will tend to reduce m. We will only consider the a priori more plausible case in which a_{12} is positive, i.e. a higher value of r raises the demand for seigniorage relative to its supply. (Note that we also assume throughout that the nominal interest rate is positive.) The coefficient a_{11}, already discussed, will be positive if the inflation elasticity of money demand is less than unity in absolute value, negative otherwise. Without a seigniorage Laffer curve, the AA_0 curve is downward-sloping as shown in Figure 13.2. The AA_1 schedule represents the unimodal long-run seigniorage Laffer curve generated by an inflation elasticity of money demand which is below unity in absolute value for low values of π and rises monotonically with π, crossing unity for some finite value of π.

The slope of the BB schedule in π–r space is given by

$$\left.\frac{\mathrm{d}\pi}{\mathrm{d}r}\right|_{BB} = \frac{-a_{22}}{a_{21}}.$$

Homotheticity is consistent with any sign for η', as long as $1 - \eta + i\eta' \geq 0$. In what follows it is assumed that $\eta' \geq 0$, i.e. given total comprehensive consumption of goods and money services, an increase in the real price of money services does not reduce the demand for goods. This implies $a_{21} \geq 0$.

The coefficient a_{22} will be positive if, *ceteris paribus*, a higher real interest rate raises absorption relative to output. Assuming that the marginal product of private capital exceeds the real growth rate ($f_1 > n$), the last term on the right-hand side of Equation (13.38e) will be positive. $\eta' \geq 0$ makes the first term on the right-hand side of Equation (13.38e) non-negative. A higher value of r also tends to raise the ratio of comprehensive consumption, q, to disposable wage income (if $n + \delta < 2r$), so the second term on the right-hand side of Equation (13.38e) is positive. Human wealth is lower, however, when r is higher and this will make the third term on the right-hand side of Equation (13.38e) negative. Figure 13.2 shows both the case where a_{22} is positive (the downward-sloping curve B_0B_0) and the case where a_{22} is negative (the upward-sloping curve B_1B_1). For reasons of space we only consider the case where, in the low-inflation (seigniorage revenue-efficient) equilibrium at E_0, the B_0B_0 curve cuts the AA_0 (or AA_1) curve from above.[15]

A cut in public consumption spending shifts the long-run seigniorage equilibrium schedule A_0A_0 to the left in Figures 13.3a and 13.3b. (We consider the case of the unimodal long-run seigniorage Laffer curve). If a higher real interest rate raises long-run absorption relative to long-run output ($a_{22} > 0$), the long-run output-absorption equilibrium schedule is negatively sloped. It shifts to the right when c^G is cut as in Figure 13.3a. In the seigniorage-efficient region, the equilibrium moves from E_0 to E_1: inflation falls and the real interest rate rises. Note that an increase in the real interest rate is required in the long run because, with $a_{22} > 0$, a higher real interest rate is required to boost absorption and reduce output, thus restoring output-absorption balance following the cut in public consumption spending. In the seigniorage-inefficient region the stationary equilibrium in Figure 13.3a moves from $\bar{E}_0$ to $\bar{E}_1$. The inflation rate rises while the effect on the real interest rate is ambiguous. If, given q, a rise in the nominal interest rate has only a small effect on the consumption of goods, i.e. if $\eta' c/\eta$ is small, the output-absorption equilibrium schedule will be near vertical and r will increase.

Figure 13.3b shows the case where $a_{22} < 0$ and a higher value of r reduces absorption relative to output. In the seigniorage revenue-efficient region the equilibrium moves from E_0 to E_1 or E_1'. The real interest rate falls and the inflation rate either falls (at E_1) or rises (at E_1'). In the seigniorage revenue-inefficient region the stationary equilibrium moves from $\bar{E}_0$ to $\bar{E}_1$ or $\bar{E}_1'$.

An increase in lump-sum taxes will shift the long-run seigniorage equilibrium schedule to the left if $b_{13} = [\sigma/(w - \tau_0 - \varrho^G k^G)] - 1 < 0$, as seems plausible empirically. This is shown both in Figure 13.4a and in Figure 13.4b. If $a_{22} > 0$ (a higher real interest rate raises long-run absorption relative to long-run real output) the absorption output equilibrium schedule shifts to the right, as shown in Figure 13.4a. If $a_{22} < 0$, the absorption-output equilibrium schedule shifts to the left, as in Figure 13.4b. In Figure 13.4a the seigniorage revenue-efficient equilibrium shows a higher real interest rate and a lower rate of inflation.

(a)

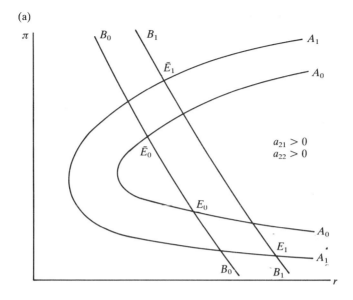

(b)

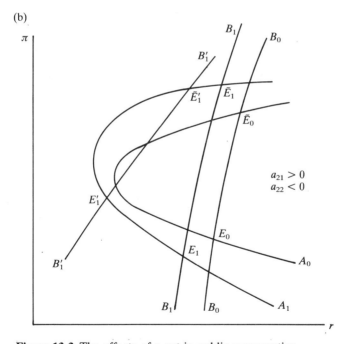

Figure 13.3 The effects of a cut in public consumption

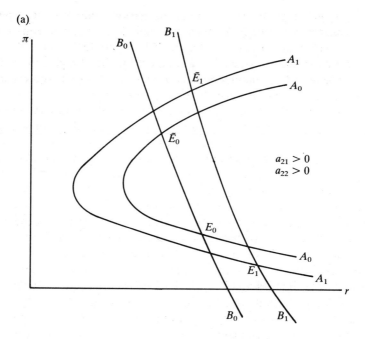

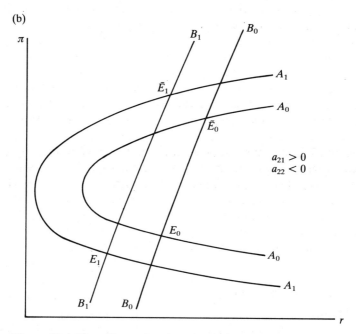

Figure 13.4 The effects of an increase in lump-sum taxes

A lower rate of public sector capital formation, unlike a cut in public sector consumption spending, need not shift the long-run equilibrium seigniorage schedule to the left. Figures 13.5a and 13.5b show the case where the expenditure effect is dominated by the direct and indirect revenue effects and the money demand effect, i.e. $b_{12} < 0$, and the long-run equilibrium seigniorage schedule shifts to the right.

The direction of the shift of the long-run output-absorption equilibrium schedule as i^G decreases is ambiguous. There is the direct expenditure effect on absorption (the term -1 in Equation (13.38j)) which is reinforced by the reduction in long-run private consumption due to the lower real wage associated with the lower stock of public sector capital (the second term in Equation (13.38j)). Absorption will be stimulated by lower user charges, if $\varrho^G > 0$. Finally, there is the depressing effect on absorption due to the lower long-run rate of private capital formation, reflecting the lower value of k that accompanies a lower value of k^G (the term f_{12}/f_{11} in Equation (13.38j)). Absorption is therefore likely to decline. Output, however, also falls, both through the direct effect of a lower value of k^G and through the depressing effect on k of a lower value of k^G (the term $1/n(f_2 - f_1 f_{12}/f_{11})$ in Equation (13.38j).

In Figure 13.5a we consider the case where a_{22} is positive (a higher real interest rate raises long-run absorption relative to long-run output) and b_{22} is positive (i.e. a lower value of i^G reduces output by more than absorption). The output-absorption equilibrium schedule shifts to the left in this case, moving the seigniorage revenue-efficient equilibrium from E_0 to E_1. The long-run responses of both the inflation rate and the real interest rate in the seigniorage revenue-efficient region are unambiguous: a cut in public sector capital formation leads to a higher rate of inflation and a lower real interest rate. The higher rate of inflation is needed to extract the larger real seigniorage that is required and the lower real interest rate raises output relative to absorption.

In Figure 13.5b we continue to assume that a_{22} is positive, but b_{22} is now assumed to be negative: a cut in public sector capital formation lowers absorption more than output. The output-absorption equilibrium schedule moves to the right in this case. In the seigniorage revenue-efficient region the response of the inflation rate and the real interest rate are ambiguous. It is possible for the inflation rate to rise and the real interest rate to fall (the case of a very small shift to the right of the output-absorption equilibrium schedule, not shown in Figure 13.5b). The inflation rate can rise while the real interest rate rises (from E_0 to E_1 in Figure 13.5b) or the inflation rate can fall while the real interest rate rises (from E_0 to E_2 in Figure 13.5b).

With $a_{22} < 0$ we obtain in the seigniorage revenue-efficient region an unambiguously positive effect of a cut in public sector capital formation on

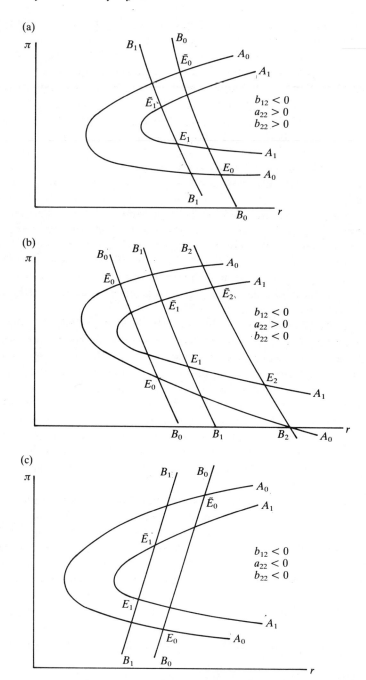

Figure 13.5 The effects of a cut in public sector capital formation

the rate of inflation when $b_{22} < 0$, i.e. when a cut in public sector capital formation reduces absorption by more than output. The real interest rate could rise if η' is large and the output-absorption equilibrium schedule shifts to the left only slightly; a lower real interest rate is more likely, however. It is easily checked that with $a_{22} < 0$ and $b_{22} > 0$, a cut in public sector capital formation lowers the real interest rate and has an ambiguous effect on the rate of inflation in the seigniorage revenue-efficient region.[16]

The two cases where a cut in public sector capital formation unambiguously raises the long-run rate of inflation are depicted in Figures 13.5a and 13.5c. In each case the seigniorage revenue-efficient equilibrium is considered, i.e. $a_{11} > 0$. In addition a cut in public sector capital formation is assumed to raise (at given values of r and π) the 'demand for seigniorage' relative to the 'supply of seigniorage', i.e. $b_{12} < 0$. Finally, we have one of the two following output-absorption equilibrium configurations: either the case of Figure 13.5a in which a higher real interest rate raises absorption relative to output ($a_{22} > 0$) and a cut in public sector capital formation reduces absorption by less than output ($b_{22} > 0$), or the case of Figure 13.5c in which a higher real interest rate raises output relative to absorption ($a_{22} < 0$) and a cut in public sector capital formation reduces absorption by more than output ($b_{22} < 0$). Note that these are sufficient conditions only. As Figure 13.5b shows, they are not necessary.

13.5 STABILITY AND DYNAMIC ADJUSTMENT

13.5.1 Perfect capital mobility

Under perfect capital mobility, the dynamic adjustment of the economy is given by Equations (13.39)–(13.44).

$$\dot{q} = (r^* - \delta)q - \delta na \tag{13.39}$$

$$\dot{a} = (r^* - n)a + (1 - \theta)\omega\left(k\left(\frac{r^*}{1 - \theta}, k^G\right), k^G\right)$$
$$- \tau_0 - \varrho^G k^G - q \tag{13.40}$$

$$\dot{k}^G = i^G - nk^G \tag{13.41}$$

$$\dot{m} = c^G + i^G - \tau_0 - \theta f\left(k\left(\frac{r^*}{1 - \theta}, k^G\right), k^G\right)$$
$$- \varrho^G k^G + (r^* - n)d - (n + \pi)m \tag{13.42}$$

$$m = \left(\frac{1 - \eta(r^* + \pi)}{r^* + \pi}\right)q \tag{13.43}$$

$$\pi = \varepsilon + \pi^*. \tag{13.44}$$

Exogenous are r^*, ϱ^G, τ_0, θ, i^G, c^G, n and δ. Note that with the real interest rate fixed exogenously, q, a and k^G are determined independently of m, π and ε.

The subsystem represented by Equations (13.39), (13.40) and (13.41) governing q, a and k^G is (locally) a saddlepoint with one unstable and two stable roots (governing the non-predetermined state variable q and the predetermined state variables a and k^G)[17] provided

$$r^*(r^* - (n + \delta)) < 0. \tag{13.45}$$

Since we assume that the real interest rate is positive, this is the viability condition $r^* < n + \delta$ required for positive steady-state consumption.[18]

From Equations (13.42), (13.43) and (13.39) we can, solving out m and $\dot{m}$, obtain $\dot{\pi}$ as a function of π, q, a, k^G and the exogenous variables. The coefficient of $\dot{\pi}$ on π in the linear approximation to this $\dot{\pi}$-equation is also the fourth characteristic root of the linearized $\{q, a, k^G, \pi\}$ system (the root 'governing' π). This coefficient, Ω_1 say, is given by

$$\Omega_1 = \frac{(1 - \eta)i}{1 - \eta + i\eta'} - (n + \pi). \tag{13.46}$$

It is easily checked that, provided $n + \pi > 0$, Ω_1 is positive if and only if a_{11} is positive. The coefficient a_{11} given in Equation (13.38b) is positive at a seigniorage revenue-efficient stationary equilibrium, negative otherwise. Around a seigniorage revenue-efficient stationary equilibrium the dynamic system governing q, a, k^G and π will have two stable and two unstable characteristic roots. There is a unique continuously convergent solution trajectory and, after any shock, a unique set of initial values of q and π that are consistent with convergence to the new seigniorage revenue-efficient long-run equilibrium. Around a seigniorage revenue-inefficient long-run equilibrium, Ω_1 is negative and there is a local continuum of initial values for π (but not for q) that are consistent with convergence to the seigniorage revenue-inefficient long-run equilibrium. Note that this analysis is applicable both to the freely floating exchange rate case and to the managed exchange rate case outlined in Section 13.3.1.

13.5.2 Zero capital mobility

With zero international capital mobility, the behavior of q and a is only independent of the behavior of the inflation rate if aggregate consumption of goods, $c = \eta(i)q$, is independent of the nominal interest rate ($\eta' = 0$). Unless this is the case, goods market equilibrium and thereby capital formation will depend on π. With k dependent on π, a and q also can only by determined simultaneously with π. The relevant dynamic system is given in Equations (13.47)–(13.52):

$$\dot{q} = ((1 - \theta)f_1(k, k^G) - \delta)q - \delta na \tag{13.47}$$

$$\dot{a} = ((1 - \theta)f_1(k, k^G) - n)a + (1 - \theta)\omega(k, k^G) - \tau_0 - \varrho^G k^G - q \tag{13.48}$$

$$\dot{k}^G = i^G - nk^G \tag{13.49}$$

$$\dot{k} = f(k, k^G) - nk - \eta((1 - \theta)f_1(k, k^G) + \pi)q - c^G - i^G \tag{13.50}$$

$$\dot{m} = c^G + i^G - \tau_0 - \theta f(k, k^G) - \varrho^G k^G + ((1 - \theta)f_1(k, k^G) - n)b$$
$$\quad - (n + \pi)m \tag{13.51}$$

$$m = \left[\frac{1 - \eta((1 - \theta)f_1(k, k^G) + \pi)}{(1 - \theta)f_1(k, k^G) + \pi}\right]q. \tag{13.52}$$

As the analytical characterization of the unrestricted five-dimensional dynamic system given in Equations (13.47)–(13.52) is too messy and complicated, I restrict the analysis to the case where $\eta' = 0$ and the classical dichotomy holds.

Note that when $\eta' = 0$, real per capita seigniorage, σ, increases (decreases) with the inflation rate if $r > n$ ($r < n$). We only consider dynamically efficient equilibria with $r > n$. This means that the long-run equilibrium seigniorage schedule is always downward-sloping in π–r space: there is no seigniorage revenue-inefficient segment. The output-absorption equilibrium schedule is vertical when $\eta' = 0$. Changes in c^G, i^G and τ_0 will however shift this vertical schedule as before. In the linearized version of the dynamic model, the characteristic root governing π (or m) is $r - n$.[19] With $r > n$ this root is therefore unstable, as desired for a locally unique solution.

The linear approximation to the subsystem governing q, a, k and k^G is given in Equation (13.53).

$$\begin{bmatrix} \dot{q} \\ \dot{a} \\ \dot{k} \\ \dot{k}^G \end{bmatrix} = \begin{bmatrix} r - \delta & -\delta n & q(1 - \theta)f_{11} \\ -1 & r - n & -(1 - \theta)((k - a)f_{11} + k^G f_{12}) \\ -\eta & 0 & f_1 - n \\ 0 & 0 & 0 \end{bmatrix}$$

$$\begin{matrix} q(1 - \theta)f_{12} \\ -(1 - \theta)((k - a)f_{12} + k^G f_{22}) - \varrho^G \\ f_2 \\ -n \end{matrix} \begin{bmatrix} q \\ a \\ k \\ k^G \end{bmatrix} \tag{13.53}$$

The root governing k^G is again $-n$. For there to be a saddlepoint configuration that matches the structure of one non-predetermined state variable (q) and three predetermined ones (a, k and k^G), two of the other three roots should be stable and one unstable. The determinant of the three-by-three submatrix obtained by deleting the last row and column of the coefficient matrix in Equation (13.53) should therefore be positive, i.e.

$$\frac{(n - f_1)}{f_{11}(1 - \theta)}(n + \delta - r)r - \eta\delta n\left[k + k^G\frac{f_{12}}{f_{11}}\right] - c(n + \delta - 2r) < 0$$

(13.54)

Provided $n + \delta > r$ (which is required for positive steady-state consumption), Equation (13.54) is equivalent to the condition $a_{22} < 0$ (see Equation (13.38e) with $\eta' = 0$). When the output-absorption equilibrium schedule is vertical, therefore, the situation depicted in Figure 13.5a cannot arise when the dynamic system has, locally, the appropriate saddlepoint configuration. This leaves the configuration shown in Figure 13.5c as the only one for which inflation unambiguously rises as public sector capital formation is reduced. The intuition is clear. Private capital deepening ($\dot{k} > 0$) means a lower real interest rate. Unless a lower real interest rate raises absorption relative to output ($a_{22} < 0$), the rate of private capital formation increases further, setting off an unstable process. (When $\eta' > 0$, the condition that a_{22} be negative is not necessary for saddlepoint stability).

The eigenvalues of a matrix are continuous functions of the coefficients of that matrix. Small perturbations of η' from zero will therefore not cause a qualitative change in the local saddlepoint configuration just discussed. For η' far from zero (including any model with a seigniorage revenue-inefficient region) numerical simulation methods are required to determine local (and of course global) stability characteristics.

13.6 CONCLUSIONS

The answer to the question 'can public spending cuts be inflationary?' is a clear 'yes'. This paper specifies the conditions under which a cut in public spending can permanently raise the rate of inflation. Monetary financing is taken to be the 'residual' financing mode. Real public spending per capita (current and capital) is taken to be exogenous. So are the share of income-related taxes in GDP, GDP-independent real per capita taxes and the real per capita public debt, both internal and external. This set-up helps us pose the issue clearly (it is one of the two fiscal-financial regimes considered in Sargent and Wallace, 1981) and it also may be a quite reasonable approximation to the real-world situation of a number of highly indebted semi-industrial countries such as Mexico, Argentina and Brazil.

These countries face the need to reduce the public sector deficit. They tend to be credit-rationed in the private international financial markets and are unable or reluctant to add to the internal public debt burden. Raising revenues (which tend to be a low proportion of national income relative to those found in most industrial countries) often appears to be politically or administratively infeasible. Barring internal or external debt repudiation (or economically equivalent capital levies on public debt holders), this leaves public expenditure cuts as the only instrument of fiscal retrench- ment. This paper emphasizes and elaborates the important distinction between cuts in public consumption expenditure which will tend to reduce the deficit[20] and cuts in public sector capital formation which may have the perverse effect of increasing the deficit. This will happen if the expenditure effect is swamped by the direct and indirect effects of a reduced public sector capital stock on government revenues.

If they increase the (inflation-and-real-growth-corrected) public sector deficit, the cuts in public sector capital formation will raise the 'demand for seigniorage revenue'. Such cuts are also likely to lower the demand for money (at a given inflation rate and real interest rate) by reducing the scale factor (real income) in the money demand function. This reduces the 'supply of seigniorage revenue'. In the seigniorage revenue-efficient por- tion of the 'seigniorage Laffer curve', the price of seigniorage, i.e. the rate of inflation, will increase.

When the domestic real interest rate is governed by the world real inter- est rate, the empirical information required to determine whether an econ- omy finds itself in the situation just outlined, is rather limited. Estimates are needed of the high-powered money demand function, including an estimate of the effect of the public sector capital stock on the 'scale factor' in the money demand function; of the production function (which includes the contribution of the public sector capital stock);[21] and of the govern- ment revenue function. When the domestic real interest rate is endogenous, things are considerably more complicated as private consumption and equilibrium in the domestic credit market now have to be modeled.

A major caveat in interpreting these results is that they are concerned with long-run (steady-state) effects. The adjustment dynamics which sup- ported the long-run comparative statics in addition did not allow for any kind of non-Walrasian equilibrium in the labor market, the output market or the credit market. Demand-deficient, Keynesian temporary equilibria in response to public expenditure cuts were not considered, but may well be an important part of the story in the larger semi-industrial debtor countries.

The assumption made in this paper that real government revenue is in- dependent of the rate of inflation is unrealistic. With low rates of inflation, 'bracket creep' in income tax systems that are progressive in nominal terms makes for a positive relationship between the price level and the real tax burden. This is unlikely to be important in most of the semi-industrial debtor countries, as they tend not to have (*de facto*) progressive tax structures. More important is the erosion of real tax receipts at high rates of inflation due to tax collection lags and a failure to charge and/or collect the appropriate interest rate on overdue taxes (see Tanzi, 1978).

Finally, when public sector capital formation is interpreted in its broadest possible sense (as it should be for the purposes of this paper) as any public outlays that yield a stream of future returns, it is likely that some of the expenditure on communications, transportation, education, and so on, which are classified as current will in fact enhance the future revenue-raising capacity of the government. Indeed some current spending (on public administration and law enforcement) may have an immediate effect on current public revenues.

While it is not difficult to come up with horror stories about instances of wasteful or socially undesirable public expenditure, it may not be as simple to ensure that the broad-brush cuts so often proposed (and occasionally implemented) do in fact achieve their declared purpose of achieving a lasting reduction in the public sector deficit and a lower rate of inflation.

13.7 NOTES

1. Running down foreign exchange reserves is included in net external borrowing by the public sector.
2. In the cases of the linear or log-linear money demand functions the absolute value of the elasticity of money demand with respect to the nominal interest rate increases with the nominal interest rate. The long-run seigniorage Laffer curve (holding constant the real interest rate and the real scale variable in the money demand function) is unimodal in this case.
3. In Hall (1987), the real rate of return on high-powered money is kept constant through policy by varying the nominal interest rate on base money with the (expected) rate of inflation.
4. Exceptions in the form of Keynesian models with more than 100 per cent 'financial crowding-out' are reviewed, for example, in Buiter (1985).
5. Some authors refer to πm or to $(n + \pi)m$ as the inflation tax.
6. $\omega_1 > 0$ and $\omega_2 > 0$ follow from $F_{LK} > 0$ and $F_{LK^G} > 0$, respectively.
7. The socially efficient solution would, of course, be to have a single firm ($N = 1$) and to choose K^G, K and L such that $f_1 = f_2 = r$ (ignoring the distortionary tax rate θ).
8. If the instantaneous utility function is of the constant elasticity of marginal utility or constant relative risk aversion variety with constant of relative risk aversion $1 - \gamma$, $\gamma < 1$, comprehensive consumption would be given by

$$q(t) = \lambda(t)(a(t) + h(t)),$$

where

$$\lambda(t) = \left[\int_t^\infty \exp\left(- \left[\frac{\gamma}{\gamma - 1} \int_t^v r(u)\mathrm{d}u + (v - t)\frac{1}{1 - \gamma}\delta \right] \right)\mathrm{d}v \right]^{-1};$$

in a steady state with constant r.

$$\lambda = \frac{\gamma}{\gamma - 1}r + \frac{\delta}{1 - \gamma}$$

provided this expression is positive. The logarithmic utility function considered in most of the paper corresponds to the special case $\gamma = 0$.

9. Since $\sigma \equiv \dot{m} + (n + \pi)m$ and in steady state $\dot{m} = 0$.
10. When $n = 0$, steady-state equilibrium with positive and bounded per capita consumption exists only if $r = \delta$. Steady-state non-human wealth, a, is 'hysteretic' in this case, i.e. it cannot be determined from the steady-state conditions alone but depends on the initial conditions and the values of the exogenous variables during the adjustment process to the steady state. For reasons of space we do not consider this case here. $n + \delta > r$ is a viability condition for this economy, ensuring positive long-run consumption provided after-tax disposable wage income is positive.
11. Alternatively, the government could run down reserves with B^* constant but B declining. The private sector would in that case reduce its foreign indebtedness.
12. The distinction between *ability* to service external debt and *willingness* to service this debt is irrelevant here. Voluntary default or repudiation risk creates external credit rationing, but no special role for a subcategory of external assets labeled 'reserves'.
13. The elasticity of money demand with respect to the nominal interest rate is $-(1/(1 - \eta))(1 - \eta + i\eta')$.
14. It is easily checked that, in the long run,

$$a = \frac{(r - \lambda)}{(n + \lambda - r)r}(w - \tau_0 - \varrho^G k^G),$$

where λ, the ratio of comprehensive consumption to total (human plus non-human) wealth is (from note 8) given by

$$\lambda = \frac{\gamma}{\gamma - 1}r + \frac{\delta}{1 - \gamma}, \gamma < 1.$$

Therefore,

$$a = \frac{(r - \delta)}{[(1 - \gamma)n + \delta - r]r}(w - \tau_0 - \varrho^G k^G).$$

The change in the ratio $a/(w - \tau_0 - \varrho^G k^G)$ as r changes is

$$\frac{d\left[\dfrac{a}{w - \tau_0 - \varrho^G k^G}\right]}{dr} = \frac{(r - \delta)^2 + \delta(1 - \gamma)n}{\{[(1 - \gamma)n + \delta - r]r\}^2} > 0.$$

Also,

$$q = \frac{\lambda n}{r(n + \lambda - r)}(w - \tau_0 - \varrho^G k^G)$$

or

$$q = \frac{(\delta - \gamma r)n}{[(1 - \gamma)n + \delta - r]r}(w - \tau_0 - \varrho^G k^G),$$

so

$$\frac{d\left[\dfrac{q}{w - \tau_0 - \varrho^G k^G}\right]}{dr} = \frac{-n[((1 - \gamma)n + \delta - 2r)\delta + \gamma r^2]}{\{[(1 - \gamma)n + \delta - r]r\}^2}.$$

when $\gamma - 0$ (i.e. in the logarithmic case considered in the body of the paper) $d(q/w - \tau_0 - p^G k^G))/dr$ will be positive if $n + \delta < 2r$. This will hold if the economy is dynamically efficient ($r > n$) and if $r > \delta$, which is necessary for $a >$ 0 (if $q > 0$).

15. If a_{12} is positive, this will certainly be the case if $a_{21} \geq 0$ and $a_{22} < 0$. In Section 13.5 it is shown that if $\eta' = 0$ (i.e. $a_{21} = 0$) $a_{22} < 0$ is necessary for the appropriate kind of saddlepoint stability.

16. It is even possible for the long-run inflation rate to rise (in the seigniorage revenue-efficient region) in response to a cut in public sector capital formation when b_{12} is positive, i.e. when the long-run seigniorage equilibrium schedule shifts to the left. This will occur for sufficiently large shifts to the left of the output-absorption equilibrium schedule. We do not consider this case for reasons of space.

17. Note that $a \equiv m + b + k + s + f^{*p}$ will jump discontinuously at a point in time if $m \equiv M/PL$, $b \equiv B/PL$, $f^{*p} \equiv EF^{*p}/PL$ or s jump discontinuously. (Since the law of one price holds, $E/P = 1/P^*$, so even with a freely floating exchange rate, f^{*p} will not move discontinuously when the exchange rate jumps.) Any jump in a can be reduced to the underlying jumps in E and s using the wealth identity. See Buiter (1984) for some linear examples.

18. Note that public sector capital formation is, with i^G exogenous, governed by the single stable root $-n$. More generally, we could represent i^G by a first-order partial adjustment process such as $i^G = \alpha(\bar{k}^G - k^G) + nk$, with $\alpha > 0$ and $\bar{k}^G > 0$.

19. This is the special case of Ω_1 in Equation (13.46) with $\eta' = 0$.

20. When $a_{22} < 0$, as shown in Figure 13.3b, the real interest rate may fall so much that inflation actually increases.

21. In our model the production function provides the relevant information on the scale factor in the money demand dunction.

13.8 REFERENCES

Blanchard, O. J. (1985) 'Debt, deficits and finite horizons', *Journal of Political Economy*, 93, April, pp. 223–47.

Blinder, A. S. (1987) 'Credit-rationing and effective supply failures', *Economic Journal*, 97, June, pp. 327–52.

Buiter, Willem H. (1977) 'Crowding out and the effectiveness of fiscal policy', *Journal of Public Economics*, 7, June, pp. 309–28 (also Chapter 6, this volume).

Buiter, Willem H. (1984) 'Saddlepoint problems in continuous time rational expectations models: a general method and some macroeconomic examples', *Econometrica*, 52(3), May, pp. 665–86.

Buiter, Willem H. (1985) 'A guide to public sector debt and deficits', *Economic Policy*, 1 (1), November, pp. 14–79 (also Chapter 3, this volume).

Buiter, Willem H. (1986) 'Fiscal prerequisites for a viable managed exchange rate regime', in *Wisselkoersen in de veranderende wereld*. Preadviezen van de Vereniging voor de Staathuishoudkunde, Stenfert Kroese, Leiden.

Buiter, Willem H. (1987) 'Borrowing to defend the exchange rate and the timing and magnitude of speculative attacks', *Journal of International Economics*, 23, pp. 221–39.

Buiter, Willem H. (1988a) 'Death, birth, productivity growth and debt neutrality', *Economic Journal*, 98, June, pp. 279–93.

Buiter, Willem H. (1988b) 'Structural and stabilisation aspects of fiscal and financial policy in the dependent economy', *Oxford Economic Papers*, 40, pp. 220–45.

Feltenstein, A. and S. Morris (1987) 'Fiscal stabilisation and exchange rate instability: a theoretical approach and some policy conclusions using Mexican data', mimeo, November.

Flood, R. and P. Garber (1984) 'Collapsing exchange rate regimes: some linear examples', *Journal of International Economics*, 17, pp. 1–13.

Hall, R. E. (1987) 'Equilibrium analysis of monetary non-neutrality', mimeo, October.

Jarque, Carlos M. (1987) 'An empirical study of the determinants of production in Mexico', mimeo, May.

Jung, W. S. (1987) 'Asset demands in Mexico', mimeo, September.

Krugman, P. (1979) 'A model of balance of payments crises', *Journal of Money, Credit and Banking*, August, pp. 311–25.

Obstfeld, M. (1986) 'Rational and self-fulfilling balance of payments crises', *American Economic Review*, 76, (1), March, pp. 72–81.

Sargent, T. J. and N. Wallace (1981) 'Some unpleasant monetarist arithmetic', *Federal Reserve Bank of Minneapolis Quarterly Review*, 5, Fall.

Tanzi, V. (1978) 'Inflation, real tax revenue and the case for inflationary finance: theory with an application to Argentina'. *IMF Staff Papers*, 25, September.

Weil, P. (1985) 'Essays on the valuation of unbacked assets', Ph.D. thesis, Harvard University.

PART V

FISCAL AND FINANCIAL POLICY IN DEVELOPING COUNTRIES

14 · SOME THOUGHTS ON THE ROLE OF FISCAL POLICY IN STABILIZATION AND STRUCTURAL ADJUSTMENT IN DEVELOPING COUNTRIES

14.1 INTRODUCTION

The processes of stabilization and structural adjustment in developing countries and the fiscal policy options that are available can be understood only by recognizing the often extreme initial conditions facing many of the countries concerned. These initial conditions are macroeconomic disequilibrium, both internal and external, and structural disequilibrium.

Macroeconomic disequilibrium is a syndrome containing many or most of the following ingredients: a large (and often unsustainable) public sector financial deficit; a large stock of external debt (often public or *de facto* publicly guaranteed), and severely restricted further access to external credit on commercial terms; a history of capital flight, resulting in a stock of external assets that is beyond the reach of the domestic fiscal authorities; a large incipient current account deficit, sometimes repressed by external credit rationing and by foreign exchange controls imposed by the domestic authorities; an overvalued real exchange rate; a high, although sometimes

Many of the participants at a World Bank (WDR) workshop on fiscal policy in the OECD and in the developing countries (on 30 October 1987) made helpful comments on an earlier draft of this paper which was written as a background paper for the 1988 WDR. Among them were Guillermo Calvo, Vito Tanzi, Sweder van Wijnbergen, Alain Ize and Brian Pinto. Gus Ranis also made a number of helpful suggestions on an earlier draft. The World Bank does not accept responsibility for the views expressed herein which are those of the author and should not be attributed to the World Bank or to its affiliated organizations. The findings, interpretations, and conclusions are the results of research supported by the Bank, they do not necessarily represent official policy of the Bank. The designations employed, the presentation of material, and any maps used in this document are solely for the convenience of the reader and do not imply the expression of any opinion whatsoever on the part of the World Bank or its affiliates concerning the legal status of any country, territory, city, area, or of its authorities, or concerning the delimitation of its boundaries, or national affiliation.

partially repressed, rate of inflation and significant recourse to the inflation tax as a source of public sector revenue; a large internal public debt (in the more advanced developing countries) competing for scarce domestic savings in a generally repressed domestic financial system; a narrow and often inequitable and inefficient public sector revenue base; and real wages in excess of market-clearing levels (and freqently highly index-linked) in the formal or the urban sector and widespread unemployment and under-employment of labor (see, for example, Ahamed, 1986; Dervis and Petri, 1987; Sachs, 1987).

Structural disequilibrium refers to the need for significant changes in the patterns of resource allocation, production and absorption; for major changes in the *modus operandi* of important markets, including the domestic financial markets, the foreign exchange market (and the terms of private access to external credit), the domestic labor market and the domestic goods markets; for far-reaching changes in the system of property rights, rules, regulations and laws that govern production, exchange and distribution; and for changes in the size and scope of the tasks performed by the public sector.

These twin disequilibria, which often interact and reinforce each other, tend to occur against a background of mass poverty, rapid population growth, and major social, cultural and political transformations. Political stability is often in doubt, both as regards the survival of incumbent admini-strations and as regards the viability of the very institutions of government. Credible pre-commitments to any long-term economic strategy are hard to come by in such an environment. Scarce administrative and managerial skills create further obstacles to the design and implementation of economic reforms.

Many of the disequilibria and policy dilemmas just referred to have been encountered also in the industrial countries. The United States today is characterized by unsustainable fiscal and external current account deficits. Hyperinflations occurred in Austria, Germany, Hungary and Poland in the 1920s. Many Western European economies have been diagnosed as suffer-ing during the 1970s and 1980s from a whole array of structural rigidities, sometimes referred to collectively as 'Eurosclerosis', that prevent a full utilization and efficient (re)allocation of resources.

The range and severity of the stabilization and structural adjustment problems faced today by, for example, the IMF's 15 highly indebted coun-tries[1] and by a large number of sub-Saharan African countries[2] are such, however, that a fresh restatement and adaptation of conventional macro-economic analysis focused on these countries' problems seem warranted.

This paper is both selective and eclectic in its coverage and is only intended as a catalyst for a wider-ranging and deeper discussion of the issues (see Buiter, 1986, for an analysis focused on developing country responses to a range of external shocks). The variety of economic systems, stages of economic development, problems and policy issues among the developing and new industrial countries is such that it is very hard indeed to find a useful middle ground between the Scylla of 90-odd book-length country studies and a dozen exhaustive comparative analyses and the Charybdis of ahistorical, institution-free abstractions. Section 14.2 covers the external and internal transfer problems. Section 14.3 considers possible causes for the breakdown of the internal and external transfer processes. Section 14.4 deals with national solvency and Section 14.5 with government solvency. In Section 14.6 the inflation tax is considered in some detail and in Section 14.7 a recent quantitative approach used by the World Bank to evaluate the consistency of certain aspects of a government's fiscal, financial and monetary strategy is evaluated.

14.2 FISCAL POLICY AND THE EXTERNAL AND INTERNAL TRANSFER PROBLEMS

In what follows we consider alternative policies for achieving a given reduction in the external trade deficit. The motivation for seeking this reduction does not matter for the analysis. It may or may not be the sensible or optimal thing to do. Countries (perceived to be) in a situation of unsustainable external imbalance and facing a cut-off of external credit flows may, of course, have no alternative to an increase in net exports, if all other means of obtaining external resources have been exhausted.

To reduce the external current account deficit or to increase the surplus is to increase the *external transfer*. To realize this increased transfer of real purchasing power to the rest of the world an internal reallocation of real resources is required: production and productive resources must be moved from the non-traded goods sector to the traded goods sector, i.e. to the production of exports or import-competing goods. This requires a decline in the relative price of non-traded goods and, if the country has any international market power, a lower relative price of exports: the increased external transfer can be effected only through a lower real exchange and a worsening of the terms of trade. It has by now become established (if sloppy) usage, to refer to the *increase* in the external transfer as the external transfer. I reluctantly adopt this usage where it does not lead to ambiguity or error.

In many developing countries (and indeed in such industrial countries as the United States), an unsustainable or undesirable external deficit tends to be associated, both statistically and causally, with an unsustainable or undesirable public sector financial deficit. The reduction of the external deficit in such cases requires the reduction of the public sector deficit.[3] This can be achieved either through cuts in public spending or through an increase in public sector current revenues: taxes, income from tariffs, public sector fees and charges, and so on. The expression (*internal*) *fiscal transfer* will be used to refer both to government revenue increases and to public spending cuts.[4]

The fundamental economy-wide financial balances identity in Equations (14.1) is a good place to start an analysis of the central role of fiscal policy in stabilization and structural adjustment:

$$S^P - I^P + S^G - I^G \equiv CA \tag{14.1a}$$

$$CA \equiv TB + \frac{EA^*}{P} - i^* \frac{E}{P}[D^* - R^*] \equiv \frac{E}{P}\Delta(R^* - D^*).^{5} \tag{14.1b}$$

S^P is private saving, I^P private domestic capital formation, S^G public sector saving, I^G public sector domestic capital formation, CA the current account surplus on the balance of payments, and TB the trade balance surplus, all measured in terms of real GDP units. A^* is net foreign aid and other current transfer receipts (such as remittances),[6] D^* the stock of foreign debt, and R^* the stock of foreign exchange reserves, all denominated in terms of foreign currency. E is the nominal spot exchange rate, P the domestic GDP deflator, and i^* the foreign nominal interest rate.

It is sometimes informative to present the financial flows in Equations (14.1) 'corrected' or 'adjusted' for asset revaluations, i.e. for capital gains and losses on outstanding stocks of assets and liabilities. In practice this means correcting for the effect of inflation on the real value of nominal assets and liabilities and for the effect of exchange rate changes and inflation on the real value of foreign-currency-denominated financial claims. While there are no issues of principle involved in these measurement or presentational conventions, it is often helpful, since economic theory specifies preferences and production technologies as defined over real commodities, to express our uses and sources of funds in the same manner. Similarly, measuring these asset revaluations-corrected stocks and flows relative to some 'scale variable', such as (trend) real GDP, is helpful when the scale variable is, implicitly or explicitly, used to define a solvency constraint or other feasibility constraint. These issues are considered further in Sections 14.4 and 14.5.

Equations (14.2) introduce the distinction between private and public external debt. This distinction has often been more important formally than substantively. The debt crisis since 1982 has been a recent reminder of the fact that many *de jure* or formally private liabilities are *de facto* publicly guaranteed. Private foreign assets often escape the grasp of the domestic fiscal authorities. Whether one labels this (privately rational) external portfolio diversification or capital flight, one of its consequences is that the tax base becomes narrower, implying the need for higher tax rates on the remaining tax base, increased recourse to seigniorage (the inflation tax) or increased borrowing.

Private and public saving, S^P and S^G, are defined as follows:

$$S^P \equiv Q - J - T + i\frac{B}{P} - i^*\frac{ED^{*P}}{P} - C^P \qquad (14.2a)$$

$$S^G \equiv J + T + \frac{EA^*}{P} - i\frac{B}{P} - i^*\frac{E}{P}(D^{*G} - R^*) - C^G \qquad (14.2b)$$

Q is domestic income or product; J is the cash return on the public sector capital stock; i is the nominal interest rate on domestic-currency-denominated public debt, B, assumed to be held only by the domestic private sector (the central bank is included in the consolidated public sector identity (14.2b)). T is domestic taxes net of current domestic transfers and subsidies; C^P is private consumption and C^G public sector consumption. Q, J, T, C^P and C^G are all measured in real GDP units. D^{*P} is private external debt (including private sector arrearages and D^{*G} public external debt (including public sector arrearages). Note that

$$D^* \equiv D^{*P} + D^{*G}. \qquad (14.3)$$

The trade balance surplus, TB, is the excess of the value of exports over the value of imports. Let X and M denote export and import volume respectively and P_X, P_M and P_N the domestic currency prices of exports, imports and non-traded goods. Then

$$TB \equiv \frac{P_X}{P}X - \frac{P_M}{P}M \qquad (14.4)$$

where

$$X \equiv Q_X - (C_X^P + I_X^P + C_X^G + I_X^G) \qquad (14.5a)$$

and

$$M \equiv C_M^P + I_M^P + C_M^G + I_M^G - Q_M.^7 \qquad (14.5b)$$

Also, ignoring imported raw materials and imported intermediate inputs

$$Q \equiv (P_X Q_X + P_M Q_M + P_N Q_N)P^{-1}. \qquad (14.6)$$

For simplicity, we approximate the GDP deflator, P, with a Cobb–Douglas weighted average of the prices of traded goods, P_T, and non-traded goods, P_N, where α is the share of non-traded goods in GDP:

$$P = P_T^{1-\alpha} P_N^{\alpha} \qquad 0 \leqslant \alpha \leqslant 1. \qquad (14.7)$$

The traded goods GDP deflator is also approximated with a Cobb–Douglas weighted average of the prices of exports and imports, where β is the share of importables production in the total production of traded goods:

$$P_T = P_X^{1-\beta} P_M^{\beta} \qquad 0 \leqslant \beta \leqslant 1. \qquad (14.8)$$

From Equations (14.1) and (14.2) we obtain the familiar absorption identities in Equations (14.9), that the current account surplus is the excess of national income over domestic absorption and that the trade balance surplus equals the excess of domestic income over domestic absorption:

$$Q + \frac{EA^*}{P} - i^* \frac{E}{P} (D^* - R^*) - (C^P + I^P + C^G + I^G) \equiv CA \quad (14.9a)$$

$$Q - (C^P + I^P + C^G + I^G) \equiv TB \quad (14.9b)$$

From Equations (14.1a) and (14.9a) we see that an increase in the current account surplus requires an increase in the combined private and public sector financial surpluses or, equivalently, an increase in national income relative to domestic (private plus public) absorption. This underlines the likelihood of a *fiscal dimension* to a current account improvement: most models of private consumption behavior suggest that, holding constant taste, technology and external parameters, public revenue increases and/or spending cuts will in general be necessary and sufficient to increase the sum of the public sector financial surplus and private saving. The main exceptions are those models of private consumption behavior that exhibit debt neutrality such as representative agent models or overlapping generations models with operative intergenerational gift and bequest motives. Such models are extremely unlikely to describe accurately private consumption behavior in developing and semi-industrial countries. Ignoring them in what follows, and assuming that public revenue increases or spending cuts do not boost private capital formation, fiscal retrenchment will reduce national absorption relative to national income.

Equation (14.9a) underlines the desirability of achieving a current account improvement via an increase in income rather than through a reduction in absorption. Three channels are potentially available for this: increased domestic output; increased foreign aid; and a reduction in foreign interest obligations, either by reducing the interest rate on the external debt or by writing down the debt.

A boost to domestic output, Q, can be achieved either by taking up any slack due to deficient aggregate demand or by fiscal or other measures aimed at boosting aggregate supply. Since output and absorption need not be behaviorally independent of each other, it is essential to adopt a general equilibrium approach when evaluating alternative policies to improve the current account. For example, successful supply-side measures, by raising both current and permanent income, can be expected to stimulate private consumption. They may also induce a positive response of domestic private investment. The net effect on the current account need not be positive, absent further measures to restrain absorption.

Fiscal measures to stimulate output under conditions of Keynesian excess capacity will involve expansionary actions such as tax cuts, public spending increases or expansionary monetary or credit policy measures that (subject to well-known qualifications concerning the exchange rate regime and the degree of international capital mobility) are likely to worsen the current account.

Increased foreign aid will only improve the current account, given output, if some fraction of the aid inflow is not spent. If the increased aid relaxes a foreign exchange bottleneck and if the additional external resources are dedicated to the importation of essential foreign productive inputs, it can boost supply. To the extent that the increased volume of production does not generate a matching increase in private or public spending, this will improve the current account.

Exactly the same holds as regards the current account consequences of a reduction in external interest payments. The one-for-one improvement in the current account caused by interest rate or debt relief at given levels of output and absorption, will be augmented by any positive supply response in countries where production is foreign-exchange-constrained. It will be correspondingly diminished by any positive effect of debt relief on public or private spending.

Equation (14.9a) also emphasizes that, even if a reduction in absorption is the current-account-improving policy of choice, there are still a number of ways of skinning that cat, each of which will have different short-run and long-run supply consequences and distributional implications. Absorption cuts can be aimed at public spending or at private spending and, within each of these categories, at consumption or at investment. Private spending can be cut by raising taxes or tariffs, by cutting subsidies or by raising the cost and/or availability of credit to the private sector. Taxing imported luxury consumer durables will have very different distributional implications from cutting subsidies on the staple foods consumed mainly by the poor. The distributional consequences of changes in exhaustive public spending (education, health, and so on) may be as important as those of variations in transfer payments or taxes. They should be considered together with the allocative consequences and, in demand-constrained sectors of the economy, the Keynesian, cyclical output effects.

These distributional effects of absorption-reducing policy measures can be reinforced or offset by changes in the distribution of factor incomes (wages of different types of labor, rental incomes from the ownership of different types of land; profits accruing to the owners of different types of capital and rentier incomes). This is considered briefly in Section 14.3.

The fiscal dimension of a current account improvement can only be understood properly by recognizing that policies to influence the current account are *ipso facto* concerned with the nation's intertemporal allocation of resources. Intertemporal relative (shadow) prices such as the real interest rate, the rates of return on other assets and, in repressed financial systems with widespread credit rationing, both the cost and availability of credit, will play a central role in the transmission mechanism between fiscal policy actions and current account outcomes. When, for example, the domestic financial markets are not perfectly integrated with the global financial markets, bond-financed fiscal tightening will tend to result in lower domestic real interest rates or less severe credit rationing. Even when domestic asset returns are fixed by the rest of the world, the nation's solvency constraint and that of the public sector (discussed in Sections 14.4 and 14.5) imply that fiscal tightening today implies fiscal relaxation (relative to what otherwise would have been the case) in the future.

Equations (14.4) and (14.5) bring out the static relative price and resource reallocation dimensions of a current account improvement. In the short run, given the foreign interest rate, the net stock of external debt and the aid flow, a current account improvement is the same thing as a trade balance improvement.[8] A trade balance improvement requires an increase in the production of tradables and/or a reduction in the absorption of tradables. This will in general require changes in the real exchange rate (the relative price of traded and non-traded goods) and, if the country in question has some international market power, in the terms of trade (the relative price of exports and imports).

Fiscal tightening (an increase in taxes or a cut in public sector absorption) will almost certainly reduce the demand for non-traded goods at the initial real exchange rate. Income tax or indirect tax increases will reduce private consumption, part of which will fall on non-traded goods. Higher taxes on profits and tighter private sector credit rationing will discourage private investment which often has a significant non-traded goods component. Public spending cuts are also likely to fall to a significant extent on non-traded goods. In a well-functioning economy with a flexible relative price of traded to non-traded goods and resource mobility between the traded and non-traded goods sectors, a fiscal contraction will reduce the relative price of non-traded goods and cause a movement of resources into the traded goods sector. This eliminates the incipient excess supply of non-traded goods at the old real exchange rate.

The non-traded goods market equilibrium condition, given in Equation (14.10), permits one to summarize the proximate determinants of the real exchange rate in a convenient manner:

$$Q_N = C_N^P + I_N^P + C_N^G + I_N^G. \tag{14.10}$$

Given the economy-wide resource endowments and the degree of intersectoral resource mobility, Q_N is a decreasing function of the real exchange rate $\pi \equiv P_T/P_N$, and Q_T is an increasing function (see, for example, Dornbusch, 1980). The concave production possibility frontier is the curve AB in Figure 14.1.

Given aggregate real private consumption, private consumption of non-

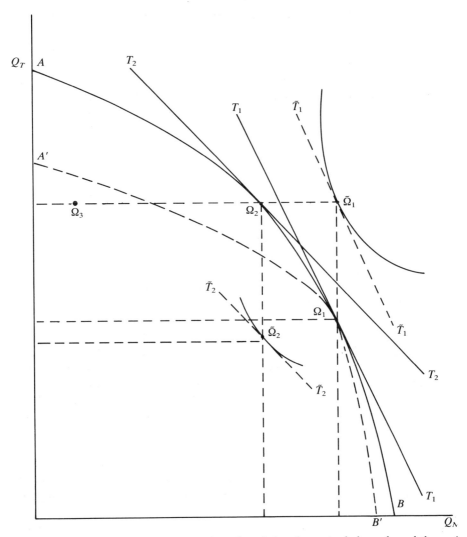

Figure 14.1 Production and consumption of traded and non-traded goods and the real exchange rate

traded goods is an increasing function of the real exchange rate. In the Cobb–Douglas (constant expenditure shares) case this yields:

$$C_N^P = \tilde{a}\pi^{(1-\tilde{a})}C^P \qquad\qquad 0 < \tilde{a} < 1. \qquad (14.11)$$

The share of non-traded consumption in total consumption is denoted $\tilde{a}$.[9]

A current tax increase reduces aggregate consumption (barring debt neutrality). In Figure 14.1, this causes a movement of production from a point such as Ω_1 to a point such as Ω_2.[10] Absorption would move from a point such as $\bar{\Omega}_1$ (with a trade balance deficit measured by the vertical distance $\bar{\Omega}_1 - \Omega_1$) to a point such as $\bar{\Omega}_2$ (with a trade balance surplus measured by the vertical distance $\Omega_2 - \bar{\Omega}_2$). The relative price of non-traded goods (measured by the absolute values of the tangents to the production possibility frontier (T_1T_1 and T_2T_2) and the indifference curves ($\bar{T}_1\bar{T}_1$ and $\bar{T}_2\bar{T}_2$)) falls, i.e. π rises. The same qualitative effects follow from a cut in public spending on non-traded goods; even if this were tax-financed, the marginal private spending share on non-traded goods is less than 100 per cent.

Restrictions on factor mobility, but still unrestricted flexibility of factor prices and relative goods prices, would result in a production possibility frontier such as $A'B'$ that lies everywhere inside the 'full mobility frontier' AB, except at the initial status quo position Ω_1.

Rigid relative prices or the emergence of Keynesian demand-constrained equilibria would show up as movements inside the production possibility frontier in response to a contraction of aggregate demand. For example, in the small-country case where traded goods output is never demand-constrained, one could get a production equilibrium at Ω_3 instead of at Ω_2 after a fiscal contraction: excess capacity and unemployment emerge in the non-traded goods sector. Where the country has some market power in the markets for its tradables, demand-deficient excess capacity and unemployment can emerge also in the traded goods sector following a fiscal contraction.

An issue requiring both more empirical and more analytical research concerns those characteristics of countries that render them more likely to experience 'Keynesian' or demand-constrained excess capacity and unemployment when subjected to policies aimed at reducing absorption. The existence of a large modern or 'formal' non-traded goods sector with production for the market rather than for subsistence or, in the traded goods sector, a downward-sloping rather inelastic world demand schedule for exportables, seems necessary for the emergence of demand-constrained equilibria. So is the existence of nominal inertia or stickiness of money wages or output prices. The larger and more developed Southern Cone countries, and countries such as Korea and Taiwan, therefore seem more likely to undergo episodes of Keynesian excess capacity when fiscal and/or monetary policy are tightened than the poorer and smaller developing countries with less extensive formal sectors. Even in the Latin American and East Asian NICs, wage and price flexibility could reduce the likelihood and severity of demand-deficient recessions. Little is known of the peculiarities of wage and price determination in developing countries, and of the extent to which the industrial country parables based on nominal or real wage rigidities need to be adapted to fit the institutions and experiences of about 100 very heterogeneous developing and new industrial countries.

Within the traded goods sector, changes in the composition of production and demand are likely in response to a fiscal contraction (see, for example, Buiter, 1988, for a recent theoretical analysis using an intertemporal model). Figure 14.2a shows an initial production equilibrium for importables and exportables at Ω_1 on the QQ locus. Domestic demand for exportables and import-competing good is at $\tilde{\Omega}_1$, with a trade balance deficit (measured in imports) of $B\tilde{\Omega}_1$. The fiscal contraction moves resources out of the non-traded goods sector into the traded goods sector. The production possibility frontier for exportables and importables moves to $Q'Q'$. In the small-country case considered in Figure 14.2a, the terms of trade are unchanged. If the resources released by the non-traded goods sector do not favour either the exporting or import-competing sector, the new production point will be one like Ω_2 in Figure 14.2a: both export production and import-competing production will increase.

The fiscal contraction which started off the whole process will reduce the demand for imports as well as for exportable goods (barring very different income effects on the demand for exportables and imports). The new domestic demand point is at $\tilde{\Omega}_2$ with a trade balance surplus (measured in imports) of $\tilde{\Omega}_2 B'$.

A country facing a downward-sloping export demand schedule would experience a worsening in its terms of trade as resources moved into the tradables sector. Compared with the constant terms of trade case, the increase in the production of tradables would favor import-competing goods rather than the production of exportables. In Figure 14.2b the production point would move from Ω_1 to a point such as Ω_2' rather than Ω_2 which would have been chosen at constant terms of trade.[11] Domestic demand (not shown in Figure 14.2b) would be moved towards exportables and away from import-competing goods, compared to what would happen at constant terms of trade.

14.3 BREAKDOWNS IN THE INTERNAL AND EXTERNAL TRANSFER PROCESSES

What can go wrong in the external–internal transfer process? First, it may be economically or politically impossible to effect the internal fiscal transfer. This means either that the government's fiscal instrumentarium is insufficient or that it is unwilling or unable to use it in the manner and to the extent required.

On the public expenditure side, there is little point in a government committing itself to a program of spending cuts if any attempt to implement such cuts leads to the fall of the government and its replacement by a government unwilling to contemplate serious cuts. For example, severe cuts in spending on the military raise the danger of a military coup. Cuts in food subsidies, in public sector civilian pay or employment or in Treasury subsidies to loss-making state enterprises, can lead to unrest, especially among the urbanized, unionized and better-educated sections of society capable of undermining or toppling governments. Debtor country governments often play the 'political constraints on public spending cuts' card quite skilfully in their negotiations with multilateral lending agencies, and foreign private and official creditors. While these constraints may be real, they are not independent of the past, present and anticipated future actions of the governments in question and the scope for strategic behavior is considerable.

Raising current revenues is difficult in most developing countries, given their narrow tax base. For decades, widening the tax base (through a more broadly-based income tax; through more effective enforcement of existing income tax rules; through a broadly-based sales tax; through expenditure taxes, and so on) has been a standard recommendation from anyone considering options for fiscal reform in developing countries, but relatively little has happened thus far. The recommendation is nevertheless repeated here.

Figures 14.3, 14.4 and 14.5 and Table 14.1 show how the overall tax burden and its composition differ across developing countries and between developing and industrial countries. The greater role of direct taxes on labor income (including social security taxes) in the industrial countries stands out, as does the quite important role of taxes on international trade in the developing countries, especially the poorest and the more open ones.

Capital flight is another factor contributing to a narrow revenue base. While capital flight occurs partly in response to macroeconomic mismanagement (such as the maintenance of an overvalued exchange rate) part of it is likely to be motivated by a desire to evade taxes. The industrial countries that are the recipients of much of this flight capital could strengthen the fiscal position of many developing countries by reporting foreign investment income to the fiscal authorities of the developing countries or even by acting as their agents in collecting taxes that are due.

Through asset sales, including privatization of publicly owned industries, the government can achieve an apparent once-off improvement of its revenue. If these assets yielded a positive net cash flow to the government, the short-run improvement of its financial position will be reversed in the longer run. The asset sale is a financing item and, like public sector borrowing, belongs 'below the line'. There may, of course, be excellent reasons for wishing to privatize, including hoped-for positive incentive effects leading to efficiency and productivity gains in the privatized industries. Revenue considerations should, however, not play a role except

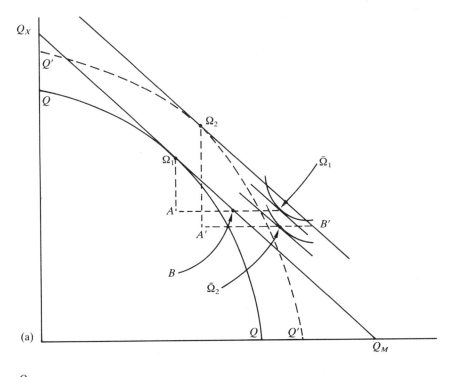

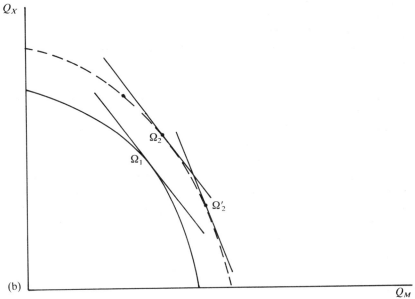

Figure 14.2 Production and consumption of exportables and import-competing goods and the terms of trade

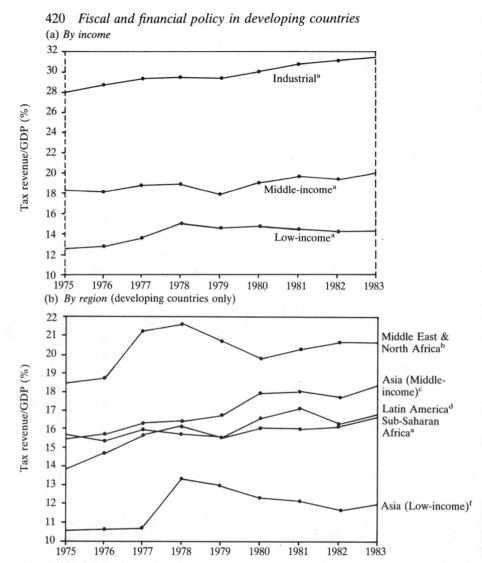

Figure 14.3 Trends in tax to GDP ratios, 1975–83

Note: Figures are unweighted, representing the average pattern for countries in the sample. The period, 1975–83, yields the largest comparable sample based on available data.
[a] Industrial sample includes 17 countries, middle-income includes 34 countries, and low-income includes 11 countries.
[b] Includes Burkina Faso, Burundi, Cameroon, Liberia, Kenya, Mali, Senegal, Tanzania, Zaire, and Zimbabwe.
[c] Includes Indonesia, Korea, Malaysia, Singapore, and Thailand.
[d] Includes Argentina, Brazil, Chile, Colombia, Costa Rica, Dominican Republic, Guatemala, Mexico, Nicaragua, Panama, Paraguay, Uruguay, and Venezuela.
[e] Includes Egypt, Iran, Israel, Morocco, Oman, Syria, Tunisia, Turkey, and Yemen.
[f] Includes India, Nepal, Pakistan, and Sri Lanka.
Source: IMF. *Government Finance Statistics*, 1986. Reproduced from World Bank, *World Development Report*, 1988.

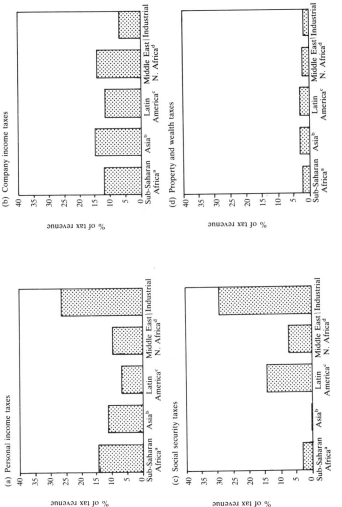

Figure 14.4 Regional variation in direct taxes, 1983

Note: Figures are unweighted, representing the average pattern for countries in the sample. The period, 1975–83, yields the largest comparable sample based on available data.
[a] Sub-Saharan Africa includes Burkina Faso, Burundi, Cameroon, Gambia, Lesotho, Liberia, Mali, Senegal, Tanzania, and Zaire.
[b] Asia includes India, Indonesia, Korea, Malaysia, Nepal, Pakistan, Singapore, Sri Lanka, and Thailand.
[c] Latin America includes Argentina, Barbados, Brazil, Chile, Colombia, Costa Rica, Dominican Republic, Guatemala, Guyana, Mexico, Nicaragua, Panama, Paraguay, Uruguay, and Venezuela.
[d] Middle East/North Africa includes Egypt, Iran, Israel, Morocco, Tunisia, Turkey, and Yemen (Arab Republic).
[e] Industrial includes WDR industrial market economies except Japan and New Zealand.
Source: as Figure 14.3.

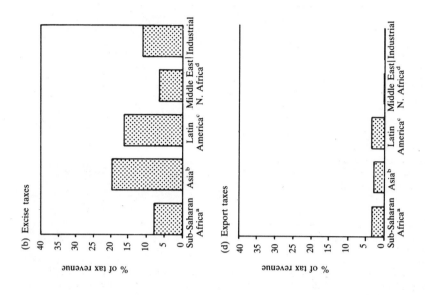

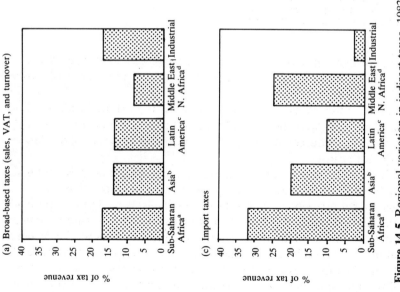

Figure 14.5 Regional variation in indirect taxes, 1983

Note: see Figure 14.4
Source: as Figure 14.3

Table 14.1 Variations in tax composition for various countries, grouped by income, 1975 and 1983

	Low-income[c]		Middle-income[d]		Industrial[e]	
Tax category[b]	1975	1983	1975	1983	1975	1983
Domestic income	19.6	19.9	30.5	31.4	34.0	33.3
Individual	(9.9)	(9.6)	(9.4)	(10.7)	(26.4)	(26.2)
Corporate	(8.4)	(8.4)	(13.1)	(13.5)	(7.3)	(7.1)
Other direct taxes	7.9	7.3	18.5	17.0	31.7	33.1
Social security	(1.0)	(2.2)	(12.9)	(10.1)	(28.2)	(29.6)
Property	(3.4)	(2.5)	(2.8)	(2.6)	(2.1)	(1.8)
Domestic commodity	29.0	35.8	26.6	30.8	29.9	30.6
Sales, VAT, turnover	(11.1)	(18.8)	(7.9)	(10.5)	(16.0)	(16.6)
Excises	(11.1)	(13.1)	(13.1)	(13.3)	(10.9)	(11.1)
International trade	43.6	37.0	24.4	20.8	4.5	2.9
Import	(32.9)	(32.6)	(19.6)	(16.2)	(4.4)	(2.7)
Export	(7.7)	(3.8)	(3.5)	(1.4)	(0.1)	(0.2)

Source: Government Finance Statistics. Reproduced from World Bank, *World Development Report 1988*.
Notes:
a. Figures are unweighted representing the average pattern for countries in the sample.
b. Figures for subcategories do not add up to the figure for each category due to the presence of smaller unallocated taxes.
c. Low-income sample includes 11 countries.
d. Middle-income sample includes 36 countries.
e. Industrial market includes 19 countries.

to the extent that the government can sell the assets to the private sector at a price in excess of the present discounted value of future net cash flows under continued public ownership.

Even if the internal fiscal transfer is effected, the external transfer may not materialize because there is full financial crowding-out (or crowding-in) or because resources do not flow in the right direction and relative prices do not adjust.

The financial crowding-out mechanism is likely to be quite different in a financially repressed, credit-rationed developing country than it is in an industrial country where interest rates and financial asset prices approximate the market-clearing paradigm more closely. With private spending constrained by the availability of rationed credit, the effect on the current account of an increase in taxes would, with a marginal propensity to spend of unity, not be offset (even in part) by a reduction in private saving. 'Debt neutrality', the independence of private consumption and investment of the government's mix of borrowing and tax financing[12] would a priori seem extremely unlikely in credit-rationed developing countries. The preliminary findings of Haque (1986) and of Haque and Montiel (1987), which do not reject the null hypothesis of debt neutrality for a number of developing countries, are therefore very surprising. With debt neutrality, government deficit reductions brought about through tax increases would lead to an equal reduction in private saving, leaving the current account unchanged. Permanent cuts in 'exhaustive' public spending also would merely result in an equal increase in private consumption and no effect on the trade balance. It seems extremely unlikely that developing countries (or indeed industrial countries) exhibit debt neutrality, but more robust empirical evidence on the nature and degree of 'financial crowding-out' on the demand side would be most useful.

Economists of the structuralist school have long emphasized the possibility of supply-side financial crowding-out and this possibility has also been recognized more recently in 'mainstream' macroeconomics (see, for example, Blinder, 1987). The simplest version of this involves an 'Austrian' production model with lags between the application of inputs and the emergence of saleable output. Such lags create a need for working capital to finance the process of production; the cost and availability of this working capital can affect (or even constrain) supply. Reductions in public sector borrowing permitted by lower public sector deficits brought about through spending cuts can therefore boost supply even in the short run. The effect of this supply-side stimulus on the current account will depend on the extent to which it induces an increase in private absorption. (What is good news for the economy need not be good news for the current account.)

The resource reallocation from the non-traded goods sector to the traded goods sector may not take place to the required extent, or at all. Where intersectoral resource immobility reflects real economic rigidities (skill mismatch, spatially separated labor markets, and so on) without serious externalities there is no prima-facie case for policy intervention on efficiency grounds. Where inefficient laws, rules and regulations in labor markets, housing markets and credit markets unnecessarily restrict the mobility of labor and other resources, the usual first-best policy prescriptions apply: eliminate the sources of the inefficiency.

The implications of fiscal adjustment for factor prices (and the distribution of 'primary' incomes) depend both on the degree of intersectoral factor mobility and on the factor intensities of production in the different sectors. Owners of factors 'specific to' the contracting sectors (typically the non-traded goods sector in the case of a fiscal contraction) will suffer a loss of rents to these fixed factors. Even where and when factors are mobile and priced competitively, the owners of factors used relatively intensively in the contracting sectors will suffer a fall in real income. If these potential losers are well organized or easily mobilized and if they cannot be bought off with an acceptable compensation scheme, they may be able to block the policy changes and prevent the necessary adjustment.

Even if compensation of losers is feasible, it is likely to be distortionary and the efficiency losses involved in the side-payments mechanisms should be taken into account in a comprehensive cost–benefit analysis.

Rent-seeking behavior may become especially intense when the status quo is threatened; the real resource cost of directly-unproductive (DUP activities) will have to be added to the cost of failing to implement the fiscal program, if the activities are successful.

The signal that both indicates the need for resource movements and motivates them is often (but not always) a change in relative prices. The adjustment process following a fiscal contraction can be frustrated by the failure to achieve a sufficiently large depreciation of the real exchange rate, i.e. a decline in the relative price of non-traded goods. This is not too surprising once one realizes that a depreciation of the real exchange rate tends to be associated with a reduction in real consumption wages.[13]

Rigid real wages in excess of market clearing values are often maintained in the formal sector through a combination of union pressure, public sector employment and pay rules and a high degree of index-linking of money wages to the cost of living. Achieving a real depreciation in such a setting means rather more than implementing a nominal 'maxi-devaluation' and validating this through appropriate supporting fiscal policies (see, for example, Khan and Lizondo, 1987; van Wijnbergen, 1986). It means achieving a change in the balance of power in the labor market by weakening organized labor and strengthening employers, private and public, through legislation and other measures. Having altered the fundamental determinants of industrial bargaining (and lobbying) power (a process likely to involve significant political and social conflict), a nominal maxi-devaluation may well, of course, be helpful in achieving any target real devaluation at least cost. For a nominal devaluation to be superior to a nominal wage and price reduction, some form of nominal inertia in wage or price determination must be present, or the asset revaluations associated with nominal maxi-devaluations must be less disruptive (or contractionary) than those associated with reductions in domestic nominal costs and prices. The rigidities stressed in most discussions of developing countries' labor markets are, however, real, not nominal rigidities. Nominal inertia (both in the level and rate of change of money wages and prices) may, however, result from lags in the indexation process, staggered, overlapping wage contracts and slow adjustment in inflationary expectations. Possible short-run contractionary effects of maxi-devaluations have been stressed by many experts (see, for example, Diaz-Alejandro, 1965; Krugman and Taylor, 1978; van Wijnbergen, 1986; Edwards, 1986). Even as a facilitating instrument in a real exchange rate adjustment that is warranted by the fundamentals, nominal maxi-devaluations do not appear to be an automatic policy choice.

Note that 'once-off' maxi-devaluations are quite distinct from choosing a higher rate of crawl in a crawling peg exchange rate regime. If the government's fiscal and financial policy choices imply a permanently higher rate of monetary growth and (eventually) a permanently higher rate of inflation, a higher rate of depreciation of the nominal exchange rate is implied, eventually. Different rates of (anticipated) inflation imply different amounts of seigniorage or (anticipated) inflation tax extraction. The fiscal aspects of the inflation tax are considered in Section 14.6 below.

Incomes policy, i.e. direct wage (and possibly price) controls, too, will not be helpful in achieving a lasting real depreciation unless it changes the underlying balance of power in the labor market. It may, of course, still be helpful in facilitating the transition from a high rate of inflation (or even a hyperinflation) to a lower rate of inflation at least cost in terms of output and employment forgone, by breaking the vicious 'after-you' equilibrium of oligopolistic wage and price determination and, perhaps, by adding to the credibility of the accompanying fiscal–monetary–exchange-rate policy package. Both incomes policy and nominal exchange rate policy can be used to 'signal' government intentions and to 'break' a non-cooperative wage and price setting equilibrium by acting as a co-ordinating device for oligopolistic unions and firms.

Finally, even if the right fiscal correction is undertaken, *and* the private financial surplus does not decline one for one with the public sector financial deficit, *and* the real exchange rate depreciates *and* resources flow out of the non-traded into the traded goods sector, the resulting improvement in the trade balance may have the wrong composition as regards increases in exports versus reductions in imports. Without detailed information on the productive technologies, economy-wide factor supplies, intersectoral factor mobility, global and domestic demands, it is impossible to determine whether the resources flowing into the traded goods sectors should be allocated to the production of exportables or of import-competing goods. The 1987 WDR suggested that, as an empirical matter, many developing countries had contravened their true international comparative advantage by favoring import competition over export promotion through overvalued exchange rates, tariffs, non-tariff barriers to trade, selective use of subsidies and credit rationing, and so on. Even where this is true, the magnitude of the corrective policy response that is required is by no means obvious. The identification and pursuit of comparative advantage in a highly distorted economy is very difficult, not only politically, but also as a narrowly technical or conceptual issue.

14.4 THE SOLVENCY OF A NATION

In this section the solvency of a national economy is studied not because solvency is necessarily (or even frequently) a binding constraint on external borrowing strategies, but because the 'forward-looking' accounting framework involved in solvency assessments can be used to evaluate the internal consistency of any set of plans for external borrowing, debt service, exports, imports and other current external transactions.

Time-consistent external debt strategies, i.e. plans for external borrowing and repayment which are at each instant in the perceived self-interest of the sovereign borrowers and the creditors (absent 'third party' enforcement of the laws of contract, including the laws of bankruptcy), may well lie strictly in the interior of what would be the feasible set in the presence of credible, binding commitments by debtors and creditors. Even such (socially suboptimal) time-consistent plans must, however, be feasible or internally consistent. This section and the next focus almost exclusively on the narrow issue that current and future plans should 'add up'. For the analysis of the positive and normative issues of sovereign borrowing, ability and willingness to pay, see, for example, Eaton and Gersovitz, 1981a; 1981b; 1983; Eaton *et al.*, 1986; Kletzer, 1984.

Consider the current account identity in Equation (14.1b). Let $F^* \equiv R^* - D^*$ be the nation's stock of net foreign assets, $f^* \equiv EF^*/PQ$ the stock of net foreign assets as a fraction of GDP, $tb \equiv TB/Q$ the trade balance surplus as a fraction of GDP and $a^* \equiv EA^*/PQ$ foreign aid and other current transfers from abroad as a proportion of GDP. Let n be the proportional growth rate of real GDP, π the domestic rate of GDP inflation, π^* the world rate of GDP inflation, ε the proportional rate of depreciation of the nominal exchange rate, γ the proportional rate of depreciation of the real exchange rate (defined here as the ratio of the foreign GDP deflator times the nominal exchange rate to the domestic GDP deflator) and r^* the foreign real interest rate.[14] It follows that

$$\gamma \equiv \varepsilon + \pi^* - \pi$$

and

$$r^* \equiv i^* - \pi^*.$$

Using these notational conventions, Equation (14.1b) can be rewritten as:

$$\Delta f^* \equiv tb + a^* + (r^* + \gamma - n)f^*. \tag{14.12}$$

Note that a depreciating real exchange rate ($\gamma > 0$) raises the domestic real resource cost of any given foreign real interest rate. The 'asset-revaluations-and-real-growth-corrected' current account identity in Equation (14.12) implies the intertemporal national budget constraint, present value national budget constraint or national solvency constraint given in Equation (14.13).

$$-f^*(s) \equiv PV(s; tb + a^*; r^* + \gamma - n). \tag{14.3}$$

$PV(s; tb + a^*; r^* + \gamma - n)$ denotes the present discounted value, at time s, of the entire planned or expected future stream of trade balance surpluses plus net foreign current transfers (as fractions of GDP) $tb + a^*$, where the discount rate is the real-exchange-rate-depreciation-corrected foreign real interest rate $(r^* + \gamma)$ minus the growth rate of real GDP, n. Equation (14.13) means that the present discounted value of future trade balance surpluses plus net inflows of foreign aid and remittances (as a proportion of GDP) is just equal to the nation's current net external debt (as a proportion of GDP).[15] The sum of the trade balance surplus and the net current transfers will be referred to henceforth as the nation's *primary surplus*.

The nation's primary surplus is occasionally called the nation's net resource transfer. In principle names do not matter, although poorly chosen names can sometimes confuse the unwary. The primary surplus is the excess of *domestic* income over national absorption. The current account surplus is the excess of *national* income over national absorption.

The primary surplus measures the nation's net resource transfer to the rest of the world when domestic income is taken as the 'bench-mark' or 'origin' relative to which transfers are measured. The current account surplus measures the nation's net resource transfer to the rest of the world if national income is taken as the bench-mark or origin. The first transfer concept emphasizes the *location* of resources and the income streams they yield within the nation's boundaries. The second concept focuses on the *ownership* of resources and the associated income streams by national residents, irrespective of the location of the resources.

An emphasis on the 'territorial' definition over the 'ownership' definition (or vice versa) is sometimes adopted by those with strong views on the (il)legitimacy or priority of foreign ownership claims on national resources (directly or through the tax system). It is (fortunately) not necessary for what follows to become sidetracked any further into these semantic discussions.

Equation (14.13) follows from the asset-revaluations and real-growth-corrected current account identity (14.12) only if the following rather technical-sounding condition holds. The present discounted value of the nation's net external debt in the very distant (strictly speaking infinitely far) future is zero.[16] What this means is that, ultimately, the external debt–GDP ratio has to grow at a rate less than $r^* + \gamma - n$, or, equivalently, that the real external debt ultimately has to grow at a rate less than $r^* + \gamma$, or again that the foreign currency value of the external debt ultimately should grow at a rate below i^*. Ultimately, therefore, the country will have to run primary surpluses in order to service (pay the interest on) its debt. Solvency does not require that the debt be repaid, only that it is not possible indefinitely to finance the interest bill through further borrowing: at some stage primary surpluses must be achieved and any further borrowing will not be sufficient to pay the entire existing interest bill. The nation cannot play a successful Ponzi game.

A debtor country (with $f^* < 0$) facing a real interest rate on its debt in excess of the real growth rate need, in principle, never achieve any *current account surpluses* in order to pursue a strategy consistent with solvency;[17] it must be capable of generating, at some point, primary surpluses. A rising debt–GDP ratio is not by itself evidence of imminent or ultimate insolvency; only a debt–GDP ratio scheduled to rise indefinitely at a rate in excess of $r^* + \gamma - n$ would spell eventual default or repudiation.

Given the existing debt, the primary surpluses projected for the future and the projected future interest rates, expressions such as (14.13),[18] can be used to assess the consistency of the external debt strategy. If, under current policy projections, Equation (14.13) is violated (specifically if the left-hand side exceeds the right-hand side) this does not mean that default is inevitable, only that the strategy under consideration will not work. What will 'give' to achieve equality in Equation (14.13) is what the debate during the current debt crisis is all about. The lenders would like to see larger trade balance surpluses by the borrowers (larger tb values in Equation (14.13) and indeed current account surpluses to reduce the creditors' exposure in the debtor countries). The borrowers would like to see some combination of more aid (larger a^*), lower interest rates (lower r^*), better terms of trade (negative γ), higher growth (larger n) or a write-down or write-off of (part of) the debt (a smaller absolute value of $-f^*$).

Capital flight introduces an important further dimension to Equations (14.12) and (14.13). Net foreign assets, F^*, consist of official foreign exchange reserves, R^*, and, in many developing countries, of a large amount of private foreign claims or assets $-D^{*P}$ against which is set a large amount of public or publicly guaranteed debt, D^{*G}. The income from the private overseas asset holdings often either stays abroad or, if repatriated, manages to escape the domestic fiscal authorities. Similarly, new private capital outflows are often beyond the control of the domestic authorities. Much of the debt crisis debate then effectively focuses on the left-hand side of the rearranged balance of payments Equation (14.14):

$$\Delta D^{*G} \equiv \Delta R^* - \left[\frac{PTB}{E} + A^*\right] + i^*(D^{*G} - R^*) + (i^*D^{*P} - \Delta D^{*P}). \tag{14.14}$$

The lenders are concerned with the developing country's debts (D^{*G}), not with its unattachable assets. Income from these assets tends to stay abroad (i^*D^{*P}, which is negative, automatically 'disappears' into $-\Delta D^{*P}$). Even the building-up of reserves by the monetary authorities is often viewed with suspicion, as being 'at the expense of' debt service or, worse, in anticipation of a post-repudiation cash-in-advance international trading regime for the country.

Other critics have pointed out causal links between ΔD^{*G} and ΔD^{*P}, with new foreign lending to the public sector of highly indebted developing countries disappearing virtually instantaneously as private capital flight,

Table 14.2 Some estimates of capital flight in new industrial countries ($ billion)

	1979	1980	1981	1982	1983	1984
Argentina	2.2	3.5	4.5	7.6	1.3	−3.4
Brazil	1.3	2.0	−1.4	1.8	0.5	4.0
Korea	−0.5	−0.7	−0.8	0.5	−0.7	−0.6
Mexico	−1.1	2.2	2.6	4.7	9.3	2.6
Philippines	0.0	−0.1	1.3	0.0	−1.5	−1.8
Venezuela	3.0	4.8	5.4	3.2	3.1	4.0

Notes: These estimates use Wm. Cline's definition of capital flight as computed by Cumby and Levich (1987).

and at times returning to the lending banks by return of electronic mail.

In the limit, capital flight and the associated tax evasion mean that, effectively, the nation's private external assets cease to be part of its true economic base and certainly of its public sector revenue base, leaving only the public external liabilities. This threatens the solvency of potentially viable nations. That the problem is serious can be inferred from Table 14.2 which reproduces some estimates by Cumby and Levich (1987) of the extent of flight capital for a number of countries.

14.5 THE SOLVENCY OF THE PUBLIC SECTOR

The discussion of 'national solvency' in the previous section should not lead one to think of any country, developing or industrial, as being well characterized by a single representative, national agent, i.e. a behaviorally consolidated private-cum-public sector with full command over all national resources. As the external transfer in most developing countries is mediated through the public sector, separate consideration of the financial accounts, solvency constraint, spending program and revenue basis of the public sector is in order.[19]

Equation (14.15) gives the budget identity of the consolidated public sector, i.e. general government, central bank and state enterprises.

$$\frac{\Delta H}{P} + \frac{\Delta B}{P} + \frac{E}{P}(\Delta D^{*G} - \Delta R^*) \equiv C^G + I^G - \frac{EA^*}{P} - T - J + \frac{iB}{P}$$

$$+ \, i^* \frac{E}{P}(D^{*G} - R^*). \tag{14.15}$$

H is the nominal stock of high-powered money or reserve money, i.e. the monetary base. It consists of coin and currency held by the public and reserves held by the commerical banking system and bears a zero nominal interest rate. Gross public sector capital formation, I^G, the public sector capital stock, K^G, and the depreciation rate of the public sector capital stock, δ, are related by

$$\Delta K^G \equiv I^G - \delta K^G.$$

$F^{*G} \equiv R^* - D^{*G}$ is the government's net stock of foreign assets. The government's gross return from the public sector capital stock, J, can be written as the product of the capital stock K^G, and its gross rate of return, η, i.e.

$$J \equiv \eta K^G.$$

We also define the following ratios to GDP:

$$h \equiv H/PQ$$

$$k^G \equiv K^G/Q$$

$$b \equiv \frac{B}{PQ}$$

$$c^G \equiv \frac{C^G}{Q}$$

$$i^G \equiv \frac{I^G}{Q}$$

$$\tau \equiv \frac{T}{Q}$$

$$f^{*G} \equiv \frac{EF^{*G}}{PQ}$$

$$d^{*G} \equiv \frac{ED^{*G}}{PQ}$$

$$\varrho^* \equiv \frac{ER^*}{PQ}.$$

The government budget identity (14.15) can then be rewritten as:

$$
\begin{aligned}
\Delta b - \Delta f^{*G} - \Delta k^G \equiv c^G &- (a^* + \tau) \\
&+ (r^* - n)(b - f^{*G} - k^G) \\
&+ (r - r^*)b - \gamma f^{*G} + (r^* - (\eta - \delta))k^G \\
&- [\Delta h + (n + \pi)h].
\end{aligned}
$$

Let D denote the net non-monetary liabilities of the government, and d their ratio to GDP, i.e.

$$D \equiv \frac{B}{P} - \frac{EF^{*G}}{P} - K^G$$

and

$$d \equiv \frac{D}{Q}.$$

The budget identity can then be written more compactly as in Equation (14.16):

$$\Delta d \equiv c^G - (a^* + \tau) + (r^* + \gamma - n)d + \ell - \sigma \tag{14.16}$$

where

$$\ell \equiv (r - (r^* + \gamma))b + (r^* + \gamma - (\eta - \delta))k^G \tag{14.17a}$$

and

$$\sigma \equiv \Delta h + (n + \pi)h. \tag{14.17b}$$

The increase in the public sector's net debt–GDP ratio can, from Equation (14.16), be expressed as the sum of four components. The first is $c^G - (a^* + \tau)$, the basic public sector primary (non-interest) current (or consumption account) deficit as a proportion of GDP. The second, $(r^* + \gamma - n)d$, is the real interest payments on the debt corrected for the growth of real GDP, as a proportion of GDP. The real interest rate imputed to the debt is the world real interest rate, $r^* \equiv i^* - \pi^*$, plus the proportional rate of depreciation of the real exchange rate, γ. The third, ℓ, consists of the additional interest losses (which may, of course, be negative) accruing on the various assets and liabilities due to the fact that the real rate of return on these assets and liabilities differs from the world real interest rate corrected for real exchange rate changes. If domestic debt pays a real interest rate in terms of home goods (r) in excess of the world real interest rate corrected for real exchange rate depreciation ($r^* + \gamma$) then ℓ increases by an amount $(r - (r^* + \gamma))b$. If the foreign real interest rate corrected for real exchange rate depreciation exceeds the net real rate of return on public sector capital, $\eta - \delta$, ℓ increases by an amount $(r^* + \gamma - (\eta - \delta))k^G$. Finally, the larger σ, real seigniorage or the real value of the increase in the nominal high-powered money stock (as a proportion of GDP), the smaller the increase in the debt–GDP ratio will be.

From Equations (14.16) and (14.17) a few obvious facts stand out.

14.5.1 Substituting domestic debt for foreign debt

The substitution of domestic debt, b, for foreign debt $(-f^{*G})$, will worsen the budgetary position of the government if the domestic real interest rate exceeds the foreign real interest rate corrected for real exchange rate depreciation. Both Turkey and Brazil have in recent years pursued such a strategy, which may not have been very sensible (see Anand and van Wijnbergen, 1987).

If the substitution of domestic government debt for foreign public debt takes the form of a 'stock-shift' open-market swap, the nation's total net foreign indebtedness at that instant will not, of course, have been affected. Private external indebtedness must have increased by the same amount as the reduction in foreign indebtedness. The government's balance sheet will have been weakened while that of the private sector has become stronger. This creates a problem if and to the extent that the government has trouble effecting the increased internal fiscal transfer required to service its costlier debt.

If the substitution of more expensive domestic public debt for foreign public debt takes the form of the government financing a larger share of its flow deficit by borrowing domestically, there will be, as time passes, first-order effects on the evolution of the nation's net external indebtedness, first, through the higher future public sector deficits that would result because $r > r^* + \gamma$ (even if seigniorage, the primary deficit, and the rest of ℓ are unchanged); and second, through any effects of the change in the internal–external financing mix on private saving and investment. If the private sector cannot borrow abroad (or cannot increase its borrowing abroad), the increased government borrowing in the domestic capital markets will crowd out private investment, either by pushing up domestic real interest rates or by tighter credit rationing. The response of private saving is less clear-cut, but, under the conditions just stated, the private sector financial surplus will have to increase by the full amount of the switch of government borrowing from the external to the internal financial markets. When private access to the international financial markets is limited but non-zero, the short-run response of the current account is still likely to be an improvement, although it again is likely to have been purchased at a cost in terms of domestic investment. Over time, the government would also encounter the more acute internal fiscal transfer problems discussed before.

14.5.2 The debt burden and the real exchange rate

As was discussed in connection with national solvency in Section 14.4, a depreciating real exchange rate ($\gamma > 0$) increases the real domestic resource cost of servicing foreign debt (at any given world real interest rate r^*). This confronts debtor countries with the unpleasant dilemma that they must achieve an improved level of competitiveness in order to generate the trade surpluses required to service their debt, while the very process of improving their competitiveness increases the real burden of that debt.

14.5.3 The return on the public sector capital stock

The implications of different rates of return on the public sector capital stock[20] can be brought out most easily by considering two extremes. The first, optimistic, scenario has the net rate of return, $\delta - \hat{\delta}$, equal to the opportunity cost of government borrowing, $r^* + \gamma$. If in addition $r = r^* - \gamma$, the primary deficit driving the debt dynamics in this case is simply the current or consumption account deficit, $c^G - (a^* + \tau)$.

The second, pessimistic (or realistic?), scenario has the gross rate of return η equal to zero. Capital effectively ceases to be an asset and gross investment $(i^G \equiv \Delta k^G + (\delta + n)k^G)$ is like public consumption expenditure. Let net public debt excluding capital as a proportion of GDP be $\tilde{d} \equiv (B - EF^{*G}/PQ)$. If, in addition, we have $r = r^* + \gamma$, the budget identity becomes

$$\Delta \tilde{d} \equiv c^G + i^G - (a^* + \tau) + (r^* + \gamma - n)\tilde{d} - \sigma. \tag{14.18}$$

The primary deficit driving the debt dynamics now includes gross public sector capital formation. With $\eta < 0$, the true primary deficit, $c^G - (a^* + \tau) + \ell$ would be even larger.

14.5.4 The solvency constraint of the public sector

From Equation (14.16) we can obtain the intertemporal budget constraint, present value budget constraint or solvency constraint of the public sector in the same way as was done for the nation as a whole in Section 14.4. It is given by

$$d(s) = PV(s; \tau + a^* - \ell - c^G; r^* + \gamma - n) + PV(s; \sigma; r^* + \gamma - n). \tag{14.19}$$

The present discounted value of future primary government surpluses (including ℓ, the drain on public sector revenues caused by costly domestic debt and low-yielding public sector capital) plus the present value of future resources appropriated by printing money should be equal to the outstanding net public debt.[21]

As in Section 14.4, the solvency constraint (14.19) should be viewed as an *ex ante* consistency check on the government's spending, revenue raising and monetization plans, given its initial outstanding debt.

When spending and revenue projections are made and evaluated, it is important to be aware of the spending and revenue implications of various structural adjustment policies.

Trade liberalization, when it takes the form of reducing tariffs or export taxes and when the revenue base is less than unit-elastic with respect to tax and tariff rates, will reduce revenues and weaken solvency unless future primary deficits are reduced or future seigniorage revenues are boosted. If neither occurs, the debt will not be serviced in full and we will see either explicit (partial) repudiation or capital levies and the like. This is not necessarily a bad thing, although it is likely to affect adversely the government's future ability to borrow. The case for a more explicitly contingent public debt (internal and external) has been made forcefully by, among others, Dornbusch (1986, pp. 131–50, 175–6). Provided the contingenceis are clearly defined and observable and not under the control of the borrowing government, the case for making debt-holders share (with labor and the owners of capital) in the burden of adjusting to internal and external exogenous shocks would seem to be a strong one.

Replacing quotas and import licenses (which typically are not auctioned off competitively) by uniform tariffs, as is currently being recommended by the World Bank, will raise government revenue, in addition to having allocative or efficiency effects, and may reduce the returns to rent-seeking activity.

The consequences of internal and external financial liberalization for the government's ability to extract seigniorage will be considered in Section 14.6.

14.6 SEIGNIORAGE AS A TAX

Seigniorage, σ, the increase in the nominal high-powered money stock (as a proportion of GDP) can be written in a number of ways, as shown in Equation (14.20):

$$\sigma \equiv \frac{\Delta H}{PQ}$$

$$= \Delta h + (n + \pi)h \tag{14.20}$$

$$= \mu V^{-1} \equiv \mu h$$

$\mu \equiv \Delta H/H$ is the proportional rate of growth of the nominal high-powered money stock and $V \equiv PQ/H$ is the income velocity of circulation of high-powered money.

As can be seen from the second line of Equation (14.20), total seigniorage can be broken down into two components, the reduction in the ratio of high-powered money to GDP that would occur as a result of nominal GDP growth, holding constant the nominal stock of high-powered money $((n + \pi)h)$ and the change in the high-powered money-GDP ratio $(\Delta h \equiv - \Delta V/V^2)$. If money demand equals money supply, $(n + \pi)h$ can be interpreted as the growth in nominal money demand due to inflation and real GDP growth at a given velocity. Δh is the increase in real money demand due to declining velocity. The two components will often move in opposite directions. Higher *actual* inflation will, *ceteris paribus*, increase $(n + \pi)h$. Directly and via higher nominal interest rates, higher *expected* inflation will also tend to increase velocity (reduce money demand at any given level of income). The third line of Equation (14.20) provides a decomposition of seigniorage (or the inflation tax) into an inflation tax *rate*, $\mu \equiv \Delta H/H$, and an inflation tax *base*, $h \equiv V^{-1}$. A higher inflation tax rate will, given the tax base, raise seigniorage revenue. To the extent that a higher value of μ raises the expected rate of inflation (and for increases in μ that are perceived as permanent, it will do so sooner or later), it will also raise velocity and reduce the tax base. Only if the elasticity of velocity with respect to μ is less than unity, will seigniorage revenue go up as μ increases.

Consider the monetary base demand function

$$h = f(i, Q; \varphi) \qquad\qquad\qquad f_i < 0. \qquad\qquad (14.21)$$

φ is a set of variables such as expected inflation, expected nominal exchange rate depreciation, foreign interest rates, official bank reserve requirements, capital controls, and so on, that may influence the demand for base money in addition to i and Q.

f_Q will be positive (negative) if the elasticity of real money base demand with respect to real income is greater than (less than) unity. For the moment, assume a unitary income elasticity and a real interest rate that is independent of the rate of inflation. In the long run, $\pi = \mu - n$. For a number of commonly used money demand functions such as the linear one in Equation (14.22a) and the log-linear one in Equation (14.22b), the long-run relationship between monetary growth and real seigniorage has the 'Laffer curve' shape shown in Figure 14.6.[22]

$$h = a - bi \qquad\qquad a, b > 0; \quad i < ab^{-1} \qquad (14.22a)$$

$$\ln h = \bar{a} - \bar{b}i \qquad\qquad \bar{b} > 0 \qquad\qquad\qquad (14.22b)$$

For the linear demand function, shown in Figures 14.4a and 14.6b, and for the log-linear demand function, shown in Figures 14.6c and 14.6d, there is a unique, finite, long-run seigniorage-maximizing rate of inflation ($a/2b$ in the linear case, $1/\bar{b}$ in the log-linear case). No rational policy-making process would drive the long-run inflation rate beyond this point as, in addition to the costs of higher inflation, there would be a reduction in inflation tax revenues. Many past and recent hyperinflationary or near-hyperinflationary episodes nevertheless saw the rate of inflation pushed well beyond the point of negative seigniorage returns. The political economy of such monetary irrationality is not very well understood.

The importance of seigniorage as a source of government revenue varies widely across countries at a point in time and over time for any given country. Only the cross-sectional variation is shown in Table 14.3. Note that all these data understate seigniorage revenue, as they only refer to currency outside banks. Currency held by the banks as 'till money' and reserves held either as cash or in the form of bankers' balances with the central bank are omitted because the data tend to be very unreliable.

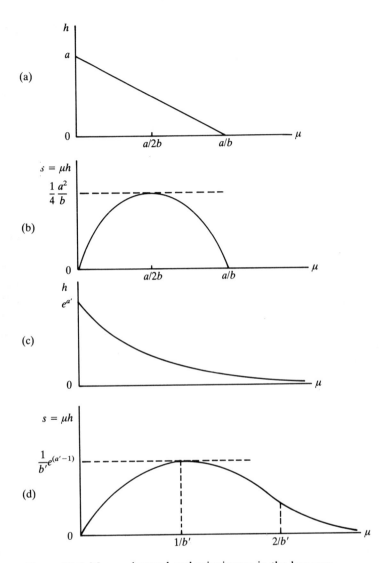

Figure 14.6 Money demand and seigniorage in the long run

The seigniorage tax base can be affected powerfully by direct international currency substitution ('dollarization') and by domestic financial developments and reforms. Domestic financial deregulation and the development of deposit-taking institutions paying attractive interest rates will shrink the demand for currency held outside the banking system (*Cur*). With a given reserve requirement (θ) against deposits (*Dep*) (assumed

Table 14.3 Revenue from seigniorage on currency (average 1980–5)

	Seigniorage revenues (increase in currency as per cent of GDP)	Ratio of currency holdings to GDP (per cent)	Currency growth (per cent) per year	Inflation (per cent) per year
High seigniorage revenues				
Argentina	4.0	3.8	269	274
Bolivia	6.2	6.1	438	506
Ghana	2.2	6.1	45	54
Sierra Leone	2.4	7.7	35	43
Moderate seigniorage revenues				
Brazil	1.0	1.4	129	147
Israel	1.1	1.3	165	181
Mexico	1.5	3.7	50	58
Peru	1.9	3.1	92	97
Turkey	1.2	3.8	38	46
Low seigniorage revenues				
Bangladesh	0.6	4.0	16	12
Colombia	0.8	4.7	18	22
Dominican Republic	0.7	4.6	16	15
Ivory Coast	0.7	9.2	8	7
Korea	0.5	4.3	13	9
Nigeria	0.8	7.2	13	16
Venezuela	0.4	4.5	8	12

Source: IFS. Reproduced from World Bank, *World Development Report*, 1988.
Notes: The first column is calculated as the end-of-year currency outside banks (IFS line 14a) minus the end-of-year value of the previous year, divided by the current year GDP. The second column is the ratio of the average of beginning-of-year and end-of-year currency outside banks to current GDP. The third column is the percentage change in currency outside banks from end-of-year to end-of-year. The final column is the percentage change in CPI (IFS line 64) from December to December. The geometric average of growth rates is used for columns 3 and 4; the arithmetic average of ratios is used for columns 1 and 2.

binding), the reserve component of the monetary base (*Res*) will grow when bank deposits grow, as

$$Res \equiv \theta Dep.$$

Since $H \equiv Cur + Res$, even the *sign* of the net effect of domestic financial deregulation and the growth of bank deposits on the seigniorage tax base is an empirical matter. Flight out of domestic currency and out of domestic bank deposits into foreign currency and/or foreign bank deposits in response to international interest differentials and/or expectations of exchange rate depreciation will unambiguously shrink the seigniorage tax base. More quantitative information on the demand for high-powered money as a function of expected inflation, domestic and foreign interest rates, expected exchange rate depreciation, the development and degree of sophistication of the banking system, and the tightness and effectiveness of exchange controls would be very helpful.

In an economy in which all sources of government revenue are distortionary, optimal policy will minimize the unavoidable dead-weight losses involved in raising a given total revenue by using all available revenue instruments, including the inflation tax. More reliable knowledge concerning the effect of changes in the inflation tax rate on the inflation tax yield is required if this instrument is to be used properly.

Seigniorage as defined here can be viewed as the *expected* inflation tax. If the government has a significant amount of long-dated nominally denominated (non-index-linked) debt outstanding, it can, in addition, use unanticipated inflation as a capital levy on the holders of this debt. Since the external debt is denominated in foreign currency and much of the domestic debt is effectively index-linked, this may not be as important a source of revenue as it could be in many of the industrial countries. In addition, this policy suffers from the defect that repeated use will lead to inflation risk premiums being built into the nominal yields on newly issued nominal debt.

Finally, inflation will affect the real yield of other taxes and revenue sources (specific duties, charges, tariffs, and so on) and the real value of public spending because many spending programs, tax schedules, etc., are not index-linked and adjust to inflation only with a lag.

The biases do not always go in the same direction. Inflation will raise the real yield of a progressive income tax when the progressive rate schedule is not index-linked and adjusted to inflation only with a lag. Delays in the collection of taxes can, unless the right interest penalty for arrearages is imposed, reduce the real tax take significantly in an inflationary environment. Again our quantitative knowledge of the effect of inflation on real public spending and revenues is very incomplete, although Tanzi's (1978) work suggests that very high rates of inflation unambiguously and significantly reduce real public sector revenues.

What is clear is that the pursuit of reductions in the rate of inflation in the range where this reduces seigniorage may have serious fiscal consequences. If no matching reduction in the primary government deficit is achieved, the growth of interest-bearing public debt (internal or external) will be increased. If taxes are raised or spending cut to prevent an increase in the growth of the public debt, the demand-depressing effect of the monetary tightening will be augmented by a contractionary fiscal impulse and a serious recession may result. While this may be judged to be a price worth paying for a reduction in the inflation rate, the choice should be made in full awareness of the entire range of likely consequences.

14.7 THE CONSISTENCY OF INFLATION TARGETS AND FINANCEABLE DEFICITS

Recently the World Bank has developed a 'short-hand consistency check' on certain aspects of a government's fiscal, financial and monetary strategy. This approach, based on the work of Anand and van Wijnbergen (1987), Knight (1986) and Coutinho (1986; 1988) within the Bank and closely related to some recent work of mine (Buiter, 1983a; 1983b; 1985; 1987a; 1987b), can be interpreted readily using the accounting framework of the previous sections and this one.

Let z denote the real-growth-corrected operational deficit as a proportion of GDP, i.e. the sum of the primary deficit and the asset-revaluations-and-real-growth-corrected interest paid on the debt, as a proportion of GDP:

$$z \equiv c^G + i^G - (a^* + \tau) + \ell + (r^* + \gamma - n)(b + d^{*G} - \varrho^*). \quad (14.23)$$

The public sector budget identity given, for example, in Equation (14.18) can be rewritten as

$$\sigma \equiv z - (\Delta b + \Delta d^{*G} - \Delta \varrho^*). \quad (14.24)$$

This identity can be used in a number of ways. One is to treat monetary financing, σ, as the residual. To implement this, projections are provided for z, i.e. for the primary deficit and the interest payments on the outstanding stocks of internal and external public debt. This requires projections of *real* interest rates, i.e. of domestic and foreign nominal interest rates, of domestic and foreign inflation rates and of changes in the real (or nominal) exchange rate. The 'financeable deficit' is then calculated, basically the desired (or permitted) changes in domestic indebtedness, Δb, external indebtedness, Δd^{*G}, minus any desired increase in external foreign exchange reserves, $\Delta \varrho^*$. This uniquely determines σ, the value of the real resources (as a percentage of GDP) that the government will have to appropriate by running the printing presses.

With the required amount of seigniorage from Equation (14.24), plus a set of equations relating base money to inflation (typically centered around a high-powered money demand function) the inflation rate implied by the fiscal-financial program on the right-hand side of Equation (14.24) can be determined. A popular candidate used in World Bank analyses is the long-linear base money demand function (in the example considered here, the income elasticity of money demand is constrained to equal unity). The inflation rate is the only other argument in this function. In Equation (14.25) h denotes the desired or long-run demand for base money as a fraction of GDP:

$$h = \exp(\bar{a} - \bar{\beta}\pi) \qquad\qquad \bar{\beta} > 0. \qquad (14.25)$$

The actual inflation rate π is assumed to exceed (fall short of) the expected, inertial or 'core' inflation rate $\hat{\pi}$ whenever h exceeds $\hat{h}$. This relationship can be perturbed by additive exogenous shocks, x.

$$\pi = x(h - \hat{h}) + \hat{\pi} + x. \qquad\qquad x > 0. \qquad (14.26)$$

Finally, inertial inflation, $\hat{\pi}$, is assumed to be a simple function of past inflation, say,

$$\hat{\pi} = \lambda\pi(-1) \qquad\qquad 0 < \lambda \leqslant 1. \qquad (14.27)$$

Given σ from Equation (14.24) and Equations (14.25), (14.26) and (14.27), we can calculate the inflation rate consistent with the deficit scenario and the assumptions about the financeable deficit. This implied or consistent rate of inflation can then be compared with the target rate of inflation (and with the inflation assumptions that are implicit in the projections made to obtain the right-hand-side of Equation (14.24)).

The converse approach is to start with a target path for inflation and to derive the path it implies for seigniorage σ given Equations (14.25), (14.26) and (14.27). Given the amounts that can be borrowed at home and abroad and given the target change in international reserves, this implies a path for the operational deficit. This can then be compared with the actual plan for the operational deficit.

Any inconsistencies (in practice most likely to take the form of an implied inflation rate in excess of the target rate or an implied deficit in excess of the target one) will have to be reconciled by some combination of revisions in inflation projections, cuts in the primary deficit, reductions in the internal or external interest burden, increased internal or external borrowing (including arrearages) or lower foreign exchange reserves.

Note that from the public sector solvency constraint given in Equation (14.19), given the initial net debt and the projected path of future (corrected) primary deficits and of future real interest rates and growth rates, the present discounted value of future seigniorage required to make these projections consistent with government solvency can be calculated. This present discounted value can, of course, be achieved with many different time paths for σ. The approach outlined in this section picks among these many feasible time paths for σ by specifying paths for $\Delta b + \Delta d^{*G} - \Delta \varrho^*$ (i.e. for the financeable deficit).

I consider this approach (basically a simple 'uses and sources of funds' accounting exercise for the consolidated public sector with minimal behavioral fill-in — just the base money demand function and the inflation equations — to be potentially useful bacause it imposes the essential discipline of looking at the totality of plans for public sector outlays, receipts and financing. Such an integrated approach is the only one that makes sense. Granted this 'global' approval of the method, I have some worries about misleading inferences that might be drawn from its prima-facie low behavioral content. There also are, inevitably, serious problems with any actual empirical implementation.

14.7.1 Nothing from nothing

The approach carries with it the danger that a casual reader or careless user might infer that in order to engage in macroeconomic policy evaluation all one needs is a base money demand function and an inflation equation. (If prices were perfectly flexible, one could even dispense with the separate inflation equation.) In fact, in order to do the exercise, a vast amount of (implicit) economic and econometric modeling is required to produce projections for the right-hand side of Equation (14.24). There we find a number of key *endogenous* variables whose determination requires (implicitly or explicitly) the kind of general equilibrium macroeconometric modeling that the consistency check appears to short-cut.

Among these key endogenous variables are the domestic real interest rate, the real exchange rate (through γ) and the growth rate and level of real economic activity. The latter enter through n and because real tax receipts and other current revenues and outlays are functions of, among other things, the levels of output and employment. The consistency check should in principle be extended to include these variables. When this is not done, the danger exists that changes in policy that are intended to eliminate an *ex ante* inconsistency between inflation plans and budget deficit plans will only do so by enlarging the inconsistency between the inflation and deficit projections, on the one hand, and the real interest rate, real exchange rate and real economic activity assumptions, on the other hand.

14.7.2 The base money demand function

Having estimated base money demand functions for the United Kingdom and United States for the period since the Second World War, it is easy to become impressed (and depressed) with the instability of this relationship.

Much of this can no doubt be explained (*ex post*) as reflecting irregular spurts of financial innovation and development. In addition, there are likely to be episodes of (dis)intermediation in response to changes in regulatory policy. In a new industrial country such as Brazil all these sources of instability are likely to be present in force, plus some others. Variations in the degree of stringency of capital controls are likely to be reflected in variations in the degree of (direct) international currency substitution. Changes in reserve requirements are also likely to shift a simple base money demand function such as the one given in Equation (14.25).

14.7.3 The inflation function

Equations (14.26) and (14.27) define a completely 'backward-looking' inflation and price process. There is no room for announcement effects, credibility, and so on, to affect the rate of inflation other than through the shift dummy, x. There is also no room in the equation (again except through x) for a role for *indexation arrangements*, direct or indirect effects of *exchange rate behavior* or *cost pressures* (domestic or imported). While it is easy to criticize any piece of empirical work for errors of omission (and errors of commission), these specific criticisms are born not out of a scholarly thirst for purity, but out of worries resulting from the fact that these particular omitted factors are widely recognized as having played (and continuing to play) a major role in the economic processes governing contemporary Brazil, Argentina, Mexico, and other states.

14.7.4 The seigniorage Laffer curve

As was pointed out in Section 14.6, many theoretically and empirically acceptable money demand functions have the property that there is more than one rate of inflation that can generate any given amount of seigniorage. This is most easily seen if we consider stationary equilibria in which the (actual and expected) rate of inflation is constant over time. (Not all plausible money demand functions have this property; for example, the hyperbolic function $h = a''/(b'' + \pi)$, with a'', $b'' > 0$, has seigniorage independent of the rate of inflation; the constant velocity version, $h = a > 0$, has seigniorage increasing with inflation for ever; other reasonable functions yield many local seigniorage peaks and troughs.)

The log-linear function often used in the World Bank's analyses has the unimodal long-run seigniorage Laffer curve depicted in Figures, 14.6c and 14.6d. When the inflation rate is calculated that yields a given amount of seigniorage, the *lower* of the two rates is typically chosen in Bank analyses. While this may be good prescriptive economics (no rational policy-making process would drive the rate of inflation beyond the point at which it yields maximal revenue), it is likely to be bad positive economics. Every hyperinflation in history clearly put the country experiencing it on the revenue-inefficient side of the seigniorage Laffer curve. The same is likely to have been true with the very high rate of inflation seen in a number of Southern Cone countries in recent years.

14.7.5 Inflation and the primary deficit

It is likely to be empirically important to allow for the effect of inflation on the primary deficit. As pointed out in Section 14.6, we know from the work of Tanzi (1978) and others that with very high rates of inflation, government real tax revenues will decline, quite often dramatically. If there are any elements of nominal progression in the income tax structure, this real revenue-raising effect will be swamped by the effect of collection lags and lags in the inflation adjustment of specific duties, etc. Less is known about the effect of high (and variable) rates of inflation on government expenditures. Empirical studies must allow for feedback from the inflation rate to be the first term on the right-hand side of Equation (14.24).

14.7.6 More lack of superneutrality

Different rates of inflation may affect the right-hand side of Equation (14.24) not only through the primary deficit but also through the real interest rate and the depreciation of the real exchange rate. I do not know how to evaluate the quantitative significance of this point.

14.7.7 Unwise budget cuts

It may be unnecessary to point out that even within the primary deficit total, the various spending and revenue components are not independent of each other, in either the short or the long run. Spending cuts that depress activity also depress output- or income-sensitive receipts. Even without extreme Lafferian responses, supply-side-friendly tax cuts or subsidies may recoup part of the initial budgetary cost. Cuts in productive public sector capital formation may damage the supply side of the economy, conceivably to the point that the public deficit rises rather than falls (see Buiter, 1987b). While these problems are not specific to the approach under consideration, they are important when the policy response to an 'inconsistency verdict' is being pondered.

15.8 CONCLUSION

This paper is a non-systematic perusal of some of the key issues in the design and conduct of fiscal policy for stabilization and structural adjustment in developing countries. Its coverage is undoubtedly subject to both Type I and Type II errors. I nevertheless hope that its focus on the external and internal transfer problems, national solvency and public sector solvency (with a fairly extended discussion of the inflation tax and the consistency of fiscal, financial and monetary plans) does provide a useful starting point for further discussion.

14.9 NOTES

1. These are Argentina, Bolivia, Brazil, Chile, Columbia, Ecuador, Ivory Coast, Mexico, Morocco, Nigeria, Peru, Philippines, Uruguay, Venezuela and Yugoslavia. The World Bank's group of 17 'heavily-indebted countries' adds Costa Rica and Jamaica. Further major debtors are South Korea, Thailand and Turkey.
2. The World Bank's World Development Report identifies 24 countries as low-income sub-Saharan Africa and ten more as (lower) middle-income sub-Saharan Africa.
3. A reduction in the private sector financial deficit will, *ceteris paribus*, also improve the current account deficit. Where this can be achieved through an increase in the savings rate, it will in general be welcome. In many of the poorer developing countries, the scope for this is rather limited. A reduction in the private sector financial deficit through a cut in private sector capital formation is unlikely to be desirable.
4. Again this ought to be called the *increase* in the (internal) fiscal transfer, but established usage and verbal hygiene conflict here, too.
5. It is assumed for simplicity that the interest rate on foreign exchange reserves is the same as that on foreign debt.
6. For simplicity all net external current transfers are assumed to accrue to the government. This assumption is most inappropriate in the case of private remittances.
7. Q_X, Q_M and Q_N are domestic production of the exportable good, the importable good and the non-traded good respectively. C_j^k and I_j^k ($k = P$, G; $j = X, M, N$) are domestic demands for the three goods by the private (P) and public (G) sectors, respectively.
8. In the long run, a smaller stock of external debt obtained as the result of a period of cumulative current account surpluses permits a country to run a sustainable smaller trade balance surplus or a larger deficit.
9. Note that C^P is aggregate consumption spending measured in GDP units, i.e. $C^P \equiv [P_X C_X^P + P_M C_M^P + P_N C_N^P]P^{-1}$.
10. Private investment spending on non-traded goods is held constant in this thought experiment and the next one involving changes in public spending on non-traded goods.
11. The production of exportables need not fall absolutely, as in Figure 14.2a.
12. Given the volume and the composition of the government's 'exhaustive' public spending program on goods and services, and ignoring the distortionary effects of non-lump-sum taxes.
13. If the money wage is W, the real consumption wage $\bar{w}$ is defined by:

$$\bar{w} \equiv \frac{W}{\bar{P}}$$

$$\bar{P} = \bar{P}_T^{1-\tilde{a}} P_N^{\tilde{a}} \qquad 0 < \tilde{a} < 1$$
$$\bar{P}_T = P_X^{1-\tilde{\beta}} P_M^{\tilde{\beta}} \qquad 0 < \tilde{\beta} < 1.$$

$\bar{P}$ is the (Cobb–Douglas) consumer price index; $\bar{P}_T$ is the consumer price index for traded goods. $\tilde{\beta}$ is the share of imports in traded goods spending and $\tilde{a}$ the share of non-traded goods in total consumption spending. If the non-traded goods price is a mark-up on unit labor cost then $P_N = (1 + \mu) WL_N/Q_N$, where μ is the proportional mark-up and L_N is labor employed in the non-traded goods sector. This implies

$$\bar{w} = \frac{Q_N}{L_N(1 + \mu)} \left[\frac{P_N}{\bar{P}_T}\right]^{1-\tilde{a}}.$$

If there are no intersectoral differences in factor intensities (so Q_N/L_N is independent of Q_N), and if the mark-up is constant then a decline in the relative price of non-traded goods lowers the real consumption wage. This will be reinforced if the average product of labor in the non-traded goods sector declines as $P_N/\bar{P}_T$ declines and Q_N contracts, which is likely to happen if the non-traded goods sector is relatively labor-intensive.

14. Measured in terms of foreign GDP.
15. In 'long-hand' algebra.

$$PV(s; tb + a^*; r^* + \gamma - n) \equiv \int_s^\infty [tb(v) + a^*(v)]$$
$$\exp\left(-\int_s^v [r^*(u) + \gamma(u) - n(u)]du\right)dv.$$

Two equivalent ways of writing Equation (14.13) are:

$$-\frac{E(s)F^*(s)}{P(s)} = PV\left[s; TB + \frac{EA^*}{P}; r^* + \gamma\right] \qquad (14.13a)$$

and

$$-F^*(s) = PV\left[s; \frac{PTB}{E} + A^*; i^*\right]. \qquad (14.13b)$$

Equation (14.13a) has the current real value of the external debt matched by the present discounted value of future real primary surpluses, using the real exchange-rate-depreciation-corrected foreign real interest rate $r^* + \gamma$ to discount the future primary real surpluses. Equation (14.13b) has the current foreign currency value of the nation's external debt matched by the present discounted value of future primary surpluses measured in foreign currency, using the foreign nominal interest rate $i^* \equiv r^* + \pi^*$ to discount the future primary foreign currency surpluses.

16. Technically, the condition is:

$$\lim_{\tau \to \infty} - f^*(\tau)\exp\left(-\int_s^\tau [r^*(u) + \gamma(u) - n(u)]du\right) = 0$$

or

$$\lim_{\tau \to \infty} - \frac{E(\tau)F^*(\tau)}{P(\tau)}\exp -\int_s^\tau [r^*(u) + \gamma(u)]du = 0$$

or

$$\lim_{\tau \to \infty} - F^*(\tau)\exp -\int_s^\tau i^*(u)du = 0$$

17. I am concerned with solvency only, not with optimal or time-consistent borrowing strategies. It may well be optimal, under certain conditions, to run current account surpluses or even to become a net external creditor.
18. Or (14.13a) or (14.13b) from note 16 above.
19. This section draws on Buiter (1983a; 1983b, 1985) and Anand and van Wijnbergen (1987).
20. Depending on the accounting conventions one adopts, J could include the operating surpluses (deficits) of the state enterprise sector. Alternatively one could include these in τ. Note that it is *cash returns* that enter into the accounts through ϱ, not the implicit social rate of return.
21. There is again a transversality or terminal condition to get from Equation (14.16) to Equation (14.19) given by

$$\lim_{\tau \to \infty} d(\tau) \exp\left(- \int_s^\tau [r^*(u) + \gamma(u) - n(u)]du \right) = 0$$

22. For simplicity $r = 0$ and $i = \pi = \mu$ in Figure 14.6.

14.10 REFERENCES

Ahamed, L. (1986) 'Stabilization policies in developing countries', *World Bank Research Observer*, 1, January, pp. 79–110.

Anand, R. and S. van Wijnbergen, (1987) 'Inflation and the financing of government expenditure in Turkey: an introductory analysis', World Bank mimeo, revised June.

Blinder, A. (1987) 'Credit rationing and effective supply failures', *Economic Journal*, 97, June, pp. 327–52.

Buiter, Willem H. (1983a) 'Measurement of the public sector deficit and its implications for policy evaluation and design', *IMF Staff Papers*, 30, June, pp. 306–49 (also Chapter 4, this volume).

Buiter, Willem H. (1983b) 'The theory of optimum deficits and debt', in Federal Reserve Bank of Boston, *The Economics of Large Government Deficits*, Conference series no. 27, October, pp. 4–69.

Buiter, Willem H. (1985) 'A guide to public sector debt and deficits', *Economic Policy*, 1, November, pp. 14–61 (also Chapter 3, this volume).

Buiter, Willem H. (1986) 'Macroeconomic responses by developing countries to changes in external economic conditions', *NBER Working Paper*, no. 1836, February.

Buiter, Willem H. (1987a) 'The current global economic situation, outlook and policy options with special emphasis on fiscal policy issues', Centre for Economic Policy Research, Discussion Paper no. 210, November.

Buiter, Willem H. (1987b) 'Can public spending cuts be inflationary?', mimeo (also Chapter 13, this volume).

Buiter, Willem H. (1988) 'Structural and stabilisation aspects of fiscal and financial policy in the dependent economy', *Oxford Economic Papers*, 40, pp. 220–45.

Coutinho, R. (1986) 'Public sector deficits and crowding out: a consistency model for Brazil', mimeo, World Bank, December.

Coutinho, R. (1988) 'Public deficits, financeable deficits and stabilization', mimeo, World Bank, February.

Cumby, R. and R. Levich (1987) 'On the definition and magnitude of recent capital flight', *NBER Working Paper*, no. 2275.

Dervis, K. and P. Petri (1987) 'The macroeconomics of successful development: what are the lessons?', mimeo, March.

Diaz-Alejandro, C. (1965) *Exchange Rate Devaluation in a Semi-industrialised Economy: The Experience of Argentina, 1955–61*, MIT Press, Cambridge, MA.

Dornbusch, R. (1980) *Open Economy Macroeconomics*, Basic Books, New York.

Dornbusch, R. (1986) *Dollars, Debts and Deficits*, MIT Press, Cambridge, MA.

Eaton, J. and M. Gersovitz (1981a) 'Debt with potential repudiation: theoretical and empirical analysis', *Review of Economic Studies*, 48, pp. 289–309.

Eaton, J. and M. Gersovitz (1981b) *Poor Country Borrowing and the Repudiation Issue*, Princeton Studies in International Finance no. 4.

Eaton, J. and M. Gersovitz (1983) 'Country risk: economic aspects' in R. J. Herring (ed.) *Managing International Risk*, Cambridge University Press, New York.

Eaton, J., M. Gersovitz and J. Stiglitz, (1986), 'The pure theory of country risk', *European Economic Review*, 30, pp. 481–513.

Edwards, S. (1986) 'Are devaluations contractionary?' *Review of Economics and Statistics*, 68, August, pp. 501–8.

Haque, N. (1986) 'Fiscal policy and private saving behaviour in developing countries', World Bank Discussion Paper Report No. DRD. 209, December.

Haque, N. and P. Montiel (1987) 'Ricardian equivalence, liquidity constraints, and the Yaari–Blanchard effect: tests for developing countries', World Bank DRD mimeo, May.

Khan, M. and J. Lizondo (1987), 'Devaluation, fiscal deficits, and the real exchange rate', *The World Bank Economic Review*, 1, January, pp. 357–74.

Kletzer, K. (1984) 'Asymmetric information and LDC borrowing with sovereign risk', *Economic Journal*, 94, pp. 287–307.

Knight, P. (1986) 'Brazil, structural adjustment, stabilization and growth', 1986 Country Economic Memorandum, World Bank.

Krugman, P. and L. Taylor (1978) 'Contractionary effects of a devaluation', *Journal of International Economics*, 8, August, pp. 445–56.

Sachs, J. (ed.) (1987) *Developing Country Debt*, NBER Conference Report.

Tanzi, V. (1978) 'Inflation, real tax revenue and the case for inflationary finance: theory with an application to Argentina', *IMF Staff Papers*, 25, September.

Wijnbergen, S. van (1986) 'Exchange rate management and stabilization policies in developing countries' in S. Edwards and L. Ahamed (eds), *Economic Adjustment and Exchange Rates in Developing Countries*, University of Chicago Press, Chicago.

INDEX

Abel, A., 185–6, 190
accommodation, monetary, versus
    monetary, crowding out, 290–3
accounting *see* measurement of public
    sector deficit
actual fiscal impulse, 85–9
adaptive expectations in stability in full
    employment model, 285–6
Africa *see* developing countries
aggregate demand
    and fiscal policy, 85, 89, 100–1
    long-run effects on *see under* fiscal and
    monetary policies
aggregation and OLG model, 290–11
Ahamed, L., 408
aid, foreign, 413
Akerlof, G., 5
allocative and stabilization aspects of
        budgetary and financial policy,
        3–6, 25–46
    public expenditure
        financing, 35, 36–42
        on goods and services, 29–36
amortization of public debt, 115–22
    closed economy, 115–18
    open economy, 118–22
    through inflation, 54–9
Anand, R., 19, 432, 440, 447
announcement date, 79
annuities markets missing, 213–16
anticipated future fiscal changes, 79–80
appreciation
    currency, amortization of public debt
        through, 115–22
    jump-appreciation, 80
Arena, J.J., 242
arithmetic
    of government budget constraint, 95–6

monetarist and hyperdeflations,
    16–18, 359–67
of solvency *see under* solvency
Asia, 416
    see also developing countries; Japan
assets, public sector
    growth, budget growth and inflation,
        340–1
    as imperfect substitutes, 305–7
    implicit, 125–6
    markets and capital formation and
        economic activity, 314–19
    public sector, 62–3, 65–6, 418
    see also measurement of public sector
        deficit
assymetric information paradigm, 27
Atkinson, A.B., 25, 26, 39
Attiat, F., 111
Auerbach, A.J., 6
Austria, 408

Babbs, S., 68
Bagwell, K., 14
Baily, M.N., 323
balance sheet of public sector, 65–7
    see also measurement of public sector
        deficit
balanced budget
    money-capital model of steady-state
        equilibrium, 344–6
    multiplier theorem, 41
Bank of England, 53
Barr, N.A., 26
Barro, R.J., 1
    on crowding out, 168
        demand, 178
        government bonds, 169, 177, 185,
        229

Barro, R.J. (*continued*)
  population growth and
    intertemporal inefficiency, 179
  ultrarationality, 163
  on debt and deficits, 48
  on debt neutrality, 72–3, 129, 230
  overlapping generations, 234
    savings, 234, 235, 243, 245, 246
  on fiscal and monetary policies, 297,
    302, 323
  on interest rate smoothing, 4
  on intergenerational gifts, 12
base money demand function, 442–3
Basevi, G., 71
Belgium: public sector debt and deficits,
  47, 71
bench mark, 84, 89
Benjamin, D.K., 134
bequests *see* overlapping generations
  model
Bernheim, B., 14
birth rate, positive, in OLG model, 185, 223
Blanchard, O.J.
  on debt neutrality, 38, 186, 207, 223
    OLG model, 13, 185–6, 211–16, 223
  on fiscal stance/taxation, 39, 83
    measure of, 85–9, 100–1
  on interest rates, 9, 78
  on monopolistic competition, 5
  on consumption, 377
  on rational expectations, 78, 81
Blinder, A.S., (with Solow) 26, 42, 325,
  341, 370, 424
  fiscal and financial policy, 9, 15, 26, 42,
    75, 83–4
    crowding out, 164, 168, 179
  long-run equilibrium model of fiscal
    effects, 76, 255–9, 270, 286
bonds
  bond-financed deficits and tax cuts, 74,
    75–6, 77–8
  and crowding out, 168–76
  open market purchase of, 269–71
borrowing, 427
  and crowding out, 163, 177
  direct, 165
  and tax cuts, 82–3
  and taxation, 231–3
  to finance public spending, 36–8,
    40, 48
  see also measurement of public sector
    deficit; public sector borrowing
    requirement
Boskin, M.J., 47, 108
Bosworth, B., 242
Bowen, W.G., 233
Branson, W.H., 77
Brazil, 443

Bretton Woods, 122
Brittan, S., 133
Buchanan, J.M., 179, 230, 232–4
budget balance, asset growth and
  inflation, 340–1
budgetary and financial policy *see*
  allocative and stabilization;
  crowding out; debt and deficits;
  developing countries; inflation;
  measurement
budgetary policy and monetary growth,
  122–5
  closed economy, 122–4
  open economy, 124–5
Buiter, W.H., 447
  on allocation and stabilization, 3
  on crowding out, 9, 11, 12, 124, 129,
    139, 187, 324, 400
    indirect, 73
    long-run, 75, 76, 77, 164, 168
    measurement, 116
    public expenditure, 34, 370
    taxation, 82, 83
  on debt and deficits, 3, 5, 7, 124, 139,
    440, 444, 447
  on debt neutrality, 12, 14, 38, 59, 92,
    129, 184, 204
  on demand and supply, 5
  on developing countries, 7, 408, 417
  on end-of-period equilibrium models,
    16
  on fiscal and monetary policies, 316,
    325, 340–1
  on hyperdeflations, 7, 158
  on intergenerational and overlapping
    generations models, 13, 184–8,
    191, 193, 223–4, 234, 297
  on measurement, 5, 116
  on public spending, 48, 377
    cuts, 7, 440
  on rational expectations models, 28,
    82, 402
  on real interest rate, 90
  on Sargent and Wallace, 7, 124, 359
  on seigniorage, 151
  on solvency, 11, 65, 383–4
  on Thatcher, 43, 139
Burbridge, J., 185, 204
burden of debt, 233

Cagan, P., 17–18, 165, 235, 244, 366
Canada
  public sector debt and deficits, 51
  solvency, arithmetic of, 149–51,
    156–7
capital
  flight, 418, 429–30
  formation, 31–3

Capital (*continued*)
  and fiscal and monetary policies, mix
    336–7
  levy, 69–71
  market imperfections, heterogeneous
    survival rates and discount rates,
    213–19
  mobility
    perfect international, 385–6
    zero international, 387–95
  output and factor demand, 374–7
  public sector income on, 62–3
  stock in developing countries, 433–4
  stock and solvency, arithmetic of, 151–2
Carlson, K.M., 168, 230
Carmichael, J.
  on debt neutrality, 38, 129, 185, 204
  on interest and inflation rates, 90
  on OLG model, 13, 187, 191, 193
Cass, D., 234
central banks, 151
children and parents *see*
  intergenerational; overlapping
Chow, G., 164
Christ, C., 75, 164, 168, 325, 340
classicism *see* New Classicism
Cline, W., 430
closed economy
  amortization of public debt, 115–18
  budgetary policy and monetary
    growth, 122–4
  and capital formation and economic
    activity, 328–38
  and crowding out, 78–9, 81
    in full employment model, 163,
      167–76, 178
  fixed-price unemployment model of
    crowding out, 166–7
Clower, R.W., 178
Cohn, R.A., 64
Committee on National Debt and
  Taxation, 70
comparative dynamics, 164
comparative statics, steady state, debt
  neutrality and, 200–4
competition
  between public and private sectors *see*
    crowding out
  imperfect, 27
complementarity, direct, 34
conplements problem and crowding out,
  177
conditional taxes and debt neutrality,
  299–300
constant net worth deficit, 68
constraints
  budget, 55, 75–7
  liquidity, and debt neutrality, 300–1

solvency, 62–7
  in developing countries, 434–5
consumers
  heterogeneity *see under* debt neutrality
  and OLG model, 188–9, 207–9
consumption
  and crowding out, 168–76, 177
  in developing countries, 419
  direct, 165
Cooper, R., 5, 72, 91
cooperative sibling gift behavior, 191
corners problem and crowding out, 177
corporate finance *see* Modigliani–Miller
Coutinho, R., 440
crowding in, 341–2
crowding out, 2–3, 6, 9, 11–16, 33–4,
  71–83
  and capital formation and economic
    activity, 288–96
    financing government expenditures,
      293–6
    government purchases of goods and
      services, 290
    versus monetary accommodation,
      290–3
  in developing countries, 423–4
  effectiveness of fiscal policy, 12,
    163–82
    examples in closed-economy
      full-employment model, 163,
      167–76, 178
    problem areas, 177–8
    see also taxonomy
  neutrality of debts and deficits, 72–3
    see also debt neutrality
  old fashioned long-run, 75–7
  old fashioned short-run, 73–5
  portfolio, 77–8
  rational expectations–augmented and
    impossibility of cutting taxes,
    81–3
  rational expectations–augmented
    Keynesian, 78–81
  and steady-state equilibrium, 341–2
  see also debt neutrality; fiscal and
    monetary policies, capital
    formation; fiscal and monetary
    policies, long-run effects
Cuba, 71
Cumby, R., 430
currency appreciation, amortization of
  public debt through, 115–22
Currie, D., 325, 340
cyclically corrected fiscal impulse, 85–9

David, P.A. (with Scadding, J.L.)
  on crowding out, 179
  on Dension's Law, 234

David, P.A. (*continued*)
  on future taxes, 229
  on public consumption, 168
  on ultrarationality, 163, 180, 234,
    239–40, 242
Davis, R.G., 233
de Larosière, J., 26
Deane, P., 49–50
debt and deficits, public sector, 6–9,
    47–101
  arithmetic of government budget
    constraint, 95–6
  in developing countries, 407–17
    financeable, 440–4
    and real exchange rate, 433
    substituting domestic debt for foreign
      debt, 432–5
  inflation, 6–8, 54–62
  measures of fiscal stance, 9, 84–9,
    100–1
  negative impact multipliers from
    budget deficits in Keynesian
    model with rational expectations,
    9, 97–9
  solvency, 6, 9, 62–71
  and solvency, arithmetic of, 145–56
  UK statistics, 48–54
  see also crowding out; inflation;
    measurement of public sector
    deficit
debt neutrality, 38, 47–8, 72–3
  and capital formation and economic
    activity, 296–302
    endless chain of intergenerational
      gifts and bequests, 297–8
    future taxes, 298–9
    heterogeneity of households,
      portfolio and distributional
      effects, 301–2
    liquidity constraints, 300–1
    lump-sum and conditional taxes,
      299–300
  in developing countries, 444
  doctrine and evidence, 15, 229–51
    empirical findings, 234–46
    historical perspective, 229–34
    positive irrelevance and normative
      relevance of, 129–38
    redistribution and consumer
      heterogeneity, 12–14, 183–222
    and capital market imperfection,
      heterogeneous survival rates and
      discount rates, 213–19
    finite horizons and uncertain
      lifetimes irrelevant for, 207–13
  see also overlapping generations
Vickrey and 'single tax' of George, 14,
    223–8

debt service, 50–1, 69
debt-financed government expenditure,
    259–68
deficit budget money-capital model of
    steady-state equilibrium, 346–9
deficits *see* debt and deficits
deflation *see* hyperdeflations
demand
  private, effective and notional, 178
  see also aggregate demand
demography, 34, 179
Denison, E.F., 180, 234, 240–1
Dervis, K., 408
devaluation: maxi-devaluation, 425
developing countries, 61, 71
  stabilization and structural adjustment,
    18–19, 407–48
    inflation targets and financeable
      deficits, 440–4
    seigniorage as tax, 435–40
    solvency *see under* solvency
    transfer *see under* transfer
  see also under debt and deficits
Diamond, P., 5, 13, 45, 193, 194, 202, 233
Diaz-Alejandro, C., 425
Dilnot, A.W., 44
direct complementarity, 34
direct crowding out (ultrarationality), 73,
    164–6, 177–9
  in full-employment model, 163,
    167–76, 178
direct revenue effect, 369
direct substitution, 34
disaggregation of government budget
    identity, 62–3, 95–6
discount, rates and capital market
    imperfections, 213–19
discount rates, and heterogeneous
    survival rates, 213–19
disequilibrium, 407–8
distributional effects and debt neutrality,
    301–2
domestic debt substituted for foreign
    debt, 432–3
Dornbusch, R., 360, 435
Dwight, M., 134
dynamic adjustment *see* stability and
    dynamic adjustment

Eaton, J., 72, 91, 427
Edwards, S., 425
effective private demand, 178
effectiveness of fiscal policy *see under*
    crowding out
elasticities of marginal utility, time
    preference rates and
    heterogeneous survival rates,
    216–19

empirical findings on debt neutrality, 234–66
government deficits and current taxes, 235–9
savings
out of different kinds of income, 242–6
stability of private rate, 239–42
employment, 35
see also full employment; unemployment
equilibrium
market, in OLG model, 194–200
see also under steady-state
equivalence theorem, 230–2
Europe
European Economic Community, 26
'Eurosclerosis', 408
hyperinflation, 408
public sector debt and deficits, 47, 51–2, 70–1
solvency, arithmetic of, 148–51, 155–8
'eventual monetization', 64–5
exchange rate, 122
and amortization of public debt, 55–6
and crowding out, 78–9
and developing countries, 415, 427, 433, 442
fixed, policy effects with, 352–3
floating, 55–6
policy effects with, 354–5
regime *see under* seigniorage
exhaustive public spending, and debt neutrality, 204–7
exogenous variables, 78, 80
expectations, adaptive, in stability in full employment model, 285–6
external borrowing, 232

factor demand and capital, 374–7
Fair, R.C., 324
Federal Reserve *see* United States
Feldstein, M.
on future taxes, 230
on population growth and intertemporal inefficiency, 179
on public consumption, 168
on savings and social security, 234, 242–4, 245–6
on ultrarationality, 163
Feltenstein, A., 6, 368
Ferguson, J., 184, 233
financial policy *see* budgetary and financial policy
Financial Statement and Budget Report, 29
financing/revenue, 35, 36–42, 48, 55, 62–4, 293–6

see also borrowing; measurement of public sector deficit; seigniorage; taxation
finite horizons and uncertain lifetimes
irrelevant for debt neutrality, 207–13
aggregation, 209–11
and government, 211–13
individual consumers, 207–9
fiscal and monetary policies
capital formation and economic activity, 15–16, 287–356
asset markets and macroeconomic policies model, 314–19
crowding out and neutrality, 288–96
debt neutrality: critique of Ricardian theory, 296–302
neutrality and superneutrality, 302–14
short-run and long-run effects of model, 327–56
long-run effects on aggregate demand, 15, 252–86
Blinder-Solow models, 257–9
debt-financed government expenditure, 259–68
fiscal policy with full employment and flexible prices, 273–9
monetary policy, 268–73
stability in full employment model, 281–6
see also developing countries
fiscal roots of inflation *see under* inflation
fiscal stance, measures of, 9, 84–9, 100–1
Fischer, S., 309, 323, 324, 360
Fisher, hypothesis, 115
fixed-price, closed-economy unemployment model of crowding out, 166–7
Fleming, J.M., 167
Flemming, J.S., 133
flexible prices and fiscal policies with full employment, 273–9
Flood, R., 383
flow-of-funds accounting, 107
see also measurement of public sector deficit
Foley, D.K., 16, 164, 168, 316
foreign exchange
running down, 55
and solvency, arithmetic of, 151
see also exchange rate; overseas
foresight, perfect *see* myopic perfect foresight
France
public sector debt and deficits, 47, 51, 70
solvency, arithmetic of, 148–51, 156–8

Frenkel, J., 76–7, 83, 186, 207
Friedman, B., 77–8
Friedman, M./monetarists, 1, 179
  on crowding out, 164
  on growth of money stock, 293
  on inflation effects of fiscal policy,
    252, 253
  language, 252
  on natural rate of unemployment, 323
  on permanent income, 295
  on public consumption, 168
  on public spending, 174
  on tax burden, 230
full employment, 75, 84
  in closed economy model and crowding
    out, 163, 167–76, 178
  fiscal policy with, 273–9
    and flexible prices, 273–9
    impact effects, 277–9
    long-run equilibrium, 274–7
    stability, 279, 281–6
  model short-run effects in, 334–6
  see also employment
future taxation, 230, 232, 243
  dependence on current deficits and
    expectation, 298–9

Garber, P., 383
generations *see* overlapping generations
George, H., 227
Germany *see* West Germany
Gersovitz, M., 72, 91, 427
Ghosh, A.R., 72, 91
Giavazzi, F., 71
gift behavior *see* intergenerational;
  overlapping generations model
Gordon, R.J., 178
government
  and OLG model, 211–13
  see also public sector; public spending
GPSR *see* gross private savings ratio
Great Depression, 292, 306
Greenwald, B., 72
gross domestic product
  and debt service, 50–1
  in developing countries, 420
  and government consumption, 30
  and national debt, 49, 51–3, 84, 89
  and solvency, 66–7
  and solvency, arithmetic of, 145–6
  see also output
gross national savings ratio, 240–1, 247
gross private savings ratio, 234, 239–41,
  247
Grossman, S.J., 27, 72
GSSR *see* gross national savings ratio
Gurley, J.G., 232

Haberler, G., 232
Hall, R.E., 15, 370, 400
Hansen, L.P., 15
Hart, O.D., 27, 72
Haque, N., 423
Heller, W., 254
Henderson, H.D., 163, 168
heterogeneity
  consumer *see under* debt neutrality
  of households and debt neutrality,
    301–2
  survival rates and capital market
    imperfections, 213–19
Hicks, J.R., 106, 168
high-powered money, income-velocity
  of circulation of, 61
Hills, J., 65, 66, 91
historical perspective of debt neutrality,
  229–34
Hungary, 408
hyperdeflations, fiscal theory of, 16–18,
  359–67

IMF *see* International Monetary Fund
imperfect competition, 27
imperfect substitutes and monetary
  finance, 305–7
implementation date, 79
implicit assets and liabilities, 125–6
income
  and direct crowding out, 165
  national *see* financing; gross domestic
    product
  policy, 426
  –velocity of circulation of high-
    powered money, 61
inconsistent fiscal-financial-monetary
  plans, 67–8
index-linked debt, 59
indirect crowding out, 166–7, 168,
  178, 180
indirect revenue effect, 369
inflation
  amortization of public debt through,
    115–22
  corrected fiscal impulse, 85–9
  'corrected' PSBR, 54
  and crowding out, 168–76
  debt and deficits, public sector, 6–8,
    54–62
    amortizing public debt through,
      54–9
    and monetization, 7, 59–62
  in developing countries, 439
    and primary deficit, 444
    targets and financeable deficits,
      440–4

Inflation (*continued*)
  expectations
    and closed economy model, 337–8
    and monetary finance, 307–9
    fiscal roots of, 12–13, 16–18
    see also hyperdeflations
  public spending cuts and, 18, 368–403
    long-run effects, 384–95
    model, 371–9
    seigniorage and exchange rate
      regime, 380–4
    stability and dynamic adjustment,
      395–8
  and solvency, arithmetic of, 156, 158
  steady, long-run effects of, 309–14
  steady-state and budget balance and
    asset growth, 340–1
information paradigm, asymmetric, 27
interest payments
  in developing countries, 413
  on public debt, 30
  and solvency, arithmetic of, 147, 153,
    155–6
interest rates
  and amortization of public debt, 56,
    59
  and crowding out, 78–80
  in developing countries, 442
  and monetization of public debt, 61
  and solvency, 63–5
intergenerational relationships, 39,
    230–1, 233–4, 242–5
  endless chain of, 297–8
  see also overlapping generations
international capital mobility
  perfect, 385–6
  zero, 387–95
International Monetary Fund, 9, 25
  and debt and deficits, 408
  and measurement of fiscal stance,
    84, 85–7
  and measurement of public sector
    deficit, 109
international reserve sufficiency:
    seigniorage and exchange rate
    regime, 380–3
investment
  and closed economy model, 337–8
  and crowding out, 78–80, 168–76, 177
  subsidy, 74
irrelevance, positive, and normative
    relevance of debt neutrality,
    129–38
IS–LM diagrams, 73–5, 78–9
  and crowding out, 165–7, 172–6
  and fiscal and monetary policies,
    316–17
  aggregate demand, 254–80

Italy
  public sector debt and deficits, 47,
    51–2, 70
  solvency, arithmetic of, 148–51, 156–8

Japan
  public sector debt and deficits, 51–2
  solvency, arithmetic of, 149–51
    155–7
Jarque, C.M., 368
John, A., 5
Johnson, H.G., 164, 168, 247
Jones, H.G., 49
Jones, R.W., 77
jump-appreciation, 80
Jung, W.S., 368
Juster, T.G., 165, 235, 244

Katona, G., 165, 235, 244–5, 247
Kenen, P.B., 77
Keynesianism, 4–5, 9
  countercyclical budget deficits, 1
  crowding out, 83, 163–4, 168, 400
    long-run, 75–7
    rational expectations-augmented,
      9, 78–81, 85, 97–9
    short-run, 73–4, 75
    two-set model, 77–8
  and developing countries, 413, 416
  failures of goods and labour markets,
    10
  fiscal and monetary policies, 15
    aggregate demand, 254–5, 257, 262
    capital formation and economic
      activity, 287, 289, 290, 294, 300,
      302, 316–17, 320
  fiscal stabilization, 40
  on Great Depression, 292, 306
  measurement of fiscal stance, 100
  measurement of public sector deficit,
    108
  revenue effect, 18
  solvency, 65, 70
  unemployment, 83, 134
Khan, M., 425
Kimball, M., 13, 14, 185, 187–94
Kindleberger, C.P., 70–1
King, R.G., 28
Kiyotaki, N., 5
Kletzer, K., 427
Knight, P., 440
Kochin, L.A., 163, 168, 180, 230, 234–7
Kopf, D.H., 233
Korb, L.J., 167
Korea, 416
Kotlikoff, L.J., 6, 9
Krugman, P., 383, 425
Kuznets, S., 241

Kydland, F., 4, 39

Laffer curve, 158, 443–4
seigniorage, 7, 17
Laffont, J.J., 72
land, taxation on, 223–7
Latin America, 71, 368, 416
see also developing countries
Leiderman, L., 15
Lerner, A.P., 232, 294
Levhari, D., 164
Levich, R., 430
levy, capital, 69–71
liabilities
implicit, 125–6
public sector *see* public spending
see also measurement of public sector
deficit
life assurance markets missing, 213–16
lifetimes
uncertain *see* finite horizons
see also overlapping generations
Lipsey, R.E., 165
liquidity constraints, and debt neutrality,
300–1
Lizondo, J., 425
LM curves *see IS–LM* diagrams
long-run consistency and seigniorage and
exchange rate regime, 380–3
long-run crowding out, 75–7, 164
long-run effects on aggregate demand
see under fiscal and monetary
policies
long-run effects of monetary growth and
steady inflation, 309–14
long-run effects of public spending,
384–95
perfect international capital mobility,
385–6
zero international capital mobility,
387–95
long-run equilibrium and fiscal policy
with full employment, 274–7
long-run monetary policy, 268–75
fiscal expansion with money-financed
debts, 271–3
open market purchase of bonds,
269–71
long-run policy effects and asset markets,
317–18
long-run policy neutrality and steady-
state equilibrium, 342–4
Lucas, R.E., 6, 323
lump-sum taxes and debt neutrality,
299–300

McCulloch, J.R., 229, 230–1
macroeconomic disequilibrium, 407–8

macroeconomic policies model and
capital formation and economic
activity, 314–19
Mankiw, N.G., 4, 74
marginal tax rates, 75
marginal utility, elasticities,
time preference rates and
heterogeneous survival rates,
216–19
market equilibrium
and external accounts, 378–9
in OLG model, 194–200
maturity structure of public debt, 60
Meade, J.A., 233
measurement of public sector deficit,
2, 9–10, 105–44
amortization of public debt, 115–22
budgetary policy and monetary
growth, 122–5
implicit assets and liabilities, 125–6
public sector accounts and private
behavior, 127–38
stylized set of public sector accounts,
108–14
see also arithmetic; solvency,
arithmetic of
measures of fiscal stance, 9, 84–9, 100–1
Medium-Term Financial Strategy, 47
Mexico, 368
Miller, M.H.
on macroeconomics, 45, 168, 179, 234
on measurement of public sector
deficit, 110, 119, 139
on public sector debt, 68
Minford, P., 7
minimizing excess burden of non-lump-
sum taxes, 39–42
Mishan, E.J., 233
Mishkin, F.S., 242
Mitchell, B.R., 49–50
mobility, capital
perfect international, 385–6
zero international, 387–95
Modigliani, F., 64, 184, 233
Modigliani–Miller theorem, 38, 130,
140, 230, 255, 302, 329
monetarists *see* Friedman;
hyperdeflations
monetary finance and capital formation
and economic activity: neutrality
and superneutrality, 302–14
inflation expectations and short-run
effects, 307–9
long-run effects of growth and steady
inflation, 309–14
money, government debt and other
assets, 305–7
open market operations, 303–4

monetary growth and budgetary policy, 122–5
monetary policy, long-run *see* long-run monetary policy
money
  base money demand function, 442–3
  –capital models of steady-state equilibrium, 344–9
  creation *see* seigniorage/money creation
  demand effect, 369
  –financed debts, fiscal expansion with, 271–3
  high-powered, income-velocity of circulation of, 61
  and monetary finance, 305–7
  monetization
    of deficit, eventual, 122–5
    and inflation, 7, 59–62
    and solvency, arithmetic of, 156–8
  quantity of, changes in, 256, 268–73
Montiel, P., 423
Morris, C.N., 44
Morris, S., 368
MTFS (Medium-Term Financial Strategy), 47
multidimensional concept, crowding out as *see* taxonomy of crowding out
multiplier theorem, balanced budget, 41
Mundell, R.A., 164, 167
Munnell, A.H., 234, 242
Musgrave, P.B. and R.A., 26
myopic perfect foresight in stability in full employment model, 282–5

Nash behavior, 190–1
National Institute of Economic and Social Research, 43, 86–8
natural resources, income from ownership of, 62–3
negative impact
  effect of tax cuts, 79–80
  multipliers from budget deficits in Keynesian model with rational expectations, 9, 97–9
net savings ratios, 241, 247
Netherlands, 47
neutrality
  and capital formation and economic activity *see under* monetary finance
  of debts and deficits, 72–3
    see also debt neutrality
  and steady-state equilibrium, 342–4
    see also crowding out and capital formation; superneutrality
New Classicism, 4, 28, 230, 234

NIESR *see* National Institute of Economic and Social Research
non-lump-sum taxes, minimizing excess burden of, 39–42
normative, relevance, and positive irrelevance of debt neutrality, 129–38
Norway, 138
nothing from nothing, 442
notional effective private demand, 178
NPSR and NSSR *see* net savings ratios

Obstfeld, M., 383
OECD *see* Organization for Economic Cooperation and Development
old-fashioned crowding out, 73–7
OLG model *see* overlapping generations model
open economy
  amortization of public debt, 118–22
  asset markets and macroeconomic policies, 319
  and budget constraint, 77
  budgetary policy and monetary growth, 124–5
  and crowding out, 79, 81
  extension to fiscal and financial policies model, 349–56
open market
  operations and monetary finance, 303–4
  purchase of bonds, 269–71
opportunity sets, public and private, difference between, 38
Organization for Economic Cooperation and Development, 26
  measurement of fiscal stance, 84, 85–9
  public sector debt and deficits, 51–2
  solvency, arithmetic of, 148–57
Ott, D.J., 111, 167
output, 253
  and anticipated future tax cut, 79
  and crowding out, 167
  in developing countries, 412, 415, 417, 419, 442
  and factor demand and capital, 374–7
  and national debt, 52
  and solvency, 64
  see also gross deomestic product
overlapping generations model, 5–6, 13, 37, 184–5, 223, 233–4
  and corners, 177
  with finite lifetimes and intergenerational gifts and bequests, 188–207
  consumer's problem, 186–90
  debt neutrality, 204–7
  gift behavior, 190–1

Overlapping generations model (*continued*)
  market equilibrium, 194–200
overseas sector accounts, 127–9
  see also exchange rate; foreign
    exchange

parents and children *see*
    intergenerational; overlapping
    generations
Patinkin, D., 164, 179, 232–3, 247
PBSR *see* public sector borrowing
    requirement
Peltzman, S., 163, 165, 168, 180
perfect capital mobility, 395–6
  international, 385–6
perfect foresight, myopic, 282–5
permanent adjustment, 68
permanent deficit, 67–9
Pesek, B., 247
Petri, P., 408
Phelps, E.S., 7, 323, 325
Pigou, A.C., 232
Poland, 71, 408
policy evaluation and design *see*
    measurement of public sector
    deficit
Ponzi game, 64, 75
portfolio
  behavior, 377–8
  crowding out, 77–8
  effects and debt neutrality, 301–2
positive birth rate in OLG model, 185,
    223
positive irrelevance and normative
    relevance of debt neutrality,
    129–38
Prescott, E.C., 4, 39
Prest, A.R., 26
prices
  flexible: fiscal policies with full
    employment, 273–9
  see also inflation
primary deficit, real
  and amortization of public debt, 56, 57
  and monetization of public debt, 60
primary surplus, 428–9
  and solvency, arithmetic of, 152–4,
    157–8
private activity displaced *see* crowding
    out
private behavior
  consumption, 377–8
  and public sector accounts, 127–38
private demand, effective and notional,
    178
private and public opportunity sets,
    difference between, 38
private savings and debt neutrality,
    239–46

production
  and market equilibrium in OLG
    model, 194–5
  see also output
PSFD *see* public sector financial deficit
public expenditure *see* public spending
public and private opportunity sets,
    difference between, 38
public sector
  accounts
    and private behavior, 127–38
    stylized set of, 108–14
  borrowing requirement, 7, 44,
    53–4,137–8
  debt and deficits *see* debt and deficits
  financial deficit, 7, 53, 67
  see also budgetary and financial policy;
    debt and deficits; public spending
public spending, 66–7
  and crowding out, 168–76, 178,
    179–80
  cuts, 399
    in developing countries, 417–18, 444
    inflationary *see under* inflation
  debt-financed, 259–68
  exhaustive and debt neutrality, 204–7
  future, 85
  on goods and services, 29–36, 290
  see also debt and deficits; financing;
    public sector

quantity of money changes, 256, 268–73

rational expectations, 9, 97–9
  –augmented crowding out
    and impossibility of cutting taxes,
    81–3
  Keynesian, 78–81
Razin, A., 15, 83, 186, 207
redistribution and consumer
    heterogeneity *see under* debt
    neutrality
reference specification *see* bench mark
relevance, normative, and positive
    irrelevance of debt neutrality,
    129–38
repudiation, debt, 69–71
reserves, sufficiency and seigniorage and
    exchange rate regime, 380–3
revenue *see* financing/revenue
Ricardo, D./Ricardian, 12, 15, 70
  critique of, 296–302
  and debt neutrality, 229–34, 243, 247,
    290, 303, 307
  equivalence theorem, 230–2
Roley, V.V., 78
Rotemberg, J.J., 5
Russell, T., 134

Sachs, J., 72, 91, 408
Sadka, E., 39
Samuelson, P.A., 233
Sandmo, A., 39
Sargent, T.J. (with Wallace, N.)
  on fiscal theory of inflation, 16–17,
    359–66
  on money, 140
  om measurement, 124, 158
  on public sector debt and deficits,
    6–7, 54, 59
  on rational expectations, 323
Saving, T.R., 247
savings
  out of different kinds of income, 242–6
  and social security, 234, 242–6
  stability of private rate of, 239–42
Scadding, J.L. *see* David
seigniorage/money creation
  and amortization of public debt, 56–7
  defined, 55
  demand for, 371–4
  in developing countries
    and inflation targets and financeable
      deficits, 443–4
    as tax, 435–40
  and exchange rate regime, 380–4
    international reserve sufficiency,
      383–4
    long-run consistency, 380–3
  and solvency, arithmetic of, 147, 151,
    156, 158
  as source of public revenue, 38, 41,
    63–4
  see also Laffer curve
service industries, 35
Shaw, E.S., 232
Shell, K., 325
Shleifer, A., 5
shocks, anticipated, 80
short-run crowding out, 73–5, 164
short-run debt, amortization of, 59
short-run effects
  of fiscal and financial policy, 351–2
  in full employment model, 334–6
  and monetary finance, 307–9
  policy, and asset markets, 317–18
  in unemployment model, 332–4
sibling gift behavior, 191
Sidrauski, M., 90, 164, 168, 309, 324
Siegel, J.J., 139
'single tax' on land, 227
Singleton, K.J., 15
Smith, A., 229, 230, 247
SNA *see* System of National Accounts
social security and savings, 234, 242–6
Solow, R.M. *see* Blinder
solvency
  arithmetic of, 11, 145–59

debt, deficits, and 145–56
  monetization and, 156–8
debt and deficits, public sector, 6, 9,
  62–71
  constraint, 62–7
  debt repudiation, 69–71
  'permanent deficit', 67–9
  sustainable fiscal-financial-monetary
    plans, 67
  in developing countries
    of nation, 426–30
    of public sector, 430–5
Soviet Union, 71
Spencer, R.W., 168, 230
Sraffa, P., 229, 231
stability
  and dynamic adjustment, 395–8
    perfect capital mobility, 395–7
    zero capital mobility, 396–8
  in full employment model, 281–6
    adaptive expectations, 285–6
    myopic perfect foresight, 282–5
    static expectations, 281–2
  of private rate of savings, 239–42
stabilization policy, 107–8
  see also allocative and stabilization
    aspects of budgetary and financial
    policy; developing countries
static expectations: stability in full
  employment model, 281–2
stationary market equilibrium in OLG
  model, 195–200
steady-state
  and debt neutrality, 200–4
  equilibrium, 338–49
    budget balance, asset growth and
      inflation, 340–1
    crowding out and crowding in, 341–2
    fiscal and financial policies model,
      355–6
    money-capital models, 344–9
    neutrality, super-neutrality and
      other long-run policy neutrality,
      343–4
Stebbing, P.W., 90
Stein, J.L., 164
Stiglitz, J.E., 25, 26, 27, 36–7, 39, 72,
  134, 230
Stokey, N.L., 6
structural adjustment *see* developing
  countries
structural disequilibrium, 408
stylized set of public sector accounts,
  108–14
substitutes/substitution
  debt, 432–3
  direct, 34
  imperfect, and monetary finance,
    305–7

Substitutes/substitution (*continued*)
  problem and crowding out, 177
Summers, L.H., 74
superneutrality
  and capital formation and economic
    activity *see under* monetary
    finance
  lacking in developing countries, 444
  and steady-state equilibrium, 342–4
surplus, primary, 428–9
  and solvency, arithmetic of, 152–4,
    157–8
survival rates, heterogeneous, and capital
  market imperfections, 213–19
sustainable fiscal–financial–monetary
  plans, 67
System of National Accounts, 107, 111
system-wide crowding out *see* indirect
  crowding out

Taiwan, 416
Tanzi, J., 82
Tanzi, V., 8, 91, 399, 439, 444
taxation
  and borrowing, 231–3
  and crowding out, 168–76, 180
  current, and empirical findings on debt
    neutrality, 235–9
  cuts, and closed economy model,
    337–8
  cuts and crowding out, 74–5, 79–81
    anticipated future, 79
    impossibility of, 81–3
  in developing countries
    seigniorage as, 435–40
    and transfer processes, 409–17,
      418–24
  financing public spending, 36–42, 48,
    55, 63
  see also measurement of public
    sector deficit
  future, 230, 232, 243
    dependence on current deficits and
      expectations, 298–9
  increase after cut, 81–2
  on land, 223–7
  rate as instrument of fiscal policy, 256,
    259–68
  varied rate, 268
taxonomy of crowding out, 163, 164–7,
  179
  short-run and long-run, 164
  see also direct crowding out; indirect
    crowding out
Taylor, C.T., 139
Taylor, J.B., 323
Taylor, L.D., 165, 235, 243, 425
Terray, A., 70

Thatcher, M., 30, 43, 139
Thompson, E.A., 233
Threadgold, 139
time preference rates, heterogeneous
  survival rates and elasticities of
  marginal utility, 216–19
Tobin, J., 183
  on crowding out, 9, 179
    long-run, 75, 77, 90, 164, 168
    taxation, 83
  on debt neutrality, 12, 129, 184,
    232–3, 234
  on fiscal and monetary policies, 9,
    12, 15
    aggregate demand, 252, 253, 254
    capital formation and economic
      activity, 287, 309, 323, 325, 340–1
transfers
  problems in developing countries,
    409–17, 428
    breakdown, 417–26
  see also intergenerational; social
    security
Turnovsky, S.J., 28

ultrarationality *see* direct crowding out
unanticipated inflation, 58
uncertain lifetimes *see* finite horizons
unemployment, 253
  in debt-financed government
    expenditure model, 256, 259–68
  in fixed-price closed economy model of
    crowding out, 166–7
  model, short-run effects in, 332–4
  in monetary policy in long-run model,
    256, 268–73
'uniform taxation' theorem, 39
United Kingdom, 1
  base money demand function, 442
  capital formation, 31–2
  crowding out, 85–9, 91
  government-owned capital, 138
  inflation, 57–62
  measures of fiscal stance, 85–9
  public expenditure, 30–1, 33–5
    cuts, 28, 29, 42
    financing, 43
  public sector debt and deficits, 7, 44,
    47, 48–54, 91
    measurement, 18–19
    see also crowding out; inflation;
      above and solvency *below*
  solvency, 66–7, 71
    arithmetic of, 147, 149–51, 155–8
United Nations, System of National
  Accounts, 107, 111
United States, 1, 8
  base money demand function, 442

United States (*continued*)
  crowding out, 82
  debt neutrality, 230, 234–9
    private savings, 239–45
  fiscal and monetary policies, capital
    formation and economic activity,
    288–323 *passim*
  government-owned capital, 138
  measures of fiscal stance, 85–8
  public sector debt and deficits, 51, 91,
    408, 409
    measurement, 118, 120
  'single tax', 227
  solvency, arithmetic of, 148–51, 152–8
Upton, C.W., 168, 179, 234
utility *see* marginal utility

van Wijnbergen, S., 19, 425, 432,
  440, 447
Vickrey, W., 223, 230, 233
Vishny, R.W., 5
von Furstenberg, G.M., 247

Wachtel, P., 324
Wagner, R.E., 234
Wallace, N. *see* Sargent
Walrasian equilibrian, 4–5
WDR *see under* World Bank

wealth, and direct crowding out, 165
Webb, D.C., 27, 37, 45, 72, 134, 142
Weil, P., 377
  OLG model, 13, 185–6, 193, 211–13.,
    216, 223
Weiss, A., 27–8, 37, 72, 134
Weitzman, M.L., 27
West Germany
  hyperinflation, 408
  public sector debt and deficits, 47,
    51, 70–1
  solvency, arithmetic of, 148–51, 156–8
Williamson, S.D., 72
World Bank
  consistency check, 440
  World Development Report (WDR,
    1988), 11, 18–19, 407n, 409, 426,
    443, 445

Yaari, M., 207, 234
  OLG model, 3, 185–6, 211–16, 223
Yellen, J., 5
Yohe, W.P., 168
Yoo, J.H., 111

Zaire, 71
zero capital mobility, 396–8
  international, 387–95